THE
REVELATION
OF
JESUS CHRIST

THE
REVELATION
OF
JESUS CHRIST

WHICH GOD GAVE TO HIM TO SHOW TO HIS
SERVANTS WHAT MUST SOON TAKE PLACE
(REVELATION 1.1)

MARGARET BARKER

T&T CLARK
EDINBURGH

T&T CLARK LTD
59 GEORGE STREET
EDINBURGH EH2 2LQ
SCOTLAND

www.tandtclark.co.uk

First published 2000

ISBN 0 567 08716 6

British Library Cataloguing-in-Publication Data
A catalogue record for this book is available from the British Library

Typeset by Fakenham Photosetting Limited, Fakenham, Norfolk
Printed and bound in Great Britain by Bell & Bain Ltd, Glasgow

For Richard

The crisis of the fall of Jerusalem explains the relation of the
Apocalypse and the Gospel.
In the Apocalypse, that 'coming' of Christ was expected, and
painted in figures: in the Gospel the 'coming' is interpreted.

B. F. Westcott, *The Gospel According to St John* (1894)

According to the Kabbalists, the Messiah has only one name,
the ineffable YHWH.

Johann Reuchlin, *On the Art of the Kabbalah* Book 1 (1517)

CONTENTS

PREFACE

If 'apocalyptic was the mother of all Christian theology', then the Book of Revelation should be put at the centre of New Testament study. In *The Revelation of Jesus Christ* I have done this, showing that the Book of Revelation is not a late text from Asia Minor but the earliest material in the New Testament.

The book is unique among New Testament texts insofar as a date and place of origin are recorded in tradition. The book itself claims to have been written on Patmos, and Irenaeus, writing about 180 CE, says it was seen by John at the end of the reign of Domitian. The internal evidence of the book, however, seems incompatible with both of these. Although few have questioned that it came from Patmos and was sent to Asia Minor, scholars long ago recognized that the cryptic allusions to contemporary events pointed not to the reign of Domitian but to 68–70 CE and that the 'John' of the Book of Revelation wrote a very different Greek from the 'John' of the Fourth Gospel. At the end of the nineteenth century, the great New Testament scholars such as Westcott, Lightfoot and Hort gave weight to the internal evidence and favoured the earlier date. In the twentieth century, although there was no new evidence, there was a new fashion and so Charles, who published his great commentary in 1920, favoured the external tradition and accepted the later date.

At the end of the twentieth century there *is* new material to bring to the study of the Book of Revelation. There has never been evidence for the persecution of Christians in Asia Minor in the first century CE apart from the Book of Revelation itself, but the Dead Sea texts now offer ample evidence of the situation in Palestine in the years preceding the war against Rome. It was a time of religious and nationalist fervour fuelled by the visions of priestly mystics, and the Book of Revelation belongs with these texts which depict the crimes of the wicked priest and the war of the sons of light against the sons of darkness. Jesus was described in the Letter to the Hebrews as the great high priest, the new Melchizedek, and the Book of Revelation presents itself as his teaching: 'The revelation of Jesus Christ which God gave him to show to his servants what must soon take place'.

The Book of Revelation is oracles and visions collected and preserved by John the beloved disciple and his brethren the prophets, the greatest of whom had been Jesus himself. Jesus spoke of what he had seen and heard in heaven (John 3.32), but people did not believe his *marturion*, his testimony. This testimony, defined in Revelation 1.2 as 'all that he saw', is preserved in the Book of Revelation. As the years passed, the prophets interpreted contemporary events in the light of these visions and oracles. These were the people whom Josephus dismissed as the 'pretended messengers of the deity who led the wretched people astray' (*War* 6.286) and inspired the war against Rome with their conviction that the LORD would return to his city. There is a remarkable similarity between the portents and oracles reported by Josephus and those in the Book of Revelation.

In order to understand the Book of Revelation, it must be recognized that the problems at the end of the second temple period originated when the exiles returned from Babylon in the sixth century BCE. Accusations followed: the priests had lost their spiritual sight, the new temple was impure, and the new city was no longer a holy city. There were many who distanced themselves from the new Jerusalem and longed for divine judgement on the faithful city who had become a harlot (Isa. 1.21). They kept alive the memory of the first temple which had been heaven on earth, and of the anointed priest-king, who had been the presence of the LORD with his people. In their writings, the rituals of the old temple became their descriptions of heaven, and they remembered how the priest-king had entered the holy of holies as a man but returned as the LORD to establish his kingdom and judge his enemies. These priestly writings are now known as apocalypses, and have been preserved by Christian scribes.

The court scenes in the Book of Revelation are not modelled on those of the Roman imperial cult; how could a Christian prophet have seen such things? The imperial cult may have been identified as the dark antitype of true worship, but the detail was drawn from priestly memories of the temple ritual. This must have been the first temple with its cherub throne, since the holy of holies in the second temple was empty. The harlot of the Book of Revelation was not Rome; she had been Jerusalem since the time of Ezekiel, even though later interpreters of the prophecy identified Rome as the harlot of their own time. Nor is there any evidence that Patmos was used as a penal settlement in the first century CE: it is quite possible that 'the word of God and the testimony of Jesus' that brought John to Patmos were the very visions and prophecies which had fuelled the troubles in Jerusalem from which he had been able to escape. The seven letters were given by the LORD in visions to his prophets in Jerusalem, and sent by the pillars of the church to the communities in Asia Minor. They were warnings about Paul whom they described as Balaam, the false prophet. Since the language of the Jerusalem Christians was Aramaic and their Scriptures were in Hebrew, it is unlikely that Greek was the original language of the Book of Revelation. The Book of Revelation was translated into Greek, which explains why its style is not that of the Fourth Gospel.

Just before the final disaster overtook Jerusalem, John received his own personal experience of the return of the LORD, recorded in the Book of Revelation as vision of the Mighty Angel coming in a cloud from heaven (10.1). He gave John new teaching, some of it to be kept secret, and from that time, John began to reinterpret the teaching of Jesus and to present the new understanding of his return.

The study of apocalyptic texts has been an area of rapid growth, especially since the non-biblical materials have become available in

English. The key question must be: Why is all this material 'outside' the Old Testament when it was clearly so central to the Dead Sea texts and the New Testament? If, as some suggest, apocalyptic was imported into Judaism during the second temple period, and is evidence for the hellenization and syncretism with oriental cults, this could explain why is was not accepted into the canon. If, however, the apocalypses were the priestly writings of the second temple period which preserved the theology and imagery of the ancient royal cult and inspired the writers of the Dead Sea texts, there must have been a compelling reason to exclude this most 'orthodox' of literature when the canon of Hebrew Scriptures was being defined after the fall of Jerusalem. The apocalypses must have been excluded because of the part they had played in that disaster, and the Christians who preserved the apocalyptic texts must have had good reason to do this.

The Revelation of Jesus Christ is the culmination of many years' work; all my publications have been leading in this direction, and their conclusions form the foundation of this book. I have summarized these points in the first three chapters. Ideally, I should like to have written a much longer work, engaging in debate with others who work in this field, but the realities of time and publishing make this impossible. What I offer is my reading of the Book of Revelation.

There have been two significant moments in the development of ideas; the first was when I bought a copy of the New Testament in (modern) Hebrew and read the Book of Revelation; and the second was when I first read J. M. Ford's *Anchor Bible Commentary on Revelation* (1975), the most exciting contribution to this field in recent years. She had the courage to suggest a new approach, but her book was not given the recognition it deserved. Although there are many points on which I would disagree with her, she sowed ideas in my mind, the sure sign of a good book.

I should like to thank the staff of the libraries where I work: the University Libraries in Cambridge and Nottingham, and the library of St John's College, Nottingham. I should like to dedicate this book to my husband, who has lived among piles of paper for a very long time.

Margaret Barker
Epiphany 1999

Note. All biblical references are to the English system of numbering chapters and verses, not the Hebrew.

1
JESUS

The four New Testament Gospels are the best known sources for the life of Jesus. The Synoptic Gospels, Matthew, Mark and Luke, although they differ in emphasis and detail, give a broadly similar picture. Jesus was a wandering teacher and preacher who performed miracles. He proclaimed that the kingdom of God was at hand, gave a new interpretation to many of the traditional purity laws and antagonized the authorities by causing a disturbance in the temple and disrupting the traders there. He was crucified when Pontius Pilate was governor of Judea but the charge is not clear: blasphemy or treason. On the third day his disciples and close friends saw him alive and proclaimed that he had risen from the dead.

Apart from the claim to resurrection, the life of Jesus is not so different from that of other teachers and holy men in Palestine at the time. There had been other wandering teachers and faith healers, and others had claimed to be the Messiah and been put to death. None, however, was the cause of a new and powerful religious movement.

Another Picture

John's Gospel gives a different picture. His Jesus teaches and performs miracles and causes a disturbance in the temple, but he also delivers long discourses and claims to speak of what he has seen and heard in heaven. 'He who comes from above is above all; he who is of the earth belongs to the earth, and of the earth he speaks; he who comes from heaven is above all. He bears witness to what he has seen and heard, yet no one receives his testimony . . .' (John 3.31–32); 'all that I have heard from my Father I have made known to you' (John 15.15).

It has recently been fashionable to regard the picture in the Synoptic Gospels as the more authentic. Even though the pious reflections of first-generation Christians can be detected in the way some of the stories are told, when these are removed, we are told, the Jesus of history reappears, but he was no messianic figure nor did he claim to be Son of God. All this and more was added to the simple story by Greek converts to the new religion. John's Gospel, apparently, is even further removed from the Jesus of history. The mysterious sayings of the heavenly Jesus are evidence for gnostic tendencies and a sure sign of (relatively) late and corrupted tradition.

But is this so? The last fifty years have seen a great increase in the number of ancient texts from which we can reconstruct the earliest 'picture' of Jesus. The *Gospel of Thomas,* the *Apocryphon of James* and the *Dialogue of the Saviour,* all found in the gnostic library discovered at Nag Hammadi in 1945, are thought to derive from early

Christian oral tradition. They suggest that John's Jesus, the enigmatic figure who spoke of what he had seen and heard in heaven, was in fact the Jesus of history.

There are many unanswered questions about the earliest years of Christianity and what the first Christians believed: Paul, for example, speaks of the conflict with heavenly powers: '[Jesus] disarmed the principalities and powers ...' (Col. 2.15). 'For I am sure that neither death, nor life, nor angels, nor principalities, nor things present, nor things to come, nor powers, nor height, nor depth, nor anything else in all creation, will be able to separate us from the love of God in Christ Jesus our LORD' (Rom. 8.38–39). He speaks of mysteries and of things which cannot be told: 'I tell you a mystery. We shall not all sleep, but we shall all be changed' (1 Cor. 15.51); 'I know this man who was caught up into Paradise ... and he heard things that cannot be told, which man may not utter' (2 Cor. 12.3–4). Is this a sign that Paul deserted the teaching of Jesus and turned Christianity into a Greek mystery cult? This has often been suggested, but there is another possibility: that all the teaching of Jesus was not recorded in the New Testament Gospels. Some was lost through the uncertainties of oral transmission but some, the teaching about angels and other heavenly matters, was deliberately kept secret and never written down. Basil of Caesarea, writing in the middle of the fourth century CE emphasized that many of the most important church teachings were not written in the New Testament but had been transmitted secretly through the tradition of the apostles (*On the Holy Spirit* 66).

Ignatius, the martyr-bishop of Antioch, writing in the early years of the second century CE, was a champion of orthodoxy who warned his flock against 'the teachings and time worn fables of another people' (*Magn.* 8). He also claimed to know about 'celestial secrets and angelic hierarchies and the dispositions of the heavenly powers and much else both seen and unseen' (*Trall.* 5). How did he, a bishop, know all this? It is not in the New Testament, although the Book of Revelation is clearly a similar body of teaching.

Towards the end of the second century CE Irenaeus, Bishop of Lyons, was worried by the growth of alien ideas in the church. He wrote a long work *Against Heresies* but he also wrote a shorter summary of essential Christian belief, The *Demonstration of the Gospel,* so that his people could 'hold to the rule of faith without deviation' (*Demonstr.* 3). The first section of the book described the seven heavens, the powers and the archangels, the relationship of the cherubim and seraphim to the Word and Wisdom of God and the role of the sevenfold Spirit. Furthermore, he knew that this teaching had been encoded in the symbolism of the temple. For Irenaeus these things were the fundamentals of Christian teaching. They are similar to the material in the Book of Revelation, alluded to elsewhere in the New Testament, but not recorded in full. Is it likely that what Irenaeus regarded as the first fundamentals of Christian teaching had not come from Jesus? *And if the teaching about*

*heavenly powers had come from Jesus, why is there nothing, appar-
ently, in the New Testament Gospels?*

The Hidden Tradition

The answer to these questions may lie in the widely held belief
that Jesus gave secret teaching to his disciples; the Gospels record that
he sometimes spoke to crowds of people but also gave additional
teaching to his disciples in private. The Gospels do not say what this
teaching was, but it concerned the true meaning of the parables which
most people would not understand. 'And when he was alone, those who
were about him with the twelve asked him concerning the parables. And
he said to them, "To you has been given the secret of the kingdom of
God, but for those outside everything is in parables" ' (Mark 4.10–11).
Since Mark summarized Jesus' preaching as 'The time is fulfilled, and
the kingdom of God is at hand; repent, and believe in the gospel' (Mark
1.15), it is very significant indeed that the core of this message, 'the
secret of the kingdom' was not revealed to everyone. The 'secret
teaching', however, was not lost and there are several places in early
Christian writings which suggest that this was the teaching about the
heavenly places and the angels.

Clement of Alexandria wrote at the end of the second century CE that
Jesus taught 'knowledge of the past, present and future' (*Misc.* 6.7). He
knew of mysteries concealed in the Hebrew Scriptures, handed down by
oral tradition but revealed by Jesus to his closest disciples (*Misc.* 5.10).
He does not reveal how Jesus learned these secrets. 'The knowledge
itself is that which has descended by transmission to a few, having been
imparted unwritten by the apostles' (*Misc.* 6.7).

Origen of Alexandria, who wrote in the first half of the third century
CE, also knew of *forbidden, secret and ineffable teaching that was
related to the temple visions of the prophet Ezekiel.*

Our prophets knew of greater things than any in the scriptures which they did not
commit to writing. Ezekiel, for example, received a scroll written within and
without ... but at the command of the Logos he swallowed that book in order that
its contents might not be written and so made known to unworthy persons. John is
also recorded to have done a similar thing (Rev. 10.9). Nay, Paul even heard
unspeakable words which it is not lawful for a man to utter (2 Cor. 12.4). (*Cels.*
6.23)

It is related of Jesus who was greater than all these that he conversed with his
disciples in private and especially in their secret retreats concerning the gospel of
God; but the words he uttered have not been preserved because it appeared to the
evangelists that they could not be adequately conveyed to the multitude in writing
or speech. (*Cels.* 6.6)

The secret things, then, concerned past, present and future and were
encoded in the Hebrew Scriptures, especially in the temple visions of

Ezekiel. In his commentary on the Fourth Gospel, Origen wrote: 'The Jews used to tell of many things in accordance with secret traditions reserved to a few, for they had other knowledge than that which was common and made public' (*On John* 1.31). Elsewhere, Origen revealed that Jesus 'beheld weighty secrets and made them known to a few' (*Cels.* 3.37).

The High Priest

Where did Jesus see these secret things? The earliest Christian writings suggest that this was temple tradition, that what Jesus 'saw' was a vision in the holy of holies, in other words, that he was initiated into the tradition of the high priesthood. Clement of Alexandria distinguished between true and false teachers by saying that the false 'make perverse use of the divine words ... they do not enter in as we enter in, through the tradition of the LORD by drawing aside the curtain' (*Misc.* 7.17). 'Drawing aside the curtain' implies entering the holy of holies, the presence of God. Only the high priest did this. Ignatius of Antioch, writing early in the second century CE, knew how Jesus had acquired the secret teaching; 'To Jesus alone as our high priest were the secret things of God committed' (*Phil.* 9).

Jesus knew the secret teaching because he was a high priest. Were these early authors the only evidence we had, we could prove very little, *but the picture of Jesus as the great high priest in all his roles and aspects appears throughout the New Testament and is the key to understanding all early Christian teaching about him.* Contemporary beliefs about the role of the high priest became the basis for the proclamation of who Jesus was and what he had accomplished by his death and resurrection.

It is important to consider all the early evidence for Jesus; considered piecemeal there is bound to be distortion. In addition to the New Testament Gospels we have to take into account the writings of the first Christians. All these must be treated with respect and the evidence they offer pieced together to reconstruct Jesus as he was. It is, however, unwise to label early writings as heretical just because they do not conform to later beliefs. Many of the so-called gnostic texts, for example, preserve real memories of Jesus, and many of the difficulties encountered in the quest for the real Jesus are difficulties of our own making. If we only accept as evidence the writings which depict Jesus as a teacher and faith healer, then of course it will be difficult to explain how he came to be worshipped as the Messiah and Son of God. Nor is it wise to be too certain about the context in which Jesus preached. The fact that the Qumran texts not only illuminated but radically altered the picture of first-century Palestine shows how inaccurate that picture had been, and yet this traditional picture is still the context of much New Testament interpretation.

The figure who emerges from a more broadly based reconstruction is far from just a teacher and miracle worker. *He is the great high priest.* The Qumran Melchizedek Text (11QMelch) shows that this was the figure who was expected to appear in the first week of the tenth Jubilee to teach about the end of the age, to rescue the children of light from the power of Satan, to set people free from the debt of iniquity, to establish the Kingdom of God and to perform the great atonement sacrifice of the last days. It has been fashionable to cast a wide net throughout the ancient Mediterranean world to find explanations for the earliest Christian claims about Jesus; pagan ideas, apparently, were incorporated into the new faith by Greek converts. This explanation is not necessary. Everything that was claimed for Jesus was part of the established belief about the great high priest and we need look no further. According to the traditional reckoning, Jesus 'appeared' when Melchizedek was expected to appear; he was baptized in the first week of the tenth Jubilee and he claimed to have fulfilled the Jubilee prophecy in Isaiah 61 which was associated with Melchizedek (Luke 4.21, see pp. 48–49).

We can be certain that the first Hebrew Christians in Palestine knew about the high priests. The fundamentals of the faith proclaimed from the very beginning were all rooted in contemporary beliefs about the anointed high priest. Nor is there any need to suggest that the first Christians pieced together a whole variety of ideas and created, for the first time, a composite figure whom they declared Jesus to be. The essence of their preaching was that Jesus had fulfilled expectations; he was the one they had been waiting for, and the Qumran Melchizedek text shows that the one they were waiting for was the high priest. The Letter to the Hebrews, even if we cannot be certain who these Hebrew Christians were, describes Jesus as their great high priest (Heb. 4.14), fulfilling the ancient rites of the temple and offering himself as the great atonement sacrifice (Heb. 9.1–28). Jesus even spoke of himself as the heavenly high priest 'whom the Father consecrated and sent into the world' (John 10.36), 'consecrate' being the technical term used in Leviticus 8.12 for making the high priest. The evidence, even at this great distance in time, fits perfectly.

The Sacrificial Death

When Paul was first instructed in Christian belief, he learned that the Christ had died 'for our sins' (1 Cor. 15.3) and he passed this on to his converts in Corinth as the original faith of the church. This echoes the statement in Hebrews 9.12, that the Christ was the high priest who offered his own blood on the Day of Atonement, the greatest of all the sin-purging rites. In the actual temple rituals, the high priests had offered the blood of goats and bulls, but this was recognized as a substitute for the self-offering of the high priest himself. The belief that Jesus made the true high priestly atonement sacrifice was deeply embedded in early Christian belief. He was identified as the mysterious

Servant in the prophecies of Isaiah, the one who would 'make himself an offering for sin' (Isa. 53.10). In the temple ritual this was enacted by pouring out blood, the symbol of the life or soul, and so Isaiah's Servant Song continues 'he poured out his soul to death' (Isa. 53.12). A fragment of an early Christian text quoted by Paul in his Letter to the Philippians proves that this high priestly imagery was used by Christians from the very beginning. Jesus, he said, 'emptied himself and took the form of a servant' (Phil. 2.7), and Paul exhorted the Christians of Philippi to follow their LORD's example. When he wrote to the Christians of Rome, he expressed the same idea in a different way: 'present your bodies as a living sacrifice, holy and acceptable to God, which is your spiritual worship' (Rom. 12.1).

Until recently, the question of the sacrificial death of Jesus has been the subject of a great debate: Did Jesus really intend to sacrifice his life, or did the disciples just offer this interpretation to come to terms with the disastrous death of their leader? Those who adopted the latter view maintained that Jesus' predictions of his own death were not genuine. It was the creative mind of Mark, they said, which invented such sayings as: 'the Son of man must suffer many things, and be rejected by the elders and the chief priests and the scribes, and be killed' (Mark 8.31), and 'the Son of man came not to be served but to serve, and to give his life as a ransom for many' (Mark 10.45). The idea of a suffering Messiah was unknown before the Christian proclamation, it was said, and so the account of Jesus explaining to the disciples from the Law and the Prophets that 'it was necessary for the Messiah to suffer to enter his glory' (Luke 24.26–27) must also have been a fiction.

Such desperate and ingenious measures are not necessary. The great Isaiah scroll found at Qumran shows that at least some people in Jesus' time knew a slightly different version of the fourth Servant Song. The mysterious Servant was not 'marred beyond human semblance' (Isa. 52.14) but one who had been anointed and no longer looked like an ordinary human being. It was this transformed (perhaps transfigured?) Anointed One who was to make himself a sin offering and pour out his soul. He would then see the light (of God's glory?); another slight difference which the scroll offers at Isaiah 53.11. This must be one of the texts Jesus was expounding to his disciples on the road to Emmaus. The Qumran Melchizedek text describes the heavenly high priest coming in the last days to make this great atonement sacrifice. 'To give his life a ransom for many' (Mark 10.45) points to just such an action and there is no reason why Jesus should not have believed this about his own vocation. 'Ransom' may not be the best way to translate the Greek at this point, since the English word 'ransom' has particular associations. In the LXX of Exodus 30.12 the same word is used to describe the means whereby Israelites protected themselves from plague and in the original Hebrew, the word is one associated with atonement. Every line of enquiry leads directly to the high priesthood and the rites of atonement.

This all suggests that Jesus saw himself as the heavenly high priest Melchizedek, called by God in the last days to make the great atonement offering and thus bring judgement on evil and the renewal of the creation. Although there can be no proof of this, it is likely that Jesus originated the teaching which the disciples later proclaimed. The alternative is to suggest that he spent his whole ministry teaching something else and that his disciples invented all the ideas about being the Messiah, Son of God, and offering his life as a sacrifice. Put another way: Did Jesus know who he was and what he was doing? Or did his followers develop all these ideas after his death? This latter, unbelievable though it may seem, has in one form or another been the interpretation offered by many New Testament scholars in the twentieth century.

The Miracles

Jesus as the high priest illuminates many other aspects of the Gospels. The fourth Servant Song implies a ritual whereby the high priest absorbed sin and sickness (the ancient world did not always distinguish between these two) in order to restore his people to wholeness: 'By his knowledge shall the righteous one, my servant, make many to be accounted righteous, and he shall bear their iniquities' (Isa. 53.11). Jesus' miracles are the high-priestly work of taking away sickness or disability or uncleanness which were believed to cut people off from the community. Matthew shows this clearly: 'That evening they brought to [Jesus] many who were possessed with demons; and he cast out the spirits with a word, and healed all who were sick. This was to fulfil what was spoken by the prophet Isaiah, "He took our infirmities and bore our diseases"' (Matt. 8.16–17, quoting Isa. 53.4).

Jesus forgave sins, a claim which scandalized the Pharisees (e.g. Luke 5.21), but this too was the role of Melchizedek and was linked in the Gospel stories to acts of healing. Thus, when the paralysed man was brought to him, Jesus said first, 'Man, your sins are forgiven you', and then, after the Pharisees had accused him of blasphemy, he offered healing: 'Which is easier, to say, "Your sins are forgiven you," or to say "Rise and walk"?' (Luke 5.23). This was the role of Melchizedek, to set free from the debt of iniquities.

Jesus removed ritual impurities, restoring the excluded to full participation in the community: lepers were cleansed (e.g. Luke 5.12–14) and the bleeding woman was healed (Luke 8.42–48). The miracles described in the Gospels are not general acts of healing; Jesus did not mend broken bones. The miracles all have a ritual significance and present Jesus as the restoring high priest. Paul presents the same ideas in a different way; the work of Christ brings sinners back into the community (he uses the term 'justification') and then no supernatural powers are ever again able to separate them and cut them off (Rom. 8.38–39). The Melchizedek text predicts that the great high priest will rescue the children of light from power of Satan's spirits; Jesus exorcized and offered this as proof that the kingdom of God was already present. 'If it is by the finger of God that I cast out demons, then the kingdom of God has come upon you' (Luke 11.20).

The Worship of Jesus

The high priest was believed to be the visible presence of the LORD with his people (see pp. 34–40) and this explains why several Gospel stories recorded by a Jewish writer say that Jesus was worshipped. A Jew of that time was prepared to die rather than worship anyone but his own LORD and yet a leper knelt before Jesus to ask for healing (Matt. 8.2); a ruler of the synagogue (the other Gospels name him Jairus) knelt to ask Jesus to restore his dead daughter (Matt. 9.18); the disciples worshipped after Jesus had calmed the storm (Matt. 14.33); a Canaanite woman knelt to beg exorcism for her daughter (Matt. 15.25); and some of the disciples worshipped the resurrected LORD on the mountain in Galilee (Matt. 28.17).

The Resurrected Ones

The high priest was believed to be resurrected, by which was meant that he was an angel figure, a son of God. Jesus himself understood that resurrection was the process by which one became a son of God, an angel; '... they cannot die any more because they are equal to angels and are sons of God, being sons of the resurrection' (Luke 20.36).

Although Jesus was at this point telling the story of people resurrected after death, there was a widespread belief in first-century Palestine that some people were 'resurrected' before their physical death. Some of the Qumran Hymns tell of people who have already stood with the angels and other texts describe how humans have been transformed. Enoch was taken up in a mystical experience, set before the heavenly throne and transformed into a messenger of the Great Holy One (1 En. 14 and 71). Another Enoch text describes how he stood before the throne; 'And the LORD said to Michael, "Go, and take Enoch from his earthly clothing and anoint him with my delightful oil and put on him the clothes of my Glory". And Michael did just as the LORD had said to him. He anointed me and clothed me ... And I looked at myself and I had become like one of his glorious ones' (2 En. 22). The earthly clothing here means the earthly body and the heavenly clothing is the heavenly body. Anointing transformed Enoch into a Messiah, a Christ (that is what the word means), an angel who had been raised up into the presence of God. He was then initiated into the heavenly knowledge and sent to earth as a messenger. He had been raised up, resurrected. The story of the Transfiguration (Luke 9.28–36) describes a similar transformation, and John's Gospel is full of Jesus' claims to have heavenly knowledge: 'He who comes from above is above all ... he bears witness to what he has seen and heard (John 3.31–32).

The priest kings in Jerusalem had all been 'raised up' and declared to be sons of God and Melchizedek priests. 'You are my son, today I have begotten you' (Ps. 2.7); 'Sit at my right hand ... You are a priest for ever after the order of Melchizedek' (Ps. 110.1, 4) described a mystical ascent, and these were the texts used by the first Christians to describe Jesus' resurrection; this is how they must have understood it. The texts which speak of resuscitation of dead bodies, texts such as Isaiah 26.19: 'Thy dead shall live, their bodies shall rise', are not used in the New Testament.

There was a widespread belief in the early church that Jesus had given his most important teaching after his resurrection. Eusebius, writing early in the fourth century, quoted from a lost work of Clement of Alexandria: 'James the Righteous, John and Peter were entrusted by the LORD after his resurrection with the higher knowledge. They imparted it to the other apostles and the other apostles to the seventy, one of whom was Barnabas' (Eusebius, *History* 2.1). Many of the so-called gnostic texts claim to record this higher teaching. The *Apocryphon of James,* for example, perhaps written early in the second century, takes the form of a letter written by James the Righteous: 'You asked me to send you the secret teaching which was revealed to me and Peter by the LORD ...' It goes on to describe how the LORD appeared to them 550 days after his resurrection. Peter and James ascended to heaven with the LORD where they saw the angelic hosts but were not permitted to ascend to the heavenly throne itself.

There are many texts which describe post-resurrection teaching and the heavenly ascent of the inner circle of disciples. Eusebius knew of many who had received such revelations: 'Paul ... committed nothing to writing but his very short epistles; and yet he had countless unutterable things to say, for he had reached the vision of the third heaven, had been caught up to the divine Paradise itself and had been privileged to hear there unspeakable words. Similar experiences were enjoyed by the rest of the Saviour's pupils ... the twelve apostles, the seventy disciples and countless others' (*History* 3.24). What has happened to all these experiences? There must be a major element of early Christianity missing from our usual picture of its origins.

There are hints of such an experience in the early baptism hymns known as the *Odes of Solomon.* A speaker, presumed to be Christ, practises mystical ascent.

[The Spirit] brought me forth before the LORD's face
and because I was the Son of Man
I was named the Light, the Son of God;
Because I was the most glorious among the glorious ones,
And the greatest among the great ones ...
He anointed me with his perfection
And I became one of those who are near him. (*Ode* 36)

Baptism was associated with the mystical experience of heavenly ascent, and traces of Jesus's own baptism experience of ascent are still discernible in Revelation 12. The tradition of post-resurrection teaching is in fact a memory of the secret teaching Jesus gave to his disciples, the inner group who knew that Jesus' personal experience of resurrection had been his baptism when he saw the heavens open and heard the voice saying 'You are my Son' (Luke 3.22).

Once we are alerted to this way of reading the New Testament, several familiar texts acquire a new significance. Who, for example, were the teachers whom Jesus met in the temple when he was twelve years old (Luke 2.46–47)? Memories of the temple preserved in the (much later) *Hekhalot Rabbati* (#225–28) describe mystics who contemplated the *merkavah*, the chariot throne of God. They lived in Jerusalem and practised in the temple, with their closest disciples forming an inner group and others listening at a distance. There are several anachronisms in the account (rabbis named who lived at a much later date), but there must have been some foundation for the story. Rabbi Neḥunyah ben Ha-Qanah, we are told, used to sit 'expounding all the matter of the Merkavah, the descent and the ascent, how one descends unto and how one ascends from the [Merkavah]'. It would be tempting to read Luke's story about Jesus and the temple teachers as one of Mary's memories, significant not because the young Jesus was missing for a while, but because this was his first contact with the mystics. Nor must we forget that the priest Zechariah, the father of John the Baptist, had an angel speak to him in the temple (Luke 1.11–20).

The priests and their tradition passed into the young church; a number were 'obedient to the faith' (Acts 6.7). John, the beloved disciple, one of the three disciples especially associated with the secret tradition, was 'known to the high priest' (John 18.15). He himself later became a 'priest wearing the [high priest's] *petalon*' (Eusebius, *History* 3.31). This astonishing statement must mean that John had the role of high priest in the church, which might explain why he was entrusted with the secret tradition recorded in the Book of Revelation. James the Righteous (not James son of Zebedee, who was killed by Herod, Acts 12.2), was the first bishop of the Jerusalem Church. He wore priestly robes of linen and used to enter the holy of holies alone to pray for the forgiveness of the people's sins (Eusebius, *History* 2.23). This is immediately recognizable as the role of the high priest on the Day of Atonement, and yet James was the bishop of the Jerusalem Church. Eusebius drew this information from Hegesippus, a second-generation Christian, and it is almost certainly accurate. (Epiphanius, using the same source, says that James, like John, wore the *petalon*. *Pan.* 1.29.4.) Eusebius also quoted Hegesippus' account of the martyrdom of James. Having testified to a crowd in the temple courts that Jesus was the Son of Man, sitting in heaven and about to return on the clouds of heaven, some of his hearers climbed onto the temple parapet where he was standing and threw him down to his death. The Roman devastation of

Jerusalem, which soon followed, was believed to be divine punishment for his murder (*History* 2.23). A group of native Palestinian Christians who called themselves the Ebionites, the Poor, used a book called the *Ascents of James*. Nothing more is known of it, but, if James had been a high priest, it is yet another indication of their being guardians of the mystical tradition.

Jesus the Great High Priest, the Resurrected One who had stood before the divine throne and learned the secrets of heaven, passed on to his chosen disciples what he had seen. As the Anointed One he would make the great atonement sacrifice and then return on the Day of the LORD as the judge of all who were living on the earth. This explains the urgency of the prophecies, and this is why the last book of the New Testament opens with the words: *The Revelation of Jesus Christ which God gave him to show to his servants what must soon take place.*

2

THE TEMPLE

In the fourth year of his reign, Solomon began to build the house of the
LORD (1 Kgs 6.1) and it took seven years to complete the work (1 Kgs
6.38). In 950 BCE, or thereabouts, the temple was consecrated and the
Glory of the LORD filled the house (1 Kgs 8.11). This temple, attacked
and looted many times, destroyed by the Babylonians and then rebuilt,
dominated the city of Jerusalem for a thousand years and was the heart
of Israel's life and worship. Even after the second destruction in 70 CE
its memory and its symbolism continued to shape the thought of both
Judaism and Christianity, the two religions to which it gave birth.

The Building

In the Hebrew Scriptures there are two accounts of how Solomon built
the temple (1 Kgs 6–7; 2 Chron. 2–5). They differ slightly but between
them give a good picture of what it looked like. There are also two long
descriptions of the tabernacle Moses had built in the desert (Exod.
25–31; 35–40) and there is Ezekiel's vision of the new temple (Ezek.
40–43). Since he had been a priest in the temple before the Babylonians
destroyed it, his vision probably included memories of the original
building. Nobody knows how the pattern of the desert tabernacle and
that of Solomon's temple related to each other. Clearly they were
similar, the temple being simply a larger version of the tabernacle. It is
possible that those who compiled the final form of Exodus allowed their
own memories of the temple to colour what they said of the tabernacle,
but in essentials they were the same. Aristeas, an Egyptian Jew who
visited Jerusalem in the second century BCE, left a description of the
temple, but a disproportionate amount of it is devoted to its plumbing
which seems to have fascinated him (*Aristeas* 83–99). There is the
Temple Scroll found at Qumran, which describes an ideal temple to be
built in Jerusalem, and there are passages in the visions of *1 Enoch*
which clearly have the temple as their setting. Josephus described the
temple he knew in the middle of the first century CE as a huge structure
of marble and gold, recently rebuilt by Herod the Great and adorned
with gifts from foreign rulers (*War* 5.184–227). These caused great
controversy (*War* 2.411–13), and in the Book of Revelation the temple
was described as a harlot.

Solomon's temple was rectangular, 20 cubits wide and 70 long, that
is about 10 metres by 35. Compared to the great cathedrals built in
medieval Europe, it was quite small. The building itself was surrounded
by courtyards, originally just an inner and an outer courtyard but these
were altered over the years. The outer court of Ezekiel's temple, for
example, was 500 cubits square (Ezek. 42.15–20) and there was an

inner court 100 cubits square (Ezek. 40.47). The court envisaged by the Temple Scroll was 1600 cubits square, about half a mile! Whatever their dimensions, the courtyards in both real and ideal temples had a similar meaning. They indicated degrees of holiness and, because the temple was built on a hill, the holier the place, the higher it was situated. These degrees of holiness culminated in the temple building itself, where only priests could enter after ritual washings, and the holy of holies where only the high priest could go once a year, after elaborate purification.

The temple building was divided into three areas: at the eastern end was a porch, ten cubits deep, then the *hekal*, the great hall, which was 40 cubits deep, and finally, at the western end, the *d^{e}bir*, the holy of holies which was a perfect cube of 20 cubits (1 Kgs 6.20). This perfect cube is important for understanding Revelation 21.16, where the entire heavenly city becomes one great holy of holies for the redeemed, the new high priesthood, and is therefore described as a perfect cube. In the older translations of the Bible (AV, RV), *d^{e}bir* used to be rendered 'oracle' on the assumption that it derived from *dbr*, speak. Most examples in the LXX simply transliterate the word as *dabeir* and both Aquila and Symmachus understood it to mean oracle. Modern scholarship now favours the meaning 'inner or hinder place', but the role of the *d^{e}bir* as the place of oracles, where the voice of the LORD was heard, gives powerful support to the traditional view. The *Lives of the Prophets*, a collection of legends compiled perhaps in the first century CE, shows what was believed about ancient *d^{e}bir*, since the murder of Zechariah the priest at the end of the ninth century, the priests no longer saw visions of angels or gave oracles there, nor could they enquire the LORD's will by the ephod and the sacred stones (*Lives* 23). The *d^{e}bir* was often described as a tower or high place, perhaps because it was raised slightly higher than the rest of the temple. Various words are used to describe it, e.g. tower or watchtower, and it was the place where the prophets stood to receive visions (e.g. Hab. 2.1). This may be why the Book of Revelation describes the temple as 'the temple of the tent of witness'. When this phrase occurs in Exodus 40.2, 6, 29 it is usually understood to mean 'the tent of meeting', but the LXX and the Book of Revelation thought otherwise (see p. 266). *It was the place where visions were seen.*

Between the great hall and the holy of holies was a curtain woven of blue, purple and scarlet thread and fine white linen, 'separating the holy place from the most holy' (Exod. 26.31–33). It was decorated with cherubim. Behind the curtain in the tabernacle was the ark of the covenant, the box of acacia wood covered in gold which had been made to carry the tablets of the ten commandments (Exod. 25.10–16). Over it was a thick slab of gold, the *kapporet*, often translated *the mercy seat*, but the name probably meant 'place of atonement'. The holy of holies is called 'the house of the *kapporet*' (1 Chron. 28.11) indicating that this was the most important item in the holy of holies. At each end of the *kapporet* was a golden cherub, the two facing each other with wings stretched out over the *kapporet*. This was the place of the LORD's presence; where Moses heard the voice of God: '. . . from above the *kapporet*, from between the two cherubim that are upon the ark of the testimony, there I will speak with you' (Exod. 25.22). In the tabernacle, the *kapporet* had been the throne. In the temple, the cherubim had been different; behind the curtain had stood two giant cherubim, carved from olive wood and covered in gold (1 Kgs 6.23–28). They stood side by side, facing down into the great hall, their outstretched wings reaching across the whole width of the holy of holies and covering the ark of the covenant. Together they formed a chariot throne (1 Chron. 28.18), which Isaiah saw in his vision as the throne of the LORD (Isa. 6.1). The LORD was 'enthroned above the cherubim' (Isa. 37.16) and this was where the king sat when he was enthroned on the throne of the LORD (1 Chron. 29.23).

Little else is known of the holy of holies; it was lined with pure gold and had upper chambers, also overlaid with gold. These upper chambers may account for the difference in height between the holy of holies (20 cubits) and the rest of the temple building (30 cubits). The holy of holies was built over the great rock where King David saw the angel of the LORD standing between earth and heaven with a drawn sword in his hand (1 Chron. 21.16 and 22.1). One account says the rock protruded through the floor of the holy of holies to the breadth of three fingers and the high priest rested the incense burner there while he sprinkled the blood on the Day of Atonement (*m. Yoma* 5.2)

The interior of the great hall in Solomon's temple was lined with cedar wood overlaid with gold (1 Kgs 6.21–22) and the walls of both great hall and holy of holies were decorated with carved figures of cherubim, palm trees and open flowers (1 Kgs 6.29). The description in 2 Chronicles 3.5–7 adds that the walls were inlaid with precious stones. The great hall was in fact a jewelled garden where the angels lived, and in Enoch's vision there were stars on its ceiling. The great hall was furnished with a small golden incense altar, which stood in front of the curtain, a table for the bread of the presence and ten golden lamps (1 Kgs 7.48–50). The other account mentions an incense altar, *ten* tables for bread and ten lamps (2 Chron. 4.7, 8, 19). The greatest detail, albeit slightly different, is found in the account of the desert tabernacle where there was a table of acacia wood overlaid with gold, *one* seven-branched lampstand of pure gold made to represent an almond tree, and an incense altar, also of acacia wood overlaid with gold (Exod. 37.10–28). The table stood on the north side of the tabernacle and the lampstand on the south (Exod. 40.22–24).

The furnishings of the temple interior were made of gold, but outside in the courtyard they were made of bronze. Two bronze pillars stood before the entrance of the temple. They were named Jachin and Boaz, but nobody knows why (1 Kgs 7.15–20). To the south-east of the temple, in the innermost courtyard, stood the bronze sea, an enormous basin supported on twelve bronze oxen. Ten cubits across, it was half as wide as the temple itself (1 Kgs 7.23–26), and held water for ritual washings (2 Chron. 4.6). Such an enormous vessel must have had a ritual significance and its name suggests it was the sea which appeared in the visions of the Man. Daniel saw the great sea from which the monsters emerged (Dan. 7.2–3), and 'Ezra' saw the Man, the Son of the Most High, rise from the sea and then fly on clouds (2 *Esdr*.13.3, 32). The bronze sea was probably used in the royal rituals which enacted the visions of the Man. There were also ten smaller bronze lavers for washing the sacrificial offerings, five on each side of the court (1 Kgs 7.38).

In front of the temple was the altar of burnt offerings. At some periods it was made of bronze (2 Kgs 16.10–16), but the tradition is that it was made of unhewn stones (Exod. 20.25), and there was certainly a stone altar in the second temple. Josephus says it was 15 cubits high and 50 cubits square (*War* 5.225), in other words a stone structure 25 metres square and 7.5 metres high. There was a ramp on the southern side so that the priests could walk up to the top with the offerings. Other accounts say that it was a stepped pyramid of three stages, the area for the altar fire being 24 cubits, i.e. 12 metres, square (*m. Middoth* 3.1). Beneath the altar was a great pit where the libations of blood, water and wine flowed away.

The outermost court of the second temple was open even to Gentiles, the second area was the furthest that women were allowed. Beyond this was a small area for men, separated by a low stone partition from the inner court of the priests. Aristeas described the plumbing of the temple courts which was an elaborate system of water outlets at the base of the great altar, to wash away the blood. The strength of the priests also impressed him, as they threw large sacrificial offerings with absolute accuracy into the altar fire. They worked, he said, in complete silence, with reverence and 'in a way worthy of the great God' (*Aristeas* 96).

King Josiah's Purge

The story of the temple and its priests is one of conflict and rivalry. The accounts of the temple in the Hebrew Scriptures give one point of view, but the accounts in other ancient texts tell a very different story.

The text which most closely resembles the Book of Revelation is *1 Enoch*. Embedded in it are fragments of older texts, two of which form a stylized history of Israel, the *Apocalypse of Weeks* (*1 En.* 91.12–17; 93.1–10). Each period of history is a 'week': in the fifth 'week' the temple was built, 'the house of glory and dominion', and in the sixth 'week', those who lived in the temple *became blind* and *forsook Wisdom*, and then the temple was burned. The seventh week, when the temple was rebuilt, was a time of apostasy. Another alternative history in *1 Enoch* describes the second temple as a place of polluted and impure offerings, a place of blinded sheep (*1 En.* 89.73–74). This period of blindness, pollution and apostasy is described in conventional accounts of the period as 'King Josiah's Reform'! To understand the Book of Revelation it is important to keep in mind this other view of the temple, that it had become a place of polluted apostates. The true temple had been the first temple, a place of vision and Wisdom.

In the Hebrew Scriptures there are two broadly similar accounts of this period of change, one in 2 Kings and the other in 2 Chronicles. The first 'reformer' of the temple was King Hezekiah, (715–687 BCE), who broke up a bronze serpent which had been an object of worship, presumably in the temple (2 Kgs 18.4), and reacted violently against the ways of his father King Ahaz. He removed the high places with their pillars and sacred trees, and had the priests and Levites purify the temple and take out all the 'uncleanness' (2 Chron. 29.16). The biblical writer says 'He did right in the eyes of the LORD' (2 Kgs 18.3), but a contemporary observer sought to demoralize the people of Jerusalem by warning that their LORD would no longer protect them because the king had destroyed his high places and altars (Isa. 36.7). The LORD 'forsook their house and their tower' (*1 En.* 89.56) and left them to the seventy angels of the nations (see p. 226).

Half a century later there was another 'reform', when King Josiah (640–609 BCE) began to restore the temple and made major changes after an old 'book of the covenant' came to light (2 Kgs 23.1–14). All the temple vessels associated with Baal, the goddess or the angels were removed. Priests who had burned incense at high places to the sun, the moon, the stars and host of heaven, i.e. to the angels, were deposed. The sacred tree symbol of the goddess was removed and burnt, and the places where the women wove robes for her were broken down. The king also removed horses and chariots dedicated to the sun and the roof altars of the upper chamber.

The purge, however, was not effective. The priest-prophet Ezekiel visited the temple on a spirit journey in 591 BCE (Ezek. 8.1–18) and described the image of the goddess in its place by the north gate, seventy elders burning incense in rooms painted with 'creeping things and loathsome beasts', and men facing east to worship the rising sun. Ezekiel warned that such worship would bring punishment from the LORD and this was his explanation of the disaster in 586 BCE. Jeremiah, another prophet of the period, records a different point of view. He travelled to Egypt, perhaps with refugees, and heard them blaming the disaster on neglect of the goddess. 'Since we left off burning incense to the queen of heaven and pouring out libations to her, we have lacked everything and have been consumed by the sword and by famine' (Jer. 44.18). In these conflicting accounts we see the situation to which *1 Enoch* bears witness; a bitter division over what was acceptable in the temple. *What was 'reform' to some was blindness and folly to others.*

The 'reformers' left their mark in the Book of Deuteronomy. Their Moses described how Israel was to worship: their Wisdom was to be the Law, they saw no form of the LORD at Sinai but heard only his voice, they saw no storm as the LORD appeared, only fire, they were to make no graven images and were to have no dealings with the host of heaven (Deut. 4.6–19). Nor were they to enquire after secret things which belonged only to the LORD (Deut. 29.29). Their duty was to obey the commandments brought down from Sinai and not to seek someone who would ascend to heaven for them to discover remote and hidden things (Deut. 30.11).

What Deuteronomy forbad and what the 'reformers' removed is what exactly appears in works such as the Book of Revelation and 1 Enoch. These tell how certain chosen people ascended to heaven to learn secret things from the LORD, they tell of angels who were the host of heaven, and of the cherubim who were the graven images at the very heart of the temple in the holy of holies. Above all, they keep an honoured place for the goddess, Wisdom, and they describe visions of the LORD on the heavenly throne.

We can only conclude that a great deal of information about the first temple has been deliberately suppressed. Evidence survives in such texts as escaped the reformers and this shows that *where the Book of Revelation seems bizarre and alien to the biblical world, this is not proof of a late pagan influence but rather evidence that Israel's older faith had survived.*

The Symbolism

When Moses was on Sinai, he was given the ten commandments and then told to build a tabernacle after the pattern or archetype he had been shown on the mountain (Exod. 25.40). It is possible that Moses had seen a vision of a heavenly temple which he had to copy on earth, but most indications are that he saw a vision of the whole creation, and this is what the tabernacle and temple were to replicate. There is a similar tradition about King David and the temple; he gave his son Solomon a detailed plan of the temple which had to be built: 'all this he made clear by the writing from the hand of the LORD concerning it, all the work to be done according to the plan' (1 Chron. 28.19). It is well known that the later storytellers made Moses more king-like when there were no more kings in Jerusalem. Receiving the plan of the tabernacle/temple may well be an early example of this tendency.

Cosmas Indicopleustus, so called because he had travelled as far as India, lived in Egypt in the sixth century CE. He wrote a book, *A Christian Topography*, in which he argued that the creation was rectangular and constructed like a huge tent, and he reached this conclusion after careful study of the Scriptures. Moses, he said, had been commanded by God to build the tabernacle as a copy of the whole creation which he had been shown in a vision: 'When Moses had come down from the mountain, he was ordered by God to make the Tabernacle, which was a representation of what he had seen on the mountain, namely an impress of the whole world . . .' The creation Moses had seen was divided into two parts:

Since therefore it had been shown him how God made the heaven and the earth, and how on the second day he made the firmament in the middle between them, and thus made the one place into two places, so Moses, in like manner, in accordance with the pattern which he had seen, made the tabernacle and placed the veil in the middle and by this division made the one Tabernacle into two, an inner and an outer. (2.35)

This simple statement is the key to understanding the world of the temple and the apocalypses which were the writings of the temple mystics. Part of the creation was not visible but was concealed behind a curtain. The few who were able to pass beyond the curtain were able to give a revelation (that is what apocalypse means) of what they had seen and heard there.

Cosmas went on to explain that the outer part of the tabernacle represented the visible world and that the sacred objects placed in it symbolized aspects of that world. There was a golden table where loaves of bread were offered, representing the fruits of the earth, and a seven-branched lampstand representing what he called 'the lights of heaven'. Cosmas did not invent this view; it originated in remote antiquity and its importance lies not so much in his description of the shape of the world as in its implications for understanding how the heirs to the temple tradition imagined the spiritual and material worlds to be related. The divine was present in the creation but concealed behind a curtain. 'Let them make me a sanctuary that I may dwell in their midst' (Exod. 25.8). The same temple imagery appears in a much older text, the *Clementine Recognitions*. 'In the beginning, when God made the heaven and the earth as one house ... he divided into two portions that fabric of the universe, although it was but one house ... that the upper portion might afford a dwelling place to angels and the lower to men' (*Clem. Rec.* 1.27).

Other sources also suggest that what Moses saw on Sinai was not a vision of the heavenly temple but a vision of heaven and earth. An ancient version of Genesis which has survived in the Scriptures of the Ethiopian Church, the *Book of Jubilees*, says that Moses on Sinai was told to record the six days of the creation, including the details of Day One which are omitted from the account in Genesis (*Jub.* 2.1–3). The seven works of the first day, which can be deduced from Genesis 1.1–5 were the heaven and the earth, the waters, the angels, the abyss, darkness and light. This cannot have been ordinary darkness and light, since the sun had not been created, but *the cosmic light and darkness*. The Mishnah says that this part of the creation story was forbidden for public reading as was Ezekiel's description of the chariot throne. 'The story of the creation may not be expounded before two persons nor the chariot before one alone, unless he be a wise man who understands of his own knowledge. Whoever gives his mind to four things: what is above, what is beneath, what is before time and what will be hereafter, ... it were better he had not come into the world ... (*m. Ḥagigah* 2.1).

Thus the works of Day One, i.e. the secrets of the creation, the angels of heaven and the chariot throne of God, were all part of the hidden world, and when Moses was commanded to reproduce what he saw in the form of the tabernacle, he had to conceal the works of Day One behind a curtain. The holy of holies in the tabernacle represented eternity within the creation, and those who entered the world of the holy of holies could know both past and future. This is why the history incorporated in apocalyptic writings records both past and future events. In *Jubilees* the angel of the presence wrote for Moses all the future history of his people that was being revealed to him on Sinai (*Jub.* 1.27). The events depicted in the Book of Revelation, then, are not all predictions of the future; some describe the time of the myths which is the eternal present and some describe the past. The Mishnah which forbad knowledge of the creation and knowledge of the chariot throne also forbad enquiring into what was above and below, what was past and future because these also belonged to the world beyond the veil, beyond time.

Nowhere in the Hebrew Scriptures does it say in so many words that the tabernacle represented the creation, with the veil separating the visible world of time and matter from the hidden world beyond. The evidence, however, points that way. Consider the words of Isaiah:

Have you not known? Have you not heard?
Has it not been told you from the beginning?
Have you not understood from the foundations of the earth?
It is he who sits above the circle of the earth,
and its inhabitants are like grasshoppers;
who stretches out the heavens like a curtain,
and spreads them like a tent to dwell in;
who brings princes to naught,
and makes the rulers of the earth as nothing. (Isa. 40.21–23)

This is the language of one who had entered the holy of holies. He had witnessed the creation and the foundation of the earth ('told you from the beginning', i.e. on Day One), he had seen the heavens as a curtain (or perhaps the curtain as the heavens) and he knew that those in the holy of holies saw a panorama of history before them, seeing princes and rulers deposed. These words were written in the sixth century BCE, during the exile and before the second temple was built. *They must be the tradition of the first temple.*

When Moses received the instructions to build the tabernacle, it was to be done, like the original creation which he had seen, in six days. On the seventh day the people were to rest because in six days the Lord made heaven and earth (Exod. 31.17). A short account of building the tabernacle appears in Exodus 40.17–32, and if we compare this with the account of the creation in Genesis 1, bearing in mind that both passages probably passed through the hands of editors and reformers, remarkable similarities are still apparent.

Like God at creation, the people began to build the tabernacle on the first day of the year. On Day One was created the basic structure of heaven and earth, waters, abyss, light, darkness and heavenly powers; on the first day of building, the frame and covering of the tabernacle were set up, establishing the basic structure. On the second day, the firmament was created and in the tabernacle the ark was screened from view by the veil. By implication, the ark and the veil represented heaven, just as Cosmas said several centuries later. On the third day, God created the dry land and its vegetation (Gen. 1.9–13; *Jub.* 2.7 says he created the Garden of Eden), and in the tabernacle a table was set up in the outer area where bread, the fruit of the earth, was offered. On the fourth day, the LORD created the sun, moon and stars (Gen. 1.14–19), and the seven-branched lampstand was set in the tabernacle which the people knew was a symbol of the sun, moon and planets (Philo, *On Gen.* I.10). After this point the pattern is not so clear, but there can be little doubt that the whole creation had a heavenly archetype and that both were represented in microcosm in the temple and tabernacle. The human, Adam, created on the sixth day, was the high priest.

The rituals of the temple were creation rituals, renewing and sustaining, replicating on earth the divine reality of heaven. Some of the hymns discovered at Qumran confirmed what had been suspected for some time: the priests in the temple were the counterparts of the angels and the high priest was the image of the LORD on earth.

The Veil of the Temple

In order to appreciate the temple setting of the Book of Revelation, it is necessary to look in more detail at one aspect of the symbolism: the veil which Moses set in place on the second day, corresponding to the screening of the ark, the sign of God's presence. The veil marked the boundary between earth and heaven, between visible and invisible worlds. Woven from red, blue and purple thread (probably wool) and white linen, the fabric symbolized the weaving together of the four elements from which the creation was formed: blue for the air, red for fire, purple, made from seashells, for water, and linen, which was a plant, for earth. Josephus, who wrote at the end of the first century CE, knew the significance of the colours, and he also revealed that the cherubim embroidered on the veil were 'a panorama of the heavens' (*War* 5.212–13). Philo, his older contemporary, knew a similar tradition about the colours and fibres; the veil which screened God's presence represented matter. 'It is right, he said, that the divine temple of the creator of all things should be woven of such and so many things as the world itself was made of, the world being the universal temple which existed before the holy temple was constructed' (*On Exod.* II.85).

Those who passed through the veil passed beyond the limitations it represented; they passed beyond space and time into eternity, the place beyond. The Hebrew word for conceal, *'alam,* is closely related to this word for eternity, *'olam*, which in fact means antiquity and futurity as well as continuous existence. The mystic beyond the veil made contact with the timeless concealed place, and the veil filtered out from his perception the dimensions of time and place. When Luke records that Jesus was shown 'all the kingdoms of the world in a moment of time' (Luke 4.5), this indicates a similar experience.

From the enigmatic writings which describe passing through the veil we are able to glimpse something of the spiritual world of the temple. *1 Enoch* is an anthology of these texts from many periods, although none can be dated with certainty. *1 Enoch* 14, thought to be among the oldest, told how Enoch was swept upwards into heaven, which he described as a great house surrounded by tongues of fire. Within the house was a second house whose floor and ceiling were made of fire, and in it was a great cherub throne. The Great Glory sat there, and so great was the splendour that even angels could not enter. The LORD summoned Enoch to enter where angels could not go, and there he heard the LORD speak to him. For Enoch, the holy of holies came alive, and he became a part of that world.

The Songs of Sabbath Sacrifice (4Q400–407; 11Q17) found at Qumran and at Masada give a similar picture. Like *1 Enoch*, they cannot be dated, so it would be unwise to suggest that their picture of the temple is a late development. Masada was a Zealot stronghold (*War* 2.447) and the texts found there presumably belonged to those committed to the purity of the temple. The Songs depict beings called 'the gods' and their worship in the holy of holies before the throne. They are 'luminous spirits, spirits of mingled colours, figures of the shapes of divine beings engraved ... glorious images' (4Q405). Even the fragmentary state of the texts cannot obscure what these hymns are describing; the holy of holies come alive, and the angels worshipping the LORD on his heavenly throne.

Nobody can date any of these texts with confidence, but the experience they describe is clearly that of Isaiah 6, which dates from 742 BCE, some thirty years before Hezekiah's 'reform'. 'In the year that King Uzziah died, I saw the Lord, sitting upon a throne high and lifted up and his train filled the temple. Above him stood the seraphim; each had six wings: with two he covered his face, and with two he covered his feet, and with two he flew. And one called to another and said: "Holy, holy, holy is the LORD of hosts; the whole earth is full of his glory" (Isa. 6.1–3). Isaiah had a temple vision. He saw beyond the veil because he saw the throne and the angels. The creatures of the holy of holies had come alive, and Isaiah became part of their world. One of the seraphim touched his mouth with a burning coal from the incense altar and Isaiah became their messenger, their angel.

Those who were able to pass through the veil passed beyond the limits of the material world. Since only the high priest was permitted to enter the holy of holies, this suggests a high priestly tradition. Early Christian writers confirm that this was so with Jesus. Ignatius, Bishop of Antioch early in the second century CE, wrote: 'Our own high priest ... has been entrusted with the holy of holies and to him alone are the secret things of God committed' (*Phil.* 9). Clement of Alexandria, writing at the end of the second century CE, also used significant imagery: 'those who have the truth enter in through the tradition of the LORD by drawing aside the curtain' (*Misc.* 7.17).

The mystics were conscious that they had passed beyond the limits of ordinary experience and therefore of human language. Sometimes the temple texts contain lists of words which make no sense at all, or long lists of superlatives to describe the presence of the LORD. Sometimes they used what seem to be contradictions. When Enoch entered the holy place, for example, he could not adequately describe the sensation: 'I entered that house and it was hot as fire and cold as ice' (*1 En.* 14.13). Daniel saw in his vision a river flowing from the throne which he describes as a stream of fire, yet other mystics said it was water. One of the hymns found at Qumran has it both ways: 'a fountain' ... but 'of bright flames' (1QH XIV formerly VI). The holy of holies beyond the veil must have been a place of complete darkness, and yet the visionaries entered a place of intense brightness and flaming fire. 'None of the angels could enter by reason of the magnificence and the Glory and no flesh could behold him' (*1 En.* 14.21). Perhaps the most familiar of these opposites is the story of the creation of humans. God, a plural noun in Hebrew, in the heavenly holy of holies decided to create a human image to be the high priest (Gen. 1.27), and yet to realize this on earth, i.e. outside the veil, two people had to be made, a male and a female. The high priest, the male who represented the male-female LORD-and-Wisdom, had to be married, and if his wife died, he had to marry again before entering the holy of holies (*m. Yoma* 1. 1).

The brightness of the holy of holies was the light of Day One, before the visible world had been created. This was not the light of the sun, which was not created until the fourth day, but the light of the Glory. Those who entered the holy of holies entered this place of light, beyond time and matter, which was the presence of 'the King of kings and LORD of lords who alone has immortality and dwells in unapproachable light' (1 Tim. 6.16). This was the place of glory to which Jesus knew he would return after the crucifixion, 'the glory which I had with thee before the world was made' (John 17.5). In the *Gospel of Thomas*, Christians are described as the new high priesthood who enter the light, and Jesus instructed his disciples to say to the guardians (the cherub guardians of Eden?) 'We came from the light, the place where the light came into being on its own accord and established itself ...' (*Thomas* 50). Everything in the holy of holies was radiant with this light. Gnostic texts later described it as a place with no shadows 'because the immeasurable light is everywhere within it' (CG II.5, OOW 98); ... 'the whole kingdom of Son of Man, the one who is called Son of God ... full of ineffable and shadowless joy and unchanging jubilation because they rejoice over his imperishable glory' (CG III.4, *Wisdom* 105).

Those who entered were transfigured and wore the bright robes of angels. These garments of glory were the resurrection body, part of the world beyond time and matter which was sometimes visible to those outside the veil. Philo described these two worlds when he explained the significance of the two accounts of creation in Genesis 1–3. They were not duplicates, as modern scholars suggest, but accounts of the two processes of creation. The first described the creation of the incorporeal and invisible world and the second, the visible, material world. 'When God willed to create this visible world, he first fully formed the intelligible world in order that he might have the use of a pattern wholly God-like and incorporeal in producing the material world as a later creation, the very image of the earlier' (*Creation* 16). This was a world of invisible light (*Creation* 31). He understood Genesis 2.4–5 to refer to this first creation:

This is the book of the genesis* of heaven and earth, when they came into being, in the day in which God made the heaven and the earth and every herb of the field before it appeared on the earth, and all the grass of the field before it sprang up. Is he not manifestly describing the incorporeal ideas present only in the mind by which, as by seals, the finished objects that meet our senses were moulded? (*Creation* 129)

Philo's is the most obvious and literal way to understand both the Hebrew and the Greek text, but it has been discounted on the grounds he must have been retelling the stories in terms of Plato's forms, the creation of an invisible world before the visible, material world was made. It is said that this could not possibly have been what the writer of Genesis actually intended. Philo's system, however, was not drawn from Plato but from the ancient priestly traditions of Israel (he was himself of a priestly family), and his exposition of the creation stories is entirely in accord with the ancient belief that Moses saw the creation in his vision on Sinai and replicated this on earth when he built the tabernacle. There were two Jerusalems, the heavenly and the earthly, and in the Book of Revelation it was the heavenly Jerusalem that was the home of the first-resurrected (see pp. 338–43).

Just as there were two creations, so there were two bodies for each human being. The one described in the second story, formed 'from the dust of the ground' (Gen. 2.7) was 'vastly different' from the one in the first story, made 'in the image' of God (*Creation* 134). The one from the dust was body, *soma,* and soul, *psuche,* man or woman, and by nature mortal. The one 'after the image' was incorporeal, neither male nor female and incorruptible. These two are described elsewhere as the two Adams, the heavenly, 'made after the image and without part or lot

---

*The Hebrew here can mean *the genealogies* and so the LXX *book of the genesis* is a literal translation.

in corruptible or terrestrial substance', and the earthly one made of clay (*All. Int.* I.31). When Paul contrasts the physical body and the spiritual body he uses this terminology. The physical body, *soma psuchikon*, is raised as a spiritual body, *soma pneumatikon*. In other words, the resurrection body is the body of the first creation, incorporeal, invisible, made after the image and incorruptible (1 Cor. 15.42–50). It is neither male nor female, just as Paul elsewhere described those who are baptized into Christ (Gal. 3.28).

The language of the holy of holies was characteristic of John's writing; John's Jesus taught that only those who are born again/ born from above, i.e resurrected, can see or enter the Kingdom (John 3.3–5). In the prologue to the Gospel he wrote of the light of Day One coming into the world when the Word was made flesh (John 1.1–14), in the first letter he contrasted the ways of light and darkness (1 John 1.5–7), and in the Book of Revelation he described the heavenly city as a place where no light was needed because it was one huge holy of holies whose light was the presence of the LORD (22.4–5) and whose citizens were the first-resurrected (20.4–6). It was the heavenly city which had become visible (see p. 317).

Sometimes the temple mystics used the language of forms ('likenesses'), but this had been their way of speaking long before it was adopted by Plato in the fourth century BCE. Ezekiel, a priest in the early sixth century BCE, spoke of 'the likeness of a throne, in appearance like sapphire; and seated above the likeness of a throne was a likeness as it were of a human form. And upward from what had the appearance of his loins I saw as it were gleaming bronze, like the appearance of fire ... Such was the appearance of the likeness of the glory of the LORD' (Ezek. 1.26–28). In Revelation, the figure on the heavenly throne was described as 'like jasper and carnelian' and round the throne there was a rainbow 'like an emerald' (4.3). Each form had an earthly counterpart: the LORD on his throne was the high priest, the heavenly host were the priests. 'On earth as it is in heaven' best describes this world view. When heaven and earth were not in harmony, demonic distortion threatened the cosmos and this is why the visionaries so often used a pattern of type and antitype. The Christ and the antichrist are the best known examples of this in the Book of Revelation, but there are many more (see pp. 230–1).

Rabbi Ishmael, a famous Palestinian scholar, was often called 'R. Ishmael the high priest' even though he lived after the temple had been destroyed by the Romans and could never have served as a high priest. To him is attributed a whole collection of remarkable texts (known as Merkavah, that is Chariot, texts) describing what he saw when he stood beyond the veil and before the chariot throne, and what he saw on the veil itself. He met the great angel Metatron who became his guide: 'Metatron said to me: Come I will show you the veil of the All Present One, which is spread before the Holy One, Blessed be He, and on which are printed all the generations of the world and all their deeds whether done or not yet done, until the last generation. I went with him and he pointed them out to me with his fingers, like a father teaching his son ...' (3 *En.* 45). R. Ishmael had passed beyond time and he saw the veil of the temple from the other side, so to speak. It appeared to him as a vast picture of everything past, present and future, a panoramic history of his people. Moses too, it was believed in the first century CE, was shown on Mount Sinai 'wondrous things and the secrets of the times and the ends of all things' (2 *Esdr.* 14.5).

Those who entered eternity became wise. One of the recurring themes of temple texts is that the mystic acquired all knowledge, often listed as a summary of the scientific knowledge of the day, but just occasionally we glimpse the older temple lore and the forbidden accounts of Day One before there was time and matter. When Enoch entered heaven, God revealed to him the great secrets: 'Before anything existed at all, from the very beginning, whatever exists I created from the non-existent, and from the invisible the visible ...' (2 *En.* 24). The *Gospel of Philip* includes the line 'The veil at first concealed how God controlled the creation ...' In the Merkavah texts this is a recurring theme. Rabbi Nehuniah saw the very bonds of the covenant 'the mysteries and secrets, the bonds and wonders ... the weaving of the web that completes the world' (*Hekhalot Rabbati* ..., # 201), Rabbi Akiba reported: 'I had a vision and observed the whole inhabited world and saw it as it is' (*Hekhalot Zutarti*, # 496).

Texts such as these confirm that what Moses saw on Sinai was not the vision of a heavenly temple, but a vision of the creation of the world.

Icons

The liturgies of the church and the buildings designed for their setting have retained the distinction between the two sacred areas originally separated by the veil. In churches of the Catholic tradition, there is a division between the holy place for the altar and the nave where the congregation stands. The floor of the holy place is at a higher level and a screen or rail marks the boundary. The survival of the temple veil is most obvious in an Orthodox church, where a screen of icons separates the holy of holies from the congregation.

Icons are the characteristic art form of the Orthodox churches and the traditional process by which they are made is in itself significant. The wooden surface to be painted is prepared with a ground of white gesso which reflects light even through the opaque pigments which are superimposed. Thus the icon depicts a saint through whom the light of the other world may be glimpsed.

The complex symbolism and characteristic style of these icons derive directly from the belief of the temple mystics about the world beyond the veil. The icon painters attempt, with their pictures, to make visible a spiritual truth and offer a glimpse beyond the veil. The essential qualification for an icon painter is 'a personal experience of the higher states in which such a world does indeed become a reality'.

> The world in which we ordinarily live is bound by certain laws; laws of time and space, laws of perspective, laws of light and shade ... But the icon painter is not concerned with these laws because he is not concerned with depicting the world in which we live. The icon painter represents a world of higher reality, the world of eternal truth. In his world there is no time except the present, the eternal now ... In the illuminated world of the icon there are no shadows since the source of light is not outside as it is in the world but emanates from within. Icons are a language to describe what is indescribable, to make visible what is invisible.*

Icon painters evolved special techniques to convey a sense of the spiritual just as the temple mystics were conscious of the limits of language when describing the world beyond the veil.

On the other hand, both icon painters and mystics recognized the fundamental similarity between the visible and invisible worlds. Jesus spoke of 'On earth as it is in heaven' and he taught in parables. The visions of Enoch in the holy of holies are also called Parables. Both the stories Jesus told and the terrifying visions of Enoch depict the timeless reality which underlies contemporary events. *1 Enoch* records three visions in the holy of holies when he sees a heavenly figure enthroned and the rulers of the earth judged. These are visions of the Day of the LORD, and they are exactly like the visions recorded in the Book of Revelation, not necessarily predictions of the future, although they could be. They are descriptions of reality, the eternal world beyond the material world. When the other world breaks through into the temporal, material world, we perceive it as history. Time is but the moving image of eternity. Thus the illustrations used by Jesus are also called parables, not in his case visions but incidents in everyday life – seeds growing, a woman baking bread – which point to an eternal truth: 'The kingdom of God is like a mustard seed ...' (Mark 4.30–32).

The Jesus who speaks in the *Gospel of Thomas* describes the enormous power available to those who are able to join the inner and outer worlds. 'When you make the two one, and when you make the inside like the outside, and the above like the below and the male and the female one and the same ... then you will enter the kingdom' (*Thomas* 22). 'When you make the two one, you will become sons of man [heavenly beings] and when you say Mountain move away, it will move away (*Thomas* 106).

*R Temple, *Icons, A Search for Inner Meaning*, London 1982, p. 43.

3

THE PRIESTS OF ISRAEL

The priesthood was hereditary; only a man who had been born into a priestly family was permitted to enter the temple and burn incense (1 Chron. 23.13). Others could not enter the holy place; men were allowed to proceed as far as the court of Israel, within sight of the temple building but separated from it, and women were restricted to an outer court.

Although the priesthood was one of Israel's most ancient institutions, it is not easy to reconstruct its history. The sources have differing emphases and many have been rewritten and updated several times. Status, rights and duties were clearly matters of great importance, but some texts describe one set of arrangements, others another. Since the texts can neither be dated nor set in order relative to each other, it is impossible to know exactly what happened in any given period.

Men Set Apart

The priests of Israel were drawn from the tribe of Levi. A tradition in the *Book of Jubilees* says that when Rachel was pregnant with Benjamin, Jacob counted his sons from the youngest upwards and Levi, the tenth, was offered as a tithe to the LORD. He became a priest, and his father vested him and gave him incense (*Jub.* 32.3). Another tradition is that the Levites were offered to the LORD to redeem the firstborn sons of all the other tribes (Num. 3.45). How the Levites as a whole related to the high priestly family of Aaron is another problem: one account says they were appointed as Aaron's assistants (Num. 3.6), another that they were appointed by the LORD to kill those who had followed Aaron in worshipping the golden calf (Exod. 32.25–29). Another tradition in Deuteronomy 10.6–9 says the Levites were not set apart for sacred service until after the death of Aaron. Several incidents in the Pentateuch must record disputes between branches of the priesthood and their respective claims to rights and duties, but all we have now are the stories whose significance is, for the most part, lost.

The simplest account would be that the tribe of Levi had charge of the tabernacle. As the twelve tribes moved through the desert, the Levites transported the tent and its furnishings, and when they settled in any place, the Levites had to camp near the tabernacle to ensure that nobody came too near the holy place. Any trespass brought divine wrath on the whole people (Num. 1.49–54). It was the Levites who carried the ark across the Jordan (Josh. 3.17), and seven of their number blew ram's horn trumpets before the ark as it was carried around the city of Jericho. When the Israelites took possession of the land, the Levites were given no territory; the LORD was their portion (Num. 18.20) and the priesthood of the LORD their inheritance (Josh. 18.7). They lived off the tithes which were brought to the holy place. Their duty was to serve there and 'to bear iniquity', in other words, to take away, and thus forgive, the effects of sin. Leviticus (the name means *The Levites' Book*), describes their rituals, but much of the meaning is now lost.

Chief among the Levites were the family of Aaron who were consecrated as priests. The LORD said to Moses: 'Then bring near to you Aaron your brother, and his sons with him, from among the people of Israel, to serve me as priests – Aaron and Aaron's sons, Nadab and Abihu, Eleazar and Ithamar. And you shall make holy garments for Aaron your brother, for glory and for beauty' (Exod. 28.1–2). They were consecrated with blood and oil (Exod. 29.1–35) and they alone were permitted to enter the holiest part of the tabernacle or temple. They were 'the keepers' of all matters concerning the altar and within the veil (LXX Num. 3.10, also MT Num. 18.7). Their 'hands were filled' with incense, the sign of priesthood. Exodus 28.41 reads, literally, 'you shall anoint them and fill their hands and consecrate them, that they may be priests to me'. No man with any physical imperfection was allowed to be a priest. 'He shall not come near the veil or approach the altar, because he has a blemish, that he may not profane my sanctuaries' (Lev. 21.23). The list was long: no blind man or lame, nor anyone with a facial abnormality or an injured foot or hand, no one too tall or too short, or with blemished skin. In the Mishnah the list is even longer (*m. Bekhoroth* 7.1–6). The regulations for sacrificial animals applied equally to priests; only the unblemished were good enough for the service of the holy place.

The priesthood was hereditary and so the genealogies of the priests were carefully kept, or, as seems likely in some cases, adjusted. Some of the power struggles within the priestly clans can still be glimpsed in the Pentateuch. Korah, the great grandson of Levi, challenged the authority of Moses and claimed equality with the family of Aaron and the right to offer incense. The earth opened up and swallowed the rebels, a sure sign that they had no right to the priesthood (Num. 16.1–40). Aaron's pre-eminence was confirmed when his was the only rod to blossom and bear almonds (Num. 17.1–11). A story records why the priesthood passed from Aaron to only two of his sons, Eleazar and Ithamar. The other sons, Nadab and Abihu, even though they had ascended Sinai with Moses and Aaron (Exod. 24.9), had erred in the matter of the incense 'offering unholy fire before the LORD' (Lev. 10.1) and were devoured by fire from the LORD. The line then passed through Eleazar's son Phineas, who ran his spear through an Israelite man and the Midianite woman he had married in defiance of the Law. Thus, we are told, he protected the whole people from the LORD's wrath. Phineas was then given 'the covenant of peace ... the covenant of perpetual priesthood', and his action in averting the LORD's wrath was described as 'making atonement' (Num. 25.6–13). According to the genealogy in 1 Chronicles 6.4–15, his family were priests in Jerusalem until the exile.

When David organized the priestly houses in Jerusalem before the temple was built, the descendants of both Aaron's sons were holding office. There were sixteen families of the sons of Eleazar and eight of the sons of Ithamar, and these became the twenty four priestly houses (1 Chron. 24.1–6). As David drew near to death, each of the two priestly clans supported a rival claimant to the throne: the Ithamar priests, in the person of Abiathar, supported Adonijah, and the Eleazar-Phineas priests, in the person of Zadok, supported Solomon. Solomon won, and the Ithamar priests were banished to Anathoth, thus fulfilling the curse brought on their house by the wicked sons of Eli at Shiloh (1 Kgs 2.27; cf. 1 Sam. 3.11–14). A famous son of the Ithamar family was the prophet Jeremiah (Jer. 1.1).

In addition, there was the royal priesthood of Melchizedek, probably the pre-Israelite priesthood of Jerusalem, since Abraham met Melchizedek the priest-king of Jerusalem (Gen. 14.18–20). This priesthood belonged to the Davidic kings as rulers of the city. Psalm 110 describes the enthronement of a Davidic king, when he was declared to be the LORD's son (Ps. 110.3 is obscure but seems to mean this) and then installed 'as a priest for ever after the order of Melchizedek'. At the LORD's right hand, he would judge nations and shatter kings. Solomon was depicted as a royal priest, blessing the congregation (2 Chron. 6.3) and consecrating the temple court before offering sacrifice there (2 Chron. 7.7). (The mysterious Melchizedek is not mentioned elsewhere in the Hebrew Scriptures but he became a key figure for the early church because Jesus is described as Melchizedek in Hebrews 5.5–10. The silence about Melchizedek is a most eloquent silence.)

From time to time there was conflict between the priests and the palace. A story told of King Uzziah probably marks a decisive stage in the relationship between the priests and the king, or maybe how the later writer would like it to have been. Uzziah had entered the temple to burn incense, but was driven out by Azariah the chief priest and 'eighty priests of the LORD who were men of valour' (2 Chron. 26.16–22). Uzziah's offence was that he had burned incense in the temple on the altar of incense. He was expelled: 'It is not for you, Uzziah, to burn incense to the LORD, but for the priests, the sons of Aaron who are consecrated to burn incense' (2 Chron. 26.18). Uzziah was punished and died a leper. The same story was told differently by the Deuteronomists who had another agenda. They wrote to show that a king was punished if he permitted sacrifice and incense other than in Jerusalem. Uzziah (they called him Azariah) tolerated other places of worship and so was smitten with leprosy (2 Kgs 15.1–5). The Chronicler, however, had been writing about the claims and aspirations of the priesthood and the exclusive right of the Aaronite priests to offer incense in the temple.

When the Babylonians destroyed the temple in 586 BCE, the chief priest and the second priest were put to death. No priests are mentioned among those taken into exile but they must have been among the chief men who were taken. Ezekiel, who prophesied in Babylon, was a priest

(Ezek. 1.3), and when the exile was ended, priests and Levites were among those who returned to Jerusalem to rebuild the temple (Ezra 1.5). Some who could not prove their descent in the priestly genealogies were excluded from the priesthood (Ezra 2.62), but Joshua ben Jozadak with his fellow priests and the Levites managed to rebuild the temple and re-establish worship there.

The early years of the second temple period are crucial for under-standing what happened to both priesthood and temple in the following centuries. There were disputes about purity and legitimacy, 'Satan' challenging the right of Joshua the Zadokite to be high priest (Zech. 3.1–5). There were expulsions, for example when a son of the high priestly family married a 'Horonite' (Neh. 13.28). Contemporary evidence from the Yeb Papyri shows that the 'Horonite' family were worshippers of the LORD, and presumably the bride had been deemed by some to be suitable. Rules and definitions were in a state of flux at this time and it is impossible to reconstruct what happened. Ezekiel 44.9–16 distinguished between the Levites who had served as priests in the ancient high places and the sons of Zadok who served in the temple. When Josiah abolished all other places of worship, the Levites came to Jerusalem to serve, but were barred from priestly duties. They were tainted by their former service in the high places and were demoted to temple servants.

There were plenty of people with priestly claims who were excluded from the service of the second temple; Jeremiah's Ithamar family could well have challenged the right of Joshua the Zadokite to the high priesthood. The Levites could well have complained about their new and inferior status. There were some who would have no dealings at all with the restored worship in Jerusalem, 'the apostate generation whose deeds are apostate' (1 En. 93.9). The Third Isaiah spoke for these people and accused the returned exiles of polluting the temple by their attitude of superiority to their brothers. Their careful rituals were in fact the worst form of idolatry. 'He who slaughters an ox is like him who kills a man, he who sacrifices a lamb like him who breaks a dog's neck' (Isa. 66.3). The ox was the high priest's offering (Lev. 16.11). Nobody knows what happened to the people who rejected the cult of the second temple. Their traditions, those of the first temple, have been preserved in 1 Enoch, and the remains of several copies of this book have been found among the Qumran scrolls. Perhaps the owners of the scrolls were some of the disaffected priests, 'the teachers who had been hidden and kept secret' (11QMelch).

In the far south of Egypt, at Yeb, there is evidence of some priests who separated themselves from Jerusalem. Letters and other documents have been found there dating from the fifth century BCE from a community who worshipped the LORD and offered sacrifice. Their temple, modelled on Solomon's, was destroyed in 410 BCE. Nobody knows how they came to be there or what happened to them after their temple was destroyed. It is possible they had been refugees from

Manasseh's reign of terror in the seventh century BCE. Their archaic practices suggest they came to Egypt before the changes introduced by King Josiah in about 620 BCE. Another temple community was established in the north of Egypt in the second century BCE. Josephus (*War* 7.422–32) says it was founded by Onias III, the legitimate high priest in Jerusalem who was ousted by his brother Jason (2 *Macc.* 4.7–17). Onias obtained permission from the rulers of Egypt to build a temple at Leontopolis, claiming this would fulfil the prophecy in Isaiah 19.19, that there would be an altar to the LORD in the midst of Egypt (*Ant.* 13.64). There were also Samaritan priests with their temple on Mount Gerizim, although nobody can be certain when or why it was built.

Thus there were several temples and many branches of the priesthood due to the turbulent history of the second temple period. Most remained loyal to the ideal of the temple in Jerusalem, but all rejected the actual cult and priesthood there. Most remain a mystery to us, but many of the Qumran scrolls depict varieties of belief and custom, hitherto unknown, which were probably the traditions of the ancient priesthood. So little is known of the priesthood in the second temple period that any account is bound to be speculative. The figures and patterns of the Book of Revelation, however, show that it was closely related to these priestly texts and thus an important witness to the last days of the priesthood.

The Scrolls speak of a Wicked Priest who was the enemy of the Teacher of Righteousness and amassed wealth in Jerusalem, defiling the temple with his evil deeds (1QpHab I). It is testimony to the corruption of the priesthood that scholars cannot agree who the Wicked Priest might have been because there are so many possibilities. It was strife between Hyrcanus and Aristobulus, two claimants to the high priesthood, that first drew Rome into the affairs of Jerusalem. Pompey came to establish order and he besieged and took the city in 63 BCE. Josephus remarked that as a result of this power struggle 'we lost our liberty and became subject to the Romans' (*Ant.* 14.77). The high priests continued to act as the rulers of Judea but were forbidden to wear a crown (*Ant.* 20.244); Rome appointed Hyrcanus II as high priest and permitted him to rebuild the walls of Jerusalem which Pompey had destroyed (*Ant.* 14.144). Hyrcanus was later disqualified from the high priesthood in 40 BCE when Antigonus, a rival claimant, 'cut off his ears and thereby ensured that he should not hold the high priesthood again since the Law required that this high office could only be held by those who are unblemished' (*Ant.* 14.366). Antigonus was, in turn, deposed when the Idumean Herod became king in Jerusalem in 37 BCE. Ineligible himself to be the high priest, he appointed a weak but legitimate Babylonian, but he kept the vestments, as a means of further controlling the high priest. They were only released seven days before a major festival, to be purified for the occasion (*Ant.* 18.93–94). Herod was then persuaded, against his better judgement, to appoint as high priest a young man named Aristobulus, the grandson of Hyrcanus II. He became a focus for Jewish nationalist feelings, reminding them of the glorious priest-kings of former times. Herod could not bear the thought of a legitimate king of the Jews and ordered him to be killed. (This was the Herod who reacted so violently to the question 'Where is he who is born King of the Jews?' (Matt. 2.2) and then murdered the children in Bethlehem.) Herod's policy was to separate political and religious power, and to subordinate the latter.

Religion and politics were, however, inextricably interconnected. Josephus explained that Moses had appointed the high priest as chief prophet in order to outlaw the evil practices of false prophets (*Ant.* 3.214). He gave his oracles in two ways, both by means of the gemstones in the breastplate. Two engraved onyx stones were worn on his shoulders (Exod. 28.9–12) and the one on the right shoulder shone when the LORD was present (*Ant.* 3.214; 4Q376). These two stones were probably Urim and Thummim, whose names were understood by the LXX to mean 'Explanation and Truth'. Later tradition believed that the use of Urim and Thummim had ceased with the destruction of the first temple (*b. Sotah* 48ab). All twelve stones in the breastplate shone when the LORD promised victory in battle, and this is why the LXX called the breastplate 'the oracle of judgement' (Exod. 28.30). Josephus believed that the breastplate and the onyx stone oracle had ceased to shine 200 years before his time, because God was displeased at the transgression of the Law (*Ant.* 3.214–18; also 4.311).

The stories of the judges and the early kings show these oracles were remembered. The judges and kings never set out to fight a holy war until they had enquired of the LORD (e.g. Judg. 1.1–2; 18.5–6; 1 Sam. 14.36–37; 2 Sam. 5.22–25). 1 Samuel 23.9–12 shows that this was done by means of the ephod: 'David knew that Saul was plotting evil against him and he said to Abiathar the priest "Bring the ephod here" '. After questioning the LORD by means of the ephod, he received answers to his two questions. This method of divination was to remain Israel's ideal. The Temple Scroll commands the leader of the army to consult the high priest before any mission: 'he may not go out before he has come before the high priest and has sought on his behalf the decision of the Urim and the Thummim ...' (11QT LVIII). Herod's policy of releasing the high priest's vestments only seven days before a festival may have been to prevent further war oracles from the traditional source.

The corruption of the high priesthood was believed to be a sign of the end times. The *Assumption of Moses* condemns the kings who called themselves priests of the Most High God, (the Hasmoneans) and yet performed impious acts in the temple. The 'king not of a priestly family' who followed them, clearly Herod the Great, persecuted these priests and brought on them the judgement they deserved. 'He killed them in secret places and no one knew where their bodies were' (*Ass. Mos.* 6.3). After his death and the reign of his heirs, a king of the west would come and burn the temple. Further information about Herod and the priests is preserved in the Slavonic text of Josephus. During Herod's campaign against the Arabs in 32 BCE, the priests in Jerusalem met in secret to discuss the crisis caused by the new king. They were waiting for the Anointed One but agreed he could not be Herod because the Law forbad a foreign king (Deut. 17.15). Ananus, the priest, never thought that God would permit Herod to rule in Jerusalem; it was a sign, he concluded, that the end was at hand and that the prophecy of desolation (Dan. 9.24–27) was being fulfilled. They were looking for a Holy of Holies, i.e. a high priest, and nobody could consider Herod as that Holy One. (Jesus was acclaimed with this title, Mark 1.24; Luke 4.34, the ancient title for the LORD, e.g. Isa. 1.4). An informer reported this discussion to Herod who had all the priests killed and then appointed others. The morning after the slaughter, there was an earthquake (*War* 1.364–70, Slavonic text). This was the massacre described in the *Assumption of Moses* 6.3.

When Valerius Gratus became procurator of Judea in 15 CE he assumed the right to appoint and depose the high priest, and four men held the office during his eleven-year term. When he was succeeded by Pontius Pilate, Caiaphas was high priest (John 11.49). In 41 CE the emperor Claudius confirmed Herod Agrippa I as king of Judea and he immediately appointed a new high priest. The first was Simon, son of Boethus, the father of one of Herod's many wives, but in the space of three years he was deposed and replaced by Jonathan, who in turn resigned in favour of his brother Matthias (*Ant.* 19.297–316). When Agrippa died, his brother who was the king of Chalcis, was given the right to appoint the high priests and he appointed and deposed as he thought fit. By the end of the 50s, there was open hostility between the high priests and the lesser orders of priests. Josephus records that after Agrippa II had appointed Ishmael ben Fabi as high priest in 59 CE, there were riots in Jerusalem. The high priests used to send their henchmen to the threshing floors to seize the tithes that were due to the priests, so that some of them died of starvation (*Ant.* 20.179–81, 207). The Qumran *Commentary on Habakkuk* describes 'the last priests of Jerusalem who amass money and wealth by plundering the peoples', and the 'Wicked Priest who robbed the poor of their possessions' (1QpHab IX, XII). Some of these poor were the Hebrews, the holy brethren who looked to Jesus as their true high priest (Heb. 3.1); they had been abused and plundered (Heb. 10.32–34). Agrippa appointed several other high priests, and one of them, Ananus, had James the Righteous murdered in the temple. Since Christian tradition remembers James not only as the first bishop in Jerusalem, but also as a high priest (see p. 10), this may be yet another episode in the history of the high priesthood of which too little is known. James, too, had complained of 'the cries of the harvesters which had reached the ears of the LORD', of the labourers who had not been paid, and of the rich who lived in luxury (Jas 5.1–5). During the 60s the corruption became worse and when the revolt finally flared, it is not surprising that the anger of the Zealots turned first against the king and the high priest. Their houses, and all records of debt, were burned (*War* 2.426–27). The corn which had been seized as tithes was also burned (*War* 5.25–26), an indication of the hatred felt towards the high priesthood, since the consequence of burning the corn was famine in the city.

Jews remembered this period with bitterness; the Babylonian Talmud records:

Woe is me because of the house of Boethus, because of their staves [they beat people]. Woe is me because of the house of Hanin, woe because of their whisperings [they were conspirators]. Woe is me because of the house of Kathros, woe is me because of their pens. Woe is me because of the house of Ishmael ben Fabi ... For they are high priests and their sons are treasurers and their sons in law are trustees and their servants beat the people with staves. (*b. Pesaḥim* 57a)

Proverbs 10.27 was interpreted as a contrast between the first and second temples.

'The fear of the LORD prolongs life' refers to the first holy of holies which remained standing for four hundred and ten years in which there served only eighteen high priests. 'But the years of the wicked will be short' refers to the second holy of holies, which lasted for four hundred and twenty years in which more than three hundred high priests served. Take away the forty years that Simeon the Righteous served, the eighty years that Johannan the high priest served, the ten that Ishmael ben Fabi served, or, as some say, the eleven years of Rabbi Eleazar ben Harsum. Count, and you will find that none of them completed his year in office. (*b. Yoma* 9a)

Josephus, himself a priest, gave an equally grim assessment of the period. 'The number of high priests from the days of Herod until the time when Titus took the temple and the city and burned them, was, in all, twenty-eight. The length of time was one hundred and seven years' (*Ant.* 20.250).

The Book of Revelation marks the transition between the second temple and the Christian claim to be the new temple of living stones. They saw themselves as heirs to both the temple and the true priesthood.

The Great Angel

The LORD told Moses to build a tabernacle and to copy on earth everything he had seen in his vision on Sinai. Those who served in the tabernacle replicated those who served in heaven; in other words, the priests were the angels, as can be seen from Malachi 2.7: 'a priest ... is the angel of the LORD of hosts' ('angel' and 'messenger' are the same Hebrew word). Fragments of hymns and liturgies found among the Dead Sea Scrolls show how vivid was this belief and how important to them.

Thou hast raised me to everlasting height.
I walk in limitless level ground

and I know there is hope for him
whom though hast shaped from dust
for the everlasting council.
Thou hast cleansed a perverse spirit of great sin
that it may stand with the host of the holy ones
and that it may enter into community
with the congregation of the sons of heaven. (1QH XI, formerly III)

May you be as an Angel of the Presence in the abode of holiness
to the glory of the God of [Hosts].
May you attend upon the service in the temple of the Kingdom
and decree destiny in company with the Angels of the Presence. (Blessings 1QSb IV)

'On earth as it is in heaven' meant that the priests and their liturgies were those of heaven, and we cannot know how literally this was believed in the first century CE. If the priests were angels, the host of heaven, then the high priest must have been the LORD of hosts. This conclusion, which seems startling at first, is amply borne out by the evidence and explains why Jesus was proclaimed both as the LORD and as the Great High Priest. The high priest was the chief of the angels, the Mighty Angel, the Great Angel. He was the key figure in the Book of Revelation, emerging from heaven, that is, from the holy of holies.

In the religion of the first temple, the LORD had been one of the seventy sons of El Elyon, God Most High. When the Most High allocated the nations of the earth among his seventy sons, Israel was given to the LORD, the firstborn, who became Israel's patron angel and national God (Deut. 32.8). After the changes introduced by the Deuteronomists, the question of Israel's second God became for some a sensitive issue, and so two versions of this text are known. The MT, which was the basis for most English translations, has 'The Most High ... fixed the bounds of the people according to the number of the sons of Israel', but the Qumran text (4QDeut[q]) has 'according to the number of the sons of God' and the LXX is similar. This suggests that the Hebrew text was changed after the LXX was translated. The MT makes little sense, but having seen the Qumran text, it is easy to see why a change might have been made, especially after the advent of Christianity.

In the cult of the first temple, the king was anointed and became the Firstborn Son: 'He shall cry to me Thou art my Father ... And I will make him the Firstborn, the Highest of the kings of the earth' (Ps. 89.26–27). He was Melchizedek (Ps. 110.4), the Man who was the Image of God, and the Servant/Lamb (see pp. 130–1). The LORD was Israel's second God, the one who was present with his people in human form, originally as the Davidic king and later as the high priest. Disentangling evidence for the earlier religion is a complex process, but so much in later texts begins to make sense if there had originally been a sacral kingship which manifested the national God, and also a High God. It would explain, for example, why there was more than one throne in Daniel's vision of the Man who ascended to heaven on clouds (Dan. 7.9). The Talmud records an explanation of the two thrones attributed to R. Akiba, a significant figure in the second war against Rome in 135 CE. One throne was the throne for God and the other, he said, for David (*b. Ḥagigah* 14a). Thus R. Akiba believed that one throne in heaven was for a human king, but other rabbis condemned him for holding this view. The second throne in heaven was clearly a sensitive issue a century after the advent of Christianity, perhaps because the Man enthroned as Israel's second God was central to the Book of Revelation.

When Moses received instructions how to consecrate the priests, he was told in minute detail how to make their vestments; the high priest had eight items and the priests four. Their names are variously translated: breast piece, ephod, robe, coat, girdle, turban and breeches were prescribed for the high priest (Exod. 28.40, 42), but only coats, girdles, caps and breeches for the priests (Exod. 28.40, 42). In addition, the high priest wore on the front of his turban a gold ornament, the *ṣiṣ*, which was probably an almond flower (Exod. 28.36). Exodus 39.30 adds that the *ṣiṣ* was on the holy crown of pure gold. (When Aaron's rod blossomed it produced first a bud, then a *ṣiṣ*, and then almonds, Num. 17.8. The *ṣiṣ* was the sign of the high priesthood.) The golden flower was engraved 'with the engravings of a seal sacred to the LORD', in other words, it was engraved with the Name. Many translations say that it was a seal engraved with the words 'Holy to the LORD', but the evidence of other sources shows that this was not the case. Aristeas, who visited Jerusalem in the first century BCE, wrote that the high priest wore the Name inscribed in sacred letters on a plate of gold (*Aristeas* 98). Philo, who came from a priestly family, says the same; the priest wore the four letters of the Name 'which only those whose ears and tongues are purified may hear or speak in the holy place and no other person nor in any other place at all' (*Moses* II.114). Josephus, who was a priest, has Ananus the high priest say: 'I who wear the high priest's vestments am called the most honourable of venerated names' (*War* 4.163).

Those who wore the Name became the LORD. This is implicit in parts of the Hebrew Scriptures, but quite clear in the later mystical texts which preserved the traditions of the temple. Enoch, who appears in several of them, was depicted as a high priest; in his vision, he entered the holy of holies to intercede for the fallen angels (*1 En.* 14.8–15.2). What happened to Enoch in the holy of holies is what happened to the high priest in the holy of holies. He described how he was anointed and vested in garments of glory; he became an angel, and the wisest of the archangels then instructed him in the secrets of the creation (*2 En.* 22). Thus in the holy of holies he was given wisdom and became divine. In 3 Enoch, R. Ishmael ascended to heaven and questioned the Great Angel Metatron. How did he come to bear the Name of his Creator? Metatron, whose name probably means 'The Sharer of the Throne' (see pp. 109–10) explained that he had formerly been Enoch, but the LORD took him up to heaven to be a witness against a sinful generation. He was made the greatest of the heavenly princes and the ruler of the heavenly host. He was given the title Servant, *na'ar*, but this was later reinterpreted as Youth to distance the text from any Christian association (*3 En.* 3–4). The text is somewhat disordered, but the gist is clear.

Enoch/Metatron then described his transformation, how he was given a throne like the throne of glory which was set at the door of the seventh palace. He was confirmed as the Servant King of heaven and instructed in all wisdom, the mysteries of the creation and the secrets of history. He was given a glorious robe, and a crown on which were written the letters by which everything was created. These were the four letters of the Name, because he was then proclaimed as the angel who bore the Name (*3 En.* 10–13). All the great angels fell prostrate before him (*3 En.* 14). He was transformed into fire (*3 En.* 15) and, looking back towards the world he had left, saw all history depicted on the curtain which separated the great hall from the holy of holies (*3 En.* 45).

Controversy surrounded this apotheosis of Enoch. Immediately after the account of Enoch/Metatron's enthronement, in the present form of the text, there is the story of how he was removed from his throne at the command of the Holy One, beaten sixty times with lashes of fire, and made to stand. This must be an insertion into the text, as it directly contradicts all that has been said about the exalted Enoch. The reason for this punishment and change of status was that R. Elisha ben Abuyah, a contemporary of R. Akiba, came before the throne in a mystical ascent and saw Metatron on his throne surrounded by angels. 'When he saw me seated upon a throne like a king, with ministering angels standing beside me as servants ... he opened his mouth and said "There are indeed two powers in heaven" ' (*3 En.* 16.2–3). Two powers in heaven was, by that time, unthinkable, and so R. Elisha ben Abuyah was condemned as a heretic and Metatron was dethroned and punished. Whoever recorded the original Enoch texts, however, must have believed that there were 'two powers in heaven' and that one of them was an exalted Man.

The Enoch texts describe the making of the high priest; what they depict had originally described the coronation and apotheosis of the king. (The name 'high priest' only occurs in the second temple; the few references in the first temple (2 Kgs 12.10; 22.4, 8; 23.4) are generally held to be anachronistic insertions.) The sacral nature of the Davidic monarchy was deemed incompatible with the post-exilic understanding of monotheism which had been inspired by the Second Isaiah and promulgated by the Deuteronomists, and so only a few details have survived the later editors and censors. In the first temple, the king had become the LORD at his coronation and the people worshipped him. The Chronicler's account of Solomon's coronation is unambiguous on this point even if some English translations are not; he sat on the throne of the LORD as king (1 Chron. 29.23) and the people 'bowed down to

the LORD, the king' (a literal translation of 1 Chron. 29.20). Psalm
89.19–27 describes what happened: the king received a vision and was
raised up (to heaven); he was given the crown and anointed and
declared to be the firstborn son, the highest of the kings of the earth.
Psalm 110.3–4 describes how he was born among the holy ones and
made the Melchizedek high priest. Thus the king, and, in the second
temple, the high priest who replaced him, was the Anointed, the
Firstborn, the One who saw the heavenly throne, and the LORD.
Hecataeus of Abdera, a writer in the fourth century BCE, described the
high priest as 'an angel of the commandments of God'. The Jews, he
said, used to fall to the ground and worship, *proskunein*, him. This
alone does not prove that the high priest was believed to be the LORD,
but it is compatible with what other texts lead us to conclude. Similarly,
the description of Simon, high priest around 200 BCE, seems to indicate
that he was worshipped (*Ben Sira* 50, see p. 181).

Philo, a contemporary of the prophets who wrote the Book of
Revelation, used all these terms and titles to describe the Logos, the
Word, whom he identified as the God of Israel seen by Moses on Sinai
(Exod. 24.10; *Tongues* 95–97). The Logos was the high priest, the
Firstborn (*Dreams* I.215), the Logos was high priest and king (*Flight*
118), the Logos was the Name of God and the Man after his Image, and
he passed between earth and heaven. He was the apostle and high priest
(cf. Heb. 3.1) who stood on the border that separated creator from
creature, and he was both intercessor for his people and a messenger
from God (*Heir* 205). Philo also described the Logos as the second God.
At times he said this plainly: 'Nothing mortal can be made in the
likeness of the Most High One and Father of the Universe, but in that
of the second God who is his Logos' (*On Gen.* II.62). At other times he
moderated his language: 'He that is truly God is One, but those who are
improperly so called are more than one'. He went on to explain that
there was a distinction between 'the God', with the article, which
indicates the One God, and 'God', without an article, which indicates
the Logos (*Dreams* I.229–30). Elsewhere he distinguished between God
who is pure being and 'that Power of his by which he made and ordered
all things', also called God (*Tongues* 137). Philo could not have
invented this idea of a second God; too many ambiguous texts in the
Hebrew Scriptures point in the same direction. Further, Philo was
chosen as spokesman by the Jews of Alexandria when they sent an
embassy to Rome, and so he is unlikely to have been heretical in his
views.

Philo revealed more about the beliefs of his day. Not only was there
a second God, but this second God could have male or female form (see
pp. 108–12). He used the same titles for Wisdom as he did for the
Logos: 'The sublime and heavenly Wisdom is of many names, for he
calls it Beginning and Image and Vision of God' (*All. Int.* I.43). He even
explained that gender was not important: 'Let us pay no heed to the
discrepancy in the gender of the words, and say that the daughter of

God, even Wisdom, is not only masculine but father, sowing and begetting in souls aptness to learn' (*Flight* 52). He knew the ancient role of Wisdom as queen consort: 'The high priest is not a man but a divine Logos ... his father being God, who is likewise Father of all, and his mother Wisdom, through whom the universe came into existence' (*Flight* 110).

A clear statement of these beliefs in found in a text usually designated gnostic, but probably a product of the Hebrew priests, which teaches about an invisible world beyond the material world of human experience and describes the divine beings:

Before the universe, the First was revealed. In the boundlessness he is a self-grown, self-constructed father who is full of shining ineffable light. In the beginning he decided to have his form come to be as a great power. Immediately the beginning of that light was revealed as an immortal androgynous man. His male name is [the Begetting of the] Perfect One and his female name All Wise Begettress Sophia. It is also said that she resembles her brother and her consort. (CG III.3, *Eugnostos* 76–77)

This was adapted as a Christian text and presented as the teaching of the risen LORD. The 'immortal, androgynous man' became the 'immortal, androgynous man through whom they might attain their salvation ...' (CG III.4, *Wisdom* 101).

The vestments of the high priest symbolized his role as the visible presence of the LORD in the world, but also as the Great Angel in the holy of holies. There is nothing in the Hebrew Scriptures about the symbolism of the vestments, but Philo and Josephus both give similar accounts of them which must have been the explanation current in the first century CE. The vestment worn outside the holy of holies, i.e. in the world, was woven from the same fabric as the veil of the temple: scarlet, blue, purple and white (Exod. 28.6; cf. 26.31). In other words, it represented the material world (see pp. 20–1). Vested in this way, the high priest was the incarnation of the LORD, the LORD made visible in the material world. Josephus, a priest, said that the garment 'denoted universal nature which it had pleased the LORD to make of four elements' (*Ant.* 3.184); and another first-century writer described Aaron's vestment as a long robe on which the whole world was depicted (*Wisd.* 18.24). The writer to the Hebrews described the veil of the temple as the flesh of Jesus; both were torn at his death (Heb. 10.20). The vestment worn in the holy of holies, however, was white linen, the dress of angels and the garment of glory. Philo explained that linen was chosen because 'it was not, like wool, the product of creatures subject to death' (*Laws* I.84). As the high priest passed into the holy of holies, he became divine. This explains why Philo read Leviticus 16.17: 'There shall be no man ... when [the high priest] enters the holy place to make atonement until he comes out' as 'When he enters the holy place to make atonement he shall not be a man until he comes out' (*Dreams* II.189, 231).

The most ancient understanding of the LORD was as a manifold divinity with both male and female natures, but nevertheless one: 'The LORD our God is One LORD' (Deut. 6. 4). (It is not hard to see how the ancient belief in God Most High and the second God with male and female aspects became the Christian Trinity.) Thus when humans were created in the image, they had to be made male and female (Gen. 1.27). When Christians were baptized into Christ the LORD, they were 'no longer Jew and Greek, slave and free, male and female' (Gal. 3.28). The writer of the *Wisdom of Solomon* told how the history of Israel had been guided not by the LORD but by Wisdom (*Wisd.* 10.1–11.14). The high priest was the incarnation of both the male and female aspects of the divinity; he was the LORD incarnate and he was also Wisdom incarnate. Ben Sira used the same imagery to describe both Wisdom (*Ben Sira* 24.1–34) and Simon the high priest (*Ben Sira* 50.1–21). Like the high priest, Wisdom ministered in the holy tabernacle (*Ben Sira* 24.10). Both were compared to a cedar and a cypress and roses. Wisdom and the priests were compared to palm trees. Wisdom was the oil used to anoint the high priest (*Ben Sira* 24.15; cf. Exod. 30.22–25) because anointing gave Wisdom, and she was the incense of the holy of holies with which the high priest's hands were filled (*Ben Sira* 24.15; cf. Exod. 30.34). Like Aaron's rod which confirmed his high priesthood, Wisdom budded, blossomed and bore fruit. Most curious of all, she invited her devotees to eat and drink her (*Ben Sira* 24.21, cf. Jesus' words at the Last Supper). This male-female high priesthood appears several times in the Book of Revelation (see pp. 112–13), and in 1 Corinthians 1.24 where the Messiah is said to be both the Power and the Wisdom of God.

* For Philo, Wisdom and Logos seem to be identical, and it is often said that they are 'personifications' of older abstractions. Since anthropomorphism was suppressed by the temple 'reformers', it is unlikely to have given rise to personification and so these figures must have been a vestige of the old cult. Both Wisdom and Logos were associated with the menorah (see pp. 84, 205). Wisdom was the image of God's goodness (*Wisd.* 7.26), Logos the Image of God (*Laws* I.81). Wisdom and Logos were both the Firstborn (Prov. 8.24; *Dreams* I.215). Wisdom and Logos were both the agents of creation (Prov. 8.30; *T.Ps. Jon.* and *T.Neof. Gen.* 1.1; *Migration* 6). Wisdom penetrated all things (*Wisd.* 7.24), Logos was the bond of the universe (*Flight* 112). Both were the God of Israel (*Wisd.* 10–11; *Tongues* 96).

The high priest 'was' the incarnation of the LORD. When the Christians first proclaimed Jesus as the LORD, they combined this with several other titles: Son of God, Most High, Anointed, Melchizedek, Lamb of God, Son of Man and Servant. This was not a sign of their creative theologizing, drawing elements from formerly disparate sources to create the new identity of the Christian Messiah. It was an accurate recollection of the ancient royal titles, from the period before the LORD had been declared to be the only God. The Book of Revelation is steeped

in the imagery of high priesthood. A man was raised up and transformed into the LORD, the Son of God. He was enthroned and given the
incense of the high priesthood. John knew of the throne of the LORD,
the Son, and he distinguished this from the great white throne and the
One who sat upon it (20.11).

The Eternal Covenant

The priests had to maintain the Eternal Covenant; this was the
commission to Phineas, the grandson of Aaron, and he maintained
the covenant by the ritual of atonement. 'Phineas ... has turned back
my wrath from the people of Israel ... Behold I give to him my covenant
of peace; and it shall be to him, and to his descendants after him, the
covenant of perpetual priesthood, because he was jealous for his God,
and made atonement for the people of Israel' (Num. 25.11–13). It is not
easy to translate the Hebrew terms $b^e rit$ 'olam, eternal covenant, and
$b^e rit$ salom covenant of peace: $b^e rit$ has links to the word for binding,
barah, and also to the word for creating, bara' which is only used of
divine creativity, never human. Eternity, 'olam, can mean eternal or
ancient, and the consonants of šalom, peace, wholeness, integrity, can
also be read as šillum, retribution. In Numbers 25.12 'my covenant of
retribution' would be a more appropriate rendering. All these elements
are present whenever the eternal covenant is mentioned.

In the Hebrew Scriptures there are several covenants: with Noah,
with Abraham, with Moses and with David, and Jeremiah looked
forward to a new covenant. The Eternal Covenant was the oldest and
most fundamental of all and was envisaged as the system of bonds
which restrained cosmic forces and maintained an ordered creation
where people could live in peace and safety. Nowhere in the Hebrew
Scriptures is the establishing of this covenant described, but there are
many places where it is assumed. The covenant with Noah was the
everlasting covenant to maintain the natural order so that all creatures
could live in safety (Gen. 9.14–16). The guarantee of Jeremiah's new
covenant, that Israel would never be destroyed, was the security of
the natural order. 'If this fixed order departs from before me, says the
LORD, then shall the descendants of Israel cease from being a nation
before me for ever' (Jer. 31.36). The LORD set bounds for the sea and
made bonds for the stars to keep them in their orbits (Job 38.10, 31).
The *Prayer of Manasseh* 3 described the process vividly: 'Thou who hast
made heaven and earth with all their order; who hast shackled the sea
by thy word of command, who hast confined the deep and sealed it with
thy terrible and glorious Name'. The sea appears in the Book of
Revelation as one aspect of the red dragon, the ancient serpent (see pp.
216–19).

The bonds were sealed by the Name, and the one who bore the
Name literally held the covenant, the creation, in being. The high priest
wore the sacred seal engraved with the Name, and in the ritual he

became the seal of the bonds of the creation. The heavenly prince who corrupted his wisdom and was thrown from the garden of Eden was a high priest (see p. 104). He had been 'The seal of perfection, full of wisdom, perfect in beauty, in Eden the garden of God ...' (Ezek. 28.12–13). Isaiah's mysterious Servant was 'given as a covenant of the people' (Isa. 42.6; 49.8), possibly 'appointed as the eternal covenant', since 'covenant of the people' *brt l'm* and 'eternal covenant' *brt 'lm* are very similar letters and the phrase 'covenant of the people' is not known elsewhere. This is how it was understood at the end of the second temple period; it was the divine plan for the fullness of time to unite all things in heaven and earth in the Anointed One (Eph. 1.9–10) and Jesus the true high priest was the beloved Son, the image of the invisible God, the One in whom all things hold together (Col. 1.17). In Revelation 19.12 he is the warrior priest who rides from heaven wearing a diadem engraved with the Name which no one knows but himself. After his triumph over the beast and the kings of the earth (19.11–21), the ancient serpent is sealed in a pit for a thousand years (20.1–3), so that the creation can be restored as the millennium kingdom.

The Name was also described as the great oath by which the creation was bound, for example, in a fragment of poetry embedded in the Parables of Enoch, in which one of the evil angels tried to learn the secret Name so as to have power over the creation, but Michael would not reveal it. This was the oath which suspended the heavens and founded the earth, created the fountains, set bounds to the sea and determined the courses of the sun, moon and stars. 'This oath is mighty over them and through it ... their paths are preserved and their course is not destroyed' (*1 En.* 69.25). These four – the heavens and the stars, the earth, the fresh water of fountains and rivers, and the salt water of the sea – are a pattern by which the theme of the Eternal Covenant may be identified, for example, in the fourfold pattern of the destruction of the creation in Revelation 8.7–13, when the first four trumpets destroy earth, sea, fresh water and heaven, or in the destruction brought by the first four bowls of wrath poured on earth, sea, fresh water and the sun (Rev. 16.2–9, see pp. 173, 248).

God's laws showed how to live within this covenant bond, and if the laws were broken, the bonds of the covenant were also broken. 'Wrath' broke in and the security of the created order was at risk; the natural world and human society might return to the state of chaos which existed before the Eternal Covenant was established. Isaiah gave the most vivid description of the broken covenant:

The earth mourns and withers,
the world languishes and withers;
the heavens languish together with the earth.
The earth lies polluted under its inhabitants;
for they have transgressed the laws,

violated the statutes,
broken the everlasting covenant.
Therefore a curse devours the earth,
and its inhabitants suffer for their guilt. (Isa. 24.4–6)

Jeremiah depicted what happened when everything returned to its precreated state, when the bonds had gone and chaos had returned.

I looked on the earth, and lo, it was waste and void;*
and to the heavens, and they had no light.
I looked on the mountains, and lo, they were quaking,
and all the hills moved to and fro.
I looked, and lo, there was no man,
and all the birds of the air had fled.
I looked, and lo, the fruitful land was a desert,
and all its cities were laid in ruins
before the LORD, before his fierce anger. (Jer. 4.23–26)

There are several such passages in the Hebrew Scriptures, but nowhere is there any description of how the Eternal Covenant was first broken by rebel angels. *1 Enoch* has preserved this myth of the fallen angels which is mentioned briefly in Genesis 6.1–4. Some of the oldest Enochic material describes how Azazel, also named Semḥaza, led a rebellion against the Great Holy One. (Angels in the Qumran texts can have more than one name, e.g. the evil Melchiresha' says he has 'three names', but two are not clear (4Q544).) The rebellion of the angels took the form of coming to earth, taking human wives and revealing their heavenly knowledge to humans. Used without the restraint of divine Law, the heavenly knowledge – of metalworking and the manufacture of weapons, of drugs and enchantments, of cosmetics and jewellery, of astrology – was used to corrupt the earth. 'There arose much godlessness and they committed fornication, and they were led astray and became corrupt in all their ways' (*1 En.* 8.2). The lawlessness led to blood being shed on the earth, and eventually the cries of the victims were heard in heaven. The four archangels reported to the Great Holy One what was happening on earth, and he sent them out to bind Azazel and imprison him in the desert.

Cast him into the darkness ... make an opening in the desert and cast him therein ... and on the day of the great judgement he shall be cast into the fire. And heal the earth which the angels have corrupted and proclaim the healing of the earth that they may heal the plague ... And then shall the righteous escape ... and then shall the whole earth be tilled in righteousness ... Cleanse the earth from all oppression and all unrighteousness and from all sin and from all godlessness. (*1 En.* 10.4–7; 17–18)

---

*Waste and void is the description of the earth in Genesis 1.2, before God created the light of Day One.

There are several significant points in this passage: Azazel is cast into a pit in the desert until the final fire of judgement, which is the fate of the ancient serpent in Revelation 20. The corruption of the fallen angels brings plague on the earth, which has to be healed by the archangels. After the judgement the earth is restored to fertility and the righteous are safe, as in the millennium kingdom.

Although this myth of the fallen angels and their breach of the Eternal Covenant is not told in detail in the Hebrew Scriptures, it is presupposed by the earliest chapters of Isaiah. The Jerusalem which Isaiah condemns and warns of impending punishment, is full of horses and chariots, gold and silver idols (metalworking), has diviners and soothsayers, magicians and experts in charms, (astrology), and wanton women with jewellery and fine clothes (Isa. 2.6–3.26). He warns that the Strong One* and all his works will be burned (Isa. 1.31). In other words, the myth of the fallen angels was part of the world of the first temple.

The broken covenant was restored and renewed by atonement; the priests acted to prevent wrath breaking out on the people as a consequence of their sin. The Levites were installed to 'atone' in case anyone came too near to the holy place and thus risked plague (Num. 8.19). When Korah revolted, those who continued to support him were threatened with wrath from the LORD; a plague began but was stopped by Aaron with his high priestly incense. It was his priestly service that prevented the spread of the plague (Num. 16.47). The *Wisdom of Solomon* shows how this incident was understood towards the end of the second temple period; Aaron's priestly service of prayer and atonement with incense withstood the wrath and showed that he was the Servant of the LORD. He intervened and the Destroyer yielded, overcome by the glory of the Name which Aaron wore on his diadem (*Wisd.* 18.20–25). Two points should be noted in this account. First, that *therapon*, the word chosen for 'servant' is one which also means healer, and here that choice was apt; the rite of atonement was the rite of healing. (One possibility for the priestly Essenes is that their name means the healers; this is implied by Philo who relates them to the Therapeuts, the community of 'healers' in Egypt (*Cont. Life* 1).) Second, the high priest withstood the Destroyer, the dark and hostile aspect of the LORD. There are several passages in the Hebrew Scriptures where the LORD seems to be depicted as a hostile force, for example in the story of the tenth plague: 'I will smite all the firstborn' is followed by 'I will not allow the Destroyer to enter your houses' (Exod. 12.12, 23). The LORD and the Destroyer are closely identified, an important element in the ritual of the Day of Atonement. In the Book of Revelation, the LORD is the *Strong Angel*.

Another example of atonement is the story of Phineas. He made

---

*The chief of the fallen angels has many names but 'zz, 'be strong' is a common feature. Lev. 16.8 'z'zel conceals 'zz'l, 'strong god'.

atonement when he killed the apostate Israelite who had married a Midianite woman and thereby breached the covenant. Israel was at risk from the plague which began to break out, and by his prompt action, Phineas, the grandson of Aaron, protected them. As a result, the Lord gave him the covenant of *šlm*, wholeness. The letters *šlm* have a whole range of meanings, peace and retribution being but two of them. They indicate whatever is necessary to restore the state of completeness and wholeness. Phineas is given the task of maintaining the covenant (Num. 25.6–13). It is possible that Phineas was not *given* the covenant but was himself appointed to 'be' the covenant, the one who held the bonds secure like Isaiah's mysterious Servant who was *given as the Eternal Covenant* (Isa. 42.6; 49.8).

Different again was the Community Rule which said that the council of the community made atonement by acts of justice and by bearing affliction (1QS VIII). The whole community saw themselves making atonement 'to obtain loving kindness for the land' without offering burnt offerings and sacrifices. Prayer and right living were to be offered instead (1QS IX).

The great ritual of atonement was the Day of Atonement, described in Leviticus 16 and in the Mishnah. Two goats were chosen, identical in all aspects according to the ruling in *m. Yoma* 6.1. One of these was chosen by lot 'for the LORD' and the other 'for Azazel' (Lev. 16.8). When the Hebrew is translated in this way, this prescription has caused many problems for interpreters because it implies an offering made to Azazel, the chief of the fallen angels. Origen, the third-century Christian scholar who had close contacts with the Jewish scholars in Caesarea, understood the Hebrew differently and in a way that better explains the Day of Atonement prescriptions. The Hebrew preposition *le* can mean 'for' or 'as' and so *lyhwh* can mean 'for the LORD' but also 'as the LORD'. Origen understood it to be the latter and said that the goat driven into the desert was not 'for Azazel' but 'as Azazel'. The second goat 'was' Azazel and so the Day of Atonement ritual was one of banishing and imprisoning the leader of the fallen angels (*Cels.* 6.43). This corresponds to the account of the Day of the LORD in *1 Enoch*, when the archangels were sent out to bind and imprison Azazel and then to cleanse and heal the earth.

The cleansing and healing elements were supplied by the other goat, the one chosen by lot 'as the LORD'. This animal was sacrificed and his blood taken by the high priest into the holy of holies. Blood used in atonement rites was 'life' (Lev. 17.11). The logic of the ritual was that the blood/life of the goat was a substitute for the blood/life of the high priest who 'was' the LORD, as implied by the argument of the Letter to the Hebrews. Jesus, the great high priest, secured eternal redemption by taking his own blood into the holy of holies. Others had taken only the blood of animals, substitutes, so what they effected was only temporary and had to be repeated every year (Heb. 9.11–14). The high priest took a substitute for his own blood into the holy of holies, the only time that anyone ever entered the innermost part of the temple; there he sprinkled some blood on the *kapporet*, the place of atonement which in the first temple had probably been the throne. The rite of atonement then moved outwards from 'heaven' into the visible creation, with the high priest sprinkling blood in particular places to cleanse and to hallow (Lev. 16.19). The meaning of this is clear: the LORD himself renewed the creation every year by the gift of his own life. The creation was renewed by the creator. He was the Saviour (Isa. 43.3, 14, 15).

When the high priest emerged from the tent/temple, he put his hands on the head of the Azazel goat and transferred to him all the transgressions and sins of Israel. The goat bearing the sins, the scapegoat, was then driven away into the desert. The logic of the ritual implies that, for the high priest to be able to transfer the sins of Israel to the goat, he himself must have been carrying them as he emerged. The result of atonement was that iniquity was 'carried' by the high priest. The Hebrew word *naśa'* means both 'to carry' and, in the older texts of the Hebrew Scriptures, 'to forgive', but this is often obscured in English translations. A person 'carries' his own guilt when he deliberately breaks a law (Lev. 19.8), but the priests 'carry' the guilt of the sinner after they have performed the atonement ritual (Lev. 10.17). When the subject of the verb is the LORD, however, it is usually translated 'forgive'; e.g. 'Who is a God like you forgiving sin?' i.e. carrying sin (Mic. 7.18). 'Why do you not forgive' i.e. carry 'my transgression and cause my guilt to pass away?' (Job 7.21). The picture that emerges is that iniquity was carried by the priests, by the scapegoat and by the LORD. In the ritual of atonement, the scapegoat 'was' the aspect of the LORD which carried away the sins.

The guilt was borne in two ways: when the priests ate the flesh of the sin offering they absorbed the sin into themselves, as implied in Leviticus 10.17, when the priests were rebuked concerning the sin offering: 'Why have you not eaten the sin offering ... it has been given to you that you might carry the iniquity of the congregation to make atonement for them before the LORD?' Above all, the high priest absorbed iniquity when he wore the Name: '[The Name] shall be on Aaron's forehead and Aaron shall take upon himself any guilt incurred in the holy offering ...' (Exod. 28.38). In other words, the high priest as the LORD bore/forgave the sins of Israel. Psalm 32.1 expresses well what was understood by atonement: 'Blessed is the man carried in respect of his transgressions and covered in respect of his sin' (translating literally).

The outstanding description of the high priest is in the Isaiah's Servant Songs: he is 'the eternal covenant' (Isa. 42.6; 49.8); he is to restore the scattered people (Isa. 49.6) and he performs the great rite of atonement (Isa. 52.13–53.12). He 'sprinkles' many nations (Isa. 52.15); other translations offered, e.g. 'startles' have altered the Hebrew in some way. He carries the people's sickness and weakness (Isa. 53.4). He pours out himself, i.e. his life/blood, as a sin offering, *'ašam*, a word used elsewhere to describe the offering made by the Philistines to avert the plague of divine wrath and be healed from the plague (1 Sam. 6.3–4; Isa. 53.10). The enigmatic words 'chastisement that made us whole' could also be translated 'the covenant bond of our peace' (Isa. 53.5b).

This picture of the high priest as the sin-bearer and renewer of the creation is assumed in the New Testament depiction of Jesus: Matthew quotes 'he took our iniquities and bore our diseases' to explain the significance of the healing miracles (Matt. 8.17); Peter's sermon describes Jesus as 'the Holy and Righteous One, the Author of Life' (Acts 3.14–15). Jesus emptied himself as the Servant, i.e. he poured out his life/blood (Phil. 2.7); and he was the bond of cosmic unity 'in him all things hold together' (Col. 1.17; Eph. 1.10). The words at the Last Supper (Matt. 26. 26–28) are Jesus' renewal of this cosmic covenant, his own ritual of atonement: 'Eat my body' casts the disciples as the new priesthood eating the sin offering, and 'my blood of the new covenant' ['or the blood of my new covenant'], 'poured out' gives the context. What had formerly been sprinkled around the temple of stone was given to the new living temple of his disciples. (There is a problem as to what was done with the flesh of the sin offering on the Day of Atonement at this period: some sources say it had to be burnt (Lev. 16.27; *m. Yoma* 6.7), but the first-century CE *Letter of Barnabas*, a Levite, quotes from an unidentified 'prophet': 'Let all the priests, but no one else, eat of [the goat's] inward parts, unwashed and with vinegar' (*Barn.* 7). This is the only contemporary source which illuminates the command at the Last Supper: 'Take, eat this is my body'.)

As a result of the act of atonement, the covenant bond was renewed, the creation restored, and those who excluded themselves through sin were brought back within the community. Originally no doubt an annual ritual of social renewal, it was reinterpreted by the prophets of the exile. Ezekiel described how the LORD would recreate his exiled people through a great act of atonement; they had despised the oath and broken the covenant (language reminiscent of *1 En.* 69.16–25, the great oath which binds the creation in its place), but the LORD would re-establish the everlasting covenant when he atoned all they had done (Ezek. 16.59–63). The LORD would be king over his people, judge them, bring them back from all the countries where they had been scattered, purge out all rebels and transgressors and then bring them back within the bond of the covenant (Ezek. 20.33–38). Here Ezekiel was presenting a future hope for the exiles in Babylon in terms of the ancient rite of atonement. The Second Isaiah did something similar, but ascribed to the Servant (the LORD in his human manifestation as the royal high priest) the role of bringing back the scattered people (Isa. 49.6).

The ingathering of the people and the return of the exiles was a practical expression of atonement formalized in the Sabbath and Jubilee years. Every seventh year was observed as a Sabbath year when the land was allowed to rest, Hebrew slaves were released and debt to fellow Hebrews was cancelled (Exod. 21.2; 23.10–11, developed in Lev.

25.2–7 and Deut. 15.1–18). After seven times seven years a Jubilee was proclaimed by a trumpet call on the Day of Atonement; all returned to their own land and possessions. There is disagreement as to whether the Jubilee was observed in the forty-ninth year or the fiftieth, the traditional compromise being that it was fifty years in the first temple period, but forty-nine in the second. Leviticus 25.21, 'I will command my blessing and the land will bring forth fruit for three years' (not two), implies that the fallow Jubilee year followed the seventh Sabbath year. The ideal of restoration, each to living a life without working for food, each to a state of freedom and each to his own land, shows that it was a return to the Eden conditions of the sixth day of creation. After six days, when creation was completed and God saw that it was good (Gen. 1.31), he rested and presumably creation enjoyed the good state in which God had left it, before being marred by sin. It was only later, after disobedience, that food had to be won from the soil by human toil (Gen. 3.19). Just as atonement was the rite of renewal and recreation, so the Sabbath year and the Jubilee were practical expressions of that ideal.

The temple was a microcosm of the creation, and so Jubilee came to be associated with the restoration of the temple. Ezekiel's new year vision in the twenty-fifth year of his exile, i.e. 572 BCE, was a Jubilee vision; there would be a restored temple and priesthood (Ezek. 40–44) with the LORD returning to his place in the temple (Ezek. 43.1–5), and the land returned to the twelve tribes (Ezek. 47.13–48.29). Reckoning back a fifty-year Jubilee for the first temple period, Josiah's temple refurbishment fell in a Jubilee year, 622 BCE (2 Kgs 22.1–6), the Jubilee year 722 BCE fell in the reign of Ahaz who made several alterations to the temple (2 Kgs 16.10–18), the Jubilee year 822 BCE fell in the reign of Joash who restored the temple (2 Chron. 24.4–14), the Jubilee year 872 BCE fell in the reign of Jehoshapat who removed high places and Asherim (2 Chron. 17.6). Reckoning a Jubilee from Ezekiel's vision gives the year 522 BCE, a possible date for the return of Joshua and Zerubbabel to rebuild the temple as the work was frustrated by local opposition until the second year of Darius, 520 BCE (Ezra 4.24). Reckoning forty-nine years for second temple Jubilees, there would have been a Jubilee in 424 BCE and one possible date for Ezra's mission to re-establish Jerusalem is 428 BCE, presumably in time for the Jubilee year. Ezra's controversial covenant at that time, when many Jews were forced to abandon their 'foreign' wives caused great bitterness (Ezra 10.2–5) and the excluded worshippers of the LORD looked back to this time as the beginning of an evil era. There were changes which they could not accept, and which would bring the LORD'S judgement on the restored temple (Isa. 66.3–6).

Daniel's prophecy of the Great Atonement, which would put an end to sin and destroy both Jerusalem and the temple, reckons seventy weeks of years from 'the going forth of the word to restore and rebuild Jerusalem' (Dan. 9.25). Seventy weeks of years, 490 years, can also be reckoned as ten Jubilees, and in the Melchizedek text (11QMelch) there is a similar expectation of the Great Atonement and judgement after ten Jubilees. Only fragments have survived, which begin by quoting the Jubilee laws of Leviticus 25 and Deuteronomy 15, interpreting them for 'the last days'. The captives who are to return are people whose teachers have been 'hidden and kept secret' and these 'people of the inheritance of Melchizedek' will return. There is insufficient text for certainty, but this could be a group who have been secretly preserving the teachings of the first temple, when there was a Melchizedek priesthood. In the tenth Jubilee Melchizedek would reveal 'the end times of the world' and his people would return, (perhaps to the temple as priests?) The liberty of the Jubilee is interpreted as release from iniquities and from the power of Belial and his horde, and it is the beginning of the atonement which was to occur on the Day of Atonement at the end of the tenth Jubilee. The return of the high priest and the release were to happen in the first week, i.e. the first seven years, of the tenth Jubilee. Melchizedek would take his place in the heavenly council, fulfilling Psalm 82.1, and the judgement of the tenth Jubilee would begin. Throughout the Melchizedek text there is allusion to Isaiah 61, the one anointed by the Spirit 'to proclaim liberty', the Jubilee prescription in Leviticus 25.10.

Reckoning from Ezra's Jubilee in 424 BCE gives the date 66 CE for the end of the tenth Jubilee, and so the first week of that Jubilee would have fallen between 18 and 24 CE. Now if Jesus was born between 12 and 6 BCE (Herod the Great died in 4 BCE when Jesus was a child, Matt. 2.19), then his baptism at the age of thirty (Luke 3.23) would have occurred, *during the first week of the tenth Jubilee*. Jesus believed himself to be the Melchizedek high priest, the anointed one who was to appear in the tenth Jubilee. After his baptism he began to preach. 'The time is fulfilled' (Mark 1.15) and he claimed that the prophecy of Isaiah 61 was fulfilled (Luke 4.16–21), that he was the one anointed by the Spirit to bring the Jubilee. The Book of Revelation records the prophecies of the tenth Jubilee, when the kingdom of God was at hand and the Day of the LORD was expected within fifty years. Jesus was proclaimed as Melchizedek (Heb. 7.11), he took his place in the heavenly council (Rev. 5.6–14, fulfilling Ps. 82.1), and the judgement was about to take place. The Book of Revelation was Melchizedek's teaching about the end times, and begins 'The revelation of Jesus Christ which God gave him to show to his servants what must soon take place'. It is a record of the prophecies of the tenth Jubilee and their fulfilment during the first generation of the church.

The Book of Revelation describes the process of the great atonement as it was realized in history in first-century Palestine. The Christian hope of the return of the LORD was identical with the hope for the culmination of the tenth Jubilee and the restoration of the creation for the time of the Messiah. It was John, the beloved disciple, who extricated a new interpretation of the return of the LORD from the carnage of the war against Rome (see p. 183).

The Warrior Priests

The LORD, the God of Israel, was a warrior; there had been a Book of
the Wars of the LORD, of which only a few lines survive in Numbers
21.14–15. One ancient poem incorporated into the story of the Exodus,
proclaims: 'The LORD is a man of war ... thy right hand O LORD
shatters the enemy' (Exod. 15.3, 6). The LORD fights for his people on
a cosmic scale; the floods congeal, the earth swallows their enemies.
Another ancient poem celebrates the defeat of the kings of Canaan in
the time of Deborah. 'When the LORD appeared, the earth trembled and
the heavens dropped, yea the clouds dropped water' (Judg. 5.4). The
stars in heaven and the torrent of Kishon joined in the battle against the
kings, and the tribes of Israel sent men to help the LORD in the struggle.
The battle was against the enemies of the LORD (Judg. 5.31) and the
people of Israel went freely to help. Habakkuk described his vision of
the LORD going forth for the salvation of his people and his Messiah
(Hab. 3.13). As the Holy One emerged, his glory filled the heavens;
plague and pestilence attended him as he measured the earth and shook
the nations. The creation writhed, warriors were crushed.

The Psalms are full of these pictures of conflict and triumph; they
describe triumph over the powers of chaos, the waters, so that the LORD
can establish the creation and rule as King on his holy mountain. The
cosmic phenomena of the creation break into the actual history of
Israel. The king is enthroned in triumph over his enemies (Ps. 2), but
also over the floods (Ps. 29). Similar patterns can be seen in Psalms 9,
24, 46, 47, 48, 68, 76, 77, 89, 97, 98, 104. Similar scenes are depicted
in the texts from Ugarit. Baal is equipped with two mighty maces,
Expeller and Driver, to fight against Yam-Nahar, the sea deity; he fells
him with his mace and dries him up (KTU 1.2.iv). A palace, i.e. a
temple, is then built for him and a banquet prepared (KTU 1.4.v–vi).
When Baal speaks, the earth quakes and the mountains are in fear (KTU
1.4.vii).

Isaiah advocated faith in the warrior God rather than in the political
alliances which the rulers of Jerusalem favoured. He exhorted Ahaz to
trust in the LORD (Isa. 7.4–9), he condemned any practical preparations
to protect the city (Isa. 22.8–11) and denounced those who sought
alliance with Egypt (Isa. 31.1–3). 'The LORD of hosts will come down
to fight upon Mount Zion and upon its hill. Like birds hovering, so the
LORD of hosts will protect Jerusalem; he will protect and deliver it, he
will spare and rescue it' (Isa. 31.4–5). When Jerusalem was threatened
by the armies of Assyria, the city was miraculously delivered: 'The angel
of the LORD went forth and slew a hundred and eighty-five thousand in
the camp of the Assyrians'. (Isa. 37.36).

Just as the LORD was a warrior, so too were his priests (c.f. 2 Chron.
26.17). Melchizedek, the royal high priest, was described in terms
reminiscent of the warrior Baal. He had a mighty sceptre which was sent
out from Zion to rule over his enemies. The LORD was to stand beside

his high priest to shatter kings and execute judgement, piling up corpses and shattering heads (Ps. 110.6). Since the high priest was himself the manifestation of the LORD, he must have been a warrior and the leader in holy war. Stories were told of heavenly warriors who appeared; the angel of the LORD with his sword drawn, confronted Balaam (Num. 22.31), the angel of the LORD slew the Assyrian army, a mounted warrior with weapons of gold repulsed a robber from the temple treasury (2 Macc. 3.25–26), Judas Maccabeus was protected by heavenly warriors. His enemies saw five heavenly warriors at the head of the Jewish armies (2 Macc. 10.29) and as they approached Jerusalem, a horseman clothed in white and brandishing weapons of gold appeared at the head of the column (2 Macc. 11.8). The War Scroll describes the day of the last battle, when the archangel Michael would appear:

This is the day appointed by him for the defeat and overthrow of the prince of the kingdom of wickedness and he shall send eternal succour to the company of his redeemed by the might of the princely angel of the kingdom of Michael ... he will raise up the kingdom of Michael in the midst of the gods and the realm of Israel in the midst of all flesh. (1QM XVII)

In the *Assumption of Moses* the great warrior priest emerges from his holy place to bring vengeance on Israel's enemies and banish Satan (*Ass. Mos.* 10. 1–4). The Melchizedek text (11Q Melch) describes the warrior priest appearing in the first week of the tenth Jubilee, rescuing his own people 'from the powers of Satan and the spirits who rebelled by turning away from the precepts of God'.

Phineas the high priest led Israel in war against the Midianites and Balaam the false prophet. One thousand soldiers from each tribe were assembled to fight and Phineas went with them taking the vessels of the holy of holies and the trumpets for alarm (Num. 31.6). These appear in the Book of Revelation as the seven trumpets and the seven bowls of wrath. They killed the five kings of Midian and the false prophet (Num. 31.8). The Hebrew Christians identified Paul as the Balaam of their time (see pp. 99–100), and when he visited Jerusalem for the last time it is clear that he was in danger from those Christians who were zealous for the Law of Moses (Acts 21.20–24). The crowd accused him of teaching what was contrary to the Law and of defiling the temple (Acts 21.28).

When Israel went to war, it was as the host of the LORD; they had to remain in a state of ritual purity 'because the LORD your God walks in the midst of your camp to save you and give up your enemies before you' (Deut. 23.14). It was not that the people were fighting for their God but that the LORD was fighting for them against their enemies. The warriors described in the War Scroll had to observe the same rules; no one with a blemish or impurity could be part of their host and everyone had to serve of his own free will, 'perfect in spirit and body and prepared for the Day of Vengeance' (1QM VII). The priests were part of the battle formation.

When the battle formations are marshalled facing the enemy, formation facing formation, seven priests of the sons of Aaron shall advance from the middle gates to the place between the formations. They shall be clothed in vestments of white cloth of flax, in a fine linen tunic and fine linen breeches and they shall be girdled with a fine cloth of flax embroidered with blue, purple and scarlet thread, a many coloured design worked by craftsmen. And on their head they shall wear mitred turbans. (1QM VII)

All those [who are ready] for battle shall march out and shall pitch their camp before the king of the Kittim and before all the host of Satan gathered about him for the day [of revenge] by the sword of God. The high priest shall rise with the [priests] his brethren, and the Levites and all the men of the army, and shall recite aloud the prayer in time of war. (1 QM XV)

The War Scroll, with its detailed prescriptions for the final war against the host of Satan and the Kittim, shows that there was more to the bitter struggle against Rome than Josephus records. He depicts a small group of fanatical revolutionaries who took advantage of the instability following the death of Nero in 68 CE. As he had himself defected to the Romans, he can hardly be regarded as an impartial reporter of what happened. He does, however, give some clues as to what motivated the rebels. He frequently mentions prophets – he calls them false prophets – in the revolutionary politics of the time. He described them as 'villains with purer hands' [than the actual assassins], 'but with more impious intentions who no less than the assassins ruined the peace of the city. Deceivers and impostors, under the pretence of divine inspiration fostering revolutionary changes, they persuaded the multitude to act like madmen' (*War* 2.259). Reflecting on the final destruction of the temple he wrote:

They owed their destruction to a false prophet who on that day proclaimed to the people in the city that God commanded them to go up to the temple court to receive there tokens of their deliverance. Numerous prophets, indeed, were at this period suborned by the tyrants [i.e. the revolutionaries] to delude the people, by bidding them await help from God, in order that desertions might be checked ... Thus it was that at that time the wretched people were deluded by charlatans and pretended messengers of the deity. (*War* 6.285–6, 288)

From the other point of view, the revolutionaries would have been described as people expecting divine intervention to assist them in the struggle, people who were inspired by prophets and angels ('messengers of the deity'). Far from seizing the moment afforded by the death of Nero, these were people who believed they were living at the end of the tenth Jubilee, when they would be released from servitude to a foreign power and restored to their own land. Theirs was the faith of Isaiah, that the LORD himself would come down to fight upon Mount Zion, to protect and deliver Jerusalem. They could well have been the saints of the Book of Revelation, exhorted to endure and keep the faith of Jesus (14.12–13). During the 50s, the young churches were expecting the imminent return of the LORD, after Caligula's attempt in 40 CE to desecrate the temple with a statue of himself (*War* 2.184–203). This was part of the mystery of lawlessness which Paul knew was working towards its inevitable conclusion, the Day of the LORD (2 Thess. 2.2–8). The letters to the seven churches were written at this time and show clearly what was expected: 'I will keep you from the hour of trial which is coming upon the whole world, to those who dwell upon the earth. I am coming soon. Hold fast to what you have' (3.10–11).

Several of the prophets were messianic figures who led people out into the wilderness, hence the warning: 'False Christs and false prophets will arise ... so if they say to you "Lo he is in the wilderness" do not go out (Matt. 24.24–26). Retreat into the wilderness was symbolic of the new exodus from the corrupted city, the Egypt which had become another name for Jerusalem (11.8). After Pompey took Jerusalem by force in 63 BCE, 'those who loved the assemblies of the devout fled from them ... refugees in the wilderness to save their lives from evil' (*Pss Sol.* 17.16–17). The mysterious Taxo took his seven sons to live in a cave rather than break the commandments (*Ass. Mos.* 9.6–7). There was an Egyptian who led a large group out into the wilderness to prepare to recapture Jerusalem (Acts 21.38; *War* 2.261). James, the first bishop of Jerusalem, led 5000 Hebrew Christians out of the city to the region of Jericho after he had been attacked in the temple by Saul's henchmen (*Clem. Rec.* 1.71). These were probably the Hebrews who had been abused in Jerusalem (Heb. 10.32–35) and left 'Egypt' to wait for their final Sabbath rest in the wilderness (Heb. 3.16–4.10). John the Baptist had fulfilled the prophecy 'In the wilderness prepare the way of the LORD' (Isa. 40.3), and the woman clothed with the sun had fled to the wilderness to escape from the great serpent (12.14). Passover became a sensitive time, when Jerusalem was crowded with pilgrims celebrating their earlier liberation from Egypt. The chief priests were wary of arresting Jesus at this time 'lest there be a tumult among the people' (Matt. 26.5), and the angels who poured out the bowls of wrath poured out the plagues of the first Exodus: sores, water turned to blood, darkness, frogs and hail (16.1–21). They were to mark the new liberation.

The Day of the LORD was believed to be imminent, and so people sought protection from the wrath. This was the original significance of the line in the LORD's Prayer: 'Do not bring us to the time of trial but deliver us from evil'. Some sought baptism to protect themselves (Luke 3.7; Acts 2.37–40). Words attributed to Peter show that the protection was believed to extend even to earthly warfare:

Everyone who, believing in this Prophet who had been foretold by Moses, is baptized in his name, shall be kept unhurt from the destruction of war which impends over the unbelieving nation and the place itself; but those that do not believe shall be made exiles from their place and kingdom, that even against their will they may understand and obey the will of God. (*Clem. Rec.* 1.39)

Whatever the date of this text, it shows either that the young church gave a political significance to baptism or was believed to have done so, another indication that those whom Josephus called the false prophets, those who encouraged people to believe that God would protect them from disaster, were Christian prophets.

Others sought to follow the example of Phineas the grandson of Aaron who averted the wrath of the LORD by killing those who had broken covenant laws. Phineas was zealous for his God (Num. 25.13), and so these new guardians of the covenant were called Zealots. Phineas was remembered and praised as a hero (Ps. 106.28–31) and his zeal for the LORD became the inspiration for the Maccabees, another priestly family who had led a war of liberation in the 160s BCE. Mattathias, a priest of the sons of Joarib, left Jerusalem because of the blasphemies committed there (1 Macc. 2.6). The holy place was given over to aliens, and the city had become a slave. When he saw a fellow Jew about to offer a sacrifice according to the command of the pagan king, Mattathias killed the Jew and the king's officer and tore down the altar. 'Thus he burned with zeal for the law as Phineas did against Zimri the son of Salu' (1 Macc. 2.26). He exhorted his sons to remember the nature of true priesthood: 'Phineas our father, because he was deeply zealous, received the covenant of everlasting priesthood' (1 Macc. 2.54). His son Judas 'went through the cities of Judah: He destroyed the ungodly out of the land; thus he turned away the wrath from Israel ... he gathered in those who were perishing' (1 Macc. 3.8–9). The issue was priesthood, true priesthood, and what this entailed. The Maccabees exemplify the traditional role of the priest as a warrior protecting the people: the Servant of the LORD, keeping the temple pure so that the LORD could dwell in the midst of his people, turning away the wrath as did Aaron in the wilderness, and gathering in those who were lost. The theme of the letters to the seven churches was true priesthood, as was the reassurance that the redeemed had become the new royal priesthood (1.6; 5.10; 20.4–6).

From the time of the Maccabees, the purity of the temple had been a major concern of movements against foreign rule, and the conduct of those foreign rulers shows why this was so. Antiochus Epiphanes in 169 BCE entered the holy of holies and looted the temple furniture (1 Macc. 1.20–24), later setting up a statue of Zeus on the great altar (1 Macc. 1.54), 'the abomination that makes desolate' (Dan. 11.31). In 63 BCE Pompey had entered the holy of holies although he took nothing (War 1.152). Crassus had plundered the temple treasury in 53 BCE to fund his expedition against the Parthians (War 1.179). When Herod finally gained entrance to Jerusalem in 37 BCE, he managed to restrain his Roman allies and prevent further violation of the temple (War 1.354), but towards the end of his reign he himself violated it by erecting a golden eagle over the main gate. He did not live to see the trouble this caused. During Passover that year his successor Archelaus let his army loose on the protesting crowds and 3000 were killed. In 26 CE Pontius Pilate brought military standards into the temple, each bearing an image of Caesar, but mass protest forced their removal (*War* 2.169–74). Caligula ordered his statue to be set in the temple in 40 CE but died before the order could be carried out and so another crisis was averted (*War* 2.184–203). When Gessius Florus stole seventeen talents from the temple treasury in 66 CE, he ignited the rebellion against Rome (*War* 2.293). The revolt began in the temple itself, during August of that year. Sicarii, i.e. Zealots, burned the houses of the high priest and of Agrippa and Bernice, the rulers who had collaborated with Rome. They then burned all records of debt, showing that this was a Jubilee rebellion (*War* 2.427). The Day of Atonement at the end of the tenth Jubilee was two months away.

The Zealots saw themselves as the true priests, upholding the Law and protecting the holiness of the temple. They strove to turn away the wrath from Israel and, like Phineas, chose direct action against offenders. It is against such a background of holy war that the Book of Revelation – indeed the whole New Testament – must be read. The Fourth Gospel links a 'Zealot' text to Jesus' cleansing of the temple: 'Zeal for thy house will consume me' (John 2.17, quoting Ps. 69.9) and, although there is insufficient evidence to say how far Hebrew Christians were involved in the struggle against Rome, there is overwhelming evidence that they were concerned with the true priesthood and good reason to believe that some at least were Zealots. Simon, son of John, (John 1.42; 21.15) for example, appears also as Simon Barjona (Matt. 16.17). The Aramaic word *barjona* (plural *barjone*) appears in the Babylonian Talmud as the name for the Zealots in Jerusalem. When Rabbi Johannan ben Zakkai managed to escape from the city and went to talk to Vespasian, he was asked, 'Why did you not come sooner?' He replied: 'The *barjone* among us did not let me' (*b. Gittin* 56a). Similarly, there is Simon the Zealot (Luke 6.15; Acts 1.13) who was also known as Simon the Cananean (Mark 3.18; Matt. 10.4). The most likely explanation of Cananean is that it was a transliteration of the Aramaic *qan'ana'*: Zealot. There was also Judas Iscariot whose name probably derived from *sicarius*, an assassin who used a dagger and Josephus' name for the rebels against Rome in 66 CE (*War* 2.254). The Talmud named the leader of the *barjone* in Jerusalem as Abba Sikera, literally Father of the Sicarii (*b. Gittin* 56a). So many similarities cannot be coincidence; there must have been Zealots among Jesus' disciples.

Some people chose baptism and others chose direct action, but their objective was the same; protection from the wrath. Jesus believed he was Melchizedek, the high priest who would finally turn away the wrath from Israel by offering himself as the atonement sacrifice of the tenth Jubilee. There is insufficient evidence to show how the various groups related to each other. The martyrs under the altar are clearly part of the Great Atonement (see p. 154), but why they died is not clear. There is no evidence that they died for their Christian beliefs although the last of their number may have been James the Righteous. Some could have been Christian Zealots who were, according to Josephus, deluded by false prophets in their struggle against Rome. It was not only Christians who refused to worship Caesar. Josephus records that even under torture, the Zealot refugees in Egypt refused to confess Caesar as their master (*War* 7.418). From the beginning of the struggle, the resistance movement founded by Judas the Galilean in about 6 CE had maintained that God was their only ruler and master. No fear of death could induce them to alter this belief (*Ant.* 18.23). This was a century earlier than Pliny's letter from Bithynia which described how Christians were compelled to offer incense to Caesar. It is often argued that a similar worship of Caesar was required of Christians in Asia Minor at an earlier date and that this persecution of the churches, *for which there is no evidence*, was the occasion of the Book of Revelation.

The concerns of the Zealots were freedom from Rome, a true and pure priesthood, a purified holy city and atonement to protect themselves from the wrath of judgement. Like the holy warriors of old, they had an unshakeable belief that the LORD would fight with them against their enemies, and this is exactly the concern of the Book of Revelation. The Benedictus could well be a Zealot song, sung by Zechariah the priest to celebrate the prophet of the Most High who was to herald the Anointed One:

... that we should be saved from our enemies,
and from the hand of all who hate us;
to perform the mercy promised to our forefathers
and to remember his holy covenant,
the oath which he swore to our forefather Abraham
to grant us that we, being delivered from the hand of our enemies,
might serve him without fear,
in holiness and righteousness before him
all the days of our life. (Luke 1.68–79)

The very familiarity of these words should not obscure what they actually say, nor that these sentiments were deemed by Luke to be the appropriate preface to his Gospel.

4

THE WORDS OF THIS BOOK

The traditional view of the Book of Revelation is that St John was in exile on the island of Patmos and on one Sunday ('the LORD's Day', 1.10), he saw the visions – all of them – and then wrote them down. The history of the book is rather more complicated than this. John, the beloved disciple and church elder, was responsible for the final form of the text, and his inspiration to write it down in this way could well have come to him on Patmos, but the words of this book were already ancient when John gave them their final form.

The Temple Tradition

The oldest material in the Book of Revelation is a series of temple visions similar to those preserved in the Parables of Enoch, which are three parallel accounts of the throne vision: the Man who ascends to the throne and presides on the Day of the LORD. The three do not form a chronological sequence, but each describes a different aspect of the same scene. A great deal has been added to the texts so that the original structure is far from clear. In the first Parable (1 *En*. 38–44), the Righteous One appears and the godless are judged. The seer stands before the throne where he sees the four archangels, hears the song of the heavenly hosts and learns the secrets of the creation. The text is fragmented and there are several obvious insertions. The second Parable (1 *En*. 45–57), describes how the Man goes up to the throne, the heavenly counterpart of the Day of Atonement ritual in the temple. The blood of the Righteous One and the prayers of the righteous on earth are offered in heaven, and the books are opened for the judgement to begin. The third Parable (1 *En*. 58–71), recounts more secrets of the creation and then describes the judgement of the earth and the final blessed state of the righteous. The names of the fallen angels are listed and their deeds recorded. There is also a fragment of poetry about the whole creation being bound together by a great oath.

The framework of the three Parables is the testimony of Enoch whose name means 'the initiated or consecrated one'. He bears witness that he has been given Wisdom and eternal life (1 *En*. 37.4) and has then been shown the three visions. *This important information shows who received such visions; it was those who had already received eternal life, that is, who had been resurrected.*

There are several features of the Parables which illuminate the Book of Revelation. First, Enoch is a high priest. He is not any particular high priest, but a representative figure. In the earliest Enoch text, he enters the heavenly temple to stand before the throne (1 *En*. 14); in Jubilees he offers incense before the LORD (*Jub*. 4.25), and in the Parables he sees visions of the Day of the LORD and learns the secrets of the creation. In other words, he is the one permitted to enter the holy of holies and, like the psalmist (Ps. 73.12–20), to see there the fate of the wicked. The strangest feature of the Parables is their last chapter (*1 En.* 71) which seems to describe how Enoch himself was transformed into the Man, the process of apotheosis by which the high priest came to be the LORD. This transformation is more clearly described in *2 Enoch* where Enoch stands before the throne, is anointed and then becomes an angel: 'Take Enoch from his earthly clothing and anoint him ... and put on him the clothes of my glory ... And I looked at myself and I had become like one of his glorious ones' (*2 En.* 22.8–10). Here the ritual of anointing, becoming a Messiah, is linked to putting on the garments of glory, that is, putting on the resurrection body of an angel. In *3 Enoch*, a much later Enoch text which incorporates earlier tradition, it is quite clear that Enoch has ascended to heaven and been transformed into the greatest of the angels, the one who bears the Name: 'He set the crown upon my head and he called me The Little LORD in the presence of his whole household in the height, as it is written My Name is in him' (*3 En.* 12.4–5). Here Enoch has not only been anointed and resurrected, he has been given the Name. Sensitivities and confusions in the second temple period resulted in both El Elyon and his Son being named as the LORD. This can be seen in Ben Sira's prayer 'to the LORD, the Father of my LORD' (*Ben Sira* 51.10), and in 'Isaiah's' account of his vision where he saw 'how my LORD and the angel of the Holy Spirit worshipped and both together praised the LORD' (*Asc. Isa.* 9.40).

The Book of Revelation is a similar anthology of high priestly material describing mystical experiences in the holy of holies. This was the knowledge given to the resurrected. The Book of Revelation must be read in the light of Josephus' evidence that portents were seen and voices heard in the temple by those who served there (*War* 6.288–309). The visions of the Book of Revelation have a temple setting and the obvious conclusion to draw is that they came from priests and high priests, in some cases interpreting the very portents which Josephus records (see pp. 247–50).

The visions were interpreted by priest-prophets who had insights into the mysteries. The *Ascension of Isaiah*, a thinly veiled account of the activities of Christian prophets in Palestine, describes how they used to assemble to hear the words of their master.

There were about forty prophets and sons of the prophets and they came from the neighbouring districts and from the mountains and from the country when they heard that Isaiah was coming ... They came that they might greet him, and that they might hear his words, and that he might lay his hand on them and that they might prophesy ... They all heard a door being opened and the voice of the Spirit. (*Asc. Isa.* 6.3–6)

The prophets wrote out and kept the account of what Isaiah had seen concerning 'the judgement of the angels, the destruction of this world, the robes of the saints, and their going out* and their transformation and the persecution and ascension of the Beloved' (*Asc. Isa.* 1.5). This is not recognizable as a description of the Book of Isaiah, but bears a striking resemblance to the Book of Revelation which is steeped in allusions to Isaiah. One wonders if this later 'Isaiah' was drawn from life, and has preserved a genuine glimpse of the Christian prophets in Palestine and their leader. 'When Isaiah saw the great iniquity which was committed in Jerusalem', he left the city and went to live 'on a mountain in a desert place', where many other prophets came to join him, 'the faithful who believed in the ascension into heaven'. They lived the life of desert hermits, clothed in sackcloth and eating wild plants (*Asc. Isa.* 2.7–11). The *Ascension of Isaiah* could well preserve the story of James the Righteous who ascended to receive visions (see pp. 193–4).

Qumran texts are full of references to a person or persons who claimed similar experiences of visions and mysteries: 'who have heard the voice of majesty, who have seen the angels of holiness, whose ear has been unstopped and who have heard profound things' (1QM X). 'Thou hast made me . . . a discerning interpreter of wonderful mysteries' (1QH X, formerly II). 'Thou hast given me knowledge through thy marvellous mysteries' (1QH XII, formerly IV). 'In thy marvellous mysteries . . . thou hast granted me knowledge' (1QH XV, formerly VII). The Qumran texts also speak of *rz nhyh*, perhaps to be translated 'mystery of existence' or perhaps the 'mystery which is to come': for example 'he has opened your ears to the mystery of existence' (4Q416), 'meditate on the mystery of existence' (4Q417). We can only guess what this might have been, but the seventh trumpet was to bring the fulfilment of 'the mystery of God as he announced to his servants the prophets' (10.7). Cryptic allusions in the Gospels show that Jesus knew these mysteries and, like 'Enoch', believed he had been anointed and transformed into the Man at the centre of the visions. They became the pattern for his own role and ministry, hence 'He bears witness to what he has seen and heard, yet no one receives his testimony' (John 3.32).

The leader of the community described in the Qumran scrolls was the *meᵇbaqqer,* often translated 'the Guardian'. His duty was 'to make wise the Many in the matter of the works of God . . . and tell them the happenings of eternity and their interpretations . . . he shall love them as a father loves his children and shall carry them in their distress like a shepherd his sheep' (CD XIII). The name given to this teacher is significant, meaning literally 'the one who seeks out'. In Ezekiel 34.11–12 it is 'the one who seeks out' his flock, the good shepherd, but in Psalm 27.4 there is the more common meaning of the word, 'to enquire' (after the LORD) in his temple. It seems that the Guardian of the camps did both; he told his people about the happenings of eternity and he was their pastor. In each of these two examples, the LXX renders the word by a part of the verb *episkopein,* whence the more familiar

---

*Cf. Luke 9.31, Jesus' 'going out' in Jerusalem.

episkopos, bishop. The *m^ebaqqer*, the Guardian of the camps who was both teacher and pastor, was probably the model for the Christian bishop.

The Myths of Israel

Myth is a difficult word, avoided by biblical scholars because of unfortunate popular usage. The myths of ancient Israel were the stories which described and explained their view of creation and the structures of their society. Some of their myths were drawn from the stories we read as Israel's history, for example the Exodus, which was used as one explanation of the Sabbath (Deut. 5.12–15). Others are less familiar to us but were very like those of neighbouring cultures, for example, of Ugarit.

Since a chance discovery in 1928, scholars have been rediscovering the ancient city of Ugarit on the Syrian coast. Clay tablets from about 1500–1200 BCE record the myths of one of Israel's neighbours, and their strange poetry reveals a world quite alien to modern ways of thinking but remarkably similar to that of the Book of Revelation. Their king was described as the son of the high god El and the sun goddess. He had a dual nature, both male and female, and he was called the Morning Star and represented by two goats. Both the dual nature and the title Morning Star appear in the Book of Revelation and the two goats suggest a link to the Day of Atonement. At his enthronement the king ascended to heaven where he received royal power and then returned to earth to rule. Similar patterns elsewhere in the Ancient Near East show that the king was taught the wisdom of the gods while in heaven. The king had to battle with the forces of chaos in order to assert his authority on earth and this was described as a struggle with a great sea monster, using weapons he had been given in heaven.

Traces of these myths break the surface in the Hebrew Scriptures, most clearly in the vivid imagery of the prophets and the psalms. The king is born from the womb of the Dawn (Ps. 110.3), he rules over the sea and the rivers (Ps. 89.25), and the LORD himself cut Rahab in pieces and pierced the dragon (Isa. 51.9). These were more than just imagery; through these myths we glimpse the world view of ancient Israel which was very similar to that of ancient Ugarit.

The Book of Revelation has the same myths. It would be incorrect to say that the people who composed these oracles and their interpretations *used* the myths in the sense that it was a conscious literary device on their part. The prophets of Israel, even in the first century CE, simply thought in that way. They wrote history and commented on current events in terms of a dragon (12.3) and beasts (13.1, 11), or of a royal child born from the womb of the Dawn (12.1–2, the woman clothed with the sun).

Revelation 4–11 is recognizable as the myth of the royal ascent to heaven in its Hebrew form, ritualized at the start of each year, when the king ascended to heaven and then returned to renew the creation. It opens with the throne vision and then describes the enthronement of the Lamb who is the Servant King. He opens the scroll with seven seals, the secrets of heaven, and there is silence in heaven when he prepares to emerge as the angel high priest. The sequence of the seven trumpets is inserted to mark the delay in his return, and finally, he appears on earth as the Great Angel (10.1) to establish his kingdom as the anointed one (11.15–18). This was the Day of the LORD and so 'I was in the Spirit on the LORD's Day' (1.10) means that the seer received a vision of the Day of the LORD.

In the royal cult of the first temple, the priest-king offered in the holy of holies a substitute for his own life-blood – perhaps he submitted to a symbolic death before being enthroned – which appears in the cult of the second temple as the Day of Atonement ritual with the two goats who were the ancient emblems of the king. The king then emerged to atone the land, that is, to heal it and remove the effects of sin. He brought judgement on his enemies and restored his people. In the Song of Moses, a piece of ancient poetry mentioned in Revelation 15.3, there is a description of this scene: the LORD emerges to bring judgement and atonement: 'to avenge the blood of his sons ... and to atone the land' (Deut. 32.43; 4QDeut^q). Isaiah's great Servant Song (Isa. 52.13–53.12) depicts a high priest who pours out his soul, i.e. his blood, as a sin offering: 'he makes himself an offering for sin ... he poured out his soul to death' (Isa. 53.10, 12). Both these texts are ancient, from the first temple period, and both were emphasized by the early church in their claims about Jesus (Heb. 1.6 quotes from the Song of Moses; Phil. 2.7 alludes to Isa. 53.12). The original meaning of the texts had not been forgotten, even if it is impossible to show by whom it had been preserved and where.

Another piece of temple tradition underlies Revelation 12.1–2 which originally described the coronation of a new king, his ritual 'birth' as Son of El and the Dawn and his ascent to the heavenly throne. This is described in several places in the Hebrew Scriptures. In Psalm 2.7 the new king declares he has heard the LORD acknowledge him as his Son. 'You are my Son today I have begotten you.' In Psalm 89.19–37, the LORD speaks to the king in a vision, raises him up on high, anoints him and makes him ruler of the kings of the earth with power over the waters. God crushes his enemies and the king calls God his Father. The last words of King David also describe how he was raised on high and anointed so as to speak the words of the LORD (2 Sam. 23.1). The most remarkable and enigmatic witness to the 'birth' of the king is Psalm 110, another text much used by the early church. The LXX of verse 3, which is clearer than the Hebrew, says that the LORD 'begot' the king and then made him a priest for eternity in the manner of Melchizedek. This belief appears also in the Messianic Rule: 'When God begets the (priestly) Messiah, he will come [ ] the head of the whole congregation of Israel' (1QSa II).

The remainder of the Book of Revelation describes the king's conflicts with the monsters who oppose his rule, the dragon and the beasts. Eventually he triumphs, establishes his authority and renews the creation.

If all the libraries of the Ancient Near East had survived and all the myths were known, it would doubtless be possible to identify other elements in the Book of Revelation and place them accurately in the overall picture. As it is, there is sufficient evidence only to show that the ancient myths still shaped the world view of some people in the first century CE. Patterns in the Book of Revelation invite speculation: the seven seals, the seven trumpets, the seven bowls. The quartet: heaven, earth, sea and rivers/fountains recurs, but in random order, describing the creation at 14.7 (also in Ps. 104 and Prov. 8) and also the destruction of the creation by the first four trumpets (8.7–12) and the first four bowls (16.2–9). There are several fragments of text as in the Parables of Enoch. Duplicate passages, such as the redeemed before the throne (7.1–8; 14.1–5), are a sign that earlier collections of oracles were incorporated intact into the final form of the Book of Revelation. Several passages are very similar to material found at Qumran: for example, the coming of the warrior angel (19.11–16) resembles the War Scroll (1QM) and the vision of the New Jerusalem (21.10–21) is similar to the New Jerusalem Text reconstructed from fragments found in Caves 1, 2, 4, 5 and 11.

The Language of the Visions

These are priestly writings, steeped in the Hebrew Scriptures and their densely packed images are a language of their own. The visionaries do not quote the Scriptures but they lived, thought and wrote in the world of the temple and its mythology. Their interpretations of Scripture must be deduced from their allusions, their juxtapositions and, above all, by their subtle changes to the text they had received. They could describe their enemy Paul as Balaam the false prophet, a perceptive comment on his conversion experience when he, like Balaam, had a vision of the LORD in his path. They could describe Lydia as Jezebel (see p. 100) with a bitterness one can almost describe as wit. They created Scripture; the differences from other known versions are not signs of ignorance or mistakes. Thus John describes the risen LORD in 1.5 using the words of Psalm 89, a royal psalm, but he alters them slightly to indicate his new interpretation. The Davidic king in Psalm 89.27 is the Firstborn, whereas the risen LORD is the Firstborn 'from the dead'. The blessed state of the redeemed is described in 7.15–17 in words drawn from Isaiah 49.10, but subtle changes make it clear that the enthroned shepherd is the Lamb. The whole of the Book of Revelation is written in this way and shows that the visionaries were those who produced new Scriptures rather than commenting on existing texts. They felt free to change what they had received rather than simply preserve it. *The*

Book of Revelation is the only text in the New Testament which claims divine inspiration. The customary curse is threatened on anyone who alters the text (22.18–19, see pp. 370–71)

Revelation was intended for a small group of initiates who were able to understand the symbolism, 'your brethren the prophets and those who guard the words of this book' (22.9). The blessing on those who read the prophecies aloud and on those who hear them (1.3) does not necessarily imply a public reading. The book may have been more widely known and heard after it was declared to be complete, when further additions and interpretations were forbidden (22.18–19). The symbolism, layer upon layer, suggests that the authors and their intended readers were a learned group, mystics and almost certainly priests. It was a highly visual tradition rather than verbal, and so one idea or image could be described in many ways. Parallels and interrelationships cannot be identified simply by looking for occurrences of a particular word. The outstanding example of this must be the many words used to describe the royal figure: Servant, Youth, Lamb, Son. Treating them as distinct figures has created many problems for interpreters of these texts. The 'Branch', one of the messianic titles is another example; it appears as *neṣer* (Isa. 11.1) or *ṣemaḥ* (Zech. 3.8; 6.12), as *'anap*, branch, whence Anaphiel Yahweh 'branch of God Yahweh' the name of the chief angel in the *Hekhalot Rabbati*, the prince 'whose name is called out before the throne of glory three times each day ... in whose hand is the seal of heaven and earth' (#241); and as *maqqel*, the rod of almond (Jer. 1.11) which became the Stave, the Interpreter of the Law, in the Damascus Document (CD VI). The holy of holies was described as a 'tower or high place', but several words were used: *migdal*, the tower in a vineyard, yet interpreted to mean the holy of holies (Isa. 5.2) or *maṣor*, a watch tower, but the place of prophetic visions and so the holy of holies (Hab. 2.1).

The Book of Revelation has inspired many artists, but attempts to depict say, the Lamb with seven horns and seven eyes (5.6), hinder rather than enhance any understanding of the visions. The number seven, whether the seven thunders or the seven angels, or, in this case, the seven eyes and horns, is making a statement about temple theology using temple language. The Lamb with seven horns means that he has been transfigured with the sevenfold light of Day One of creation.

Other aspects of the code are easier to describe. In the drama of heaven and earth, animals represent human beings – the Lamb, or the sheep and the goats in Jesus' parable of the Judgement (Matt. 25.31–46). Men are angels, as can be seen from Luke's account of Easter Day when the women at the tomb saw two men in white and this was reported later as a vision of angels (Luke 24.4, 23). This strange convention, humans as animals and the gods as humans, can also be seen in the Ugaritic texts, for example when Baal seduces a heifer who gives birth to 'a bull calf' and his father then clothes him (KTU 1.5.v.15). There are also several places where cryptic allusions should be read alongside equally cryptic lines in say, *1 Enoch* or the Qumran Hymns. Only then can we hope to approach what the visionaries were writing without our own forced and unnatural interpretations of the text.

Fundamental to the world view of the temple and the writings of its mystics was the correspondence between heaven and earth: 'On earth as it is in heaven'. This was not Platonism, it being attested in Isaiah long before the time of Plato, but rather the world of the ancient wise men, who sought comparisons. The Proverbs, which were their characteristic mode of teaching, were comparisons; that is what the Hebrew *mᵉšalim* 'proverbs' literally means. The same word, however, appears as the 'Parables' of Enoch, which are 'visions of Wisdom' (*1 En.* 37.1). What Enoch saw in heaven had its counterpart on earth. Conversely, Jesus' parables make comparisons to teach about heaven: 'the kingdom of heaven is like . . .' The correspondence of earth and heaven is central to understanding the Book of Revelation. The visions interpret and explain contemporary events in Palestine in terms of the timeless realities of heaven, and the writer reveals the significance of these events by the very fact that he sees in them the fulfilment of prophecies and the realization of visions. This was the hope of Daniel 9.24: 'to fulfil the visions and the prophecies and to anoint the holy of holies'. The armies of heaven were believed literally to be involved in the struggles of first-century Palestine.

When the visionaries described evil, they employed a system of antitypes. If the divinely appointed ruler in Jerusalem was the Messiah, then any other ruler was an antimessiah, the exact opposite of everything that was believed about the legitimate ruler. These patterns of type and antitype, good and evil, harmony and perversion, pervade the Book of Revelation and often assist in interpreting the visions. There is a true and a false prophet, there is a true and a false ruler of Jerusalem, there is a true and a false high priest, there are the harlot and the bride, which are both descriptions of Jerusalem, and so forth. Often the comparisons have been worked out with a remarkable degree of sophistication, as can be seen in the complex depiction of the beast from the sea as the false messiah, the antichrist.

The Book of Revelation is both visions and their interpretations. Ancient material, some far older than the Christian movement which adopted and preserved it, has been interwoven with interpretations, some pre-Christian, some from Jesus himself, but most from Christian prophets of the first and second generations. They believed that they were living in the last days, and so they wrote their history in that way, blending myth and contemporary comment, prophecy and fulfilment, culminating in their vision of the kingdom established on the Day of the LORD.

The Visions of Jesus

Sayings attributed to Jesus in the Gospels show that he knew this tradition: he had visionary experiences (Luke 4.5); at his baptism he saw the heavens open and he heard himself addressed as the Son (Mark 1.10–11) and he experienced the angels and the creatures of the throne (Mark 1.13). He taught his disciples about the events of the seven seals in the passage which has come to be called the Synoptic Apocalypse (Mark 13), and Josephus refers to one of these sayings as an oracle in the records of the ancient prophets (*War* 6.110 refers to Mark 13.12–13). This suggests that Jesus was quoting from a lost text, possibly the Book of the LORD (see p. 67). Jesus knew that he had to cast fire on the earth like the Great Angel (Rev. 8.5; 16.17, cf. Luke 12.49) and he had seen Satan fall from heaven as in Revelation 12.11 (Luke 10.18). He told a parable about the angel reapers (Matt. 13.36–45) and he prophesied the fall of Jerusalem (Luke 19.41–44).

Where Jesus learned of this material, or even what it was, we can only guess, but there are some significant passages in Luke which do not occur in the other Gospels. Only Luke records the mystic's timeless moment when Jesus was in the desert and saw 'all the cities of the world in a moment of time' (Luke 4.5). Only Luke says that he saw Satan fall from heaven (Luke 10.18) and that he had come to cast fire on the earth (Luke 12.49). Luke also implies that the transfiguration was Jesus' own experience of transformation as the disciples were asleep and awoke to see that his appearance had changed (Luke 9.32). Distinctive readings in an ancient version of Luke's Gospel (Codex Bezae) say that Jesus heard the words of Psalm 2 at his baptism: 'today I have begotten you', words originally addressed to the king (Luke 3.22), and that he saw an angel in Gethsemane (Luke 22.43). These passages suggest that Luke's source of information knew of Jesus' contact with the mystics who had preserved the traditions of the first temple, and gives added significance to two other incidents recorded only by Luke: first that Jesus met the temple teachers when he was only twelve years old and made a great impression on them (Luke 2.41–51); and second, that when he read from the scroll of Isaiah in his home synagogue, he claimed that he was fulfilling the Jubilee prophecy (Luke 4.21).

Jesus could read – this in itself is an important indication of what might have been available to him – and his home synagogue possessed a scroll of Isaiah. Scrolls were expensive items; small communities would have had scrolls of the Law and perhaps the Psalms, and then whatever else they could afford. Jesus was steeped in the words and imagery of Isaiah, presumably because he had known the scroll in his youth and the Gospel writers confirm this insofar as they quote from, or allude to, Isaiah more than any other book in the Hebrew Scriptures.

The Book of Revelation also draws its major themes from Isaiah: the heavenly throne (4.1–11, cf. Isa. 6); the destiny of the faithful as priests (1.6; 5.10, cf. Isa. 61.6); the Servant/Lamb (5.1–14, cf. the Servant Songs in Isa. 42, 49, 50, 52–53); the Day of the LORD (6.1–7, cf. Isa. 2.12–22; 34.4; 50.3); the ingathering of Israel (7.1–8, cf. Isa. 4.2–6; 49.6); the blessed state of the redeemed (7.15–17, cf. Isa. 25.8; 49.10); the great star falling from heaven (8.10, cf. Isa. 14.12); the mystery revealed to the prophet (10.7, cf. Isa. 24.16, but see on 10.7 for this translation of Isa. 24.16); the Gentiles trampling the temple (11.2, cf. Isa. 63.18); the birth of the Messiah (12.5, cf. Isa. 7.14); the Lamb on Zion (14.1–5, cf. Isa. 31.4); the voice from the temple announcing the judgement (16.1, cf. Isa. 66.6); the desolate state of the fallen city (18.2–3, 22–23, cf. Isa. 21.9; 24.8–13); the proud queen of cities (18.7, cf. Isa. 47.8–9); the new heaven and earth (22.1, cf. Isa. 66.22); the new Jerusalem and her jewels (21.10–14, cf. Isa. 54.11–12). The titles for the LORD are also taken from Isaiah: 'the First and the Last' (1.17, cf. Isa. 44.6) and 'LORD God Almighty' translates a title characteristic of Isaiah, LORD God of Hosts.

The similarities are even more apparent when the Book of Revelation is compared to the Isaiah Targum. The Targums were originally oral translations into Aramaic which accompanied the reading of the Hebrew text in the synagogue. They were not literal translations but incorporated an element of interpretation and comment on contemporary issues. Eventually the Targums were fixed in written form, but the Targums known today contain material from many different periods of interpretation. In the Isaiah Targum there are several passages which comment on the temple and its priests which can only have been relevant before the temple was destroyed in 70 CE. These interpretations were probably known to Jesus. Isaiah 22.15–25, for example, is a condemnation of the steward Shebna and the prediction that he would be replaced by Eliakim: 'And I will place on his shoulder the key of the house of David; he shall open and none shall shut; and he shall shut and none shall open' (Isa. 22.22). This was originally a glimpse of palace politics in the eighth-century BCE, but was interpreted in the Targum to describe the removal of a corrupt high priest, a thinly veiled allusion to the state of the high priesthood in the first century CE. He would be replaced by another who would be faithful in his office. An allusion to this Targumic interpretation best explains Revelation 3.7, 'The words of the Holy One, the True One, who has the key of David, who opens and no one shall shut, who shuts and no one shall open'. This is claiming Jesus as the new high priest. Isaiah 28 was originally an oracle against Ephraim, the corrupted northern kingdom which fell to Assyria in 723 BCE. In the Targum it too became an oracle against the high priest, and Ephraim, by implication, was the corrupted priesthood. This is exactly like the Qumran texts where Jerusalem was 'the city of Ephraim, those who seek smooth things during the last days, who walk in lies and falsehood' (4Q169.II); 'the wicked of Ephraim and Manasseh' would be 'delivered into the hands of the violent among the nations for judgement' (4Q171.II). Isaiah 24.16, opaque in the Hebrew original, became in the Targum: 'The prophet said: The mystery of the reward of the righteous is visible to me, the mystery of the retribution for the wicked is revealed to me', as in Revelation 10.7: 'that in the days of the trumpet call to be sounded by the seventh angel, the mystery of God, as he announced to his servants the prophets, should be fulfilled'.

The earliest material in the Book of Revelation may have been the

Book of the LORD, a text mentioned in Isaiah 34.16. The context in Isaiah suggests that this was an authoritative description of the Day of the LORD and the prophet could appeal to it to authenticate his own words of warning against Edom. No text is known which has this title and there are no references to it elsewhere. The discoveries at Qumran, however, are a constant reminder that many ancient texts whose existence was not even suspected because there is no mention of them elsewhere, were known and used in first-century Palestine. The Book of Hagu, for example, a most important text according to the Damascus Document (CD XIV), is completely lost. The Book of the LORD was an ancient Hebrew book known to Isaiah, that is, a book from the first temple period. It is not impossible that the material which now forms the basis of Revelation 4–11 was this Book of the LORD, describing the enthronement of the king who became the LORD, the terrors which preceded his appearance and his triumph over his enemies. It is all too easy to read into the first-century situation the later idea of a canon of Scripture.

The Book of Revelation has many similarities to the prophecies of Ezekiel, not because there was a conscious imitation of the earlier prophet, but because both books were the product of temple priests (Ezek. 1.3) and stood in the same tradition. There is the heavenly throne (4.1–8, cf. Ezek. 1.4–28); the sealing of the faithful with the sign of the LORD (7.3, cf. Ezek. 9.4); the enthroned Lamb as the Shepherd (7.17, cf. Ezek. 34.23–24); the coals thrown onto the wicked city (8.5, cf. Ezek. 10.2); eating the scroll (10.10, cf. Ezek. 3.1–3); measuring the temple (11.1 and 21.15, cf. Ezek. 40.3); the seven angels of wrath (16.1–21, cf. Ezek. 9.1–11); the harlot city (18.9, cf. Ezek. 26.17–18); the riches of the wicked city (18.12–13, cf. Ezek. 27.1–36); the fate of Gog (19.17–21 and 20.8, cf. Ezek. 39.1–20); the vision of Jerusalem (21.9–27, cf. Ezek. 40.1–43.5); the river flowing from the temple and the tree of life (22.1–2, cf. Ezek. 47.1–12).

The visions were not necessarily spontaneous or original to Jesus, but if he was steeped in their imagery, they would have become his natural way of thinking. His own inspiration would have been expressed by incorporating it into the account he had received, either as an element of the vision or as its interpretation. Identifying with a text or the account of a vision can be a very real and powerful experience and is in no way to be compared simply to the close scrutiny of a text in scholarly study. *Any suggestion that the many authors of the Book of Revelation drew consciously on ancient texts and compiled their work in the manner of a piece of modern research misunderstands completely the mind of a seer.*

Jesus often taught his disciples in private, and there is widespread evidence for a secret tradition of teaching which was not recorded in the Gospels. The recurring theme of John's Gospel: 'He bears witness to what he has seen and heard and yet no one receives his *testimony*' (John 3.32) cannot be lightly dismissed. The community persecuted by the red dragon, the other children of the woman clothed with the sun, described themselves as 'those who keep the commandments of God and have the *testimony* of Jesus' (12.17, translating literally). In each case it is the same Greek word for 'testimony' and the Book of Revelation itself defines what that word means: 'the *testimony*' of Jesus Christ, 'what he saw', and John bears witness to this (1.1). Thus the Christians in Palestine identified themselves as those who kept the commandments of God 'and had the *testimony*, i.e. the visions of Jesus' which others had not accepted.

Something similar is implied by an anonymous ruling recorded in Tosefta Yadaim 2.13: 'The *gilyonim* and the books of the heretics do not defile the hands'. By 'defile the hands' was meant that these texts were not sacred, not inspired. The word *gilyon* usually means an empty space or a margin, but in this instance it is more likely to be wordplay and derive from the word *galah,* meaning reveal. The *gilyonim* must have been *the revelations* which the heretics regarded as Scripture. The Book of Revelation in Syriac begins with a similar word: the *gelyana* of Jesus Christ, the *revelation* of Jesus Christ. A later account attributes to R. Meir and R. Joḥanan some bitter wordplay on the Greek word for gospel: *evangelion.* R. Meir called it *aven gilyon* meaning worthless revelation, and R. Johannan called it *avon gilyon*, iniquitous revelation (*b. Shabbat* 116a, a line censored from many texts). This suggests that the claims made in the Book of Revelation and the Christian appropriation of this book, gave rise to particular bitterness. Ascent experiences were forbidden (see p. 261) and any enquiry into hidden matters was forbidden (*m. Ḥagigah* 2.1).

Jesus warned that the Day of the LORD was imminent; 'the blood of all the prophets ... shall be required of this generation' (Luke 11.51). This is a clear reference to the Qumran text of Deuteronomy 32.43 (4QDeut^{q}) where the LORD appears 'to avenge the blood of his sons, take vengeance on his enemies and atone the land of his people'. The kingdom was at hand (Mark 1.15), and the disciples were sent out to warn what was to come. They would not have time to go through all the towns of Israel before the Man came (Matt. 10.23). On the Day of the LORD the temple would be destroyed but Jesus' prophecy of its destruction would endure: 'There will not be left here one stone upon another that will not be thrown down ... Tell us, when will this be? ... Truly this generation will not pass away before all these things take place. Heaven and earth will pass away but my words will not pass away' (Mark 13.2, 30–31). Before the end came, the gospel had to be preached to all nations (Matt. 24.14). It would be a time of endurance for the faithful; no explanation was offered as to why such sufferings were necessary (Mark 13.13, and parallels in Matt. 24.13; Luke 21.19). As the predicted sequence of signs took place, so the time of the great Day of Atonement and the tenth Jubilee drew nearer: 'Now when these things begin to take place, look up, and raise your heads, because your redemption is drawing near' (Luke 21.28). Matthew, Mark and Luke do not give identical accounts of Jesus' predictions but elements from all three can be seen in the Book of Revelation, showing that each Gospel writer recorded the predictions important for his own community.

The Book of Revelation shows the same sense of urgency and imminence. The visions known to Jesus were 'to show his servants what must soon take place' (1.1), 'for the time is near' (1.3). The fragments of prophecy collected at the end of the book have the same message: 'what must soon take place' (22.6), 'I am coming soon' (three times: 22.7, 12, 20); 'the time is near' (22.10). There is the same sequence of signs as the seals are opened, the same command to endure (6.11), and Revelation 18 describes how the temple city was destroyed.

The Pillars of the Church

The Acts of the Apostles is the only history of the early church included in the New Testament. Others were written and extracts have survived in, for example, the writings of Eusebius. Most of Acts is devoted to the missionary work of Paul. Of the twelve apostles there are only glimpses, which raises the question: what were they doing?

The life and mission of the early church was centred on Jerusalem. When Philip had been making converts in Samaria, the apostles in Jerusalem immediately sent Peter and John (Acts 8.14). When Paul was converted, he went to Jerusalem and was vouched for by Barnabas (Acts 9.26–27). When Peter had baptized the Gentile Cornelius, he had to face criticism from the strict Hebrew Christians in Jerusalem (Acts 11.1–3). When Paul was brought back from Tarsus to Antioch, prophets from Jerusalem immediately appeared on the scene (Acts 11.27). After the first missionary journey, when Paul and Barnabas had made converts among the Gentiles, 'men from Judea' confronted them on their return (Acts 15.1). They had to attend the council of elders in Jerusalem, where James, the bishop, issued a statement defining the terms on which Gentiles could join the church. This was sent as a *letter* to Antioch (Acts 15.22) which Paul had to deliver to all the other churches he visited (Acts 16.4).

It is clear from Acts that the Jerusalem elders led by James had an effective system of communicating with other churches and disciplining them. They knew what had happened in Asia Minor during Paul's first missionary journey. On Paul's final visit to Jerusalem, when he again reported on his work among the Gentiles, he was told 'You see brother how many thousands there are among the Jews of those who have believed; they are all zealous for the Law, and they have been told about you, that you teach the Jews who are among the Gentiles to forsake Moses ...' (Acts 21.20–21). His life was in danger and Paul was being watched.

At the start of his second missionary journey, the 'Holy Spirit' forbad him to return to Asia Minor and the 'Spirit of Jesus' barred him from Bithynia (Acts 16.6–7). Paul's preaching was longer welcome in the very areas which were to receive the letter of Peter (1 Pet. 1.1) and the seven letters of the Book of Revelation, in other words, communications from the Pillars in Jerusalem. The seven letters mention Lydia ('Jezebel', 2.20) whom Paul was to meet on his second missionary journey, so the letters in the Book of Revelation cannot have been the reason for Paul's avoiding Asia Minor at the start of that journey. His later reluctance to visit Ephesus (Acts 20.16) and remarks in letters to his converts in Asia Minor ('the faithful brethren', Eph. 1.1; Col. 1.2) indicate that something decisive happened shortly afterwards. Writing to the Galatians, Paul justifies 'his' gospel by saying that he (i.e. he *also*), learned it through a 'revelation of Jesus Christ' (Gal. 1.12). He cursed anyone who taught another gospel, even 'an angel from heaven' (Gal. 1.8). The Galatians had originally received him (i.e. him *also*) 'as an angel of God' (Gal. 4.14). The 'other gospel' was Hebrew Christianity: the works of the Law, a special calendar and circumcision (Gal. 3.2; 4.10; 5.2).

In the interval between Paul's preaching to the Galatians and his writing to them, they had received from Jerusalem the seven letters. The risen LORD from heaven had revealed to the churches how they should live, shunning the teaching of Balaam the false prophet, that is, Paul, and abhorring his concessions to the Gentiles, namely food sacrificed to idols and immorality (2.14). The seven letters date from the early 50s, when the LORD's return was believed to be imminent. The seven letters had the desired effect. Paul (or someone writing in his name) could say later: 'All who are in Asia have turned away from me' (2 Tim. 1.15). The fathers of the Asian churches recalled instead how they had learned from John the beloved disciple, who spent his last years among them in Ephesus.

The Christian Prophets

The first generation of Hebrew Christians looked for the fulfilment of Jesus' predictions in their own generation. He had warned that not even he knew exactly when the signs would begin and so his disciples were told: 'Watch, for you do not know when the time will come' (Mark 13.32–33). The disciples' pressing last question, according to Luke's account of the Ascension, was: 'LORD will you at this time restore the kingdom to Israel?' (Acts 1.6), and Jesus replied that this too was something they were not allowed to know. They were expecting the Day of the LORD, 'the time', but this was also a political expectation, the kingdom restored to Israel. It is important to bear this in mind when reading the Book of Revelation. The struggles against Rome may not have been the persecution of Christians for which there is little evidence in the first century, apart from Nero. A more likely setting is the struggle of the Jews who wanted to liberate their land from Roman rule, and the fervour of the tenth Jubilee is the context of the early years of the church.

The Christians interpreted the prophecies in the light of

contemporary events, as did the Qumran community, and as the prophecies were fulfilled, so they recorded this in the book of prophecies. These additions can be seen where the original pattern or sequence is broken or unbalanced. Thus the words of the third seal predict a great famine, and then add: 'A quart of wheat for a denarius and three quarts of barley for a denarius but do not harm the oil and the wine' (6.6). These are probably the words of Agabus a prophet from Jerusalem 'who foretold by the Spirit a great famine over all the world and this took place in the days of Claudius' (Acts 11.28). The enigmatic words have the style of authentic prophecy and mark the fulfilment of the words of the third seal. The additions to the prophecy of the fifth seal may have been made when James bar Zebedee was killed by Herod (Acts 12.1–2), but a more likely occasion was the martyrdom of James the Righteous in 62 CE (see on 6.9–11), an event not recorded in Acts. The events of the fifth seal appear also in *1 Enoch* 47.2: the righteous whose blood has been shed pray to the LORD 'That judgement may be done, that they may not have to suffer for ever'. The original text for the fifth seal was only 6.9–10, to which the Christian prophet added a word of comfort for the martyrs, telling them to rest a little longer, the time was not yet fulfilled. Another seal, however, had been opened. The additions to the sixth seal were from the time of Nero's persecution of Christians in Rome. A multitude of Gentiles in white robes 'from all tribes and peoples and tongues' was standing before the throne and identified as 'those who were coming out of the great tribulation' (7.14). The persecution in Rome, which followed the great fire in July 64 CE, was interpreted as fulfilment of the sixth seal.

The Hebrew Christians would by that time have been expecting the imminent return of the LORD, at the end of the tenth Jubilee, but in the final compilation of the Book of Revelation the delay in his return was marked by the seven trumpets, which proclaimed the Jubilee (Lev. 25.9) and announced his coming (Rev. 8–9). The angel high priest is made ready in heaven and the first four trumpets sound. The eagle rises in heaven, a traditional motif, and then the fifth and sixth trumpets describe contemporary events in great detail. They are a thinly veiled account of the months which preceded the Jewish revolt in 67 CE. The seventh trumpet announcing the LORD still did not sound and he did not return.

The visions of Jesus had not been entrusted to John alone; others 'had' them. The children of the woman clothed with the sun had the 'testimony' (12.17) as did a group called 'his brethren' (19.10). These are the 'keepers' of the words of the book. The word 'keep' is *tereo*, which means both to 'preserve' and also to 'observe closely'. These 'keepers' were the disciples watching for the Day of the LORD, keeping the words and speaking with angels (22.9) to learn new interpretations of the visions. In Revelation 1.1 this is described as the second stage in the formation of the book; an angel (the Spirit of Truth, John 16.13) was sent to John 'to make known' the revelation which Jesus had seen, to interpret the visions for his own time and to cause the disciples to 'remember' the real significance of events in the life of Jesus (John 2.22; 12.16).

The disciples of the ancient prophets had kept their words and visions in the same way. The Book of Isaiah, for example, was compiled over some three centuries. The words and visions of Isaiah of Jerusalem were interpreted by his disciples for new situations. The oracles prompted by the crisis of 701 BCE, when Jerusalem was threatened by the army of Assyria, were re-used a century later when the enemy was Babylon. The trauma of the exile in Babylon led a disciple in that period to make a formal collection of the master's words and their interpretation, and he added more in the same manner for his own time.

The Book of Revelation was formed as a book of prophecy, the one collection of prophecy to survive from the Palestinian period of the church. Only those who had been closest to Jesus were permitted to interpret the prophecies; later tradition remembered them as recipients of special knowledge: 'James the Righteous, John and Peter were entrusted by the LORD after his resurrection with the higher knowledge. They imparted it to the other apostles and the other apostles to the seventy, one of whom was Barnabas' (Clement of Alexandria, quoted in Eusebius, *History* 2.1). Clement makes clear that the James was not James son of Zebedee, in other words, that those who received the higher knowledge were not all drawn from the Twelve. It is possible that the John mentioned was not one of the twelve either.

Those who received the higher knowledge did not make public all they knew. John was forbidden to write down what the Mighty Angel called out when the seven thunders sounded (10.3–4). The revelation had to be sealed up. Later writers knew there had been things John could not reveal. Origen (died 253 CE) knew that the sound of the seven thunders was knowledge he could not reveal (*On John* 13.33); he knew that the little scroll which John ate was a sign of knowledge which had to be kept from the unworthy (*Cels.* 6.6)

John, the beloved disciple, was a key figure in the church's expectations. He had been a follower of John the Baptist and was the unnamed disciple in John 1.37. Two of the Baptist's disciples are mentioned in this incident, but only one, Andrew, is named (John 1.40). The other disciple, who wrote the Gospel, knew that John the Baptist had recognized Jesus as the Lamb of God (John 1.35–36) and had revealed this to Jesus himself. He knew Jerusalem and the temple well, and was almost certainly a priest. He was the person later described as 'John the elder' who named himself as the writer of 2 and 3 John. There is no way of knowing if he was also John, son of Zebedee. He wrote the Fourth Gospel and was responsible for the preservation and final form of the Book of Revelation. Much has been written about the relationship between the Gospel and the Book of Revelation, and whether they could have been the work of the same writer, because the two books are written in very different styles of Greek. If, however, the Book of

Revelation was not written in Greek but translated by an Asian Christian at a later date, comparison of Greek styles is irrelevant. In subject matter and allusions, as will be seen in the detailed commentaries, there is considerable similarity.

John's original Gospel ended at John 20.31, but chapter 21 was added to correct the mistaken belief that John would live until the LORD's return (John 21.23). John was also a key figure in helping the church come to terms with the delay in the LORD's return, as can be seen in his compilation of the Book of Revelation. John was called to further prophecy in the vision of the mighty angel, the LORD, handing him the little scroll (10.1–11). The heavenly high priest did come with the clouds (10.1), as the church was expecting (1.7; Acts 1.11), but he appeared only to John with a further message. The seventh and final trumpet would indeed establish the kingdom on earth, but John was called to a further period of prophesying before this would happen. The scroll which he ate was at first sweet in his mouth, but in his stomach it was bitter. There follows an account of the last days of Jerusalem (Rev. 11).

A Christian prophet in Palestine had described in Revelation 13 the beast from the sea and the beast from the land, another account of events in Palestine during the early years of the church. Several layers of interpretation are apparent in these verses, for example, the final identification of the beast as Nero. A prophet also saw Jerusalem as the harlot on the seven hills (Rev. 17), and the angel offered to tell him the mystery of the woman and the beast. Several layers of interpretation follow here also, and these would probably have been written in Aramaic.

In the preface to his *Jewish War* (*War* 1.3) Josephus said that his original book was written in the language of his own country* and only later was a Greek translation made. The same was true of the Book of Revelation. The older Hebrew material was interpreted and expanded, and only later was the entire book put into Greek. One of the clearest indications of a Hebrew or Aramaic original is the frequent use of 'and' to start a sentence. Over half of the sentences in Revelation begin with 'and', an over-literal translation of the normal Hebrew style but strange in the Greek. There are several difficulties in the Greek text which disappear if we assume that a Hebrew or Aramaic word has been misread or misunderstood. Revelation 11.1–2, for example, is an oracle about measuring: the temple, the altar and the worshippers, but not the outer court. We should expect the boundary of the sacred area to be measured if everywhere outside it was to be left unprotected, but where 'boundary' is expected, we find 'worshippers'. In Aramaic the two words are similar and could easily have been confused. The special name for the boundary which divided the court of the Gentiles from the sacred area was the *soreg*, a word which could well have been unknown to a Christian in Asia. Written *srg*, it resembled the word for worship,

---

*He does not say whether this was Hebrew or Aramaic.

sgd, as *r* and *d* are almost identical letters. It has been suggested that the translator saw an appropriate word for this temple context and thus the oracle became 'measure the temple, the altar and *the worshippers*'.

There are several places where the prophecies in the Book of Revelation correspond with those recorded by Josephus. He says that zeal for the Jewish war against Rome was prompted by an ambiguous oracle in their sacred writings 'that one from their country at about that time should become governor of the habitable earth' (*War* 6.312–14). Josephus himself claimed prophetic powers and said that Vespasian, at that time the military commander in Palestine, would rise to become emperor of Rome (*War* 3.400–402). What Josephus interpreted in Vespasian's favour was probably this same oracle about a world ruler arising in Palestine, the Hebrew Christian oracle about the return of Jesus to establish the kingdom. The Christians condemned Josephus as a false prophet, destined for the lake of fire (19.20). They knew from their prophets that the fifth and sixth trumpets had sounded and that the time of the seventh and last trumpet was near, when the kingdom of the world would become the kingdom of the LORD and his Anointed. Josephus says that this oracle was in the sacred writings of the people who had risen against Rome: *he, a Jew, does not claim it was in the Jewish Scriptures*, he does not say 'one of our oracles', but one 'written in their sacred oracles'. The prophecy in question appears in Revelation 11.15–18 as the vision of the seventh trumpet. It was this fervour for bringing the seventh trumpet, the third woe, that John had to quell with his new period of prophecy, and it was bitter in his stomach.

Another oracle warned the Christians to leave Jerusalem because the judgement was imminent: 'Come out of her my people, lest you take part in her sins, lest you share in her plagues; for her sins are heaped high as heaven and God has remembered her iniquities' (18.6). Eusebius records that this oracle was 'given by revelation to acceptable persons in Jerusalem', in other words, to the recognized prophets of the church. He had heard a story that the community left the city and fled to Pella, east of the Jordan (*History* 3.5), but some must have gone west to the coast where they saw Jerusalem burning and recorded that the prophecies of Jesus about the destruction of the city had been fulfilled (18.17–18). The guardian of the prophecies took them with him as he fled, perhaps to Asia Minor and eventually to Patmos where he found himself 'on account of the word of God and the testimony of Jesus' (1.9). Josephus records that during the summer of 70 CE, Titus offered safe conduct out of Jerusalem to any who would avail themselves of the offer. Many left the city at that time, including several members of high priestly families (*War* 6.114). John was probably among these.

The third and final stage of the formation of the Book of Revelation is illuminated by a passage in *2 Baruch*, a book written after the fall of Jerusalem to try and explain the disaster. After listening to the account of his visions and their interpretation, the people come to Baruch with a request; they ask him to write to their brothers in the dispersion because the teachers in Jerusalem have all died. 'Write also to our brothers in Babylon a letter of doctrine and a scroll of hope so that you might strengthen them also before you go away from us. For the shepherds of Israel have perished and the lamps which gave light are extinguished and the fountains from which we used to drink have withheld their streams' (2 *Bar.* 77.12–13). Letters of doctrine and a scroll of hope describes exactly the Book of Revelation in its final form. The letters of the risen LORD given through John and the prophecies were compiled into one scroll, perhaps by John himself on Patmos, and sent to the churches of Asia Minor. Like the letter of Baruch, they were probably 'read carefully in their assemblies' (2 *Bar.* 86.1).

In this third stage, John was commanded to write what he had seen and send it to the churches (22.16). He told the history of the LORD and his followers by means of the oracles and their fulfilment, interpreting the events of the previous fifty years. The prophecy was to be unsealed for all to read and hear, and no longer restricted to the circle of Christian prophets (22.10). Nobody in the future would be permitted to add interpretation or to take anything away (22.18–19) because the time of the prophets was over. A new understanding of the faith was emerging, for which the Fourth Gospel was written. Thus the Parousia prophecies found no place in the final form of the Book of Revelation, but were collected together in the fragments at the end.

When Jerusalem fell and the Palestinian Christians were scattered, the Hebrew churches in Asia lost touch with their roots and with the world of the temple which had shaped the earliest faith. The Book of Revelation was translated into Greek which soon became the language of the Mediterranean churches, and even the titles of the biblical books were no longer understood. A curious fragment of early church history has survived in the library of the Greek Patriarchate in Jerusalem, a list of the books of the Hebrew Scriptures in Aramaized form, but written in Greek letters. People who could no longer read the Hebrew script needed help even to pronounce the names of the biblical books.

Who, When and Where?

Most early Christian writers say that the Book of Revelation was written in the reign of Domitian, about 95 CE. Irenaeus, writing about a century later, was the first to mention this date. 'It was seen . . . almost in my own lifetime, at the end of Domitian's reign' (*AH* 5.30). Clement of Alexandria (*Rich Man* 42) and Origen (*On Matt.* 16.6) both mention that John was banished to Patmos, but neither names the emperor responsible. Victorinus of Pettau, who died in 305 CE, was the first to write a full commentary on the Book of Revelation. John, he said, saw the Revelation when he was on Patmos, condemned to the mines by Domitian (*On the Apocalypse* 10). Although he does not name them, Eusebius wrote that 'our ancient ones' taught that the apostle John returned to Ephesus at the end of Domitian's reign, 'after his exile on the island' (*History* 3.20).

The evidence of the book itself, however, suggests it was not written at any one time. The final form of the Book of Revelation may date from the reign of Domitian, when it was translated into Greek and first made known to the churches. The Book of Revelation is a collection of prophecies and their interpretation, with the oldest material pre-Christian and all the rest clearly antedating the separation of Judaism and Christianity. It mattered to the churches at Smyrna and Philadelphia that their enemies claimed to be Jews when in fact they were a synagogue of Satan (2.9; 3.9). The threat to the seven churches was not emperor worship; the only possible reference to it is the throne of Satan in Pergamum (2.13), and only two of the seven churches faced persecution (Smyrna, 2.10 and Pergamum, 2.13). The danger was false teaching, almost certainly that of Paul, as he tried to convert Hebrew Christians to his gospel, and the churches expected the imminent return of the LORD. None of these indicates a date in the reign of Domitian.

The most detailed interpretations of prophecy – the sixth seal and the sixth trumpet – depict events in the mid-60s: Nero's persecution of the Christians in Rome in 64 CE and Gessius Florus' reign of terror in Palestine in 66 CE. The name of the beast as Nero and the elaborate identification of the head and horns of the beast both point to the same period, i.e. to the end of Nero's reign and the accession of Vespasian. These are not the only interpretations of prophecy: there are thinly veiled references to earlier events such as the famine in the reign of Claudius (41–54 CE), to the death of James and to the whole era of Roman rule in Palestine. It is possible that the prophecies of the New Jerusalem date from after the fall of the city in 70 CE. Isaiah 49.17 in both the Qumran Hebrew and the LXX reads: 'Those who destroyed it shall rebuild'. The *Letter of Barnabas* saw this as a mistaken hope to rebuild the temple: 'after their armed rebellion it was pulled down by their enemies and now they themselves are about to build it up again, as subjects of their foes' (*Barn.* 16). The Christian interpreters of the prophecies were looking for the heavenly Jerusalem to appear. When the grandsons of Jude were arrested in the time of Domitian, they explained that their hope was for a heavenly kingdom and so they were released as harmless (Hegesippus, quoted in Eusebius, *History* 3.20).

Just as the components of the Book of Revelation were written over many years, so too, there was no one author. Early Christian testimony that 'John' saw the visions must refer to his status as the chief of the prophets, the authorized interpreter of the tradition and compiler of the final form of the book. There are many references to the author of the book, but the most valuable must be those of the Christians of Asia Minor to whom it was sent.

First there is Papias, Bishop of Hierapolis early in the second century CE. He had lived near Laodicea and Philadelphia only a few years after the traditional date assigned to Revelation, 95 CE. Papias wrote a five-volume work *The Sayings of the LORD Explained*, of which only a few short passages survive as quotations in Eusebius. Papias wrote that he 'carefully learnt from the elders ... And whenever anyone came who had been a follower of the elders, I enquired into the words of the elders, what Andrew or Peter had said, or Philip or Thomas or James or John or Matthew, or any other disciple of the LORD, and what Aristion and the elder John were still saying' (*History* 3.39). He seems to mention two Johns; Eusebius certainly understood the passage in this way and concluded that it was the second John who saw the Revelation. He says there were the tombs of two Johns in Ephesus and pointed out that Papias learnt from 'the followers' of the Twelve, but from the elder John himself.

Many scholars have followed Eusebius in holding that it was John the elder who wrote the Book of Revelation. Eusebius may, however, have misread Papias, who could have been drawing the distinction between those of the twelve elders who were no longer teaching, and John the elder who was still alive. Only John is called an elder, not Aristion. Further, he seems to have taken his story about the two tombs from a letter of Dionysius, Bishop of Alexandria in the mid-third century CE: 'I think there was another John among the Christians of Asia as there are said to have been two tombs at Ephesus, each reputed to be John's' (*History* 7.25).

Eusebius gives other information about Papias which is more significant for any enquiry into the origin of the Book of Revelation

Papias reproduces other stories communicated to him by word of mouth, together with some otherwise unknown parables and teachings of the Saviour and other things of a more mythical character. He says that after the resurrection of the dead there will be a period of a thousand years when Christ's kingdom will be set up on this earth in material form. I suppose he got these notions by misinterpreting the apostolic accounts ... (*History* 3.39)

If Papias did not misunderstand what the apostles had said, then he attributes to Jesus material which is presently found not in the Gospels but in 20.4–6, the millennium kingdom. Presumably he learned about this from the elder John.

Second there is Justin, who was martyred in 165 CE and had lived in Ephesus before moving to Rome. He said that the Book of Revelation came from 'John, one of the apostles of the Christ' (*Trypho* 81), but he gave no more details.

Third, there is Irenaeus, who was brought up in Asia Minor but sent as bishop to Lyons in southern Gaul after the persecutions there in 177 CE. He recalled how, as a boy, he had listened to the teaching of Polycarp, the Bishop of Smyrna who had been martyred in 155 CE. 'I remember how he spoke of his close companionship with John and with the others who had seen the LORD, how he repeated their words from memory ... To these things I listened eagerly at that time ... not committing them to writing but learning them by heart' (*Letter to Florinus*, quoted in *History* 5.20). The significance of this remark becomes apparent when he writes elsewhere of some teachings of Jesus not found in the Gospels.

As the elders remember, which saw John the LORD's disciple, that they heard from
him how the LORD taught concerning those times, and said: The days shall come
wherein vines shall grow each having ten thousand branches and on each branch
ten thousand shoots and on every shoot ten thousand clusters and on every cluster
ten thousand grapes ... These things Papias also, a hearer of John and an associate
of Polycarp, testifies in writing in the fourth of his books. (AH 5.33)

The teaching attributed to Jesus continues with descriptions of the
fertility of the earth, with huge harvests of grain and fruit, and all
animals at peace with each other and with humans. This teaching is not
in any Gospel or in the Book of Revelation, but similar material can be
found in other apocalypses. Some of the oldest material in 1 Enoch
describes the fertility of the earth after the judgement on the fallen
angels: 'Every seed that is sown, one measure will yield a thousand and
one measure of olives will yield ten measures of presses of oil' (1 En.
10.19). 2 Baruch has lines almost identical to those attributed to Jesus:
'the Anointed One will begin to be revealed ... the earth will also yield
fruits ten thousand fold and on one vine will be a thousand branches
and one branch will produce a thousand clusters and one cluster will
produce a thousand grapes and one grape will produce a cor of wine
...' (2 Bar. 29.3, 5). This passage continues with the promise of manna,
words attributed to Jesus in the letter to Pergamum (2.17). The material
which Irenaeus attributes to Jesus draws on Isaiah 11.6–9 and Isaiah
65.25, the animals at peace with each other and with humans. Such use
of Isaiah was characteristic of Jesus and increases the likelihood of these
being genuine sayings. Note that both Papias and Irenaeus say that it
was 'John' who handed on the 'apocalyptic' teaching of Jesus that is not
in the Gospels, yet resembles material in the Book of Revelation.
    The writer of the Book of Revelation is described as one of 'the
brethren who keep the testimony [i.e. the visions] of Jesus' (19.10, translating literally) and the whole book is prefaced, like the other books of
Hebrew prophecy, with the name of the prophet. What is unusual about
the Book of Revelation is that it gives two names. It was 'the Revelation
of Jesus Christ', showing that Jesus was the original prophet, and it was
authenticated and interpreted by John, 'who bore witness to the ...
testimony [i.e. visions] of Jesus, to all that he saw' (1.1–2, translating
literally). John writes himself into the Book of Revelation as the interpreting elder who reveals the fulfilment of the earlier visions. Just as he
conceals himself in the Fourth Gospel as the unnamed beloved disciple,
so in the Book of Revelation he conceals himself as the elder who interprets the visions. He it was who revealed to the church that Jesus had
been the Lamb who was opening the seals (5.5), and he identified Nero's
persecution as the sixth seal (7.14). The interpreting elder does not
appear in the later material, that is, in the new oracles nor in the
separate sequences incorporated into the final text. The words of
the other prophets are anonymous and like the words of Isaiah's
disciples, simply included under the name of their master.

John was a priest. A member of the high priest's family named John is mentioned in Acts 4.6, but John was a popular name and this could be a coincidence. The John of the Book of Revelation knew too much about the temple traditions and the material in other high priestly texts such as *1 Enoch* to have been just a fisherman. Whether or not he was John, son of Zebedee, cannot be known, but he was the beloved disciple, the one known later as the elder. In the Fourth Gospel he knew the name of the high priest's servant (John 18.10) and was able to gain admission to the court of the high priest for himself and Peter simply by speaking to one of the servants there (John 18.15–16). He knew of Caiaphas' sarcasm when chief priests and Pharisees conferred about the problem of Jesus and decided to put him to death (John 11.47–53). This can hardly have been a public meeting. Polycrates, bishop of Ephesus writing about 190 CE, described John as 'a priest who wore the *petalon*', the golden plate which bore the Name. In other words, John was a high priest (Eusebius, *History* 3.31). This is entirely consistent with the contents of the Book of Revelation. John was one of those in the temple at Passover who saw the great light shine in the small hours of the morning and was one of the 'sacred scribes' who correctly interpreted this as a portent of evil. He was one of the priests in the temple itself who heard the voices at Pentecost, both omens being reported by Josephus (*War* 6.290–99).

He introduces himself as a fellow sufferer who was on Patmos on account of the word of God and the testimony of Jesus. This could be a reference to the original John's place of refuge after he had fled from Jerusalem. Later tradition, based on this passage, repeats the story about exile on Patmos, but there is no contemporary evidence that Patmos was used as a place of exile. Pliny says only that it was an island some 30 miles in circumference (*Natural History* 4.23), and Strabo says that it was near the island of Cos (*Geographies* 10.5.3). There are no other contemporary references to Patmos. Tacitus says that islands were sometimes used as places of exile (*Annals* 4.30). There is no reason however, why John should not have been in exile on the island, except that he would have been very old indeed in the reign of Domitian.

Where and when might it have been compiled? The obvious place, in view of its contents and concerns, would have been John's place of refuge after escaping from Jerusalem in 70 CE. John assembled into one scroll the prophecies and evidence of their fulfilment. Having himself inspired the fervent expectation of the LORD's imminent return after the sixth seal, with his pronouncement that Nero's persecution marked the opening of the sixth seal (7.14), he indicated the delay by incorporating after the sixth seal the older Sounding of the Seven Trumpets, also completed as far as the sixth scene. The LORD did not return and John eventually received the vision of the mighty angel wrapped in a cloud (10.1–11), his personal vision of the return of the LORD, 'coming with the clouds' (1.7), but every eye did not behold him, only John. The seven thunders were the heavenly voice revealing to him that the return of the LORD would not be as the Christians had expected. This was the secret he could not reveal. He was told to warn of the destruction of Jerusalem. Having learned that the return was not imminent, he had to leave Jerusalem in order to continue his prophetic ministry among others (10.11), which is why he left Jerusalem and moved to Asia Minor. This seems to have been a place of refuge for those escaping from Jerusalem. Justin reports that the Jew Trypho was in Ephesus as a refugee from the Bar Kochba war in 135 CE and was trying to find his family there (*Trypho* 1, 3).

The compiler of the Book of Revelation had knowledge of older material such as the Sounding of the Seven Trumpets and, from some place on the coast, had seen Jerusalem burning. All this was put together after the pattern of the ancient priestly curses at the end of the holiness lawcode (Lev. 19–26). Those who spurned the LORD's statutes could expect a sevenfold punishment four times: these became the seven seals, the seven trumpets, the seven bowls of wrath and finally the destruction of Jerusalem. In the holiness code was written: 'If in spite of all this you will not hearken to me I will chastise you again sevenfold for your sins' (Lev. 26.18); the punishment was famine. 'If you walk contrary to me and will not hearken to me, I will bring more plagues upon you sevenfold as many as your sins' (Lev. 26.21); the punishment was wild beasts. 'And if by this discipline you are not turned to me ... I myself will smite you sevenfold for your sins' (Lev. 26.23); the punishment was pestilence and the sword. The final sevenfold punishment was a graphic foretelling of the fate of Jerusalem in 70 CE:

You shall eat the flesh of your sons,
and you shall eat the flesh of your daughters.
And I will destroy your high places,
and cut own your incense altars,
and cast your dead bodies on the dead bodies of your idols;
and my soul will abhor you.
And I will lay your cities waste,
and make your sanctuaries desolate,
and I will not smell your pleasing odours.
And I will devastate the land,
so that your enemies who settle in it shall be astonished at it.
And I will scatter you among the nations,
and I will unsheathe the sword after you;
and your land shall be a desolation,
and your cities shall be a waste. (Lev. 26.29–33)

As a priestly writer, the patterns of history were significant to him. At the centre of his scroll he positioned the elders, of whom he was one, singing their song of triumph which formed the overall pattern of the Book of Revelation.

We give thanks to thee Lord God Almighty, who art and who wast,
that thou hast taken thy great power and begun to reign. (11.17)

This was the material in the first half of the scroll; the enthronement of the Lamb as it had been described perhaps in the Book of the LORD.

The nations raged, but thy wrath came,
and the time for the dead to be judged,
for rewarding thy servants, the prophets and saints,
and those who fear thy name, both great and small,
and for destroying the destroyers of the earth. (11.18)

This summarized the remainder of the scroll: the beast and his armies, the final battle, the day of the LORD and the millennium kingdom and finally, the resurrection, last judgement and new creation.

THE MAN AMONG THE LAMPS

I John, your brother, who share with you in Jesus the tribulation and the kingdom and the patient endurance, was on the island of Patmos on account of the word of God and the testimony of Jesus. I was in the Spirit on the LORD's Day, and I heard behind me a voice like a trumpet saying, 'Write what you see in a book and send it to the seven churches, to Ephesus and to Smyrna and to Pergamum and to Thyatira and to Sardis and to Philadelphia and to Laodicea.' Then I turned to see the voice that was speaking to me, and on turning I saw seven golden lampstands and in the midst of the lampstands, one like a son of man, clothed with a long robe and with a golden girdle round his breast. (Rev. 1.9–13)

The Man among the Lamps

The Book of Revelation is a series of visions set in the temple; there is the heavenly throne in the holy of holies (4.2), the altar of sacrifice (6.9), the golden incense altar (8.3), the ark of the covenant (11.19) and there are angel priests with censers (8.3), trumpets (8.6) and libation bowls (16.2–17). The seven lamps which John sees must originally have been the menorah, the lamp with seven branches which stood in the outer part of the temple, the great hall. This is confirmed by the movement in the vision. After he has met the Man among the seven lamps and received the letters from heaven, the seer is summoned to enter the higher place where he sees the throne. In other words, he moves in his vision from the great hall to the holy of holies.

The menorah was a stylized almond tree of pure gold, with lamps at the top of its seven branches (Exod. 25.31–37). Moses had been commanded to stand it in the outer part of the tabernacle, together with a table for the bread of the Presence (Exod. 25.23–30). The description of the temple in 1 Kings 6–7 does not mention it, nor does the later account in 2 Chronicles 3–5, leading some to conclude that there was no menorah in Solomon's time, that the ten golden lamps described in 1 Kings 7.49 were the only lamps in the temple. In a psalm attributed to King David, however, we read: 'Thou art my lamp, O LORD' (2 Sam. 22.29), and there is much in the Hebrew Scriptures to suggest that not only had there had been a lamp in Solomon's temple but that it had been a symbol of the LORD's presence with his people. It had become a sensitive issue because of the danger of idolatry and its association with the goddess* (see p. 205).

When the prophet Haggai was exhorting the people to rebuild the temple after their return from Babylon in the sixth century BCE, his contemporary Zechariah received visions which had a temple setting.

*Perhaps it was the Asherah removed by Josiah (2 Kgs 23.6).

He described a seven-branched lamp in the temple and he knew that it represented the presence of the Lord. This must have been his memory of the first temple. Twice he says this: the seven individual lamps are the seven eyes of the LORD (Zech. 4.10) and the lamp which he sees between two olive trees is the LORD standing between his two anointed ones (Zech. 4.14). It passed into Jewish tradition that the Holy One dwelt with mortals in the light of a lamp (*Num. Rab.* XV.9), and yet the sages who compiled the great commentaries on the holy books were curiously silent about that lamp. They discussed the significance of every detail of the tabernacle but said very little about the menorah.

The Man in the midst of the lamps was the central part of the one, composite lamp, rather than a distinct figure surrounded by seven free-standing lamps as often depicted. The seven-branched lamp as a whole was the presence of the LORD with his people, the seven spirits before the throne (1.4) who were all present in the Anointed One. 'The spirit of the LORD shall rest upon him, the spirit of wisdom and under-standing, the spirit of counsel and might, the spirit of knowledge and the fear of the LORD' is how Isaiah had expressed the idea of the Spirit as a sevenfold presence (Isa. 11.2). Even though the Spirit of the LORD is described as a separate entity, it was nevertheless part of the seven. It was one and seven, just as the Man was part of the lamps.

The greeting to the seven churches is another composite description of the heavenly LORD, as one and three: 'Grace to you and peace from him who is and who was and who is to come, and from the seven spirits who are before his throne, and from Jesus Christ the faithful witness, the first born of the dead and the ruler of the kings of the earth' (1.4). The visions show that Jesus is identified as 'the one who was and is and is to come' (1.8, cf. 22.13), and that he was also the one in whom was the sevenfold spirit (5.6). These complex and cumulative descriptions of one being are characteristic of the Book of Revelation and are important for understanding its theology.

Another important element is the relationship between the temple and the pattern of creation. The six days of creation recorded in Genesis 1 were replicated in the building of the tabernacle (see pp. 19–20). The fourth day of creation, when the sun, moon and stars were created (Gen. 1.14–19) corresponded to the LORD's fourth command, to set up the golden lampstand (Exod. 40.24). The menorah was not only a golden tree; it was also the great lights of heaven. Philo, writing in the first century CE, knew this twofold meaning (*On Gen.* I.10).

There was yet another aspect to this most complex of temple symbols. It was the tree and the lights of heaven, but it was also the sevenfold presence of the LORD with his people, one branch of it representing the Davidic king. Ahijah prophesied that King David would always have one of his dynasty as a lamp before the LORD in Jerusalem (1 Kgs 11.36); David's soldiers begged him not to out to battle lest he 'put out the lamp of Israel' (2 Sam. 21.17). A suffering king, whom Isaiah described as the LORD's Servant, was compared to 'a damaged branch of the lamp, a dimly burning wick that would not be put out' (Isa. 42.3, translating literally). The royal family as a whole was described as a great tree and the expected Messiah as one of its branches. The Branch, *ṣemaḥ*, is how Zechariah describes the Messiah (Zech. 3.8; 6.12). Isaiah uses another word for Branch, *neṣer* (Isa. 11.1) which explains the otherwise unknown prophecy of Jesus fulfilled in Matthew 2.23: not 'He shall be called a Nazarene', but 'He shall be called the Nezer', the Branch (see p. 63).

Philo tells us something more about the menorah. He says that the central branch represented the Logos, the Word (*Heir* 215), just as Isaiah had distinguished between the Spirit of the LORD and the six other elements, all of which together were the indwelling Spirit. Philo says a great deal elsewhere about the Logos, the Word: he is 'the Archangel' (*Heir* 205), 'the Mediator and Judge' (*On Exod.* II.13), 'God's viceroy' (*Dreams* I. 241), 'the High Priest and King' (*Flight* 118), 'God's Firstborn Son' (*Agriculture* 51). Some of these are recognizable as titles of the Davidic king; the Psalms described him as 'high priest' (Ps. 110.4), 'son' (Ps. 2.7) and 'firstborn' (Ps. 89.27). Philo's writings suggest that the royal high priest was still remembered as an angelic being, the central shaft of the menorah which symbolized the presence of the LORD. The first chapter of the Book of Revelation describes the glorious Man in the same way: 'I saw seven golden lampstands and in the midst of the lampstands, one like a son of man'.*

Originally the Man had been the central stem of the lamp and the description of his appearance shows that he was the archangel high priest of whom Philo wrote. He wore a long robe with a golden girdle round his breast, exactly how Josephus describes the dress of the high priest. 'He wore a linen vestment, made of fine flax, doubled ... This vestment reaches down to the feet ... and it is girded to the breast a little above the elbows' (*Ant.* 3.153–4). The long robe is a problem; the word used here, *poderes* (1.13) is often used in the LXX to describe the high priest's vestments, although, curiously, it is used for several different garments, e.g. the breastplate (Exod. 25.7) or the ephod (Exod. 28.31). In Ezekiel 9.2, 3 and 11 the word is used for the linen garment worn by the chief angel, and in Zechariah 3.4 it is the rich apparel of the newly vested high priest. We are not told the colour of the long robe; Philo uses *poderes* for the long coloured robe which the high priest removed before he entered the holy of holies (*All. Int.* II.56; *Moses* II.118) and *Aristeas* 96 uses the same word to describe the coloured vestment of the high priest Eleazar. On balance, we should probably assume that the robe in Revelation 1.13 was the white linen worn by the high priest when he entered the holy of holies as no other vestments are mentioned. Had it been the long coloured robe worn elsewhere, he would have been wearing over it the embroidered tunic, the ephod, and the breastplate set with twelve gem stones. These are not mentioned. The Man wore

---

*Son of man is just an idiom for a man.

just a long robe with a golden girdle round his breast, but the golden girdle shows that he was the high priest. Any priest would wear a multicoloured sash of red, blue, purple and white, but only the high priest wore a sash interwoven with gold (*Ant.* 3.159). The prescription in Leviticus 16.4 is that the high priest has to wear four linen garments when he enters the holy of holies: the loincloth, the coat, the sash and the turban; and at the end of the second temple period, it was still the custom to enter the holy of holies wearing white linen (*m. Yoma* 3.6). The Man in the vision has no linen turban (his white hair is visible) but, like the priests who served in the temple, he is barefoot (his feet are like burnished bronze). The Man in the midst of the seven lamps is the high priest on the Day of Atonement who has just emerged from the holy of holies into the great hall. His face is radiant because he has been in the divine presence which has transformed him into the LORD.

People who had stood in the presence of God became divine. Moses' face was shining when he came down from Mount Sinai because he had been with God (Exod. 34.29). When Simon the High Priest emerged from the holy of holies, he looked glorious, said Ben Sira, 'like the morning star among the clouds, like the moon when it is full, like the sun shining upon the temple of the Most High' (*Ben Sira* 50.6–7). The temple mystics gave enigmatic descriptions of what happened before the throne, presumably the priests' own profound experiences in the holy of holies. Enoch was anointed with holy oil and dressed in garments of glory; he saw that he had been changed into an angel (2 *En.* 22.8–10). When Jesus was praying his clothes became dazzling white and his face altered. This must be Jesus' own description of his experience while praying because Luke notes that the disciples were asleep. 'When they woke up', they saw that his appearance had changed (Luke 9.32, reading the actual Greek text. Some English versions – e.g. the NRSV – alter this verse even though there is no authority for it in any ancient version).

The figure in the midst of the seven lamps was the fiery Man, the Great Angel. Daniel had seen such a figure standing on the banks of the River Tigris, a Man clothed in linen, whose loins were girded with gold of Uphaz. His body was like beryl, his face like the appearance of lightning, his eyes like flaming torches, his arms and legs like the gleam of burnished bronze and the sound of his words like the sound of a multitude. Daniel was overcome at the sight and fell prostrate before him (Dan. 10.5–9). A radiant heavenly figure was described in other writings: there was Iaoel, whose head was wreathed with a rainbow (*Ap. Abr.* 11.3) and there was the fiery human form with the brightness of a rainbow, whom Ezekiel saw on the chariot throne and described as the likeness of the Glory of the LORD (Ezek. 1.26–28).

There was also the Ancient of Days (Dan. 7.9) who sat on a fiery throne and received the Man. The Ancient of Days, a title not used elsewhere in the Bible, was the enthroned LORD, and Daniel's vision was a memory of the apotheosis in the ancient kingmaking. The Man became the Enthroned One (see pp. 121–23), and so the LXX translated 7.13 'He came *as* the Ancient of Days', *hos,* recognizing the apotheosis, but the post-Christian translation of Theodotion, because this had become a sensitive issue, offered 'He came *to* the Ancient of Days', *heos*. Here in 1.14–16 the fiery Man is already divine: white hair, eyes of fire and shining face.

The seer in the Book of Revelation reacted as the others had done: 'I fell at his feet as though dead' (1.17). Daniel fell on his face in a deep sleep (Dan. 10.9), Abraham became like stone and fell face down on the earth (*Ap. Abr.* 10.2) and Ezekiel fell upon his face as he heard the voice (Ezek. 1.28). *The Man was no ordinary angel* (cf. Heb. 1.1–8). John was forbidden to worship the angel who showed him the later visions: 'I John am he who saw and heard these things. And when I heard and saw them, I fell down to worship at the feet of the angel who showed them to me; but he said to me, "You must not do that! I am a fellow servant with you and your brethren the prophets and with those who keep the words of this book. Worship God"' (Rev. 22.8–9, with a similar verse at 19.10). The Man among the lamps, however, did not forbid worship, but told John not to be afraid, the reassurance given to seers in the presence of the LORD. Daniel was told 'Fear not' (Dan. 10.12). Enoch fell prostrate at the sight of the Glory but the LORD summoned him: 'Do not fear, Enoch ... come near to me and hear my voice' (*1 En.* 15.1). In *2 Enoch* there is a similar account. When Enoch saw the LORD he fell prostrate and the LORD called to him: 'Fear not. Stand up and stand before my face for ever' (*2 En.* 22.5).

A Living Book

The first chapter of the Book of Revelation illustrates well the process by which an older collection of visions was interpreted and reinterpreted by the young churches as they realized the abiding significance of the prophecies. Any attempt to peel away the layers of a biblical text is bound to be speculative to some extent, and finding the earlier version of a text does not in any way imply that this is the correct version, the best version or the most authentic version. Prophecy was a living tradition and those who used it incorporated their own insights into what they had received. The Book of Revelation is no different in this respect from the prophecies of Isaiah, Jeremiah or Ezekiel; the present form of these biblical books includes reflection and insight from later generations of the prophets' disciples.

A glance at the chapter shows that it is has been put together from several texts; it has a formal opening at verse 1 and also at verse 4, there is a concluding *Amen* in verse 6 and in verse 7, there are commands to write in verse 11 and in verse 19. Three stages can be detected: first, the original vision of the Man which was the vision known to Jesus; second, the interpretation of the Christian prophet who added emphases to make clear that Jesus had become that Man; and third, the material incorporated from the seven letters when the letters and the visions were put together as one scroll.

The earliest text recoverable from the first chapter of the Book of Revelation is a temple vision of the angel high priest emerging from the holy of holies on the Day of the LORD. This is what was enacted every year on the Day of Atonement and many non-biblical texts describe what the ritual represented. The *Assumption of Moses*, a text whose present form dates from the first century CE also describes the emerging high priest:

Then his kingdom will appear throughout his whole creation
And the Satan shall be no more ...
Then the hands of the angel shall be filled*
Who has been appointed chief
And he shall forthwith avenge them of their enemies
For the heavenly one will arise from his royal throne
And he will go forth from his holy habitation
With indignation and wrath on account of his sons. (*Ass. Mos.* 10.1–3)

This priest figure is a warrior who emerges from his holy place to bring the Judgement. There follows a description of mountains falling, the sun being darkened and the moon turning to blood, the prophets' descriptions of the Day of the LORD which appear in the Book of Revelation as the terrors of the sixth seal and the first four trumpets. Scholars agree that this passage in the *Assumption of Moses* is based on the final section of the Song of Moses (Deut. 32.43), showing how those enigmatic verses were understood in the first century CE. In the biblical text, the one who emerges to bring judgement is the LORD, the God of Israel, but in the *Assumption of Moses* the same figure is described as the angel high priest, the heavenly warrior. This means that when the Book of Revelation was a living book of prophecy, the LORD was being described as a warrior high priest who would come from his holy place to bring the Day of the LORD. The Melchizedek text found at Qumran has a similar theme, describing the emergence of the heavenly Melchizedek, the great high priest. He was to take his place in the heavenly council, (the scene described in Rev. 5), and then wreak vengeance on the horde of Satan and rescue the sons of light. *1 Enoch* begins in a similar way: 'The Holy Great One will come forth from his dwelling ... and all shall be smitten with fear ... And the high mountains shall be shaken and the high hills shall be made low, and shall melt like wax before the flame' (*1 En.* 1.3, 5, 6).

The oldest part of Revelation 1 was just such a vision of the LORD emerging as the high priest from the holy of holies: it was known to Jesus and thus forms the introduction to his visions:

---

*This means filled with incense, i.e. made a priest, here the high priest.

(1) The revelation of Jesus Christ, which God gave him to show to his servants what must soon take place (3) for the time is near. (7) Behold, he is coming with the clouds, and every eye will see him.* (8) 'I am the Alpha and the Omega', who is and who was and who is to come, the Almighty. (12) Then I turned to see the voice that was speaking to me, and on turning I saw seven golden lampstands and in the midst of the lampstands one like a son of man, clothed with a long robe and with a golden girdle round his breast; his head and his hair were white as white wool, white as snow; his eyes were like a flame of fire, his feet were like burnished bronze, refined as in a furnace, and his voice was like the sound of many waters; in his right hand he held seven stars, from his mouth issued a sharp two-edged sword, and his face was like the sun shining in full strength. When I saw him, I fell at his feet as though dead. But he laid his right hand upon me, saying, 'Fear not, I am the first and the last, and the living one. (4.1) After this I looked, and lo in heaven an open door . . .

It is clear from the visionary texts that for the mystics there were two degrees of involvement, perhaps stages of initiation. Some, like Daniel, were only observers of the heavenly world, watching as the Man went up to the heavenly throne (Dan. 7.13–14). This is the case here, where the seer watches as the Man speaks to him. Other texts show that the mystics themselves became part of the vision; Enoch, for example, describes how he was taken up to stand before the throne (1 En. 14) and was then declared to be the Man whom he had seen (1 En. 71, although this is a difficult text). 2 Enoch and 3 Enoch say unambiguously that Enoch was transformed into an angel. A damaged text from Qumran (4Q491) is an unknown person's account of his own incomparable glory and exaltation among the 'elohim, the gods, of the holy place. He has 'a throne of strength in the congregation of the 'elohim and nobody can stand against the power of his words'. Jesus had had this experience of transformation; initially he had been an observer, seeing the Man and speaking of the Son of Man as if he were someone else who would come in the future. At his baptism he became the enthroned Man and accepted that the central figure of the visions (the Man, the Lamb/Servant) was to be the pattern for his life. The voice from the cloud told this to the disciples who experienced the Transfiguration (Mark 9.8–9), and they were the ones remembered by later Christian writers as recipients of Jesus' secret teaching.

The only comparable account of an appearance of the LORD in his temple has survived in the book of the priest-prophet Ezekiel who had known the first temple. At the climax of his vision of the throne chariot, the prophet saw a fiery human figure, surrounded by the brightness of a rainbow, exactly the description of the high priest Simon (Ben Sira 50.7) and the Mighty Angel in 10.1. For Ezekiel (and presumably for the later writers who used the same words), this was 'the appearance of the likeness of the glory of the LORD', the most startling piece of

---

*In Daniel 7.13 the Man is ascending with clouds, but in Revelation 10.1 he returns.

anthropomorphism in the Hebrew Scriptures (Ezek. 1.26–28). By the first century CE it was forbidden to read this passage in public, so strange and dangerous were its descriptions believed to be. The fiery Man on the throne chariot then transported Ezekiel in his vision to the temple in Jerusalem where he showed him all its abominations. Six angels of judgement appeared at the northern gate of the temple and were told to destroy everyone in the city who did not bear the mark of the LORD. 'Begin', said the Man, 'at my sanctuary' (Ezek. 9.6), so there can be no doubt about the identity of the Man. It is easy to see here in the judgement scenes of Ezekiel an ancient parallel to the Book of Revelation. The Man in the midst of the lamps is the LORD walking in his temple, dressed as the high priest, with the sword of judgement in his mouth. He is about to conduct the seer into the holy of holies to see the angels of judgement sent out against Jerusalem. Like Enoch (1 En. 14.24–25), the seer is summoned into the holy of holies (4.1).

The Man speaks of himself as the one 'who is and was and is to come', the Almighty (1.8), titles used in the greeting to the churches (1.4) and also used by the living creatures in heaven as they worship around his throne (4.8). 'Who is and was and is to come' is an elaborate version of the Name' (see p. 125) and so he names himself as the LORD of hosts. He declares himself to be 'the First and the Last', the title of the LORD used by Isaiah. 'Thus says the LORD , the King of Israel, and his Redeemer, the LORD of hosts: I am the First and I am the Last; besides me there is no God' (Isa. 44.6). 'I am He. I am the First and I am the Last' (Isa. 48.12). (These titles also appear among the fragments collected at the end of Revelation 22: 'Behold I am coming soon, bringing my recompense to repay everyone for what he has done. I am the Alpha and the Omega, the Beginning and the End, the First and the Last' (22.12–13).) The LORD warns that the time is at hand. This is exactly what is described in the *Assumption of Moses* 10: the warrior angel, the high priest, emerging from his holy place to bring judgement on those who have persecuted his people.

At first Jesus' mission had been to warn: 'The time is fulfilled, the Kingdom of God is at hand, repent and believe the good news' (Mark 1.15) but later he wept over Jerusalem, because the city did not recognize when the LORD came to her (Luke 19.41–44). He warned his disciples that he had come to bring 'a sword to the earth' (Matt. 10.34), that he had come to bring 'fire to the earth' but was held back until he had undergone his 'baptism', his death (Luke 12.49–50). Jesus knew that his own death would be the final atonement sacrifice to inaugurate the Day of the LORD, after which he would emerge from heaven and return as the warrior high priest. In John's Gospel, Jesus speaks of what he has seen and heard in heaven: 'If I have told you earthly things and you do not believe, how can you believe if I tell you of heavenly things'? (John 3.12). John the Baptist told his own disciples of Jesus' visionary experience: 'He bears witness to what he has seen and heard yet no one receives his testimony' (John 3.32). John, the beloved disciple, also bore witness to what Jesus had seen and heard (1.2), and this eventually became the Book of Revelation.

The first Christians knew Jesus as the heavenly high priest. The crucial verse in the Song of Moses (Deut. 32.43), which describes the LORD emerging to bring vengeance, became a proof text to demonstrate who Jesus was (Heb. 1.6 quotes from the longer original text, known in the LXX and found at Qumran). The crucifixion was recognized as his atonement sacrifice (Heb. 9.11–12). He had entered not the holy of holies but heaven itself. *The first generation were waiting for their high priest to emerge and complete the Great Atonement.* Peter preached about this in Jerusalem. There was only a little time left before the LORD, by whom he meant Jesus, would come from his holy place to bring judgement on evil and renewal for the whole creation, the fulfilment of the prophecies. 'Repent and turn again that your sins may be blotted out, that times of refreshing may come from the LORD and that he may send the Anointed One appointed for you, Jesus, whom heaven must receive until the time for establishing all that God spoke through the mouth of his holy prophets from of old' (Acts 3.19–21). (This is fulfilled at the end of the Book of Revelation in the description of the millennium kingdom.)

The second stage in the formation of the Book of Revelation was when the Christian prophets believed Jesus' prophecies and visions were being fulfilled. John described as 'the Spirit of Truth' the special inspiration which enabled him to interpret the prophecies for his own time. 'When the Spirit of Truth comes, he will guide you into all truth; for he will not speak on his own authority, but whatever he hears he will speak, and he will declare to you the things that are to come. He will glorify me, for he will take what is mine and declare it to you' (John 16.13–14). John first explained his own role in transmitting the vision: '[Jesus Christ] made it [the revelation] known by his angel [the Spirit of Truth] to his servant John, who bore witness to the word of God and to the testimony of Jesus Christ, even to all that he [Jesus] saw. Blessed is he who reads aloud the words of the prophecy and blessed are those who hear, and who keep what is written therein' (1.1b–3). The collection of prophecies had become the visions of Jesus Christ, and their interpretation was shown to John by means of the angel (the Spirit of Truth). John guaranteed that this was indeed what Jesus had seen, and the time had come to make it known. The prophecy would bring blessing both to those who read it and to those who listened and kept, that is, guarded, the words. The 'keepers of the testimony of Jesus' are mentioned elsewhere: in 12.17 they are the children of the woman clothed with the sun who are persecuted by the dragon, and in 19.10 they are described simply as John's brethren.

The second command to write (1.19) belongs to this stage of the Book. John has become one of the revealers, like Enoch and Jesus (and R. Neḥunya who instructed his disciples to write down what he spoke to them after his ascents, see p. 116). The importance of this role can be seen in the *Book of Jubilees*, where Moses, too, is depicted as a revealer, not just of the plan for the tabernacle, but of the whole plan of history. 'Write down all the matters which I shall make known to you on this mountain, what was in the beginning, and what will be at the end, what will happen in all the divisions of the days which are in the Law and testimony and throughout their weeks (of years) according to the jubilees for ever, until shall descend and dwell with them in all the ages of eternity' (*Jub.* 1.26). This is exactly what appears in the Book of Revelation, what will be at the end until the LORD comes to dwell with his people for all the ages of eternity. What had been transmitted orally was to be fixed in writing and John was told to write about the present and the future. To 1.7 he added a few words from Zechariah 12.10 to make it clear who coming the LORD would prove to be: 'Everyone who pierced him, all the tribes of the earth will wail on account of him', a free rendering of the Hebrew text and not a quotation from the LXX. To the words of the Man he added 'I died and behold I am alive for ever more and I have the keys of Death and Hades' (1.18).

This declaration, both here and by implication elsewhere in the Book of Revelation, that Jesus is the LORD, the God of Israel, is the most remarkable testimony to early Christian belief. 'Jesus is LORD' was the earliest declaration of the new faith, and by this was meant that Jesus was the God of Israel (see p. 40). Verses of Hebrew Scripture about the God of Israel were applied to Jesus not only in the Book of Revelation. but in many early writings. The words of the prophet Joel, for example, 'Everyone who calls on the Name of the LORD will be saved' (Joel 2.32), were used of Jesus by Paul. R. Johannan ben Zakkai, a contemporary of the first Christians, taught: 'Three were called by the Name of the Holy One ... the righteous, the Messiah and Jerusalem (b. *Baba Bathra* 75b).

John's first task as the interpreter of the prophecies had been to announce that Jesus had been the Lamb who was worthy to open the scroll, the Servant whose sacrifice inaugurated the great Day of Atonement of the last days. Once the process of opening the seals had begun, the prophets looked for their fulfilment. The most likely time for John to announce the imminent fulfilment of the final prophecies was from 64 CE onwards, when Nero was persecuting the Christians in Rome and the Jews were about to revolt against Rome as the tenth Jubilee drew to a close. This would account for the reference to Nero's persecution in Revelation 13, and to the burning of Jerusalem in Revelation 18. The vision of the little scroll in Revelation 10, indicates the final phase of interpretation, as the Parousia is delayed and Jerusalem is about to fall.

The third and final version of Revelation 1 incorporated the letters which John had sent to the seven churches of Asia during the 50s, the first crisis caused by Paul's Gentile mission. The greeting to the seven churches, 1.4–6, had originally been the introduction to the seven letters and John then recounted how he had received a revelation while on Patmos (1.9). This was probably his inspiration to combine the letters and the visions and send them openly to the churches (1.11). Each letter begins with an emphatic reference to the heavenly Jesus as its author, showing that these letters were as authentic a communication from the LORD as the other visions and prophecies in the book.

It is impossible to date the final form of the Book of Revelation and thus the present form of the first chapter. There is insufficient evidence from external sources to know how the churches in Asia Minor fared during the latter part of the first century CE. Various attempts have been made to reconstruct Roman persecutions in the area, but they depend for their evidence on the supposed setting of the Book of Revelation. Thus many arguments for dating the Book of Revelation prove to be circular.

6

THE LETTERS TO THE SEVEN CHURCHES

John to the seven churches that are in Asia: Grace to you and peace from him who is and who was and who is to come, and from the seven spirits who are before his throne, and from Jesus Christ the faithful witness, the firstborn of the dead, and the ruler of kings on earth. To him who loves us and has freed us from our sins by his blood and made us a kingdom, priests to his God and Father, to him be glory and dominion for ever and ever. Amen. (Rev. 1.4–6)

The seven churches of Asia were in Ephesus, Smyrna, Pergamum, Thyatira, Sardis, Philadelphia and Laodicea. These words stand as a greeting to all of them and, in the final form of the text, the 'letter' is the whole of the Book of Revelation. Most of the letters in the New Testament begin with a similar greeting: 'Grace and peace from God the Father and the LORD Jesus Christ'. In the letter to the Galatians there is an addition indicating the subject of the letter: 'Grace and peace from God the Father and our LORD Jesus Christ who gave himself for our sins to deliver us from the present evil age' (Gal. 1.4). The greeting to the seven churches is the most elaborate of all and implies a degree of learning and sophistication on the part of the recipients.

'Grace to you and peace from ... Jesus Christ the faithful witness', shows that he was an example for martyrs, 'the firstborn of the dead' shows that he gave hope for life beyond death, 'and the ruler of the kings of the earth' shows that he was greater than any Roman emperor. John is alluding here to Psalm 89, a royal psalm. This verse is a good example of how the Hebrew Scriptures are used throughout the Book of Revelation, and, we must assume, in the earliest churches. There is constant allusion, not actual quotation. The Christian prophets did not have the Hebrew Scriptures before them as they pieced together new oracles; they were steeped in the imagery of the Scriptures and spoke in their language.

Psalm 89, here translated literally, describes the enthronement of the Davidic king.

Of old thou didst speak in a vision to thy pious ones and say
I have set the help* on the mighty one,
I have raised up high one chosen from the people.
I have found David my servant;
with my holy oil I have anointed him ...
And I will appoint him the firstborn
the highest of the kings of the earth ...
His seed shall be for ever
and his throne like the sun before me.

* '*zr*, but a similar word *nzr* means crown.

Like the moon it shall be established for ever;
and a faithful witness in the clouds. (Ps. 89.19–20, 27, 37)

In his greeting to the churches, John adapts this psalm and describes Jesus as 'the firstborn', but adds 'of the dead', a reference to the resurrected state, and also as 'the ruler of kings on earth'. This is not the LXX, which renders the Hebrew quite literally as 'highest among the kings of the earth'. John paraphrases the Hebrew, and this was later translated into Greek. Paul uses an even looser paraphrase in Colossians 1.18: 'the first born from the dead so that in everything he might be pre-eminent', suggesting that this was an established interpretation of that psalm in the early church and not one of John's innovations.

Jesus is also described as 'the faithful witness', not 'a faithful witness in the clouds' (as in the Hebrew of Psalm 89) or 'in heaven' (as in the Greek of Ps. 89). There may be interpretation here too, since Jesus the faithful witness in heaven would originally have meant Jesus the faithful reporter of what he had seen and heard in heaven, as can be seen in 1.2, 'the witness of Jesus Christ, all that he saw', but it also meant 'martyr' since Jesus was one of the two martyrs described in 11.3–13. 'Witness' came to have the meaning 'martyr' rather than simply 'witness' as can be seen in 2.13, where Antipas, who has died for his faith, is also described as 'my faithful witness'. In his use of Psalm 89, John is paraphrasing, alluding to the Scriptures and interpreting for the new situation: the firstborn 'from the dead', the faithful 'martyr' (see also on 3.14).

The seven churches are reminded that they have nothing to fear from the imminent judgement. 'He has *freed* us from our sins by his blood'. Some ancient versions have here *washed,* i.e. *lousanti* instead of *lusanti,* but the meaning is the same as can be seen from 7.14 'they have washed their robes in the blood of the Lamb'. They are the royal priesthood on earth, 'a kingdom, priests to his God and Father' (1.6). This is also the theme of the new song in heaven (5.9–10) and of the millennium kingdom (20.6).

The new and even universal priesthood was important in the Book of Isaiah which was such a formative influence on Jesus and hence also in the early church (see pp. 65–6). The themes of Isaiah recur as those of the Book of Revelation, and the promises to those who had been excluded and dispossessed when the second temple was established became the aspirations of the Christians. They would become priests in the temple and inherit the double portion of the firstborn:

Aliens shall stand and feed your flocks,
foreigners shall be your ploughmen and vinedressers;
but you shall be called the priests of the LORD,
men shall speak of you as the ministers of our God ...
Instead of your shame you shall have a double portion. (Isa. 61.5–7)

[Isaiah 44.21: 'I formed you, you are my servant; O Israel, you will not be forgotten by me', became in the Targum: 'I have prepared you to be a servant serving before me: O Israel, you will not forget my fear'.]

The question of the true and legitimate priesthood was very real in the first century CE, and the claim that Jesus was the great Melchizedek and his followers the new priesthood, 'the living stones of a spiritual house and a holy priesthood' (1 Pet. 2.5) must be the context of this greeting. This is no ordinary priesthood; as in 1 Peter 2.9, the claim in the Book of Revelation is to 'a royal priesthood', the more ancient order of Melchizedek, the priest of God Most High (Gen. 14.18). The awkward Greek of 1.6, which gives the English 'a kingdom, priests to his God and Father', echoes not only Exodus 19.6 'You shall be to me a kingdom of priests and a holy nation', but also the additional lines in Exodus 23.22 which appear only in the LXX but not (no longer?) in the Hebrew. 'All the earth is mine and you will be for me a royal priesthood and a holy nation'. 'Royal priesthood' is how the LXX translates 'a kingdom of priests' in Exodus 19.6. The royal priesthood is the theme of each of the seven letters, and the seven churches regard themselves as fellow-heirs with Jesus to the ancient temple priesthood.

There may have been other elements in this claim. Philo understood royal priesthood (Exod. 19.6, LXX *basileion hierateuma*) to mean 'palace and priesthood', that the holy people were themselves God's palace, the sanctuary (*Sobriety* 66). In view of the living temple theme in the New Testament and at Qumran, this is a significant contemporary understanding of the text. The preface to 2 *Maccabees* shows that the universal royal priesthood had become part of the nationalist hope. 'It is God who has saved all his people, and has returned the inheritance to all, and the kingship and priesthood and consecration, as he promised through the law' (2 *Macc.* 2.17–18).

The seven individual letters, however, are not in the form of letters; they are oracles delivered in the style of the Hebrew prophets and reveal John as a prophet. There are examples in the Hebrew Scriptures of prophets speaking in the name of the LORD, but communicating their oracles by letter: Elijah wrote to King Jehoram, 'Thus says the LORD ...' and warned him of the fearful plague he was bringing on his family and his people by his wicked acts (2 Chron. 21.12–15); Jeremiah wrote from Jerusalem to the elders of the exiles in Babylon 'Thus says the LORD' and then warned them against false prophets (Jer. 29.4, 31). John writes in a similar way. Each of the seven letters begins: 'The words of him who' ... and the speaker then identifies himself as the LORD. That this was oracular style can be clearly seen by comparison with some texts from Isaiah, which first name the speaker and then identify him by one of his characteristics. 'Thus says God, the LORD who created the heavens and stretched them out ...' (Isa. 42.5); 'Thus says the LORD who created you, O Jacob' (Isa. 43.1); 'Thus says the LORD , the King of Israel and his Redeemer ...' (Isa. 44.6). The style both in the classical Hebrew prophets and in the seven letters is unmistakable. Each characteristic of the LORD which appears at the head of the letter relates closely to the exhortations that follow.

The History of the Seven Churches

The Acts of the Apostles is Luke's account of Paul's work in the Roman province of Asia, but it says nothing of the other missionaries who must have worked there. Of the seven churches of Asia, Paul was three years in Ephesus (Acts 20.31) and had links to Laodicea through Epaphras, one of his friends who taught there (Col. 4.13). None of the other five churches is associated with Paul's work, and so we must assume that they were founded by others, perhaps from the Jerusalem church.

There are many gaps in our knowledge of the early years of the church, but James the Righteous One seems to have been head not only of the church in Jerusalem but also of churches elsewhere. It was 'men from James' who condemned Paul's work in Antioch (Gal. 2.12), suggesting that James had received reports of what was happening there. It was a letter from James and the elders in Jerusalem which was sent to 'the brethren of the Gentiles in Antioch and Syria and Cilicia', imposing certain requirements of the Law of Moses on the new churches (Acts 15.23). This is important information for understanding the situation in which the seven letters were sent to the Asian churches. Just as the authority of James was recognized far afield in churches from which he had received reports, so too the authority of John, another 'pillar' of the church in Jerusalem (Gal. 2.9), could have been accepted in churches he had not known personally. Reports of their situation could have reached him; he need not necessarily have visited them.

The New Testament letters attributed to the other pillars Peter and James, are addressed in a distinctly Jewish style to whole groups of churches: Peter writes to 'the exiles of the dispersion in Pontus, Galatia, Cappadocia, Asia and Bithynia' (1 Pet. 1.1), James to 'the twelve tribes in the dispersion' (Jas 1.1). These suggest that there were Christians in the area other than Paul's converts, Hebrew Christians far removed from Palestine. In other words, there were conversions to Hebrew Christianity as a result of missionaries other than Paul, perhaps Jews who had visited Jerusalem as pilgrims, or perhaps Peter who went 'to another place' after his miraculous release from prison (Acts 12.17), or perhaps those unknown Christians who had taught Apollos in Alexandria. He had been 'instructed in the way of the LORD in his own country' (Acts 18.25, according to Codex Bezae). It was these people of whom James spoke to Paul: 'many thousands among the Jews of those who have believed, all zealous for the Law, they have been told about you that you teach all the Jews among the Gentiles to forsake the Law of Moses ...' (Acts 21.20–21).

Few details survive of the early years of Christianity in Asia Minor and what there are suggest conflict between Paul and another group. His early missionary work in Galatia to the south was dogged by opposition from people whom Luke calls Jews (Acts 13.50; 14.19). Paul's letter to the Galatians, however, shows they were not Jews but Hebrew Christians, 'men from James', who did not like what Paul was preaching about freedom from the Law of Moses. He told his Galatian converts how he had resisted the demands of the Hebrew Christians when they insisted that the Law be kept (Gal. 2.11–12). Paul was very conscious that the Jerusalem church did not accept him as a genuine apostle; what he taught was suspect (Gal. 1.11–12; 2 Cor. 11.21–22). How he countered this accusation is very interesting. He said that his gospel came through a revelation of Jesus Christ (Gal. 1.12) suggesting that a revelation from Jesus Christ was recognized by his opponents as the source of authentic teaching, as in Revelation 1.1. Paul was emphatic that even 'an angel from heaven' (Gal. 1.8) should not turn them away from his teaching. He was alarmed at the success the Hebrew Christians had had among his Galatian converts, and one wonders whether it was a claim to heavenly revelation, like that in the seven letters, which had been so influential. 'Who has bewitched you? How can you turn back again to the weak and beggarly elemental spirits whose slaves you want to be once more? You observe days and months and seasons and years! I am afraid I have laboured over you in vain' (Gal. 3.1, 4.9–10).

On his second missionary journey Paul avoided the area of the seven churches, 'forbidden by the Holy Spirit to speak the word in Asia' (Acts 16.6). Had the churches there received instructions from Jerusalem? He eventually spent three years in Ephesus, where Apollos, an Alexandrian Jew and disciple of John the Baptist, had already been teaching about Jesus (Acts 18.24–25). Aquila and Priscilla, two Jews from Pontus, converted him to another view of Jesus having 'expounded to him the way of God more accurately' (Acts 18.26), and Apollos then became a Pauline missionary in Achaea. When he arrived in Ephesus, Paul himself baptized Apollos' disciples.

All was not well. Paul spoke of Ephesus as a place of 'many enemies' (1 Cor. 16.9) where he had 'fought with beasts' (1 Cor. 15.32), and he did not visit the city on his final journey to Jerusalem. Presumably the seven churches had by then received their seven letters. He called instead at Miletus, a city some 50 miles to the south, and asked the church elders from Ephesus to meet him there. He warned them of troubles ahead in the church; fierce wolves would threaten the flock and even members of the church would speak perverse things (Acts 20.29–30) Later he (or perhaps a disciple writing in his name) wrote to Timothy saying that all in Asia *had turned away from him* (2 Tim. 1.15).

Paul does not name his opponents in Asia but hints in his letters show that they, too, were Hebrew Christians. His friend Epaphras had been the Pauline missionary in Colossae, Laodicea and Hierapolis, and in his letter to the Colossians, Paul warned them against certain errors: 'empty deceit and human tradition, the elemental spirits of the universe, circumcision, food and drink, festivals, new moons and Sabbaths' (Col. 2.8–16). Circumcision, food laws and Sabbaths indicate a Jewish group and the other characteristics – making allowance for his anger and his rhetoric – suggest angels and a special calendar. He condemned such observances as 'the appearance of wisdom and asceticism' (Col. 2.23). Paul's own followers were about to be expelled from the church: 'Let no one disqualify you, insisting on self-abasement and worship of angels, taking his stand on visions' (Col. 2.18). 'The mystery hidden from ages and generations' had been made known to Gentiles (Col. 1.26–27). Paul emphasizes that he has revealed something very important to the Gentiles. This is reminiscent of some lines in the Qumran Community Rule, where such a thing is forbidden. 'He shall not rebuke the men of the Pit nor dispute with them. He shall conceal the teaching of the Law from men of injustice' (1QS IX); 'I will conceal knowledge with discretion and will prudently hedge it within a firm bound' (1QS X); 'My eyes have gazed on that which is eternal, on wisdom concealed from men' (1QS XI).

Paul's letter is addressed to 'the saints and faithful brethren' (Col. 1.2), a form of words found elsewhere only in the letter to Ephesus (Eph. 1.1), suggesting that Paul was writing to those who had not joined the Hebrew Christian group in Asia Minor. The letter to Timothy in Ephesus also warned against those who taught a different doctrine, 'promoting myths, genealogies, speculations and the Law of Moses' (1 Tim. 1.3–7). These people forbad marriage and kept food laws (1 Tim. 4.3) and indulged in godless chatter that was falsely called knowledge (1 Tim. 6.20).

A picture emerges of the Hebrew Christians in Asia. They kept the Law in all its aspects, they revered angels, visions and revealed knowledge which they called wisdom, they placed great emphasis on their calendar and they adopted an ascetic and celibate lifestyle, expelling those who did not keep to the rules. *In another context, such a group would be identified with some confidence as the Qumran community.* The evidence suggests that some of the Qumran group lived in the wider community, 'the assembly of the towns of Israel' (CD XII), keeping to the rules of the group but avoiding contact with Gentiles and other Jews. Each community was a 'camp', cf. 20.9, where the saints live in a 'camp' and are attacked by the horde of Satan. Each camp was in the care of a *mbqqr,* usually translated 'Guardian', but the Greek equivalent would have been *episkopos,* 'bishop', as can be seen by comparing the Hebrew and Greek of Ezekiel 34.11 'the one who seeks out' his flock. The 'bishop' had 'to instruct the congregation in the works of God ... recount all the happenings of eternity to them ... love them as a father loves his children and carry them in all their distress like a shepherd his sheep' (CD XIII). A camp was divided into small groups of ten or more men, each under a priest who was 'learned in the Book of Hagu and in all the judgements of the Law' (CD XIV). This Book of Hagu is unknown but the name probably means 'The Book of Meditation'. It is interesting to note that the community persecuted by the dragon (12.17) described itself as the children of the woman clothed with the sun who took refuge in the desert, those who (translating literally) 'guard the commandments of God and have the testimony of

Jesus', testimony being defined in the introduction (1.2) as 'the testimony of Jesus which he saw'. Thus the community which kept the Book of Revelation also revered the Law and a Book of Visions. The seven letters are oracles in the same style as the visions, sent to the angel priests who had charge of the communities in Asia. The parallels with the Qumran community are interesting.

Anyone who broke the rules of the community was punished; challenging the authority of the community or betraying it meant expulsion (1QS VII). 'As a rebel he shall be dismissed from the community ... and all [the inhabitants] of the camps shall assemble in the third month and curse him who turns aside' (4Q266.11). The angel of Ephesus was warned that he might be expelled because he had fallen away from the works he did at first (2.5), and Paul's followers were threatened with expulsion (Col. 2.18).

Of the seven churches in Asia, Acts mentions only Ephesus and records two significant details of Paul's activity. First, that there were disciples of John the Baptist in the city, John 'who was in the wilderness until the day of his manifestation to Israel' (Luke 1.80), perhaps living at Qumran. Paul converted these disciples to his gospel and baptized them. Second, there were itinerant exorcists who also used the name of Jesus, 'seven sons of a Jewish high priest named Skeva' (Acts 19.1–20). It would be interesting to know more about these men. Seven sons of a high priest suggests a formal group rather than a family, and they were exorcizing in the name of Jesus. In other words, there were seven Hebrew Christians whose leader was Skeva, a high priest. Skeva is a strange name, but very similar to the Aramaic word for a seer, *sakya* and the related verb *sky* meaning look, expect, wait, hope. It is possible that the 'father' of the seven exorcists was a high priest known as the Seer or one who was keeping the prophecies in expectation. John, the beloved disciple and seer, was also remembered as a high priest; Polycrates, bishop of Ephesus, writing at the end of the second century CE, described John 'as a priest wearing the *petalon*' (i.e. the golden plate engraved with the Name, Eusebius, *History* 3.31). It seems that Paul's enemies in Ephesus were the Hebrew Christians who kept to the temple traditions and retained the title 'high priest' for their leader.

The seven letters reflect the conflict between Paul's churches and the Hebrew Christians. The letters mention 'Nikolaitans' active in Ephesus (2.6) and Pergamum (2.15), 'the synagogue of Satan' in Smyrna (2.9) and Philadelphia (3.9), a false teacher named 'Balaam' in Pergamum (2.14), a false prophetess named 'Jezebel' in Thyatira (2.20), and Satan dwelling in Pergamum with his throne (2.13). There were teachers in Ephesus who 'claimed to be apostles', but were not (2.2). It has been suggested that these are all colourful descriptions of the same group, the followers of Paul.

The story of Balaam is told in Numbers 22–25. Balaam the son of Beor was summoned by the king of Moab to curse the Israelites, but on the way he had a vision of the angel of the LORD standing in his path.

'I have come forth to withstand you because your way is perverse before me.' Balaam repented of his plan to curse the Israelites and was told by the angel. 'Only the word which I bid you, that shall you speak' (Num. 22.32–35). Paul was called Balaam because he, too, was struck down by a vision of the LORD as he travelled to Damascus to persecute the Christians there. He was converted and became a missionary to the Gentiles (Acts 9.1–19). Paul later put great emphasis on this experience; the vision was proof, he said, that his was the true gospel. It had come to him through the revelation of Jesus Christ (Gal. 1.11–17). In the letter to Ephesus, he was the 'one who called himself as apostle and was not' (2.2). The story of his conversion must have been well known to the Hebrew Christians of the churches of Asia as Paul wrote to tell his churches of the vision which was the basis of his preaching. A fragment of text from Qumran (4Q339) lists 'the lying prophets who arose'; the first of them is the son of Beor, that is Balaam. This Balaam appears again in 2 Peter 2.15 and also in the letter of Jude, where he is compared to Cain who made an unacceptable offering and then killed his brother (Gen. 4.8–16); and to Korah, who led a rebellion against Moses and against the authority of the priesthood, declaring that all the congregation had equal status with them: 'For all the congregation are holy, every one of them, and the LORD is among them. Why then do you exalt yourselves above the assembly of the LORD?' (Num. 16.3). This is a striking parallel to the situation with Paul and his rebellion against the authorities in Jerusalem. Both 2 Peter and Jude, who mention Balaam, also use imagery drawn from the Enoch tradition, the fallen angels and the last judgement, exactly as in Revelation and in the Damascus Document (CD II), suggesting that they had a common origin. The Babylonian Talmud records a midrash that Israel had three enemies at the time of the war against Rome: Titus, Jesus and Balaam (*b. Gittin* 56b–57a). Presumably this reflects the threats from Rome, and from the two groups within the church, the followers of Jesus and the followers of Paul.

Jezebel, the false prophetess in Thyatira, was Lydia, whom Paul had met in Philippi. She was a seller of purple goods from the city of Thyatira (Acts 16.14) and had been baptized together with her whole household. Paul, Silas and Luke stayed with her while they were in Philippi. A merchant dealing in purple goods implies that she was a woman of some wealth, and her trade implies an association with the city of Tyre which was famous for its purple dyes. Paul's wealthy convert in Thyatira became known as Jezebel, the princess of Tyre who had tried to draw Israel into foreign ways in the time of King Ahab. She had been confronted by Elijah who challenged her prophets to a contest on Mount Carmel. 'How long', he said to the assembled people, 'will you go limping with two opinions? If the LORD is God, follow him; but if Baal then follow him' (1 Kgs 18.21). This was the situation in the Asian churches, with a new Jezebel trying to draw Israel into new ways.

Her teachings are the same as Balaam's; they both allow their people to eat food sacrificed to idols and they permit immorality (2.14, 20). These had been forbidden by the Council of Jerusalem; the Gentile churches did not have to keep the whole Law, but they did have 'to abstain from what has been sacrificed to idols, and from blood and from what is strangled and from unchastity' (Acts 15.29). Paul had interpreted this rather liberally, arguing that, since idols do not exist, the food offered to them could not be any different from ordinary food. A Christian should abstain from eating only if to eat would cause anxiety to a weaker brother: 'Food will not commend us to God' (1 Cor. 8.8; this was an important issue, and Paul also deals with it in 1 Cor. 10 and Rom. 14). Immorality probably meant marriage outside the strict rules of Judaism, but it could have meant any departure from a code of which we now know nothing. The churches of Asia Minor continued to observe the apostolic decree (Acts 15.29), but Trypho (mid-first century CE) bears witness to the fact that some continued to follow Paul's more permissive teaching. He complained to Justin that some people who called themselves Christians ate meat which had been offered to idols. Justin said these people were not true Christians: 'Such men pretend to be Christians ... yet do not profess Christ's doctrine. They follow spiritual error' (*Trypho* 55).

The enemies were 'the synagogue of Satan, those who claimed to be Jews but were not' (2.9; 3.9). Paul had explained at great length to the Galatian Gentiles that they were the true Israel: 'it is the men of faith who are the sons of Abraham' (Gal. 3.7); 'Now we, brethren, like Isaac, are children of promise' (Gal. 4.28); 'For neither circumcision counts for anything, nor uncircumcision, but a new creation' (Gal. 6.15). His letter to the Ephesians puts it even more strongly: 'Therefore remember that at one time you were Gentiles in the flesh, called the uncircumcision by what is called the circumcision, which is made in the flesh by hands – remember that you were at that time separated from Christ, alienated from the commonwealth of Israel, and strangers to the covenants of promise ...' (Eph. 2.11–12). The Qumran community also identified their enemies as 'an assembly of deceit and a horde of Belial' (1QH X, formerly II), a synagogue of Satan.

The 'Nikolaitans' have long been a mystery. Some early writers (Tertullian, Irenaeus) speculated that they were the followers of Nikolaus the deacon, the proselyte from Antioch (Acts 6.5). Some modern scholars have suggested that the name is linked to Balaam, which was thought to mean the ruler of the people (*b'l 'm*) and Nikolaitans would then derive from the Greek words *nikan*, conquer, and *laos*, people. If, however, 'Nikolaitans' was a name used by the Hebrew Christians to describe their enemies, then the Semitic name underlying 'Nikolaitans' would have been significant. The name must have come from *nkl*, which means *deceive* in both Hebrew and Aramaic. Satan was the Deceiver (12.9 and 20.2). The enemies in 2 Peter 2.13 are described as 'revelling in their deceits' (translating literally). Paul protests in an early letter that he has preached in the face of great opposition and that he did not 'deceive' his hearers (1 Thess. 2.2–3). An element in the debate in 2 Corinthians was deceit: Who was deceiving whom? 'We refuse to practise cunning or to tamper with God's word' (2 Cor. 4.2). Paul maintained that it was his enemies who were the deceivers: 'Such men are false apostles, deceitful workmen, disguising themselves as apostles of Christ' (2 Cor. 11.13). This was also a name which the Qumran community gave to their enemies; there was 'a Spouter of Lies who led many astray' (1QpHab X), and the Hymns tell of 'teachers of lies and seers of falsehood' who offer 'smooth things' to the people (1QH XII, formerly IV). The opponent of the Teacher of Righteousness was the Liar (CD VIII). Perhaps the Hebrew Christians of Asia adopted a traditional name for their enemies, 'the deceivers', just as they knew Satan as the Deceiver (12.9; 20.2). Or perhaps the Nikolaitans were the common enemy of the Hebrew Christians and the Qumran community, bearing in mind that Paul had formerly been the agent of the high priest in Jerusalem (Acts 9.1–2), whom the Qumran community regarded as the Wicked Priest. At Paul's first meeting with the Hebrew Christians in Jerusalem, they were afraid of him, did not believe that he was truly converted and tried to kill him (Acts 9.26–29). Paul's converts might have received similar treatment.

What we glimpse in the seven letters, then, are the communities whom Paul described as his enemies, the Hebrew Christians. These are very early texts, written in reaction to Paul's mission in Asia Minor, at a time when the Parousia was still thought to be imminent: 'I will come soon (2.16); Hold fast what you have until I come' (2.25); 'I will come like a thief and you will not know at what hour I will come upon you' (3.3); 'I will keep you from the hour of trial which is coming upon the whole world, to try those who dwell upon the earth.* I am coming soon, hold fast what you have' (3.10–11).

The Royal Priesthood

John addresses the leaders of the seven churches as the royal priesthood; each is described as the angel of his church and the oracle is to him personally. The seven oracle-letters were combined with the Book of Visions; in other words the visions are important for understanding the situation in the churches. The royal priesthood in Asia would have identified with the royal priesthood in the visions to define their role and their future hope.

In the visions there are distinct ranks of people in the heavenly temple: the high priest who appears in the midst of the lamps (1.12–13), or emerges with a cloud (10.1); the various angels who stand in the temple or emerge from it often carrying trumpets or incense or libation bowls (8.1–3; 16.1); the 144,000 celibates who bear the Name on their foreheads and stand before the throne (7.1–8; 14.1–5), and the great

---

*A reference to the Day of the LORD when the living would be judged (see p. 343).

multitude from all nations who wear white robes and also stand before the throne. They have come through the Great Tribulation and washed their robes in the blood of the Lamb (7.13–17). These four groups resemble the four classes in the only priestly community of which we know anything at this period: the Qumran community described in the Damascus Document. 'They shall all be enrolled by name: first the Priests, second the Levites, third the Israelites and fourth the proselytes' (CD XIV). It is possible that the Hebrew Christian churches had a similar structure.

Each letter is addressed to the angel, the priest, (perhaps bishop, m^ebaqqer) who is the guardian of his church. 'The lips of the priest should guard knowledge ... for he is the angel of the LORD of hosts', said the prophet Malachi (Mal. 2.7) and this exactly is how the Qumran priests continued to describe themselves. One of their blessings for the priests, the sons of Zadok, is: 'May you be as an angel of the Presence in the abode of holiness to the glory of the God of [hosts]' (1QSb IV).

There is some confusion in the imagery of the lamps and the stars; the explanation in 1.20, that the stars in the Man's hand are the angels and that the lamps are the seven churches, is a departure from temple tradition, which regarded both stars and lamps as symbols of angels. This explanatory material was probably inserted by the translator who shows elsewhere that he does not understand temple tradition and terminology (see p. 187). The threat to the angel of Ephesus, that his lamp would be removed, makes more sense if the lamp represents him. Isaiah had described the Servant of the LORD as a damaged lamp: 'a bruised lamp, he will not be broken off, a dimly burning wick, he will not be put out' (Isa. 42.3; the Hebrew word qnh translated 'reed' also means the 'hollow branch of a menorah'). The presence of the Servant of the LORD was a sign of hope for his people. Isaiah also described what happened if the guardian figures of the people were removed from their holy place. 'The mediators of Israel', their royal high priests, had transgressed, and so the LORD had 'profaned', i.e. cast out, 'the princes of the sanctuary' (Isa. 43.27–28). When this happened, the Babylonians were able to take Jerusalem. The presence of the priest was the presence of the guardian angel; priests who failed were cast out, and with them went their dependent people. Removing the lamp of the angel of Ephesus would have meant the destruction of his people.

John is told to send a message to each angel, and this again is a traditional motif. Enoch the high priest had entered the holy of holies to intercede for the fallen angels, and the LORD told him to take them instead a message of judgement: they would have no peace (1 En. 15). The messages to the angels of the seven churches do contain a strong element of judgement and enable us to glimpse the very human leaders of these early communities. The angel of Ephesus has fallen from his first love and should repent if his lamp is to stay in its place (2.4–5). The angel of Pergamum has tolerated false teaching in his church and is told to repent or face the sword of the LORD's words (2.14–16). The angel of Thyatira tolerates Jezebel the false prophetess (2.20), and the angel of Sardis has been neglecting his flock. He is more dead than alive and his people have fallen into bad ways (3.1–4). The angel of Laodicea has become apathetic; he has become rich in material things but lost sight of his true condition. His money would be better spent on true riches, a white garment of glory and ointment for his failing spiritual sight.

Each letter ends with a promise of reward for 'the one who conquers', (or perhaps this should be 'the one who is worthy', the Aramaic would have been identical) just as the Lamb has 'conquered' or was 'worthy' to open the scroll (see on 5.5). This may refer to overcoming death, or it may refer to keeping the faith in a time of persecution, or to keeping the faith in the face of false teaching. All are mentioned in the letters: the angel of Sardis is suffering tribulation and poverty, and the devil is about to put some of the flock into prison (2.10); the angel of Pergamum has held to the faith even though one of his flock has been killed (2.13). The angels of Ephesus, Pergamum, Thyatira and Philadelphia have had false teachers in their midst.

The rewards are the rewards for faithful priests; each is linked in some way to status in the temple.

The angel of the church at Ephesus is promised 'To him who conquers I will grant to eat of the tree of life which is in the Paradise of God' (2.7). Adam and Eve had been barred from the fruit of the tree of life, as punishment for their disobedience. Eating the fruit would have given them eternal life (Gen. 3.22). The human pair were driven from Eden and as they left the LORD's presence they became mortal. The cherub with a flaming sword guarded the way into Eden and prevented Adam's return (Gen. 3.24). The story of Adam's expulsion from Eden was originally the story of corrupt angel priests being expelled from the mountain of God and condemned to mortality, as can be seen from the older version of the story in Ezekiel 28. The Prince of Tyre described there was originally the Prince of Zion (the words 'Tyre' and 'Zion' look very similar in Hebrew, and a prophet's words were often reused, as can be seen in the Book of Revelation itself). The Greek of Exodus 39.10–13, which describes the high priest's jewelled breastplate in more detail than the Hebrew text at this point, makes it clear that Ezekiel's angel prince wore the jewels of the high priest. Leaving Eden was how Ezekiel described the ancient high priests leaving the first temple. The climax of the Book of Revelation describes their return (22.1–5, see p. 327).

After generations of decline and corruption in the priesthood, it was believed that the LORD would raise up a new priest: 'and he shall open the gates of Paradise, he shall remove the sword that has threatened since Adam, and he will grant to the saints to eat of the tree of life' (*T. Levi* 8.10). This pre-Christian text may have been expanded by a Christian writer, but it confirms that the new priest would give to the saints the fruit of the tree of life and so restore to them eternal life. Enoch saw the tree of life on his heavenly journey and asked the angel what it was: 'And as for this fragrant tree, no mortal is permitted to touch it till the great judgement when ... it shall be given to the righteous and holy. Its fruit shall be for food for the elect: it shall be transplanted to the holy place, the temple of the LORD, the eternal King' (*1 En.* 25.4–5). Fragments of this chapter have been found at Qumran (4Q205). Thus the angel of the church in Ephesus is promised eternal life and access to the heavenly sanctuary from which Adam had been barred. The church was the ancient priesthood restored.

The angel of the church at Smyrna, which is to face tribulation and imprisonment, is promised a crown of life (2.10). The crown, *stephanos*, is described by James: 'Blessed is the man who endures trial, for when he has stood the test he will receive the crown of life which God has promised to those who love him' (Jas 1.12). Peter exhorted the church elders to tend their flocks: 'And when the chief Shepherd is manifested you will obtain the unfading crown of glory' (1 Pet. 5.4), and the Community Rule at Qumran promised to the faithful 'healing, great peace in a long life and fruitfulness together with everlasting blessing and eternal joy in life without end, a crown of glory and a garment of majesty in unending light' (1QS IV). It has been suggested that this image derived from the victor's crown at the games, but it is more likely to be a reference to the high priest's golden diadem which was worn around his turban (*Ben Sira* 45.12; *1 Macc.* 10.20). Philo described it as 'a piece of gold plate, wrought in the form of a crown, with four incisions showing a Name ... which has four letters' (*Moses* II.114); and a similar crown given to the heavenly Enoch bore the 'letters by which heaven and earth were created' (*3 En.* 13). The angel of Smyrna is also promised that he will not be harmed by the second death. The first death was physical death from which only the martyrs would rise at the first resurrection to reign with Christ for a thousand years: 'Blessed and holy is he who shares in the first resurrection! Over such the second death has no power, but they shall be priests of God and of Christ, and they shall reign with him a thousand years' (20.6). After the thousand years would come the Last Judgement, when those whose names were not in the Book of Life would be thrown into the lake of fire, the second death (20.14–15 see p. 360). The angel of Smyrna would be safe.

The angel of the church at Philadelphia is warned to be steadfast so that nobody can seize his crown (3.11). In the visions, crowns are worn by the false Messiah (6.2), by the locusts (9.7) and by the woman clothed with the sun (12.1). The crowns promised to the angels of Smyrna and Philadelphia, however, are probably those of the son of man (14.14) and the twenty-four elders (4.4, 10), insignia of the royal priesthood.

The angel of the church at Pergamum is promised the hidden manna, the food which the Israelites ate during their forty years in the wilderness (Exod. 16.31–36). A golden jar of manna was kept in the ark (Heb. 9.4), but there was no ark in the second temple. It was believed to be hidden away until the age of the Messiah (*Num. Rab.* XV.10) or until God would again gather his people together and show them mercy (2 *Macc.* 2.7). In the visions, however, the ark is revealed in the heavenly temple, so the manna is also available (11.19). The almost contemporary vision of Baruch says that when the Messiah is revealed, the earth will enjoy miraculous fertility 'its fruit ten thousandfold', and the treasury of manna shall again descend from on high and be given to those who have come to that time of fulfilment (2 *Bar.* 29.1–8). One of the *agrapha* (unwritten sayings of Jesus, i.e. not recorded in the four Gospels) says that Jesus also taught about a time of miraculous fertility:

Some elders who had known John the beloved disciple heard from him how the LORD taught concerning these times and said: The days shall come wherein vines shall grow each having ten thousand branches, and on one branch ten thousand shoots and on every shoot ten thousand clusters and on every cluster ten thousand grapes. (Irenaeus, *AH* 5.33.3)

Note that it was John, the beloved disciple, who knew this additional teaching. If Jesus taught about the time of great fertility exactly as in 2 *Baruch*, it is possible that the promise of the manna was also one of his sayings. Manna was known as the bread of angels (2 *Esdr.* 1.19), and so would have been an appropriate food for the angel priests of the messianic kingdom (see on 20.4–6).

The angel of the church at Pergamum is also promised the gift of a white stone, inscribed with a secret name known only to himself. The letters were sent with the visions which describe the Word of God riding out from heaven (c.f. *Wisd* 18.15), with a name known only to himself inscribed on his diadem (19.12), and since he is the heavenly warrior priest and the name is on his diadem, it must be a form of the sacred Name. The secret name on the white stone given to the angel of Ephesus is this sacred Name, and the gift of such a stone had been part of Joshua's consecration as high priest (Zech. 3.1–9), when the LORD came from his holy place and appeared as an angel to vest his high priest in the temple. He ordered attendant angels to give Joshua the turban and the garments of high priesthood, and then assured him that, if he walked in the ways of the LORD, he would have the right to enter the holy place. He then set before Joshua an engraved stone with seven 'eyes' and said that he would remove the guilt of the land in a single day. The Hebrew text here is obscure but resembles the instructions given to Moses for making Aaron's high priestly vestments, tying to the front of the turban a golden seal engraved with the sacred Name. When Aaron wore it, he would be empowered to bear away the guilt, that is the impurity, of any offering brought to the holy place (Exod. 28.36–38). In other words, wearing the Name enabled the high priest to remove guilt. The engraved stone given to Joshua, the high priest, had the same power to remove guilt from the land and the seven eyes engraved on it were a symbol of the LORD, perhaps the menorah which was 'the seven eyes of the LORD' (Zech. 4.10). The angel of the church of Pergamum is also promised this stone engraved with the Name, making him a high priest with power to effect atonement (see also on 19.12).

The angel of the church at Thyatira is promised power over the nations, using words from Psalm 2, a coronation psalm: 'You shall rule them with a rod of iron and dash them in pieces like a potter's vessel'. Jesus had heard some words of this psalm at his baptism: 'You are my Son' (Mark 1.11), and had wrestled with the meaning of this sonship during his time in the desert. How would he come to rule over the nations? Satan offered him an easier way to have power over all the kingdoms of the world: 'If you will worship me, it shall all be yours' (Luke 4.7), but Jesus resisted the ways of Satan. The faithful in Thyatira have also rejected 'the deep things of Satan' (2.24), the easier way offered by Paul, and to each one who overcomes this temptation, the promised reward is the same: enthronement as Jesus was enthroned. 'And I will give him the Morning Star' reveals that the writer of these letters was not a native speaker of Greek. 'I will give' is a Hebrew way of saying 'I will appoint' (as in Ps. 89.27), and here it has been over-literally translated into Greek. The one who conquers and is enthroned will also be appointed as the Morning Star, a title which Jesus uses elsewhere of himself (22.16). The title is a mystery; it appears in Psalm 110.3, another coronation psalm which has been damaged in trans-mission and is no longer readable. The translator of the LXX recognized in verse 3 the title 'Morning Star' and rendered the line 'I begot you from the womb before the Morning Star'. 'I begot you' is certainly one way to read the Hebrew *yldtyk* and so it is possible that this psalm once described the temple ritual for the divine birth of the king who was then appointed as Melchizedek and the Morning Star. The parallel structure of Hebrew poetry, where the second line duplicates the meaning of the first, shows that the Sons of God who sang for joy at the creation were also known as Morning Stars (Job 38.7). Perhaps this was an ancient title for a Son of God as it had been for the kings of Ugarit.

The angel of the church at Sardis and his people are promised the white garments of the sanctuary: 'they shall walk with me in white for they are worthy' (3.4). A great multitude in white robes stood before the throne of the Lamb and joined with the angels and the elders in worship. They had made their robes white with the blood of the Lamb. Soiled garments were a sign of sin (3.4) and only those who had been freed from sin by the blood of the Lamb (1.5) would join the throng in the heavenly temple. White linen garments were worn by the high priest in heaven when he entered the holy of holies on the Day of Atonement. They were the dress of the angels. The men in dazzling clothes, whom the women saw at the tomb on Easter morning, were later described as angels (Luke 24.4 and 23). The white garments were the garments of glory and represented the resurrection body. Josephus says they were worn by the Essenes (*War* 2.123) and they probably had this meaning for them, too. An early Christian mystical text describes how Isaiah ascended to the seventh heaven and saw 'Enoch and all with him stripped of robes of the flesh and I saw them in their robes of above and they were like angels who stand there in great glory' (*Asc. Isa.* 9.9).

2 Corinthians 5.4 is similar; Paul speaks of death as taking off clothes and then being reclothed, 'so that what is mortal may be swallowed up by life'. He who conquers is promised resurrection.

The angel of the church at Sardis is also assured that his name is still in the Book of Life to be opened at the Last Judgement (20.12). It was an ancient belief that the LORD had a book in which he wrote the names of his faithful people. When Israel sinned, Moses offered the LORD his own life as a sacrifice for their forgiveness: 'Blot me, I pray thee, out of thy book which thou hast written. But the LORD said to Moses: Whoever has sinned against me, him will I blot out of my book' (Exod. 32.32–33). Whoever conquered knew that his name would be in the Book of Life, that he would be safe at the Last Judgement: 'I will confess his name before my Father and before his angels' (3.5). Similar words are attributed to Jesus at several places in the Gospels, anticipating the persecution of his disciples: 'Every one who acknowledges me before men, the Son of man also will acknowledge before the angels of God; but he who denies me before men will be denied before the angels of God' (Luke 12.8–9; also Matt. 10.32; Mark 8.38; Luke 9.26).

The angel of the church at Philadelphia is promised an important place in the living temple (see p. 325). He is to be a pillar. This temple image appears in other letters to the churches of Asia and must have been well known to them. Paul's letter to the Ephesians exhorts them to grow into a holy temple to the LORD, which has apostles and prophets as its foundations and Jesus Christ as its cornerstone (Eph. 2.20–22). Peter, writing to all the churches of the area, exhorts them to become living stones built into a spiritual house (1 Pet. 2.5). *Pillar* was also a title for the leaders of the Jerusalem church as can be seen from Paul's bitter remarks about Peter, James and John, who were 'reputed to be pillars of the church' (Gal. 2.9). Irenaeus was later to speak of the twelve pillared foundation of the church, by which he meant the twelve apostles (*AH* 4.21.3). The Qumran community described themselves as a holy of holies: 'a house of holiness for Israel ... a most holy dwelling for Aaron' (1QS VIII).

The angel of the church at Philadelphia is to be marked with the new Name of the fiery Man and the Name of his God, not two names but one, since the Man and his God both had the sacred Name (see p. 36). Lines quoted by Paul, possibly from an early hymn, describe the risen Jesus and his new Name: 'God has highly exalted him and bestowed on him the Name which is above every Name' (Phil. 2.9). The heavenly Jesus, who sent his words to the seven churches, bore the Name, and this would be given to the angel of the church in Philadelphia. This must be understood in the light of Revelation 14, the vision of 144,000 standing before the Lamb on Mount Zion, with the Name of the Lamb and of his Father on their foreheads. The angel of the church in Philadelphia would also have the name of the new Jerusalem. This again was the sacred Name, first used of Jerusalem by the priest-prophet Ezekiel when he described the gates of a new temple city (Ezek. 48.35). The line is usually translated 'The name of the city henceforth shall be, The LORD is there' (*yhwh s'mh*), but the seer of Revelation read the same Hebrew letters as 'The LORD is its name' (literally 'her name', because city is a feminine noun). A Qumran psalm is similar: 'Jerusalem ... the Name of the LORD is called on her' (4Q380). Thus the LORD, the heavenly Jesus and the heavenly city all have the same Name, and this would be given to the faithful bishop. R. Joh.annan ben Zakkai, a contemporary of the first Christians, taught that three were called by the Name: The Righteous, the Messiah and Jerusalem. Of Ezekiel 48.35, he said: 'Do not read "there" but "its name"' (*b. Baba Bathra* 75b). 'As to the name of the city, from that day it shall be "the LORD"' (cf. Dan. 9.19).

In the early years of the second century CE, Ignatius, the old bishop of Antioch, passed through Asia on the way to his martyrdom in Rome. He wrote letters to the churches of Asia describing the bishop and clergy as though they were the high priest and the priests of the temple: *The bishop was God and the clergy were his heavenly council* (*Magn.* 6, *Trall.* 9). This is a remarkable confirmation that the churches of Asia modelled themselves on the temple and its hierarchy; the bishop was the LORD with his people, exactly the reward promised to the faithful bishops of the seven churches.

In the male–female nature of the LORD we glimpse one of the strangest aspects of temple tradition. The holy city was also the goddess, as in Revelation 21.9–10, where the heavenly Jerusalem is the bride of the Lamb/Messiah. The goddess was also the mother of the Messiah, as in Revelation 12.1–5, where the woman clothed with the sun gives birth to the royal child. After so many centuries we cannot be certain what Israel meant by 'the LORD', but it does seem that even in the first century CE they could think of the God of Israel as both male and female, manifested in the royal high priest and in the city, identified with both so closely that, when the royal high priest was expelled from the holy place, the city also perished. When Jesus, the true high priest, was put to death, the city was doomed, and when the true high priest appeared from heaven, so, too, did the heavenly Jerusalem (19.7–16). This, as we have seen, was the warning given to the angel of the church at Pergamum, that his fate would be shared by his church. Here, the angel of Philadelphia is promised that he will be the presence of the LORD with his people, like Jesus the Anointed One who was both the (male) Power and the (female) Wisdom (1 Cor. 1.24). This is the dual nature, known more than a thousand years earlier in the texts from Ugarit, which surfaced in Genesis 1.26–27 when the male and female were created in the divine image.

The angel of the church at Laodicea is promised a place on the heavenly throne. Just as Jesus had conquered and taken his place (the vision of the slain Lamb in Rev. 5) so, too, the victor would be enthroned. The implication of this promise is that Jesus was the first of many who would all become one with him in his heavenly state. 'In Christ' is the familiar term for this state of union. Just as the martyrs under the altar (6.9–11) were united with Jesus in the Great Atonement; so too the conquerors would be one with him in the final exaltation. They were 'in Christ, the body of Christ', the heavenly LORD who, when he made humans in his image on earth had to make them both male and female (Gen. 1.26). In the new body, however, there was neither male nor female nor any other human distinction because they were the body of the heavenly LORD. This is what Paul wrote to the neighbouring churches of Galatia (Gal. 3.27–28).

Sharing the heavenly throne was the reward of the high priest who entered the holy place. This is a recurring theme of later Jewish mystical texts. Enoch is taken to heaven and transformed there into the Great Angel Metatron, a name which probably means 'the throne sharer'. In *3 Enoch* Rabbi Ishmael, also described as a high priest, ascends to heaven and meets Metatron. 'Why', he asks, 'are you called by the name of your creator?' Metatron has received the Name inscribed on the crown, the letters by which the world was created (*3 En.* 13). He then explains to Ishmael that he has been appointed Prince and Ruler among the angels (*3 En.* 4: 'appointed' is literally 'given' as in 2.28: 'I will give/appoint you the Morning Star'). Metatron is also given a throne, and then a herald is sent out to proclaim that Metatron, the Servant, has been appointed Prince and Ruler over the heavenly hosts (*3 En.* 10). The similarities to Paul's lines about Jesus are obvious: 'God has highly exalted him [the Servant] and bestowed on him the name that is above every name, that at the name Jesus every knee should bow, in heaven and on earth and under the earth' (Phil. 2.9). *3 Enoch*, however, is a Jewish text with a temple setting. Even though it cannot be dated (perhaps it was penned in Babylon in the fifth century CE), the description of the exalted Enoch/Metatron which is so like the description of Jesus in Philippians 2, will not have been borrowed from the New Testament by a Jew. Whatever has been preserved in *3 Enoch* must have originated in the same pre-Christian milieu as the Book of Revelation, among the temple mystics. Eusebius, writing in the fourth century CE, described the God of Israel as the one who was anointed and became the Christ, the one who was the Beloved of the Father and his Offspring, the eternal Priest and the being called 'the Sharer of the Father's throne' (*Proof* 4.15). This was the promise made to the angel of Laodicea; he, too, would become like Enoch and like Jesus, exalted and enthroned.

The LORD of the Letters

Each letter begins with a description of the one who sends it. The Man in the midst of the seven lamps is described in some detail as a human figure whose face shines like the sun. He has white hair, fiery eyes, feet like burnished bronze and a voice like many waters. He is dressed like the high priest, with a two-edged sword in his mouth and seven stars in his right hand. He proclaims himself the First and the Last, the Living

One who has died and is alive for evermore. He has the keys of Death and Hades. Each of the seven letters begins with similar descriptions of the LORD, and most, but not all of them, correspond to the description of the Man among the lamps. The details at the head of each oracle relate in some way to the oracle itself, that is, each picture of the LORD defines what his followers should do and be.

The letter to Ephesus comes from the one 'who holds the stars and walks among the lamps'. The threat to the angel of Pergamum is that 'his lamp will be removed', that he will be thrown from the holy place which was Eden. The sevenfold lamp also represented the tree of life in the Garden of Eden and so the conqueror is promised that he will be allowed to eat its fruit.

The letter to Smyrna comes from the one who is 'the First and the Last who died and came to life' and so he promises that the faithful will win the 'crown of life' and not be harmed by 'the second death'.

The letter to Pergamum comes from one like the Servant of the LORD in Isaiah 49.2 who 'has the two-edged sword' and he threatens to use this sword in judgement against those who follow false teachers.

The letter to Thyatira comes from the Man with fiery eyes and glowing feet, 'the Son of God'. This latter is the key to the rest of the letter, although the link is not so obvious as in the oracles to Ephesus, Smyrna and Pergamum. The priest-king was declared to be 'Son of God' at his enthronement, and the promises made to the divine Son at that time are recorded in Psalm 2. The same promises are made in this oracle to the one who conquers: 'he will rule the nations with a rod of iron and shatter them like earthen pots' and he will also receive the same royal title as Jesus, the Morning Star (22.16). Whoever wrote these letters knew more about the temple tradition than we do.

The letter to Sardis comes from the Man who has the seven stars and the 'seven spirits of God'. The sevenfold Spirit was to rest on the Messiah (Isa. 11.2) and this had been given to Jesus at his baptism (Mark 1.10), making him the divine Son. The earliest known records of baptismal practice of the Syrian churches show that Jesus' baptism in the Jordan was re-enacted for each new convert. The bishop represented the LORD and declared to each one who emerged from the water the words of Psalm 2: 'You are my son, I have today begotten you'. The newly baptized were then robed in white as a sign of their new heavenly life after the gift of the Spirit. Here, the one who has the seven spirits speaks 'to those whose baptismal garments are still white' and assures them that he will acknowledge them as his own at the Last Judgement (see p. 362).

The letter to Philadelphia comes from the Holy and True One who 'holds the key of David' and 'he has opened a door' before them that nobody can shut. The Isaiah Targum 22.22 illuminates this enigmatic line. The original text referred to the appointment of a new palace steward after his corrupt predecessor had been removed, but the Targum interprets it of a corrupt high priest, whose turban would be taken away. The new high priest is to rule over the priests and Levites and have the key to open and shut the sanctuary. As the holy and true high priest, the Man promises that the one who conquers will become a pillar in the temple.

The letter to Laodicea comes from 'the faithful and true witness', a title for the LORD in Jeremiah 42.5, 'a true and faithful witness' (see also on 1.5). There may be an allusion to Proverbs 14.5: 'A faithful witness does not lie, but a false witness breathes out lies', and to Proverbs 14.25: 'A truthful witness saves lives, but one who utters lies is a betrayer'. The contrast of the witness and the liar is almost certainly intentional, given the situation in the seven churches and their conflict with the deceivers.

He is also 'the Amon, the beginning of God's Creation' (3.14). What must have originally been *'amon* appears in the Greek text as *Amen*, a more familiar word and another sign that the Book of Revelation was translated into Greek. The original would have been *'amon*, a word found in Proverbs 8.30 but nowhere else in the Hebrew Scriptures. As a result, nobody can be sure what it meant: 'child' has been suggested, but LXX understood it to mean 'carpenter', one 'who joins things together' (a reference to the bonds of the cosmic covenant) and so the meaning is probably the same as *'aman*, which means a craftsman. The Man is described as this craftsman, the first created. Paul wrote in the same way: 'He is the image of the invisible God, the first-born of all creation ... He is before all things, and in him all things hold together (Col. 1.15, 17).

The original poem in Proverbs 8.22–31 is one of the strangest passages in the Hebrew Bible. It describes a female figure, Wisdom, who was begotten before the visible world was created. She was 'brought forth' before the earth was formed and was witness to the creation: 'When he marked out the foundations of the earth, I was beside him like a master workman'. This is the female figure with whom the Man identifies himself, the dual nature again. In John's Gospel, this figure is described as the Word: 'He was in the beginning with God; all things were made through him and without him was not anything made that was made' (John 1.2–3). In the Parables of Hermas, the same figure is male: 'the Son of God is older than all his creation so that he was the Counsellor of his creation to the Father' (*Sim.* 9.12.2).

Like Wisdom, the Man offers reproof and counsel to those he loves (3.19, cf. Prov. 1.23) and because he is Wisdom, the Man 'knows the works' of the angel of Laodicea, and knows that he has a false wisdom. The angel thinks he is rich and prosperous but in fact he is wretched and pitiable, poor, blind and naked. Wisdom offers him counsel, that he should buy the best gold to relieve his poverty, white garments for his nakedness and salve for his blinded eyes. These three, true riches, white garments and restored vision, are the traditional gifts of Wisdom. Wisdom is better than silver and gold (Prov. 3.14; 8.10; cf. Job 28.12–19) and wealth is nothing compared to Wisdom (*Wisd.* 7.8). 'If riches are a desirable possession in life, what is richer than Wisdom who makes all things?' (*Wisd.* 8.5). This is the gold refined by fire which the Man offers to the angel of Laodicea. He also offers white garments, the garments of glory which are the clothes of the baptized, the resurrected, the angels. Wisdom made humans like God and opened their eyes (Gen. 3.5); Wisdom conferred immortality (*Wisd.* 8.13), or, in the language of the temple, gave them the white garments of glory. Those who 'godlessly forsook Wisdom' at the end of the first temple period became 'blind' (*1 En.* 93.8), a graphic description of the seventh-century 'reformers' who altered the ways of the temple. Here it is a description of the wretched angel of Laodicea who was in danger of falling away. Wisdom's anointing would open his eyes. Since her rejection from the temple, Wisdom had looked in vain for a home on earth: 'Wisdom went forth to make her dwelling among the children of men, and found no dwelling place' (*1 En.* 42.2). Here in Laodicea, however, Wisdom knocks at the door and asks to enter and make a home again.

The Faith of the Hebrew Christians

The world of the Hebrew Christians in Asia was remarkably similar to that of the Qumran community. More than that we cannot say. They had similar customs and used similar turns of phrase, making allowance for the fact that the letters to the seven churches are in Greek and the Qumran materials are in Hebrew and Aramaic. *The letters are evidence for a mystical understanding of the heavenly Jesus in the earliest years of the Palestinian church.* He promised to each of his angels, if they remained faithful, that they would become one with him, enthroned in heaven as the anointed high priest, the LORD.

No ancient source explains the connection between the Qumran community, said by Pliny to be Essenes (*Natural History* 5.73), and the Essenes described by Philo (*Every Good Man* 75–91) and Josephus (*War* 2.119–61) who lived in small communities or their own quarters in larger towns. What cannot be known is how widespread these communities were; Philo implies that there were some in Egypt and if there, why not in Asia Minor also? They could have been 'the exiles of the Dispersion in Pontus, Galatia, Cappadocia, Asia and Bithynia' (1 Pet. 1.1), 'the twelve tribes in the Dispersion' (Jas 1.1). The Essenes shared their possessions, cared for each other's needs and studied ancient writings: 'with the help of these and with a view to the treatment of diseases, they make special investigations into medicinal roots and the properties of stones' (*War* 2.136). Philo says they were known as the Essenes or Holy Ones (*Every Good Man* 91), doubtless linking by sound the Greek words *Essaioi* and *hosioi*, holy ones, but suggesting that the name may have derived from the Hebrew *hasidim*, the pious ones. The Christian communities also called themselves the holy ones, *hagioi* (albeit using the word *hagioi* translated 'saints', e.g. 1 Cor. 1.2; 2 Cor. 1.1; Eph. 1.1; Phil. 1.1; Col. 1.1). Philo also implies that the Essenes he describes in *Every Good Man is Free* live an active life whereas the Therapeuts are a contemplative group within the same movement who live in a desert community (*Contemplative Life* 1, 21–22). The name Therapeuts, however, means healers, but whether this meant medical healers as well as spiritual cannot be known. They cultivated 'the sight which alone gives knowledge of truth and falsehood ... and desired the vision of the One who Is' (*Contemplative Life* 10–11). Eusebius believed that the Therapeuts were a Christian community, the first desert monks and nuns (*History* 2.17). This view is frequently dismissed by modern scholars, but the connection between the Book of Revelation and the Qumran texts, the Qumran texts and the Essenes, the Essenes and the Therapeuts and the Therapeuts with Christian monasticism cannot be mere coincidence.

THE CHARIOT THRONE OF GOD

After this I looked, and lo, in heaven an open door! And the first voice, which I had heard speaking to me like a trumpet, said, 'Come up hither, and I will show you what must take place after this.' At once I was in the Spirit, and lo, a throne stood in heaven, with one seated on the throne! And he who sat there appeared like jasper and carnelian, and round the throne was a rainbow that looked like an emerald. Round the throne were twenty-four thrones, and seated on the thrones were twenty-four elders, clad in white garments, with golden crowns upon their heads. From the throne issue flashes of lightning, and voices and peals of thunder, and before the throne burn seven torches of fire, which are the seven spirits of God; and before the throne there is as it were a sea of glass, like crystal.

And round the throne, on each side of the throne, are four living creatures, full of eyes in front and behind: the first living creature like a lion, the second living creature like an ox, the third living creature with the face of a man, and the fourth living creature like a flying eagle. And the four living creatures, each of them with six wings, are full of eyes all around and within, and day and night they never cease to sing,
'Holy, holy, holy is the LORD God Almighty
who was and is and is to come!'
And whenever the living creatures give glory and honour and thanks to him who is seated on the throne, who lives for ever and ever, the twenty-four elders fall down before him who is seated on the throne and worship him who lives for ever and ever; they cast their crowns before the throne, singing,
  'Worthy art thou, our Lord and God,
  to receive glory and honour and power,
  for thou didst create all things,
  and by thy will they existed and were created.' (Rev. 4)

The Book of Revelation is an anthology of visionary and prophetic material compiled according to the traditional pattern. It is clear that the first three chapters are set in the outer part of the temple, the great hall where the menorah stood, because the seer describes the Man amidst the seven lamps. He then hears a voice like a trumpet summoning him to a higher place to learn what must take place in the future, and the vision moves into the holy of holies ('lo! in heaven an open door').

The Door in Heaven

The holy of holies was beyond time, the place where the seer could learn of the past, the present and the future. Such practices were forbidden at that time (*m. Ḥagigah* 2.1). Even 'Ezra' the first-century visionary who spoke with angels, denied that he had ever ascended into heaven (2

Esdr. 4.8), and the Mekhilta of R. Ishmael dismisses Christian claims such as John 1.14, 'We beheld his Glory'. He wrote thus on Psalm 115.16: 'The heavens are the heavens of the LORD but the earth has been given to the children of men. Neither Moses nor Elijah ever went up to heaven, nor did the Glory ever come down to earth'. It was in this climate that the Book of Revelation was written: 'I saw in heaven an open door ... "Come up hither and I will show you what must take place after this ..." ' (4.1).

A similar description of a door into heaven is found in the *Ascension of Isaiah*. Although said to be about the prophet, Isaiah, it is a thinly veiled account of an early Christian prophet, and the detail given is remarkable. When the seer of Revelation writes 'I was in the Spirit ... I heard a loud voice ... I looked and lo! in heaven an open door' (1.10; 4.1), we have to envisage a situation like that described in the *Ascension*. Several important people were sat with Isaiah, and forty other prophets had assembled from the surrounding region to hear his words:

They all heard a door being opened and the voice of the Spirit ... And when they all heard the voice of the Holy Spirit, they worshipped on their knees and they praised the God of righteousness ... They ascribed glory to the One who had thus graciously given a door in an alien world, had graciously given it to a man. And while he was speaking with the Holy Spirit in the hearing of them all, he became silent and his mind was taken up from him and he did not see the men who were standing before him. His eyes indeed were open but his mouth was silent and the mind in his body was taken up from him, for he was seeing a vision. And the angel who was sent to show him the vision was not of this firmament, nor was he from the angels of glory of this world, but he came from the seventh heaven. And the people who were standing by, apart from the circle of the prophets, did not think that the holy Isaiah had been taken up. And the vision which he saw was not from this world but from the world which is hidden from the flesh. (*Asc. Isa.* 6.6–15)

In the *Hekhalot Rabbati* there is a similar account, recorded much later but naming a first-century teacher. R. Neḥunya sat on a marble bench in the temple precincts, and fire and torches were seen around him (#202–203). His disciples sat, an inner group and an outer group, and they were instructed to write down what he said to them: 'Behold, see, learn and write down what I [some versions have *we*] say and what we hear' (#228).

(The *Acts of Thomas* 6–8 describes how the apostle travelled to India and one day, at a wedding feast, he anointed himself and then went into a trance as a Hebrew flute girl was playing. He began to sing what seems to be a hymn in praise of Wisdom, the Bride (see p. 321). She is the daughter of light, and with her servants and attendants, she awaits her bridegroom. There is to be a wedding feast where the eternal ones are guests, clad in bright robes and royal garments. They praise the Father of truth and the Mother of wisdom. When Thomas had finished his song he sat in silence but his appearance had altered. Only the flute girl had understood him because he sang in Hebrew.)

The seer in the Book of Revelation stands in his vision before the throne. Once in the holy of holies, he is able to see the curtain of the holy of holies depicting the whole history of the world, past, present and future. Just as 'Isaiah' learns about the future descent of the LORD into the world to become the Christ, the seer of Revelation watches as the scroll is unsealed. Everything is fore-ordained, and those who enter the holy of holies are able to learn the secrets of the future.

There is a description of the curtain in *3 Enoch* 45, written long after Revelation, but in the same tradition of temple visions. 'R. Ishmael (said to be a high priest) said: Metatron (the transformed heavenly Enoch) said to me: Come and I will show you the curtain of the Omnipresent One, which is spread out before the Holy One, Blessed be He, and on which are printed all the generations of the world and all their deeds, whether done or to be done unto the last generation.' This is implied in the vision of Habakkuk, written long before the Book of Revelation.

I will take my stand to watch,
and station myself on the tower,*
and look forth to see what he will say to me,
and what I will answer concerning my complaint.
And the LORD answered me:
Write the vision;
make it plain upon tablets,
so that he may run who reads it.
For the vision awaits its time;
it hastens to the end – it will not lie.
If it seem slow, wait for it;
it will surely come, it will not delay. (Hab. 2.1–3)

The *Testament of Levi* describes a vision in which Levi was taken through the heavens, and the angel who went with him said: 'You shall stand near the LORD, you shall be his priest and you shall tell forth his mysteries to men' (*T. Levi* 2.10). Levi ascended. 'At this moment the angel opened for me the gates of heaven and I saw the Holy Most High sitting on the throne. And he said to me, "Levi, to you I have given the blessing of the priesthood until I shall come and dwell in the midst of Israel." And then the angel led me back to the earth' (*T. Levi* 5.1–3).

The mysteries entrusted to the priesthood are described in the Qumran texts; the Teacher of Righteousness was to be a priest (4Q171) to whom God would reveal all the mysteries of the words of the prophets (1QpHab VII). Wisdom writings exhort the reader to consider the *raz nihyeh*, the 'mystery of existence', or perhaps it means 'the mystery to come' (4Q416). There are frequent references to the *raz*

---

*The visionaries' word for the holy of holies.

nihyeh; those who ponder it will learn 'the birth time of salvation' and who is 'to inherit glory or trouble' (4Q417). Piecing together two fragments (4Q417 21 and 4Q418 43) shows that the *raz nihyeh* is knowledge of the God of the Awesome Ones, knowledge of past, present and future, of truth and iniquity, of wisdom and foolishness. The Hymns thank God for 'marvellous mysteries' and knowledge (1QH XV, formerly VII). Melchizedek was to reveal 'the ends of the ages' (11 QMelch).

1 Enoch gives more detail of how the seer is taken first into the great hall and then summoned to the inner holy of holies:

And lo! there was a second house, greater then the former, and the entire portal stood open before me and it was built of flames of fire ... And I looked and saw therein a lofty throne: its appearance was as crystal and the wheels thereof as the shining sun, and there was the vision of cherubim. And from underneath the throne came streams of flaming fire so that I could not look thereon. And the Great Glory sat thereon, and his raiment shone more brightly than the sun and was whiter than any snow. None of the angels could enter and behold his face by reason of the magnificence and glory and no flesh could behold him ... And until then I had been prostrate on my face, trembling: and the Lord called me with his own mouth, and said to me: 'Come hither Enoch, and hear my word.' And one of the holy ones came to me and waked me, and he made me rise up and approach the door: and I bowed my face downwards. (*1 En.* 14.15, 18–21, 24)

This is some of the oldest material in *1 Enoch*; it cannot be dated with certainty, but a very similar throne vision occurs in Isaiah 6, precisely dated 'In the year that king Uzziah died', i.e. in 742 BCE.

In the year that King Uzziah died, I saw the Lord sitting upon a throne, high and lifted up; and his train filled the temple. Above him stood the seraphim; each had six wings: with two he covered his face, and with two he covered his feet, and with two he flew. And one called to another and said:
'Holy, holy, holy is the LORD of hosts',
the whole earth is full of his glory.' (Isa. 6.1–3)

This is one of the oldest texts in the Hebrew Scriptures and yet evidence for the same temple mysticism as we find in Revelation. R. Ishmael, Levi and Enoch were all priest figures; Isaiah was probably a priest. *The seers of the Book of Revelation were priests.*

The Cherubim

Around the throne were four living creatures: one like a lion, one like a calf, one with a human face and one like an eagle. In later Christian tradition, these four were to represent the four evangelists, but in the earliest temple ritual they were probably the masked priests depicting heavenly guardians of the holy of holies, the creatures who appear in the later gnostic texts. In the Untitled Apocalypse in the Codex Brucianus, for example, there are guardians at the four gates of the holy of holies which is the heavenly city (see p. 325). They were also closely related to the four archangels who were the agents of the LORD's judgement (*1 En*. 10.1–12), and believed to be aspects of the LORD. In the Book of Revelation the living creatures summon the four riders as the four seals are opened (6.1–7), and one of them hands the seven golden bowls of wrath to the angels as they emerge from the temple (15.7). They are probably also the four angels with power to destroy (7.1–2) and the four who had been prepared to kill one third of mankind (9.14–15).

Ezekiel identified the living creatures as the cherubim: in the first description of the chariot throne, the attendants are the four living creatures, winged human forms with four faces and bovine feet (Ezek.1.5–6), but in the second account they are called cherubim and Ezekiel (or his editor) makes it quite clear that the living creatures are the same as the cherubim (Ezek. 10.20–22). Perhaps this was an innovation, and the living creatures had formerly been distinct from the cherubim, the living creatures being the guardians of the holy of holies and the cherubim the bearers of the throne. In the later *Merkavah* texts, which preserved so much temple lore, the living creatures and the cherubim are distinct: in the *Hekhalot Zutarti* the cherubim kiss the king and the living creatures carry him (# 411) and in *3 Enoch* the angel Hayli'el YHWH is in charge of the living creatures, and Kerubi'el YHWH in charge of the cherubim (*3 En*. 20.1; 22.1). In the later biblical texts, however, the creatures and the cherubim do seem to have coalesced.

The cherubim had originally been the huge human-headed monsters who appear frequently in the art of the Ancient Near East. Two of these winged creatures, cherubim carved from olivewood and overlaid with gold, were placed in the holy of holies of Solomon's temple (1 Kgs 6.23–28; 2 Chron. 3.10–14). They stood wing-tip to wing-tip behind the temple veil, reaching from one wall of the holy of holies to the other and formed a huge throne. Two smaller cherubim of hammered gold were set face to face on the mercy seat above the ark (Exod. 25.18–20). We do not know how Israel reconciled these great statues with the commandment to make no images.

In the earliest traditions, the cherubim were the winds on which the LORD rode to help his people.

He rode on a cherub and flew;
he came swiftly upon the wings of the wind. (Ps. 18.10)

The parallelism of Hebrew poetry, the second line paraphrasing the first, indicates that the cherub and the winds were one and the same. There is a vivid description of the chariot throne and its attendants in Psalm 104:

Thou art clothed with honour and majesty,
who coverest thyself with light as with a garment,
who hast stretched out the heavens like a tent,

who hast laid the beams of thy chambers on the waters,
who makest the clouds thy chariot,
who ridest on the wings of the winds,
who makest the winds thy messengers [i.e. 'angels', it is the same word]
fire and flame thy ministers. (Ps. 104.1–4)

Thus the cherubim who bore the throne were also clouds and winds and angels.

Details of the vision in the holy of holies were modified over the centuries, e.g. Ezekiel's four creatures seem to have four faces each (Ezek. 1.10), whereas in Revelation each creature has only one, but in essentials the throne visions were unchanged. Thus the vision in the Book of Revelation is recognizably that of Ezekiel in the fifth year of King Jehoiachin's exile, 592 BCE:

As I looked, behold, a stormy wind came out of the north, and a great cloud, with brightness round about it, and fire flashing forth continually, and in the midst of the fire, as it were gleaming bronze. And from the midst of it came the likeness of four living creatures. And this was their appearance: they had the form of men, but each had four faces, and each of them had four wings ... As for the likeness of their faces, each had the face of a man in front; the four had the face of a lion on the right side, the four had the face of an ox on the left side, and the four had the face of an eagle at the back. (Ezek. 1.4–5, 10)

There were no cherubim in the second temple; according to Josephus, the holy of holies was empty (*War* 5.219). They are not listed with the temple treasures which the Babylonians removed (2 Kgs 25.13–17; Jer. 52.17–23). Although there is no record of what happened to them, they were not forgotten. In the age of the Messiah, it was said, five things would be restored to the temple: the fire, the ark, the menorah, the Spirit and the cherubim (*Num. Rab.* XV.10). *Their memory was preserved, however, in the writings of the second temple period, showing how ancient was the imagery used in these texts.* The golden cherubim of the holy of holies appear in the Qumran Sabbath Songs, but the living creatures are not mentioned. There are chariots in the holy of holies whose cherubim and wheels join in the worship (4Q403) and another fragment shows that the cherubim were the same as the living creatures in the holy of holies.

The cherubim prostrate themselves before him and bless. As they rise, a whispered divine voice is heard, and there is a roar of praise. When they drop their wings there is a whispered divine voice. The cherubim bless the image of the chariot throne above the firmament and they praise the majesty of the luminous firmament beneath his seat of glory. (4Q405.20, reconstruction and translation by Geza Vermes)

This bears a striking resemblance to Revelation 4.8–9 where the four living creatures praise the LORD day and night, giving glory and honour and thanks. The Sabbath hymns at Qumran used the same imagery as early Christian prophecy and both drew on the traditions of the first temple.

The One Enthroned

The imagery of the throne visions originated in the first temple, and so this is the primary context in which they must be understood. Only the interpretation of the visions reflects the situation in which they received their present written form. In the first temple, the LORD was believed to be present with his people in the person of the priest-king, and Psalm 68 describes a procession into the temple.

Thy solemn processions are seen, O God,
the processions of my God, my King, into the sanctuary –
the singers in front, the minstrels last,
between them maidens playing timbrels. (Ps. 68.24–25)

This text clearly equates God and King. The Chronicler, when he describes how Solomon was made king, says that 'he sat on the throne of the LORD as king' (1 Chron. 29.23) and that the people worshipped him: 'And all the assembly blessed the LORD the God of their fathers and they bowed their heads and worshipped the LORD and the King' (1 Chron. 29.20). Many English translations obscure this remarkable piece of information by translating the verse differently, e.g. 'they worshipped the LORD and did obeisance to the king' (thus RSV), distinguishing the two acts. The Hebrew does not say this, and *this smallest of emendations to the text obscures the most important piece of evidence in the Hebrew Scriptures for understanding the Book of Revelation.*

The human figure enthroned was both LORD and King, and the image of a man going up to the holy of holies, i.e. ascending to heaven, was indelibly imprinted in Israel's memory of the temple, whence it passed into early Christian imagery. To be granted this vision was a great privilege: in Daniel 7 it was the vision of the One like a Son of Man going on the clouds to his enthronement, and King David thanked the LORD that he had been granted the vision of *the Man ascending* (1 Chron. 17.17, translating literally). Israel prayed to the one on the cherub throne (Ps. 80.1), Moses heard the LORD speak from between the cherubim in the tabernacle (Exod. 25.22), but the LXX Habakkuk 3.2 understood the cherubim to be the living creatures: 'Be known in the midst of the two living creatures ...' When the Assyrians were threatening Jerusalem, King Hezekiah, himself believed to be the LORD with his people, went to the temple and prayed, 'O LORD of hosts, God of Israel, who art enthroned above the cherubim, thou art the God, thou alone, of all the kingdoms of the earth ...' (Isa. 37.16). The reasoning by which Israel understood the priest-king to be both the LORD and the one who prayed to the LORD must be the reasoning by which the first Christians understood the divine and human roles of Jesus.

When Isaiah saw the LORD enthroned in the holy of holies, he did not describe the figure on the throne; all we are told is that his voice shook the temple (Isa. 6.1–8). Ezekiel, however, did attempt a description, and it is surely no coincidence that the passage became forbidden reading:

'They may not use the chapter of the chariot as a reading from the prophets', and 'The chapter of the chariot [may not be expounded] before one alone unless he is a sage who understands of his own knowledge' (*m. Megillah* 4.10 and *m. Ḥagigah* 2.1). Ezekiel the priest described a fiery Man:

And above the firmament over their heads [the four living creatures] there was the likeness of a throne, in appearance like sapphire; and seated above the likeness of a throne was a likeness as it were of a human form. And upward from what had the appearance of his loins I saw as it were gleaming bronze, like the appearance of fire, enclosed round about; and downward from what had the appearance of his loins, I saw as it were the appearance of fire, and there was a brightness round about him. Like the appearance of the bow that is in the cloud on the day of rain, so was the appearance of the brightness round about. Such was the appearance of the likeness of the glory of the LORD. And when I saw it, I fell upon my face, and I heard the voice of one speaking. (Ezek. 1.26–28)

When he described the chariot throne after it had left the polluted temple, Ezekiel revealed more about the One on the throne. The Fiery Man appeared to him in Babylon and took him on a spirit journey to Jerusalem (Ezek. 8.1–3, reminiscent of the spirit journeys in Rev. 17.3 and 21.10 and in Luke 4.5–12). Then the Fiery Man identified himself as the LORD, summoned six angels to destroy Jerusalem and a scribe to mark the foreheads of those who were to be spared (Ezek. 9.1–4). The Man told them: 'Begin at my sanctuary' (Ezek. 9.6), in other words, the LORD's judgement on Jerusalem was sent out from the holy of holies, just as the wrath came out of the holy of holies in the time of Aaron (Num. 17.42–50). In Revelation, the four horsemen in chapter 6, the seven angels with trumpets in chapters 8–9 and the seven angels with bowls of plague in chapters 15–16 all emerge from holy of holies; the tradition did not change. Finally, in Ezekiel's vision, the chariot throne left the temple and Jerusalem was destroyed (Ezek. 11.22–25). In chapters 17–18, the great harlot city was judged and overthrown. Josephus reported strange phenomena in the temple just before its destruction: 'a commotion and a din and then the voice as of a host "We are departing from this place"' (*War* 6.300).

    Daniel 7 is the only other description of the throne in the Hebrew and Aramaic Scriptures: 'As I looked',

thrones were placed
and one that was Ancient of Days took his seat;
his raiment was white as snow,
and the hair of his head like pure wool;
his throne was fiery flames,
its wheels were burning fire. (Dan. 7.9)

This account, which reached its present form in the middle of the second century BCE, differs from those in Isaiah and Ezekiel insofar as it describes how a Man came to be enthroned. He approached with the clouds of heaven, and was given everlasting dominion and a kingdom which would never be destroyed. There are no details of the Man's appearance and no more is said about the Ancient of Days. The throne visions are reticent about describing the figures, but the focus is always on the one ascending as though there had been some recollection that the human figure was the only visible form of the One on the throne. This accounts for Jesus' reply to Philip's question: 'LORD show us the Father'. 'He who has seen me has seen the Father' (John 14.9).

In *1 Enoch* there are several throne visions, and again the One enthroned before the advent of the Man is not fully described. He is the 'Great Glory', whose raiment shines and whose face is too glorious to behold (*1 En.* 14.20–21; 71.10); his wings shelter the Man (*1 En.* 39.7); he has hair like white wool (*1 En.* 46.1); and he is seated on the throne of glory (*1 En.* 47.3). The key figure in each of the visions is not the Great Glory but the Man, and in seven distinct places (*1 En.* 45.3; 47.3; 51.3; 55.4; 61.8; 62.2–5; 69.27–29) the Man is seated on the throne of God as was Solomon: 'And the Elect One shall in those days sit on My throne' (*1 En.* 51.3). The holy of holies visions of *1 Enoch* preserved the royal traditions of the first temple; the Man who ascended the throne was believed to become the One already enthroned.

The Twenty-Four Elders

The worship in the temple was the counterpart of the worship in heaven; the priests were the angels and the priest-king was the LORD. The homage of the living creatures followed by the adoration of the twenty-four enthroned elders (4.9–11) is reminiscent of the homage of the cherubim and the praises of the heavenly beings in the Qumran Sabbath Songs which describe 'chariots with cherubim and 'elohim', (gods, 4Q403.1). Gods and chariots, i.e. chariot thrones (plural) in the holy of holies is a remarkable piece of evidence, and suggests that the enthroned elders of Revelation 4 would have been familiar to those who sang the Sabbath Songs, those who read Daniel 7 with its description of thrones in heaven and the holy ones (saints) of the Most High to whom judgement was given (Dan. 7.27), and those who heard Paul's letter (Col. 1.16).

The twenty-four elders with their white robes and golden crowns, seated on chariot thrones around the great throne, are probably the angel counterparts of the heads of the twenty-four courses of priests. David and Solomon are said to have chosen twenty-four chief men from the sons of Aaron (1 Chron. 24.1–6), and their descendants became the twenty-four courses of priests who took turns to serve in the temple, one week at a time. At the three great festivals of Passover, Pentecost and Tabernacles, however, all the courses of priests were present in the temple (*m. Sukkah* 5.7) and this would account for their twenty-four angel counterparts being present around the throne. In the first century CE these leading priests were known as 'the elders of the priesthood' (*m. Yoma* 1.5). In the vision they wear the white robes of the holy of holies, the dress of angels, and their golden crowns are a sign of their rank. As priests, the elders offer incense and prayers before the throne (5.8) and they are privy to the secrets of heaven (5.5; 7.14). The elders are mentioned on several occasions (throughout chapters 4 and 5; also at 7.11; 11.16; 14.3; and 19.4), always worshipping. John the beloved disciple was also known as John the elder and remembered as a high priest. *He wrote himself into the visions as one of these elders who saw the mysteries of the holy of holies (5.5; 7.14).*

The tradition of the elders in the heavenly holy of holies was known to Isaiah:

On that day the LORD will punish
the host of heaven, in heaven
and the kings of the earth, on the earth.
They will be gathered together
as prisoners in a pit;
they will be shut up in a prison,
and after many days they will be punished.
Then the moon will be confounded,
and the sun ashamed;
for the LORD of hosts will reign
on Mount Zion and in Jerusalem
and before his elders he will manifest his glory. (Isa. 24.21–23)

The ultimate origin of the council of elders may lie in the assembly of heavenly beings mentioned in Psalm 82.1:

God has taken in place in the divine council;
in the midst of the gods he holds judgement.

This text had a special significance in the time of Jesus, as it was thought to be a prophecy about the last days. The Melchizedek text (11QMelch) tells how the Great High Priest would come for the final Day of Atonement and fulfil Psalm 82.1 by taking his place as judge in the midst of the gods, the elders of the vision. He would be the Anointed One, the messenger of good tidings who would rescue his own people from the power of Satan and come to Jerusalem as the Anointed Prince to establish the kingdom of God. This sequence is still apparent in Revelation: the Lamb, i.e. the Anointed One, takes his place in the heavenly council (5.8), the judgement begins (Rev. 6), the redeemed are saved (Rev. 7) and the kingdom of the Anointed One is established (11.15–18).

This was the tradition Jesus knew and he believed he had been called to fulfil the prophecies and set the predicted events in motion. The world of the temple mystics became the world of the young church. At the Last Supper, Jesus promised his disciples that they would sit with him on the Day of LORD on their twelve thrones (Luke 22.28–30). Paul knew the pattern of type and antitype which characterizes this tradition. The antitype of Melchizedek, the Righteous One enthroned as LORD in the holy of holies, was 'the man of lawlessness the son of perdition who takes his seat in the temple of God proclaiming himself to be God' (2 Thess. 2.3–4). The Satanic mystery was already at work, and once the Restrainer had gone, probably James the Righteous One (see p. 192), the LORD himself would return to destroy the man of lawlessness. Paul reminded the Christians in Corinth that they would one day judge the world (1 Cor. 6.2). The risen LORD, who sent the letters, promised the angel of Laodicea that those who conquered would share his throne, 'as I myself conquered and sat down with my Father on his throne' (3.21). The climax of Revelation describes all the servants of the Lamb in the holy of holies, worshipping before the throne and 'seeing his face' (22.4). The Lamb, by his blood, had made them all a kingdom of priests (1.6 and 5.10) and in his millennium kingdom they became judges on their thrones (20.4). The *Ascension of Isaiah,* which reached its final Christian form at the end of the first century CE, describes how the prophet Isaiah ascended through a door to the seventh heaven and saw the righteous of past ages wearing their white robes. They were the resurrected ones, but had to wait for their thrones and crowns of royal priesthood until the LORD Christ had returned from the earth (*Asc. Isa.* 9.17–18).

The Songs of the Holy of Holies

Music was an important part of temple worship; musicians are listed along with priests and Levites as temple personnel (1 Chron. 25.1). Psalm 150 describes the praise of the LORD in the holy of holies and lists the instruments played. Isaiah heard the seraphim calling, 'Holy, holy, holy is the LORD of hosts' (Isa. 6.3), and Enoch heard 'those who sleep not saying holy, holy, holy is the Lord of Spirits' *(1 En. 39.12).* The songs in Revelation probably reflect temple practice with the song of the living creatures: 'Holy, holy, holy is the LORD God Almighty' (4.8b) being the greatest of the holy of holies songs. ('Almighty' is one of the ways that the LXX translates the Hebrew *Sabaoth* (of hosts), for example throughout Zechariah). The second line of the song (4.8c) shows what the Name was thought to mean: 'Who was and is and is to come'. It occurs also at 1.8: 'I am the Alpha and the Omega says the LORD God, who is and who was and who is to come, the Almighty'.

When the Name was revealed to Moses at the burning bush (Exod. 3.14), it was not the form of the Name found elsewhere in the Hebrew Scriptures, *yhwh,* but *'ehyeh 'ašer 'ehyeh,* and there has always been a problem translating this. The customary English rendering is *I AM WHO I AM* and the LXX opted for the very similar 'I am the One who is', but another possibility has now to be considered. It has been suggested that the unique form of the Name at Exodus 3.14 means 'I call into being what will be', in other words 'I create'. The simple form of the Name found elsewhere, usually rendered Yahweh or Jehovah, would then mean not 'He Who Is' but 'He Who Causes To Be, He Who

Creates'. The Palestinian Targums of Exodus 3.14, confirm this by rendering the Name: 'He who said to the world from the beginning, "Be there", and it was there, and is to say to it, "Be there", and it will be there' (Fragment Targum; Neof. and Ps. Jon are similar). The Name is expanded into past and future aspects, like the threefold form in Revelation 4.8, where the living creatures praise the One 'who was and is and is to come'. As this is the Greek translation of a Hebrew or Aramaic original, the forms 'Was and Is' could well have be understood to mean 'Caused to be' and 'Cause to Be', as in the Targum. The song of the living creatures would then be praising not the One who always exists but the One who created and continues to create, which is the theme of the second song: 'Thou didst create all things and by thy will they existed and were created' (4.11). One of the Qumran hymns is similar: 'By thy wisdom [ ] eternity, and before creating them thou knewest their works for ever and ever ... All things [ ] according to [ ] and without thee, nothing is done' (1QH IX, formerly I). The secrets of the creation, Day One, were some of the hidden things of the holy of holies, and so the songs of the holy of holies extol the power of the creator. This was the *raz nihyeh*, the mystery of existence (see p. 59).

Jesus knew that the Creator continued to create. When criticized for healing on the Sabbath, Jesus replied: 'My father is working still and I am working' (John 5.17). The creation was not yet completed and the great Sabbath which marked its completion was still to come (see p. 350).

The Heavens Opened

All four Gospels agree that Jesus' ministry began at his baptism when the Spirit came upon him. Mark's is probably the earliest account:

In those days Jesus came from Nazareth of Galilee and was baptized by John in the Jordan. And when he came up out of the water, immediately he saw the heavens opened and the Spirit descending upon him like a dove; and a voice came from heaven, 'Thou art my beloved Son; with thee I am well pleased.' The Spirit immediately drove him out into the wilderness. And he was in the wilderness forty days, tempted by Satan; and he was with the wild beasts; and the angels ministered to him. (Mark 1.9–13)

Jesus saw the heavens opened, he heard a voice from heaven, he was driven by the Spirit, he was served by angels and he was with the wild beasts. The account of the baptism, when he saw the heavens opened, and the account of the temptations, when he was alone in the desert, can only have come from Jesus himself. These few lines in Mark's Gospel indicate that Jesus claimed a throne vision at his baptism. Being with wild beasts may imply no more than the presence of desert animals during the forty days, but the reference to wild beasts and serving angels together with open heavens and a heavenly voice suggests rather more. In the Greek, the words for 'beasts' in Mark 1 and 'living creatures' in Revelation 4.6 are different; but the Hebrew word *ḥayyah* would have been used for both a wild animal (Gen. 8.1) and one of the throne creatures (Ezek. 10.15).

The other Gospels add significant details: during his time in the desert, Jesus looked down from a mountain top and saw 'all the kingdoms of the world in a moment of time' (Luke 4.5); he also felt himself on a pinnacle of the temple (Luke 4.9). Both these are holy of holies experiences, mentioned by other mystics: Habakkuk was set on a watch-tower in the temple to see his vision (Hab. 2.1); the angel Metatron, the transformed Enoch, showed Rabbi Ishmael all history depicted on the curtain of the heavenly holy of holies (3 En. 45).

Echoes of this experience can be detected in the earliest Christian writings. Origen, in the first half of the third century CE, compared Ezekiel's vision of the chariot throne to the open heavens at the baptism of Jesus, implying that what the prophet saw, Jesus also saw (Origen, Homily 1 on Ezekiel). Jesus, he said, first ascended to heaven at his baptism and brought down to earth the spiritual gifts which he gave to his followers. Justin Martyr, writing early in the second century CE, described how a fire appeared in the Jordan when Jesus was baptized (Trypho 88). There is other evidence for this fire, including two of the Old Latin translations of the New Testament which include: 'a huge light shone around from the water' (Matt. 3.15 in Codex Vercellensis and Codex Sangermanensis), and Ephraem's Commentary on the Diatessaron.

The temple mystics believed it was necessary to pass through the river of fire, the ultimate purification, in order to become an angel and enter the holy of holies. This was the baptism of fire. Malachi prophesied that the LORD would 'purify the sons of Levi', the priests, with fire (Mal. 3.2–3), there was a river of fire flowing from the throne in Daniel's vision (Dan. 7.10) and Paul alludes to the belief: 'each man's work will be made manifest; for the Day will disclose it, because it will be revealed with fire and the fire will test what sort of work each one has done' (1 Cor. 3.13). Later mystical texts described the angels purifying themselves in a river of fire before joining the heavenly worship in the holy of holies (3 En. 36). Perhaps the most remarkable parallel to the fire in the Jordan is a story told of Rabbi Johannan ben Zakkai, a contemporary of the first Christians. He saw a fire burning around one of his disciples as he expounded the mysteries of the chariot throne (see p. 194). The references to fire and open heavens were intended for those who knew the secret tradition and what these phenomena really implied.

A variant reading in some ancient versions of Luke's Gospel provides another link to the throne vision of Revelation 4. In Matthew and Mark, the voice from heaven speaks words from a coronation psalm, 'You are my Son' (Ps. 2.7), and from a Servant Song, 'with whom I am well pleased' (Isa. 42.1), thus linking the traditions of king and servant. The text of Luke 3.22 in the Codex Bezae, however, has only Psalm 2.7: 'You are my son, today I have begotten you', linking the baptism experience unambiguously to the coronation ritual, the moment when the king entered the holy of holies, i.e. ascended to heaven, and was enthroned as Son of God. The vision of the throne in Revelation 4 is followed by the description of the Lamb approaching the throne.

The evidence in early Christian tradition is only explicable if the baptism had been remembered, perhaps only by the inner group of initiates, as the moment when Jesus ascended to heaven, experienced the throne vision and accepted that he was the one called to be enthroned. At first he resisted – the temptations in the desert record that he had doubts that he was the Son of God – but then he accepted the calling with all that this entailed. 'The kingdom of heaven', he later taught, 'is like a merchant in search of fine pearls, who, on finding one pearl of great value, went and sold all that he had and bought it' (Matt. 13.45–46).

8

THE SACRIFICED LAMB

And between the throne and the four living creatures and among the elders, I saw a
Lamb standing, as though it had been slain, with seven horns and with seven eyes,
which are the seven spirits of God sent out into all the earth ...

Then I looked, and I heard around the throne and the living creatures and the elders
the voice of many angels, numbering myriads of myriads and thousands of
thousands, saying with a loud voice, 'Worthy is the Lamb who was slain, to receive
power and wealth and wisdom and might and honour and glory and blessing!' And
I heard every creature in heaven and on earth and under the earth and in the sea,
and all therein, saying, 'To him who sits upon the throne and to the Lamb be
blessing and honour and glory and might for ever and ever!' And the four living
creatures said, 'Amen!' and the elders fell down and worshipped. (Rev. 5.6, 11–14)

The Lamb is the key figure in the visions of Revelation. His first
appearance is here, approaching the heavenly throne where he is
worshipped by the living creatures and the elders. Later he conquers the
agents of the beast and has the title 'King of kings and LORD of lords'
(19.16), he marries the heavenly Jerusalem (21.9) and sits on the
heavenly throne (22.1–5). Christian readers of the Book of Revelation
have recognized in the Lamb the person of Jesus, the risen LORD,
because Jesus identified himself as this figure, hearing the words of
Isaiah 42.1 at his baptism. Whereas the original text of Isaiah 42.1
reads, 'Behold, my servant whom I uphold ... he will bring forth justice
to the nations', the Targum changes it to 'Behold my servant, I will
bring him near* ... my judgement shall he reveal to the nations'.

The ascending figure was well known to the mystics as the royal high
priest who would offer himself as the Great Atonement sacrifice of the
last days. He is the Man who appears in Daniel 7, ascending with clouds
of heaven to be offered to the Ancient of Days and enthroned. Since
Jesus had associated with the mystics for some time before his baptism
(Luke 2.46–47), their visions and expectations were familiar to him.
They were of two types: visions such as Daniel 7, where an observer
describes the ascent of another figure; and visions such as 1 Enoch 14,
where the mystic is the one who ascends and describes his own
experience. Before his baptism Jesus knew the visions only as an
'observer' (see p. 150).

It was believed at that time that the Messiah was 'unknown and did
not even know himself and had no power until Elijah came to anoint
him and reveal him to Israel' (Justin, Trypho 8). The moment of
personal revelation for Jesus was at his baptism when John said:

---

*Bring near is a priestly term for approaching the LORD with an offering, showing that the
Servant is understood to be a priest, or an offering, like the Man in Dan. 7.13 (see p 382).

'Behold, the Lamb of God who takes away the sin of the world ... I myself did not know him but for this I came baptizing with water, that he might be revealed to Israel ... And I have seen and borne witness that this is the Son of God' (John 1.29, 31, 34). This was the point at which Jesus recognized that he was called to be the Lamb, with all that that implied. He was to be the key figure of the visions. At first he resisted the call, as can be seen from the temptations in the desert: Was he God's Son? (Luke 4.3, 9). Then he accepted his calling and began to live out in his ministry the role of the Lamb, eventually accepting even the sacrificial death in Jerusalem (Mark 10.33).

The reaction of John the Baptist's disciples to this revelation shows what their circle already believed about the Lamb: he was the 'Anointed One' (John 1.41), the 'Son of God, the King of Israel' (John 1.49). The fullest account of contemporary beliefs about the Lamb, however, is in the Book of Revelation.

The Lamb

The visionaries used a complex code of symbols; in order to distinguish heavenly beings from earthly, they referred to angels as 'men, or men in white' (as in Luke 24.4, 23) and to human beings as animals (as in Matt. 25.31–46, the parable of the sheep and the goats). The code is even clearer in *1 Enoch*, where three 'men in white' take Enoch onto a high tower, i.e. into the holy of holies, to watch a panoramic vision of the history of Israel in which all the human characters are depicted as animals: bulls, sheep, wolves, camels and so forth (*1 En.* 86.1–87.4). The visionaries also believed that certain great men in Israel's history had been taken into God's presence and transformed into heavenly beings. When Moses came down from Sinai with the ten command-ments, for example, he had been transformed by the experience of God's presence. Exodus 34.29 says, 'the face of his skin shone because he had been talking with God', but *1 Enoch* 89.36 says Moses had been changed from an animal into a human: 'I saw in this vision until that sheep became a man and built a house for the Lord of the sheep' (i.e. built the tabernacle). The presence of the Lamb in the throne vision indicates a similar transformation. He appears later in the visions as the Mighty Angel, for example in 10.1 as the Mighty Angel wrapped in a cloud who comes down from heaven. In the holy of holies visions, one figure can appear under several names. In the holy of holies vision of Joshua being vested as high priest, for example, Joshua stands before 'the angel of the LORD', he is addressed by 'the LORD' and then 'the angel' gives orders to his attendants (Zech. 3.1–5). The angel of the LORD, the LORD and the angel are all the same figure.

The Lamb's apotheosis is confirmed by two curious details of his appearance: seven eyes and seven horns. 'Sevenfold' indicated divine fullness or completion, and so in the Enochic *Apocalypse of Weeks*, at the end of the seventh week 'there shall be chosen the elect, for witness to righteousness ... who would be given sevenfold wisdom and knowledge' (4Q En^g, *1 En.* 93.10). The seven eyes are said to be 'the seven spirits of God sent out into the earth' (5.6) who are also the 'seven spirits before the throne', the menorah lamps which are the seven archangels (1.4). Zechariah had seen them as the seven eyes of the LORD ranging through the whole earth (Zech. 4.10). Each of these archangels was one aspect of the presence of the LORD; the name Raphael, for example, means 'God heals', Uriel means 'God illuminates' and so forth. Together, they were the one LORD ('the LORD our God is One LORD', Deut. 6.4), and so the sevenfold lamp represented the full presence of the LORD who was to rest in his sevenfold spirit on the expected Messiah (Isa. 11.2). The seven eyes of the Lamb indicate the presence of the sevenfold spirit. Paul, using plainer language, said: 'For in him all the fullness of God was pleased to dwell' (Col. 1.19). The Lamb with seven eyes was the human being who had become the LORD, not just one aspect, an angel.

The seven horns are another indication of his transformation. When Moses came down from Sinai, the skin of his face shone (Exod. 34.29–30), but the Hebrew word 'shone' is the same as the word for a 'horn' *(qrn)*, presumably in this context a ray of light. Just as the horn of Moses indicated the radiant light of someone transfigured, so the seven horns of the Lamb indicate an even greater radiance, the sevenfold light. One of the Qumran Hymns has the same idea;

I thank thee, O LORD,
For Thou hast upheld me by thy strength,
Thou hast shed thy holy Spirit upon me ...
And I shall shine in a sevenfold light
In [ ] Thee for Thy glory
For Thou art an everlasting heavenly light to me. (1QH XV, formerly VII)

The sevenfold radiance was the divine light which shone on Day One of creation, before the sun, moon and stars had been made. It was the light which shone in the invisible world which, in temple symbolism, was the holy of holies beyond the temple veil. Those who entered the holy of holies, heaven, entered the presence of God and also Day One (see p. 22). They were in the place of sevenfold light, beyond both time and the material world. When Pseudo-Philo described Moses' descent from Sinai, he used this language of temple light mysticism: 'And when he had been bathed with invisible light, he went down to the place where the light of the sun and moon are, and the light of his face surpassed the splendour of the sun and the moon and he did not know this. And when he came down to the sons of Israel they saw him but they did not recognize him. But when he spoke they recognized him' (*LAB* 21.1, cf. Luke 24.28–31). Light mysticism was well known: the resurrected believed that they would shine like stars (Dan. 12.3) and angels wore dazzling garments. The sevenfold light of the Lamb indicates more than mere resurrection; his was the light of Day One, the light of the Firstborn.

What was this light? The Targum Neofiti to Exodus 12.42 links the story of the Exodus to the creation: 'the world was without form and void and darkness was spread over the face of the abyss and the Word of the LORD was the light and it shone ...' In other words, the second divinity who was present at the creation, known variously as the Word or the Son or Wisdom, was the original light. In the prologue to his Gospel, John chose not to tell the story of the Messiah's human birth in Bethlehem, but rather of his ultimate origin as this light of Day One.

In the beginning was the Word, and the Word was with God and the Word was God. He was in the beginning with God; all things were made through him, and without him was not anything made that was made. In him was life and the life was the light of men ... And the Word became flesh and dwelt among us, full of grace and truth; we have beheld his glory, glory as of the only Son from the Father ... (John 1.1–4, 14)

It was this sevenfold light which appeared upon the Lamb as he approached the throne and returned to the place whence he had come. John's Jesus speaks of this glorious light in his prayer after the Last Supper, often called the High Priestly Prayer: 'And now Father, glorify thou me in thy own presence with the glory which I had with thee before the world was made' (John 17.5). Jesus then prays that his disciples may also come to the place of light: 'Father I desire that they also, whom thou hast given me, may be with me where I am, to behold my glory which thou hast given me in thy love for me before the foundation of the world' (John 17.24). At the climax of the Book of Revelation all the baptized do enter this place of light, standing before the throne with the LORD God as their light (22.3–5).

This hope of returning to the holy of holies, Day One of creation and the place of light, appears also in the *Gospel of Thomas*. When instructing his disciples how they will enter the holy of holies Jesus explains first how to answer the guardian angels who guard the way to the tree of life (Gen. 3.24): 'If they say to you, "Where do you come from?", say to them, "We came from the light, the place where the light came into being on its own accord, and established [itself] and became manifest through their image." If they say to you, "Is it you?", say, "We are its children and we are the elect of the living father" ' (*Thomas* 50). This saying is not in the Synoptic Gospels, but John, who knew the secret tradition preserved in Thomas, attributed similar sayings to Jesus. They can best be explained by reference to the imagery of the Book of Revelation. As the chosen ones return to the holy of holies, to the timeless place before the visible world was created, so they pass into the presence of God and are resurrected. Hence another of the sayings in Thomas: 'The disciples said to Jesus, "Tell us how our end will be." Jesus said, "Have you discovered then the beginning that you look for the end?" For where the beginning is, there the end will be. Blessed is he who takes his place in the beginning; he will know the end and not experience death" ' (*Thomas* 18). As they pass beyond time, they are able to see all history, to know the beginning and the end. Those who entered the holy of holies worshipped in the presence of God and so Jesus said 'When you see one who was not born of woman, prostrate yourselves on your faces and worship him. That one is your father' (*Thomas* 15). Those who had entered were known as the sons of light.

The Servant

Wordplay was characteristic of the prophets and visionaries. The Aramaic word *tly'* can mean either 'Lamb' or 'Servant'. The primary meaning is 'young one', but it was used for boy, child, Servant, and Lamb. There is no exact equivalent in Greek, although *pais* conveyed some of the meaning insofar as it was used for both 'child' and 'servant' (Acts 3.13; 4.27). The Lamb of the vision signifies the Servant, the enigmatic figure who appears throughout the Hebrew Scriptures, and was one of the first titles the Jerusalem Christians gave to Jesus. Peter, addressing a crowd in the temple after healing the lame man said: 'The God of Abraham and of Isaac and of Jacob, the God of our fathers glorified his servant Jesus ...' (Acts 3.13). When Peter and John had been released from prison, the Christians praised God for his mighty acts: 'thou stretchest out thy hand to heal and signs and wonders are performed through the name of thy holy servant Jesus' (Acts 4.30). John the Baptist identified Jesus as the Lamb of God (John 1.29), by which he must have meant the Servant.

Many important figures in the Hebrew Scriptures were called 'the Servant'. Abraham (Gen. 26.24) and Moses (some forty examples) probably acquired the title when the Pentateuch reached its final form after the exile. The most interesting example is where Moses 'my Servant' is distinguished from other prophets: 'With him I speak mouth to mouth, clearly, and not in dark speech; and he beholds the form of the LORD' (Num. 12.8). This implies that the Servant was someone who had seen the LORD. In most cases, however, the Servant was the king who ascended to the holy of holies.

Of old thou didst speak in a vision,
to thy faithful one, and say:
I have set the crown* upon one who is mighty,
I have exalted one chosen from the people.
I have found David, my servant;
with my holy oil I have anointed him. (Ps. 89.19–20)

When Ezekiel prophesied the restoration of the monarchy after the exile, he spoke of the Servant King: 'My servant David shall be king over them and they shall all have one shepherd' (Ezek. 37.24). Haggai proclaimed Zerubbabel the Servant of the LORD, the Chosen one and

*MT has 'help'.

the Seal (Hag. 2.23). His contemporary Zechariah referred to a mysterious figure 'my servant the Branch' (Zech. 3.8).

Most of the evidence for the Servant is found in the prophecies of
Isaiah. There are four passages, usually known as the Servant Songs,
which describe him (Isa. 42.1–4; 49.1–4; 50.4–9 and 52.13–53.12).
The first three depict the Servant as someone chosen and upheld by the
LORD to bring forth justice and to be a light to the nations. He was
endowed with the Spirit, his mouth (i.e. his teaching) was like a sharp
sword (cf. Rev. 1.16) and he was to reveal the Glory of the LORD. He
had to bring back God's people (i.e. at the Jubilee), and, although
despised and abhorred, would eventually be acknowledged by rulers
and princes. He would also suffer at the hands of tormentors.

The fourth Song gives the fullest description of the Servant, and several
details reveal that he is a high priest. He is raised up and becomes wise
(Isa. 52.13; 'prosper' in many English versions is better rendered 'become
wise'). Then, if we follow a Qumran text of Isaiah, he is anointed and his
appearance changes. There is one extra letter in 1Q Isaª 52.14, giving
mšḥty 'I have anointed' instead of *mšḥt* 'disfigured'. Astonished earthly
kings recognize him for his true self, and he *sprinkles* many nations (Isa.
52.15). He suffers and his suffering is eventually recognized as that of the
sin-bearer, the one who carries away the sins of his people and enables
the sinner to be restored to the community, made righteous (Isa. 53.11).
He offers himself as an atonement sacrifice by pouring out his own blood
('he poured out his soul to death', Isa. 53.12). After his ordeal he 'sees
the light' (Isa. 53.11, reading with the Qumran text and the LXX).

The fourth Song was originally inspired by the sufferings of King
Hezekiah who almost died of plague when Jerusalem was threatened by
the Assyrian army in 701 BCE (Isa. 38.1–6). Behind Isaiah's poem,
however, we glimpse the Servant figure to whom Hezekiah was
compared. He was the royal high priest, raised up to God's presence,
anointed and transfigured. This was his first ascent to heaven. He became
wise and was taught the secrets of heaven. He was then not only the
LORD with his people, but also the key figure who 'sprinkled' the blood
on the Day of Atonement. Although an animal was offered as a
substitute, the blood represented the life-blood of the high priest, taken
into the holy of holies. This represented another ascent to heaven. When
he emerged with the blood, it was sprinkled to remove the effects of sin
from the temple, i.e. to repair the bonds of the covenant and to renew the
creation for another year (see pp. 45–7). Hence John the Baptist's words:
the Lamb/Servant of God 'who takes away the sin of the world', and the
description of the Lamb in the vision 'as though it had been slain' (5.6).

Vestiges of this survived as the Day of Atonement rituals of the second
temple, but the true meaning of the earlier rites can best be seen in the writings
which preserved the traditions of the first temple. The Servant in these texts
is far from being the humbled and suffering figure which some scholars find
in the Servant Songs. The Parables of Enoch preserve a Day of Atonement
vision and all the elements of this are present in Revelation 5–6: the prayers

and praise of the holy ones in heaven, the prayers of the righteous ascending to heaven (1 En. 47.1–2), the Head of Days seated on the throne in glory and the books opened (1 En. 47.3). Even the cry of the martyrs is the same. In 1 Enoch it is a Man, chosen by the LORD of Spirits, who judges the kings and the mighty, reminiscent of the Son of Man vision of Daniel 7, but in the Book of Revelation he is called the Lamb. The setting is clearly the temple; the Chosen One is under the wings of the LORD of Spirits (1 En. 39.7), seated on the throne of glory (1 En. 61.8) and heavenly beings sing 'Holy, holy, holy' (1 En. 39.12). The key figure is Anointed and Chosen, the Righteous One endowed with the spirit to establish justice, a light to the peoples before whom kings are humbled. This Servant is a triumphant royal figure.

The Isaiah Targum also understood the Servant to be a triumphant royal figure, the Messiah, as can be seen from the interpretations added to the text in comparison with the RSV translation of the MT:

52.13 My Servant the Messiah shall prosper ...	MT My Servant shall prosper
52.15 ... he shall scatter many peoples ...	MT He shall sprinkle many nations
53.2 ... his appearance is not a common appearance, and his fearfulness is not an ordinary fearfulness, and his brilliance will be a holy brilliance ...	MT He had no form or comeliness that we should look at him, and no beauty that we should desire him ...
53.5 he shall build the sanctuary which was profaned for our sins, handed over for our iniquities ...	MT He was wounded for our transgressions, bruised for our iniquities
53.7 ... the strong ones of the people he will hand over like a lamb to the sacrifice ...	MT like a lamb that is led to the slaughter
53.8 From bonds and retribution he will bring our exiles near ...	MT By oppression and judgement he was taken away
53.9 and he will hand over the wicked to Gehenna ...	MT and they made his grave with the wicked
53.10 Yet before the LORD it was a pleasure to refine and to cleanse the remnant of his people in order to purify their soul from sins; they shall see the kingdom of their Messiah.	MT It was the will of the LORD to bruise him, he has put him to grief; when he makes himself an offering for sin, he shall see his offspring he shall prolong his days.

The triumphant figure in the Targum and the Parables of Enoch, judging the kings of the earth, bears a strong resemblance to the triumphant Lamb of Revelation.

The Servant in the New Testament

The Lamb is the key figure in the Book of Revelation and the Servant is the key figure in other parts of the New Testament. Jesus is depicted as the Servant. At the baptism, Jesus heard the voice from heaven speaking the words of the first Servant Song: 'Thou art my beloved son, with thee I am well pleased' (a version of Isa. 42.1, quoted in Mark 1.11). *John the Baptist identified Jesus as the Lamb, but Jesus himself heard the words of the Servant Song.* When he began his ministry of healing and exorcism, Matthew explained that this was the role of the Servant in the fourth Song: 'He took our infirmities and bore our diseases' (Isa. 53.4, quoted in Matt. 8.17). At the Transfiguration, Peter, James and John heard the words that Jesus had heard at his baptism; this was when they realized that Jesus was the Servant (Mark 9.7). When John explained why Jesus' miracles made no impression on many people, he quoted the fourth Song, that many would not recognize the Servant: 'LORD, who has believed our report, and to whom has the arm of the LORD been revealed?' (John 12.38, quoting Isa. 53.1)

Above all, the crucifixion was recognized as the self-sacrifice of the Servant. On the road to Emmaus, Jesus explained to the two disciples that it was necessary for the Anointed One to suffer and enter his glory (Luke 24.26); this must refer to the Qumran version of the fourth Servant Song, *since there is no other passage in the Hebrew Scriptures which speaks of a suffering Anointed One.* Christ the Servant was the example for persecuted Christians to follow; he was the sin-bearer who brought back the straying sheep (1 Pet. 2.21–25). Paul told the Christians in Corinth of the first instruction he received after his conversion: 'Christ died for our sins in accordance with the scriptures' (1 Cor. 15.3), which must be a reference to Isaiah 53. The Ethiopian eunuch asked Philip to explain the meaning of the fourth Servant Song which he happened to be reading. 'Then Philip opened his mouth, and beginning with this scripture, he told him the good news of Jesus' (Acts 8.35), in other words, that Jesus was the Servant. A glance at these examples will show that they come from Matthew, Mark, Luke, John, Paul and Peter, that is, from all the major authors of the New Testament. *Jesus as the Servant was not a minority viewpoint, but the original claim of the Christians.*

There is a remarkable correspondence between the Lamb of Revelation 5 and the Servant depicted in Philippians 2. Paul seems to be quoting, possibly from a hymn, when he exhorts the Christians of Philippi to follow the example of the Servant:

[he] emptied himself, taking the form of a servant,
being born in the likeness of men.
And being found in human form he humbled himself
and became obedient to death, even death on a cross.
Therefore God has highly exalted him
and bestowed on him the name that is above every name,

that at the name of Jesus every knee should bow,
in heaven and on earth and under the earth,
and every tongue confess that Jesus Christ is LORD
to the glory of God the Father. (Phil. 2.6–11)

The Servant in this hymn has emptied himself, i.e. poured out his blood to make the atonement. *Therefore God has exalted him.* For those who used this hymn, exaltation followed the atonement sacrifice, and not only exaltation, but also the gift of the Name above every name. The one exalted was given the sacred Name, he was called the LORD, he became divine. Once Jesus had been given this Name and had become the LORD, all in heaven, on earth and under the earth, worshipped him and acknowledged that Jesus was the LORD. This is exactly what is implied by the account the coronation in 1 Chronicles 29: *Solomon sat on the throne of the LORD as king and all Israel worshipped him.*

In Revelation 5 the Lamb has been slain and taken up to heaven. He approaches the throne and takes the book with seven seals (this must correspond to 'receiving the Name'). In the royal ritual it must have been the moment when the king received the *'edut,* usually translated 'testimony', but exactly what he received is unknown (2 Kgs 11.12).* Then the four living creatures and the elders fall down before him, singing a new song, and the whole creation joins in the worship of the Lamb on the throne, 'every creature in heaven and on earth and under the earth and in the sea and all therein ...' This is royal ritual, for the Lamb is also named as the Lion of Judah and the Root of David (5.5). 'The Lion of Judah' is taken from Jacob's blessing of his twelve sons, when Judah is described as a lion's whelp, the one destined to hold the sceptre and the ruler's staff (Gen. 49.9–10). 'The Root of David' is a title taken from Isaiah. The Suffering Servant in Isaiah 53.2 is described as 'a sucking child, a root from dry ground', even though the English versions prefer the alternative meaning 'a young plant, a root from dry ground'. Isaiah 53.1 could be translated: 'To whom has the *offspring/seed* of the LORD been revealed?' rather than 'To whom has the *arm* of the LORD been revealed?' This gives a cluster of titles for the Servant – offspring, sucking child, root – and accounts for the similar description of Jesus in 22.16: 'I Jesus ... am the root and the offspring of David, the bright morning star'. Isaiah 53 describes the suffering of the Root of David, but in Isaiah 11.10–11, which are later interpretations added to the great messianic prophecy in Isaiah 11.1–9, the 'Root of Jesse' is a triumphant figure, the banner to which all nations will be drawn on the day when Israel is gathered together again. On that Day also, the LORD will redeem the remnant of his people from all lands, assemble the outcasts of Israel and gather the dispersed of Judah at the great Jubilee (Isa. 11.11). A comparison with the new song (5.9) shows that this prediction, too, has been fulfilled by the Lamb who has

---

*Jesus also received a 'testimony', *martyria,* something he saw (Rev. 1.3), the LXX translation of *'edut* in e.g. Num. 1.50, 53; 10.11.

redeemed men from every tribe and tongue and people and nation. In other words, these visions are steeped in the language and imagery of Isaiah and record the expectations of Israel.

An elder interprets the vision (5.5), an indication that a new meaning is being given to older material. Here he reveals who has become the LORD with his people. This is not the vision of Ezekiel who received an opened scroll, but something that preceded it, the opening of the scroll by the LORD. *The revelation of Jesus Christ which God gave to him to show his servants what must soon take place* (1.1). In 5.5 John the elder reveals to his community the interpretation of the Servant/Book vision. John the elder had been the unnamed disciple of John the Baptist (John 1.35–40), to whom the Baptist had revealed the identity of the Servant: 'He looked at Jesus as he walked and said "Behold the Lamb of God"' (John 1.36). After Easter, John had revealed this to a wider circle of followers, and in so doing had proclaimed that the events of the end time had been set in motion because the book was being opened.

Several such contemporary interpretations of the Hebrew Scriptures have been found at Qumran and there are examples of communities who met together to study the Scriptures. According to the Damascus Document, the *mᵉbaqqer* (the guardian/bishop of the community) had to instruct the Many in the mighty acts of God: 'He shall recount before them the things of eternity' [the *'olam*, which probably meant the secrets of the holy of holies] 'and their interpretation' (CD XIII). The Community Rule prescribed that the community should 'watch for a third of every night of the year, to read the Book and to study the Law and to bless together' (1QS VI). Closest to the picture in the Book of Revelation is Philo's description of the Therapeuts, a religious community who lived on the Mediterranean coast of Egypt, west of the delta. They lived a communal and ascetic life, spending six days in the private study of Scripture and then on the seventh assembling together: 'The elder among them who has the fullest knowledge of the doctrines they profess . . . gives a well reasoned and wise discourse' (*Contemplative Life* 31). At Pentecost 'they assemble, white robed' (66) and after their common meal the president discussed 'some question arising in the holy scriptures' (75). When he had finished speaking, hymns were sung (80–87), modelled on the choir led by Moses and Miriam after they had passed through the sea (Exod. 15.1, 21). It is interesting to note that whenever the elder in the Book of Revelation speaks to interpret the vision (5.5; 7.14) there follows a hymn, exactly the custom of the Therapeuts. Eusebius (*History* 2.17) had no doubt that the Therapeuts were Christian communities, and, although it has been fashionable recently to doubt Eusebius' judgement, the interpreting elder and the hymns in the Book of Revelation make it likely that he was correct. We have to envisage a group of priest-prophets, living an ascetic life in the desert, studying their Scriptures and giving interpretations to their communities.

The Synoptic Gospels depict Jesus hiding his true identity (e.g. Mark 1.34, 44; 5.43) and even his closest disciples were forbidden to reveal what they knew until later (Mark 9.9). This has been explained as a literary fiction, the so-called Messianic Secret. Jesus himself, it is said, had made no claims to be the Messiah and so when the church proclaimed him as the Messiah, they had to explain why so few had recognized him during his ministry. The evangelists overcame the problem by inventing the Messianic Secret, that Jesus had forbidden his disciples to reveal his true identity until later. The role of John the elder, however, 'making known the revelation of Jesus Christ' (1.1) shows that there had indeed been a Messianic Secret – albeit not as described by modern scholars. John had known who Jesus was and he 'made known' what Jesus had revealed to him (and to other close disciples), when the time came to reveal it. The risen LORD was not revealed to everyone, said Peter, but only to those who 'were prepared beforehand as witnesses' (Acts 10.40–41, translating literally).

Not all the important texts from this period have survived, and so the Lamb text which John was interpreting is not extant, but it will have been the vision known to Jesus in his baptism and wilderness experiences. (The Book of Hagu, a key text for the Qumran community which the 'bishop' had to expound, is also completely lost). In 7.13–14 there is a similar interpretation by the elder of older material. An older vision of the ingathering of Israel, perhaps inspired by Isaiah, has been reinterpreted as the ingathering of the Roman Christians into the church as the result of their sufferings under Nero. In the style of the Qumran commentaries the incident would have been recorded: 'Interpreted, this concerns those who are coming out of the Great Tribulation', but here the inspiration of the new interpretation has been acknowledged, and the elder speaks from heaven. Note that it in each case it is an elder who has the authority to interpret the vision. This is John concealing himself in the book and indicating where he gave or revealed new teaching to the churches. Here in 5.5 he confirms that Jesus was the expected royal figure, who would inaugurate the end times. This teaching is found also in the Fourth Gospel where he says that the disciples did not at first understand the royal significance of Palm Sunday, but later 'remembered' the real meaning of what had happened (John 12.15–16, see p. 189). The Holy Spirit, said John's Jesus, would teach all things and 'bring to your remembrance all that I have said to you' (John 14.26)

The Lamb on the Throne

Once the Lamb is enthroned, he is worshipped. Some texts are ambiguous, but 7.17 is quite clear; the Lamb 'in the midst of the throne' will be their shepherd, cf. 'in the midst of the fire' (Ezek. 1.5). The worship of the enthroned Lamb shows that he has become the LORD and the vision of Revelation 5 is a scene of apotheosis, corresponding to temple ritual underlying Psalm 2 and Psalm 110.

'I have set my king on Zion, my holy hill.'
I will tell you of a decree of the LORD:
He said to me, 'You are my son,
today I have begotten you ...' (Ps. 2.6–7)

Psalm 110.3–4 is an obscure text but a possible reconstruction has been suggested:

... in the glory of the holy ones, (or perhaps holy place)
from the womb of the Dawn I have begotten you.
The LORD has sworn
and will not change his mind
You are a priest for ever,
After the manner of Melchizedek.

At the enthronement, the Servant/Lamb is born as the Son and becomes the high priest Melchizedek.

The 'ambiguous' texts in Revelation confirm that this enthronement ritual was apotheosis. Their present form is probably the result of transferring a Semitic idiom into Greek. The account of Solomon's coronation (1 Chron. 29.20, 23), shows how the ambiguity might have arisen. Solomon sat on the throne of the LORD as king, and the people worshipped the LORD and the king. Since Solomon was occupying the throne of the LORD, this must mean that Solomon was worshipped as the LORD, and the Hebrew does in fact say: 'They gave worship to the LORD and to the King'. A similar double designation, first the divinity and then the human, occurs in the 'ambiguous' texts of Revelation. 'Salvation belongs to our God who sits on the throne and to the Lamb' (7.10) is followed by 'they fell on their faces and worshipped God' (no mention of the Lamb, 7.11). 'To him who sits upon the throne and to the Lamb' be blessing and honour and glory and might for ever and ever (5.13) is a similar construction. There are 'firstfruits' 'for God and the Lamb' (14.4, see p. 243), there is 'the throne of God and of the Lamb' (22.1, 3) followed by 'his [singular] servants shall worship him, they shall see his face'. Similarly there is 'the kingdom of our LORD and his Christ' (11.15) followed by 'and he [singular] shall reign for ever and ever'. They will be 'priests of God and of Christ' (20.6) followed by and 'they shall reign with him [singular] a thousand years'. Early scribes sometimes found this a problem and as a result, there are two versions of 6.16–17. One says: 'Fall on us and hide us from the face of him who is on the throne, and from the wrath of the Lamb; for the great day of *their* wrath has come'; and the other says: 'the great day of *his* wrath has come'. The singular 'his' is more likely to be the original, as one can understand a scribe altering to the plural in this context, but not changing a plural into a singular (see p. 369, where the Spirit and the Bride is a similar double naming).

The Lamb, like Solomon, sat on the throne of the LORD and was worshipped. Exactly the same was said of Moses by one Ezekiel (not the prophet, but nobody knows exactly when this Ezekiel lived) who wrote a Greek-style play about the life of Moses. Only extracts have survived, quoted by Eusebius (*Preparation* 9.29). Here, Moses tells his father-in-law about a dream, and Ezekiel has clearly transferred to Moses some of the old traditions about the king:

Methought upon Mount Sinai's brow I saw
A mighty throne that reached to heaven's high vault
Whereon there sat a man of noblest mien
Wearing a royal crown; whose left hand held
A mighty sceptre; and his right to me
Made sign, and I stood forth before the throne.
He gave me then the sceptre and the crown,
And bade me sit upon the royal throne,
From which himself removed. Thence I looked forth
Upon the earth's wide circle, and beneath
The earth itself and high above the heaven.
Then at my feet, behold a thousand stars
Began to fall, and I their number told,
As they passed by me like an armed host.

Moses ascended and stood before the heavenly throne; he became the enthroned one, and watched the host of heaven pass at his feet. Philo said something similar when he described Moses' experience on Sinai using terms drawn from temple beliefs about the king entering the holy of holies:

For he [Moses] was named God and King of the whole nation, and entered, we are told, into the darkness where God was, that is, into the unseen, invisible, incorporeal and archetypal essence of existing things. Thus he beheld what is hidden from the sight of mortal nature ... (*Moses* I.158)

Revelation 5 describes the moment when the Lamb entered heaven and became God and King.

Fragments of a Qumran text attest a similar belief, but this time the writer claims the enthronement for himself 'a throne of strength in the congregation of the gods ... my glory is incomparable, and apart from me none is exalted ... I am reckoned with the gods and my dwelling place is in the congregation of holiness ...' (4Q491). Jesus described his desert experience in this way. When Mark records that 'He was with the wild beasts and the angels served him' (Mark 1.13), this must have been Jesus' own account of what happened when he was alone after his baptism: 'I was with the beasts and the angels served me'.

The Lamb as the LORD

In Philippians 2, the Servant is exalted after his death and receives the Name. Then he is worshipped as the LORD. In Revelation this worship of the Servant/Lamb as the LORD is confirmed by the pattern of the doxologies. When the elders around the throne worship him who lives for ever and ever, they sing: 'Worthy art thou our LORD and God to receive glory and honour and power, for thou didst create all things and by thy will they existed and were created' (4.11). When the whole host of heaven worships the Lamb they use similar words: 'Worthy is the Lamb who was slain to receive power and wealth and wisdom and might and honour and glory and blessing' (5.12). When the whole creation joins in worship they say: 'To him who sits upon the throne and to the Lamb be blessing and honour and glory and might forever and ever' (5.13). The two, now one, are worshipped (cf. John 10.30).

A comparison of the two doxologies also shows that these were hymns for the Day of Atonement when the covenant bond was restored and the creation renewed by the blood which was the life of the LORD (see p. 45). The first doxology praises the LORD as creator, 'For thou didst create all things and by thy will they existed and were created' (4.11); the second praises the Lamb as redeemer who recreates with his own blood, 'for thou wast slain and by thy blood thou didst ransom men for God ... and hast made them a kingdom and priests' (5.9–10). Although 'ransom of blood' has long been the accepted understanding of these words, their context, and the awkward Greek word *egorasas*, meaning 'bought in the market', suggest a poorly translated Hebrew original. The original was probably *qnh*, which can mean 'to buy' (e.g. Exod. 21.2), but also 'to redeem' (e.g. Ps. 74.2) or 'to create/beget' (e.g. Deut. 32.6). The same word is found at 14.4, where the firstborn have been 'redeemed' from the earth (see p. 244). The Lamb is praised because he has been slain (*esphages* a word used specifically of sacrificial slaughter, used to describe the Servant in the LXX of Isaiah 53.7, like a lamb that is led to the 'slaughter'). The Lamb's blood, the life of the LORD, has been used as on the Day of Atonement, to restore and renew the creation, and to create a kingdom of priests, the assembly of the firstborn (see on 14.4). In other words, the Lamb who approaches the throne is the LORD returning to his holy place after he has made the Great Atonement. 'But when he had offered for all time a single sacrifice for sins,* he sat down at the right hand of God, then to wait until his enemies should be made a stool for his feet' (Heb. 10.12–13). The sequence which follows, from Revelation 6.1–11.18 describes the time of waiting until the time for the defeat of his enemies, the Day of the LORD.

The Book of Revelation, apart from these scenes of worship, confirms that the Lamb was the LORD. We shall look at these passages in more detail later, but at this point note only the following:

The wrath is the wrath of the Lamb (6.17), but also the wrath of God (15.7).

---

*Cf. here the description of the Man in Daniel's vision. He came in the clouds of heaven and was 'offered before' the Ancient of Days before being enthroned. The verb in Dan. 7.13 usually translated 'present' is *qrb*, but in a temple context this means 'to offer'.

The redeemed are marked with the Name of the Lamb and of his Father (14.1), but this mark was also the seal of the living God (7.2–3) in other words, the Name.
The Lamb has the book of the living, the book of life (13.8; 21.27), but in the Hebrew Scriptures this is the LORD's book (Exod. 32.32; Ps. 69.28).
The Lamb is the warrior, the LORD of lords and King of kings, with a secret Name inscribed on his crown (17.14; 19.12).
The new Jerusalem is the bride of the Lamb, whereas Isaiah had described her as the bride of the Lord (21.9–10; Isa. 54.5).

The picture is consistent: the Lamb has the sevenfold spirit and the sevenfold light of the first day, and he becomes the LORD, enthroned in the midst of the beasts and the elders.

9

THE BOOK WITH SEVEN SEALS

And I saw in the right hand of him who was seated on the throne a book written within and on the back, sealed with seven seals; and I saw a strong angel proclaiming with a loud voice, 'Who is worthy to open the book and break its seals?' And no one in heaven or on earth or under the earth was able to open the book or to look into it, and I wept much that no one was found worthy to open the book or to look into it. Then one of the elders said to me, 'Weep not; lo, the Lion of the tribe of Judah, the Root of David, has conquered, so that he can open the book and its seven seals.' And between the throne and the four living creatures and among the elders, I saw a Lamb standing, as though it had been slain, with seven horns and with seven eyes, which are the seven spirits of God sent out into all the earth; and he went and took the book from the right hand of him who was seated on the throne. And when he had taken the book, the four living creatures and the twenty-four elders fell down before the Lamb, each holding a harp and with golden bowls full of incense, which are the prayers of the saints; and they sang a new song, saying:

Worthy art thou to take the book and to open its seals,
for thou wast slain and by thy blood didst ransom men for God
from every tribe and tongue and people and nation,
and hast made them a kingdom and priests to our God,
and they shall reign on earth. (Rev. 5.1–10)

The Lamb takes the book with seven seals and immediately the elders and the creatures worship him. *Taking the book must be the moment when he becomes divine.*

The Strong Angel who asks, 'Who is worthy to open the book?' is the one seated on the throne, the LORD. He appears again in 10.1 and is often described in the Hebrew Scriptures as 'the angel of the LORD', or simply as 'the angel'. In Zechariah 3, for example, all three designations occur together for the same figure: the LORD, the angel of the LORD and the angel. In Judges 2.1 it is not the LORD but the angel of the LORD who brings Israel out of Egypt and makes a covenant with them, and in the story of Manoah and his wife, the angel of the LORD, a man of God and the LORD are all one figure (Judg. 13.3, 6, 22). Wherever a Strong/Mighty Angel is mentioned in the Book of Revelation, it is the LORD. The LORD is the angel with the great seal (7.2); he is the heavenly high priest with the incense preparing to come from heaven on the Day of the LORD (8.3); he comes down from heaven after the sixth trumpet to give the open book to John (10.1), and in chapter 18 he appears twice to announce the destruction of the wicked city (18.1, 21). In chapter 5 he appears as the one on the throne who gives the book to the Lamb (5.1–2) and the Lamb then becomes the LORD, receiving his names and titles.

The earliest evidence for a royal ritual in which a human becomes the LORD is the enigmatic prophecy in Isaiah 9.6:

For to us a child is born, to us a son is given;
and the government will be upon his shoulder, and his name will be called
'Wonderful Counsellor, Mighty God,* Everlasting Father, Prince of Peace.'

These lines, like Psalm 2.7, describe the 'birth' of the king as son of God and then list his throne names. 'Mighty God' suggests he was more than a human figure. In the LXX, however, all these titles are summarized as one, and the new king is to be called 'Angel of Great Counsel' or, more likely, 'Angel of Great Council', as the Greek can mean either. The new king has become the angel who presides in the heavenly assembly, the LORD, the Son.

In the Book of Revelation he is called the Strong/Mighty Angel, almost certainly *El Gibbor*, and in most cases he is described as *another* angel (7.2; 8.3; 10.1; 18.1). This, however, is a mistranslation which has given the impression that there were several of these Mighty Angels. If the word in the original was *'ḥr,* then it is a word with two meanings in both Hebrew and Aramaic. It can mean 'another', but it can also mean 'afterwards'. The original text was not 'I saw another angel ascend', but 'Afterwards I saw the angel ascend' (7.2), and similarly elsewhere. There are not many Mighty Angels, just one: the LORD.

The Mighty Angel on the throne asks, 'Who is worthy to open the book?' and the interpreting elder says that the Lion of Judah, the Root of David 'has conquered to open the book' (translating literally). This is strange Greek but suggests an Aramaic original for the elder's words, as the word *zkh* (also spelled *zk'*) can mean 'to be victorious' or 'to be worthy' or 'to be pure'. In view of the Mighty Angel's question, 'Who is worthy?' and the new song which follows, 'Worthy art thou to take the book', we should expect the elder's interpretation to be 'The Lion of Judah and the Root of David is worthy to take the book'. His original saying was probably understood in that way. Since the final form of the Book of Revelation was for churches who feared imminent persecution, the other meaning of the word was found in the verse, and the Lamb who 'was worthy' became the Lamb who 'has conquered'. Such wordplay did not transfer to the Greek and so it had to be spelled out by using a different word. Similar wordplay probably underlies the promises in the seven letters to 'those who conquer' (e.g. 2.7), and explains the strange Greek of 15.2 (see p. 261).

The Servant in Philippians 2.9–10 was worshipped after he had been exalted and received the Name. Isaiah's Servant, however, was not worshipped but 'became wise' after he had been exalted and anointed. The MT is not clear (Isa. 52.13–14), but the Qumran text seems to say that after the Servant had been lifted up and 'made wise', his appearance and form altered because he had been 'anointed'. This is very different

*Translating *El Gibbor*.

from the version usually given, that his appearance was altered because his face was disfigured. In the Qumran Isaiah, the change in his appearance was a sign that he had become divine, and possessing 'knowledge' was a vital part of this. It enabled him to bear (i.e. forgive) sin and redeem the lost. 'By his knowledge shall the righteous one, my servant, make many to be accounted righteous, and he shall bear their iniquities' (Isa. 53.11). Isaiah's poem is dense with imagery from the royal cult and much of it remains obscure. One aspect of this heavenly knowledge, however, can be deduced from the court room scene where the gods of the nations are challenged to prove their divine power by demonstrating their knowledge of the future: 'Tell us what is to come hereafter, that we may know that you are gods' (Isa. 41.21–24). As it is the LORD alone who has this knowledge, he is the only God:

Thus says the LORD, the King of Israel and his Redeemer, the LORD of hosts: 'I am the first and I am the last; besides me there is no god. Who is like me? Let him proclaim it, let him declare and set it forth before me. Who has announced from of old the things to come?* Let them tell them what is yet to be'. (Isa. 44.6–7)

The Lamb has the knowledge of the future which proves he is divine, as does Melchizedek, who was to instruct his people about 'all the ends of the age' (11QMelch 20).

The Book

The book was sealed with seven seals, probably to emphasize how firmly it was closed. Daniel, who interpreted for his own times the temple vision of the Man ascending to the heavenly throne (Dan. 7), was told by an angel: 'Shut up the words and seal the book until the time of the end' (Dan. 12.4). We are not told what was in this book, but it may have concerned the fate of Jerusalem and the temple in the end time. Daniel's prophecies addressed the crisis in Jerusalem in the second century BCE, and are clearly an interpretation of earlier material for that situation: 'Then the LORD spoke to Daniel: "Go your way, Daniel, for the words are shut up and sealed until the time of the end. Many shall purify themselves and make themselves white, and be refined; but the wicked shall do wickedly; and none of the wicked shall understand; but those who are wise shall understand" ' (Dan. 12.9–10). The sealed book was to be opened at the end time, and only the wise would understand.

There have been many attempts to explain how a book with seven seals could be opened one seal at a time, and no explanation is convincing. The book was also written 'within and on the back', and again, there have been many attempts to explain what this means. In the Book of Revelation it probably means a book was envisaged written on

*The Hebrew is not clear here.

both sides of the page, as opposed to a scroll.* It would, however, have been a scroll written within and without that had been offered to Ezekiel, after he had seen the chariot throne and the Fiery Man. He had had no problem with seven seals as the scroll he saw was already open.

> And when I looked, behold, a hand was stretched out to me, and, lo, a written scroll [literally 'scroll of a book'] was in it; and he spread it before me; and it had writing on the front and on the back, and there were written on it words of lamentation and mourning and woe. And he said to me, 'Son of man, eat what is offered to you; eat this scroll, and go, speak to the house of Israel.' So I opened my mouth, and he gave me the scroll to eat. (Ezek. 2.9–3.2)

There is a tradition of the Ethiopian Church that the outside of the scroll was knowledge not to be revealed and the inside was knowledge for public reading, but the Ezekiel Targum suggests that the scroll was an overview of Israel's history: 'And he spread it before me and behold it was inscribed on the face of it and on the reverse of it, that which was from the beginning and that which is destined to be in the end'. Ezekiel, like Daniel, was concerned with the future of Jerusalem. The 'open' scroll which Ezekiel saw written on the front and on the back corresponds to the open book in Revelation 10 and John, too, was told to eat the open book. Scholars have now concluded that the sealed book which the Lamb takes and opens is the book which he, described as the Mighty Angel, the LORD, later gives to John (10.2, 8).

The two 'scroll' visions of Revelation 5 and 10 are summarized in Revelation 1.1 which records how the visions were handed down and interpreted: 'The revelation of Jesus Christ which God gave him to show to his servants what must soon take place' is the visionary experience of Jesus himself, warning what would happen to Jerusalem in the near future. This is the vision of the Lamb opening the book as he becomes the LORD (Rev. 5). 'And he made it known by sending his angel to his servant John.' In the visions, the Mighty Angel of 10.1 is the LORD entrusting this book of revelation to John, and telling him what is to be revealed. 'Made known' is a word characteristic of John and includes the idea of explaining a sign or enigmatic saying as in John 18.32: 'This was to fulfil the word which Jesus had spoken to make known by what death he was to die'. The risen LORD of Revelation 1 communicates with John through a vision ('the Spirit of Truth', John 16.13) and this enables John to interpret Jesus' visions for the churches of his own time. He 'bore witness to the word of God and to the testimony of Jesus Christ, even to all that he saw'. John now bears witness that he knew of the visions and heavenly testimony of Jesus, all that Jesus himself had seen.

Thus the Book of Revelation in the form we know it today comprises the visions which Jesus knew and which inspired his ministry, and the interpretation of them which John gave to the persecuted churches of the next generation. The final form of the book was prefaced with the

---

*In the Book of Revelation 'scroll' and 'book' are probably identical.

seven letters and sent to the seven churches of Asia, after the church in Palestine had been dispersed by the war against Rome.

Early in the third century CE, Origen compared Ezekiel's vision of the open scroll and John's:

Our prophets did know of greater things than any in the scriptures which they did not commit to writing. Ezekiel, for example, received a roll written within and without ... but at the command of the Logos he swallowed the book in order that its contents might not be written and so made known to unworthy persons. John also is recorded to have seen and done a similar thing. (*Cels.* 6.6)

According to this Christian scholar of the Hebrew Scriptures, the Fiery Man on the throne, who had given the open scroll to Ezekiel, was the Logos. The Mighty Angel who brought the open book to John was the same figure, the Fiery Man, wrapped in a cloud with a rainbow over his head (10.1). This implies that in both cases the LORD had opened the book before handing it on to his prophet, which accords with our earlier deduction: that the Mighty Angel who also appears in 5.2, 8.3 and 18.21 is the LORD and that the Lamb became the LORD when he took the book.

Heavenly Knowledge

There are two attitudes towards heavenly knowledge in the Hebrew Scriptures: that of the reformers, that is, the Deuteronomists, and that of the older temple tradition. The Book of Revelation reflects the older tradition which originated in the royal cult of the first temple.

The 'reformers' were responsible for the Eden story in Genesis 2–3 which teaches that humans sinned because they wanted knowledge, i.e. wisdom. They warned against any desire for heavenly knowledge and the serpent, they taught, tempted humans to take what was forbidden. They recognized that 'the secret things belong to the LORD our God' (Deut. 29.29), but emphasized that humans did not need to know them. 'The things that are revealed belong to us and our children for ever, that we may do all the words of this law' (Deut. 29.29). Israel had the Law and that was all they needed. 'It is not in heaven, that you should say, "Who will go up for us to heaven, and bring it to us, that we may hear it and do it?"' (Deut. 30.12). Knowledge about heaven or brought from heaven existed, but it brought trouble. It was forbidden even to read Ezekiel's description of the heavenly chariot in public, or to expound it for students (*m. Megillah* 4.10 and *m. Hagigah* 2.1). Those who forbad study of the chariot were those who denied the value of heavenly knowledge. It is not their teachings that we find in Revelation where someone does go up to heaven to bring back heavenly knowledge. This implies that the vision of taking the scroll, or something very similar, must have been known to the writer of Deuteronomy.

In the older tradition, however, knowledge/wisdom had been the great gift which made humans like God. The words of the serpent reflect the older tradition: 'When you eat [of the tree of knowledge] your eyes will be opened and you will be like God, knowing good and evil' (Gen. 3.5). Joab had flattered King David when he said to him, 'My LORD has wisdom like the wisdom of the angel of God to know all things that are on the earth' (2 Sam. 14.20). The mysterious heavenly being, the King of Tyre, was thrown from Eden because of his pride and his abuse of wisdom. Being wise was part of his heavenly perfection: 'You were full of wisdom and perfect in beauty. You were in Eden, the garden of God': (Ezek. 28.12–13). The Servant in Isaiah 52.13 was 'made wise, exalted and lifted up' (translating literally), and it was his knowledge which enabled him to bear/forgive the iniquities of the people (Isa. 53.11). 'The lips of a priest guard knowledge' (Mal. 2.7).

The Enoch books preserved the older temple traditions, and show the heavenly knowledge in its original setting. Enoch was taken up to heaven and stood before the throne. The LORD told Michael to anoint him and give him the robes of glory. As he was anointed, Enoch saw himself transformed into an angel 'like one of his glorious ones' (2 En. 22.10). An archangel then brought the books about the great secrets of God, which God revealed and related to Enoch and he 'spoke with him face to face' (2 En. 24.1). In 3 Enoch, the angel Metatron, the transformed heavenly Enoch, was enthroned as 'my Servant, a prince and ruler over all the denizens of the heights ...' (3 En. 10.3). Metatron said to Rabbi Ishmael: 'The holy one, blessed be he, revealed to me from that time onward (when he was enthroned) all the mysteries of wisdom ... All the mysteries of the world and all the orders of nature stand revealed before me as they stand revealed before the creator. From that time onward I looked and beheld deep secrets and beheld wonderful mysteries' (3 En. 11.1–2). 1 Enoch is largely devoted to accounts of this secret knowledge. Enoch saw the secrets of the creation and the secrets of the angels, 'for the angel who went with me showed me all the hidden things' (1 En. 40.2). When he asked the angel about the Man figure in heaven he was told: 'This is the Son of Man who hath righteousness, with whom dwelleth righteousness, and who revealeth all the treasures of that which is hidden, because the LORD of Spirits hath chosen him' (1 En. 46.3).

The Qumran texts also speak of this heavenly knowledge; in the Hymns we find: 'These things I know by the wisdom which comes from thee for Thou hast unstopped my ears to marvellous mysteries', (1QH IX, formerly I). 'Thou hast made me ... a discerning interpreter of wonderful mysteries' (1QH X, formerly II).

I, the Master, know Thee, O my God,
By the spirit which Thou hast given me,
and by thy Holy Spirit I have faithfully hearkened
to Thy marvellous counsel
In the mystery of Thy wisdom
Thou hast opened knowledge to me,
and in Thy mercies
[Thou hast unlocked for me] the fountain of Thy might. (1QH XX, formerly XII)

One of the Songs of the Sabbath Sacrifice describes the Princes in their heavenly holy of holies and 'the seven mysteries of knowledge' (4Q403). The text is fragmented, but the seven mysteries may account for the seven seals on the Lamb's book. One of their prayers for the Day of Atonement mentions the hidden and revealed things: 'Prayer for the Day of Atonement. Remember O LORD, the feast of mercies and the time of return ... Thou knowest the hidden things and the things revealed ...' (4Q508). The Teacher of Righteousness, the priest whom 'God chose to stand before him' (4Q171.3) was the one to whom God made known all the mysteries of the words of his servants the prophets: 'The final age shall be prolonged and shall exceed all that the prophets have said; for the mysteries of God are astounding' (1QpHab VII).

John's Portrait of Jesus

John concealed himself in the Fourth Gospel as the beloved disciple. His portrait of Jesus cannot be considered secondary and less authentic than those of Matthew, Mark and Luke, who were not among the closest disciples, and yet this is what is usually done. The enigmatic teacher whom John depicts is said to be far removed from the real Jesus and John's Jesus is said to be a fantasy figure created by Gentile converts to Christianity who had not fully shaken off their pagan ways.

The Jesus whom John portrays, however, is someone who claims to have ascended to heaven and he could have been the unnamed seer in Revelation 4.1 who saw the visions of the throne and the Lamb. After the words of John the Baptist at his baptism, Jesus knew it was his vocation to be the Lamb and realize the visions on earth: 'Thy kingdom come, on earth as it is in heaven'.

Jesus speaks to Nicodemus about those born from above who are able to see the kingdom and those born of water and Spirit who are able to enter the kingdom. Two stages: seeing and entering. At first Jesus had seen the visions, then he had become a part of them.* When Nicodemus does not understand, Jesus says, 'We speak of what we know, and bear witness to what we have seen; but you do not receive our testimony. If I have told you earthly things and you do not believe, how can you believe if I tell you heavenly things?' (John 3.11–12). Nicodemus does not accept Jesus' testimony to what he has seen, whereas the prologue to Revelation says that John did accept and bear witness to the testimony of Jesus Christ, 'to all that he saw' (Rev. 1.2). John the Baptist also knew of Jesus' ascent experience and told his own disciples: 'He bears witness to what he has seen and heard, yet no one receives his testimony' (John 3.32). Since John the Baptist was executed shortly after Jesus' baptism, this must refer to a visionary experience at the very start of Jesus' ministry. The baptism is the obvious occasion, when he saw the heavens open (Mark 1.10).

---

*1 En. 71 seems to describe Enoch seeing the holy of holies, being taken up by Michael and appointed as the Man.

When Jesus was teaching in the temple at the Feast of Tabernacles, people marvelled at his knowledge, 'How is it that this man has learning when he has never studied?' So Jesus answered them, 'My teaching is not mine but his who sent me' (John 7.15–16). He spoke time and again of being the messenger sent from God: 'He who sent me is true and I declare to the world what I have heard from him' (John 8.26); 'I speak of what I have seen with my Father' (John 8.38); 'For I have not spoken on my own authority; the Father who sent me has himself given me commandment what to say and what to speak' (John 12.49); 'All that I have heard from my Father I have made known to you' (John 15.15). He believed that he had been 'consecrated' as the heavenly high priest and 'sent into the world' (John 10.36). He also claimed to be the Man who ascended and was enthroned as judge: '[The Father] has given him authority to execute judgement, because he is the Son of Man' (John 5.27).

Jesus spoke of his two ascents, the one at his baptism and the other after his death. After he had entered Jerusalem on Palm Sunday, Jesus was praying, 'Father glorify thy name, and a voice came from heaven "I have glorified it and will glorify it again"' (John 12.28). At the Last Supper, Jesus told his disciples that some of his teachings had yet to be explained to them: 'I have many things to say to you, but you cannot bear them now. When the Spirit of truth comes, he will guide you into all the truth; for he will not speak on his own authority, but whatever he hears he will speak, and he will declare to you the things that are to come. He will glorify me, for he will take what is mine and declare it to you' (John 16.12–14).

When John described how he had received his own insight into the vision of Jesus, 'He made it known by sending his messenger/angel to his servant John' (Rev. 1.1), he was referring to this saying of Jesus at the Last Supper. The Angel of Truth was another name for the Prince of Light, the patron angel of Israel (1QS III), and here he is the angel of the LORD who was to explain the hidden teaching of Jesus, 'what is mine', and pass it on to the disciples 'declare it to you'. This teaching concerned 'the things that are to come'. In other words, John incorporated into his account of the Last Supper an indication of how the visions would be transmitted and interpreted. John's communications from the risen LORD were written down as the seven letters and as the interpretation of the secret teaching and visions. *The risen LORD of 1.13–16 is the Mighty Angel of 10.1, in each case speaking to John in the temple.*

In his prayer after the Last Supper, Jesus speaks of himself as the Lamb of Revelation 5: 'Father, glorify thou me in thy own presence with the glory which I had with thee before the world was made' (John 17.5) refers to the vision of the Lamb as he approaches the throne, with the seven horns which are the sevenfold light of Day One. He re-enters the holy of holies, Day One, before the creation of time and matter. 'Father, I desire that they also, whom thou hast given me, may be with me where I am, to behold my glory which thou hast given me in thy love for me before the foundation of the world' (John 17.24) refers to the final vision of the Book of Revelation, the redeemed in heaven, 'beholding the face of the Lamb on the throne', and needing no other light than the light of his glory (22.3–4). Jesus knew that he bore the sacred Name, that he was the LORD visible on earth: 'I have manifested thy name to those whom thou gavest me ... (John 17.6); 'Thy name which thou hast given me ...' (John 17.12); 'He who has seen me has seen the Father' (John 14.9).

At his trial, Jesus said he had taught openly, and said nothing in secret (John 18.20), but the evidence of the other Gospels contradicts this. The parables were not for everyone to understand, and so he explained them to his disciples in private (Mark 4.10–11).

John's account of Good Friday is full of references to the high priestly sacrifice of the Servant/Lamb. 'My kingship is not of this world' (John 18.36); he was a king who suffered blows from tormentors (John 19.1–3) as did Isaiah's Servant figure (Isa. 50.6); Pilate's words 'Behold the Man' (John 19.5) recall the presentation of the Man in the vision of Enoch: 'Open your eyes ... if you are able to recognize the Elect One' (1 En. 62.1); and the protest of the crowd: 'he ought to die because he has made himself the Son of God' (John 19.7) is the final irony.

Opening the Book

As the Lamb opens the seals, so the future fate of Jerusalem is revealed. With the first four seals there emerge the four horsemen, as in Zechariah's vision (Zech. 1.8). In terms of temple furnishings, they were probably the horses of the sun which had stood at the entrance to the temple until King Josiah had them removed (2 Kgs 23.11). Here in the vision, they, like all the other temple furnishings, are alive. At the bidding of the four living creatures, they emerge from the temple.

It was an ancient belief that the LORD's punishments emerged from his holy of holies. Aaron rushed to make atonement when wrath, in the form of plague, emerged from the tent of meeting (Num. 16.46). Habakkuk described the LORD appearing:

His brightness was like the light, rays flashed from his hand;
and there he veiled his power.
Before him went pestilence, and plague followed close behind.
He stood and measured the earth; he looked and shook the nations;
then the eternal mountains were scattered, and the everlasting hills sank low.
His ways were as of old. (Hab. 3.4–7)

Plague and pestilence were a sign of the LORD's approach. Ezekiel the priest had warned Jerusalem of four sore acts of judgement, sword, famine, evil beasts and pestilence (Ezek. 14.21); and Isaiah described the wrath of the LORD against Jerusalem as devastation and destruction, famine and the sword (Isa. 51.19).

The first rider has a white horse and sets out to conquer. The second has a red horse and brings war. The third has a black horse and brings famine. The fourth has a pale horse and brings death; he is followed by Hades, and between them they have power to kill with sword, famine, pestilence and wild beasts, the four punishments known to Ezekiel. With the fifth seal, the seer sees the souls of the martyrs under the altar and with the sixth, he sees the Day of the LORD: the sun darkened, the moon red, stars falling from the sky and the mountains and islands moving.

It has often been observed that this sequence of woes is exactly like that predicted by Jesus as he sat on the Mount of Olives a few days before his death. Matthew, Mark and Luke all record this, albeit with small variations in their accounts. Matthew says Jesus taught the disciples privately whereas Mark says that only Peter, James, John and Andrew were present. In each case, it was Jesus' final teaching before his death (Matt. 24; Mark 13; Luke 21). One suggestion is that John used this teaching of Jesus and developed it into the vision of the six seals. Another is that Jesus knew an existing 'document' of predictions and John knew it too. Both suggestions are partly correct; Jesus knew the sequence of expected woes and he believed that by his death, by becoming the Lamb, he would inaugurate the sequence of woes and bring the destruction of Jerusalem.

Jesus predicted the destruction of the temple:

As he came out of the temple, one of his disciples said to him, 'Look, Teacher, what wonderful stones and what wonderful buildings!' And Jesus said to him, 'Do you see these great buildings? There will not be left here one stone upon another, that will not be thrown down.'

And as he sat on the Mount of Olives opposite the temple, Peter and James and John and Andrew asked him privately, 'Tell us, when will this be, and what will be the sign when all these things are to be accomplished?' (Mark 13.1–4)

The passage which corresponds so closely to the vision of the six seals is Jesus' reply to the question: 'When will the temple be destroyed?' The answer is given, not to a large crowd or even to the twelve, but to the inner group, privately. What we read in the Synoptic Gospels, the so-called Synoptic Apocalypse, is a summary of what was said. John, who does not record this teaching in his Gospel, gives the vision in full in Revelation 6.

The Gospel summaries enable us better to understand the figures in the vision. The first sign would be false messiahs: 'Many will come in my name, saying, "I am He!" and they will lead many astray' (Mark 13.6), in other words, there would be people who claimed to be the LORD returning. In the vision of the seals, this was the rider on the white horse who went out conquering. Unlike the other riders, he had a crown, and it has often been observed how similar this figure is to the real Messiah who returns to judge and make war, riding a white horse and crowned with many diadems (19.11–12). The similarity was intentional. There was an ancient belief that the LORD sometimes punished his people by sending them false prophets, and the false Messiah was one of them. 'A lying spirit' was put into their mouths and their false message was the punishment (1 Kgs 22.20–23). The second sign would be war and rumours of war (e.g. Mark 13.7) and the rider on the red horse was permitted to take peace from the earth. The third sign was famine, the rider on the black horse. In Matthew's version of the Synoptic Apocalypse, famine is the third devastation, but in Mark and Luke the third is earthquake and the fourth is famine. The fourth rider was death, whom Luke described as pestilence.

The fifth seal revealed the souls of the martyrs under the altar and corresponded in the Synoptic Apocalypse to Jesus' prediction of persecutions (Mark 13.9–13). No explanation of the persecution was offered, there was simply the call to endure (Mark 9.13). Since the soul was believed to be in the blood, the vision of the fifth seal was a vision of blood under the altar. On the Day of Atonement, the blood which remained after the ritual sprinkling was poured away under the great altar (*m. Yoma* 5.6), and in the vision, this blood has become the souls of the martyrs whose death has been part of the final Day of Atonement. Blood was believed to cry out for justice (Gen. 4.10), and Enoch described the souls of the victims of the fallen angels 'crying and making their suit to the gates of heaven' (*1 En.* 9.10). The cry of the martyrs under the altar: 'O Sovereign LORD, holy and true, how long before thou wilt judge and avenge our blood on those who dwell upon the earth?' (6.10) is exactly the same as in Enoch's account of the Day of Atonement in heaven. First, the Man ascends (*1 En.* 46), then the blood of the Righteous One is taken up to the throne (*1 En.* 47.1, cf. Dan 7.13; see p. 382), and finally the holy ones pray 'on behalf of the blood of the righteous which has been shed, that the prayer of the righteous may not be in vain before the LORD of Spirits, that judgement may be done for them and that they may not have to suffer for ever' (*1 En.* 47.2). The souls under the altar are told to wait a little longer as the number of martyrs is not yet complete, exactly as in *1 Enoch*.

In those days I saw the Head of Days when he seated himself upon the throne of his glory
And the books of the living were opened before him.
And all his host which is in heaven above and his counsellors stood before him,
And the hearts of the Holy were filled with joy,
Because the number of the righteous had been offered,
and the prayer of the righteous had been heard. (*1 En.* 47.3–4)

Once the number of martyrs was completed, the judgement could begin. The vision of the fifth seal implies knowledge of this idea. The number of souls under the altar was not yet complete, and the judgement could not begin. Whoever wrote this account of the fifth seal was in touch with the same traditions as appear in Daniel 7 and the Parables of Enoch.

The sixth seal brought the Day of the LORD, a time of supernatural catastrophes. The four horsemen had brought disasters on a human scale: war, famine and death, but the vision of the sixth seal was a time of cosmic upheaval: falling stars, vanishing skies and moving mountains. Such a Day had been described in the Hebrew Scriptures (see pp. 354–7). The prophet Joel had predicted first the gift of the Spirit on all flesh and then portents in heaven and on earth: 'The sun shall be turned to darkness and the moon to blood, before the great and terrible Day of the LORD comes' (Joel 2.31). Peter claimed that the Spirit had been given at Pentecost, fulfilling one element of the prophecy (Acts 2.15–21). He warned that the Day of the LORD was near; that the crucified Jesus had been exalted to heaven and made the LORD. In other words, the Lamb had been sacrificed and the events of the book set in motion. The crowd were convinced by the argument and said, ' "Brethren, what shall we do?" And Peter said to them, "Repent and be baptized" ...' (Acts 2.37–38). The seal of baptism would protect them from the imminent wrath, just as John the Baptist had taught (Matt. 3.1–12). A passage in the *Clementine Recognitions* shows how literally this was understood (or was believed to have been understood), in the first century CE: 'everyone who ... is baptized in his Name, shall be kept unhurt from the destruction of war which impends over the unbelieving nation, and the place itself [i.e. Jerusalem], but those who do not believe shall be made exiles from their place and kingdom ...' (*Clem. Rec.* 1.39).

Other details in the description of the sixth seal were drawn from Isaiah's picture: 'For the LORD of hosts has a day against all that is proud and lofty, against all that is lifted up and high ... And men shall enter the caves of the rocks and the holes of the ground, from before the terror of the LORD, and from the glory of his majesty when he rises to terrify the earth' (Isa. 2.12, 19). 'All the host of heaven shall rot away and the skies roll up like a scroll. All their host shall fall, as leaves fall from the vine, like leaves falling from the fig tree' (Isa. 34.4). The descriptions of the sixth seal are drawn from the Hebrew Scriptures, yet not quoted word for word. We have to imagine someone steeped in the language and imagery of the Scriptures who naturally draws on them to recount his own experiences. The Day brings the wrath of 'the one who sits on the throne and the Lamb'; these are not two but one, the LORD.

When Jesus was on his way to Calvary, many in the crowd were lamenting for him. He spoke to them, knowing that he was about to open the book of Jerusalem's future:

'Daughters of Jerusalem, do not weep for me, but weep for yourselves and for your children. For behold, the days are coming when they will say, "Blessed are the barren, and the wombs that never bore, and the breasts that never gave suck!" Then they will begin to say to the mountains, "Fall on us" and to the hills; "Cover us". For if they do this when the wood is green, what will happen when it is dry?' (Luke 23.28–31)

Luke puts into Jesus' mouth the words from the sixth seal vision. 'Fall on us, Cover us', an allusion to Hosea 10.8 but not a quotation, is found as a different paraphrase in Revelation 6.16: 'calling to the mountains and rocks, "Fall on us and hide us from the face of him who is seated on the throne and from the wrath of the Lamb" '.

Those who kept Jesus' prophecies recorded when they had been fulfilled. The addition to the prophecy of the third seal. 'A quart of wheat for a denarius and three quarts of barley for a denarius but do not harm the oil and the wine' are probably the oracle of the Christian prophet Agabus who predicted the great famine in the reign of Claudius (Acts 11.28). The enigmatic words 'Do not harm the oil and the wine' were probably rather different in the original. 'Harm' here translates the Greek *adikeo*, but in the LXX, words from this root are used to translate the Hebrew *'wl* which means 'to act unjustly or unrighteously' as in Psalm 58.3, Psalm 71.4 or Ezekiel 28.15. The original was probably 'Do not act unjustly in the matter of the oil and the wine'. Josephus records the original context:

When Claudius was emperor of the Romans and Ismael was our high priest, and when so great a famine was come upon us that one tenth of a measure of wheat was sold for four drachmae and when no less than seventy cori of flour were brought into the temple at the feast of unleavened bread ... not one of the priests was so hardy as to eat one crumb of it, even while so great a distress was upon the land; and this out of dread for the Law and of that wrath which God retains against acts of wickedness ... (*Ant.* 3.320–21)

'Do not act unjustly in the matter of the oil and the wine' was an exhortation to the priests to show similar restraint with regard to the other offerings brought to the temple. They were to act with righteousness. The great famine fulfilled the prophecy of the third seal.

The additions to the vision of the fifth seal could have been made after the persecution of the Jerusalem Christians when James bar Zebedee was killed and Herod 'laid violent hands on some who belonged to the church' (Acts 12.1–2). The souls under the altar, however, suggests another possibility. When James the Righteous was martyred in 62 CE, Eusebius records that he was stoned and clubbed to death in the temple court. The presence of James the Righteous was believed to protect Jerusalem from the wrath, and so his death left the city in danger as another seal was opened (see pp. 192–4). James was buried where he died, 'on the spot, by the holy of holies, and his headstone is still there by the holy of holies' (*History* 2.23). If James was interred at that spot, he was almost literally under the great altar, which stood in the court of the priests, by the holy of holies.

The vision of the sixth seal describes the time immediately before the Day of the LORD, and the great detail added to the time of the sixth seal in chapter 7 shows that the writer believed himself to be living in that time. The vision of the fifth and sixth trumpets in chapter 9 is similar insofar as it gives a detailed account of contemporary events, which the writer believed to be the days before the seventh trumpet. It was customary for the interpreters of prophecy to write in this way. Their own times were the most significant, and so contemporary events were set into the pattern of the last days. Daniel 8–12, for example, gives detailed predictions of the international situation which led to the Maccabean revolt in 166 BCE, thus indicating when the final version of Daniel was compiled. The vision of the sixth seal has been extended to the whole of chapter 7 since these were the last events before the LORD returned. The interpretation of the elder linked the sixth seal to Nero's persecution of the Christians in Rome and, since this prophecy was being fulfilled (those in white robes 'are coming' from the Great Tribulation) the time of the seventh seal and the return of the LORD was believed to be imminent. Note that it is an elder who gives the interpretation, in other words, John is at this point writing himself into the text. The declaration that the sixth seal was opened in 64–65 CE, confirmed by the interpretation of the fifth and sixth trumpets (see pp. 176–8), set the scene for the revolt against Rome. John, who made these interpretations, must have been a public figure of some importance.

Josephus records the fervour with which Palestine was waiting for the fulfilment of the prophecy of the seventh seal after the sounding of the seventh trumpet. In the Book of Revelation this appears as the loud voices in heaven proclaiming the establishment of the Messiah's Kingdom: 'The kingdom of the world has become the kingdom of our LORD and of his Christ and he shall reign for ever and ever' (11.15). In the Synoptic Apocalypse it is the coming of the Man in glory (Mark 13.26), which Jesus said was imminent: 'This generation will not pass away before all these things take place' (Mark 13.30). Josephus says that this expectation actually led to the revolt against Rome.

But what more than all else incited them to the war was an ambiguous oracle, likewise found in their sacred scriptures, to the effect that at that time one from their country would become ruler of the world. This they understood to mean someone of their own race and many of their wise men went astray in their interpretation of it. (*War* 6.312–13)

This oracle says Josephus, was *in their sacred scriptures*, which confirms that the earliest stratum of this part of the Book of Revelation was a holy book which has not survived elsewhere, but which the Christians (and probably others, too) were interpreting as prophecy. The oracle was known to Tacitus: 'The majority firmly believed that their ancient priestly writings contained the prophecy that this was the very time when the East would grow strong and that men starting from Judea would possess the world. This mysterious prophecy had in reality pointed to Vespasian and Titus ...' (*Histories* 5.13). It was also known to Suetonius: 'An ancient superstition was current in the East, that out of Judea at this time would come the ruler of the world. This prediction, as events later proved, referred to the Roman Emperor, but the rebellious Jews, who read it as referring to themselves, murdered their governor, routed the Governor of Syria when he came to restore order, and captured an Eagle' (*Vespasian* 4).

10

THE REDEEMED

After this I saw four angels standing at the four corners of the earth, holding back the four winds of the earth, that no wind might blow on earth or sea or against any tree. Then I saw another angel ascend from the rising of the sun, with the seal of the living God, and he called with a loud voice to the four angels who had been given power to harm earth and sea, saying, 'Do not harm the earth or the sea or the trees, till we have sealed the servants of our God upon their foreheads.' And I heard the number of the sealed, a hundred and forty-four thousand sealed, out of every tribe of the sons of Israel.

After this I looked and behold, a great multitude, which no man could number, from every nation, from all tribes and peoples and tongues, standing before the throne and before the Lamb, clothed in white robes, with palm branches in their hands, and crying with a loud voice, 'Salvation belongs to our God who sits upon the throne, and to the Lamb!' And all the angels stood round the throne and round the elders and the four living creatures, and they fell on their faces before the throne and worshipped God, saying, 'Amen! Blessing and glory and wisdom and thanks-giving and honour and power and might be to our God for ever and ever! Amen.' (Rev. 7.1–4 and 9–12)

When John the Baptist saw many Pharisees and Sadducees coming to him for baptism, he said: 'Who warned you to flee from the wrath to come?' (Matt. 3.7). When Peter spoke to the crowd of pilgrims in Jerusalem at Pentecost, and showed them that the events of the end time had begun, they asked, 'Brethren, what shall we do?' (Acts 2. 37). John the Baptist and Peter both offered the same protection: baptism. The redeemed of this vision are the baptized who have been protected from the imminent wrath. The multitude in white robes are Gentile Christians, but the thousands of Israel were originally those whom John the Baptist and others before him had prepared for the last times.

The Damascus Document tells of the remnant which held fast to the commandments of God, to whom were revealed 'the hidden things in which all Israel had gone astray' (CD III). This is very similar to the description of the children of the woman in 12.17; they 'kept the commandments of God and had the testimony of Jesus', i.e. guarded what Jesus had seen (c.f. the priests, p. 28). The remnant of the Damascus Document set themselves apart in the age of wrath, and the cryptic figures given, 390 years after Nebuchadnezzar had taken Jerusalem, suggest a time early in the second century BCE, when the temple was threatened by Antiochus Epiphanes and Jason, his puppet high priest. Loyal Jews were persecuted and killed, and the temple was desecrated, 'And very great wrath came upon Israel' (*1 Macc.* 1.64). The prophecies of Daniel addressed this situation, predicting Israel's ultimate triumph over monstrous foreign rulers and the Man ascending to take power over all nations (Dan. 7.14). The vision of Revelation 7.1–8 could have originated at that time, depicting the wrath from which the faithful of Israel would be saved. The martyrs from the Great Tribulation, the people of the saints of the Most High (Dan. 7.27), would stand in triumph before the enthroned Man.

In its present context, however, the visions of Revelation 7 are the visions of the sixth seal. When Jesus described the Day of the LORD, the sixth seal, he spoke first of cosmic catastrophes and then of the return of the Man who would send out his angels 'to gather his elect from the four winds, from one end of heaven to the other' (Matt. 24.31). This gathering of the elect is what we see in 7.9–17, people drawn from every nation who have come through the Great Tribulation.

The Seal of the Living God

The seer saw four angels restraining the four winds which were about to bring destruction. Enoch had learned about these winds from the angel Uriel; it was an aspect of heavenly knowledge. He saw the temple and its courts as a microcosm of the whole creation with the gates in its outer walls, three on each side, as gates in the horizon whence came the sun, the stars and the winds. Winds from north, south, east or west were winds of blessing and prosperity, but those which blew from points in between were hurtful winds: 'when they are sent, they bring destruction on all the earth and on the water upon it, and on all who dwell thereon, and on everything which is in the water and on the land' (1 En. 76.4). Enoch saw the destructive winds as four pairs; the seer of Revelation 7 sees only four, at the corners of the earth, but they are the same destructive winds, ready to harm the earth and the sea.

An angel who had the seal of the living God rose 'from the rising of the sun' (7.2). He had authority over the angels with power over the winds. From Matthew's account of gathering the elect (Matt. 24.31), we can deduce that the one who commanded the angels of the wind was the Man, the LORD. Other details confirm this: he rises in the east, as does the Glory of the LORD in Ezekiel's vision of the LORD returning to the temple: 'Afterward he [the angel guide] brought me to the gate, the gate facing east. And behold, the glory of the God of Israel came from the east; and the sound of his coming was like the sound of many waters; and the earth shone with his glory' (Ezek. 43.1–2). Both the Therapeuts and the Essenes used to face east to pray as the sun rose. Philo said of the Therapeuts: 'At sunrise they pray for a fine bright day, fine and bright in the true sense of the heavenly daylight which they pray may fill their minds' (Contemplative Life 27), and Josephus wrote of the Essenes: 'Before the sun is up they utter no words on mundane matters but offer to him certain prayers which have been handed down from their forefathers as though entreating him to rise' (War 2.128). Sunrise prayers had been a feature of the first temple, albeit one which Ezekiel had condemned (Ezek. 8.16), and in the second temple, some continued to condemn them. During the celebration of Tabernacles, those processing through the eastern gate of the temple turned back towards the west and said: 'Our fathers when they were in this place turned ... and they worshipped the sun towards the east, but as for us our eyes are turned upon the LORD' (*m. Sukkah* 5.4). The third Sibyl, however, writing a eulogy of the Jews in the middle of the second century BCE, described them as 'a sacred race of pious men ... [who] at dawn lift up holy arms toward heaven, from their beds, always sanctifying their flesh with water ...' (*Sib.* 3.573, 591–92), and praying towards the rising sun seems to have been one of the ancient customs which distinguished the Essenes and the Therapeuts from their contemporaries. They were probably praying for the LORD to return to his temple, as in the time of Ezekiel, and this vision in 7.2–3 may be their sunrise ritual. (Praying towards the east was one of the secret traditions of the church, according to Basil of Caesarea (*On the Holy Spirit* 66). The reason for this practice, he said, had been transmitted orally from the apostles and never written down.)

In the Qumran texts, the angel of Israel is called the Prince of Light(s) (CD V, 1QM XIII) and there seems to be a hymn of the Prince of Lights in 1QH XII (formerly IV). This could easily have formed part of a sunrise service:

Thou hast illumined my face by the covenant ...
I seek Thee and sure as the dawn Thou appearest as [to me] ...
Thou hast revealed thyself to me in thy power as perfect light,
and thou hast not covered my face with shame.
All those who are gathered in the covenant enquire of me ...
Through me Thou hast illumined the face of the congregation ...

The Prince of Light was the Dawn Angel, an ancient name for the LORD. In Zechariah's temple vision, the Servant of the LORD is called *ṣemaḥ*, usually translated 'Branch' (Zech. 3.8). The word literally means 'something that springs up' and during the second temple period, the word acquired another meaning 'Dawn'. When the LXX was translated, the Servant's title here was thought to be 'My Servant, the Dawn' (also LXX Jer.23.5; Zech 6.12), the light who comes from the east (cf. Isa. 9.2). This is how it was understood in the first century CE, which explains the words attributed to the Baptist's father, another Zechariah: 'you will go before the LORD to prepare his ways ... the Dawn from on high shall visit us ... (Luke 1.76, 78, translated literally). When Luke wrote his Gospel, some time after the Book of Revelation had been compiled, he knew this as the song of a priest expecting his son to prepare the way for the Dawn, the LORD. In his ministry, John warned of the imminent wrath (Matt. 3.7) and predicted the coming of a mighty one, that is, the Mighty Angel of the Book of Revelation, who would baptize with Spirit and fire, and then begin the harvest of the Day of the LORD, gathering his wheat but 'burning the chaff with unquenchable fire' (Matt. 3.11–12). These appear in the Book of Revelation as the visions of the angel in the rising sun and the reaper on the cloud (14.14). The LORD seals his chosen ones with baptism to protect them from the judgement to come, and then he gathers his harvest.

The vision of the 144,000 sealed before the wrath must have been known to John the Baptist and his priestly family, and to the people in the wilderness with whom he grew up, probably the Qumran community (Luke 1.80). Although there is no record of how John baptized, it is usually imagined as a simple immersion in the Jordan. The vision of the sealing, however, suggests that he also made a sign on their foreheads. Only the number of the sealed is revealed, 144,000, and this was the inspiration for John's ministry of baptism. To the penitent he offered protection from the imminent wrath of judgement, as described in the Qumran Community Rule which he must have known: 'And when his flesh is sprinkled with purifying water and sanctified by cleansing water, it shall be made clean by the humble submission of his soul to all the precepts of God' (1QS III). Those who joined the community were promised '... healing, great peace in a long life, and fruitfulness, together with every everlasting blessing and eternal joy in life without end, a crown of glory and a garment of majesty in unending light' (1QS IV). These are recognizable as the original multitude of 7.9–12, before John the elder gave the new interpretation (7.13–17). Those who refused to repent would endure 'a multitude of plagues by the hand of all the destroying angels, everlasting damnation by the avenging wrath of the fury of God, eternal torment and endless disgrace together with shameful extinction in the fire of the dark regions' (1QS IV). These were the disasters brought by the six trumpets (8.7–9.21). John the Baptist warned of the wrath to come, when the chaff of the great harvest would be burned in unquenchable fire. Those sealed in Revelation 7 were spared the plagues brought by the angels with trumpets, and words attributed to Peter in the *Clementine Recognitions* show how literally this protection was understood: 'Every one who ... is baptized in his Name, shall be kept unhurt from the destruction of war which impends over the unbelieving nation and the place itself' (*Clem. Rec.* 1.39, see on 6.12–17).

The angel had the seal of the living God, which other sources reveal was the Name. This seal is described in Exodus 28.36 as an important element of the high priest's regalia: 'You shall make a plate of pure gold and you shall engrave on it the engravings of a sacred seal The LORD' (translating literally). The Dawn angel had, that is wore, the seal of the Name, which shows that he was vested as the high priest. He had power to delay the wrath until the chosen were safe, one of the functions of the high priest as can be seen from the stories of Aaron and Phineas holding back the plagues of wrath (Num. 16.41–50; 25.6–13). The Dawn Angel was the One whose way John the Baptist was preparing, the Angel of the Covenant who would appear in his temple (Mal. 3.1).

Ezekiel in the sixth century BCE had known a similar vision of sealing with the Name. The LORD took him on a spirit journey from Babylon to Jerusalem where he saw the angels of destruction summoned to the temple. First, an angel was sent to mark the faithful: 'Go through the city, through Jerusalem, and put a mark upon the foreheads of the men who groan and sigh over all the abominations that are committed in it' (Ezek. 9.4). The LORD then spoke to the other six angels: 'Pass through the city after him and smite; your eye shall not spare and you shall show no pity ... but touch no one upon whom is the mark. Begin at my sanctuary' (Ezek. 9.5–6). The mark on the forehead was protection against the wrath (see p. 155).

'Mark', however, conceals what that mark was. The Hebrew says that the angel marked the foreheads with the letter *tau*, the last letter of the Hebrew alphabet. In the ancient Hebrew script that Ezekiel would have used, this letter was a diagonal cross, and the significance of this becomes apparent from a much later tradition about the high priests. The rabbis remembered that the oil for anointing the high priest had been lost when the first temple was destroyed and that the high priests of the second temple were only 'priests of many garments', a reference to the eight garments worn on the Day of Atonement (*m. Horayoth* 3.4). The rabbis also remembered that the anointed high priests of the first temple had been anointed on the forehead with the sign of a diagonal cross (*b. Horayoth 12a*). This diagonal cross was the sign of the Name on their foreheads, the mark which Ezekiel described as a letter *tau*.

The mark of the Name was known to protect. When Aaron had to protect Israel from the wrath, according to a rewritten version of Numbers 16.47, it was 'the majesty on his diadem' that is, the Name, which was the protection (*Wisd.* 18.24–25). Targum says that the mark put on Cain was the Name: 'And the LORD sealed upon the face of Cain the mark of the Name great and honourable, that anyone who might find him should not kill him when he saw it upon him' (*T. Ps. Jon. Gen.* 4.15). The *Psalms of Solomon* knew that the mark of the LORD protected the righteous from very worldly disasters: 'God's mark is on the righteous for salvation. Famine and sword and death shall be far from them' (*Pss Sol.* 15.6–7). 'Ezra', however, seemed to question the value of sealing; everything was planned by the LORD from the beginning, before the world was created, and long before the present time of sin when some 'who stored up treasures of faith were sealed' (*2 Esdr.* 6.5). The community described in the Damascus Document were expecting the wrath to come at any time, but they expected to be safe and may themselves have used the mark (perhaps in their sunrise prayers?):

The humble of the flock are those who watch for Him. They shall be saved at the time of the Visitation, whereas others shall be delivered up to the sword when the Anointed of Aaron and Israel shall come, as it came to pass in the time of the former Visitation concerning which God said by the hand of Ezekiel: They shall put a mark on the foreheads of those who sigh and groan. But the others were delivered up to the avenging sword of the Covenant. (CD VII, Ms B)

Clearest of all is the second vision of the 144,000 in Revelation 14: 'Then I looked, and lo, on Mount Zion stood the Lamb, and with him a hundred and forty-four thousand who had his name and his father's name written on their foreheads' (14.1). The mark on the forehead, the seal, was the Name which the Lamb received from his father, that is, the mark of the high priest. It was the new name promised to the angel of the church in Philadelphia: 'I will write on him the name of my God and the name of the city of my God ... and my own new name' (3.12). It was also the original sign of the cross used in Christian baptism. Thus the servants of the Lamb, who bear his name on their foreheads, are the royal priesthood, the baptized. They stand before him in the heavenly sanctuary and worship him on his throne, as did Isaiah. They see his face (22.3–4, see p. 335).

Every Tribe of the Sons of Israel

In Exodus 23.14–17, which is Israel's oldest lawcode, it is written that all males should appear before the LORD three times a year. There were three pilgrimage feasts: unleavened bread, harvest and ingathering. Over the centuries, these developed into Passover, Weeks and the group of autumn festivals: New Year, Day of Atonement and Tabernacles. In the first century CE the pilgrimage festivals were the occasion for huge crowds to converge on Jerusalem. It was the crowds at Passover which made the city authorities wary of arresting Jesus (Mark 14.1–2), and there were crowds seven weeks later at Pentecost when Peter spoke 'to devout men from every nation under heaven' (Acts 2.5).

The vision of 7.4–8 may have been inspired by one of these pilgrimage festivals. There had not been twelve tribes as such since the Assyrian deportations from the northern kingdom in the eighth century BCE, but the return of the twelve tribes and the restoration of the great assemblies became part of the national hope. There are several passages in Isaiah which testify to this; some may be as old as the original Isaiah in eighth-century Jerusalem, who had seen the deportation of the northern tribes; others were probably additions made by later scribes, showing that the hope for the ingathering did not fade with the passing of time. 'In that day, the LORD will extend his hand yet a second time to recover the remnant which is left of his people, from Assyria, from Egypt, from Pathros, from Ethiopia, from Elam, from Shinar, from Hamath, and from the coastlands of the sea' (Isa. 11.11); 'In that day a great trumpet will be blown, and those who were lost in the land of Assyria and those who were driven out to the land of Egypt will come and worship the LORD on the holy mountain at Jerusalem', (Isa. 27.13). The ingathering of the tribes had become part of the hope for the great Day of Atonement and the last Jubilee. 'That day' was the Day of the LORD (see p. 354). As a temple festival, the Day of Atonement had originally been the occasion for restoring to the community all the penitent sinners of Israel; both the people and the created order were renewed for the new year by the blood which the high priest sprinkled. When the people were dispersed through war and deportation, this scattering was seen as punishment for sin, and the return they longed for came to be seen as the great Day of Atonement and Jubilee, when the sin was atoned and the dispersed people brought back.

The royal high priest, the Servant, had performed the original rite of atonement and ingathering in the temple. When the Second Isaiah reinterpreted the role for the new situation of the exile, he said the Servant would bring back the tribes who had been dispersed throughout the nations. The white robes and palms of the great multitude (7.9), are probably the twelve tribes assembled for the Feast of Tabernacles after the great Day of Atonement.

And now the LORD says, who formed me from the womb to be his servant
to bring Jacob back to him, and that Israel might be gathered to him,
for I am honoured in the eyes of the LORD, and my God has become my strength –
he says: 'Is is too light a thing that you should be my servant, to raise up the tribes of Jacob and to restore the preserved of Israel;
I will give you as a light to the nations,
that my salvation may reach to the end of the earth.' (Isa. 49.5–6)

The Isaiah Targum even interprets the fourth Servant Song in this way, the passage which was so crucial for Jesus' self-understanding.

All we like sheep have been scattered; we have gone into exile, every one his own way; and before the LORD it was a pleasure to forgive the sins of us all for his sake ... From bonds and retribution he will bring our exiles near; the wonders which will be done for us in his days, who will be able to recount? ... Yet before the LORD it was a pleasure to refine and cleanse the remnant of his people, in order to purify their soul from sins: they shall see the kingdom of their Messiah ... they see the retribution of their adversaries. (T. Isa. 53.6, 8, 10, 11)

The Servant was expected to restore the twelve tribes. Zechariah's last prophecy describes the pilgrimage of the survivors of the nations, to keep the Feast of Tabernacles in Jerusalem (Zech. 14.16). These appear in the Book of Revelation as the survivors from the Great Tribulation in Rome, celebrating with their white robes and palm branches the end of the great harvest of the judgement. 'On that Day', said Zechariah, there would be continuous light, no longer night and day, living waters would flow from Jerusalem and there would be plagues on all who fought against her. This is the vision of Revelation 22: the river of life, no more night, and the servants of the Lamb standing before him (see pp. 333–7). John's account of Jesus cleansing the temple (John 2.14–16) makes a clear link to the enigmatic final verse of this chapter: 'There shall no longer be a trader in the house of the LORD on that day'. When Jesus drove the traders from the temple, he was beginning to bring back the remnant for Tabernacles.

John also records the remarks of Caiaphas the high priest, when the chief priests and Pharisees were plotting to kill Jesus. With an unmistakable allusion to the Servant, and doubtless to Jesus' own claim to be the Servant, he says to the Council: 'You do not understand that it is expedient for you that one man should die for the people, and that the whole nation should not perish'. John emphasizes the role of the Servant by adding: 'He did not say this of his own accord, but being high priest that year he prophesied that Jesus should die for the nation, and not for the nation only, but to gather into one the children of God who are scattered abroad' (John 11.49–52). (How could John have known what was said unless he had contacts in the high priest's household?) John's Jesus also spoke of other sheep for whom he would die: 'And I have other sheep, that are not of this fold; I must bring them also, and they will heed my voice. So there shall be one flock, one shepherd. For this reason the Father loves me, because I lay down my life, that I may take it again' (John 10.16–17). The other Gospel writers attribute similar sayings to Jesus: 'Go to the lost sheep of the house of Israel', he said to his disciples as he sent them out (Matt. 10.6); 'O Jerusalem ... how often would I have gathered your children together as a hen gathers her brood under her wings ...' (Luke 13.34). Jesus spoke of the great ingathering: 'I tell you, many will come from east and west and sit at table with Abraham, Isaac and Jacob in the kingdom of heaven, while the sons of the kingdom will be thrown into outer darkness' (Matt. 8.11); 'You who have followed me will also sit in twelve thrones, judging the twelve tribes of Israel' (Matt. 19.28).

In 'Ezra's' vision, the Man rising from the sea defeats his enemies with a stream of fire from his mouth and then calls to himself a peaceable multitude (2 Esdr. 13.3–13). The interpretation of the vision is that the multitude is the ten lost tribes dispersed even beyond Assyria, their original place of exile, and the Man would bring them home again (2 Esdr. 13.39–50). Such a home-coming is implicit in the vision in Revelation 7, where 12,000 are sealed from each of the tribes. The numbers are symbolic; even the list of the tribes is without parallel elsewhere since both Manasseh and Joseph are listed (Manasseh was a part of Joseph), and Dan is not mentioned. What is important is that this is the triumph of the Servant who has rescued a remnant from each of the tribes.

The Multitude in White Robes

Having seen the twelve tribes, 12,000 from each, the seer now speaks of a great multitude which no man can number, from every nation, from all tribes and peoples and tongues. These are clearly intended to be a group distinct from the celibates. A new interpretation of traditional material is being given, indicated by the conversation with the elder, who tells the seer who these people are. This is John, writing himself into the text and offering his interpretation of the vision that they are the martyrs in Rome, coming from the Great Tribulation.

When Daniel was reinterpreting traditional material for his contemporary situation, the new teaching was put into the mouth of an angel:

'I approached one of those stood there [one of the angels] and asked him the truth concerning all this. So he told me and made known to me the interpretation of the things' (Dan. 7.16). Daniel is then told the true meaning of the four beasts from the sea and how the saints of the Most High will triumph. The interpretation of prophecies in this way was recognized as a prophetic gift in itself; the Teacher of Righteousness, for example, was the one to whom God made known 'all the mysteries of the words of his servants the prophets' (1QpHab VII). In a Qumran commentary, the elder's words in Revelation 7.14–17 would have appeared as 'Interpreted, this means those who come out of the Great Tribulation'.

The multitude in white robes had originally been the crowd who came to celebrate the festivals in Jerusalem. Here they are holding branches, as prescribed in Leviticus 23.40, and must have been in the temple at the Feast of Tabernacles, five days after the Day of Atonement when the blood had been sprinkled and the covenant renewed. They sing 'Salvation belongs to our God who sits on the throne and to the Lamb' (7.10), probably a free rendering of the Tabernacles psalm *Hosanna* [Save us], 'O LORD, O LORD we beseech thee, give us victory. Blessed is he who comes with the Name of the LORD' (Ps. 118.25–26; 'Salvation', *hyšw'h* and 'Save us', *hyšw'h* look very similar in Hebrew). The Mishnah describes the festival in the first century CE. People went in procession to the temple carrying bunches of myrtle, willow and palm, and as they walked round the great altar, they sang Psalm 118. When they reached 'Hosanna, O LORD', they waved the branches, exactly as described in 7.9–10 (*m. Sukkah* 3.4, 9; 4.5).

John indicated in two ways his interpretation of the crowd with palms. As an elder in the vision he declares them to be the martyrs outside Jerusalem, brought into the city as the sixth seal opens to prepare for the coming of the LORD to Jerusalem. In the Fourth Gospel, when he tells the story of Palm Sunday, he says that the disciples later 'remembered' the significance of a crowd with palms coming into the city and bringing with them the king. John is the only evangelist to say that the people of Jerusalem 'went out to meet' those who came with the king to his city. They waved palms and sang the Tabernacles psalm, 'Hosanna' (John 12.12–16, see p. 189).

In the prophetic writings there are many passages which envisage such a gathering on the Day of the LORD, the final great festival when the land was renewed and the reign of the LORD established. The passages begin 'On that Day'. Zechariah described the great Feast of Tabernacles (Zech. 14.19) and some passages in Isaiah must have been the immediate inspiration for the visions in the Book of Revelation.

On that day the branch of the LORD shall be beautiful and glorious, and the fruit of the land shall be the pride and glory of the survivors of Israel. And he who is left in Zion and remains in Jerusalem will be called holy, every one who has been recorded for life in Jerusalem, when the LORD shall have washed away the filth of the daughters of Zion and cleansed the bloodstains of Jerusalem from its midst by a spirit of judgement and by a spirit of burning. Then the LORD will create over the whole site of Mount Zion and over her assemblies a cloud by day, and smoke and the shining of a flaming fire by night; for over all the glory there will be a canopy and a pavilion. It will be for a shade by day from the heat, and for a refuge and a shelter from the storm and rain. (Isa. 4.2–6)

[On that Day] He will swallow up death for ever, and the LORD God will wipe away tears from all faces, and the reproach of his people he will take away from all the earth; for the LORD has spoken. It will be said on that Day, 'Lo, this is our God; we have waited for him that he might save us. This is the LORD; we have waited for him, let us be glad and rejoice in his salvation'. (Isa 25.8–9)

I am coming to gather all nations and tongues; and they shall come and see my glory ... And some of them also I shall take for priests and for Levites, says the LORD. (Isa. 66.18, 21, see p. 336)

The Essenes regarded their white linen clothes as holy vestments and wore them only for their solemn assemblies (War 2.123, 129). Since white linen was the dress of angels (Luke 24.4, 23), and the Qumran community regarded themselves as angels on earth, their white-clad assemblies were probably assemblies of angels. The Hebrew Christians had a similar practice; they looked forward to the heavenly Jerusalem and to 'innumerable angels in festal gathering' (that is the community of the resurrected) at a time when Jesus, the high priest and mediator of the new covenant, had sprinkled the blood (Heb. 12.22–24). This would be the assembly of the firstborn, the redeemed at Tabernacles (see on 14.4).

The seer of 7.9–17 sees the expected assembly of the last days, every nation, tribe, people and tongue. The multitude in white robes, we learn from the new interpretation of the vision, are those who 'are coming' (note that this is the present tense) out of the Great Tribulation; they are the Christians in Rome, enduring persecution under Nero after the great fire of Rome in July 64 CE. A Great Tribulation had been predicted by Daniel, when many would purify themselves and become white and be refined (with fire, Dan. 12.10). Tacitus described what happened in Rome. 'Covered with the skins of beasts they were torn by dogs and perished, or were nailed to crosses, or were doomed to the flames. These served to illuminate the night when daylight failed' (Annals 15.44.6). John the elder explains this tribulation as the opening of the sixth seal, implying that the seventh, the return of the LORD, is imminent. A few months later, in August 66 CE, the records of debt were burned in the temple to inaugurate the tenth Jubilee and the final war against Rome began (War 2.425).

'They have washed their robes and made them white in the blood of the Lamb', said the elder, and here the symbolism of the visionaries is at its most opaque. When the Lamb took the book, the living creatures and the elders sang a new song, proclaiming that he had made every tribe and tongue and people and nation into a royal priesthood by his blood. The churches of Asia had been reminded that Jesus had freed/washed them from their sins by his blood and made them also into a royal priesthood (1.5–6). The multitude in white robes, from 'every nation, tribe, people and tongue', standing before the throne of God and serving day and night in the temple, are that royal priesthood. The blood of the Lamb has made their robes white; in other words, they have been given the white garments of the priests in the sanctuary, the garments of glory, the resurrection body. The blood sprinkled on the Day of Atonement cleansed and consecrated (Lev. 16.19) and so the blood made their robes into garments of priesthood, garments of glory. By their death the martyrs have also made the high priestly sacrifice and are part of the Great Atonement. This is the picture of the millennium kingdom (20.4–6). The kingdom of priests consists of those on the thrones and also – a clear addition to the text – the resurrected martyrs (see p. 341).

The One on the throne shelters them with his presence, literally 'tabernacles over them', as in Ezekiel 37.27, where the Hebrew has 'my tabernacle shall be over them'. The reference here in Revelation 7.15 is to Isaiah's picture of the assembly before the Branch of the LORD on that day: 'For over all the glory there will be a canopy and a pavilion. It will be for a shade by day from the heat, and for a refuge and a shelter from the storm and rain' (Isa. 4.5–6). Their blessed state in the kingdom is also described in lines drawn from Isaiah. The words used are not from the LXX but a free rendering from the Hebrew where Isaiah describes the work of the Servant, releasing prisoners and bringing back exiles: 'They shall not hunger or thirst, neither scorching wind nor sun shall smite them, for he who has pity on them will lead them and by springs of water will guide them' (Isa. 49.10). The corresponding piece in Revelation 7.16–17 has 'heat', rather than 'hot wind', and 'shepherd them' rather than 'lead them'. The major difference is that 'he who has pity on them' has become 'the Lamb' and he leads them not 'by' but 'to' springs of living water, a reference to the fountains of wisdom by the throne from which the thirsty would drink after the blood of the Righteous One had been offered (1 En. 48.1, cf. Rev. 21.6; 22.17).

The account of this vision was written by someone steeped in the Hebrew Scriptures, not quoting verbatim, but drawing on the parallel traditions preserved in 1 Enoch and then adapting and interpreting for the events of 65 CE. The source texts used are not chosen at random; they are all descriptions of the Day of the great assembly, when Israel would be gathered in by the LORD, *and they are all drawn from Isaiah*. Both the original visions could have been known to Jesus; he certainly spoke of gathering in the lost of Israel as this was the role of the Servant (Isa. 49.6), but it was John, the beloved disciple, who had to make this known (1.1).

11

THE SEVEN TRUMPETS

When the Lamb opened the seventh seal, there was silence in heaven for about half an hour. Then I saw the seven angels who stand before God, and seven trumpets were given to them. And another angel came and stood at the altar with a golden censer; and he was given much incense to mingle with the prayers of the saints upon the golden altar before the throne; and the smoke of the incense rose with the prayers of the saints from the hand of the angel before God. Then the angel took the censer and filled it with fire from the altar and threw it on the earth; and there were peals of thunder, voices, flashes of lightning and an earthquake. Now the seven angels who had the seven trumpets made ready to blow them. (Rev. 8.1–6)

Jesus predicted the fall of the temple during the lifetime of his disciples and told them of the signs that would precede the disaster. Mark 13 (with parallels in Matt. 24 and Luke 21) summarizes the portents of the seals and shows that the seventh seal corresponds to the Son of Man coming in clouds with great glory (Mark 13.26). In the temple ritual which corresponded to its mythology, the incense which accompanied the high priest into the holy of holies was the clouds on which the Man entered heaven. As the seventh seal is opened, the incense is prepared to form the clouds of heaven with which the high priest will emerge from the holy of holies. The trumpets announce the great Jubilee (Lev. 25.9) and the high priest eventually appears in 10.1 as the Mighty Angel wrapped in a cloud who comes down from heaven to earth (cf. 1.7).

Silence in Heaven

There is silence as the LORD prepares to emerge from his holy place. In the temple, this may well have been a silence as the people waited for the high priest to emerge safely from the holy of holies, actualizing in ritual what the Hebrew Scriptures describe; the whole earth silent as the LORD comes forth from his holy place. When Zephaniah warned that the Day of the LORD was at hand he commanded: 'Be silent before the Lord GOD' (Zeph. 1.7). Habakkuk took his stand on the tower, in the holy of holies, and waited for the LORD to emerge. 'The LORD is in his holy temple, let all the earth keep silence before him' (Hab. 2.20). What follows is a description of the Holy One as he came from Mount Paran with his heavenly host of plague and pestilence, measuring the earth (which must mean 'preparing it for destruction', see pp. 187–8) and shaking the nations. The mountains were scattered, the waters surged, and the sun and moon stood still. Zechariah described the consecration of the high priest Joshua (in Hebrew Joshua and Jesus are the same name), when the LORD vested him in the holy of holies. Immediately before this description of the vesting there was the command: 'Be silent, all flesh, before the LORD; for he has roused himself from his holy dwelling' (Zech. 2.13–3.5). In other words, vesting the high priest took place in the silence before the LORD emerged from his holy place, and this was the silence in heaven as the seventh seal was opened. The angel high priest was about to appear on earth.

The Targum to Ezekiel 1.24–25 describes the moment of silence as the chariot throne comes to rest and the Man is about to appear: 'When they stood still, their wings became silent. And at such a time, when it was his will to make the Dibbur* audible to his servants the prophets of Israel, there was voice which was heard from above the firmament which was above their heads. When they stood still, their wings became silent before the Dibbur'.

The Angel with the Incense

The angel who receives the incense is the high priest. 'To fill the hands with incense' was the Hebrew idiom for 'ordaining a priest' and here, it is the Mighty Angel who is receiving the high priesthood before emerging from the holy of holies. This is one of the places in the Book of Revelation where the original text had *'ḥr,* 'afterwards' and this was mistaken for the identical form *'ḥr,* 'another'. The angel with the incense is not 'another' angel but the Lamb himself, the Mighty Angel, who has been enthroned as the LORD and now prepares to emerge from heaven. The *Song of Moses,* a text so important that some men wore it in their phylacteries (4QphylN), describes how the LORD would emerge to atone the land and take vengeance on those who had killed his sons (Deut. 32.43). An expansion of this text in the *Assumption of Moses* shows how it was understood in the first century CE, and this passage is the key to understanding the sequence of the seven trumpets, not because the sequence of the trumpets is directly modelled on it, but because both depend on a common source, perhaps a temple ritual.

And then his kingdom shall appear throughout all his creation
And the devil shall be no more
And sorrow shall depart with him.
The hands of the angel shall be filled
who has been appointed chief
And he shall forthwith avenge them of their enemies
For the heavenly one will arise from his royal throne
And he will go forth from his holy habitation
With indignation and wrath on account of his sons. (*Ass. Mos.* 10.1–3)

The surviving text in Latin is a translation from the Greek which was in turn translated from Hebrew or Aramaic, to judge from some over-literal and unidiomatic phrases. In such a process of transmission, nuances may have been lost but the gist is clear. The preceding chapter

*Dibbur means Word.

of the *Assumption* describes a certain Taxo who exhorts his seven sons to die with him rather than break the commandments of the LORD, so the context of this passage is persecution and martyrdom. First, the kingdom appears and the devil departs, (literally 'is led away') a reference to the scapegoat being led away on the Day of Atonement, i.e. the banishment of Azazel. The angel who has been appointed chief is then made a priest ('his hands are filled with incense') and he prepares to take vengeance on the enemies of his martyrs. He rises (this word is missing in the text) from his throne and prepares to leave his holy dwelling. This is what is described in 8.3. The Lamb has been enthroned throughout the opening of the seals and now he moves to the golden incense altar to receive the incense of priesthood which he offers with the prayers of the saints. He then takes burning coals from the incense altar and throws them onto the earth (cf. Isa. 6.6–7, Isaiah's vision of the throne, where one of the angels takes a coal from the incense altar to purify the prophet's speech and Ezek. 10.2 where one of the angels is told to take burning coals from before the chariot throne and cast them over Jerusalem). The thunder, voices, lightning and earthquake (8.5) are signs that a theophany is imminent, as in 11.19, where the Queen of Heaven is about to emerge from the sanctuary, or 16.17 where the seventh angel, the LORD, brings the final judgement (see pp. 274–5).

The Seven Trumpets

The seven trumpets and their disasters prepare the earth for the advent of the Mighty Angel, the heavenly high priest. He eventually emerges in 10.1 wrapped in a cloud of incense, coming down from heaven to earth. In other words, the high priest emerges from the holy of holies into the great hall of the temple, 'Behold, he is coming with clouds' (1.7). His halo is a rainbow, the light of Day One being made visible in the material world. The rainbow was the sign of the eternal covenant (Gen. 9.16) and the emerging high priest was the Angel of the Covenant (Mal. 3.1) who was to appear in the temple to bring judgement on both priests and people. The seven angels who announce his coming are probably 'the seven ruling Princes of the sanctuary ... the angels of the king' whose role in the heavenly temple is described in the Qumran Songs for the Sabbath Sacrifices (e.g. 4Q403).

The trumpets announce the Jubilee, the fiftieth year which was the year of release (Lev. 25.10). The Melchizedek text (11QMelch), which also describes the coming of the heavenly high priest, shows the expectations of the time. He would appear at the end of the tenth Jubilee to perform the final atonement sacrifice, rescue his own from the power of Belial and take his place in the heavenly council to begin the great judgement, as does the Lamb in 5.6–14. Only part of the Melchizedek text has survived, and so we cannot know what, or how much, has been lost. The surviving text begins with a fragmented reference to the Jubilee and the remission of debt: 'each of you shall return to his property'

(Lev. 25.13) and 'every creditor shall release what he has lent to his neighbour' (Deut. 15.2), and it breaks off quoting the commandment to send out the trumpet (*shofar*, the ram's horn) on the tenth day of the seventh month, the Day of Atonement (Lev. 25.9). Given the concerns of the Zealots, namely a pure high priesthood and freedom from bondage to Rome, the hope for the Jubilee must have been crucial to the nationalist movements in first-century Judea. Josephus records an incident at the start of the war against Rome. The Sicarii joined forces with the rebels in Jerusalem and overcame the pro-Roman rulers: 'The victors burst in and set fire to the house of Ananias the high priest and the palaces of Agrippa and Bernice; they next carried their combustibles to the public archives, eager to destroy the money-lenders' bonds and to prevent the recovery of debts ...' (*War* 2.426–27). The rebels were bringing the Jubilee, proclaiming the release which would bring the great Day of Atonement as described in the Book of Revelation, with the seven trumpets announcing the appearance of the heavenly high priest, the Angel of the Covenant.

The trumpets were also the signal for holy war. Phineas, the grandson of Eliezar who became the inspiration for the Zealots because he destroyed those who broke the covenant (Num. 25.6–13), went out to war against the kings of Midian and Balaam the false prophet (Num. 31.1–12). He took with him one thousand men from each of the twelve tribes and also 'the vessels of the holy of holies and the trumpets for the alarm' (*ḥᵃṣoṣrot*, metal trumpets). These trumpets and sacred vessels which accompanied the army in holy war appear in the Book of Revelation as the seven trumpets and the seven bowls, although we can only guess how the sacred vessels were used. There may have been a ritual libation before battle began, perhaps the cursing of the enemy. Oracles against the enemies of Israel, which presumably would have been used in preparation for battle against them, were described at that time as 'a cup of cursing'. In the Isaiah Targum, for example, the original phrase 'The oracle concerning ***' became 'The cup of cursing to give to ***' (*Babylon, T. Isa.* 13.1; *Moab, T. Isa.* 15.1; *Damascus, T. Isa.* 17.1; *Egypt, T. Isa.* 19.1). The Targum's description of the curse as a cup probably indicates how a curse was cast.

The seven trumpets also appear in the account of the battle of Jericho, where seven priests walked ahead of the ark, blowing trumpets (rams' horns, Josh. 6.4). There are trumpeters in the War Scroll, seven priests of the sons of Aaron and also seven Levites 'clothed in vestments of white cloth of flax, in a fine linen tunic and fine linen breeches and they shall be girdled with a fine cloth of flax embroidered with blue, purple and scarlet thread ... and on their heads they shall wear mitred turbans' (1QM VII). These are the normal vestments for a priest, the 'coats, girdles, caps and breeches' mentioned in Exodus 28.40–42. The priests in the War Scroll carry trumpets: 'The first priests shall advance before the men of the formation to strengthen their hand for battle, and the six other priests shall hold in their hands the trumpets ... seven Levites shall accompany them bearing in their hands seven rams' horns (1QM VII). Since the LXX uses the same Greek word, *salpinx,* for both the ram's horn and the metal trumpet, and this is the word used in 8.2, it is not possible to know which type of trumpets the seven angels were blowing.

The War Scroll sets out a plan for forty years of war, with details of which campaigns would be fought in which year and how the army was to be recruited and trained (1QM II). The Sounding of the Seven Trumpets was originally a similar history of Roman rule in Palestine which has been incorporated into the Book of Revelation. Brief symbolic histories such as these are characteristic of the apocalypses. In *1 Enoch*, for example, the history of Israel is told as a series of weeks, the Apocalypse of Weeks (*1 En.* 93), with the temple being destroyed by the Babylonians in the sixth week and restored in the seventh. Here, the history of Rome's involvement in Palestine is punctuated by the trumpets but shaped by the tradition which appears also in the *Assumption of Moses*:

And the earth shall tremble, to its confines shall it be shaken,
And the high mountains shall be made low
And the hills shall be shaken and fall
And the horns of the sun shall be broken and turned into darkness,
And the moon shall not give her light and be turned wholly to blood
And the circle of the stars shall be disturbed
And the sea shall retire into the abyss,
And the fountains of waters shall fail and the rivers shall dry up. (*Ass. Mos.* 10.4–6)

Similar, but not identical, phenomena follow the first four trumpets and the first four bowls of wrath. The trumpets destroy the earth (8.7), the sea (8.9), the rivers and fountains (8.10) and the heavens (8.12). The bowls of wrath afflict the earth (16.2), the sea (16.3), the rivers and fountains (16.4) and the heavens (16.8). In the *Assumption* the earth trembles, the heavens turn to darkness, the sea withdraws to the abyss and the rivers and fountains fail. The angel who extols the creator in 14.7 cries out: 'Worship him who made heaven and earth, the sea and the fountains of water'. These three examples of the same quartet, earth and heaven, sea and fountains, describing both the power of the creator and the process by which the creation is to be destroyed, must have originated in a common source (see on 14.7, p. 248).

Tacitus summarized the Roman involvement in Palestine which eventually led to the revolt: 'The first Roman to subdue the Jews and set foot in their temple by right of conquest was Gnaeus Pompey ... The walls of Jerusalem were razed but the temple was left standing' (Tacitus, *Histories* 5.9). Josephus gives more detail: the walls were attacked first with stones, using engines which Pompey had brought from Tyre, the people in the city tried to defend the breaches in the walls by setting fire to adjacent buildings, and finally there was a great slaughter in which 12,000 Jews were killed (*War* 1.147–51). Pompey then entered the temple, something which only the high priest was allowed to do. Since the temple was a microcosm of the creation, the whole creation was defiled by his presence. The stones, the fire and the slaughter of Pompey's attack became 'hail and fire mixed with blood' which fell upon the earth as the first trumpet sounded, and as he defiled the temple and the creation was polluted, 'the earth and the trees and the green grass were burnt up'. It is odd that only one third of the earth and the trees were destroyed, but all the grass. The Hebrew letters *šlš*, 'one third', can, however, have another meaning. In the original of this passage they were probably the rare word found in Isaiah 40.12 and Psalm 80.5, the only occurrences in the Hebrew Scriptures. In Isaiah it means 'a measure', but in the Psalm it means 'in full measure': 'Thou hast given them tears to drink in full measure'. 'In full measure' is how the word should be understood in 8.7, giving: 'The whole of the earth was burnt up, and all the trees were burnt up and all of the grass'. The first trumpet was the coming of Pompey in 63 BCE.

Tacitus continued: 'Later, in the time of our civil wars, these eastern provinces fell into the hands of Mark Antony . . . [who] gave the throne to Herod'. Mark Antony lost his power at the decisive naval battle of Actium in 31 BCE, and control of the Roman world passed into the hands of Octavian who became the Emperor Augustus. Josephus records that about the time of the battle of Actium there was an earthquake in Palestine (*War* 1.370). When the second trumpet sounded a great mountain burning with fire was thrown into the sea. The fall of a great mountain indicates the fall of a ruler; Jeremiah, for example, described the fall of Babylon as the fall of a burning mountain (Jer. 51.25). The fall of Mark Antony was a great mountain falling into the sea, and there was a naval battle in which the ships were destroyed and the sea became blood and the living creatures (perhaps human beings) died in the sea.

Rome then ruled Palestine through Herod the Great who was remembered by both Jews and Christians as a tyrant. Josephus describes him 'as a man of great barbarity towards all men equally and a slave to his passions' (*Ant.* 17.191). His son Antipater tried to kill him with poison (*Ant.* 17.69) but he eventually died a dreadful death, a punishment, it was said, for his impiety. His doctors prescribed taking the waters on the eastern side of the Jordan, at Callirrhoe where there were warm baths (*Ant.* 17.171). Herod had also built a residence at Machaerus east of the Jordan where there were hot springs, some of them bitter (*War* 7.186). Herod's attempt to find relief from his illness in this way was noted by the author of *1 Enoch*, and this association of ideas is important for understanding the history of the trumpets, both here and later. The fallen angels were believed to be imprisoned under the rift valley, and the warm springs, where Herod sought relief from his afflictions, were heated by the subterranean fire which was burning the angels. Jesus spoke of the eternal fire prepared for the devil and his angels (Matt. 25.41) and the Parables of Enoch make this cryptic reference to the fate of evil kings: 'Those [warm] waters shall become in those days a poisonous drug of the body and a punishment of the spirit unto the kings ... Lust shall fill their souls so that their bodies shall be punished ... These waters of judgement are poison to the bodies of the kings' (*1 En.* 67.8–13). The death of Herod in 4 BCE was announced by the third trumpet as a great star falling from heaven, just as Isaiah had described the fall of the king of Babylon (Isa. 14.12–20). The name of the star was Wormwood, the proverbial name for poisoned justice. Amos had said 'You turn justice to wormwood and cast down right-eousness to the earth' (Amos 5.7, also 6.12), and Jeremiah had warned that the LORD would give wormwood and poisonous water to those who deserted his Law (Jer. 9.14, also 23.15). The reign of Herod had in itself been part of the LORD's punishment for those who abandoned his commandments, and so the blazing star Wormwood fell into the waters and made them bitter and many men died.

When the fourth trumpet sounded, the sun, moon and stars were darkened, as in the *Assumption of Moses* 10.5, and then an eagle flew in the mid-heaven, warning of the woes which the other three trumpets would bring. This corresponds to the next section of the *Assumption*. There is reference to an eagle and then to the fate of Israel's enemies:

Then you will be happy, O Israel,
And you will mount above the neck and wings of an eagle,
And all things will be fulfilled
And God will raise you to the heights
Yea, he will fix you firmly in the heaven of the stars,
in the place of their habitations,
And you will behold from on high
Yea you will see your enemies on the earth. (*Ass. Mos.* 10.8–10)

Josephus records an incident with an eagle which marked a further decline in the relationship between Judea and Rome. When it became known that Herod was dying, two great teachers of the Law named Judas and Matthias incited their students 'to pull down all those works which the king had erected contrary to the law of their fathers'. Their first act was to destroy the huge golden eagle which Herod had placed over the main gate of the temple. They pulled it down in the middle of the day and cut it in pieces with axes (*Ant.* 17.155). The seer heard this eagle flying up from the temple into the mid-heaven, warning of the woes to come. It was the fate of the eagle, an obvious symbol for Rome, which brought the next disasters to Judea. The dying Herod ordered the ringleaders to be burnt alive, and that very night there was an eclipse of the moon (*Ant.* 17.167). Such was the grief and anger at the death of those who had destroyed the eagle that Archelaus, Herod's heir in Judea, had to send a regiment to Jerusalem to control the crowds during Passover. This made matters worse, and the whole army was then sent into the crowded city. Three thousand were killed. When Archelaus sailed to Rome, the whole of Judea rose in a revolt which was brutally suppressed by Rome and her allies (*Ant.* 17.250–98). After ten years, the people of Judaea complained to Rome about Archelaus' barbarity and in 6 CE he was banished. Judea became part of the province of Syria, with a local governor.

The three woes suggest that the disasters of the fifth, sixth and seventh trumpets have been incorporated from another source which described the three woes of the LORD's judgement. The fifth trumpet brings an army of locusts, the sixth an army of fiery horsemen and the seventh the kingdom of the LORD and the destruction of his enemies. This threefold sequence is as old as Amos, who saw the same visions of judgement. First he saw locusts about to destroy the land, second a great fire which the LORD summoned to eat up the deep, and third the LORD with his plumb line, measuring Israel and about to destroy the polluted high places and sanctuaries (Amos 7.1–9). The LXX of Amos shows that the locusts had already been interpreted as a hostile army with an evil king; Amos 7.1 was translated: 'there was a growth of locusts in the morning and one locust was the king Gog'. The War Scroll also describes 'Gog and all his assembly gathered about him', to be chastised on the Day of Wrath (1QM XI), and the fate of the beast and his armies in 19.17–21 is that of Gog and his host in Ezekiel 39. Their flesh is eaten by the birds.

The fifth trumpet takes up again the story of Herod, the star who fell from heaven. John saw a star who *had fallen* from heaven to earth and was given the key of the shaft of the bottomless pit. He opened the shaft and released smoke like a great furnace, from which emerged locusts to torture those who did not have the seal of the Name on their foreheads. The evil cloud he released was part of the divine plan because the fallen star *was given* the key (9.1), and the motif of the Name on the forehead takes up again the theme of the sixth seal, that the seal of the living God would protect the servants of God from the Day of Wrath (7.1–3). The blazing star had fallen into the warm springs of the rift valley, where Sodom and Gomorrah had been destroyed and the smoke of their destruction had also gone up like the smoke of a furnace (Gen. 19.28). The fallen star opened up the place where the fallen angels were imprisoned in an abyss of fire (*1 En.* 67.1–13), and he released 'the Angel of Malevolence ... and all the spirits of his company, the Angels of Destruction' (1QM XIII). The Qumran Hymns describe 'the arrows of the pit' and the wrath of Satan (1QH XI, formerly III) and the descriptions of cosmic conflict in the War Scroll show that the hosts of Belial at that time were the Kittim, the Romans: 'The day when the Kittim fall ... shall be the day appointed from ancient times for the battle of destruction of the sons of darkness' (1QM I). Thus the horde released from the Pit were both the angels of destruction and the Romans. Their king was the angel of the Pit (9.11), and the name of the Pit (not the name of the angel) would have been Abaddon: 'Thou hast redeemed my soul from the Pit, and from the hell of Abaddon thou hast raised me up' (Hymns 1QH XI, formerly III).

The horde was like locusts, a description of an invading army even as early as the Ugaritic texts where King Keret's army were 'like locusts as they settled on the steppe' (KTU 1.14.iv.30). Joel had spoken of 'the cutting locust, the swarming locust, the hopping locust and the destroying locust', all descriptions of the nation who came against the land, 'powerful and without number' (Joel 1. 4–6); the Book of Judges described the Midianites and the Amalekites as locusts, swarming over the land (Judg. 6.5 and 7.12). The immediate inspiration for this description, however, was Amos 7, where the locusts were the invading army under their king, Gog. The seer indicated that these locusts were also the fallen angels released from the Pit by describing their human faces, long hair and golden crowns. They were warriors in armour, but they also had tails like scorpions.

It has been suggested that the five months of their invasion (9.5) indicates the five-month reign of terror and pillage in the time of the procurator Gessius Florus, from May to September 66 CE. Other information given by Josephus supports this suggestion; he said that Gessius Florus was the final provocation to the war against Rome and could easily have been seen as the first of the final woes: 'He filled Judaea with an abundance of miseries . . . and it was this Florus who necessitated us to take up arms against the Romans' (*Ant.* 20.252, 257). He and his soldiers swept through the land like locusts, robbing and looting:

He omitted no sort of rapine or vexation . . . He indeed thought it a petty offence to get money out of single persons so he spoiled whole cities and ruined entire bodies of men at once . . . His greediness of gain was the occasion that entire toparchies were brought to desolation and a great many of the people left their own country and fled to foreign provinces. (*War* 2.278–79)

The locusts had tails like scorpions (9.10), a reference to the whips which Florus used on his victims before he put them to death. ('Scorpions' was a biblical name for vicious whips: 'My father chastised you with whips but I will chastise you with scorpions', 1 Kgs 12.14). Josephus notes this, too, as one of Florus' outstanding barbarities: 'The soldiers caught many of the quiet people and brought them before Florus, whom he first chastised with stripes and then crucified . . . Florus ventured to do what no other had done before, that is, to have men of the equestrian order whipped and nailed to the cross . . . Although they were Jews by birth, they were nevertheless Roman citizens' (*War* 2.308).

The fifth trumpet marked the time of Gessius Florus, and it has been suggested that the sixth was the invasion which followed his reign of terror, when Cestius the governor of Syria ravaged the land for two months in the autumn of 66 CE. Information given by Josephus explains many of the details in the episode of the sixth trumpet. In order to quell the rising revolt in Palestine, Cestius brought a huge number of troops from Antioch, and received additional help from Antiochus, King of Commagene in North Syria, Soaemus, King of Emesa in North Syria and Agrippa, the puppet king of Judea. All four would have come from the north, not far from the upper reaches of the Euphrates, and

Josephus noted especially the huge numbers of cavalry they mobilized. There were four troops of horsemen from Antioch in addition to 2000 from Antiochus, 1000 from Agrippa and about 1400 from Soaemus. 'The number of the troops of cavalry was twice ten thousand times ten thousand' (9.16), showing that they were the demonic counterpart of the host of the LORD in the Hebrew Scriptures, 'twice ten thousand, thousands upon thousands came from Sinai' (Ps. 68.17). This huge army moved into Galilee and began to burn the land. They set fire to the city of Zebulon and to the outlying villages, burned the villages around Caesarea, burned the Jewish camp at Antipatris and the outlying villages there, and burned the city of Lydda (*War* 2.515). When they attempted to attack Jerusalem, however, they were repulsed by its Jewish defenders. These invading cavalry were the horsemen of fire in the vision who appeared with the sixth trumpet, when the voice from the golden altar, the voice of the Mighty Angel who was standing by the altar of incense ordered the release of the four angels bound at the Euphrates (8.13–15; cf. Amos 9.1 where the LORD stood by the altar to order destruction). The demonic cavalry breathed out fire and smoke and brimstone, another echo of the story of Sodom and Gomorrah, where the LORD's judgement on the evil cities was 'fire and brimstone and smoke like the smoke of a furnace' (Gen. 19.24, 28). It is possible that the four 'angels' bound at the River Euphrates were originally four 'kings', as 'king' and 'angel' are very similar words in both Hebrew and Aramaic. This does not affect the meaning as angels were the supernatural counterparts of kings.

The fall of Jerusalem in 70 CE came to be described in terms of the fall of the city to the Babylonians in 597 BCE. 2 *Esdras*, written as though by Ezra in Babylon in the middle of the sixth century BCE, and 2 *Baruch*, attributed to Jeremiah's scribe, were in fact attempts to explain the disaster of 70 CE. It is possible that people in the first century CE feared that history would repeat itself, and that the destruction of Jerusalem would again come from the east. The Euphrates, the River, had been a symbol of the LORD's judgement since the time of Isaiah: 'The LORD is bringing up against them the waters of the River, mighty and many, the King of Assyria and all his glory' (Isa. 8.7), and the War Scroll still lists Assyria among the enemies of Israel (1QM XVIII–XIX). Nine years of its forty-year plan were to be spent fighting against the kingdoms of the east (1QM II). The Parables of Enoch link the final judgement of Azazel and his hosts to an attack from the east by the Parthians and Medes, 'roused from their thrones, breaking forth as lions from their lairs ... treading underfoot the land of his elect' (*1 En.* 56.5–6). The ancient threat had become very real since the Parthians had defeated Crassus at the battle of Carrhae in 53 BCE, and in the sequence of the bowls of wrath, the sixth bowl dries up the Euphrates so that the kings of the east can pass over (16.12). Here, however, the detail in the terrors of the sixth trumpet suggests that the invasion by Cestius in 66 CE was seen as fulfilment of the prophecy.

The sequence of the six trumpets ends by saying that those who survived these plagues did not cease from their worship of idols, a curious conclusion. It was probably drawn from the tradition underlying both the six trumpets and the *Assumption of Moses* as the latter also mentions the destruction of idols on the Day of the LORD: 'He will come to work vengeance on the nations, yea all their idols he will destroy' (*Ass. Mos.* 10.7). The words in 9.20 echo, but do not quote, Psalm 115.4–7:

Their idols are silver and gold, the work of men's hands
They have mouths but do not speak; eyes but do not see.
They have ears but do not hear; noses but do not smell.
They have hands but do not feel; feet but do not walk,
    and they do not make a sound in their throat.

The seventh trumpet, on this reckoning, would have corresponded to Amos' third and final vision of destruction, the LORD with a line *measuring* the wall of the temple (Amos 7.7). This was realized in 10.7 where the seventh trumpet is announced, and John is told to 'measure' the temple (11.1).

I will never again pass by them;
the high places of Isaac shall be made desolate,
and the sanctuaries of Israel shall be laid waste. (Amos 7.8–9)

The sequence of the seven trumpets gives several important indications as to the origin and compilation of the Book of Revelation. First, the descriptions and allusions are drawn from the Hebrew Scriptures and would only have been intelligible to a hearer similarly steeped in the Scriptures. Second, the stylized presentation of the Roman era in Palestine shows a detailed knowledge of significant events of the previous century and not only of those which took place in Palestine itself. A similar range of knowledge was displayed by Josephus when he tried to persuade Jerusalem to surrender (*War* 5.394–419), in other words, it would have been available to an educated person of the priestly class. Third, it indicates a familiarity with ideas found in the Parables of Enoch and the Qumran writings, and suggests that the composer of the Sounding of the Seven Trumpets was from the same circle. *Fourth, it is an interpretation of events significant for Palestine as a whole and not just for the Hebrew Christians.* The Book of Revelation, whatever its final form and destination, was a book of Jewish prophecy produced by an educated, priestly group who had much in common with the writers of the Qumran Scrolls.

12

THE ANGEL IN THE CLOUD

Then I saw another mighty angel coming down from heaven, wrapped in a cloud, with a rainbow over his head, and his face was like the sun, and his legs like pillars of fire. He had a little scroll open in his hand. And he set his right foot on the sea, and his left foot on the land ...

Then the voice which I had heard from heaven spoke to me again, saying, 'Go, take the scroll which is open in the hand of the angel who is standing on the sea and the land ...'

And I took the little scroll from the hand of the angel and ate it; it was sweet as honey in my mouth, but when I had eaten it my stomach was made bitter. (Rev. 10.1–2, 8, 10)

Six seals have been opened and their prophecies fulfilled. Following the sequence in the Synoptic Apocalypse, the seventh seal was to bring the Son of Man in clouds with great power and glory (Mark 13.26). He did not appear. Within the seventh seal, the seven trumpets marked the delay. Eventually the Man did return, but only to John his seer and only in a vision to give him a further commission. John had to give further teaching that the return of the LORD would not be literally as the prophecies had predicted. There was at that time a widespread belief that the beloved disciple would live to see the return of Jesus, but after the new revelation, John had to make it clear that he did not expect this to happen. Another section was added to the Gospel: 'The saying spread abroad among the brethren that this disciple was not to die; yet Jesus did not say to him that he was not to die, but, "If it is my will that he remain until I come, what is that to you?" ' (John 21. 23).

The High Priest

The writer to the Hebrews explained that Jesus, the great high priest, had passed through the heavens (Heb. 4.14) and was enthroned in heaven, a minister in the holy of holies and true tabernacle (Heb. 8.1–12). He had offered himself as the one great atonement sacrifice and was waiting until his enemies were defeated (Heb. 10.12–13). He had been given the Name and was ranked above the angels (Heb. 1.3–4). In the near future he was to emerge from his holy place to complete the atonement and bring judgement on his enemies. Luke depicts the high priest entering the holy of holies 'a cloud took him' (Acts 1.9 cf. *1 En.* 14.8) and blessing his disciples (Luke 24.50). Peter explained the significance of events in Jerusalem. Jesus had been put to death, fulfilling the prophecies that the Anointed One would suffer. He had been taken to heaven and was waiting to return. Peter warned his listeners to repent of their sins before the Anointed One emerged (Acts 2.12–21). Peter's sermon and the Letter to the Hebrews both imply the same understanding of the crucifixion; Jesus had been the high priestly atonement sacrifice, he had taken his own blood into the holy of holies (Heb. 9.12) and was still there, about to emerge at any time to complete the final Day of Atonement when the earth would be judged and renewed. 'Repent', said Peter, 'that your sins may be blotted out, that times of refreshing may come from the presence of the LORD' (Acts 3.19).

The first generation of Christians expected the LORD to return at any time. Paul wrote that the believers in Thessalonika had 'turned from idols' in order to wait for the Son of God from heaven, 'whom he raised from the dead, Jesus who delivers us from the wrath to come' (1 Thess. 1.10). Paul expected this to happen in his own lifetime: 'We who are alive, who are left until the coming of the LORD, shall not precede those who have fallen asleep. For the LORD himself will descend from heaven with a cry of command, with the archangel's call, and with the sound of the trumpet of God' (1 Thess. 4.15–16). As the years passed and the signs of the seals were fulfilled, so it was believed that the return and the time of wrath were imminent.

John's vision of the angel wreathed in a rainbow and wrapped in a cloud was, for him, the return of the high priest, the LORD, *appearing in a cloud in his holy place* (Exod. 40.34; Lev. 16.2; 1 Kgs 8.10–11): 'Behold he is coming with the clouds' (1.7). After the sixth trumpet, he saw the Mighty Angel coming from heaven to earth. This is another occasion when *'ḥr*, 'after' was read as *'ḥr*, 'another', and so the original text would have described not 'another Mighty Angel' but the one and only Mighty Angel, the one who had been the Strong Angel on the throne in 5.1–2. The English versions translate the Greek word *ischuros* differently in these two places, but the Strong Angel of 5.2 is the same as the 'Mighty Angel' of 10.1. In 4.2–3 he was on his throne, encircled by a rainbow; in 5.7 the human figure, the Lamb, took the scroll and himself became the Mighty Angel, worshipped by the heavenly host (5.13–14). The Mighty Angel received the incense of the high priesthood in 8.3 and then prepared to emerge from his holy place. Finally, in 10.1 he came from the holy of holies, from heaven to earth, wrapped in a cloud, which was the incense of the sanctuary. He had a rainbow over his head, a halo, and his face was radiant because he has been transfigured by his anointing. This resembles Enoch's experience: 'He anointed me and he clothed me ... and I had become like one of the glorious ones' (*2 En.* 22.9–10). There is an exactly similar description of the high priest emerging from the holy of holies in *Ben Sira* 50. Simon the high priest 'was glorious when he came out of the house of the veil, like the morning star among the clouds, like the moon when it is full, like the sun shining upon the temple of the Most High, and like the rainbow gleaming in glorious clouds'. His very presence 'made the court of the sanctuary glorious' (*Ben Sira* 50.5–7, 11). All the elements are there in both descriptions: the clouds, the rainbow and the radiant face. The bow in the clouds was the sign of the covenant (Gen. 9.12–13) and of the glory of the LORD (see p. 264), and the heavenly high priest wrapped in the bow and the clouds was the sign of that covenant renewed (cf. Isa. 42.6: 'I have given you [the Servant] as the eternal covenant', see p. 42). He was the Angel of the Covenant, bringing the judgement (Mal. 3.1–5).

A similar figure appears elsewhere in the Hebrew Scriptures, in each case to warn Jerusalem of its fate. Daniel saw a Fiery Man who had come 'to make him understand what was to befall his people in the latter days' (Dan. 10.5–6, 14). Ezekiel also saw the Fiery Man who warned him of the fate of Jerusalem: 'The land is full of blood and the city full of injustice ... My eye will not spare nor will I have pity ...' (Ezek. 8.2; 9.9–10). In Daniel the figure is not named, but an early Christian commentator knew that the Fiery Man was the LORD (Hippolytus, *On Daniel* 24). In Ezekiel, there is no doubt that the Fiery Man who walks in the temple was the LORD because he told the angels of destruction: 'Begin at my sanctuary' (Ezek. 9.6). The Mighty Angel who appeared to John also warned of the disaster coming to Jerusalem; he was the LORD returning.

The Mighty Angel had a voice like a lion roaring (10.3), an ancient description of the voice of the LORD. Amos began his prophecies: 'The LORD roars from Zion, and utters his voice from Jerusalem' (Amos 1.2). The voice of the LORD was also the seven thunders. When Jesus heard the voice from heaven, some in the crowd said it was thunder, others that it was the voice of an angel (John 12.27–29). The psalmist, too, had likened the voice both to thunder and to the sound of many waters. 'The voice of the LORD is upon the waters; the glory of God thunders, the LORD upon many waters. The voice of the LORD is powerful, the voice of the LORD is full of majesty' (Ps. 29.3–4).

The Secret Teaching

At this crucial time, when he had declared the sixth seal open, the pattern in Revelation 10 suggests that John received three revelations of new teaching. The first was the seven thunders, a message which had to be sealed up, i.e. kept secret, and not written down. The second was the words of the angel, that the mystery of God announced by the prophets was about to be fulfilled. The third was the little scroll which John had to eat, i.e., keep secret. Origen made a direct link between Ezekiel's vision of the scroll and John's:

Our prophets did know of greater things than any in the Scriptures which they did not commit to writing. Ezekiel, for example, received a roll written within and without ... but at the command of the Logos he swallowed the book in order that its contents might not be written down and so made known to unworthy persons. John is also recorded to have seen and done a similar thing ... And it is related of Jesus, who was greater than all these, that he conversed with his disciples in private and especially in their secret retreats concerning the gospel of God; but the words which he uttered have not been preserved because it appeared to the evangelists that they could not be adequately conveyed to the multitude in writing or speech. (*Cels.* 6.6)

The only teaching he could reveal openly was the message of the angel that the mystery of God was about to be fulfilled, after the seventh trumpet. It is easy to identify this as the establishing of the kingdom of God and the destruction of those who had destroyed the earth (11.15–18). The rest was secret teaching which we should not expect to find in any written source, but it is likely to be the key to John's characteristic teaching and interpretation of Jesus. *Here, in the vision of the angel wrapped in a cloud, the heavenly high priest again gave secret teaching to John.* In a time of Parousia fervour in Jerusalem, when the seventh seal was expected, John's personal vision of the Parousia revealed to him another understanding of the LORD's return. It was to be the LORD's presence with his church rather than the future, but imminent, return of the warrior priest.

The early church knew that Jesus had given secret teaching to an inner group of disciples, in the first instance to just three. 'James the Righteous, John and Peter were entrusted by the LORD after his resurrection with the higher knowledge. They imparted it to the other apostles and the other apostles to the seventy, one of whom was Barnabas' (Eusebius, *History* 2.1, quoting a lost work of Clement of Alexandria, *Hypotyposes*). 'After his resurrection' means after Jesus' own experience of birth as Son of God, his baptismal anointing with the Spirit. This secret teaching was given during the ministry and is mentioned in the Synoptic Gospels, for example, by Mark: 'And when he was alone, those who were about him with the twelve asked him concerning the parables. And he said to them, "To you has been given the secret of the kingdom of God, but for those outside everything is in parables"' (Mark 4.10–11). John in his Gospel reveals more about the private teaching when he has Jesus say to Nicodemus, who came to him by night, 'unless one is born anew (or 'from above'), he cannot see the kingdom of God ... Unless one is born of water and the Spirit, he cannot enter the kingdom of God' (John 3.3, 5). The kingdom could only be seen by the resurrected, only entered by the children of God. Theirs was the secret teaching from the risen LORD, that the millennium kingdom would be for the first resurrected (see p. 339).

Other early texts show that this secret teaching was given by Jesus the high priest, which is how he is depicted in this vision. It is no coincidence that it is the high priest figure who imparts the only secret teaching mentioned in the Book of Revelation. Bishop Ignatius of Antioch, who saw himself as a guardian of the true teaching, wrote early in the second century CE: 'To Jesus alone as our high priest were the secret things of God committed' (*Phil.* 9). Clement of Alexandria, writing at the end of the second century CE, knew of secret teaching acquired by 'drawing aside the curtain' – a clear reference to the temple veil – but never written down, presumably teaching like that of the seven thunders. It was knowledge of 'past, present and future which the LORD has taught us', divine mysteries from the only begotten Son (Clement, *Misc.* 6.7–7.1). This indicates the apocalyptists' style of history; those who passed beyond the veil of the temple passed beyond time and so were able to see all history, past present and future. They also saw history in patterns by which they were able to understand what was happening, hence the pattern of the 'weeks' in *1 Enoch* (*1 En.* 93), or the 'sevens' and the motif of three and a half in the Book of Revelation.

Eusebius knew that the secret teaching had been given to the three pillars of the Jerusalem church, to James the Righteous, John and Peter. The *Apocryphon of James*, usually dated in the first half of the second century CE, is in the form of a letter written from James the Righteous to someone whose name cannot be deciphered, who had asked about the secret teaching: 'You asked me to send you the secret teaching which was revealed to me and Peter by the LORD ... Be careful and take heed not to rehearse to many this writing which the Saviour did not wish to divulge even to all of us, his twelve disciples'. The letter goes on to describe how Peter and James ascended into heaven after Jesus and saw angelic visions before the other disciples summoned them back to earth. Basil of Caesarea knew that important elements in the church's teaching – about the consecration of the Eucharist and the signing with a cross – were not written down but transmitted orally from the apostles (*On the Holy Spirit* 66).

The angel high priest also gave John an open scroll and told him to eat it, to keep its message secret. The LORD had offered Ezekiel an open scroll and told him to eat it; it was apparently, the LORD's message of judgement to the house of Israel and sweet in his mouth (Ezek. 2.8–3.4). John's was a similar experience, an open scroll from the hand of the LORD, but for John the experience was sweet and then bitter (10.8–11). He received the message of judgement that the temple would not be rebuilt and that he had to leave the city and go elsewhere. He had a further commission to prophesy about 'many peoples and nations and tongues and kings' (10.11).

The Mystery of God

Chapters 10 and 11 form a complex sequence and are the most enigmatic texts in the Book of Revelation. One element in the pattern can be recovered from the Targum to Isaiah 24 which expands the original text in a significant way. The Hebrew words *razy razy* in Isaiah 24.16, which the AV gives as 'my leanness, my leanness', the RSV as 'I pine away, I pine away', and the Good News Bible as 'I am wasting away', were understood by the targumist to have a meaning similar to the identical Aramaic word *raz* which means 'mystery'. The Targum therefore has 'The prophet said "The mystery of the reward of the righteous is visible to me, the mystery of the retribution for the wicked is revealed to me" '. It continues 'Woe to the robbers who are robbed and to the plunder of the plunderers which now is plundered'. This would be one example of bitter and sweet in the revelation, the reward of the righteous and the punishment of the wicked. Isaiah 24.16 in the original begins 'From the ends of the earth we hear songs of praise, of glory to the Righteous One', but in the Targum it became: 'From the sanctuary, whence joy is about to go forth to all the inhabitants of the earth, we hear a song for the Righteous One'. Here, then, is the holy of holies of 10.1, the setting for the emerging high priest and the revelation he brought about the mystery of reward and punishment. The Targum to Isaiah 24.17–22 describes the catastrophes that follow: one who comes out of the pit and is trapped in a net, the earth trembling and the LORD punishing the kings and the mighty hosts. Finally, as in the original Hebrew, the kingdom of the LORD of hosts is revealed in Jerusalem and he appears before the elders in his glory (Isa. 24.23), the scene in 11.15–18.

Elements in Isaiah 24.16–23, and especially in the Targum, explain several features in Revelation 10–11: the mystery revealed to the prophets, the beast from the pit (11.7), the earthquake (11.13) and finally the voices which call out in heaven, that is, in the holy of holies: 'The kingdom of the world has become the kingdom of the LORD and of his Christ and he shall reign for ever and ever' (11.15). There follow rewards and punishments, the mystery revealed to the prophet: 'the time for rewarding thy servants the prophets and saints, and those who fear thy name both small and great, and for destroying the destroyers of the earth' (11.18).

The Qumran Habakkuk Commentary shows a similar way of interpreting prophecy, with interesting correspondence in both subject matter and wording: 'The men of violence and the breakers of the covenant will not believe all they hear [ ] the final generation from the priest [ ] God set [ ] that he might interpret all the words of his servants the prophets through whom he foretold all that would happen to his people and his land' (1QpHab II).

God told Habakkuk to write down that which would happen to the final generation, but he did not make known to him when time would come to an end. And as for that which he said, 'That he who reads may read it speedily' (Hab. 2.1–2): interpreted, this concerns the Teacher of Righteousness to whom God made known all the mysteries of the words of his servants the prophets. 'For there shall be yet another vision concerning the appointed time. It shall tell of the end time and shall not lie' (Hab. 2.3): interpreted, this means that the final age shall be prolonged and shall exceed all that the prophets have said; for the mysteries of God are astounding. (1QpHab VII)

The words of the angel to John were not 'there should be no more delay', as 10.6 is sometimes translated, but 'there shall be no more time', exactly how the prophecy of Habakkuk was understood at that time. Habakkuk did not know when time would come to an end but this was revealed to John. John, like the Teacher of Righteousness, was given 'yet another vision concerning the appointed time' and, it would seem, how the 'final age was prolonged' (indicated in the Book of Revelation by the Sounding of the Seven Trumpets).

The Qumran Hymns have similar ideas:

Thou hast unstopped my ears to marvellous mysteries. (1QH IX, formerly I)

Thou hast made me ... a discerning interpreter of wonderful mysteries. (1QH X, formerly II)

Thou hast given me knowledge through thy marvellous mysteries. (1QH XII, formerly IV)

... the mystery which thou hast hidden in me. (1QH XIII, formerly V)

The Melchizedek text said he would teach about 'the ends of the age', and the Damascus Document also includes the enigmatic line: 'From the day of the gathering in of the teacher of the community until the end of all the men of war who deserted to the liar there shall pass about forty years' (CD VIII). Forty years was almost exactly the length of time from the crucifixion of Jesus to the fall of Jerusalem, and would explain the heightened expectation of the Parousia as the forty years passed.

The Isaiah Apocalypse (Isa. 24–27) forms the framework of the section, but there are other elements interwoven. The angel who swears that there will be no more time (10.5–6) is the angel described in Daniel 12.5–9. Daniel at that time saw 'a man clothed in linen', the Man who had previously appeared in Daniel 10.5–14, and whom the early Christians recognized as the pre-incarnate LORD (Hippolytus, *On Daniel* 24). The one who appeared to John swore by 'him who lives for ever' (10.6) just as the Man in Daniel 12.7 swore by 'him who lives forever'. These also suggest that the Man was the LORD, who was often depicted as swearing by his own Name: Genesis 22.16 'By myself have I sworn, says the LORD'; or Jeremiah 22.5, 'I swear by myself, says the LORD'; or Jeremiah 51.14, 'The LORD of Hosts has sworn by himself'.

Daniel then asked the LORD, 'How long shall it be to the end of these wonders?' (Dan. 12.6). and the LORD replied that it would be 'a time, two times and half a time'; when the shattering of the power of the holy people came to an end, all these things would be accomplished. 'Go your way, Daniel, for the words are shut up and sealed until the time of the end' (Dan. 12.9). The 'last king' would have power over the saints of the Most High for 'a time, two times and half a time' (Dan. 7.25). The enigmatic 'a time, two times and half a time', appears as the motif of three and a half years in Revelation 11; it was the duration of the ministry of the two witnesses and the period of time for which the nations were to trample Jerusalem (11.2–3) and it was the length of time that the woman clothed with the sun was to be in the desert (12.14). It was also the duration of the final struggle with Rome; Vespasian entered Galilee with his armies in the spring of 67 CE (*War* 3.29–34) and Jerusalem fell forty-two months later, in September 70 CE. The significance of the period three and a half or its equivalents is not so much the length of time, but the fact that it is the last time and that *at the end of that time*, something would happen to Jerusalem. Thus the focus is on the end of the time of the two witnesses, and on the end of the time of the woman's exile in the desert. The angel shows John that the Queen is returning to her city, but the harlot is in the desert (17.3).

The Song of Moses (Deut. 32), an important text for understanding the Book of Revelation (see pp. 170, 241), is the key to understanding this angel. Just before the LORD appears to bring vengeance on those who have shed the blood of his servants and to make the great atonement, he proclaims: 'I lift up my hand to heaven, and swear As I live for ever, when I whet my glittering sword* and my hand takes hold on judgement, I will take vengeance on my adversaries, and will requite those who hate me' (Deut. 32.40–41). The angel in 10.5–7 is clearly the same figure, who lifts up his hand to heaven, swears by himself and proclaims the imminent judgement. This vision in 10.5–7 was the interpretation of a portent which Josephus reported. Some time before the war began, 'a star resembling a sword stood over the city, and a comet, which continued for a year' (*War* 6.289). This was the lightning sword of the LORD which the prophets saw being held over Jerusalem, and it was interpreted as the fulfilment of the Song of Moses, that there should be no more delay (see p. 247). The sword was a well-known portent: the Sibyl had spoken in the second century BCE of fiery swords falling from heaven to earth when the great God protected his city from abominable kings (*Sib.* 3.673) and 'swords seen at night in the starry heaven' were a sign of the end times (*Sib.* 3.798). Only the mark of the LORD would protect against the sword of the covenant on the Day of Visitation (CD BVIII).

Measuring the Temple

John was given a reed to measure the temple. Such reeds were the usual way to measure, as can be seen in 21.15, where the angel has a golden reed to measure the heavenly city; or Ezekiel 40.3, where the Man who measures the new temple has a line of flax and a measuring reed; or the New Jerusalem text from Qumran (5Q15), where the measurements are also in reeds. John was told to measure the temple, *naos,* and the altar, *thusiasterion.* The word *naos* in 11.19 means the holy of holies, but here it seems to mean the whole temple building as it does in Josephus (e.g. *War* 5.204). The *thusiasterion* in 8.3 is the incense altar inside the temple. John was also told to 'measure the worshippers'. It has been suggested that the underlying Aramaic here was not *sgd*, worship, but *srg*, *soreg* being the technical name for the boundary which separated the holier parts from the court of the Gentiles, 'a latticed railing ten handbreadths high' (*m. Middoth* 2.3). The Aramaic letters 'd' and 'r' are easily confused, and such a proposal certainly explains what follows: that the court outside the temple was not to be measured as it was given over already to the Gentiles (cf. Luke 21.24). Whoever translated the Book of Revelation into Greek no longer knew all the correct terms for

*Literally 'the lightning of my sword'.

the temple buildings, and this is why too much weight cannot be put on exactly what was meant by *naos* and *thusiasterion*.

Why he was told to measure the temple is not so clear. The angel who measured the temple in Ezekiel's vision was showing the prophet exactly how the temple city should be built. This measuring revealed the dimensions. The Temple Scroll, too, gives exact dimensions and may have been the plan for the true temple which was to replace Herod's. More often, though, measuring was a sign of imminent destruction and in these cases no dimensions were given. Thus Amos saw the LORD with a plumb line and knew it was a warning of destruction (Amos 7.7); Isaiah warned that the LORD would stretch a line of confusion and a plummet of destruction over Edom (Isa. 34.11); Habakkuk saw the LORD measuring the earth and shaking the nations (Hab. 3.6); and unnamed prophets warned that the LORD would stretch the line and the plummet over Jerusalem because of the sins of Manasseh (2 Kgs 21.13). When the measurements of the heavenly temple city are given later (21.15–17), this is not a city destined for destruction. The measurements of the temple are not given in 11.1–2 suggesting that the command to measure the temple was a warning of its destruction.

It is quite possible that John did measure the temple area as far as the *soreg*. Such acted prophecies were an established practice of the Hebrew prophets, as when Ahijah tore his cloak and told Jereboam to rule over the ten tribes (1 Kgs 11.30–31) or when Jeremiah broke the pot and warned of the destruction of Jerusalem (Jer. 19.10–11). Josephus records this prophecy, which suggests that it was public knowledge. He noted that the area enclosed by the *soreg* was 'four cornered', *tetragonon*, which may mean square or rectangular (*War* 5.195) and then, when reviewing the portents and prophecies which had preceded the destruction of the temple, he wrote: 'The Jews, by demolishing the tower of Antonia, had made their temple foursquare (*tetragonon*) while at the same time they had it written in their sacred oracles "That then should their city be taken as well as their holy house, when once their temple should become foursquare (*tetragonon*)"' (*War* 6.311). This oracle is not in the Hebrew Scriptures, but what Josephus wrote next clearly refers to the oracle in Revelation 11.15. In other words, 'their Scriptures' seems to mean the writings which the Christians were using. Josephus wrote of 'an ambiguous oracle, also found in their sacred writings, how about that time one from their country should become ruler of the whole earth'. If Josephus' second prophecy is an oracle in 'their' Scriptures and corresponds to 'The kingdom of the world has become the kingdom of our LORD and of his Christ' (11.15), it is likely that the first 'oracle in their Scriptures' which warned that destruction would follow making the temple square, is a reference to John's measuring the temple in 11.1–2. He was proclaiming the fulfilment of the square temple prophecy, once the Antonia tower had been demolished. *The prophecies in the Book of Revelation were a significant factor in the war against Rome.*

The destruction and rebuilding of the temple was an important hope in the second temple period. *1 Enoch* 90.20–29 describes the judgement on the fallen angels and their followers who are thrown into the abyss of fire. The old temple is taken away and the LORD sets up a new one in its place. Jesus made the same prediction, but, because he believed himself to be the LORD, he predicted that he himself would set up the new temple. This was an accusation brought against him at his trial: 'We heard him say "I will destroy this temple that is made with hands, and in three days I will build another, not made with hands"' (Mark 14.58; also Mark 15.29 with parallels in Matt. 26.61 and 27.40). This was an important element in Christian prophecy. The Slavonic text of Josephus, having described the notices in the temple which warned foreigners not to pass beyond the *soreg*, says there was another hung above them: 'Jesus the king did not reign but was crucified because he prophesied the destruction of the city and the devastation of the temple' (*War* 5.195). The bitterness of the message of the little scroll (10.8–10) was that the temple would be destroyed but not rebuilt. Jesus' prediction about the new temple had to be reinterpreted, and so in John's Gospel we find: 'Jesus answered them "Destroy this temple, and in three days I will raise it up" ... But he spoke of the temple of his body. When therefore he was raised from the dead, his disciples remembered that he had said this ...' (John 2.19–22).

In the Fourth Gospel there are three places where John alters ('corrects') a current teaching just as there are two places where he, the unnamed elder, interprets visions in the Book of Revelation. In two of the cases in the Gospel, the disciples 'remembered' the true meaning because the Holy Spirit, whom John calls the Paraclete, taught them and enabled them to 'remember' (John 14.26). It was the Spirit of Truth who made plain the real meaning of what Jesus had taught (John 16.13) just as the Angel of Truth was to succour all the sons of light (1QS III).

(Apart from the true meaning of rebuilding the temple, the other occasion when the disciples 'remember' is the account of Palm Sunday. Matthew 21.5 and John 12.15 both quote Zechariah 9.9, 'Rejoice daughter of Zion, ... your king comes to you ... humble and riding on an ass' but John adds that the disciples did not understand what this meant. Only when Jesus had been glorified were they able to 'remember' and thus to understand what was happening at the time (see p. 166). This is a strange comment about a prophecy which Matthew quoted as though it were common knowledge. John implies that Jesus' role as the King coming to Zion was not known to all the disciples until long after the event. This is confirmed by the elder's interpretation of the vision of the Lamb approaching the throne. The Lion of Judah and the Root of David, the King, had proved himself worthy to open the scroll (5.5). Confirming the identity of Jesus was the first of the elder's revelations to those who were not the three pillars of the church. Thus by the time Matthew wrote his Gospel, it was common knowledge, and the prophecy was quoted without explanation. The third occasion when

John corrected a current teaching was where he made clear that the beloved disciple would not necessarily live until the LORD returned (John 21.23).)

At this crucial point in the history of the young church, John had three revelations of teaching: the words of the angel, i.e. the LORD, that the mystery of establishing the kingdom was imminent; the bitterness of the scroll that the temple would not be rebuilt, and the seven thunders, that the return of the LORD was not imminent. He had returned only in a vision to his prophet. The temple saying was reinterpreted to show that Jesus had not, in fact, predicted that it would be rebuilt in three days. This had been a prediction of resurrection after three days and so, joined to the prophecy of the destruction of the temple (11.1–2) there is the account of the two witnesses who were raised from the dead after three days (11.11).

The Two Witnesses

The passage about the two witnesses (11.3–13), is acknowledged to be the most obscure in the entire Book of Revelation. The great detail given shows that it was not obscure to the original readers. Our problem is that so little has survived from this period of the church in Palestine that the identity of the two witnesses has to be a matter of guesswork. (There is, for example, no record in the New Testament of the murder of James the Bishop of Jerusalem, which must have happened during the period covered by Acts.) No two characters fit the descriptions exactly. This may be a sign of a much reworked text with a variety of detail incorporated, or just that we lack the vital evidence to identify them.

The two people are described as my 'witnesses', that ambiguous word which can mean either 'one who has seen' or 'martyr'. In the opening chapter of the Book of Revelation Jesus was described as 'the faithful witness' (1.5) and John bore witness to the 'witness' of Jesus, 'to all that he saw' (1.2), showing that the element of vision cannot be excluded from the definition of 'witness'. The two witnesses in chapter 11 are appointed as prophets (11.3), they are killed by the beast (11.7), they lie unburied in the streets of Jerusalem (11.8) and there is general rejoicing over their deaths (11.10). They are then resurrected and summoned into heaven with the words 'Come up hither' (11.12) the words which the seer heard as he, too, was summoned into heaven (4.1).

First, the two witnesses died in Jerusalem, 'the great city which is spiritually called Sodom and Egypt, where their LORD was crucified (11.8)'. This latter phrase was probably added to the text at a later stage, for the benefit of a generation who were not able to identify the city known as Sodom and Egypt. The opening oracles of Isaiah make it clear that Jerusalem was known as Sodom, and why that name was given to her: 'Hear the word of the LORD, you rulers of Sodom! Give ear to the teaching of our God, you people of Gomorrah! "What to me is the multitude of your sacrifices?" says the LORD; "I have had enough of burnt offerings of rams and the fat of fed beasts ..." ' (Isa. 1.10–11)

Egypt is not a name given to Jerusalem in the Hebrew Scriptures. The Letter to the Hebrews, however, which also treats the Scriptures 'spiritually' (especially Heb. 8 and 9), shows that the Hebrews were 'holy brethren who share in the heavenly call' (Heb. 3.1) and they had left Jerusalem due to persecution. They compared themselves to Jesus who suffered outside the wall of the city in order to sanctify the people by his blood (Heb. 13.12). They looked for 'the city which is to come' (Heb. 13.14), presumably the heavenly Jerusalem described at the end of the Book of Revelation. The Hebrews had 'endured a hard struggle with sufferings, sometimes being publicly exposed to abuse and affliction ... and you joyfully accepted the plundering of your property, since you knew that you yourselves had a better possession and an abiding one' (Heb. 10. 32–34). These could have been the priests who joined the church (Acts 6.7), whose tithes had been plundered by the high priests (see p. 33). A priestly group would certainly account for the temple imagery in the letter. As a result of persecution they had, like the Israelites of old, left 'Egypt' under the leadership of their 'Moses' and were living through times of testing in the wilderness – forty years (Heb. 3.7–19). They were probably the people who left Jerusalem with James after he had been attacked by Saul, and so James was their Moses (see p. 53).

The two witnesses are also described as 'the two olive trees and the two lampstands which stand before the LORD of the whole earth' (11.4). The allusion here is to Zechariah's vision of the two olive trees on either side of the menorah, which the angel explains are the two anointed ones who stand by the LORD of the whole earth (Zech. 4.14). In 11.4 they have become two olive trees and two lampstands, implying that each witness is both a tree and a lamp. Since the seven-branched lampstand was a stylized tree, albeit an almond, this identification of lamp and tree is not a problem. What is remarkable is the implication of the text: there are two anointed ones, two Messiahs.

There are, apparently, two Messiahs named in the Qumran Community Rule. The community were waiting for the Prophet and the Messiahs of Aaron and Israel (1QS IX). The Messianic Rule also mentions the priest who takes precedence over the Messiah of Israel in blessing the bread (1QSa II). In Zechariah's vision the identity of the two anointed ones is not clear; the two key figures in the prophecies are Joshua (that is, Jesus) the high priest, and Zerubbabel, the direct descendent of King Josiah and so a Davidic prince. These two could have been the original Messiahs of Aaron and Israel, but there is no clear indication that these two were the anointed ones, due to the poor state of the text. Only Joshua was given the crowns of high priesthood (Zech. 6.11).

Since Zechariah's prophecy of the two anointed ones is all but quoted in the vision of the two witnesses (11.4), and since the only anointed one who was clearly named was Joshua/Jesus the high priest, the first of the two witnesses put to death in Jerusalem is likely to have been Jesus. He was described in the opening chapter of Revelation as the 'faithful witness' and 'the firstborn of the dead' (1.5), and he was taken up to heaven in a cloud (11.12; Acts 1.9). Jesus was also described as a prophet, not only in the Gospels 'a great prophet has arisen among us' (Luke 7.16), or 'Some say that you are John the Baptist, others say Elijah and others Jeremiah or one of the prophets' (Matt. 16.14), but also in early texts such as the *Clementine Recognitions*. Peter instructs Clement about the True Prophet (*Clem. Rec.* 1.16) and Clement speaks of his own faith in the True Prophet (*Clem. Rec.* 1.18). It was the True Prophet who had appeared in the Hebrew Scriptures, for example, to Abraham (*Clem. Rec.* 1.33). Witness, Prophet, and Anointed One killed in Jerusalem, but taken to heaven in a cloud are all descriptions of Jesus. The deaths of the two witnesses were linked to the destruction of Jerusalem and here again, Christian tradition links the death of Jesus to the fall of the city. Luke has Jesus say, as he draws near to Jerusalem and weeps over the city, 'They will not leave one stone upon another in you, because you did not know the time of your visitation' (Luke 19.44). The destruction of Jerusalem, wrote Eusebius, 'was the result of the iniquitous and wicked treatment of God's Anointed One ... After the Saviour's Passion ... disaster befell the entire nation' (*History* 3.7).

The second witness was James the Righteous, the first bishop in Jerusalem, murdered in the temple in about 62 CE. Eusebius, quoting Hegesippus, says he lived an ascetic life. He consumed neither meat nor alcohol, never cut his hair and never anointed himself (*History* 2.23). This suggests an Essene with a Nazirite vow. Even Josephus, who was no spokesman for the Christians, wrote of the destruction of Jerusalem: 'These things happened to the Jews in requital for the death of James the Righteous, who was brother of Jesus known as the Christ, for though he was the most righteous of men, the Jews put him to death'. (Quoted by Eusebius, *History* 2.23. This passage has not survived in our texts of Josephus, but Origen knew it.) The *Gospel of Thomas* shows his importance for the community which preserved the secret teachings of Jesus. 'The disciples said to Jesus, "We know that you will depart from us. Who is to be our leader?" Jesus said the them, "Wherever you are, you are to go to James the Righteous, for whose sake heaven and earth came into being"' (*Thomas* 12). James was a figure of cosmic significance.

This may explain something recorded by Hegesippus, a Christian of the first generation after the apostles. James, he said, was known as the Righteous One and also as 'Oblias, meaning in our own language Defence of the People' (quoted by Eusebius, *History* 2.23). It has been suggested that this strange name derives from the prophecy of the two rods/branches in Zechariah 11.7. (The same word *maqqel* occurs in Jer. 1.11, 'the branch' of an almond.) The two branches have names: the first is *no'am*, translated elsewhere as *beauty* of the LORD (Ps. 27.4) or his 'favour' (Ps 90.17), which would have been Jesus, the LORD; and the second is *ḥoblim*, bonds. Bonds of the people, *ḥobley ha'am* could have been the mysterious 'Oblias', and explain why the presence of James was so vital for the security of the city. He was the Bond of the Covenant for the people as was the Servant (Isa. 42.6; 49.8).

The name Oblias, 'Defence' would then link Jerusalem, 'Sodom' to the story of the original Sodom, when Abraham had pleaded with the LORD to spare the city: 'Wilt thou indeed destroy the Righteous with the wicked?' (Gen. 18.23). The LORD promised Abraham that if only ten righteous people could be found in the city he would not destroy it (Gen. 18.32). As with the original Sodom, the LORD had already visited the city, but 'they did not know the time of their visitation' (Luke 19.44). James the Righteous, by his very presence, kept Jerusalem from destruction. Paul described his presence in the city as part of the mystery: 'For the mystery of lawlessness is already at work; only he who now restrains it will do so until he is out of the way. And then the lawless one will be revealed, and the LORD Jesus will slay him with the breath of his mouth and destroy him by his appearing and his coming' (2 Thess. 2.7–8). Even when Eusebius was writing his *History* in the mid-fourth century CE, it was still known that James had protected Jerusalem by his presence: 'At that time most of the apostles and disciples, including James himself, were still alive, and by remaining in the city, furnished the place with an impregnable Defence' (*History* 3.7). Immediately after his death in 62 CE, when the true defence of the city was gone, the prophet Jesus ben Ananias came to Jerusalem during the Feast of Tabernacles and began to utter oracles of woe. These continued for seven years, until he was killed in the siege of Jerusalem (*War* 6.300–309).

When asked by the scribes and Pharisees to address the crowds in the temple and warn them not to be misled by Jesus, James replied, 'I tell you he is sitting in heaven at the right hand of the Great Power and he will come on the clouds of heaven' (Eusebius, *History* 2.23). The Ebionites are said to have used a book called the *Ascents of James* (Epiphanius, *Panarion* I.30.16) of which nothing more is known, but this would account for James' ascent (11.4). It is likely that the visionary material incorporated into the *Ascension of Isaiah* originated as the *Ascents of James* and preserves his teaching and also the account of his ascents. 'Isaiah's' disciples heard a door being opened and the prophet being summoned to ascend (*Asc. Isa.* 6.6), just as the witnesses 'heard a loud voice from heaven saying "Come up hither" and in the sight of their foes they went up to heaven in a cloud' (11.12). The *Clementine Recognitions* describe James' debates with the authorities in Jerusalem, in particular about the two comings of Christ (*Clem. Rec.* I.66–70) and how he and his 5,000 followers left the city, just as 'Isaiah' withdrew from Jerusalem with the faithful prophets (*Asc. Isa.* 2.7–11). Two of 'Isaiah's' visions do describe the first and second comings of Christ (*Asc. Isa.* 11.1–33; 4.14–20). It was when James declared: 'He is sitting in heaven at the right hand of the Great Power' (Eusebius, *History* 2.23) that the scribes and Pharisees threw him from the temple parapet, stoned him, and finally clubbed him to death. This is also the climax of 'Isaiah's' vision: 'I saw that he sat down at the right hand of that Great Glory, whose glory I told you I could not behold, and I saw the angel of the holy spirit sat on the left' (*Asc. Isa.* 11.32–33). Hegesippus concluded of James: 'He has proved a true witness to Jews and Gentiles alike that Jesus is the Christ. Immediately after this, Vespasian began to besiege them' (quoted by Eusebius, *History* 2.23). Eusebius records elsewhere that James and Jesus were both regarded as martyrs: 'James the Righteous suffered martyrdom like the LORD and for the same reason . . .' (*History* 4.22), another indication that Jesus and James were the two witnesses.

Tradition has identified the two witnesses as Enoch and Elijah, but they were taken up into the presence of God and did not die. One of the few clear details about the witnesses, however, is that they were killed in Jerusalem, and so it is unlikely that Enoch and Elijah were intended. Other details are ambiguous. Power to shut the sky (11.6) does, however, suggest Elijah who had the power to bring drought (1 Kgs 17.1: 'There shall be neither dew nor rain these years except by my word'), and the one who turned water to blood and brought plagues (11.6) was Moses (Exod. 7.20 and 8.1–11.10), perhaps a reference to James. Fire from the mouth (11.5) was a sign of the Messiah: 'He sent forth from his mouth as it were a stream of fire and from his lips a flaming breath . . . and they fell on the onrushing multitude which was preparing to fight' . . . (2 *Esdr.* 13.10–11), although is was also said that Elijah breathed fire: 'The prophet Elijah arose like a fire, and his word burned like a torch' (*Ben Sira* 48.1). Jesus was expected to return with fire and slay the lawless one with the breath of his mouth (2 Thess. 1.7, 2.8), but a more likely reference is to the mystics who were John's contemporaries. Of R. Jonathan b. Uzziel, it was said that 'fire came down when he studied the Torah' (*b. Sukkah* 28a). The Jerusalem and Babylonian Talmuds both record the story of R. Eleazar b. Arak expounding the mysteries of the chariot throne before his master, R. Johannan b. Zakkai. Fire came down from heaven and surrounded them 'the ministering angels danced before them' (*y. Hagigah* 77a), and 'fire encompassed all the trees in the field' (*b. Hagigah* 14b). A fire shone in the waters of the Jordan when Jesus was baptized (see p. 127).

The two witnesses could have been martyrs who were identified as Elijah and Moses. John the Baptist had been described as Elijah, 'I tell you Elijah has come' (Mark 9.13) and James the Righteous had led 5000 Christians out of 'Egypt'. It is therefore possible, but less likely, that John the Baptist and James were the two witnesses, the two Messiahs from Aaron and Israel. John was the son of Zechariah the priest (Luke 1.5) and James was the son of Joseph, 'of the house and lineage of David' (Luke 2.4). Both men were Nazirites: one from Aaron and the other from David.

Another interesting possibility arises from a collection of mystical texts known as *Hekhalot Rabbati*, which cannot be dated but have clear links to the Enoch literature. These and other similar texts describe the ascent of a mystic to stand before the heavenly throne, and so their relevance to the Book of Revelation is obvious. The two witnesses both experienced ascent when they were summoned into heaven (11.12) and they both had great power to punish their enemies; they enjoyed divine protection and could pour fire from their mouths, turn water into blood and afflict the earth with plagues. Their death brought destruction to the city which terrified all who survived it (11.13). *The Hekhalot Rabbati attributes similar powers to the temple mystic.* The text is obscure, but the powers seem to come from the mystic's guardian angels:

Whoever raises a hand against him and strikes him, they [the angels?] robe him with plagues, cover him with leprosy and crown him with a rash. Whoever speaks evil of him, they hurl and throw upon him blows, boils, bad wounds and bruises ... He is glorified by those above and below ... If anyone makes him fall, great evil things fall upon him from heaven. The heavenly court will raise its hand against each one who shamefully lifts a hand against him. (# 84–85)

It is possible that something similar stood in the original text about the two witnesses. If any harm befell them, fire came from their heavenly protectors and consumed their foes (11.5). It was the death of the witnesses that brought the destruction of the city.

The Seventh Trumpet

The seventh and last trumpet brings to a close the sequence which was probably based on the ancient Book of the LORD (Isa. 34.16). It began when the Lamb approached the throne and took the sealed scroll and it continued through the opening of the six seals. The seventh seal was the moment when the Servant/Lamb, who had become the enthroned LORD, prepared to emerge from his holy place to complete the great judgement and atonement. Christian prophets had marked events in the years which followed the crucifixion of Jesus and they had seen six seals open. The LORD did not return.

The great Day of Atonement at the end of the tenth Jubilee was the moment when Melchizedek the heavenly high priest, the Righteous King, was to return and bring judgement on the host of Satan. He would then proclaim to Zion, 'Your God reigns'. The Melchizedek text breaks off just as Leviticus 25.9 is quoted. The trumpets had a role in the final Day of Atonement, but we do not know what it was. The end of the tenth Jubilee must have been a period charged with political and religious significance – prisoners released, debts cancelled and the land returned to its rightful owners (see pp. 48–9).

The Melchizedek text shows that the Anointed One was the Anointed Prince prophesied by Daniel. The ten Jubilees of the Melchizedek text are the same as the seventy weeks of years foretold in Daniel 9.24: 'Seventy weeks of years are decreed concerning your people and your holy city, to finish the transgression, to put an end to sin, and to atone for iniquity, to bring in everlasting righteousness, to seal both vision and prophet, and to anoint a most holy place'. This verse is obscure as the text has been damaged in transmission, but it describes the final Day of Atonement. The beginning of the text should probably be read as 'to confine rebellion, to seal up sin and to atone iniquity. To bring in everlasting righteousness' probably conceals Melchizedek, and 'to anoint a most holy place' was traditionally understood as a prophecy of the Messiah, that is 'to anoint a Most Holy One'. The Righteous and Holy One, designations of this Anointed One, are found in Acts 3.14 as descriptions of Jesus: 'You denied the Holy and Righteous One . . .' The enigmatic words 'to seal up the vision and the prophet' were understood by the translator of the LXX as 'to complete the vision and the prophet', that is, to fulfil the prophet's vision. The Hebrew for 'to seal' is *lhtm* and for 'to complete' is *lhtm*, hence the confusion. The Melchizedek high priest was to come and fulfil the prophecies.

There are further problems in this important passage in Daniel: 'an anointed one shall be cut off, and shall have nothing; and the people of the prince who is to come shall destroy the city and the sanctuary' (Dan. 9.26). The text is obscure at this point, even opaque, and one has to ask why. Prophecies are by their nature enigmatic, but there is more than enigma here. It seems to say that the Anointed One will be killed and then return 'the prince who is to come', to destroy both Jerusalem and the temple. If this is how it was understood, that the Anointed One would himself return to destroy Jerusalem and the temple, it would have been a text much favoured by the early church. It would explain the very different and possibly polemical translation of this verse made in the second century CE by a Jewish scholar, Theodotion: 'He shall destroy the city and the holy place together with the prince who is to come'.

In addition to fulfilling the prophecies of Daniel, the Melchizedek text promises comfort to those who mourn (Isa. 61.2), and then begins to explain the trumpets. It was in such a context of political and messianic fervour that the Book of Revelation was compiled. Seven trumpets had already been used as a framework for the stylized history of Roman rule in Palestine. When the Book of Revelation was compiled, the seven trumpets became the trumpets of the Day of Atonement announcing the LORD's coming, but also marking his delay. The prophet Joel had described the trumpet which warned of the Day of the LORD: 'Blow the trumpet in Zion; sound the alarm in my holy mountain! Let all the inhabitants of the land tremble, for the day of the LORD is coming, it is near' (Joel 2.1). Finally, the seventh trumpet sounded.

Paul knew of the seventh and last trumpet, and what it would bring. Presumably the churches to whom he was writing knew about it too. In his first letter to the Thessalonians – his earliest surviving letter written about 50 CE – he wrote:

We who are alive, who are left until the coming of the LORD, shall not precede those who have fallen asleep. For the LORD himself will descend from heaven with a cry of command, with the archangel's call, and with the sound of the trumpet of God [cf. Rev. 11.15]. And the dead in Christ will rise first; then we who are alive, who are left, shall be caught up together with them in the clouds to meet the LORD in the air; and so we shall always be with the LORD. (1 Thess. 4.15–17, cf. Rev. 11.18)

Paul expected the last trumpet to sound in his own lifetime, the dead to be raised and the reign of the LORD to begin. About five years later, writing to the church in Corinth, he said: 'Lo! I tell you a mystery. We shall not all sleep, but we shall all be changed, in a moment, in the twinkling of an eye, at the last trumpet. For the trumpet will sound, and the dead will be raised imperishable, and we shall be changed' (1 Cor. 15.51–52). The last trumpet was the moment of resurrection and 'change'. Matthew described the return of the high priest in the same way. The Man would come on the clouds of heaven, as did the Mighty Angel in Revelation 10.1, 'and he will send out his angels with a loud trumpet call and they will gather his elect from the four winds, from one end of heaven to the other' (Matt. 24.31).

When the seventh trumpet sounded, the LORD would begin to reign with his elect, the first-resurrected ones. A longer account of this appears in the description of the millennium kingdom (20.4–6), where the seer has a vision of thrones (20.4), that is the elders as in 4.4, and then the resurrected martyrs: 'They came to life and reigned with Christ for a thousand years' (20.4). In 11.15–18 the original prophecy of the kingdom is incorporated into the praise of the elders.

Josephus wrote of a prophecy in 'their' sacred scriptures – so not in the Hebrew Scriptures – that at that time one from their country would become ruler of the world (*War* 6.312). The Slavonic text continues: 'Some understood that this meant Herod, others the crucified wonder worker Jesus and others again Vespasian'. Josephus believed that it was a prophecy of Vespasian's being proclaimed emperor while he was in Palestine, and this interpretation was to appear in the writings of both Tacitus (*Histories* 5.13) and Suetonius (*Vespasian* 4, see p. 157). The people of Jerusalem, however, understood it to refer to someone of their own race and Josephus said 'many of their wise men went astray in their interpretation of it'. This indicates that the prophecy was messianic and a significant factor in the war against Rome, as were the interpretations of Christian 'wise men'. Eusebius knew that Josephus had been wrong to interpret the oracle in favour of Vespasian: 'But Vespasian did not rule over the entire world, but only the part under Roman rule. It would be more justly applied to Christ of whom the Father had said: Ask of me and I will give the heathen world for your inheritance, and for your possession the ends of the earth' (*History* 3.8). Eusebius believed that the oracle in question was Psalm 2 which he quoted; but Josephus, a Jew from a high priestly family, would never have referred to the Psalms as 'their' scripture. The oracle which heightened the messianic fervour and fuelled the war against Rome was whatever lay behind 11.15. The original may simply have been: 'The kingdom of the world will become the kingdom of the LORD and his Anointed'. Doubtless it was based on and related to Psalm 2.7–8, especially as the conspiracy of Herod and Pilate against Jesus had been interpreted as the fulfilment of Psalm 2.2, the kings of the earth and the rulers taking council together 'against the LORD and his Anointed'. Identical words appear in 11.15, 'the kingdom of our LORD and his Anointed'. The Chronicler had described the enthronement of Solomon in the same way: 'All the assembly blessed the LORD, the God of their fathers and they worshipped the LORD and the king ... And Solomon sat on the throne of the LORD as king ...' (1 Chron. 29.20, 23). The original oracle about the one who was both LORD and anointed king was probably the climax of the Book of the LORD. In the vision of the seventh trumpet, the elders proclaim 'the kingdom of our LORD and of his Anointed One', but they fall down and worship just one, the LORD God Almighty (11.15–16).

The praise of the elders marks the centre of the Book of Revelation and summarizes its contents. 'We give thanks to thee, LORD God Almighty, who art and who wast, that thou hast taken thy great power and begun to reign' (11.17) is the first part of the book, chapters 4–11, which describes the enthronement of the Servant/Lamb in heaven and then the signs of his return to establish his kingdom. In these early chapters the coming of the LORD is an event expected in the future: 'I am the Alpha and the Omega, says the LORD God, who is and who was and who is to come, the Almighty' (1.8) occurs in the preface to the earliest stratum of the book, and the elders in heaven sing: 'Holy, holy, holy is the LORD God Almighty who was and is and is to come' (4.8). Here at last, in 11.17, after the seventh trumpet has sounded, the LORD has returned and so the elders no longer sing of his future coming: 'We give thanks to thee LORD God Almighty, who art and who wast, that thou hast taken thy great power and begun to reign'. The angel's revelation to John showed him that this had already happened, that it was no longer in the future and so the return of the LORD became, in the Fourth Gospel, the gift of the Spirit (John 20.22) and the heavenly food of his flesh and blood (John 6.52–58).

The second half of the elders' song points forward to the second half of the book: the raging of the nations and the destruction of those who are destroying the earth. There is no chronological sequence joining the two sections; 11.19 marks a new beginning and the second part begins with a resumé of history. The one destined to rule the nations is born as son of God (12.5) and Michael begins to fight with the dragon (12.7) who is thrown from heaven and begins his reign of terror. First he attacks the Woman and her children, then the beast and the false prophet join forces with him. Chapters 14–16 summarize the harvest of the earth as the great conflict proceeds, chapters 17–18 describe the harlot city and her destruction. Finally the One destined to rule the nations (12.5) emerges from heaven to conquer the beast (19.11–16).

The great battle and the last judgement follow and the destroyers of the earth are destroyed. The Book of Revelation ends by describing the reward of the servants, the prophets and the saints and those who fear the LORD.

The Targum to Isaiah 24 is so similar to this passage in 11.15–18 that there must have been some link between them. The most likely is that both targumist and seer reflected the expectation of their own times and drew on a common source:

From the sanctuary, whence joy is about to come forth unto all the inhabitants of the earth, we have heard a song of praise for the righteous. The prophet said, 'The mystery of the reward of the righteous hath been shown unto me, the mystery of the punishment of the wicked hath been revealed to me. Woe to the oppressors, for they shall be oppressed, and to the spoiling of the spoilers, for behold they shall be spoiled ... And it shall come to pass at that time, that the LORD shall punish the mighty hosts that dwell in the stronghold and the kings of the sons of men that dwell on the earth ... For the kingdom of the LORD of hosts shall be revealed in the mountain of Zion and in Jerusalem, and before the elders of his people in glory'. (*T. Isa.* 24.16, 21, 23b)

13

THE WOMAN CLOTHED WITH THE SUN

Then God's temple in heaven was opened, and the ark of his covenant was seen within his temple; and there were flashes of lightning, voices, peals of thunder, an earthquake and heavy hail. And a great portent appeared in heaven, a woman clothed with the sun, with the moon under her feet, and on her head a crown of twelve stars; she was with child and she cried out in her pangs of birth, in anguish for delivery ... she brought forth a male child, one who is to rule all the nations with a rod of iron, but her child was caught up to God and to his throne. (Rev. 11.19 and 12.1, 2, 5)

The heavenly sanctuary has been opened and the long lost ark is seen again. A Jewish tradition recorded in *Numbers Rabbah* XV.10 said that the ark would be restored to the temple in the time of the Messiah, and this is the vision of his birth. The Woman clothed with the sun is his mother, the Queen of Heaven. She is the ancient goddess of Jerusalem, venerated for centuries until banished by temple reformers in the seventh century BCE. She was also the constellation Virgo, and when the sun was in Virgo and she the reigning sign, i.e. in September, the birth of the Messiah was expected. At the Autumn Festival, the birth of her son was celebrated as the enthronement of the king and she was both his patron and his heavenly mother.

Looking into the sanctuary, beyond the veil, the visionary sees events outside time. Here the child is born and enthroned before the creation of the material world, just as Enoch describes the Man in heaven: 'And at that hour the Son of Man was named, in the presence of the LORD of Spirits and his name before the Head of Days. Yea before the sun and the signs were created, before the stars of heaven were made, his name was named before the LORD of Spirits' (*1 En.* 48.2–3).

The Queen of Heaven

The Woman clothed with the sun wears a crown of twelve stars because she is the Queen of Heaven. The twelve stars may represent the twelve tribes of Israel, as they did in Joseph's dream (Gen. 37.9), but there can be no doubt about her son. He is the royal child destined to rule the nations with a rod of iron (12.5, cf. Ps. 2.8–9). The Woman's child is caught up to the throne of God, just as the royal child was set on Zion as the LORD's king, begotten that day as his divine son.

Psalm 110 describes this birth. The LORD addresses the psalmist's king 'The LORD said to my Lord', and commands him to share the divine throne (Ps. 110.1). He becomes a priest for ever, in the manner of Melchizedek (Ps. 110.4), and the Melchizedek text (11QMelch) shows how this was understood in the first century CE. Melchizedek was a divine figure, who took his place in the heavenly council and prepared to bring the Day of the LORD. The intervening lines in Psalm 110 must describe the process by which the human king became the divine Melchizedek. He has an army prepared for holy war, 'the freely offered people (see p. 245) and he stands in the splendour of the holy ones' (following the LXX text). The rest of the obscure (obscured?) verse yields the following: 'I have begotten you, from the womb, the Morning Star, dew to you'. The dew probably refers to resurrection; 'the dew of light' brings resurrection (Isa. 26.19) and the dew was the means of resurrection in later texts. When Israel was overcome by the divine presence at Sinai, for example, the Lord brought down 'the dew that resurrects the dead' and revived them (*b. Shabbat* 88b). The process of making the Melchizedek high priest was described in the first century CE as resurrection (Heb. 7.11, see pp. 8–9) and 'Morning Star' was a title given to Jesus and promised to the faithful angel of the church at Thyatira (22.16; 2.28). *The womb* must have been the heavenly mother from whom the king was born/resurrected.

Evidence from Ancient Ugarit confirms the identity of the king's heavenly mother who was clothed with the sun. Their sun goddess, whose two aspects were named Athirat and Rahmay, gave birth to the two aspects of the king named Morning Star and Evening Star. (These geminated forms are common in the mythology of the area, and reappear in the figure of the risen LORD see p. 375). A stela from Ugarit depicts the scene when the king approaches the heavenly throne, under the wings of the sun disc, who represents his heavenly mother. The sun goddess despite being mother of the royal heir, was known as the Virgin (KTU 1.15.ii.), as well as the 'Great Lady who tramples the sea' and the 'Creatrix of the gods' (KTU 1.4.iii.34–35). The seventy sons of El, the gods of the nations, were her children, and she was the consort of El Elyon who appears in Genesis 14.20, 22 as God Most High served by the priest-king of Jerusalem named Melchizedek. The fragment of Deuteronomy 32.8–9 found among the Dead Sea Scrolls (and appearing in newer translations such as the NRSV), shows that Israel had known the sons of El. It prompts the question how there came to be two versions of such a sensitive text, since this longer version must have been the one used by the translators of the LXX, i.e. it is the older text:

When the Most High apportioned the nations
when he divided humankind
he fixed the boundaries of the peoples
according to the number of the gods
The LORD's own portion was his people,
Jacob his allotted share. (4QDeut.⁹)

A millennium and more separates the Ugaritic evidence from the Book of Revelation, but not from the cult of the first temple. The Woman clothed with the sun is not the Ugaritic goddess, but the Hebrew goddess who was worshipped in Jerusalem until the temple purges in the seventh century BCE. She is the Queen of Heaven, the consort of the King, the LORD of Hosts, whom Isaiah had seen in his vision (Isa. 6.5). The eighth-century prophets, however, spoke of her as the *'almah*, (which the LXX understood to mean Virgin), the mother of the royal child, Immanuel, God with us (Isa. 7.14) and as the woman who would give birth in Bethlehem to the mighty shepherd of Israel (Mic. 5.2–4). When Malachi warned of the Day of the Lord, he promised that the Sun of Righteousness would rise up with healing 'in her wings' (Mal. 4.2, usually translated 'its wings'). In the Book of Revelation she gives birth to her son and then flies away on eagles' wings into the desert, to escape the ancient serpent (12.14).

The Daughter of Zion

The Woman was also the genius of the city, the Daughter of Zion and mother of its citizens (LXX Ps. 87.5 describes her as 'Mother Zion', cf. 2 *Esdr.* 10.7: 'Zion the mother of us all' and Gal. 4.26: 'Jerusalem our mother'). The eighth-century prophets mention the Daughter of Zion, and it is more than just a personification of the city. 'The mount of the Daughter of Zion' (Isa. 10.32; 16.1; Mic. 4.8) should be understood as literally as 'the hill of the LORD' (Ps. 24.3). 'The kingdom of the daughter of Jerusalem' (Mic. 4.8) cannot be understood differently from the LORD's kingdom (Ps. 103.19; 145.12–13). The virgin Daughter of Zion scorned the Assyrian attempt to attack her (Isa. 37.22), but Jeremiah heard her crying out before the Babylonians: 'the cry of the Daughter of Zion, gasping for breath, stretching out her hands, "Woe is me! I am fainting before murderers!" ' (Jer. 4.31). When she was put under a cloud, the splendour of Israel was cast from heaven (Lam. 2.1), just as Ezekiel described the city of Tyre falling when her king was driven from heaven (Ezek. 28.12–19). The temple was her 'tent' (Lam. 2.4), and as her city was destroyed, the princess among cities became a widow (Lam. 1.1).

The exilic prophecies of Isaiah tell her story, an abandoned woman who claimed that the LORD had forsaken her (Isa. 49.14). The LORD told her to get up from the dust and dress herself again like the Queen (Isa. 52.1–2). The barren woman was to rejoice and no longer live as a widow (Isa. 54.1–4). 'Your Maker is your husband, the LORD of Hosts is his name' (Isa. 54.5). The woman then becomes the city, and the LORD promises to rebuild her with precious stones (Isa. 54.11–12), but the goddess imagery remains. Just as the eternal goddess had been the mother of the king and also his consort, so too the city is assured 'your sons shall marry you' (Isa. 62.5, often mistranslated 'builders', as the Hebrew words are identical). The city becomes the mother of many more children and enjoys renewed prosperity (Isa. 66.7–14).

There are two figures in these exilic prophecies of Isaiah and both are reinterpreted by him for the new situation. The male figure is the Servant (see pp. 46–7, 133), originally the royal high priest who made the atonement sacrifice. He became a symbol for the whole suffering people. The female figure, who has often been overlooked, became a symbol or personification of the restored city. She had originally been the Great Lady, the Daughter of Zion. *Both the Servant and the Great Lady in all her aspects are key figures in the Book of Revelation.* The Great Lady and her divine son had been banished from the city for centuries, and the seer looked forward to their return. As Jesus entered Jerusalem on Palm Sunday, he fulfilled the prophecy that the King would return to the Daughter of Zion (Zech. 9.9; Matt. 21.5; John 12.15).

The Lady Wisdom

The Woman had another role as co-creator of the world, and Proverbs 8 has preserved an extraordinary glimpse of the Mother at work. In this account she is the daughter of the LORD, but it is possible that the original described her as the daughter of El Elyon. Before the beginnings of the earth, on Day One or even before, Wisdom was brought forth: 'The LORD begot me' (Prov. 8.22, *qnh*; see p. 142). She was beside the Creator as he established the heavens and confined the seas, marking out the foundations of the earth 'like a master workman' (Prov. 8.30, see p. 112). The psalmist knew her role in creation: 'O LORD how manifold are thy works! With Wisdom thou hast made them all' (Ps. 104.24). When she had been banished from Israel's religion, her role in creation was denied: 'Who has directed the Spirit of the LORD . . . whom did he consult for his enlightenment?' (Isa. 40.13-14), but she was not forgotten. The Targums render Genesis 1.1 'With Wisdom the LORD created . . .'(*T. Ps. Jon.* and *T. Neof.*, see p. 40).

She was the Tree in Eden, originally one tree, since her gift of Wisdom was also the gift of eternal life (see below and p. 208). The Wisdom she offered was known to make humans like God (Gen. 3.5), but this was condemned along with the rest of her cult. The Deuteronomists turned the temple myths into history, and the Great Lady became Eve, the Mother of all living (Gen. 3.20, see p. 210) 'brought forth' from Adam without a second parent.

When Jesus ben Sira wrote his book of Wisdom in Jerusalem, early in the second century BCE, he described Wisdom as a powerful heavenly being who spoke in the assembly of God Most High (*Ben Sira* 24.2). She was created first (*Ben Sira* 24.9) and had a heavenly throne:

I dwelt in high places
and my throne was in a pillar of cloud.
Alone I have made the circuit the vault of heaven
and have walked in the depths of the abyss.
In the waves of the sea, in the whole earth,
and in every people and nation I have gotten a possession. (*Ben Sira* 24.4–6)

She was allocated Israel for her inheritance, exactly as was said of the

LORD (*Ben Sira* 24.8; Deut. 32.9). She ruled in Jerusalem and served in the temple: 'In the holy tabernacle I ministered before him' (*Ben Sira* 24.10), and she 'took root in an honoured people' (*Ben Sira* 24.12). Wisdom was described as a beautiful tree, her ancient symbol, spreading out glorious and graceful branches (*Ben Sira* 24.16). She invited her devotees to eat and drink from her, so that they would hunger and thirst for more (*Ben Sira* 24.19–22). Ben Sira's poem then changes course, and the Wisdom imagery is transferred to the Law. The original is still clear, though, and it describes Wisdom as the rivers that flowed from Eden, watering her garden, 'making instruction shine like the dawn … and pouring out teaching like prophecy' (*Ben Sira* 24.31–33).

Asherah Destroyed

In the seventh century there had been several attempts to alter the temple worship in Jerusalem (see pp. 15–17). The Deuteronomists, who brought about the changes, had taught that the Law was to be the Wisdom of the chosen people (Deut. 4.6). They had forbidden the veneration of the sun, moon, stars and all the host of heaven (Deut. 4.19), despite the fact that the most ancient title of Israel's God was the LORD of hosts. The hosts, i.e. the stars and the angels they represented, were forbidden. King Josiah sanctioned a great purge in the temple which removed not only the goddess, but also the angels. He burned the vessels made for Asherah, Baal, and all the Host of heaven. He drove out the priests. Asherah herself was taken from the house of the LORD and burned at the brook Kidron in the valley of Jehoshapat (2 Kgs 23.6), traditionally the site of the LORD's judgement (Joel 3.2, 12). Her image was not gone for long; when Ezekiel visited Jerusalem on his spirit journey some thirty years later, he saw it at the northern entrance to the inner court of the temple (Ezek. 8.3). Its identity, however, has been concealed by adding one letter to the Hebrew text. Instead of *sml hqn'h hmqnh*, the image of jealousy which provokes to jealousy, read *sml hqnh hmqnh,* and the goddess reappears: 'the image of the creatrix who causes life'. (In Hebrew *qn'* means 'be jealous' and *qnh* means 'get children'. Changing letters was a common way of conveying the editor's opinion of something he did not like, e.g. in Isaiah 19.18 the 'City of the Sun' becomes the 'City of Destruction', just by changing one letter.)

King Josiah also destroyed the chapels of her devotees (the text now describes them as prostitutes), where women wove hangings for the statue (2 Kgs 23.7). This must have been an important part of her cult as the garments of the goddess appear in the Book of Revelation (19.8). King Josiah also destroyed all traces of sun worship, the horses and chariots that the kings of Judah had dedicated in the temple (2 Kgs 23.11), and these too appear in the Book of Revelation as the four riders (6.1–8). (When Dame Kathleen Kenyon was excavating near the temple precinct itself, she uncovered a quantity of female figurines and miniature horses with sun discs on their heads.)

The worship of the goddess was long established even in the royal house. At the beginning of the ninth century, King Asa had deposed his mother, the Great Lady of the court, because she had made an image of the goddess. He had 'the abominable thing' cut down and burned by the Kidron (1 Kgs 15.13). Two centuries later, Hezekiah 'broke the pillars, cut down the Asherah and broke in pieces the bronze serpent that Moses had made', which the people had been worshipping (2 Kgs 18.4).

Attempts to purge the temple cult show that the worship of the goddess was linked to the sun and stars, but also to a bronze serpent and to something which could be cut down and burned. This may have been an image of the goddess, but there may also have been sacred trees which represented her presence. The LXX regularly translated Asherah as 'sacred grove', and this appears in the older English translations; Jezebel maintained 400 prophets 'of the groves' (1 Kgs 18.19) and Gideon cut down 'the grove' by the altar (Judg. 6.28). At the end of the second temple period, Asherah was remembered as a sacred tree; the Mishnah distinguished three kinds of Asherah: trees planted as sacred, trees trimmed and shaped to make a sacred object, and trees under which there was an idol (*m. Abodah Zarah* 3.7). The community who wrote the Qumran Hymns, however, described themselves as these trees, 'the branches of the Council of Holiness' (1QH XV, formerly VII), 'a watered garden ... a plantation of trees of life beside a mysterious fountain ... the everlasting trees ...' (1QH XVI, formerly VIII).

A tree which was specially shaped immediately suggests the menorah, the stylized golden almond tree which Moses was commanded to set in the tabernacle (Exod. 25.31–39). The 'official' accounts of Solomon's temple in 1 Kings 6–7 and 2 Chronicles 3–5 do not mention the menorah even though Zechariah, who prophesied before the second temple was built, saw in his temple vision a seven-branched lamp (Zech. 4.2), angels standing among trees (Zech. 1.10) and four horsemen (Zech. 1.8; 6.1–8). These must have been his recollection of the original temple, before the horses of the sun and the stylized tree were removed. The silence of the other accounts shows it was a sensitive issue. Although there was a menorah in the second temple, its meaning must have altered, because it was said that in the age of the Messiah, five things would be restored to the temple: the lamp, the ark, the Spirit, the fire and the cherubim (*Num. Rab.* XV. 10).

When the Deuteronomists purged the worship of Israel, they also began to rewrite and to edit the ancient texts. There are several places where their work can still be detected, but there must be many more where all trace of the goddess has gone. They described the image of Asherah as the 'abominable thing' (1 Kgs 15.13) and made subtle alterations to the older texts. The image of the goddess disappeared from Ezekiel's vision (Ezek. 8.3), she was renamed 'the sin' of Samaria (Amos 8.14 has *'šmt* instead of *'šrh*, but in Hebrew these look similar), she no longer came in glory at the right hand of the LORD but became 'flaming fire' (Deut. 33.2 has *'šdt* instead of *'šrh*, but these too look similar in Hebrew).

There are also texts where the word *'elah*, goddess, may have been read as the identical *'elah*, terebinth, because a goddess was not expected. Joshua, for example, set up a memorial stone for the Law of Moses in the sanctuary of the LORD at Shechem 'under the oak tree' or 'instead of the goddess' (Josh. 24.26, the Hebrew is identical). An almost opaque oracle from Isaiah, perhaps in response to Hezekiah's destruction of the Asherah (2 Kgs 18.4) warns that 'the Asherah' (not 'one tenth') will be burned again, 'like the goddess' and the oak tree, 'the Asherah' (not 'which') will be cast down from the high place, but the holy seed is in her stump (Isa. 6.13 cf. 11.1).

Archaeologists now recognize that accounts of Israel's religion written long after the event give an idealized picture and that there had indeed been a mother goddess in the cult of Solomon's temple, the queen consort of the LORD. Large numbers of female figurines and plaques have been discovered at Israelite sites, even in the royal palace excavated at Ramath Rachel. A graffito of the LORD and a female figure has been found at Kuntillet 'Ajrud, and there is an inscription which mentions 'the LORD and his Asherah'. It is not wise, however, to attempt to reconstruct Israel's goddess simply on the basis of what is known about the female deities of Canaan, or to match the names of their goddesses to the female figures in the Hebrew Scriptures. Just as one would not depict the LORD solely in terms of his similarity to Canaanite deities, nor use Baal figurines as primary evidence for Israel's religion, so too, Israel's goddess must be recovered from Israel's texts and traditions.

The Queen in Exile

When Jerusalem was destroyed in 586 BCE and refugees fled to Egypt, they knew what had caused the disaster: 'Since we left off burning incense to the Queen of Heaven, and pouring out libations to her, we have lacked everything and have been consumed by the sword and by famine' (Jer. 44.18). The Jews in Egypt continued to venerate the goddess, and their writings have best preserved her memory. A hoard of papyrus documents was found at Yeb in the south of Egypt, dating from the fifth century BCE and written by a community of Jews who had kept the older ways. Alongside the LORD, they worshipped a goddess with a Hebrew name, Anat-Yahu.

An anonymous Egyptian Jew who adopted the pseudonym of King Solomon, wrote a book of Wisdom at the end of the second temple period. He too recalled the ancient roles and titles of the goddess. It is possible that for him they were no more than figures of speech, but even so, the imagery is revealing. She gave 'Solomon' great knowledge because she was 'Wisdom, the fashioner of all things' (*Wisd.* 7.22). She was more beautiful than the sun and the stars, and pervaded the whole earth (*Wisd.* 7.29–8.1). The king desired Wisdom for his Bride (*Wisd.* 8.2) and she gave him immortality (*Wisd.* 8.13). He spoke of Wisdom forming humankind (*Wisd.* 9.2) and knew that she was present when the world was made (*Wisd.* 9.9). She sat beside the throne of God (*Wisd.* 9.4), but came to the king when he prayed for Wisdom to help him rule (*Wisd.* 9.10–12). Most extraordinary of all is his history of Israel, which he told as the history of Wisdom guiding her people: Wisdom protected Adam, rescued Abraham, guided Jacob, delivered Joseph and led Moses (*Wisd.* 10.1–11.14).

Philo also knew the goddess, but he used the traditions about her in allegories. Some of what he says could have been deduced from the Scriptures, for example, that Wisdom was older than the whole earth (*Virtues* 62), but most of what he says could not. *He is therefore proof that the goddess traditions were known and used by first-century Jews even though they are not in the Scriptures we have assumed they were using.* Philo knew of the divine couple who had been parents of the king and he used this imagery to describe the creation. 'Knowledge, having received the divine seed ... bore the only beloved son ... this world' (*On Drunkenness* 30). He could have deduced from Scripture that God is the Father of all things, but not that 'he is the husband of Wisdom' (*Cherubim* 49). He described the high priest as the Logos, the son of God and of 'Wisdom his mother through whom the universe came into being' (*Flight* 109). He could probably have deduced from Proverbs 8 that Wisdom was the daughter of God, but not that she was 'the first born mother of all things' (*On Gen.* IV.97).

When he wrote of the 'daughter' of God, he explained that the feminine gender only indicated her second place in the divine order, in contrast with the Maker who is masculine (*Flight* 50–51). He uses the same titles for Wisdom as he does for the Logos: 'the heavenly Wisdom is of many names ... beginning and image and vision of God' (*All. Int.* I.43, see below). Most remarkable is his complex allegory of the patriarchs and their wives, clearly derived from the tradition of Wisdom as the perpetual consort, the virgin wife and mother of each king. Abraham married Sarah, who was motherless Wisdom (*On Gen.* IV.145) and she became a virgin again after the LORD visited her and she conceived Isaac (*Cherubim* 45; *Posterity* 134). Isaac married Rebecca, who was also Wisdom, and thus he was consoled when his mother died (*On Gen.* IV.146). Philo's allegory of family relationships between God, Wisdom and the Logos is extremely complex and not always consistent; what matters is that he felt able to use the illustration of a divine family which is not in the public form of the Hebrew Scriptures known today.

In her homeland, we glimpse Wisdom calling to her children in the Book of Proverbs. The new ways of the reformers have lured them away from her teaching, and disaster has struck. The Babylonians have come but she will not answer her children's call.

You have ignored all my counsel
and would have none of my reproof,
I also will mock at your calamity;

I will mock when panic strikes you,
when panic strikes you like a storm,
and your calamity comes like a whirlwind,
when distress and anguish come upon you.
Then they will call upon me, but I will not answer;
they will seek me diligently but they will not find me. (Prov. 1.25–28)

The restored Jerusalem is compared to a loose woman who forgets the covenant (Prov. 2.16–17) and she appears in Revelation 17 as the great harlot.

Wisdom was not forgotten, and even though it is not known who preserved and transmitted the texts, her devotees told her story in *1 Enoch*. The Apocalypse of Weeks is a cryptic Enoch text which tells the history of Israel as ten 'weeks'. In the sixth week those who lived in the temple became blind and abandoned Wisdom, just before the temple was destroyed by fire (*1 En.* 93.8). The reference is unmistakable; King Josiah's purge, twenty-five years before the Babylonians burned the temple, was the time when the priests became 'blind' and abandoned the goddess. They lost their spiritual vision. A prophecy warns of the time when sinners will tempt men to think evil of Wisdom and no place will be found for her (*1 En.* 94.5), and a lament describes how she left heaven to search for a dwelling place on earth but found none and so returned to take her place among the angels:

Wisdom found no place where she might dwell,
Then a dwelling place was assigned to her in the heavens
Wisdom went forth to make her dwelling among the children of men,
And found no dwelling place,
Wisdom returned to her place
And took her seat among the angels.
Unrighteousness went forth from her chambers:
Whom she sought not, she found,
And dwelt there as rain in a desert, and dew on a thirsty land. (*1 En.* 42.1–3)

Although the Book of Enoch preserves material from many periods, the Wisdom material is consistent throughout. Most is known elsewhere, but *1 Enoch* adds that the gift of Wisdom/resurrection was to be a sign of the last times. She would be given to the chosen ones to resurrect them on the Day of the LORD (*1 En.* 5.8; 91.10). At the end of the seventh week they would receive sevenfold knowledge about the creation (*1 En.* 93.10). Those who have Wisdom will be saved at the Judgement (*1 En.* 99.10). Wisdom stands by the heavenly throne (*1 En.* 84.3) and gives Enoch eternal life which enables him to 'see' his visions (*1 En.* 37.3–4). Eden imagery is used throughout. In his visions of heaven, Enoch sees a huge fragrant tree whose fruit gives Wisdom (*1 En.* 32.3), and therefore presumably eternal life. (*1 En.* 24.4–25.6 describes 'the tree of life' whose fruit was not for mortals but for the chosen ones, clearly the same tree, see p. 329.) Enoch saw fountains of

Wisdom flowing around the throne, and the thirsty drinking from them (1 En. 48.1), *Wisdom poured out like water* before him (1 En. 49.1).

There are also fragments of Jewish liturgy preserved, with Christian additions, in the *Apostolic Constitutions*. These depict God as the 'Father of Wisdom' (7.35.10), the only Son is God the Logos, the living Wisdom, the firstborn of every creature, the angel of great counsel and the high priest (8.12.7). God spoke to Wisdom when he said 'Let us make man after our image' (7.34.6).

Non-biblical texts such as these show that Israel's second God had two aspects, male and female, but insufficient evidence has survived to form a complete picture. The fusion of El Elyon and the LORD in some post-Deuteronomic texts and the attempt to suppress all evidence of the royal cult, complicate matters further. Such evidence as survives shows that:

- Both the LORD and Wisdom were angel figures who had been allocated Israel as their heritage.
- Both the LORD and Wisdom were present in the high priest.
- Both the Logos and Wisdom were the firstborn.
- Both the Logos and Wisdom were co-creators.
- Both the LORD and Wisdom are associated with the image of the menorah.

This explains why Jesus was believed to be 'Christ, the power of God and the Wisdom of God' (1 Cor. 1.24, see pp. 109, 112).

The Holy Spirit

The goddess is most familiar in her role as the Holy Spirit. The power in creation is the Spirit moving on the face of the waters (Gen 1.2), creating all things (Ps. 104.30) and creating humans (Job 33.4). Wisdom inspired the kings (*Wisd.* 7.7), yet this was also 'the Holy Spirit from on high' (*Wisd.* 9.17). Wisdom 'passed into holy souls and made them prophets' (*Wisd.* 7.27), and yet it was the Spirit that entered Ezekiel (Ezek. 2.2). The Spirit was poured out and brought the gift of visions and prophecy as a sign of the last times (Joel 2.28); Wisdom opened the eyes and was given to the elect in the last times.

Early Christian tradition remembered the Spirit as the Mother and as the one enthroned in heaven. Origen quoted a saying of Jesus from the (now lost) *Gospel According to the Hebrews*: 'My mother the Holy Spirit took me by one of my hairs and transported me to the great mountain Tabor' (*On John* 2.12). Jerome, commenting on Isaiah 11.2 'the Spirit of the LORD shall rest upon him', quoted from the same source an account of Jesus' baptism: 'The Holy Spirit descended and rested upon him and said unto him: "My son in all the prophets I was waiting for thee ... thou art my first begotten son, that reignest for ever" '. The *Gospel of Philip* denied that Mary conceived by the Holy Spirit: 'When did a woman ever conceive by a woman?' (*Philip* CG

II.3.55). 'Isaiah' in his vision of heaven saw the ascended LORD sat at the right hand of the Great Glory and 'the angel of the Holy Spirit sat on the left' (*Asc. Isa.* 11.33).

The Queen Lives

Remarkable evidence for the goddess can be found in ancient gnosticism, of which all too little is known, but there can no longer be any doubt that it developed from the older religion of Jerusalem as it had been before King Josiah's changes. Refugees brought it to Egypt and, centuries later, we glimpse the goddess in the gnostic texts. A hoard of these was discovered in a cave at Nag Hammadi in Egypt in December 1945, and early Christian writers such as Irenaeus (who wrote at the end of the second century CE) give some, albeit largely hostile, accounts of what the gnostics believed. Wisdom/Sophia appears throughout either as the consort and counterpart of the second deity, the great Archon, or as his mother, another echo of the royal cult.

Wisdom frequently appears as the name of an angel, one half of a pair: 'Astaphaios' feminine name is Wisdom ...' (*OOW* CG II.5.106). The great Archon was called the Perfect One 'and his female name [is] all wise Begettress Wisdom. It is also said that she resembles her brother and her consort' (*Eugnostos* CG III.3.76). The second deity's consort was 'the great Wisdom', (*Wisdom of Jesus Christ* CG III.4.101).

Wisdom was enthroned: 'Sabaoth sits on a throne concealed by a great light cloud and there is no one with him in the cloud except Wisdom Faith' (*OOW* CG II.5.106). 'Wisdom Zoe who is beside Sabaoth' (*OOW* CG II.5.113). Irenaeus described her: 'from the first angel who stands by the side of the Only Begotten, has been sent forth one whom they term Wisdom' (*AH* 1.29.4).

Wisdom was the co-creator: 'The heaven was consolidated along with the earth by means of the Wisdom of Yaldabaoth' (*OOW* CG II.5.103). 'Wisdom Zoe sent her breath into Adam who was without a soul' (*OOW* CG II.5.115). 'Wisdom ... was called life [i.e. Eve] which is the mother of all living' (*Ap. Jo.* CG II.1.23; cf. Gen. 3.20).

The separation of the LORD and his female consort after the seventh-century changes to the Jerusalem cult appears in the gnostic tradition as the arrogant Archon (ruler) who claimed he was the only God because he had lost sight of Wisdom, his mother, and did not realize she existed. Like the priests described in the 'Apocalypse of Weeks', the Archon became blind and so was known as Samael, the blind God (HA CG II.4.86–87). He claimed that he alone had created the world. Wisdom despaired of all her offspring (earlier known as the sons of El) and she returned to heaven.

When these were generated, the mother Wisdom, greatly grieved, fled away, departed to the upper regions, and became the last of the Ogdoad. On her thus departing, he [the arrogant archon] imagined that he was the only being in existence. (Irenaeus, *AH* 1.29.4)

Perhaps the most remarkable of all the evidence for the survival of goddess is found in the *Kabbalah*, where she appears as the Shekinah, meaning 'the indwelling' (of God in the world). Many rituals of the Kabbalists depicted the sacred marriage of the Shekinah. She is virtually an independent being and is now in exile, separated from her LORD. The tradition of the Talmud is that the Shekinah went into exile with the children of Israel, to Babylon or wherever they went (*b. Megillah* 29a), but the Kabbalists taught that it was the Shekinah herself who was exiled at that time, that a part of God had been separated off. This is exactly what her devotees said had been the fate of the goddess. When the people of Jerusalem went into exile in Babylon, the Queen of Heaven was banished from her place in the temple cult.

The Mother of the Messiah

The Queen of Heaven in all her aspects is central to the Book of Revelation. She returns to her city, first giving birth to the divine child. The harlot who had replaced her as the genius of Jerusalem is destroyed, and the Bride can then return from heaven as the heavenly Jerusalem. She gives herself as the gift of resurrection, and her children become citizens of the heavenly city, restored to Eden and eating from the tree of life (see pp. 329–30).

Jesus knew the vision of the Woman clothed with the sun. He quoted the words of Wisdom (Luke 11.49–50) and he spoke of himself as the child of Wisdom (Luke 7.35). The tradition of the Queen of Heaven, the Bride, was known to the circle of John the Baptist (Mark 2.19–20; John 3.29) with whom Jesus associated for a while, John being himself the son of a temple visionary (Luke 1.8–23).

'She brought forth a male child and her child was caught up to God and to his throne'. Origen compared the baptism of Jesus to the experience of Ezekiel. The prophet had seen the heavens open and had seen 'visions of God' (Ezek. 1.1). He saw the chariot throne, the fiery living creatures and a radiant human form (Ezek. 1.26). Then he was commissioned as a prophet and given a scroll which he was told to eat (Ezek. 3.3). Origen implies that what the prophet saw, Jesus also saw. The Gospels encode this information in the account of the temptations in the wilderness. Jesus was 'with the creatures and the angels served him' (Mark 1.13), immediately recognizable as a Merkavah experience.

When he returned from his forty days in the wilderness, Jesus proclaimed the coming of the kingdom of God (Mark 1.15) and he began to drive out demons (Mark 1.21–28). Revelation 12.7 records that 'war began in heaven'.

WAR IN HEAVEN AND EARTH

And another portent appeared in heaven; behold a great red dragon, with seven heads and ten horns, and seven diadems upon his heads. His tail swept down a third of the stars of heaven, and cast them to the earth. And the dragon stood before the woman who was about to bear a child, that he might devour her child when she brought it forth . . .

Now war arose in heaven, Michael and his angels fighting against the dragon; and the dragon and his angels fought, but they were defeated and there was no longer any place for them in heaven. And the great dragon was thrown down, that ancient serpent, who is called the Devil and Satan, the deceiver of the whole world – he was thrown down to the earth, and his angels were thrown down with him . . .

And when the dragon saw that he had been thrown down to earth, he pursued the woman who had borne the male child. (Rev. 12.3–4, 7–9, 13)

There are three monsters in the Book of Revelation: the red dragon with seven heads, ten horns and seven diadems who appears in heaven and tries to devour the new-born child; the beast with seven heads, ten horns and ten diadems, who rises from the sea and is the agent of the dragon; and the second beast with only two horns who is the agent of the first beast. The red dragon is identified as the Devil and Satan, the Deceiver (12.9), an indication that it is a composite figure. He also incorporates Azazel, the leader of the fallen angels, and Leviathan, the sea monster. The first beast has received a mortal wound in one of its heads and is identified by the number 666 (13.3, 18). The second beast is identified as the false prophet (19.20). All three are eventually destroyed. The beast and the false prophet are captured after a battle against the Word of God and the armies of heaven, and they are thrown into the lake of fire (19.20). The ancient serpent is bound for a thousand years, and then he too is thrown into the lake of fire (20.2, 10).

The red dragon is a 'portent in heaven' (12.3), in other words, a divine being, and he is thrown down to earth (12.10). The first beast rises from the sea and is presented as the image of the dragon, because each has seven heads and ten horns (12.3, cf. 13.1). The second beast comes from the land but has only two horns (13.11). The three monsters together are the antitype of the temple cult and a comment on what it has become. The red dragon with seven heads is the antitype of the LORD, who had originally been a sevenfold deity. There are several indications of this in the Hebrew Scriptures: the seven branches of the menorah which were his eyes on earth (Zech. 4.10), the seven archangels (see p. 83, 266–7) and the sevenfold spirit which was to rest on the Messiah (Isa. 11.2, cf. Rev. 5.6). The beast from the sea is the antitype of the king who had been the human presence of the LORD with his people, his Image who rose from the Sea, 'my Son whom you saw as a man coming up from the sea' (2 *Esdr*. 13.32). The beast from the land was a prophet. A similar group of three appear in the *Ascension of Isaiah*: Belial who 'dwells' in Manasseh the wicked king, and has a false prophet, Belkira' (*Asc. Isa*. 1.9; 3.1–12; 5.1–3).

In the cult of the first temple, the roles of priest, king and prophet had been united in the Davidic king, and the ideal had been restored briefly in the person of John Hyrcanus who ruled from 135–105 BCE. Josephus wrote of him: 'He was the only man to unite in his person ... the supreme command of the nation, the high priesthood and the gift of prophecy' (*War* 1.68). For most of the second temple period the high priest was believed to have the gift of prophecy (e.g. John 11.51), but he held office under a succession of foreign overlords and so was no longer a king. This is the situation depicted by the three monsters; the separated roles of prophet, priest and king. This threefold expectation can be seen in the Qumran Community Rule which looked forward to the coming of 'the Prophet and the Messiahs of Aaron and Israel' (1QS IX).

Azazel

By the first century CE, Satan had developed into the antitype of Melchizedek. According to the Qumran fragments 4Q280 and 4Q544 Satan had three names: the first is Melchiresa', meaning 'My king is evil', whereas Melchizedek means 'My king is justice'; the second can also be read Satan, meaning 'the tempter, the accuser' (cf. 12.10), the antitype of the Paraclete, meaning 'the advocate, the intercessor'. The third name in the fragment has not survived. Perhaps it was the Prince of Darkness, as his followers are called the 'Sons of Darkness' and the followers of Melchizedek are called the 'Sons of Light'. Satan is described as dark in appearance, wearing multicoloured garments and with the face of an adder; he has become a snake.

The serpent in Eden, however, had been another figure. He was Azazel, the leader of the fallen angels, and he is one element in the composite red dragon. Azazel appears only once in the Hebrew Scriptures (Lev. 16.10), but this single appearance belies his true importance as he was a key figure in the most important ritual of the temple year, the Day of Atonement. The story of Azazel (also called Semḥaza, but both mean the same: 'mighty god/name') is found in the oldest parts of *1 Enoch*. He and his angels bound themselves into an anti-covenant (*1 En*. 6) and came to earth where they took human wives and revealed their heavenly knowledge. Their children were giants who devoured mankind, and the heavenly knowledge was used to teach about warfare, magic and other evils. The four archangels reported the corruption of the earth to the Most High, and he ordered them to act: Uriel was sent to Noah to warn him of the approaching punishment, Raphael was sent to imprison Azazel in a pit in the desert until the last judgement when he would be cast into the fire, Gabriel was sent to stir up strife among the giants so that they would destroy each other in war; and Michael was sent against the other fallen angels (1 En. 10). After the Great Judgement, the earth was cleansed from all defilement and restored to great fertility. The sin of Azazel was rebellion against the Great Holy One; he had abused the heavenly knowledge and used it to corrupt and destroy the earth. He, and those whom he swept to earth with him, were breaking the cosmic covenant whose bonds secured the created order. The role of the true high priest was to maintain the cosmic covenant and renew the creation (see p. 45). Azazel and his angels were 'the destroyers of the earth' (11.18) who were destined for destruction.

The fallen angels are mentioned briefly in Genesis 6, but this short account gives no indication of the importance of the myth. Its fuller form is known only in texts which *were later excluded from the Bible*, but the fallen angels were a foundation myth of the first temple. The oldest parts of the Book of Isaiah are based on this myth, and the evidence from Qumran shows that Enoch texts continued to be widely used. Scholars have suspected for some time that the story of the fallen angels was used in the third and second centuries BCE as a thinly disguised attack on the priests in Jerusalem. They believed themselves to be the earthly counterpart of the angels and so their opponents depicted them as fallen angels. *Since the leader of the fallen angels in the original myth was Azazel, he must have represented the high priest, the Wicked Priest who appears in the Qumran texts.* His priests would have been the antitype of the community who produced the Book of Revelation and claimed to be the true royal priesthood (1.6). This explains why the seven-headed dragon wears seven diadems (12.3), another antitype. A Qumran fragment about vesting the high priest (11Q18) shows that he wore seven crowns. These are not mentioned in the Hebrew Scriptures, but there are crowns (plural) for the high priest in Zechariah 6.9–14, and the warrior priest who emerges from heaven wears 'many diadems' (19.12).

The dream visions of Enoch (1 En. 83–90) also describe the fall of Azazel. The history of Israel is told at this point in the style of the apocalyptists, with animals standing for human beings and men for angels. After the story of Adam and Eve and their children, described as cows and bulls, Enoch sees a star fall from heaven which is Azazel coming into the Garden of Eden. Many more stars follow the first one, change themselves into bulls and begin to mate with the cows. These are the fallen angels taking human wives. Three men in white (angels) take Enoch up to a high place (i.e. he stands in the holy of holies to receive his vision, cf. Ps. 73.15–20) and he watches as the other four archangels punish the fallen stars. This is the same story as in the earlier chapters: the first fallen star is imprisoned in an abyss, the other fallen stars are also imprisoned and their sons incited to destroy each other in war. Noah is warned to build the ark and escape. The history of Israel is then told up to the time of the Maccabean revolt, the writer's own time, with the prediction that the last judgement is imminent. Immediately after the triumph of the Maccabees, the throne is set up, the books are opened, and the fallen stars are cast into an abyss of fire (*1 En.* 90.24). This is depicted also in the Book of Revelation, and so the dragon who sweeps one third of the stars down to earth (12.4) must be Azazel coming to earth with his angels. He is first bound in a pit (20.2–3) and then, after a thousand years, thrown into a lake of fire (20.10). Just as the writer of *1 Enoch* had predicted the outcome of contemporary events on the basis of the myth of Azazel, so the writer of the Book of Revelation predicts the outcome of events in his own time. *He interprets the history of his own times in terms of the ancient myths in order to show the significance of what was happening.*

(In the *Book of Jubilees*, Azazel appears as Mastema, chief of the spirits, who was permitted to keep one tenth of the evil spirits under his command, after the archangels had imprisoned the others. (*Jub.* 10.4–9). Elsewhere in *Jubilees*, he is identified as Satan.)

Satan

Satan was originally one of the angels whose role was to tempt people and test their faith. He challenged the Lord to let him test the faith of Job (Job 1.1–12) and he tempted David to take a census of Israel (1 Chron. 21.1). He even stood before the Lord in the holy of holies to challenge Joshua's right to be the high priest (Zech. 3.1). In origin, however, Satan appears to have been an aspect of the Lord himself, insofar as later texts attribute to him what had formerly been described as actions of the Lord. For example, in the earlier version of the story, it was not Satan but the anger of the Lord that tempted David to conduct the census (2 Sam. 24.1). In the *Book of Jubilees* it was Mastema (here as Satan) who persuaded the Lord to test Abraham and demand the sacrifice of his son, exactly as Satan persuaded the Lord to test Job (*Jub.* 17.16). It was Mastema who opposed Moses in Egypt (*Jub.* 48.9–12), but he was bound for five days to enable the Israelites to escape. The 'wrath of the Lord', which began to consume Israel after the rebellion of Korah, became 'the destroyer' who feared the Name on the high priest's diadem, when the story was retold in the first century BCE (Num. 16.43–50; cf. *Wisd.* 18.20–25). Isaiah knew that the Lord created both 'weal and woe' (Isa. 45.7) but this was changed at the beginning of the second temple period, and there appeared an angel whose role was to tempt and to oppose. The Chronicler rewrote the story of David's census, and Zechariah saw Satan in the holy of holies, opposing the high priest.

In the *Life of Adam and Eve*, Satan tells Adam how he and his angels were driven out of heaven. This text explains, by way of antitypes, many of the allusions in Revelation 12–13 and the account of Jesus' temptations in the wilderness. When Adam was created, God breathed into him the breath of life and made him his Image. Michael then commanded all the angels: 'Worship the Image of the LORD God, as the LORD God has instructed' (*Life* 14.1). Satan refused on the grounds that he had been created before Adam, and so Adam should worship him. When Satan and all his angels refused to worship Adam, the Image of God, they were cast down from heaven and began to take vengeance on Adam who had been the cause of their downfall (*Life* 12.1), cf. 'the devil has come down to you in great wrath ...' (12.12).

Although this episode is not recorded in the Hebrew Scriptures, there is allusion to it in the Song of Moses, which was a key text for those who produced the Book of Revelation. The MT is shorter than both the Qumran text and the LXX at this critical point (Deut. 32.43), but the longer form is the older text.

Praise, O heavens, his people,
worship him all you gods,
for he will avenge the blood of his sons
and take vengeance on his adversaries,
he will requite those who hate him
and atone the land of his people.

This is the Qumran text. The LXX is broadly similar, but has 'sons of God' and 'angels of God' instead of 'gods'. The verse describes how the hosts of heaven are commanded to worship the LORD when he appears on the Day of Atonement. This was also a key text in the Letter to the Hebrews, whose opening chapter is a catena of quotations from the Scriptures to demonstrate who Jesus is. The royal texts from Psalm 2 and Psalm 45 are used to show that he is the Son and the Anointed One, and then Deuteronomy 32.43 to show that he is the LORD who comes on the Day of Atonement. He is described as the Firstborn, another royal title (Ps. 89.27) and as he comes into the world, *the angels are commanded to worship him*. The earliest beliefs about Jesus were those of the royal cult in the first temple. The king became the LORD at his enthronement, his 'birth' as the Son, and as he came from heaven to earth, i.e. as he emerged from the mysteries of the holy of holies, he was worshipped: 'Serve the LORD, Kiss the Son at his feet' (Ps. 2.11–12); 'Let all the gods worship him' (Deut. 32.43). He had been created as the Image of God, as Adam, and was worshipped as the LORD. Some manuscripts of the *Life of Adam and Eve* retain a trace of this belief. When Satan refused to worship Adam, Michael commanded him a second time: 'Worship the Image of God, the LORD' (*Life* 14.2). When Satan refused, he was driven out.

(Satan acquired other names: in the *Book of Jubilees* he is known as Beliar and so Moses prays, 'Do not let the spirit of Beliar rule over [your people], to accuse them before you and ensnare them...' (*Jub.* 1.20).).

Leviathan

In the first temple period, Israel had envisaged the creation not as the simple ordering described in Genesis 1 but as the LORD's triumph over primeval waters to establish dry land. The seven-headed dragon had been the sea monster who represented the watery chaos, and this is the third element of the monster in Revelation 12. Conflict with the waters or the sea appears in several places in the Hebrew Scriptures, sometimes depicted as the dragon, sometimes simply as hostile waters. Triumph over either was a sign of the LORD's triumph as he became king. 'The LORD sits enthroned over the flood, the LORD sits enthroned for ever' (Ps. 29.10). Psalm 93 describes the LORD in majesty enthroned over the floods; Psalm 24 says he established the world upon the seas.

Other texts mention a sea monster by name, defeated when the LORD established the created order:

Yet God my King is from of old,
working salvation in the midst of the earth.
Thou didst divide the sea by thy might;
thou didst break the heads of the dragons on the waters.
Thou didst crush the heads of Leviathan,
thou didst give him as food for the creatures of the wilderness.
Thou didst cleave open springs and brooks;
thou didst dry up ever-flowing streams.
Thine is the day, thine also is the night;
thou hast established the luminaries and the sun.
Thou hast fixed all the bounds of the earth;
thou hast made summer and winter. (Ps. 74.12–17)

Leviathan is a name known from the mythology of Canaan. Ugaritic texts mention a creature named Litan who had seven heads and was known as the writhing serpent and the dragon: 'Because you smote Litan [i.e. Leviathan] the wriggling serpent, finished off the writhing serpent, encircler with seven heads' (KTU 1.5.ii.1); 'Surely I lifted up the dragon, I ... smote the writhing serpent, the encircler with the seven heads' (KTU 1.3 .iii.40). These bear a strong resemblance to one of Isaiah's descriptions of the Day of the LORD: 'In that day the LORD with his hard and great and strong sword will punish Leviathan the fleeing serpent, Leviathan the twisting serpent, and he will slay the dragon that is in the sea' (Isa. 27.1). The Hebrew Scriptures do not say how many heads Leviathan had, but the writer of Revelation knew he had seven, *an indication that he knew the tradition and not just the Hebrew Scriptures*. Leviathan's other name was Rahab, and so Job could describe how God smote Rahab and pierced the fleeing serpent (Job 26.12–13). Isaiah described the triumph over the waters of the Red Sea in the same way: 'Was it not thou that didst cut Rahab in pieces, that didst pierce the dragon? Was it not thou that didst dry up the sea, the waters of the great deep; that didst make the depths of the sea a way for the redeemed to pass over?' (Isa. 51.9–10).

The clearest picture of the dragon in the royal traditions of Israel is in Psalm 89. Having extolled the LORD as the greatest of the holy ones, who ruled the sea and crushed Rahab, we are told that the Davidic king shared these triumphs. 'I will set his hand on the sea,* and his right hand on the rivers.* He shall cry to me, "Thou are my Father, my God and the Rock of my salvation." And I will make him the Firstborn, the highest of the kings of the earth' (Ps. 89.25–27).

Jerusalem and its temple, the centre of the whole creation, had been established as dry land in the midst of the watery chaos. According to a tale recorded centuries later in the Babylonian Talmud, waters under Jerusalem were a threat which King David averted by throwing into the waters a potsherd inscribed with the Name. The waters subsided 16,000 cubits, but this left the city without a water supply so he sang the fifteen Songs of Ascent and brought them back up 15,000 cubits! (b. Sukkah 53b). The idea of these cosmic waters subdued beneath the city was one that persisted; it appears in Revelation as the great harlot seated on many waters (17.1), but she is also described as seated on a scarlet beast, the dragon of the waters (17.3).

The waters were subdued and bound when the LORD established the creation: 'Thou hast confined the deep and sealed it with thy terrible and glorious Name' (Prayer of Manasseh 3, see p. 41). They represented chaos and evil, and so, in the time of Noah, when 'the LORD was sorry that he had made man on the earth' (Gen. 6.6), the waters were allowed to return and destroy evil with evil. In the Book of Revelation, evil has to be bound before the millennium kingdom appears (20.1–6) and evil has to be destroyed before there can be a new heaven and a new earth but no more sea (20.10, 21.1). When the LORD established order, he set the sand of the seashore as the boundary which the sea could not pass; the dragon stood on the sand of the sea to watch the beast rising (12.17, see p. 230).

Sometimes the waters themselves indicate hostile forces or enemies:

O God of our salvation
who art the hope of all the ends of the earth,
and of the farthest seas;
who by thy strength hast established the mountains,
being girded with might;
who dost still the roaring of the seas,
the roaring of their waves,
the tumult of the peoples;
so that those who dwell at the earth's farthest bounds
are afraid at thy signs. (Ps. 65.5–8)

Isaiah described the King of Assyria as the River that would flood Judah (Isa. 8.7), not a reference to the great rivers of Mesopotamia, but to the hostile waters of ancient mythology. Daniel prophesied that a flood

---

*Prince Sea and Judge River are the two names for a defeated monster in other Ugaritic texts: the god Baal defeated someone with these titles before he was proclaimed king. He dried them up (KTU 1.2.iv.25), cf. Revelation 12.16: 'The earth opened its mouth and swallowed the river which the dragon had poured from his mouth'.

would destroy Jerusalem and the sanctuary (Dan. 9.26), and reconstructed lines from the Qumran Commentary on Nahum show that
waters continued to be the symbol for hostile forces. The interpretation
of Nahum 1.4 'He rebukes the sea and makes it dry' is: 'The sea is all
the Kittim [the Romans] who are ... to execute judgement against them
and destroy them ...' (4Q169). In Revelation 17.15 the identification is
explicit: 'The waters that you saw, where the harlot is seated, are
peoples and multitudes and nations and tongues'.

Texts such as these, and there are many more, shaped the thought and
language of the temple visionaries even in the first century CE. It was not
a question of conscious borrowing or imitation or even quoting from
Scripture. As they expressed ideas about evil and the political situation
of their time, so the features of the monsters were altered, but always
within the limits of their tradition.

The Red Dragon

Several incidents in the ministry of Jesus must be understood as his
conflict with the red dragon in his three aspects: Leviathan, Satan and
Azazel.

First, there is the conflict with Leviathan, depicted in 12.4 as the red
dragon with seven heads lying in wait for the new-born royal child
before he can be taken up to the heavenly throne. Psalms 29, 74 and 93
describe the LORD conquering the waters before ascending his throne,
and the early church believed that this had been fulfilled in Jesus'
baptism in the Jordan. All the Gospel accounts of the baptism allude to
the ancient king-making, with the heavenly voice addressing Jesus as the
Son, the Servant. The Codex Bezae text of Luke 3.22, however, has
the heavenly voice declare the whole coronation text: 'You are my Son,
today I have begotten you' (Ps. 2.7). Since the earliest account of the
baptism makes it clear that the vision was Jesus' personal experience,
'He saw the heavens opened ... You are my beloved Son' (Mark
1.10–11), it must have been Jesus himself who interpreted his
experience as the king-making and then spoke of it to his disciples.
What is extraordinary is that the church came to describe his baptism
as the time when Jesus fulfilled Psalm 74.13 and defeated the dragon
with seven heads. In other words, it was known that when Jesus was
'born' as Son of God he defeated the dragon of the waters, exactly as
depicted in Revelation 12. This must have come from Jesus, too.

The *Odes of Solomon*, thought to be early baptismal hymns, also
describe how Jesus defeated the dragon with seven heads and the hostile
waters:

He who caused me to descend from on high
and to ascend from the regions below ...
He who overthrew by my hands the dragon with seven heads,
And set me at his roots that I might destroy his seed ... (*Ode* 22.1, 5)

But the chasms were submerged in the submersion* of the Lord. (*Ode* 24.7)

Hippolytus, writing early in the third century CE, knew that Jesus defeated the waters at his baptism: 'For the waters saw him and were afraid ... We have seen the Creator of all things in the form of a Servant ... Jesus hid the dignity of his divinity to elude the snares of the dragon' (Hippolytus, *On the Holy Theophany*, 2.4). Baptism as the defeat of the dragon was mentioned by many early Christian writers and passed into baptism services. This is an early Greek prayer: 'You sanctified the streams of the Jordan having sent your Holy Spirit from heaven and shattered the head of the dragon writhing there'. A prophecy in the *Testament of Asher* (possibly a Christian addition to an earlier text) told of a man who would crush the dragon's head in the water and save Israel (*T. Asher* 7.3)

This tradition of triumph over the waters can only have been transmitted through the vision in Revelation 12; there is no hint in the Gospel accounts of the baptism. The only Gospel allusion to the dragon of the waters is after the storm on Galilee: 'Who then is this, that even the wind and sea obey him?' (Mark 4.41). The defeated waters occur, however, in two other places in Revelation: in the vision of the new heaven and the new earth there is 'no more sea' (21.1) and in the vision of the risen LORD, when he is described as the heavenly high priest wearing a long robe with a golden girdle around his breast (1.13). Josephus tells us the significance the high priest's girdle: 'This vestment reaches down to the feet and sits close to the body; ... it is girded to the breast a little above the elbows by a girdle often going round, four fingers broad, but so loosely woven that you would think it the skin of a serpent ... And the girdle which encompassed the high priest round signified the ocean ...' (*Ant.* 3.154, 185). The risen LORD wears the ocean like the skin of a dead snake, the encircler with seven heads!

Second, there is Jesus' conflict with Satan in the wilderness after his baptism. Satan in his ancient role as the tempter, tried to convince him that he was not the Son, when the Spirit had revealed that he was. The framework of the narrative is still Psalm 2. 'I have set my king on Zion my holy hill' (Ps. 2.6) became Jesus standing on the pinnacle of the temple, perhaps originally the 'tower', the holy of holies (Matt. 4.5//Luke 4.9) and 'Ask of me and I will make the nations your heritage' (Ps. 2.8) became Satan offering Jesus all the kingdoms of the world in return for his homage (Matt. 4.8–9//Luke 4.6–7). Psalm 2.11b–12a is a difficult text but it probably means 'Serve the LORD with fear, with trembling kiss the Son at his feet'. The Hebrew is obscure, but 'Serve the LORD' and 'Kiss the Son' are clear. After his enthronement as Son and King, the rulers of the earth were commanded to pay homage, which explains Satan's offer to Jesus, another antitype: 'Worship me and you shall rule the earth'.

---

*The word might mean 'sealing', but either meaning indicates baptism.

Piecing together this evidence from Psalm 2 and Deuteronomy 32.43, both proof texts used in the Letter to the Hebrews, and from the *Life of Adam and Eve*, the context of the other beasts begins to appear. The story of the creation of Adam explains the allusions in Revelation 13.14–15, where the beast from the land bids the dwellers on earth make an image: 'It was allowed to give breath to the image ... and to cause those who would not worship the image to be slain'. This is another set of antitypes. We can only guess who or what was meant by the image but the striking similarity of this passage and the *Life of Adam and Eve* – the image brought to life by the breath of God, Satan refusing to worship him and being thrown to earth as a result, his subsequent hostility to Adam – cannot be coincidence.

The child who was to rule the nations with a rod of iron (12.3 drawing on Ps. 2.9, see on 19.15) was caught up to God and his throne. Satan's refusal to worship him is not mentioned; we are told only that there was war in heaven (12.7). Michael and his angels fighting Satan and his angels is described in the Qumran texts where Melchizedek, another name for Michael, fights against Satan and his horde to rescue the Sons of Light (11QMelch), and where Michael was expected to defeat the Prince of the kingdom of wickedness, his triumph in heaven being the triumph of Israel on earth (1QM XVII). In 12.10 Michael has already triumphed: the kingdom of God and his Anointed One has begun with Satan's expulsion from heaven: 'Thy Kingdom come, Thy will be done, On earth as it is in heaven'.

In the Synoptic Gospels, the war in heaven is worked out on earth in Jesus' ministry of healing and exorcism. Immediately after his experience of conflict with Satan in the desert, Jesus returns to Galilee and proclaims: 'The time is fulfilled and the kingdom of God is at hand' (Mark 1.15). The royal priest Melchizedek has come, and the Sons of Light are to be rescued. The first miracle at Cana is an exorcism, rescuing a man from the power of Satan (Mark 1.23–27). Then the demons at Gadara recognize him and complain: 'Have you come to torment us before the time?' (meaning 'the time set for the Judgement', Matt. 8.29). When challenged that his power over demons was in itself demonic, Jesus replied to his critics: 'If it is by the finger of God that I cast out demons, then the kingdom of God has come upon you' (Luke 11.20). After the seventy disciples returned from their mission and reported: 'LORD even the demons are subject to us in your name' (Luke 10.17); Jesus replied: 'I saw Satan fall like lightning from heaven'. This must refer to 12.9; Jesus and his seventy disciples were Michael and his angels, the seventy sons of God, and this was the simultaneous warfare in heaven and earth depicted in the War Scroll (1QM XVII).

Paul told the Christians in Rome that God would 'crush Satan under their feet' (Rom. 16.20); he wrote of Jesus' triumph over 'principalities and powers' (Col. 2.15) and of the sons of disobedience who still followed the prince of the power of the air. Christians, he said, were formerly like that, destined for the wrath like the rest of mankind, but

'God had [already] raised them up to heavenly places as he had raised up Jesus (Eph. 2.1–7). He reminded them: 'We are not contending against flesh and blood, but against the principalities, against the powers, against the world rulers of this present darkness, against the spiritual hosts of wickedness in the heavenly places' (Eph. 6.12).

It was in his aspect as Azazel, the chief of the fallen angels and the Wicked Priest, that the red dragon pursued into the wilderness the Woman clothed with the sun (12.13–14). She was given the wings of the great eagle to escape into the desert, an ancient motif drawn perhaps from Isaiah 40.31, that the LORD rescues those who wait for him and they rise up with the wings of an eagle, but more likely, given the prominence of the text elsewhere in the Book of Revelation, from Exodus 19.4–6. Those who fled from Egypt were carried on eagle's wings to 'become a kingdom of priests and a holy hation' (see on 1.6 and 5.10). A Qumran fragment uses the same imagery: 'Like an eagle ... which spreads out its wings, takes [a nestling] and carries it on [ ], so we dwell apart and are not reckoned among the nations ...' (4Q 504.6).

The woman stayed in the desert for 'a time, times and half a time' (12.14), the cryptic three and a half years which is also the duration of the Gentile trampling of the temple court (11.2, 'forty-two months') and the ministry of the two witnesses (11.3, 'one thousand two hundred and sixty days'), and the reign of the beast (13.5, see p. 186). There are echoes here of the Eden story when the LORD told the serpent: 'I will put enmity between you and the woman, and between your seed and her seed; he shall bruise your head* and you shall bruise his heel' (Gen. 3.15).

The flight of the Woman into the desert is a reference to the persecuted Christians leaving Jerusalem after the death of Stephen (Acts 8.1), or after the attack on James (see below and on 11.3–13). The original reference was probably to a faithful community who fled from the corruption in Jerusalem, perhaps the Sons of Light in the War Scroll who described themselves as 'exiles in the desert' preparing to fight against the company of Satan (1QM I). The Woman pursued by the river from the dragon's mouth is strikingly similar to the opening of the Damascus Document; after God had raised up the Teacher of Righteousness, the Scoffer arose who 'shed over Israel the waters of lies' (CD I). The flood of water was the dragon's ancient watery chaos, but the LORD protected his people, and, like Baal in the ancient texts from Ugarit, he dried up the flood (KTU 1.2.iv.25). The words of 12.16, 'the earth opened its mouth and swallowed the river', confirm that those who pursued the Woman were both 'men of Egypt' and the wicked priests. In the Song of Moses, the Egyptians who pursued the escaping

*Hence the head wound of the beast (13.3). Those who preserved the temple tradition would have known that Wisdom, the Woman and Eve the mother of all life, were one and the same (see pp. 203, 210).

Israelites met this fate (Exod. 15.12) and when Korah and some other priests rebelled against his authority, Moses told the people how the LORD would show whom he had chosen: 'If the ground opens its mouth and swallows them up ... you will know that these men have despised the LORD (Num. 16.30). The earth did open its mouth and swallow them, proving that they were 'wicked men' (Num. 16.26), exactly as happened to the river which came from the mouth of the dragon. The dragon then went off to attack the other children of the Woman, in other words, the high priest began to persecute the Jerusalem Christians 'who kept the commandments of God and had the testimony, i.e. the visions of Jesus' (12.17, translating literally).

Although the churches in Smyrna (2.10) and Pergamum (2.13) had experienced some persecution, the greatest threat was from false teaching; the Nikolaitans were the deceivers (see p. 101), and John warned against the antichrist whom he called the deceiver (1 John 2.22) and the liar (2 John 7). Satan in the Book of Revelation is 'the deceiver of the whole world' (12.9; 20.3). Those 'coming from the great tribulation' (7.14) were probably the Roman martyrs in the time of Nero, *but the other persecutions were at the hands of the Jerusalem priests.* Peter and John were arrested by the high priests (Acts 4.5–7), several apostles were imprisoned (Acts 5.17–18) and Saul acted as the agent of the high priest when he set out to arrest the Christians in Damascus (Acts 9.1–20). Few details of this period are recorded in Acts but another text seems to have preserved glimpses of the early days in Jerusalem. The *Recognitions of Clement* sets a series of debates and formal speeches in a framework that could well be an accurate picture of the young church in Palestine. Some of the disciples, including Peter and Thomas, were debating in the temple with Caiaphas the high priest. Peter had warned that the temple would be destroyed, that the time of blood sacrifices had passed. The debate resumed the following day, this time led by James the bishop in Jerusalem. It was disrupted by enemies, which an ancient scribe identified as Saul and his men. James was attacked with a piece of wood from the altar woodpile, thrown down the steps and left for dead.

But our friends lifted him up for they were both more numerous and more powerful than the others ... When evening came the priests shut the temple and we returned to the house of James and spent the night there in prayer. Then before daylight came we went down to Jericho, some five thousand men. After three days one of the brethren came to us from Gamaliel ... bringing us secret tidings that the enemy had received a commission from Caiaphas, the chief priest, that he should arrest all who believed in Jesus and should go to Damascus with his letters ... and make havoc among the faithful. (*Clem. Rec.* 1.71)

This is presupposed by Acts 9.1–2, which does not say how there came to be Christians in Damascus and Jericho.

John depicts in his Gospel this conflict with the dragon Azazel and his corrupted priests. He describes Jesus' enemies as 'the Jews', and commentators wonder who this particular group must have been, since it cannot have been a general designation for all the heirs to Israel's ancient faith. Josephus says that the name 'Jew' was given to those who returned from exile to rebuild Jerusalem (*Ant.* 11.173) and that the Samaritans claimed to be 'Hebrews ... but not Jews' (*Ant.* 11.344). If Josephus, a contemporary, knew the distinction between a Hebrew and a Jew, it is likely that John did also. The definition is significant because the hostility towards Jerusalem apparent in the Book of Revelation originated many centuries earlier, when the exiles returned to rebuild the city. It is very likely indeed that for the visionaries, 'the Jews' still referred to that group (see p. 30).

There had been conflict in the priesthood throughout the second temple period. The prophet Zechariah described a vision of Joshua the high priest, who had returned with the exiles from Babylon, standing before the LORD with Satan accusing him (Zech. 3.1); in other words, someone was questioning his fitness to be high priest. (It is interesting that in the LXX this became Satan challenging Jesus' fitness to be high priest, noted in Justin, *Trypho* 79.) The LORD dismissed Satan's accusation – we are not told what it was, but it was symbolized by filthy garments – and Joshua was vested in clean garments as high priest. From the very beginning of the dispute, the one who accused the high priest was described as Satan, as in 12.10, 'the accuser of our brethren'.

The Third Isaiah, who prophesied at the beginning of the second temple period, condemned the priests of the restored cult because they excluded from worship many who were worshippers of the LORD. The new emphasis on purity requirements rather than brotherly love rendered their sacrifices no better than pagan cults: the lambs, cereal offerings and incense were as bad as slaughtered dogs, pigs' blood and idolatry (Isa. 66.3). The prophet warned them: 'You shall leave your name to my chosen for a curse' (Isa. 64.15). These were the Jerusalem Jews. The enigmatic histories in *1 Enoch* give a similar picture: the temple was rebuilt and the offerings were restored but they were polluted and not pure (*1 En.* 89.73). 'In the seventh week shall an apostate generation arise, and many shall be its deeds, and all its deeds shall be apostate' (*1 En.* 93.9)

The Qumran texts give ample evidence of division and conflict between priests; the Commentary on Psalm 37 confirms that the mysterious Teacher of Righteousness was the priest 'whom God chose to stand before him' (4Q171 III), exactly as was said of Joshua in Zechariah 3, and the Commentary on Habakkuk describes the Teacher as one who would interpret all the words of the prophets 'through whom God foretold all that would happen to his people' (1QpHab II). His opponent was the proud Wicked Priest who forsook God and amassed wealth for himself. God delivered him into the hands of his enemies because of what he had done to the Teacher of Righteousness and his Elect Ones (1QpHab VIII, IX).

There are several allusions to this priestly conflict in the New

Testament. The two opposing figures in the Qumran Scrolls may have been identified with historical figures but the conflict was not limited to any one pair of opponents. The true high priest and Azazel continued their conflict. In the Fourth Gospel, this conflict takes the form of the Jews confronting Jesus who claims that he is the heavenly high priest 'whom the Father consecrated and sent into the world' (John 10.36) and that the Jews are children of the devil, 'the father of lies' (John 8.44). *Most of the confrontations are set in the temple*: after driving out the traders (John 2), after healing the lame man at the Pool of Bethsaida (John 5), at Tabernacles (John 7–8), after healing the blind man (John 9–10); and it was the chief priests who had Jesus arrested and saw to it that he was put to death (John 18.3, 40). When pressed, the chief priests declared that their only king was Caesar (John 19.15), expressed in Revelation as the red dragon in league with the beast from the sea. The Hebrews, as distinct from the Jews, proclaimed Jesus as Melchizedek, the true high priest (Heb. 5.5–10).

15

THE TWO BEASTS

And I saw a beast rising out of the sea, with ten horns and seven heads, with ten diadems upon its horns and a blasphemous name upon its heads. And the beast that I saw was like a leopard, its feet were like a bear's, and its mouth was like a lion's mouth. And to it the dragon gave his power and his throne and great authority. One of its heads seemed to have a mortal wound, but its mortal wound was healed, and the whole earth followed the beast with wonder. Men worshipped the dragon, for he had given his authority to the beast, and they worshipped the beast saying, 'Who is like the beast, and who can fight against it?'

Then I saw another beast which rose out of the earth; it had two horns like a lamb and it spoke like a dragon. It exercises all the authority of the first beast in its presence, and makes the earth and its inhabitants worship the first beast, whose mortal wound was healed.

This calls for wisdom: let him who has understanding reckon the number of the beast, for it is a human number, its number is six hundred and sixty-six. (Rev. 13.1–4, 11–12, 18)

The two beasts and their ruler, the red dragon, are the antitypes of the temple cult. The recurring theme of the Qumran texts is the opposition between good and evil: between Melchizedek and Melchiresa', between Michael and Satan, between the Wicked Priest and the Teacher of Righteousness, between the Children of Light and the Children of Darkness. This is not dualism in the strictest sense of that word, since the outcome of the struggle is never in doubt; everything remains in God's power and is part of his plan. When his agents exceed their allotted powers they are judged and destroyed. The faith of believers is tested by their endurance; they must accept their part in the plan, and continue to trust. Jesus warned: 'This must take place. The end is not yet ... But he who endures to the end will be saved' (Mark 13.7, 13), and the unnamed voice, presumably the voice from the throne, tells the martyrs that they have to wait until their number is complete (6.11). The seer himself recognizes that the call to resist the beast is a call for 'the endurance of the saints' (14.12).

The Seventy Shepherds

The history of Israel was written in many different ways. The Deuteronomists, who wrote 1 and 2 Samuel and 1 and 2 Kings, were hostile to the Davidic monarchy and blamed the kings for the fall of Jerusalem in 597 BCE. They had not maintained what the Deuteronomists believed to be the only true religion of Israel, and the city was destroyed as a result. The Chronicler wrote a very different account of the same period in 1 and 2 Chronicles, which focused on the affairs of the temple. These are the major history writings in the Hebrew Scriptures. The Enochic writings, however, have another point of view; the period of the second temple was a time of pollution and apostasy and, by implication, the golden age had been the time of the first temple. King Josiah's changes to the temple cult were the actions of blind men who had forsaken wisdom (*1 En.* 93.8). Since the imagery of the Book of Revelation is rooted in that of the first temple, it is not surprising that it has the Enochic view of history.

In the *Book of Enoch*, the history of Israel is not only the past but also the present and the future, and it is under the rule of the seventy shepherds. During the eighth century BCE, from the time of Hezekiah (2 Kgs 18.14), Jerusalem lost her autonomy and became subject to foreign powers: first the Assyrians, then the Babylonians, the Persians, the Egyptians, the Syrians, and finally the Romans and their puppet kings, the Idumean Herods. These foreign rulers were seen as agents of the LORD's punishment* and were described by Enoch as the 'seventy shepherds'. Since they are depicted as human figures they must, in the code of the visionaries, have represented heavenly beings, the patron angels of the foreign nations. When Jerusalem was subjected to the Assyrians, Enoch says the city was put into the hands of the angels of the nations, the shepherds:

And he [the LORD] called seventy shepherds and cast those sheep to them that they might pasture them ... 'I will deliver them over to you duly numbered, and tell you which of them are to be destroyed ...' And he called another [angel] and spake unto him: 'Observe and mark everything that the shepherds will do to those sheep; for they will destroy more of them than I have commanded ... record against every individual shepherd all the destruction he effects ...' (*1 En.* 89.59–64)

History then unfolds and the evil deeds of the shepherds are recorded. The Day of Judgement comes: 'And he said to that man who wrote before him ... : "Take those seventy shepherds to whom I delivered the sheep, and who taking them on their own authority slew more than I commanded them ..." And those seventy shepherds were judged and found guilty and they were cast into that fiery abyss' (*1 En.* 90.22, 25).

The shepherds had originally been the seventy 'Sons of El' who appear in the mythology of Canaan but were also known in ancient Israel. Jeremiah describes the 'shepherds' preparing to attack Jerusalem (Jer. 6.3); Zechariah threatens the 'shepherds' with the LORD's anger (Zech. 10.3). The seventy shepherd rulers were also known to the early church, not least in the Good Shepherd, which was far more than a pastoral image. One early Christian text, which purports to be a debate between Peter and Simon Magus, describes the (shepherd) angels to whom the Most High God committed the seventy nations of the world. They were the gods of those nations, yet not autonomous: '[Peter says:] For every nation has an angel to whom God has committed the

*Hezekiah had destroyed the ancient shrines (1sa. 36.7 cf 2 Kgs 18.1–4)

government of that nation; and when one of these appears, although he be thought and called God by those over whom he presides, yet being asked, does not give such testimony to himself ... Thus the princes of the several nations are called gods, but Christ is God of Princes, who is Judge of all' (*Clem. Rec.* 2.42). In another text, Simon Magus says: 'The Father, limiting the nations to seventy languages, according to the number of the sons of Israel* who entered Egypt ... gave to his own Son who is also called the LORD, and who brought into order the heaven and the earth, the Hebrews as his portion, and defined him to be God of gods ...' (*Clem. Hom.* 18.4).

This is curious reasoning, but another (older?) version of that text found at Qumran makes more sense: the nations were established according 'to the number of the sons of God'. The LORD was one of the sons of God Most High, and he was allotted Israel. The tradition that there had been seventy of these angels was not forgotten, even though it disappeared from the Hebrew Scriptures. The Targum has: 'When the Most High allocated the world to the nations ... he cast lots among the seventy angels, the princes of the nations ...' (*T. Ps. Jon. Deut.* 32.8)

The first Christians understood history in this way. Evil angel rulers had been permitted by God to rule for a certain time. When Satan tempted Jesus in the desert and offered him worldly power he said: 'It has been delivered to me and I give it to whom I will' (Matt. 4.6). Jesus knew that the time of judgement was at hand: 'Now is the judgement of this world, now shall the ruler of this world be cast out' (John 12.31). When Pilate reminded Jesus that he had power to release him or have him crucified, Jesus replied, 'You would have no power over me unless it had been given you from above' (John 19.11). The exhortation to the saints in the Book of Revelation was to endure: 'Here is a call for the endurance and faith of the saints' (13.10). These were the words of Jesus to his disciples when he warned them what would happen in the days before the temple was destroyed and the Man returned: 'He who endures to the end will be saved' (Mark 13.13). They echo the words to the martyrs under the altar (6.9–11), that they should accept the divine plan with patience and endure. The saints who keep the commandments of God and the faith of Jesus are contrasted in 14.9–12 with those who accept the mark of the beast, and they, too, are exhorted to endure. The beast is permitted to utter blasphemies and make war on the saints, and they have to accept what the LORD has planned for them. The beast, as the agent of Satan, is testing the faith of the saints just as the LORD had permitted him to test the faith of Job. 'Satan answered the LORD, ... "Put forth thy hand now and touch his bone and his flesh and he will curse thee to thy face." And the LORD said to Satan, "Behold he is in your power; only spare his life" ' (Job 2.5–6). Job was considered by the Hebrew Christians to be a man who endured rather than one who

---

*The 'seventy sons of Israel' appear in the MT of Deuteronomy 32.8 where God Most High establishes the nations 'according to the number of the sons of Israel'.

questioned the ways of God (Jas 5.11). The words of 13.10 echo those of Jeremiah 15.1–3. The punishment for the sins of Manasseh (2 Kgs 21.1–16) had been decreed and nobody could intercede to plead for mercy: 'Thus say the LORD: Those who are for pestilence, to pestilence, and those who are for the sword, to the sword; those who are for famine, to famine and those who are for captivity, to captivity'. The form of the words in Revelation 13.10b is different, 'If anyone slays with the sword, with the sword he must be slain', and is thought to reflect the words of Jesus to Peter in Gethsemane: 'All who take the sword will perish by the sword' (Matt. 26.52). The saints had to keep their faith that Jesus himself would return to destroy their enemies. Power was committed to the seventy shepherds, but not absolute power. Thus we read of the beast, who represents any one of the seventy shepherds, that 'it was given' a mouth that spoke blasphemy and that 'it was allowed' to exercise authority for forty two months (13.5), that 'it was allowed' to make war on the saints and conquer them, and that 'it was given' authority over all peoples (13.7).

The number seventy for the seventy sons of God Most High is concealed in the descriptions of the dragon and the beast; both have seven heads and ten horns. The ten-horned beast in Daniel's vision, however, had all ten horns on one head (Dan. 7.20), each horn representing one angel ruler and the head the empire or dynasty. The original monsters in Revelation 12 and 13 probably had seven heads with ten horns on each, indicating the seventy angels in their heavenly and earthly aspects who were permitted to rule Jerusalem. By describing evil as one monster with many heads and horns, the visionary shows that the individual evil powers are part of one all-pervasive unity of evil. They are the antitype of the good angels, the seventy sent out to announce the kingdom (Luke 10.1–12). These seventy were all parts of the one good; the lesser angels being aspects of the greater ones and they in turn aspects of the LORD himself. A gnostic text from (perhaps) the early third century CE expresses it thus: 'The emanation of the totalities, which exist from the one who exists, did not occur according to a separation from one another, as something cast off from one who begets them. Rather, their begetting is like a process of extension, as the Father extends himself to those whom he loves, so that those who have come forth from him might become him as well' (*Tripartite Tractate* CG I.5.73). John attributes to Jesus similar teaching about the unity of Father, Son and disciples: 'that they may all be one, even as thou, Father art in me and I in thee, that they also may be in us so that the world may believe that thou hast sent me. The glory which thou hast given to me I have given to them, that they may be one even as we are one. I in them and thou in me, that they may become perfectly one …' (John 17.21 –23). John's concept of the unity of the divine good is exactly counterbalanced by his depiction of the unity of demonic evil; one monster with many heads and horns, permitted to rule but not to triumph.

The Antitypes of Good and Evil

The beast from the sea represents any evil ruler of Jerusalem and in all details he exactly opposes the true ruler, the Messiah. He is the antichrist:

- The beast emerges from the sea, as does the Messiah in Ezra's vision: 'As for your seeing a man come up from the heart of the sea, this is he whom the Most High has been keeping for many ages, who will himself deliver his creation' (2 *Esdr.* 13.25). The vision of the ascending Man in Daniel 7.13 does not say where he came from but it is likely that he, too, came from the great sea, depicted by the great bronze 'sea' in the temple court (1 Kgs 7.23–26). There had probably been a ritual in the temple when the king was immersed in the 'sea' (see pp. 14–15).
- The Messiah is 'the image of the invisible God' (Col. 1.15), the sevenfold angel who appears in all his forms in 16.1–21 (see also on 1.12–13). He comes to mark with the Name and then returns to bring judgement. He is 'the First and the Last' (1.17; 22.13). The beast is the image of the dragon, each of them having ten horns and seven heads (13.1). The seven heads of the dragon symbolize the seven heavenly archetypes of the evil dynasties, which Enoch saw as seven evil angels burning in 'a waste and horrible place' (1 *En.* 18.13), and the crowned horns of the beast are the individual rulers on earth. The beast was one of the seven heads who would return as 'the eighth' (17.11) so he, too, was 'the First and the Last'.
- The Messiah has many crowns and wears the Name (19.12) as did the high priest; the dragon wears seven crowns (12.3), as did the high priest (see p. 306). The beast has ten crowns and a blasphemous name on its heads (13.1), just as the human manifestation of the LORD wore the Name on his forehead.
- The LORD of Spirits set the Messiah on the throne of glory to preside at the judgement (1 *En.* 61.8) and the Man in Daniel's vision was given 'dominion and glory and kingdom' (Dan. 7.14); the dragon gave his power, his throne and great authority to the beast (13.4).
- The Lamb was standing even though it had been slain; the beast had received an apparently fatal wound in the head from which it had recovered (13.3), a reference to 'God my King crushing the heads of Leviathan' (Ps. 74.14) and Eve's child bruising the head of the serpent (Gen. 3.15).
- Everyone would see the return of the Messiah who had been pierced (1.7) just as everyone would follow the beast with wonder after his wound had been healed (13.3–4). Like the LORD 'who was and is and is to come' (1.4, 8 and 4.8), so too the beast who 'was and is not and is to come' would re-emerge from the bottomless pit (17.8).
- People worshipped the LORD and his anointed king (1 Chron. 29.20); those whose names were not written in the Lamb's Book of Life worshipped the dragon and the beast to whom he gave his authority

(13.8 and 17.8). The beast was also permitted to utter blasphemy, to exercise authority, to make war on the saints and to conquer them (13.5–8).

- The poetry of Israel had proclaimed: 'Who is like thee, O LORD, among the gods?' (Exod. 15.11; also Pss 35.10 and 89.6); the followers of the beast said, 'Who is like the beast?' There is also wordplay here; the one who defeats the dragon and throws him from heaven is Michael whose name means 'Who is like God?'
- The redeemed bore the mark of the LORD (7.2–3, cf. Ezek. 9.4: 'Put a mark on the foreheads of those who sigh and groan over all the abominations . . .' see pp. 162, 269) and those who bore the mark of the beast were destined for destruction (19.20–21) and had no hope of sharing the millennium kingdom (20.4).

Interpretations of the Vision

The beast from the sea (13.1) is the one to whom the red dragon gives 'his power, his throne and great authority'. Hostile rulers had long been described as beasts and monsters, the best known being the four who emerged from the primeval sea in Daniel's vision of the Man (Dan. 7). The first was like a winged lion, the second like a bear, the third like a leopard with four heads and four wings, and of the fourth we are told only that it had iron teeth and ten horns. The four monsters at that time were understood to be Babylon, Media, Persia and Greece, the empires which preceded the advent of the glorious Man and the expected triumph of Israel in the second century BCE. The beast from the sea in Revelation 13.1–2 is a composite of all Daniel's monsters: he is lion, leopard and bear and he has ten horns. These monstrous forms are another antitype because anyone who served as a priest in the temple had to be physically perfect. There is a long list of bodily imperfections that disqualified a man from serving as a priest: the wrong shape of head, insufficient hair or eyebrows, ears, eyes or nose too small or too big, skin too dark or too pale, too tall or too short and so forth (*m. Bekhoroth* 7).

The monsters had become political ciphers long before the time of Daniel. In the Hebrew Scriptures Egypt was Rahab, the sea monster (Isa. 30.7) and the LORD threatened her with the fate of Prince Sea and Judge River:

Behold, the LORD is riding on a swift cloud and comes to Egypt;
and the idols of Egypt will tremble at his presence,
and the heart of the Egyptians will melt within them . . .
And the waters of the sea* will be dried up
and the river will be parched and dry. (Isa. 19.1, 5)

In the sixth century BCE, Ezekiel had described Egypt as a dragon:

---

*The Hebrew has Sea, not Nile as in some translations.

Behold, I am against you, Pharaoh king of Egypt,
the great dragon that lies in the midst of his streams,
that says, 'My Nile is my own; I made it.'
I will put hooks in your jaws,
and make the fish of your streams stick to your scales;
and I will draw you up out of the midst of your streams,
and all the fish of your streams which stick to your scales. (Ezek. 29.3–4)

Son of Man, raise a lamentation over Pharaoh king of Egypt, and say to him:
You consider yourself a lion among the nations,
but you are like a dragon in the seas;
you burst forth in your rivers,
trouble the waters with your feet, and foul their rivers.
Thus says the LORD God:
I will throw my net over you with a host of many peoples;
And I will haul you up in my dragnet. (Ezek. 32.2–3)

In each case the monster was to be strewn on the mountains and his flesh eaten by the birds and beasts, as in Revelation 19.17–21. In the first century CE the sea beast still represented the foreign rulers in Jerusalem, and these would have been variously identified as situations changed.

The true king in Jerusalem is a recurring theme in the Gospels. Herod, the Idumean puppet king in Jerusalem, reacts violently to the news that a child has been 'born king of the Jews' (Matt. 2.2). The deepest ironies of the Passion narrative address the issue of kingship, with the Jews saying, 'We have no king but Caesar' (John 19.15), and Pilate the Roman governor insisting on the superscription 'The King of the Jews' (John 19.19–22). Jesus warned about Caesar worship when he replied to the question about Roman taxes: 'Render to Caesar the things that are Caesar's and to God the things that are God's' (Mark 12.17), and the first Christians in Jerusalem recognized the conspiracy to kill Jesus as fulfilment of the ancient conflict: 'The kings of the earth set themselves, And the rulers take counsel together, against the LORD and his anointed ...' (Ps. 2.2, quoted in Acts 4.25–28 of the conspiracy of Pilate and Herod). The Romans would have been one manifestation of the beast, and the Herods which grew from their kingdom were the ten horns (Dan. 7.24, cf. Rev. 17.12).

The issue of divine kingship was not new in Jerusalem. It was at the very heart of the temple cult, and the Messiah was the symbol of legitimate kingship in Jerusalem. Jesus must have been aware of these issues since a statue of Augustus had been erected in Caesarea (*War* 1.414) and Pontius Pilate had attempted to bring images into Jerusalem (*War* 2.171). (The first temple to the god Caesar had been dedicated in Pergamum in 29 BCE, perhaps *the throne of Satan* mentioned in 2.13.) Jesus' words: 'Render to Caesar the things that are Caesar's and to God the things that are God's' had only one possible meaning: Do not worship Caesar. The story is told with emphasis on 'the image' of

Caesar which appeared on the coins (Mark 12.16), and this must be one element in the image of the beast (13.15).

He warned that Daniel's prophecy would be fulfilled; there would be an abomination in the temple, and the people of Judea should escape to the hills (Mark 13.14). Scholars often say that this was not a genuine saying of Jesus, that it was added later by the Christian community, but there is no reason why it should not have been Jesus' own prediction of the final sequence of events. Paul knew of such a sequence, and his earliest letters (about 50 CE) deal with problems arising from it. The Christians at Thessalonika had been warned to expect persecution and temptation (1 Thess. 2.14 and 3.4–5). The end was near and those who were still alive would be caught up in the clouds to meet the LORD (1 Thess. 4.15–17, but the pattern had still to be worked out. First there would be the great rebellion and the 'man of lawlessness [would be] revealed ... who opposes and exalts himself against every so-called god or object of worship, so that he takes his seat in the temple of God, proclaiming himself to be God' (2 Thess. 2.4). The LORD Jesus would then appear and destroy him with the breath of his mouth (2 Thess. 2.8), exactly as in Revelation 19.15, where the returning Messiah destroys his enemies with the sharp sword of his mouth. Those who taught Paul his new faith taught him these predictions, another indication that the Book of Revelation originated in Palestine.

It is pointless to try to find one ruler who fulfilled everything in these verses which depict the antitype of the Messiah. In the final form of the Book of Revelation, the beast is identified as Nero; the mortal wound in the head of the beast found fulfilment in the manner of Nero's death in 68 CE when he committed suicide after discovering a plot against him (War 4.493). Immediately in 69 CE there arose rumours that he had fled to the east and would return (Tacitus, Histories 2.8–9), hence the resurrection of the beast (13.12; 17.8). Similar rumours arose in 80 CE and 88 CE, each associating the revived Nero with the dreaded king of the Parthians. Nero did not, however, proclaim himself a god, nor did he directly defile the temple except insofar as the war against Judea began in his reign.

Most references to the beast refer only to his mark (14.9; 16.2; 19.20, 20.4), but the introduction of his 'number' is another device to indicate Nero. The name of the beast and 666, the number of its name (13.17), refer to the way that letters were also used as numbers; the first letter of the Hebrew alphabet was used for 1, the third for 3 and so on. Treated thus, a process known as gematria, the Greek name 'Neron Caesar', spelled in Hebrew letters, becomes N (50) + R (200) + W (6) + N (50) + Q (100) + S (60) + R (200), making 666. This spelling of the name is confirmed by an Aramaic document found at Murabba'at, dated 'the second year of the Emperor Nero'. This implies an interpretation of the name by people who understood Hebrew or Aramaic, even though Revelation is now written in Greek. The identification of the beast as Nero has been a commonplace among scholars since it was first suggested a century ago, long before the Murabba'at document confirmed the contemporary spelling of the name Nero. The problem is that this form of gematria is only known elsewhere using Greek letters, not Hebrew. At the end of the second century CE, however, there were some versions of Revelation which had the number of the beast as 616, a further challenge to scholars' ingenuity (Irenaeus, *AH* 5.30). It could represent the Latin form 'Nero Caesar', the final 'N' of the Greek form being dropped and thus the gematria number being reduced by 50 to 616. Or it could be conventional gematria with the Greek letters of the name 'Gaios Kaisar', and the beast could be Caligula.

By the time of Irenaeus, the end of the second century CE, the identification of the beast as Nero was not known (*AH* 5.28–30), but the fear of Nero had passed into Christian tradition, and there can be no doubt that Nero's evil reign was written into the final interpretation of the beast in the Book of Revelation. The *Ascension of Isaiah,* whose Christian version was completed towards the end of the first century CE, 'foresees' the reign of Nero:

Beliar will descend, the great angel, the king of this world ... He will descend from his firmament in the form of a man, a king of iniquity,* the murderer of his mother** and he will persecute the plant which the twelve apostles of the Beloved have planted ... By his word he will cause the sun to rise by night, and the moon also he will make to appear at the sixth hour. And he will do everything he wishes in the world; he will act and speak like the Beloved and he will say, 'I am the LORD and before me there was no one' ... And all men in the world will believe in him. They will sacrifice to him and will serve him saying, 'This is the LORD and besides him there is no other' ... And the power of his miracles will be in every city and district and he will set up his image before him in every city. (*Asc. Isa.* 4.1–12)

The beast, however, had taken many forms before it was identified as Nero. The evil reign of Antiochus Epiphanes (175–163 BCE) was also a time of the beast, as can be seen from Daniel 7.19–27 which explained that the time of the fourth and last beast had come. When a false rumour arose that Antiochus was dead, civil strife broke out in Judea and Antiochus returned to quell the trouble in Jerusalem (*2 Macc.* 5). A great slaughter followed, with 40,000 killed and a similar number sold as slaves. He robbed the temple and defiled the sanctuary by entering it and then setting up a pagan altar. Many Jews adopted his pagan ways and sacrificed to idols (*1 Macc.* 1). The Book of Daniel addressed this situation and interpreted the ancient vision of the Man ascending to heaven as a sign of hope for those troubled times (Dan. 7). There would be an abomination set in the temple, but the saints would triumph. Much of what is said about the beast in Revelation could have been said of Antiochus. Had these fragments of Revelation been discovered for the first time, abandoned in a cave, it would have been easy for scholars

---

* This must be Melchiresa' the evil king, the antitype of Melchizedek the righteous king.
** Nero had his mother Agrippina murdered in 59 CE.

to argue for a date in the second century BCE. The beast had the blasphemous name 'Epiphanes', which means 'The Manifest God'; there had been a rumour of his death but he returned to wreak havoc in Jerusalem just as the beast returned 'from the bottomless pit' to wreak havoc in Jerusalem (11.7–8); he blasphemed God's Name and his dwelling, the temple (13.6), and he both took captives and slew with the sword (13.10).

Or the beast could have been Ptolemy IV Philopator (222–205 BCE) whose story is told in *3 Maccabees* 1–2. When the Seleucid king Antiochus IV attempted to take Palestine from the Egyptians, Ptolemy drove him back, marched in triumph into Jerusalem and tried to enter the sanctuary. The high priest Simeon prayed that the sanctuary should be spared this defilement, and Ptolemy was struck down before he could enter. His bodyguards feared for his life as he was both paralysed and dumb, but he recovered and wreaked vengeance on the Jews of Alexandria. They were forced, on pain of death, to sacrifice to Dionysus. Those who did so were branded with an ivy leaf, the sign of the god, and were then granted equal status with other citizens of Alexandria. Ptolemy had received an apparently mortal blow from which he recovered. He then made war on the saints and conquered them. He too blasphemed against the Name and the temple; he too branded those in his power (13.16), and only those who had submitted to pagan worship were allowed to live as citizens.

Or the beast could have been Pompey who became involved with Jerusalem in 63 BCE after one of two rivals for the high priesthood asked him to intervene. (The red dragon summoned the beast from the sea.) He came to the city and entered the sanctuary of the temple. The *Psalms of Solomon* record bitterly what happened; an arrogant sinner broke down the walls and entered the temple, and then the people were sold as slaves. Pompey is described as 'the dragon' whom God then pierced on the mountains of Egypt as punishment for his arrogance in claiming to be 'Lord of land and sea' (*Pss Sol.* 2.25). As punishment for her sins, Jerusalem had been ruled by the Hasmoneans who despoiled the throne of David, and then Pompey the Roman had come as God's agent against them (*Pss Sol.* 8.15). At first they had welcomed him like the Messiah:

The leaders of the country met him with joy. They said to him,
May your way be blessed. May you enter in peace.
They graded the rough roads before his coming;
They opened the gates to Jerusalem,
they crowned her city walls. (*Pss Sol.* 8.16–17)

Pompey, however, had not come in peace. He poured out the blood of Jerusalem 'like dirty water' (*Pss Sol.* 8.20). The prayer of the psalmist was then for a true king, the son of David 'to rule over your servant Israel', to replace 'the lawless one' (*Pss Sol.* 17.21 and 11).

Or the beast could have been the Emperor Caligula (37–41 CE). He had a serious illness from which people were amazed that he recovered

(Philo, *Embassy to Gaius* 14–20), and he insisted on being worshipped as a god. He had the heads removed from statues of Greek gods and replaced with his own, and he branded slaves (Suetonius, *Caligula* 22 and 27). He held conversations with a statue of Jupiter, 'he made the image speak' (Rev. 13.15, cf. Suetonius, *Caligula* 22). When the Jews of Alexandria refused to worship him, an informer told the emperor that they were 'neglecting honours that belonged to Caesar . . . for these Jews alone thought it a dishonourable thing for them to erect statues in honour of him, as well as to swear by his name' (*Ant.* 18.257–58). A new governor was sent to Syria with orders to invade Judea and erect a statue of the emperor in the temple itself. The Jews protested that they would die before allowing this to happen, but the emperor was murdered by a head wound before the outrage could be committed. Some of Josephus' descriptions of Caligula are reminiscent of the beast: 'By reason of the vastness of his dominions he made himself a god and took upon himself to act in all things to the reproach of the Deity itself' (*Ant.* 18.256). Petronius, the new governor of Syria, spoke to the assembled Jews at Tiberias: 'Will you then make war with Caesar, without considering his great preparations for war, and your own weakness?' (*Ant.* 18.271). Perhaps Caligula was the beast of whom it was said: 'Who is like the beast and who can fight against it?' His reign was short, forty-six months, and he above all blasphemed against God and the temple.

A composite beast appears in Revelation 17, carrying the harlot on his back. He is red and symbolizes many waters, so he resembles the dragon yet he is called a beast. He was to ascend from the bottomless pit and go to his final judgement (17.8), as described in Revelation 20. Several layers of interpretation have accumulated in this passage also (see p. 286). The Christians were heirs to a rich tradition, and there had been all too many occasions in Judea's history when the prophecies of the beast were fulfilled.

The False Prophet

The great beast had a prophet, the second beast who came from the land. The dragon and the two beasts sent foul spirits from their mouths in the form of frogs, and these demons performed miracles (16.13–14). Jesus had predicted false prophets, wolves in sheep's clothing (Matt. 7.15) who would work signs and wonders to lead people astray before the Son of Man returned (Mark 13.21). Paul also warned of the pretended signs and wonders which would lead people astray before the day of Christ's return (2 Thess. 2.9). Moses had warned Israel about false prophets: even if they performed signs and wonders and their prophecies came true, they were false prophets if they enticed people to serve other gods. It was believed that the LORD sometimes sent false prophets to test his people's love and faith (Deut. 13.1–3) and he could send a lying spirit (1 Kgs 22.19–23).

The false prophet of the beast came from the earth, that is, 'from the land'. He was a traitor within Judea not a foreign ruler like the first beast. He looked like a lamb but spoke like a dragon (13.11) and persuaded the people of the land to worship the beast and set up his image. Those who did not worship the beast were killed, those who did not bear his mark on their right hand and forehead could not engage in trade. The false prophet performed signs and exercised the authority of the first beast.

Who was the false prophet? The pattern of type and antitype suggests that John saw this 'person as an antitype of himself, a priest-prophet who was interpreting oracles in the light of current events. *This must have been Josephus*. John was the prophet entrusted with the testimony of Jesus, and its true interpretation had been revealed to him (1.1–3). In particular, he knew the prophecies of the seals and the promise of the messianic kingdom when the seventh seal was opened. He had already identified Nero's persecution as the sixth seal (7.14), and the political situation in Palestine had become very dangerous as a result. Josephus wrote: 'What more than all else incited them to war was an ambiguous oracle found in their sacred scriptures that at that time one from their country would become ruler of the world. This they understood to mean someone of their own race, and many of their wise men went astray in their interpretation of it' (*War* 6.312–13). The Slavonic text continues: 'Some understood that this meant Herod, others the crucified wonder worker Jesus, others again Vespasian'. The Christians interpreted the oracle of the Parousia, but it was Josephus who said that the world ruler would be Vespasian.

Josephus, who would have regarded John as a false prophet, claimed prophetic gifts and saw himself as another Jeremiah, insofar as it had been revealed to him that the Romans were the divinely appointed agents of the LORD's judgement on Jerusalem. Therefore he went over to their side. He wrote of his decision to desert his people:

There came back to his mind those nightly dreams in which God had foretold to him the impending fate of the Jews and the destinies of the Roman sovereigns. He was an interpreter of dreams and skilled in divining ambiguous utterances of the Deity; a priest himself and of priestly descent, he was not ignorant of the prophecies in the sacred books. At that hour he was inspired to read their meaning and, recalling the dreadful images of his recent dreams, he offered up a silent prayer to God. 'Since it pleases thee', so it ran, 'who didst create the Jewish nation, to break thy word since fortune has wholly passed to the Romans, and since thou hast made choice of my spirit to announce the things that are to come, I willingly surrender to the Romans and consent to live. But I take thee to witness that I go not as a traitor but as thy minister.' (*War* 3.351–54)

When he had been taken prisoner by Vespasian, Josephus conveniently recalled his prophetic gifts and interpreted the oracle about the ruler from Palestine as a prediction that Vespasian would become the next emperor of Rome: 'I have come to you as a messenger of good tidings . . .

You, O Vespasian are emperor, you and your son ... You O Caesar are master not only over me but over the land and sea and all mankind' (*War* 3.400, 402). This ensured Josephus' safety and future prosperity, but would have made him a false prophet in the eyes of the Hebrew Christians.

The false prophet exercised all the authority of the first beast in its presence and made the earth and its inhabitants worship the first beast (13.12). This is a reference to Josephus' role as spokesman for Titus during the siege: 'He delegated Josephus to parley with them in their native tongue, thinking that possibly they might yield to the expostulation of a fellow countryman ... Josephus, accordingly, went round the wall ... and repeatedly implored them to spare themselves and the people, to spare their country and their temple ...' (*War* 5.361–62). God was with the Romans, he said, and they should serve them. They should worship the beast who 'was wounded by the sword and yet lived', a reference to the rumour that Nero had come back to life. Giving breath to the image and causing all who would not worship it to be slain are antitypes drawn from the Adam story (see p. 216); the beast has been created in the image of his god and all are commanded to worship him on pain of death. The reference is probably to Josephus' offer to the people of Jerusalem: 'Even at this late hour Caesar desired to offer them terms, whereas if he took the city by storm, he would not spare a man of them ...' (*War* 5.373).

Josephus offered his own interpretation of the voices in the temple at Pentecost which said: 'We are leaving this place' (*War* 6.300). He concluded his speech with the words: 'My belief, therefore, is that the Deity has fled from the holy places and taken his stand on the side of those with whom you are now at war' (*War* 5.412). Josephus was later ordered by Caesar to make another appeal to the Zealots in the city: 'Josephus, standing so that his words might reach the ears not only of John' [of Gischala, the Zealot leader] 'but also of the multitude, delivered Caesar's message in Hebrew, with earnest appeals to them to spare their country ... But the tyrant [i.e. John], after many invectives and imprecations upon Josephus, ended by saying that he could never fear capture since the city belonged to God' (*War* 6.98). This without doubt is the false prophet, scorned by the Zealots who believed that the city was protected by God. Josephus admitted that John of Gischala had never trusted him (*War* 2.590–95) and after he had become spokesman for the Romans, John had looked for an opportunity to capture him (*War* 6.112).

Josephus then taunted the people in the city: 'God himself who is with the Romans is bringing fire to purge his temple ...' (*War* 6.110). This is the false prophet 'making fire come down from heaven to earth' (13.13). He told them that one of the ancient oracles against Jerusalem was being fulfilled, that the city would be taken when one should begin to slaughter his own countrymen (*War* 6.110). The oracle is not found in the Hebrew Scriptures as we have them today, but is clearly the one spoken by Jesus when describing the signs that the temple would be destroyed: 'Brother will deliver up brother to death and the father his child, and children will rise against parents and have them put to death; and you will be hated by all for my name's sake. But he who endures to the end will be saved' (Mark 13.12–13). Josephus was an educated man, a priest who knew the ancient writings of his people, and he had a considerable interest in prophecy. He describes this saying of Jesus as an ancient oracle, and we must assume he was correct. Jesus must have been quoting from a book no longer extant, which strengthens the possibility that the rest of his sayings incorporated in the Synoptic Apocalypse were also quotations from a lost text (see p. 67), and that the Seven Seals were an ancient tradition.

Other considerations confirm that Josephus was the false prophet; he was of royal and high priestly blood (*Life* 1), 'a lamb and he spoke like a dragon' (13.11). He tried to persuade his people to accept Roman rule: 'He makes the land and its inhabitants worship the first beast ... Who is like the beast and who can fight against it?' (13.4, 12). In his autobiography, Josephus wrote: 'I laid before their eyes against whom it was they were going to fight and told them that they were inferior to the Romans' (*Life* 4). The people of Galilee accused him of betraying them to the Romans (*Life* 27), but he declared that he had been inspired by a dream to fight for the Romans (*Life* 42) and he says that he managed to persuade many people that he was 'the Benefactor and Saviour of the country' (*Life* 47). It was only when he was taken prisoner to the Roman commander Vespasian, that his prophetic gifts enabled him to reveal his captor's glorious destiny. As a result, when the land of Judea was ravaged by the Romans and Jerusalem was destroyed, Josephus prospered. The Emperor Vespasian gave him Roman citizenship, a house in Rome and an annual pension:

When those that envied my good fortune did bring accusations against me, by God's providence I escaped them all. I also received from Vespasian no small quantity of land, as a free gift, in Judea. [The emperor] punished those Jews who were my accusers ... and he also made that land which I had in Judea tax free, which is a mark of the greatest honour to him who has it. (*Life* 76)

This was the false prophet from the land.

The most popular identification of the false prophet is that he represented the priesthood of the imperial cult, practising magic and preventing Christians from engaging in trade. Unfortunately, the only evidence for the magical practices of the imperial priesthood in Asia Minor is derived from this passage in Revelation which is assumed to describe them! The letters to the seven churches of Asia do not mention the imperial cult and its priesthood, unless this is implied by the throne of Satan in Pergamum (2.13). When Ignatius, Bishop of Antioch, wrote to the church in Ephesus in 107 CE, he described the conflict between Christ and the age-old empire of evil as a time when 'magic crumbled away, spells of sorcery were broken and superstition received its death blow' (*Eph*. 19), and there had been magicians in the city who burned their books when Paul was there (Acts 19.11–20). There is nothing to link these magicians with the imperial cult. The magician whom Paul confronted on Cyprus was a Jewish false prophet named Bar Jesus, a man of some influence with the Roman pro-consul (Acts 13.6–7). Nor is there any evidence for Christians being compelled to worship Caesar until 112 CE, when a letter to the Emperor Trajan from the governor of Bythinia enquired how he was to treat Christians. He had been compelling suspects to offer incense and wine to the emperor's statue and to curse Christ in order to prove they were not Christian (Pliny, *Letters* 10).

The false prophet made everyone wear the mark of the beast on their right hands and foreheads. This mark is mentioned six times (13.7; 14.9; 11, 16.2; 19.20; 20.4) and must have been the most conspicuous way of identifying the followers of the beast. Those who did not bear the mark of the beast were subjected to economic sanctions so that no one could buy or sell unless he bore the mark (13.17). 'Those who kept the commandments of God and the testimony of Jesus' (12.17) knew only too well what was meant by the mark of the beast. As with so much else, this phrase was an allusion to the Hebrew Scriptures. The 'mark' of the beast, *charagma*, meant literally the mark of a snake bite, and in Hebrew the word for snake bite was also the word for interest paid on money, *nšk*. It was forbidden to charge interest on money (e.g. Exod. 22.25) and yet the rule of the beast was that no one could buy or sell without interest ('the mark', 13.17). Habakkuk threatened the rapacious who had plundered many nations: 'Will not those who pay you interest suddenly rise up . . .' (Hab. 2.7) and the Qumran Habakkuk Commentary interprets this verse as a prophecy of judgement on the Wicked Priest (1QpHab VIII): 'His chastisement by means of the judgement of wickedness . . . the last priests of Jerusalem who shall amass money and wealth by plundering the peoples'. The implication is the priests in Jerusalem had been amassing wealth by flouting the Law, and that the making of money had replaced the Law of Moses. When the people gained control of the temple, their first act, after burning the houses of the high priest and the Roman puppet king, was to burn all the contracts 'belonging to their creditors and thereby dissolve their obligations for paying their debts' (*War* 2.427). They were inaugurating the final Jubilee and destroying the mark of the beast. The economic tensions between Jerusalem and the surrounding country were deep-rooted. In the middle of the fifth century BCE, Nehemiah had dealt with an ugly situation caused by the Jerusalem Jews' treatment of the people of the land, 'You are exacting interest, each from his brother' (Neh. 5.7). It is not difficult to see how the mark of the beast excluded people from trading in the city. Josephus, reflecting on Judean society and the causes of the revolt concluded it was due to 'the men of power oppressing the multitude and the multitude earnestly labouring to destroy the men of power' (*War* 7.261).

In the Hebrew Scriptures, the best known story about snake bites is in Numbers 21.4–9. The Israelites spoke against the LORD and he punished them with fiery snakes whose bite was fatal. Moses was told to set up a bronze serpent on a pole and 'everyone who is bitten, when he sees it shall live' (Num. 21.8). The bronze serpent was set up in their midst and the people were protected. John's Jesus spoke of himself as the serpent lifted up in the wilderness (John 3.14–15), implying that the bite of the snake, the mark of the beast, was known to Jesus and that he offered protection. It would be interesting to know the original import of this cryptic remark and of the saying about serving two masters: 'You cannot serve God and Mammon' (Matt. 6.24; Luke 16.13).

It is thought that the wearing of phylacteries had been one sign of religious and nationalist revival during the Maccabean period (DJD VI). The marks of the beast were worn on the right hand and the forehead (13.16), in other words, they had replaced the phylacteries worn as 'a sign upon your hand and as frontlets between your eyes' (Deut. 6.8). The type and style of the phylacteries, however, was matter of some dispute. Jesus warned against the new fashion for large phylacteries (Matt. 23.5), and the variety of phylactery texts found at Qumran suggests that the verses of scripture placed inside them had a sectarian significance. Most of the examples are of traditional texts (Exod. 12.43–13.16 and Deut. 5.1–6.9; 10.12–11.21) – but phylactery N (4Q141) is the Song of Moses (Deut. 32), a text of special significance in the Book of Revelation. Those who have kept themselves pure from the beast and its image, stand before the throne and sing the Song of Moses (15.2–3) which suggests that the Song of Moses was the text by which the redeemed distinguished themselves. The community described in the Damascus Document also identified their enemies in terms drawn from the Song of Moses: 'They have wilfully rebelled by walking in the ways of the wicked of whom God said "Their wine is the venom of serpents, the cruel poison of asps" ' (Deut. 32.33; CD VIII). The bite of the snake, the mark of the beast again.

More evidence to identify the beasts lies in the events which led to the outbreak of war with Rome. After the outrages of the Roman governor Gessius Florus, the people were driven to revolt. The high priest's son refused to accept a sacrificial offering from Caesar despite protests from the temple authorities that offerings from foreign rulers had always been accepted. 'Their forefathers had adorned their temple in great part by donations bestowed on them by foreigners' (War 2.412–13). The Jerusalem authorities, the high priest and the leader of the Pharisees, tried in vain to make the people accept Roman rule:

but then perceiving that the sedition was too hard for them to subdue, and that the danger that would arise from the Romans would come upon them first of all, endeavoured to save themselves and sent ambassadors [to the Roman governor and the king] ... and they desired of them, ... that they should come with an army to the city and cut off the sedition before it should be too hard to be subdued ... (War 2.418)

Here was the dragon, the priesthood, summoning the beast, the power of Rome. The object of their wrath was the common people of Palestine who had risen against the corrupt temple rulers and their Roman allies.

16

THE HARVEST OF THE EARTH

Then I looked, and lo, on Mount Zion stood the Lamb, and with him a hundred and forty-four thousand who had his name and his Father's name written on their foreheads ... These have been redeemed from mankind as first fruits for God and the Lamb, and in their mouth no lie was found, for they are spotless ...

Then I looked, and lo, a white cloud, and seated on the cloud one like a son of man, with a golden crown on his head, and a sharp sickle in his hand. And another angel came out of the temple, calling with a loud voice to him who sat upon the cloud, 'Put in your sickle, and reap for the hour to reap has come, for the harvest of the earth is fully ripe.' So he who sat upon the cloud swung his sickle on the earth, and the earth was reaped.

And another angel came out of the temple in heaven, and he too had a sharp sickle. Then another angel came out from the altar, the angel who has power over fire, and he called out with a loud voice to him who had the sickle, 'Put in your sickle, and gather the clusters of the vine of the earth, for its grapes are ripe.' So the angel swung his sickle on the earth, and gathered the vintage of the earth, and threw it into the great wine press of the wrath of God; and the wine press was trodden outside the city, and blood flowed from the wine press, as high as a horse's bridle, for one thousand six hundred stadia. (Rev. 14.1, 4b–5, 14–20)

Chapter 14 is based on a sequence of temple festivals: the 144,000 who are the 'firstfruits', the reaper on the white cloud and then the vintage of the earth. With the 'firstfruits' already gathered on Zion, the seer watches as angels emerge from the temple to harvest the earth. These scenes correspond to the annual sequence of temple festivals: the Passover, the Feast of Weeks and then the Offering of the New Wine. The Qumran Temple Scroll has a calendar of festivals and their dates which differs from any previously known; the year was 364 days, exactly 52 weeks, and so every year began on the same day of the week. Passover, 14th Nisan, always fell on a Tuesday and the sheaf of the firstfruits mentioned in Leviticus 23.10, the Omer, had to be offered on the day after the Sabbath after the end of the Feast of Unleavened Bread. This was later than in other traditions, and meant that the sheaf was offered on 26th Nisan. Seven weeks after that, on the day after the seventh Sabbath, there was the 'new grain offering to the LORD', corresponding to the new grain offering in Leviticus 23.15–21 and serving also as a feast of the firstfruits of the wheat. This fell on 15th Sivan. The Temple Scroll then prescribes an offering not mentioned in Leviticus; seven weeks after the new grain offering, on the day after the Sabbath, new wine was to be offered by all the twelve tribes of Israel (11QT XVIII–XIX), a feast which fell on 3rd Ab. *This calendar, with the festivals falling at a slightly later date, is important for understanding Revelation 14.*

Revelation 14 duplicates oracles found elsewhere in the Book of Revelation, and Josephus suggests a reason for this. He describes a series of portents which appeared as the war progressed, but says there was disagreement as to what they meant. By the inexperienced, he wrote, they were regarded as good omens, but 'the sacred scribes interpreted them in accordance with what followed' (*War* 6.291). The prophecies preserved in the second half of the Book of Revelation come from these prophets in Jerusalem who did not always speak with one voice. The 144,000 on Zion (14.1–5) are the 144,000 in 7.1–8, and the three angels (14.6–11) correspond to the angels at 10.5–7; 18.1–3 and 18.4–8. The sequence of harvests and oracles, read in the light of Josephus, suggests that chapter 14 is an account of the last months in Jerusalem before the temple was burned, from Passover to 10th Ab in 70 CE.

The One Hundred and Forty-Four Thousand

The Lamb stands on Mount Zion, a motif found in Psalm 48, where the LORD, her great King, stands on his holy mountain in the midst of his city, and his presence terrifies the kings who try to attack. This gives a context for the vision; Jerusalem is under threat from enemy attack and the city is protected by the Lamb. The Lamb on Zion also occurs in Psalm 2: 'I have set my king on Zion my holy hill ... be warned, O rulers of the earth' (Ps. 2.6, 10) and in Psalm 110: 'The LORD sends forth from Zion your mighty sceptre. Rule in the midst of your foes ... He will shatter kings on the day of his wrath' (Ps. 110.2, 5). The Lamb on Zion is the same figure as the child destined to rule the nations with a rod of iron, who had been 'caught up' to the throne of God (12.5, based on Ps. 2.9). The kings and rulers have conspired against him and plotted in vain (Ps. 2.1), a verse fulfilled in the conspiracy of Herod and Pilate against Jesus (Acts 4.26–28). This vain conspiracy against the Lamb is the warfare on earth depicted in the Book of Revelation from the time when Satan is thrown from heaven (12.7) to the time when he is bound in the pit (20.2). Secure above the turmoil is the Lamb on Zion who rules in the midst of his foes and shatters kings. In another royal psalm the LORD promises the king:

I will crush his foes before him and strike down those who hate him ...
He shall cry to me, 'Thou art my Father, my God, and the Rock of my salvation.'
And I will make him the firstborn, the highest of the kings of the earth. (Ps. 89.23, 26, 27)

'The firstborn' is the key to understanding 14.1–5 because the multitude on Zion have been redeemed not as 'firstfruits' but as the 'firstborn'. The Greek text has *aparche*, which reveals little since the LXX used this word for a whole range of temple offerings: tithes, fat, firstfruits, or, most frequently, oblation, *terumah*, which meant any contribution or offering. Elsewhere in the New Testament it does mean firstfruits (e.g. Rom. 11.16; 1 Cor. 15.20, 23; Jas 1.18). If we assume a Hebrew original, the written form of the two words for firstfruits and firstborn is identical in the singular *bkwr* and the construct plural *bkwry*. A translator who was not well informed about temple customs could easily have confused them. *The crucial difference is that firstfruits were not redeemed but the firstborn were*, hence redeemed as the firstborn (14.4).

One of the texts placed in phylacteries was Exodus 12.43–13.16, which must have given this text a particular significance. It links possession of the land to two observances: keeping the Passover and the Feast of Unleavened Bread, and consecrating to the LORD all firstborn males, both animal and human. As a memorial of their redemption from Egypt, when the firstborn of Egypt died in the tenth plague but the firstborn of Israel were kept safe by the blood of the Passover lamb, all firstborn animals were sacrificed. The firstborn sons were redeemed (Exod. 13.15) for five silver shekels (Num. 18.16; *m. Bekhoroth* 8.7), or by a Levite offered to serve in the temple (Num. 3.41). That these 'firstfruits' on Mount Zion were in fact the firstborn is confirmed by Hebrews 12.22–23 where the assembled firstborn stand on Mount Zion: 'You have come to Mount Zion and to the city of the living God, the heavenly Jerusalem, and to innumerable angels in festal gathering, and to the assembly of the firstborn who are enrolled in heaven . . .' The vision of the 144,000 on Zion marked the spring of the year, Passover and the firstborn.

The firstborn were 'redeemed', a word used to describe the Qumran community, 'Thy Poor whom Thou hast redeemed' (1QM XI) and which also occurs in 5.9, 'by thy blood thou didst redeem men for God . . . and hast made them a kingdom and priests'. This is another reference to the multitude on Zion as can be seen from the similarity of 5.6–11 and 14.1–5 which both describe the Lamb standing, the throne with the elders and living creatures, the sound of harps and the new song. In other words, the 144,000 on Mount Zion are the new royal priesthood. A similar idea in a similar context is found in Psalm 74 which laments an earlier destruction of the temple: the enemy has destroyed everything in the holy of holies (Ps. 74.3b) and the psalmist prays: 'Remember thy congregation which thou hast gotten of old, which thou hast redeemed to be the tribe of thy heritage' (Ps. 74.2). 'Gotten' here translates well the Hebrew *qnh* which can mean either buy, redeem, create or beget (see p. 142). It is likely that the Hebrew original of 14.4 had *qnh* and described the multitude as the firstborn who had been redeemed/begotten as sons of God, like the Davidic king: 'Today I have begotten you' (Ps. 2.7, *yldtyk*) and 'I will make him the firstborn' (Ps. 89.27, *bkwr*). This emphasis on being the firstborn was important for the Hebrew Christian; James, the Bishop of Jerusalem, wrote: 'he gave birth to us by the word of truth so that we should be a kind of firstborn of his creatures' (Jas 1.18, translating literally, assuming again the confusion of firstfruits and firstborn).

The 144,000 are marked on the forehead with the Name of the Lamb and the Name of his Father (14.1), in other words they bear the sacred

Name on their foreheads as did the high priests. A comparison with the other vision of the 144,000 confirms this; they were sealed with the seal of the living God (7.2), which was the seal engraved with the Name and worn by the high priest (Exod. 28.36). This was a diagonal cross which became the mark of Christian baptism (see on 7.1–8 pp. 161–3). The multitude on Zion are the first resurrected of the millennium kingdom (20.4–5).

The triumphant Lamb on Zion appears also in 2 *Esdras*, a first-century CE Jewish text preserved and expanded by Christians. In his dream, 'Ezra' saw a Man who came up out of the sea and flew on the clouds. A huge crowd assembled to attack him but he went to stand on a great mountain and repulsed his attackers with a stream of fire from his mouth (see on 11.5). Then he summoned another multitude who met him in peace at the foot of the mountain. When 'Ezra' prayed to know the meaning of his dream, he was told that the Man was the Son of God Most High, the mountain was Zion, the enemies were the godless nations and the peaceful multitude were the dispersed ten tribes of Israel (2 *Esdr.* 13.1–11 and 25–45). The same multitude on Zion appears in the earlier vision of the tall young Man on Mount Zion, distributing crowns and palms. The angel explains: 'These are they that have put off mortal clothing and have put on immortal and they have confessed the Name of God; now they are being crowned and receive palms' (2 *Esdr.* 2.45; cf. Rev. 7.9).

The 144,000 'have not defiled themselves with women' (14.4). Since the context of the vision is war, when the Lamb and his host on Zion confront the dragon and the beast, the purity of the multitude is a sign of readiness for holy war. Warriors had to abstain from every evil thing (Deut. 23.9–10) and this included sexual acts. (This prohibition is an important part of the story of David and Bathsheba. Even though her husband Uriah had been summoned home from battle to visit his wife and thus provide cover for David's earlier seduction, he refused to sleep with her because he and his fellow soldiers were at war and he was purified for battle (2 Sam. 11.11).) The War Scroll has similar prescriptions: 'No man shall go down to battle who is impure because of his emissions' (1QM VII). The 144,000 were also spotless, literally 'without blemish', physically perfect, another indication that they were priests, since one of the qualifications for priesthood was physical perfection: 'No man of the descendants of Aaron the priest who has a blemish shall come near to offer the LORD's holy offerings by fire ... that he may not profane my sanctuaries' (Lev. 21.18–23). The War Scroll has the same rules for priestly warriors which cannot possibly have applied literally to fighting men; no blind or crippled person could have been an active soldier: 'No man who is lame or blind or crippled or afflicted with a lasting bodily blemish or smitten with a bodily impurity shall march out to war with them' (1QM VII). In addition the War Scroll prescribes: 'They shall all be freely enlisted for war', like the army that fought with Deborah (Judg. 5.2) and Melchizedek's host in Psalm 110.3: 'Your people offer themselves freely on the day of your host' and they were prepared to shatter kings on the day of wrath. In each case the same word is used: *ndbt,* freely offered.

These priestly warriors follow the Lamb wherever he goes, a motif familiar from the Gospels where it is so often associated with suffering and martyrdom, e.g. Mark 8.34: 'If any man would come after me, let him deny himself and take up his cross and follow me' (cf. Mark 10.28); or John 8.12: 'He who follows me will not walk in darkness but have the light of life'; or John 13.36: 'Where I am going you cannot follow me now, but you shall follow afterwards'.

'And in their mouth no lie was found' (14.5) could be a reference to the Servant 'there was no deceit in his mouth' (Isa. 53.9), or to Zephaniah's vision of the LORD's people in the last days: 'Those who are left in Israel shall do no wrong and utter no lies, nor shall there be found in their mouth a deceitful tongue' (Zeph. 3.13). The Lie, however, was an important theme in the Qumran texts and the Man of Lies was one description of their great enemy. There was 'the Scoffer who shed over Israel the water of lies' (CD I); 'the Spouter of lies who led many astray' (1QpHab X) and the fragment of a commentary on Micah interprets the sins of the house of Israel (Mic. 1.5) as 'the Spouter of Lies [who led] the simple [astray]' (1Q14). Some had been 'unfaithful together with the Liar' (1QpHab II), those who gave the teacher of Righteousness no help against the Liar (1QpHab IV). Satan, the red dragon, was the Deceiver of the whole world (12.9).

The 144,000 in 14.1–5 were the heavenly warriors of the Lamb, 'the armies of heaven arrayed in fine linen' who later follow him from heaven when he rides out against the Beast (19.14). They were the hosts of the LORD of hosts, the heavenly host described in the War Scroll who would 'fight from heaven' (1QM XI) and they were believed literally to be present with the army, 'the congregation of thy holy ones, among us for everlasting succour ... the King of Glory is with us together with the Holy Ones, valiant ones of the angelic host among our numbered men ... the host of his spirits with our foot soldiers and horsemen' (1QM XII). It was hopes like these in the War Scroll that inspired the resistance in Jerusalem in the summer of 70 CE: 'This is the Day appointed by him for the defeat and overthrow of the prince of the kingdom of wickedness and he will send eternal succour to the company of his redeemed by the might of the princely angel of the kingdom of Michael' (1QM XVII). Christian prophecy was similar: 'After 1332* days the LORD will come with his angels and with the hosts of the saints from the seventh heaven, with the glory of the seventh heaven' (*Asc. Isa.* 4.14). The angel told the seer that there would be no more delay before the mystery of the kingdom was fulfilled (see on 10.6–7) and John of Gischala, the Zealot leader in Jerusalem, knew that the city belonged to God and was protected by him

---

*Clearly related to the 'time, times and a half a time' of Dan. 7.25 and Rev. 12.7 (see p. 186).

(*War* 6.98). The hard-pressed defenders, however, had hurled insults at God because of his delay in punishing their enemies (*War* 6.4). Though outnumbered, they did manage to repel an attack on the city shortly after Passover (*War* 5.119).

As he saw the vision of the multitude, so the seer heard a sound (better than 'voice') from heaven like many waters and like thunder, the sound of harps before the throne (14.2). This sound of many waters is mentioned also in 1.15 and 19.6, and other visionaries reported similar sensations. When Ezekiel saw the throne he heard the wings of the heavenly beings 'like the sound of many waters, like the thunder of the Almighty, a sound of tumult like the sound of a host' (Ezek. 1.24). The Qumran Song for the twelfth Sabbath (4Q 405) describes the sound of the cherubim around the throne: 'as the cherubim rise ... there is a roar of praise'. Enoch described the sound of perpetual praise as he passed through the fourth heaven (2 *En.* 17) and a later Enoch text pictures the sounds of heaven flowing like rivers from the throne: rivers of joy, rejoicing, gladness, exultation, love and friendship, together with the sound of harps from the living creatures, drums from the wheels of the throne and cymbals from the cherubim (3 *En.* 22B, cf. 2 *Esdr.* 6.17). The extraordinary similarity is not one of words but rather of a shared experience of sound. What the seers heard they described as waters, harps, drums or thunder. In 14.3 the sound is 'a new song' which none can learn but the redeemed, reminiscent of Paul's description of a mystical ascent: 'he heard things that cannot be told, that man may not utter' (2 Cor. 12.4). A similar experience is recorded in the *Apocalypse of Abraham*, another first-century text: 'A voice was in the fire like a sound of many waters, like the voice of the sea in its uproar. And the angel said: "Worship, Abraham and recite the song which I taught you"' (*Ap. Ab.* 17.1). As he experiences the presence of the throne, so Abraham has to learn a song from the angel, a new song, in order to join in the heavenly worship.

The Three Angels

Three angels emerge from heaven with three oracles. In each case (14.6, 8, 9) 'another' should probably be read as 'afterwards' because the three angels are three appearances of the Mighty Angel, the LORD (see on 8.3). These three appearances are reported elsewhere in the Book of Revelation, but differently interpreted, showing that the prophets in Jerusalem did not speak with one voice. Among other phenomena there was a sword-shaped star which hung over the city for a year, there was a light which shone in the temple for half an hour at three o'clock in the morning just before Passover, and at Pentecost there were voices in the temple at night (*War* 6.289–300). The three angels were three of these portents, and in the same order as Josephus described them.

The 'first angel' (14.6-7), the sword-shaped star (see p. 187), is another interpretation of the portent described in 10.1 as the Mighty

Angel wrapped in a cloud. The two accounts have many similarities. Here in 14.6 the angel brings an 'eternal gospel for every nation, tribe, tongue and people', and he commands the people of the earth to worship the creator because the Day of the LORD has come. That these verses were originally in Hebrew can be seen from the fact that the phrase 'all *the inhabitants* of the earth' has been translated over-literally into Greek by *kathemenous,* those set, or settlers, rather than the expected *katoikountes,* dwellers. The LXX of Jeremiah 25.29 makes the same literal translation of the Hebrew *yšb,* literally 'settle', but idiomatic Hebrew for 'dwell'. This in itself is not a significant detail and does not affect the meaning, but it does offer the possibility that other Hebrew words may have suffered in translation from a written text. Thus 'an eternal gospel' would have been written in the same letters as 'a hidden gospel', *bśrt 'lm,* although the words would have been pronounced differently. The angel of 14.6 was probably proclaiming 'a hidden gospel' to the whole world, corresponding to 'the mystery' of God proclaimed by the angel in 10.7. Peter described the good news (gospel) as a mystery, 'things into which angels long to look', but which had been 'preached through the Holy Spirit from heaven' (1 Pet. 1.12). Thus in both 10.7 and 14.7 the angel speaks of the mystery/hidden good news about to be revealed to the whole world. The hour of judgement has come.

In each account the angel speaks of the creator: 'the creator of heaven, earth and sea' (10.6) or 'him who made heaven and earth, the sea and the fountains of water' (14.7). Heaven and earth, sea and fountains must have been traditional symbols of the creation; Wisdom was brought forth before the creation of the heavens, the fountains, the sea and the earth (Prov. 8.27–29). Conversely, the dissolution of the created order was depicted in terms of the destruction or pollution of heaven, earth, sea and fountains. The *Assumption of Moses* describes the destruction of the earth, the heavenly bodies, the sea and the sources of water as signs of the Day of the LORD (*Ass. Mos.* 10.4–6). At the sound of the first four trumpets the earth (8.7), the sea (8.8), the fountains (8.10) and the heavens (8.12) are destroyed and the first four bowls of wrath are poured on the earth (16.2), the sea (16.3), the rivers and fountains (16.4) and the heavenly bodies (16.8). Both the trumpets and the bowls of wrath announced the destruction of the old creation in preparation for the new heaven and the new earth (21.1).

The 'first angel' had been the sword-shaped star which hung over the city for a year. This was the 'angel flying in midheaven' (14.6), the LORD with his glittering sword preparing to take vengeance on his enemies, as prophesied in the Song of Moses (Deut. 32.41, see on 10.5–7). There had been a similar portent before the temple was built, when David had sinned and the city was about to be punished. 'And David lifted up his eyes and saw the angel of the LORD standing between earth and heaven, and in his hand a drawn sword stretched out over Jerusalem' (1 Chron. 21.16). David repented and the temple was later built at the place where the angel had appeared.

The 'second angel' (14.8), corresponds to the angel of 18.1–3, and was the light in the temple (see on 18.1–3). There is no indication of the great light in this account but other elements of the two passages do correspond: 'Fallen, fallen is Babylon the great' (14.8, cf. 18.2) must have been one of the oracles pronounced by the prophets against Jerusalem, echoing both the words of Isaiah 21.9, his vision of the fall of Babylon, and of Daniel 4.30, Nebuchadnezzar's proud boast about his great city which drew the wrath of God. 'The wine of her impure passion' also occurs in both passages, 14.8 and 18.3; it must have been another phrase in common use, possibly linked to the poisonous grapes of Sodom (Deut. 32.32) which described the rebellious ways of sinners in the Damascus Document (CD VIII) and to the wild grapes of the LORD's vineyard, 'bloodshed and cries of despair' when he had expected a vintage of justice and righteousness (Isa. 5.7).

The description of the 'third angel' emphasizes his voice ('he spoke with a loud voice', 14.9) and this corresponds to the voices in the temple at Pentecost (*War* 6.300). Another interpretation of this phenomenon is found in 18.4–8, giving two different interpretations of the portent: in 18.4–8 it is a warning to leave the city, but in 14.9–11 it is a warning to have no dealings with Rome, the beast. Josephus gives the context for these differing oracles in response to the same portent. On Tammuz 17 – late July, and so a few weeks after Pentecost when the voices were heard – the daily Tamid sacrifices ceased in the temple because there were no lambs to offer. Titus instructed Josephus to appeal to John of Gischala to surrender the city so that the sacrifices could be restored (*War* 6.97). He quoted a prophecy that when a man began to kill his own countrymen the city would be taken, possibly Ezekiel 38.21: 'Every man's sword will be against his brother'. This, however, does not refer to the fall of the city but to the destruction of Gog. More likely is Jesus' prophecy of the signs which would precede the destruction of the temple: 'And brother will deliver up brother to death, and the father his child, and children will rise against parents and have them put to death' (Mark 13.12), another indication of the role of 'Christian' prophecy in the war.

Many in the city were persuaded to surrender, says Josephus, but some were too terrified of the Zealot guards to leave the city, even though they knew it was doomed (*War* 6.113). Others, among them several of the chief priests and their families, did leave the city in safety and went to Jufna some ten miles north of Jerusalem. When they had gone, the Zealots spread rumours that they had been killed. The priests were then brought back and shown to be alive, 'whereupon great numbers fled to the Romans. Grouped together and standing before the Roman lines, the refugees with lamentations and tears implored the rebels as their best course to admit the Romans freely to the city and save the fatherland ... These appeals only excited fiercer opposition' [from the Zealots] 'and they retorted by heaping abuse on the deserters' (*War* 6.119–21).

This was the situation which gave rise to the two conflicting interpretations of the voices in the temple: 18.4–8 exhorted people to leave the city and interpreted the voices in the temple to this effect, whereas 14.9–11 threatened the wrath of God on any who deserted to the beast and received his mark. Similar warnings and exhortations were also attributed to Jesus. In the last days before the return of the Man, he said, 'let those who are in Judea flee to the mountains; let him who is on the housetop not go down, nor enter his house to take anything away ... For in those days there will be such tribulation as has not been from the beginning of the creation ...' (Mark 13.14–15, 19). He warned of false messiahs and false prophets showing signs and wonders to lead the chosen astray (Mark 13.22), and he promised that those who endured to the end would be saved (Mark 13.13). This suggests that some of the followers of Jesus would have left the city during the last days. Others did not, and it was to them that 14.12 was addressed. After warning apostates of the fate that awaited them, we read: 'Here is a call for the endurance of the saints, those who keep the commandments of God and the faith of Jesus', that is, those who continue to trust in Jesus. After Josephus' first speech that they should seek salvation by the surrender of the city (*War* 5.361), the Zealots kept watch more to see who was trying to leave the city than who was trying to enter, 'and whoever afforded but a shadow of suspicion was instantly slaughtered' (*War* 5.423).

The fate of those who have dealings with the beast is described in traditional terms (14.10–11) and this is an account of the abuse heaped on the deserters by those who stayed in the city (*War* 6.121). They were attacked as they left and many were killed: 'They ranged their scorpions, catapults and ballistae above the holy gates so that the surrounding temple court from the multitude of the dead resembled a common burial ground ...' (*War* 6.121). The deserters are to drink the cup of the wine of God's wrath, words found also in Jeremiah 25.15 (cf. Ps. 75.8), and they are to be tormented in fire before the Lamb and his angels, the heavenly warriors defending Jerusalem and watching the abuse of the deserters. Watching the destruction of enemies is a recurring motif: the *Book of Jubilees*, for example, promises that the servants of the LORD will drive out their enemies and 'see all of their judgements and all of their curses come upon them' (*Jub.* 23.30); Jesus told the parable of the rich man tormented after his death, who looked up to heaven and saw there the poor man whom he had failed to help (Luke 16.19–31). There would be no rest for those who worship the beast (14.11), i.e. no place in the millennium kingdom (see p. 341).

Those who remained in the city were exhorted to endurance (14.12) in a phrase reminiscent of 13.10. These are the saints who keep the commandments of God – they are observant Jews – and the faith of Jesus, that is faith in Jesus. The risen LORD had commended the angel of the church in Pergamum because he had not denied his faith in Jesus (2.13), but we can only speculate what this faith in Jesus might have been. Other sayings in the Book of Revelation suggest that it was faith in his imminent return to avenge the blood of his servants and bring the Day of the LORD. Thus the church at Pergamum was warned, 'I will come to you soon and war against them', i.e. the followers of Balaam (2.16). The church at Thyatira was exhorted to 'hold fast to what you have until I come' (2.25). The church at Philadelphia was assured 'I will keep you from the hour of trial which is coming upon the whole world, to try those who dwell upon the earth. I am coming soon; hold fast to what you have' (3.10–11). Among the fragments of prophecy preserved at the end of the Book of Revelation, there are: 'Behold I am coming soon' (22.7), 'Behold I am coming soon, bringing my recompense' (22.12), and 'Surely I am coming soon' (22.20). One of the fragments of Aramaic prayer which has survived from the Palestinian church is exactly this: 'Come our LORD, Maranatha' (1 Cor. 16.22), and Jesus taught his disciples to pray: 'Thy kingdom come, thy will be done on earth as it is in heaven ... Do not bring us to the time of testing but deliver us from the evil one' (Matt. 6.10, 13). The imminent end of the tenth Jubilee would have heightened the sense of expectation.

The faith that the LORD would return and fight for his servants was expressed by the vision of the Lamb and his army (14.1–5), one of the inspirations for the desperate last struggle in the city. Excited watchmen saw the huge stones being hurled into the city and believed they were the supernatural hail which announced the coming of the LORD. They called out 'The Son is coming' (*War* 5.272). During the critical weeks of the siege, several prominent people had taken advantage of the Roman offer to leave the city, and John the beloved disciple was probably one of them. He had been told in his vision of the angel in the cloud that the return of the LORD was not imminent and that the city and the temple would be destroyed. He was called to another ministry elsewhere: 'You must prophesy again about many people and nations and tongues and kings' (10.11).

The seer was then told to write a benediction for those who were about to die. The Spirit echoes the voice from heaven, much as the seven letters each end: 'He who has an ear let him hear what the Spirit says to the churches'. Those who are about to die ('henceforth', *ap arti*, but some texts have 'assuredly', *aparti),* are assured that they will die in the LORD, that they will rest from their labours and that their works will follow them. The first Christians expected the return of the LORD in their own lifetime: 'This generation will not pass away before all these things take place' (Mark 13.31); 'When these things begin to take place ... your redemption is near' (Luke 21.28). Paul had assured the Christians of Thessalonika that those who were alive when the LORD returned, amongst whom he included himself, would not precede those who had already fallen asleep. The dead in Christ would rise first and then the living would be caught up to meet the LORD (1 Thess. 4.15–17). Those about to die in Jerusalem had the same fear and received the same assurance that they would die in the LORD.

After endurance they were promised rest, a theme which also appears in the Letter to the Hebrews. 'The holy brethren who share in a heavenly call' (Heb. 3.1) were exhorted not to lose faith and rebel like their forefathers in the wilderness. 'We share in Christ only if we hold our first confidence firm to the end' (Heb. 3.14). Those who keep the faith will enter the final Sabbath rest. *This was not the rest of death but the world Sabbath in the holy of holies, the millennium kingdom.* They would probably have known the story of Kenaz' vision, when he saw the place of invisible light and recognized it as the place of rest of the righteous (LAB 28.10). For these Hebrew Christians, the seventh day of creation had not yet dawned and they were still fellow workers with God on the sixth day. John's Jesus had the same belief; when accused of healing on the Sabbath, he replied: 'My Father is working still and I am working' (John 5.17). For Jesus, the Sabbath rest had yet to come, and the work of creation was not completed until the end of the sixth day, the Friday when he uttered his last words, 'It is finished' (John 19.30) and then rested on his Sabbath day. The Hebrews were assured: 'There remains a Sabbath rest for the people of God; for whoever enters God's rest also ceases from his labours as God did from his' (Heb. 4.9–10). 'Isaiah' prophesied that the LORD would give 'rest to the pious' who were still alive when he came (*Asc. Isa.* 4.15).

The *Letter of Barnabas* teaches about this Sabbath, and 14.13 should probably be understood as 'Barnabas' explains it. If God finished the creation in six days, and one day in the LORD's sight is a thousand years (Ps. 90.4), 'then in six days, six thousand years that is, there is going to be an end of everything. After that, "he rested on the seventh day" indicates that when his Son returns, he will put an end to the years of the Lawless One, pass sentence on the godless, transform the sun, moon and stars, and then on the seventh day enter his true rest' (*Barn.* 15). The Sabbaths of the present age are not acceptable to the LORD (Isa. 1.13), he wrote, but only the final Sabbath when the Son would return and reign, putting an end to evil. After the era of the millennium kingdom, 'after I have set all things to rest', that Sabbath 'is to usher in the eighth day, the commencement of a new world'. This eighth day is the new creation, described in 21.1–4 as following the millennium kingdom (see p. 363).

These ideas survived and appear in an early gnostic text, the *Dialogue of the Saviour*. The chosen ones have already been baptized and seen visions, but their time of rest is yet to come:

The Saviour said to his disciples, Already the time has come, brothers, that we should leave behind our labour and stand in the rest; for he who stands in the rest will rest for ever ... These by thy sacrifice enter in with their good deeds, they who have redeemed their souls from these blind limbs in order that they might exist for ever ... Matthew said, LORD I wish [to see] that place of life ... in which there is no evil but rather it is the pure light. The Lord said, Brother Matthew you cannot see it as long as you wear the flesh.

The LORD promised that his disciples would rule over the angels when they had been clothed in light (CG III.5.120, 121, 132, 138).

Those facing certain death in Jerusalem were comforted with the assurance that they were about to enter their true Sabbath, their labours ended; they were the martyrs of 20.4 (see p. 341). Their works would accompany them (14.13) as a sign of their faith. James their bishop had written: 'Faith, if it has no works, is dead. A man is justified by works and not by faith alone' (Jas 2.17, 24) and Jesus had taught 'Lay up for yourselves treasure in heaven' (Matt. 6.20). Early in the second century CE, R. Akiba taught that his good works enabled him to stand in safety before the throne (see p. 263).

The Oracles of Isaiah

A sequence of oracles in Isaiah shows why the 'works' of the martyrs were so important. The Isaiah Targum, which shows how these texts were being understood in the first century CE, is even clearer. The Book of Isaiah and the Book of Revelation viewed history in the same way as did the Book of Enoch (see p. 227), namely that the LORD had committed the care of his people to seventy shepherds. He had also instructed an angel to record the deeds of the shepherds because they were to answer for their actions on the Day of the LORD. Isaiah described the shepherd rulers and the angel who recorded their deeds: 'Upon your walls, O Jerusalem, I have set watchmen; all the day and all the night, they shall never be silent. You who put the LORD in remembrance, take no rest and give him no rest until he establishes Jerusalem and makes it a praise in the earth' (Isa. 62.6–7). In the Targum, however, the role of the recording angels was to remind the LORD of his people's good works so that he would act to save the city: 'Behold, the deeds of your fathers, the righteous, O city of Jerusalem, are prepared and watched before me, all the day and all the night continually they do not cease. And their remembrance shall not cease before him until he establishes Jerusalem and makes it a praise in the earth' (T. Isa. 62.6–7). Thus the word of blessing and consolation for those about to die was that their good works would hasten the time of Jerusalem's deliverance.

Isaiah 62.8–9 would have spoken directly to the situation in Jerusalem during the summer of 70 CE:

The LORD has sworn by his right hand and by his mighty arm:
I will not again give your grain to be food for your enemies,
and foreigners shall not drink your wine for which you have laboured;
but those who garner it shall eat it and praise the LORD,
and those who gather it shall drink it in the courts of my sanctuary.

The Targum hardly differs from the original at this point, but in the next verse there is a significant adaptation: 'Go through, go through the gates, prepare the way for the people; build up, build up the highway, clear it of stones . . .' became: 'Prophets, go through and return by the gates, turn the heart of the people to a correct way; announce good reports and consolations to the righteous who have removed the impulsive fantasy which is like a stone of stumbling ...'(T. *Isa.* 62.10). The message of the prophets is very similar to the vision of the Lamb and his host on Mount Zion: 'Say to the congregation of Zion, Behold your saviour is revealed; behold, the reward of those accomplishing his Memra is with him, and all their deeds are disclosed before him. And they shall be called the holy people, the redeemed of the LORD ...' (T. *Isa.* 62.11b–12).

Isaiah 63.1–6, one of the most vivid and gruesome descriptions in the whole of the Book of Isaiah, was the inspiration for the grapes of wrath (14.17–20). Isaiah describes the LORD coming from Edom which he had punished by trampling them in his great wine press. The Targum, which is close to the Book of Revelation, gives here a very free rendering of the original:

He is about to bring a stroke upon Edom ... to take the just retribution of his people ... Why will the mountains be red from the blood of those killed, and plains gush forth like wine in the press? Behold, as grapes are trodden in the press, so shall slaughter increase among the armies of the peoples and there will be no strength for them before me; and I will kill them in my anger and trample them in my wrath ... For the day of vengeance is before me and the year of my people's salvation has come. (T. *Isa.* 63.1–4)

The sequence of oracles in Isaiah 62–66 is exactly that of Revelation 14–16. After the judgement on Edom, Isaiah described how the LORD shared the affliction of his people and saved them through the angel of his presence (Isa. 63.7–9), dividing the waters to lead them to safety (Isa. 63.10–14, cf. Rev. 15.2–4, see p. 265). The people pray that the LORD will return and save his people because their enemies have trodden down his holy of holies (Isa. 63.15–19). 'O that thou wouldst rend the heavens and come down ...' (Isa. 64.1). The response is the voice from the temple, the LORD rendering recompense to his enemies (Isa. 66.6), which becomes the voice from the temple in 16.1, sending out the seven angels with their bowls of wrath.

The Reaper

Fifty days after the Omer had been brought to the temple, the new wheat was offered. In the summer of 70 CE, the Romans completed the earthworks around the city at about this time (*War* 5.466), and the fighting became more desperate. All hope of escape was gone; there was famine in the city, the streets and squares full of corpses which their families had not the strength to bury (*War* 5.511–15). Some 600,000 were flung from the ramparts into the ravines around the city (*War* 5.569). At this time of acute famine, the new corn arrived for the Roman troops and was shown to the starving people in the city to weaken their resolve (*War* 5.520). The seer must have recalled the words of Isaiah 62.6–9 and the teaching of John the Baptist and Jesus about the great harvest.

Jesus had told a parable about a man who sowed good seed in his field, but while he was sleeping, an enemy came and sowed weeds. When his servants asked what should be done, he told them to allow both to grow together until the harvest. Then his servants were to gather the weeds and burn them before harvesting the good grain for his barn (Matt. 13.24–30). The disciples did not understand the parable at first and so when they were alone with him, they asked Jesus to explain. The good seed, he said, meant the sons of the kingdom and the weeds were the sons of the evil one. The harvest was the end of the age, and the reapers were the angels whom the Son of Man would send to remove all sin and evil from his kingdom (Matt. 13.37–42). These angel reapers appear elsewhere in the Gospels. John the Baptist warned the Pharisees and Sadducees that the Mighty One who came after him would gather the harvest into his granary but burn the chaff in unquenchable fire (Matt. 3.12). When the seventy were sent out, they were the angels sent into the harvest (Luke 10.1–20). As the story is told, the plentiful harvest was linked to woes of judgement on the towns of Galilee: Chorazin, Bethsaida and Capernaum. The reapers went with power to tread on serpents and scorpions, that is to trample on evil, and Jesus recognized their success as the fall of Satan from heaven. The disciples were seeing and hearing, he said, what prophets and kings had longed for but never known (Luke 10.21–22) because the mission of the seventy was one of the 'hidden things' which the wise did not understand. The angel reapers were one of the secrets of the kingdom which Jesus had revealed to his disciples privately when he explained the parable (Matt. 13.36–43; Mark 4.10–12).

The LORD's judgement had often been compared to a harvest. Jeremiah prophesied that Babylon would be like a threshing floor, 'yet a little while and the time of her harvest will come' (Jer. 51.33), and before him, Isaiah had described the defeat of Israel as a harvest, 'when the reaper gathers standing grain and in his arm harvests the ears' (Isa. 17.5). Joel had predicted a grim harvest, when the LORD would sit in judgement on all the nations who had gathered in the valley of Jehoshapat. (The name means 'The LORD Judges', and later tradition identified it as the Kidron valley, east of Jerusalem between the city and the Mount of Olives. This is an important detail because Jesus sat looking out over this valley when he taught his disciples the signs of the Day of the LORD.) Joel's words 'Put in the sickle for the harvest is ripe' (Joel 3.13), were the very words which the seer heard in the temple (14.15).

In the New Testament, however, the image of the great harvest is positive; John the Baptist had warned of the Mighty One to come who would gather his wheat into the granary but burn the chaff (Matt. 3.11–12), and in Jesus' parable of the angel reapers, the angels were told to gather the wheat into the barn, but burn the weeds. The reaper in 14.14 is the LORD himself, a Son of Man seated on a white cloud and wearing a golden crown. He himself gathers his wheat before the weeds and the chaff are burnt. This was the word of consolation to those who were facing death in the famine, watching their corn consumed by the Romans. The dialogue between the Man on the cloud and the angel who comes from the temple is the scene familiar from *1 Enoch*, when the recording angel reports to the LORD the state of the earth and he decides to act to save his people. The words are similar to the ritual for gathering the Omer.

When the crop was fully ripe, the messengers of the court used to go out on the eve of the festival day and tie the grain in bunches while it was yet unreaped to make it easier to reap ... When it grew dark he called out, 'Is the sun set?' and they answered, 'Yea!' ... 'Is this a sickle?' and they answered 'Yea!' ... 'Is this a basket?' And they answered 'Yea!' ... 'Shall I reap?' 'And they answered 'Reap!' He used to call out three times on every matter and they answered 'Yea!' 'Yea!' 'Yea!' (*m. Menaḥoth* 10.3)

The harvest of the earth was reaped as the faithful defenders of Jerusalem died in their thousands during the period from Pentecost to Tabernacles, when the firstfruits should have been offered.

The Grapes of Wrath

On the fiftieth day after Pentecost, according to the calendar of the Qumran Temple Scroll (11QT XIX), there was a festival not mentioned in the Hebrew Scriptures, the Offering of New Wine. This took place early in the month of Ab and so a few days before the date which Josephus gives for the final destruction of the temple, 10th Ab (*War* 6.250). The seer links the festival of the wine to the final judgement on the temple, the great wine press of the wrath of God from which blood flowed for about 200 miles (14.19–20).

The gathering and trampling of grapes had long been associated with the Day of the LORD, and the vintage of Jerusalem had a special significance. Isaiah had described the city as the LORD's vineyard, carefully planted and tended, in which he set up a tower, the temple. He had looked for a harvest of good grapes but found only wild ones. He had looked for justice and righteousness but found only bloodshed and cries of distress. What could the LORD of the vineyard do but abandon it and let it be trampled underfoot (Isa. 5.1–7)? One hundred and fifty years later, an unknown poet, perhaps the prophet Jeremiah, lamented the fate of Jerusalem after the Babylonians had destroyed it in 586 BCE.

He [the LORD] summoned an assembly against me
  to crush my young men;
the LORD has trodden as in a wine press
  the virgin daughter of Judah. (Lam. 1.15)

When the prophet Joel foresaw the Great Judgement in the valley of Jehoshaphat he spoke of harvesting grain and of trampling grapes. The nations would assemble there on the Day of the LORD, the sun and moon would be darkened and the stars cease to shine, and then the LORD would give his command:

Put in the sickle, for the harvest is ripe.
Go in, tread, for the wine press is full.
The vats overflow, for their wickedness is great. (Joel 3.13)

Jesus warned of a similar calamity. First he prepared his hearers by telling the chief priests, scribes and elders in the temple his own version of Isaiah's parable. The LORD of the vineyard had waited in vain for a vintage and when his servants and even his Son obtained nothing, he resolved to act: 'What will the owner of the vineyard do? He will come and destroy the tenants and give the vineyard to others' (Mark 12.9). He then left the temple and prophesied that all the wonderful buildings would be destroyed. With just four of his disciples, Peter, James, John and Andrew (Mark 13.3–4), he went to the Mount of Olives, and there they questioned him about his prophecy. When would this happen? Looking back across the very valley where Joel had foreseen the great judgement, Jesus all but repeated the prophet's words. The sun and moon would be darkened and the stars would fall from heaven. At this point, Joel's prophecy has simply the command 'Put in the sickle for the harvest is ripe', but Jesus revealed more of its context to his disciples. Mark records that he said: 'They will see the Son of man coming in clouds with great power and glory. And then he will send out the angels, and gather his elect from the four winds, from the ends of the earth to the ends of heaven' (Mark 13.26–27). John, however, has preserved more of the original vision. In Revelation 14, one like a son of man emerges with the angels from the temple (the door of the temple faced east towards the Mount of Olives). He is seated on a white cloud, wearing a golden crown and carrying a sickle ready for the harvest. Then his other angels gather the grapes to be trampled in the wine press of wrath.

The angel with power over fire (14.18) pronounced the sentence, and the vintage of the earth was pressed in the wine press of wrath. The fire angel was one of the four who, according to the *Testament of Abraham*, stood by the judgement seat of the Son of Adam (the Son of Man?, *'adam* means a human being). On the right was the angel who recorded good deeds, on the left the angel who recorded sins. A third angel weighed the soul and the fourth, 'a fiery angel, merciless and relentless', held the all-consuming fire for testing sinners (*T. Abr.* A12.1–18). The prophets had spoken of judgement by fire (Jer. 6.29; Zech. 13.9; Mal. 3.2–3) and Paul warned of testing by fire (1 Cor. 3.13). The angel of fire would have been known to the Hebrew Christians; they lived in the world which we have to piece together from the fragments of evidence that survive.

The blood from the wine press flowed as high as a horse's bridle (14.20). *1 Enoch* has a similar account of the Day of the LORD.

And the horse shall walk up to the breast in the blood of sinners,
And the chariot shall be submerged to its height.
In those days the angels shall descend into the secret places,
And gather into one place all those who brought down sin.
And the Most High will arise on the Day of Judgement,
To execute great judgement among sinners. (*1 En.* 100.3–4)

When the city fell to the Romans in 70 CE, the prophecy of the wine press was fulfilled and detail was added to the original prophecy. There would be blood for 1600 stadia, about two hundred miles.

But when they went in numbers into the lanes of the city, with their swords drawn, they slew those whom they overtook without mercy, and set fire to the houses whither the Jews had fled ... They ran everyone of them through whom they met with, and obstructed the very lanes with their dead bodies and made the whole city run down with blood to such a degree indeed that the fire of many of the houses was quenched with these men's blood. (*War* 6.404–406)

17

THE BOWLS OF WRATH

Then I saw another portent in heaven, great and wonderful, seven angels with seven plagues, which are the last, for with them the wrath of God is ended. And I saw what appeared to be a sea of glass mingled with fire, and those who had conquered the beast and its image and the number of its name, standing beside the sea of glass with harps of God in their hands. And they sing the song of Moses, the servant of God, and the song of the Lamb. (Rev. 15.1–3)

The calendar sequence from chapter 14 is continued and completed with the Day of Atonement. Seven angels emerge from the holy of holies and pour wrath on the creation – earth, sea, rivers and heaven – and the great city is destroyed. This is the LORD's vengeance on those who have shed the blood of his children (Deut. 32.43). There is another glimpse of the firstborn singing a song of triumph in heaven, and the seer is among them.

The sequence from Isaiah is also continued. After the vision of the wine press, the prophet described how the angel of the presence saved his people and brought them safely through the Red Sea (Isa. 63.7–19). The two themes of Day of Atonement and Exodus are combined to depict the final destruction of Jerusalem.

The Sea of Glass

The seer stood in the great hall of the heavenly temple and described what he saw and heard. There was a sea of glass, described in 4.6 as 'the sea of glass like crystal' before the throne where there were seven torches of fire. He saw seven angels emerging from the holy of holies, and one of the living creatures giving to each a golden bowl. A voice from the holy of holies commanded the angels to go and pour out the wrath of God on the earth, and the angel 'went' out of the temple (16.2), implying that the seer was in the temple and watched the angel 'go' (cf. 14.15 where the angel 'came' out of the temple). This was the voice Isaiah had heard, 'the voice of the LORD rendering recompense to his enemies' (Isa. 66.6).

The sea of glass was the floor of the heavenly temple which Enoch had described in his vision. When he was taken up to heaven he saw a great house built of white marble, with *a floor of crystal* and a ceiling like stars and lightning. There was a second 'inner' house, built of fire with a floor of fire, in which he saw the throne (*1 En.* 14.9–12). The interior of Solomon's temple was lined with gold (1 Kgs 6.22) and it had a golden floor (1 Kgs 6.30). Josephus described the interior of the temple, completely covered with gold so that 'the whole temple shined and dazzled the eyes of such as entered, by the splendour of the gold that was on every side of them'. Even the floor was plates of gold (*Ant.* 8.74). There is no description of the interior of the second temple; Josephus mentions only the menorah, the table and the incense altar (*War* 5.215–18). The temple was built of white marble decorated with gold, and the doors were covered with gold (*War* 5.208). 'To approaching strangers it appeared from a distance like a snow-clad mountain; for all that was not overlaid with gold was of purest white' (*War* 5.223). The description of the outer house in Enoch's vision suggests that it was inspired by this marble and gold temple for it was built of 'stones like hailstones' (*1 En.* 14.10), with interior walls of crystal mosaics and a crystal floor. The whole house was surrounded by tongues of fire, and the doors were fire. The crystal and fire of Enoch's vision correspond to the marble and gold of Josephus' description, and suggest that the 'sea of glass mingled with fire' (15.2) was the floor of the great hall, white marble with gold mosaic. The temple which the seer knew in Jerusalem inspired his description of the temple in heaven. Only a priest was permitted to enter the temple; the seer must have been a priest.

The great hall of the temple represented the Garden of Eden, and so the crystal sea must have had a place in the mythology of the original Eden, the mountain garden of God (Ezek. 28.13, 16, see pp. 20, 104). The *Life of Adam and Eve* gives a good illustration of this and confirms that the mythology of the first temple was still known and used in the first century CE. After he had been driven from Paradise, Adam was visited by the archangel Michael and taken back up to Paradise in a chariot of fire. Adam saw the LORD there, enthroned in the midst of fire and surrounded by thousands of angels. He worshipped, and then 'Michael held in his hand a rod and touched the waters which were around Paradise and they froze. I crossed over and Michael with me, and he took me to the place where he had seized me' (*Life* 29.2–3). This is temple imagery: the LORD enthroned in Paradise amongst the angels, and around his throne a frozen sea. Ezekiel had seen this in his vision; under the throne he saw a firmament 'like the gleam of the terrible ice' (Ezek. 1.22, translating literally). The crystal sea around the throne, however it was described, was known in the time of the first temple.

This ancient image of the sea does not appear in the Genesis account of Eden, but it is implicit in Ezekiel's. He had spoken of the prince of Tyre (i.e. the patron angel of the city who 'was' the king) who became proud: 'You said "I am a god. I sit in the seat of the gods in the heart of the seas ..."' (Ezek. 28.2). 'The seat of the gods in the heart of the seas' was the throne in the mountain garden of Eden from which he was expelled and thrown down to earth. Isaiah had described those who were worthy to dwell in the heights and see the king in his beauty (Isa. 33.16–17); those who walked in righteousness would see the LORD in his majesty, in a place of broad streams and rivers where no ship would sail (Isa. 33.21). In other words, he would see the throne in the midst of the sea. Psalm 24 is similar, but without mentioning the sea; whoever has clean hands and a pure heart will be able to ascend the hill of the LORD and stand in his holy place. The holy place was the garden of the LORD established in the midst of waters.

Perhaps the oldest illustration of all is the first Song of Moses, incorporated now in Exodus 15.1–18 as an account of crossing the Red Sea:

The deeps congealed in the heart of the sea ...
Who is like thee, majestic in holiness,
terrible in glorious deeds, doing wonders?
Thou didst stretch out thy right hand, ·
the earth swallowed them.
Thou hast led in thy steadfast love the people whom thou hast redeemed,
thou hast guided them by thy strength to thy holy abode ...
till thy people, O LORD, pass by,
till the people pass by whom thou hast purchased,
Thou wilt bring them in, and plant them on thy own mountain,
the place, O LORD, which thou hast made for thy abode,
the sanctuary, O LORD, which thy hands have established.
The LORD will reign for ever and ever. (Exod. 15.8b, 11b–13, 16–18)

There are many echoes of this song in the Book of Revelation: 'Who is like thee?' was said in irony of the beast (see on 13.4); the earth also swallowed the river which came from the dragon's mouth (see on 12.16); the 'redeemed' are the kingdom of priests, the firstborn (5.6, 14.4) who have been set free from Egypt (see on 11.8) and established on the holy mountain (14.1–5). They are brought across a sea which has congealed to let them pass, the crystal sea of the vision.

Those who 'are conquering the beast' (15.2, present tense) stand beside or perhaps 'on' (Hebrew or Aramaic 'al means either) the marble floor of the temple, with harps in their hands. In the earlier vision of the crystal sea it was the elders who held the harps (5.8); here it is the faithful who have become the new priesthood, those who bear the Name and look upon the face of God (22.4). They are conquering the beast and its image and the number of its name (15.2). The Greek here is strange and it has been suggested that the original word was the Aramaic zk' which can mean 'to be victorious' or 'to be worthy' or 'to be pure'. The Greek is literally 'those who are conquering from the beast', so 'conquering' should perhaps have been rendered 'pure', giving 'those who are pure from the beast and its image and the number of its name'. These would then be the spotless ones singing before the throne (14.1–5). Their harps are not harps of God ('lh'), but harps of aloes wood ('hl'), one of the scented woods mentioned among the city's imports (18.12).

The visionaries who practised the mystical ascent found themselves at the centre of considerable controversy. Members of the Qumran community hoped to be 'like an angel of the presence' (1QSb IV) and their hymns mention those 'who stand with the host of the holy ones, the congregation of the sons of heaven' (1QH XI, formerly III). The

Odes of Solomon express similar ideas: 'I became one of those who are near him' (*Ode* 36) or 'I went up into the light of truth as into a chariot' (*Ode* 38), so there can be no question that they passed early into Christianity. Deuteronomy had long forbidden any interest in such things (Deut. 29.29), and the Mishnah reinforced the prohibition. It was not permitted to enquire what was above and below, what was before and what would come after (*m. Ḥagigah* 2.1). An early commentary on Exodus 19.20 is clearly polemical: 'R. Jose says: Behold it says The heavens are the heavens of the Lord but the earth hath been given to the children of men' (Ps. 115.16). 'Neither Moses nor Elijah ever went up to heaven, nor did the glory ever come down to earth' (*Mekhilta of R. Ishmael*). The controversy appears in the *Ascension of Isaiah* as the reason for 'Isaiah' and the (Christian) prophets leaving Jerusalem: 'When Isaiah son of Amoz saw the great iniquity which was being committed in Jerusalem and the service of Satan and his wantonness, he withdrew from Jerusalem ... and many of the faithful who believed in the ascension into heaven withdrew and dwelt on the mountain. All of them were clothed in sackcloth and all of them were prophets' (*Asc. Isa.* 2.7–10).

Most of the evidence for ascents is found in collections of texts compiled long after the first century CE, but recurring themes and clusters of motifs in them bear such a striking resemblance to the Book of Revelation that they must have had a common origin. The blessed in heaven in the Book of Revelation bear the seal of the Name on their foreheads (14.1), there is the sound of many waters in their presence (14.2), they sing a new song (14.3), they are ritually pure and have told no lies (14.5), their good deeds follow them to their place of rest (14.13), they worship before the throne and see the face of God and the Lamb (22.4). Their journey to heaven is associated with the Exodus, and their vision of the throne with the crossing of the sea.

Compare this with a cryptic account in the Babylonian Talmud which warns against the practice of mystical ascent: 'Our Rabbis taught: Four men entered the Garden, namely Ben Azzai and Ben Zoma, Aḥer and R. Akiba. R. Akiba said to them: When you arrive at the stones of pure marble, say not Water, water! For it is said: He that speaketh falsehood shall not be established before my eyes' (*b. Ḥagigah* 14b). Of the three who entered the Garden, only one returned unharmed: Ben Azzai died, Ben Zoma went mad and Aḥer became an apostate. 'R. Akiba went up unhurt and went down unhurt; and of him Scripture says: "Draw me, we will run after thee". And R. Akiba too the ministering angels sought to thrust away; but the Holy One, blessed be He, said to them: "Let this elder be for he is worthy to avail himself of my glory" '(*b. Ḥagigah* 15b).

The four rabbis, who were all active in the middle of the second century CE, were entering the great hall of the temple in their mystic ascent, as did Enoch. They were entering the Garden of Eden. In the great hall they saw the marble floor but were forbidden to associate it with the water of the crystal sea. No one who spoke a lie could stand before the LORD. Other versions of the story of the four who went into the Garden do not mention the marble stones and the water. The *Tosefta Ḥagigah* 2.3–4, *y. Ḥagigah* 77b and a commentary on the Song of Songs, *Shir haShirim Rabbah*, simply describe how the rabbis entered the Garden with only R. Akiba returning in safety. Someone, however, knew of and forbad the link between the Garden and the stones of marble. This is a curious piece of polemic until read in the light of the Book of Revelation with its description of the crystal sea before the throne and the multitude who had told no lies. Those who later described the Christian prophecies as 'worthless visions' (see p. 68) and associated them with the teaching of Jesus and the disastrous war against Rome, expressed in this way their hostility to the Christian claim to heavenly ascent.

Among the Hekhalot texts, the *Hekhalot Zutarti* describes four who entered the heavenly temple, and the similarities to the Book of Revelation are clear. R. Akiba explains at one point that he was able to enter and leave in safety because of his good works, just as the wise men had taught: 'Your works will bring you near and your works will keep you distant' (#338, cf. 14.13, 'their deeds follow them'). When R. Akiba arrived at the entrance to the seventh palace, the holy of holies, he stood by the veil and the angels of destruction came out to destroy him. God spoke to them: 'Leave this elder in peace for he is worthy to look on my glory' (#346, cf. 15.5–8, the plague angels emerge from the sanctuary, and 22.4, 'they shall see his face'). Other texts suggest that the destroying angels attacked him with iron axes (e.g. #258), a direct link with the destroying angels who brought the bowls of wrath from the holy of holies. When Ezekiel described the angels who came to destroy Jerusalem (Ezek. 9.1–2), he used the ambiguous word *kly* to describe what they were carrying; it could mean 'bowls of', hence the 'bowls of wrath', or it could mean 'weapons of'. The LXX opted for 'weapon' and said the angels were carrying axes. The tradition was divided. In the Book of Revelation the angels carried bowls but in the Hekhalot texts the same destroying angels carried axes, and these were the heavenly guardians who tried to prevent R. Akiba from entering the holy place. The 'sixth palace' in the Hekhalot texts corresponded to the great hall, the original *hekhal* which gave these texts their name. It seemed to be a place of water, with thousands of waves of the sea (cf. 14.2, 'the sound of many waters'), but was really a place of pure marble. If the one who entered asked about the waters, a voice from the seventh palace (i.e. the holy of holies) declared that he was not worthy to see the king in his beauty (cf. Isa. 33.17) because he was descended from those who had worshipped the golden calf (#408). These must have been the Christians.

Later Jewish texts were not only opposed to the marble being described as water. There was also hostility to any idea that the Israelites had seen a vision of the throne at the Red Sea because those who made such a claim went on to worship the image of the golden calf. The Red Sea seems here to have been superimposed on another body of water which the Exodus episode was seeking to suppress, namely, the waters which surrounded the heavenly throne. The earliest evidence for this is from the sixth century BCE, when Isaiah prayed that the LORD would dry up the waters of the sea to make a way for his redeemed, just as he had overcome the dragon of the waters in the past (Isa. 51.9–10). These were the primeval waters over which the LORD sat enthroned in the temple (see on 17.1), the terrible ice under the throne which Ezekiel had seen in his vision, but with Isaiah they became the waters which separated Egypt from the promised land. The link between the crystal sea, the vision of the heavenly throne and the Exodus had ancient roots. The later Jewish teachers' hostility to it cannot have been because it was unscriptural; there must have been another reason, and its importance in the Book of Revelation is the most likely one.

The third object of the rabbis' concern was the rainbow. Some deduced from Ezekiel 1.28 that the Glory of the LORD was seen as a rainbow and that anyone who saw a rainbow should prostrate himself before it. Others condemned this as idolatry. Stories told of the merkavah sages, however, did not only tell of the fire that appeared while they were teaching (see on 11.5); they also described the rainbow that appeared in the cloud overhead: 'R.Joshua and R. Jose the priest were going on a journey. They said: Let us also expound the work of the merkavah ... The heavens became overcast with clouds and a kind of rainbow appeared in the cloud ...' (b. Ḥagigah 14b). The later Hekhalot texts described the Man surrounded by a rainbow (Ezek. 1.28) as 'the young one' (see p. 133), the prince who was the Angel of the presence and bore the Name. The language of these texts is often obscure, but the young one enters the most secret and glorious places, serving before the fire which consumes fire (#396). He was written (marked?) with the one letter by which heaven and earth were created and he had the signet of the name revealed at the burning bush (see p. 306). He goes under the throne, he has six men with him around the throne on the right hand side, and his body is like the rainbow that was 'round about' in Ezekiel 1.28 (#398). This is clearly the Servant, marked with the letter tau which was the sign and seal of the Name. He was also Ezekiel's seventh angel, who went under the throne to take the burning coals of destruction (Ezek. 10.2).

These three beliefs – the marble stones as water, the throne above the waters of the sea and the rainbow as the Glory of the LORD (see p. 181) – were all important in the Book of Revelation. The rabbis said they indicated an apostate who had worshipped the golden calf, the forbidden image, even though none of the three has any obvious link to the story of the golden calf. The apostasy in question must have been Christianity, and the forbidden image must have been 'the image of the invisible God, the firstborn of all creation' (Col. 1.15) whom the Christians worshipped.

Those who stood on the crystal sea and worshipped before the throne in the heavenly temple had ascended to heaven (15.2–4). They were worthy and pure and had been given the seal of the Name to protect them from the wrath of God (7.3). Among them were those who had recently died during the siege of the city and the seer, in his vision, was able to see them safe in heaven. Once they had been gathered, their number was complete (cf. 6.9–11), and the wrath of the judgement could begin.

The redeemed in heaven sang the Song of Moses and the Song of the Lamb. There are two Songs of Moses in the Hebrew Scriptures: Exodus 15.1–18 and Deuteronomy 32.1–43. The former was sung by Moses and the people of Israel after they had passed through the Red Sea (Exod. 15.1), the latter by Moses and Joshua. Since Joshua and Jesus are the same name, the Song of Moses in Deuteronomy 32 may have been understood as 'The Song of Moses and Jesus', i.e. the Lamb. No other Song of the Lamb is known.* The song of the redeemed in 15.3–4 is reminiscent of both Songs of Moses, of Exodus 15 (see above) and also Deuteronomy 32 which was the tephilim text (see on 13.16). 'I even I am he and there is no god beside me' (Deut. 32.39) is exactly the theme of the song in heaven, and the Qumran text of Deuteronomy 32.43 (4QDeut^q) is the theme of the whole of the Book of Revelation. There are also allusions to Psalm 111.2, 'Great are the works of the LORD', and to Psalm 145.17 'The LORD is just in all his ways'.

The blessed in heaven watched as the angels of wrath went out of the temple to destroy those left in the city. Like their ancestors, they had been saved from the hand of the 'Egyptians' (see on 11.8) and they, too, were about to see the bodies of their enemies. 'Israel saw the Egyptians dead upon the seashore. And Israel saw the great work which the LORD did against the Egyptians, and the people feared the LORD ...' (Exod. 14.30–31). The multitude on the sea of glass sang: 'Great and wonderful are thy deeds ... Who shall not fear and glorify thy name O LORD?' (15.3-4).

(There are two pairs of variant readings in these verses which suggest the interesting possibility that there was more than one translation of the Book of Revelation, that all our manuscripts have not come ultimately from one, but from two Greek translations of the original text. 'King of the ages' *aionon* appears in some manuscripts as 'King of the nations' *ethnon* (15.3), two very different words which can hardly be explained as a scribal error or misreading of a Greek text. In Hebrew, however, the words 'ages' *'lmm* and 'nations' *'mm* are very similar and either would have made sense in the context. Perhaps one translator read 'ages' and the other 'nations'. A similar divergence occurs in 15.6 which invites a similar explanation. The seven angels were wearing 'pure bright linen' *linon*, but some manuscripts say the seven angels were wearing 'pure bright stone' *lithon*, presumably a reference to the gemstones of the high priestly vestments. These two words

---

*Deut. 32.44 now has a unique spelling of 'Joshua', perhaps to distinguish it from 'Jesus'.

linon and *lithon* could have been confused in the Greek, but another explanation has been suggested. The Hebrew *šeš* can mean either 'fine linen' (e.g. Exod. 28.39) or 'marble' (e.g. Song 5.15), and thus the two Greek versions could indicate two translators who read *šeš* differently.)

The Seven Angels

There was a voice from the temple, commanding the seven angels to pour out the wrath on the earth, but there was no Ezekiel to pray for mercy for the land full of blood and injustice (Ezek. 9.8–9). The Third Isaiah, too, had heard the voice from the temple, the LORD bringing judgement on his enemies (Isa. 66.6). It is clear from the context that the enemies were those who had polluted the temple and cast out their brethren (Isa. 66.3–5).

To complete the great Day of Atonement, the sevenfold presence of the LORD comes from the holy of holies, but does not pour out his lifeblood to cleanse and hallow (Lev. 16.19). Instead, the seven angels carrying bowls of plague emerge from 'the temple of the tent of witness in heaven' (15.5). This awkward phrase is a literal translation of 'the tabernacle of the tent of meeting' (Exod. 40.2, 6, 29), the entire sacred tent. 'Meeting' was understood by the translators of the LXX to be 'witness or testimony', *marturion*. The written Hebrew for both 'meeting' and 'witness' is identical (*m'd*), even though the words would have been pronounced differently. In the LXX the sacred tent was described as 'the tent of the witness'. The longer phrase in Revelation 15.5 'the temple of the tent of witness' is not taken from the LXX but is an independent translation of the same three-word phrase in Exodus 40. It suggests that the prophets of the Book of Revelation also understood the temple to be a place of 'seeing' rather than a place of meeting (see p. 13), and gives a context for the introduction to the Book of Revelation: 'the testimony* of Jesus Christ, all that he saw' (1.2).

It is likely that the seven angels were robed in linen rather than stone because, being girded at the breast with golden girdles, they would then have been dressed exactly like the Man among the lamps (1.13). The angels were high priests, the sevenfold presence of the Great High Priest. Plural identity was characteristic of the temple tradition, and the LORD was a manifold deity albeit a unity. 'The LORD our God, the LORD is One', was repeated daily but the plurality of Israel's LORD was never forgotten. This can be seen in John's greeting to the seven churches: 'Grace to you and peace 1) from him who is and who was and who is to come and 2) from the seven spirits who are before his throne and 3) from Jesus Christ, the faithful witness, the firstborn of the dead and the ruler of kings on earth' (1.4–5). The one who is and was and is to come is identified throughout the Book of Revelation as Jesus, the risen LORD, and Jesus is also the one who has the seven spirits (5.6). The seven angels

---

* marturia, a synonym of *marturion*.

are the seven spirits before the throne, the seven torches of fire (4.5). They were represented in the temple by the menorah (see on 1.12–16), with the LORD as the middle one of the seven. Thus the 'three' in John's greeting are one, just as the 'seven' are one. The type and antitype of the seven angels can be seen in the seven heads of the one dragon (12.3) and the one beast (13.1, 17.10). They were the sevenfold unity of evil, and here there is the sevenfold presence of the LORD (see pp. 83, 229).

Zechariah is the earliest witness to this belief when the angel told him that the golden lampstand was 'the seven eyes of the LORD which range through the whole earth' (Zech. 4.10). These 'eyes' are a mystery because the word must have meant an angel figure both in this context and elsewhere. In Psalm 87.6–7, for example, there is a glimpse of children of Zion being recorded by a heavenly scribe. The scribe is the LORD – not a role usually associated with the God of Israel – and there follows a verse which in the English translations either makes little sense (AV, RSV, NRSV) or adds considerably to the Hebrew in order to force sense from it (Good News, NEB). The heavenly scribe records, 'Singers, dancers and all my springs of water'. Of these three 'singers' *šrm* were probably 'princes' *šrm,* as in Isaiah 43.28, the princes of the sanctuary; and 'all my springs of water' *kl m'yny* were probably 'all of them my eyes' *klm 'yny*. The 'dancers' *ḥllm* is a word with many meanings. In Ezekiel 28 alone – a chapter which describes an angel figure being thrown down from heaven and plays on the various meanings of this word – it is translated defile, slay, wound, profane, and it can also mean bore, pierce or play the pipe. A very similar word *ḥwl*, which in some forms is identical with *ḥll*, can mean whirl, dance, writhe, be firm or be strong. Of the three groups mentioned in Psalm 87.7, then, two were princes and eyes and the third cannot be identified. The point of this digression is to show that the seven 'eyes of the LORD' were probably the angel princes of the holy of holies who were the sevenfold presence of the LORD, the sevenfold Spirit. The Qumran Songs of the Sabbath Sacrifice mention the seven sovereign princes of the holy of holies (4Q403 1i) and these are the seven high priestly angels who emerge from the holy of holies in 15.6, as the sevenfold presence of the LORD.

The seven also occur in the *Shepherd of Hermas*, a book of prophecies from the church in Rome in the middle of the second century CE. Seven angels appeared to Hermas, and his guardian angel (his 'shepherd') explained who they were: 'You see the six men and the glorious and great Man in their midst ... The glorious Man is the Son of God and these six are glorious angels supporting him on the right hand and on the left' (*Sim.* 9.12.7–8). This was the pattern of the menorah, with the Man in the midst of the other lamps, and also of the Hekhalot text which described the 'young one' and his six men around the throne.

The seven angels came out of the holy of holies and as they emerged each was given a bowl of plague to pour onto the earth. Israel had always described the wrath of God as plague coming out of the sanctuary; the Levites even had to camp around the tabernacle to protect the people from any outbreaks (Num. 1.53). When Korah and his company of rebels had been swallowed by the earth (Num. 16.32), it was a plague of wrath from the holy of holies which punished their supporters: 'They turned towards the tent of meeting and behold, the cloud covered it and the glory of the LORD appeared. And Moses and Aaron came to the front of the tent of meeting, and the LORD said to Moses, "Get away from the midst of this congregation, that I may consume them in a moment" '. Moses then instructed Aaron to prepare incense to make atonement 'For wrath has gone forth from the LORD, the plague has begun' (Num. 16.42–46, cf. Num. 11.33 and Num. 25.11). All the elements of 15.5–8 are here: the cloud and the glory in the temple, and then the outbreak of wrath. When Habakkuk received his vision of the LORD coming for 'the salvation of his people and his anointed' (Hab. 3.13), he saw pestilence and plague in attendance. 'Before him went pestilence and plague followed close behind. He stood and measured the earth, he looked and shook the nations' (Hab. 3.5–6). The whole chapter describes a violent theophany as the LORD tramples the nations in his anger.

Ezekiel the priest-prophet of the first temple has left the most vivid description of the wrath emerging from the temple. He saw the seven men 'who were set over the city' (Ezek. 9.1, not 'executioners' as in RSV) and each had in his hand a vessel of destruction (verse 1) or a vessel of shattering/scattering (verse 2). The word translated 'weapon' commonly means a utensil or vessel (as in 1 Chron. 28.13–14 where it means the temple vessels) or it can be a musical instrument, so it is by no means certain that the men were carrying weapons. The seer of the Book of Revelation believed that the angels' vessels of destruction were 'bowls of wrath', and the Greek translator of the Book of Revelation chose the word *phiale,* often used in the LXX for a temple vessel, e.g. 1 Chronicles 28.17. The LXX, however, says that Ezekiel's angels carried axes, understanding 'vessels of shattering' in this way. In the Hekhalot texts, the angels who guard the seventh palace and prevent the unworthy from entering to stand before the throne were also armed with axes. They, too, must have been Ezekiel's angels of wrath.

The seventh man in Ezekiel's vision was singled out and described in detail. He stood 'in the midst of' the others (Ezek. 9.2, not just 'with them'); he was clothed in linen and apparently had the inkpot of a scribe hung at his side. The LXX read this very differently and found no scribe here, even though he was the one who put the mark on the foreheads of the faithful, the role of the LORD in Psalm 87.6. The word scribe *spr* was read as sapphire *spyr* and the figure became 'one man in the midst of them dressed in a long robe' (*poderes,* always the dress of a high priest, see on 1.12), 'with a girdle of sapphire around his loins'. In other words, the translator read the word for inkpot *qst,* as *qšt,* rainbow, a very common word, and understood the phrase to mean 'a rainbow of sapphire around his loins'. Now the word *qst,* inkpot, does not occur anywhere else in the Hebrew Scriptures, and so the translator of the LXX probably rendered the text correctly. Ezekiel had described the man in the midst of the seven angels as wearing the linen robe of a high priest, 'his loins girded with a rainbow of sapphire'. This same man appears in Ezekiel's vision of the chariot by the River Chebar, but the description there is not easy to translate: 'A likeness as it were of a human form ... and from the appearance of his loins and downwards I saw the appearance of fire and he had brightness round him'. The brightness round his loins is then described as 'like the appearance of a rainbow' (Ezek. 1.26–28). The Man in the midst of the seven was the Man who sat on the throne, the LORD. He was also the young one described in the later Hekhalot text, with a body like the rainbow and six men in attendance, who went into the secret place of fire under the throne (#398).

In Ezekiel's vision, the LORD called first to the man in the midst and told him to go through Jerusalem and mark all those who had remained faithful. The mark would protect them from the wrath (see on 7.1–4). Then the other six were directed to go through the city and 'smite' everyone who had not been marked on the forehead. 'Begin at my sanctuary ... Defile the house and fill the courts with the slain. Go forth' (Ezek. 9.6–7). The angelic visitation was described as 'pouring out wrath' on Jerusalem (Ezek. 9.8). When the Man in the midst had marked the faithful, he returned and was commanded to go under the throne between the wheels, fill his hands with burning coals from between the cherubim and scatter them over the city (Ezek. 10.2). The Man had two roles; he brought warning and gave the mark which protected the faithful, but he also delivered the final punishment on the city. *He was the First and the Last.*

The seven angels set over Jerusalem were the seven who emerged from the temple in the vision of the bowls of wrath. The seer expected such a visitation because this was how the LORD had destroyed the city in the time of Ezekiel. (His contemporaries 'Baruch' and 'Ezra' also described the destruction in 70 CE as the destruction in 586 BCE). The vessels which poured out the wrath became the bowls of wrath, and all seven angels were dressed in linen and girded like a high priest. Ezekiel does not record what the other six wore. Each angel in turn went out from the temple and delivered his plague. What follows must have been a description of the destruction of Jerusalem, and the plagues, though resembling the plagues on Egypt because this was another deliverance for those protected by the blood of the Lamb (Exod. 12.13), were in fact descriptions of life in the city during the siege of Jerusalem. The framework was traditional, as with the seven trumpets – heaven and earth, sea and rivers – but the detail was drawn from life.

The Plagues

The first plague was 'foul and evil sores' (16.2), and translated in this way it evokes the plague of boils and sores (Exod. 9.9). The primary meaning of *helkos*, however, is not 'sore' but 'festering wound' and so the first plague was foul and evil festering wounds. The second and third plagues were bloodshed. Josephus' account of the last months in Jerusalem gives ample evidence of these plagues. He described an attack on the temple courts while the Zealots were fighting among themselves: 'The dead bodies of natives and aliens, of priests and laity were mingled in a mass and the blood of all manner of corpses formed pools in the courts of God' (*War* 5.18). When the temple was set on fire and a battle ensued, 'the stream of blood was more copious than the flames and the slain more numerous than the slayers. For the ground was nowhere visible between the corpses; but the soldiers had to clamber over heaps of bodies in pursuit of the fugitives' (*War* 6.276). Josephus put special emphasis on the bloodshed in the temple; perhaps he, too, had in mind Ezekiel's destroying 'angels defiling the house and filling the courts with the slain' (Ezek. 9.7). After the third bowl of wrath, the angel of water explained the plague of blood; those who had shed blood would drink blood. Isaiah had prophesied that the oppressors of Jerusalem would drink their own blood (Isa. 49.26) and here it was the people in Jerusalem who had become the enemies of the LORD's servants. As with the plagues of Gog (see on 16.14), the punishments once threatened for their enemies became the punishments for Jerusalem. The blood of the saints and the prophets had been shed in Jerusalem, and for this the city had been condemned as an enemy. This condemnation was repeated in 18.24, when the Mighty Angel threw the millstone into the sea and the prophecies were fulfilled. Jesus had warned that all the blood of the prophets shed in Jerusalem would be required of his generation (Luke 11.50–51) and the Song of Moses warned that the LORD would avenge the blood of his servants when he came to atone the land (Deut. 32.43). Addressed by his ancient name as the Mighty Angel of Israel, the Holy One is praised for his justice (16.5–7). Here, as in 9.13, the golden altar speaks, just as the throne itself speaks in the later Hekhalot texts (#99).

The fourth plague was the unbearable heat (16.8–9) because the siege lasted throughout the summer of 70 CE until the city was burned at the end of September. The fifth plague was the destruction of the temple, which was no longer the place of the heavenly throne (cf. Ps. 11.4) but had become the throne of 'the Angel of Darkness' (1QS III), of Satan, 'the Angel of Malevolence who rules in darkness' (1QM XIII), and so of his earthly manifestation, the beast (see p. 212). The temple became a place of darkness, not light. Men gnawed their tongues in anguish (16.10). Josephus described how the famine was at its most acute in the days immediately before the temple was burned: 'Necessity drove the victims to gnaw anything and objects which even the filthiest of brute beasts would reject they condescended to collect and eat: thus in the end they abstained not from belts and shoes and stripped off and chewed the very leather of their bucklers. Others devoured tufts of withered grass' (*War* 6.197–98). One woman ate her own child. 'The starving folk longed for death' (*War* 6.213). They cursed God for their 'pain and sores' (16.11). Pain, *ponos*, can also mean distress or toil and the struggle of battle. The starving people of Jerusalem, as the temple was about to be destroyed, cursed God for the struggle of battle and their festering wounds. Josephus records this, too: 'Therefore sufferings of the people of Jerusalem grew daily worse ... they rushed out to war with the foreigners, and it seems to me they were hurling insults at the Deity for being so slow in bringing retribution [to their enemies]' (*War* 6.1, 4). The picture in 16.8–11 is accurate; the people in Jerusalem cursed God for their sufferings with no sign of divine intervention, and the prophets exhorted them to endure to the end.

The sixth plague was enemies assembling to fight against the city, and the sense must be that God was fighting with them against Jerusalem. 16.12–16 is, however, composite and this has introduced some confusion. The kings from the east (16.12) and the kings of the whole world (16.16) prepare for battle, and this is a fair description of the forces that mustered for the siege. The fifth legion approached from the west, the tenth from Jericho and Titus himself came from Caesarea with the fifteenth, and with the twelfth which he had summoned from Antioch. He also commanded 2000 men from the units in Alexandria and 3000 from the Euphrates. Marching with him were the allied kings and their armies: Antiochus IV of Commagene and Soaemus of Emesa, both kingdoms in the north of Syria (*War* 2.499–501 and 5.39–44). Titus approached Jerusalem from the north, with the kings and their armies positioned at the head of the column. They camped on Mount Scopus to the northwest of the city, and the legion from Jericho set up camp on the Mount of Olives to the east.

Their way had been prepared by the sixth angel who had dried up the waters of the Euphrates to let them pass over. This allusion is a problem. One possibility is that, since Jerusalem is described in the Book of Revelation as 'Babylon', this is a reference to the fall of Babylon in 539 BCE. Herodotus (*Histories* 1.189ff.) described how Cyrus had his engineers lower the water level of the Euphrates by diverting the river into a neighbouring marsh. His army was then able to wade across the river and take Babylon by surprise. Drying the Euphrates might allude to the massive engineering works of the Romans which enabled them to take Jerusalem. Four embankments and a new road enabled them to attack and take the Temple Mount (*War* 6.149–51) and earthworks were thrown up to the east and west of the upper city before that, too, was taken (*War* 6.374–77). There is, however, no way of knowing if the seers in Jerusalem knew how Cyrus had taken Babylon. It is more likely that the drying of the Euphrates was an antitype of the drying of the Red Sea, in view of the Exodus theme of this sequence. None of the assembled forces had had to cross the Euphrates, but if the seers were reliving events in the time of Ezekiel, they could well have described the armies as another horde of kings from the east, beyond the Euphrates.

As the kings assembled for battle, unclean spirits like frogs came from the mouths of the dragon, the beast and the false prophet (16.13). This is another antitype. Wisdom was 'the breath of the power of God, a pure emanation of the glory of the Almighty ... who passes into holy souls and makes them friends of God and prophets' (*Wisd.* 7.25, 27). The unclean spirits came from three people who regarded themselves as the friends of God and a prophet, namely the high priest (the dragon), the Roman commander (the beast) and Josephus (the false prophet), all of whom 'tried' to prevent the destruction of the temple. The high priests Joseph and Jesus had gone over to the Romans and they begged the Zealots in the city to allow the Romans in and thus save the city and the temple from destruction (*War* 6.111, 119). This was the unclean spirit from the mouth of the dragon. Titus, presenting himself as someone who wanted to protect the temple at all costs, had spoken to the leader of the Zealots and begged him to avoid destroying the city and the holy place. He should no longer pollute the holy place nor sin against God and he had permission to resume offering sacrifices (*War* 6.95). This was the unclean spirit from the mouth of the beast. Josephus, the false prophet, also begged the Zealots to surrender the city and quoted a prophecy to them, that the city would be taken when Jews were slaughtering their own countrymen (*War* 6.110, see p. 238). In fact, the dragon, the beast and the false prophet were the ones who had assembled the armies against Jerusalem.

The kings assembled at 'the place which is called in Hebrew Armageddon' (16.16). Traditionally, this has been identified as Har Megiddo – the mountain of Megiddo – but there is no such place. Megiddo was a plain (2 Chron. 35.22). It had been the site of several great battles in Israel's history: Deborah and Barak defeated the Canaanites there (Judg. 5.19); King Ahaziah was killed nearby during Jehu's revolt (2 Kgs 9.27) and King Josiah was killed there in battle, fighting against Pharaoh Neco (2 Kgs 23.29). It has been suggested that Armageddon was originally Har Mo'ed, the Mount of Assembly, the letter 'ayin often appearing in Greek transliteration as *g* (the Hebrew for Gaza begins with 'ayin). On the Mount of Assembly was the throne of God Most High; in Isaiah's taunt song against Babylon the Mount of Assembly is in the north, an echo of Canaanite mythology (Isa. 14.13), but for Israel, the mountain of God's throne was Zion. The hostile forces who massed against it came against Jerusalem and were defeated. The psalms celebrated the fate of the kings of the earth who came against the LORD and his anointed (Ps. 2.2) and extolled Mount Zion in the far north, the city of the great king, where the kings assembled and then took flight (Ps. 48.1–6).

The Great Day of God the Almighty, i.e. the LORD of hosts, was expected to be a time of triumph for Jerusalem. The War Scroll expressed the hope of the time. 'On the day when the Kittim fall, there shall be battle and terrible carnage before the God of Israel, for that shall be the day appointed from ancient times for the battle of destruction of the sons of darkness. At that time the assembly of gods and the hosts of men shall battle, causing great carnage' (1QM I). 'The Prince of Light Thou hast appointed from ancient times to come to our support' (1QM XIII). The enemies of Israel would perish like the host of Pharaoh in the Red Sea and like the host of Gog (1QM XI). A first-century CE text described this battle at the mountain. In his vision Ezra saw:

> an innumerable multitude of men gathered together from the four winds of heaven to make war against the Man who came out of the sea ... and all who had gathered together against him, to wage war with him, were much afraid yet dared to fight. And behold, when he saw the onrush of the approaching multitude, he neither lifted his hand nor held a spear nor any weapon of war; but I saw only how he sent forth from his mouth as it were a stream of fire and from his lips a flaming breath ... (2 *Esdr.* 13.5–10)

The Man from the sea is later identified as the Son of God Most High and the fire from his mouth as his words of judgement. The Christians expected Jesus to return as this Man who breathed fire, but they had a more literal expectation of what this fire would do: 'And then the lawless one will be revealed, and the LORD Jesus will slay him with the breath of his mouth and destroy him by his appearing and his coming' (2 Thess. 2.8). These were the expectations of the people besieged in Jerusalem. To depict the hordes as the sixth plague, however, implies they were to defeat Jerusalem, that the LORD would fight against Jerusalem in this battle. The city was the Egypt from which the faithful had been brought out, and the plagues destined for Gog and his horde became the plagues on Jerusalem. 'Pestilence and bloodshed' (Ezek. 38.22) describes exactly the plagues of the first five bowls, and the other terrors upon him were those of the seventh bowl.

The plagues were signs of the imminent return of the LORD and so his voice was heard, 'I am coming like a thief'. Jesus had warned that the Son of Man would come at an unexpected time, like a thief (Luke 12.39), and combined this with teachings about endurance, remaining faithful and prepared: 'Do not fear those that kill the body and after that have no more harm they can do ... You are of more value than many sparrows ... Let your loins be girded and your lamps burning and be like men who are waiting for their master ... Blessed are those servants whom the master finds awake when he comes ...' (Luke 12.4, 7, 35, 37). The social setting is also familiar: the rich man who hoarded grain and built bigger barns while the disciples were anxious about the necessities of life. Jesus was anxious to bring the judgement, when the blood shed in Jerusalem would be avenged in his generation (Luke 11.51). He had come to cast fire upon the earth and cause divisions within families as the Day drew nearer (Luke 12.49–53), fulfilling Ezekiel's prophecy of the time of Gog: 'Every man's sword will be against his brother' (Ezek. 38.21). The people who heard him did not know how to interpret the signs of their times (Luke 12.56). As with the sixth bowl (16.15), the saying is coupled with one about garments: 'Let your loins be girded ... like men waiting for their master to come home' (Luke 12.35). Matthew also associated this saying about the thief with the coming of the Son of Man: 'Watch therefore for you do not know on what day your LORD is coming. If the householder had known when the thief was coming ...' (Matt. 24.42–43) He placed it with the parables of the wise and foolish maidens, the talents, and the sheep and the goats.

Paul used the same illustration when he wrote in about 50 CE to the church in Thessalonika, explaining about the Day of the LORD. The LORD would descend from heaven, the archangel call out and the last trumpet sound. The dead would be raised, and those left alive would be caught up to heaven. Nobody knew exactly when this would happen; it would come 'like a thief in the night' (1 Thess. 5.2). The children of light had nothing to fear from the wrath; their armour was the breastplate of faith and love and the helmet of the hope of salvation (1 Thess. 5.8). The letter to the church in Sardis was written at about this time: 'I will come like a thief. You will not know at what hour I will come to you' (3.3) and this saying was also linked to one about garments (3.4). The second letter of Peter, written to Christians anxious about the delay, spoke of the Day of the LORD coming 'like a thief', a day like a thousand years and a thousand years like day (2 Pet. 3.8, 10).

The Seventh Bowl

The voice with the sixth bowl, announcing the imminent return of the LORD, makes it certain that the seventh bowl was the Parousia. The angel of the seventh bowl corresponds to the seventh angel in Ezekiel's vision of the destruction of the city. The seventh angel appeared first as the man who went through the city to mark all who would be saved from the wrath (Ezek. 9.4). While the other six angels were going through the city with their punishments, the seventh angel was at work and he eventually 'brought back word saying, "I have done as thou didst command me"' (Ezek. 9.11). This was the angel who wore the rainbow, the one whom Ezekiel had seen on the throne as 'the likeness of the glory of the LORD' (Ezek. 1.26). Once his mission was completed and the faithful were safe, he was commanded to throw burning coals over the city and bring its final destruction (Ezek. 10.2). In the Book of Revelation, the first mission of the angel was when he appeared as the Dawn and delayed the wrath until the faithful were sealed (7.2–3), and there, as here, the sealing was followed by the Parousia, when the great high priest was consecrated in heaven and eventually emerged to speak to John (see on 10.1). He was 'the First and the Last'. In chapter 16 there is a duplicate account of these events. The faithful marked with the Name (14.1) were already safe before the throne and so the judgement could begin.

The beast was the antitype of the seventh angel. He was one of the seven rulers who would make a second appearance, 'an eighth but it belongs to the seven' (17.11). He, too, had marked his faithful with his name. The Dawn Angel had first appeared in the ministry of Jesus, and Luke knew the hymn that proclaimed Jesus as the expected Dawn (Luke 1.78, see on 7.2). The angel with the seventh bowl was the return which Jesus had predicted, the Parousia, hence his saying: 'I came to cast fire on the earth' (Luke 12.49). There was a voice from the temple, 'It is done' (16.17). This was the voice which Isaiah had heard, the LORD coming in to punish those who had polluted the temple and excluded their brethren (Isa. 66.1–6). The words were the words of Ezekiel's seventh angel: 'I have done as thou didst command me', and the words of Jesus from the cross: 'It is accomplished' (John 19.30). In the timeless world of the seer, these events are one and the same.

Nor was there any problem with the figure on earth being also, and at the same time, an angel in heaven. Origen dealt with this in his *Commentary on John* and cited as evidence a text used in his time by 'the Hebrews'. There is no way of knowing the age of the text he was quoting in the middle of the third century CE, but he felt it explained how John the Baptist was believed to be simultaneously a man and an angel. The Prayer of Joseph, he wrote, showed 'that those who have something distinctive from the beginning when compared to men, being much better than other beings, have descended from the angelic to the human nature. Jacob, at any rate, says "I, Jacob, who am speaking to you, am also Israel, an angel of God and a ruling spirit" ' (*On John* 2.31). A simultaneous earthly and heavenly existence is also attested in a Targum of Jacob's dream at Bethel. The angels who were guarding Jacob ascended to heaven on the ladder and summoned the other angels to see the sleeping patriarch: 'Come see Jacob the pious whose image is on the throne of Glory' (*y. Gen.* 28.12). A commentary on Genesis has material on this passage attributed to two first-century Palestinians, R. Hiyya and R. Yannai. 'You, O Israel, in whom I will be glorified' (Isa. 49.3) was associated with Jacob at Bethel and interpreted to mean: 'You are he whose image is engraved on high. They ascended on high and saw his image, they descended on earth and saw him sleeping' (*Gen. Rab.* LXVIII.12). John's Jesus spoke of himself in the same way, when at the start of his ministry he alluded to this passage and spoke of the angels ascending and descending on the Son of Man (John 1.51). He was claiming to be like Jacob, the image in heaven on the throne and yet also a man on earth. This belief, which John attributes to Jesus himself, underlies and explains the multiple identity of the figures in Ezekiel's vision and the Book of Revelation. The Dawn Angel of 7.2 and seventh angel were both descriptions of the LORD; on earth as it is in heaven.

He poured his bowl into the air, the domain of Satan who was 'the prince of the power of the air, the spirit that is now at work in the sons of disobedience' (Eph. 2.2) and, after the voice had been heard from the temple, there were signs of a theophany: lightning, voices, thunder and earthquake. When the angel high priest was about the appear from the heavenly temple there were thunder, voices, lightning and earthquake (8.5). When the Woman clothed with the sun was about to appear from the heavenly temple, there were lightning, voices, thunder, earthquake and hail (11.19). *The appearance of the seventh angel from the heavenly temple was a description of theophany, confirming that the seventh angel was the LORD.*

The Hebrew Scriptures show that when the LORD came to rescue his people he came in a storm. Psalm 18 is one of the oldest storm theophany texts (although it is unlikely that the seers in Jerusalem were concerned with the relative age of their Scriptures). When 'David' was in danger he called on the LORD to help him.

From his temple he heard my voice,
and my cry to him reached his ears.
Then the earth reeled and rocked;
the foundations also of the mountains trembled
and quaked, because he was angry ...

Out of the brightness before him
there broke through his clouds
hailstones and coals of fire.
The LORD also thundered in the heavens,
and the Most High uttered his voice,
hailstones and coals of fire.
And he sent out his arrows and scattered them;
he flashed forth lightnings, and routed them. (Ps. 18.6–7, 12–14)

All the phenomena are here: thunder, lightning, voices, earthquake and hail. Psalm 77.16–20 described the Exodus in a similar way: thunder, whirlwind, lightning and earthquake. Some elements of the storm theophany appeared in the accounts of Sinai: thunder and lightning together with a cloud and the sound of a trumpet (Exod. 19.16, 20.18). Deuteronomy only mentions fire at the mountain, in the heart of darkness, cloud and gloom (Deut. 4.11). This could suggest that the storm theophany was part of the older temple cult they sought to suppress (see p. 16). The LORD had fought the kings of Canaan in a storm (Judg. 5.4–5) and the punishments on Gog were earthquakes, pestilence and bloodshed, rain, hailstones, fire and brimstone (Ezek. 38.19–22).

Josephus shows how literally these ancient texts were understood in his time. When the Idumeans (another element in the complex politics of the war against Rome), were camped outside the walls of Jerusalem, there was a violent storm during the night: strong winds, rain, lightning, thunder and earthquake. He commented: 'The disordering of the system of the world was a clear sign that destruction was coming on men and anyone would have thought that these were omens of no small disaster' (*War* 4.287). The Idumeans interpreted the storm as a sign of God's anger at their coming to Jerusalem, and the high priest Ananus said it was a sign that the battle had been won without fighting, because God was 'directing the battle on their behalf' (*War* 4.288). The ancient prophecies and the exhortations of contemporary prophets were a major factor in the conduct of the war, the most remarkable illustration being the reaction to the Roman bombardment. Huge white stones were hurled into the city and the watchmen interpreted these as the hailstones of a theophany. They shouted in their native tongue 'The Son is coming' (*War* 5.272).

God remembered the great Babylon. The recording angels, whose task was to report in heaven what was happening on earth, brought the sins of Jerusalem before the LORD (see on 18.5). Isaiah's words of comfort to the city were set aside and she was treated as her own worst enemy: 'Behold I have taken from your hand the cup of staggering; the bowl of my wrath you shall drink no more; and I will put it into the hands of your tormentors ...' (Isa. 51.22–23) became 'God remembered ... to make her drain the cup of the fury of his wrath' (16.19). The cup she mixed was to hold a double draught for herself (18.6), and the vision of the harlot on the seven hills revealed her with a golden cup of abominations (see on 17.4). The Hebrew Scriptures knew well the fury of the wrath of the LORD. The first destruction of Jerusalem had been caused by the LORD 'on the day of his fierce anger, when in his fierce anger he cut down the might of Israel, gave full vent to his wrath and poured out his hot anger' (Lam. 1.12; 2.3; 4.11). Ezekiel had given a lurid account of the fate of the harlot city, when the LORD sent enemies against her 'to deal with her in fury, seize her sons and daughters and devour the survivors by fire' (Ezek. 23.25). The seven bowls of wrath brought this destruction.

Jeremiah's oracle against Judah must have been in the mind of the seer as he found words to describe the seventh bowl. Jerusalem had to drink the cup of the wine of wrath (Jer. 25.17–18) because the LORD's judgement on the world would begin with his own city (Jer. 25.29). The LORD would roar from his holy habitation, like those who tread grapes (Jer. 25.30) and he would bring judgement on the shepherds, the rulers of the nations (Jer. 25.34–38). These were the seventy shepherds of the nations to whom the LORD had committed the care of his people (see p. 226), and they were to be judged first on the Day of the LORD. Seven men in white, who must have been Ezekiel's seven men, carried out the sentence.

Then the LORD called those men, the seven first white ones ... and he said to that Man who wrote before him, being one of those seven white ones ... Take the seventy shepherds to whom I delivered the sheep and who taking them on their own authority, slew more than I commanded them ... And those seventy shepherds were judged and found guilty and they were cast into that fiery abyss. (*1 En.* 90.22–25)

These shepherds appear in the vision of the seventh bowl, but have been translated as 'the cities of the nations' who fell (16.19), but this should be 'the angels of the nations', the Watchers. The ancient name for the seventy angels was the Watchers, '*rym* and the word cities is also '*rym*. The clearest illustration of this confusion can be found in Isaiah's oracle against the king of Babylon, a proud heavenly being who called himself the Morning Star, son of the Dawn, and tried to set his throne above the throne of God Most High. He was thrown down from heaven and the final curse on him was the slaughter of his sons.

May the descendants of evildoers never more be named!
Prepare slaughter for his sons because of the guilt of their fathers,
lest they rise and possess the earth,
and fill the face of the world with cities. (Isa. 14.20–21)

The slaughter was in fact to prevent the earth being infested with the evil offspring of the proud angel and the 'cities' were the Watchers.

In the vision of the seventh bowl, several heavenly beings are judged: the angels of the nations fell (and their cities with them, see on 2.5), islands fled and mountains were not found (16.20). 'Was not found' is a Hebrew idiom for 'ceased to exist' (see Ps. 37.36). It occurs also in 5.4 and 12.8 (literally no place *was found* for them in heaven); and in 14.5, 18.21 and 20.11. The destruction of the mountains and islands is not a description of cosmic catastrophe but conceals the judgement of the heavenly beings. 'Mountain' was a common designation for an angel or his royal manifestation on earth; the seven kings were seven mountains (see on 17.9–10) and the great Roman who fell to his doom was a fiery mountain falling into the sea (see on 8.8). 'Islands' also conceals the name of a hostile supernatural being, even though it is not certain exactly what this was. The Hebrew *'yym*, islands, coastlands, occurs in several passages in the Hebrew Scriptures where it clearly has another meaning. In Zephaniah 2.11 'islands' appear in parallel to 'the gods of the earth', in Isaiah 59.18 they are listed among the 'adversaries of God' and in Isaiah 41.5 they wait in fear and trembling for the judgement of the LORD. Whatever the 'mountains and islands' were who fled from the coming of the LORD, they were probably not mountains and islands! There is a similar sequence in *Sibylline* 3.702–20, where the Holy One fights for his people and *the islands and cities* acknowledge his greatness. They sing hymns and worship and send offerings to the temple.

The great city was split into three parts. Zechariah had depicted the Day of the LORD as a time of battle, 'all nations against Jerusalem', when the LORD would go out and fight against them (Zech. 14.2–3). The Mount of Olives would split into two, and the LORD would become king over all the earth (Zech. 14.4, 9). Some such expectation may have been in the mind of the seer, but Josephus suggests another possibility. Jerusalem divided into three factions: Eleazar formed a group who took possession of the temple area, John held the outer courts of the temple area and Simon held the upper city and some of the lower city. Battles between the three rivals did much to weaken the city, and Josephus commented: 'One might say that the division was a good thing among the evil men, and even a work of justice' (*War* 5.3). This was the ultimate judgement on the city, to fall as the result of internal strife while the Romans were bombarding the city. Thus the seer wrote: 'The great city was split into three parts ... and great hailstones, heavy as a hundredweight, dropped on men from heaven, till men cursed God for the plague of hail, so fearful was that plague' (16.19, 21).

18

JERUSALEM

Then one of the seven angels who had the seven bowls came and said to me, 'Come, and I will show you the judgement of the great harlot who is seated upon many waters, with whom the kings of the earth have committed fornication, and with the wine of whose fornication the dwellers on earth have become drunk.'

After this I saw another angel coming down from heaven, having great authority; and the earth was made bright with his splendour. And he called out with a mighty voice, 'Fallen, fallen is Babylon the great!' (Rev. 17.1–2, 18.1–2)

When the compilers of the Isaiah Scroll wrote the preface to their great work, they surveyed the story of Jerusalem which it recounted and concluded: 'How the faithful city has become a harlot, she that was full of justice' (Isa. 1.21). The harlot on the seven hills was Jerusalem, the antitype of the heavenly city which became the Bride of the Lamb. One of the seven angels with bowls took the seer on a spirit journey and showed him the harlot in a wilderness, seated on seven mountains (17.9). The angel also took him on a spirit journey to a high mountain and showed him another city, the Bride of the Lamb coming down from heaven (21.9–10). She was decked with jewels, but had no temple; instead, she had the presence of the LORD God Almighty, a bitter and revealing remark (21.22).

The first temple had been a harlot because of the worship of foreign gods; the second had been a harlot because foreign money was accepted for rebuilding and yet many who worshipped the LORD were excluded; and Herod's rebuilt temple city was a harlot who had grown rich with the wealth of her wantonness. One key to understanding the description of the fall of the great city is the economic situation prevailing in Judea in the first century CE. The emphasis in Revelation 18 is not primarily on infidelity, although this is mentioned, but on wealth. It is the merchants who weep.

The Harlot City

In the first temple there had been a goddess, the mother and queen consort of the LORD but also the genius of the city, the 'Daughter of Zion' (see p. 202). The changes made by the Deuteronomists make it difficult to reconstruct exactly what she was like, but there is a glimpse of her in the oracles of Micah in the eighth century BCE. He described her leaving her city in agony at the hands of her enemies, but later triumphing over them, threshing the nations like sheaves on a threshing floor (Mic. 4.10–13). She then became the mother of the great ruler who would feed his flock in the strength of the LORD and gather in his people (Mic. 5.3). This was the great Shepherd, the angel ruler of Israel.

Isaiah also spoke of the goddess: 'Behold a virgin shall conceive and bear a son and call his name Immanuel' (Isa. 7.14). The king was the son of his human father and mother, but also proclaimed as the divine Son of a heavenly father and a heavenly mother.

When Jerusalem fell to the Babylonians in 597 BCE one of her poets wrote:

How the LORD in his anger
has set the daughter of Zion under a cloud!
He has cast down from heaven to earth
the splendour of Israel. (Lam. 2.1)

Her fall was the fall of her city.

Writing during the exile which followed her fall, the Second Isaiah said Zion felt like an abandoned wife. He assured her she would one day be the mother of many children; she had not been forgotten, for the image of the heavenly Zion was always with the LORD:

But Zion said, 'The LORD has forsaken me,
my LORD has forgotten me ...'
Behold, I have graven you on the palms of my hands;
your walls are continually before me. (Isa. 49.14, 16)

Zion has not been divorced, he said, but only put away because of her children's behaviour (Isa. 50.1–3). She had been drunk with grief for her lost children, all but destroyed by the husband who has finally taken away 'the bowl of his wrath' (Isa. 51.17–23, cf. Rev. 15.1 the seven plagues which marked the end of God's wrath). She was to be released from captivity and put on fine clothes again, dressing like a queen (Isa. 52.1–2; 54.11–12). She was to enlarge her tent at the prospect of many more children (Isa. 54.1–2). Zion's sons would marry her (Isa. 62.1–5) and finally, she awaited the birth of her children (Isa. 66.7–14).

The glimpses of the woman in Micah and Isaiah are important for understanding the two female figures in Revelation. In the royal cult which these two prophets knew, the goddess had been both the mother and the consort of the king. 'Your sons shall marry you' (Isa. 62.5), and the complex imagery of the Book of Revelation can only be understood in this temple context. The Bride of the Lamb is also his mother, the Woman clothed with the sun. Her antitype is the harlot on the scarlet beast who epitomizes the corruption of the ancient ideal. The woman drunk with grief at the loss of her children is contrasted with the harlot drunk with the blood of the saints and martyrs (17.6); the bejewelled bride/city is contrasted with the harlot decked in gold and pearls (17.4); and the mother of many children is contrasted with the mother of harlots and abominations. The mother of the Messiah has fled to the wilderness (12.14); here it is the mother of abominations who is in the wilderness (cf. *1 En.* 42, see p. 208). If the underlying text here was Hebrew, there was probably wordplay: Messiah is *mšyḥ*, and corruption is *mšḥyt*. Jeremiah had called Babylon the 'corrupted' mountain whom the LORD would throw down (Jer. 51.25, LXX). Such wordplay was characteristic of the prophetic style and of the scribes who transmitted the texts. An identical wordplay can be found in Isaiah 52.14 where the Qumran Isaiah Scroll describes the Servant as 'anointed' *mšḥty*, but the MT has 'disfigured', *mšḥt*. The Woman clothed with the sun was also the mother of those who keep the commandments of God (12.17), but the harlot's children were also harlots, unfaithful like their mother (17.5).

Ezekiel was the first to paint this lurid picture of Jerusalem the harlot. She was a foundling whom the LORD had brought up and then married, lavishing on her his love and his wealth. Jerusalem had been unfaithful; she had taken her fine clothes and made them into shrines for harlotry; she took her gold and silver and made for herself idols. Her lovers were the Egyptians, the Assyrians and the Chaldeans whom the LORD would turn against her (Ezek. 16 and 23). 'Your lewdness and your harlotry have brought this upon you, because you played the harlot with the nations, and polluted yourself with their idols' (Ezek. 23.30). This is exactly what happens to the harlot in 17.16; her lovers turn against her and destroy her.

The Third Isaiah, who lived in the period when the second temple was being built by the returned exiles (Ezra 1.2–11), compared even the restored city to a harlot, but his reasons were different. According to the Book of Ezra, Cyrus king of Persia allowed the exiles to rebuild Jerusalem and restored to them the temple vessels looted by the Babylonians. The people of Judea who had not been in exile asked to help rebuild the temple as they, too, worshipped the LORD, but their offer of help was rebuffed and trouble began. The accounts are confused. Ezra describes these people as immigrants settled in the land by the kings of Assyria: 'We have been sacrificing to your God ever since the days of Esarhaddon king of Assyria who brought us here' (Ezra 4.2). The wrath of the the Third Isaiah, however, suggests they were Israelites who fell short of the stringent purity rules observed by the returned exiles (Isa. 56.1–8). The matter of the rebuilding was settled by a further royal decree which not only allowed the temple building to proceed but also made provision for it to be funded by Persian tax revenue: 'Let the governor of the Jews and the elders of the Jews rebuild this house of God on its site. Moreover I make a decree regarding what you shall do for these elders of the Jews for the rebuilding of this house of God; the cost is to be paid to these men in full and without delay from the royal revenue, the tribute of the province from Beyond the River' (Ezra 6.7–8).

This was the arrangement that drew the prophet's wrath; the LORD's ancient people were excluded as impure and yet foreign money was acceptable to rebuild the temple. In some of the bitterest language to be found in the Hebrew Scriptures, he described the city and its temple as a harlot's bed. 'Upon a high and lofty mountain you have set your bed and thither you went up to offer sacrifice' (Isa. 57.7). The whole passage is full of words with double meaning so that much of the bitterness is lost in the English versions: 'bed' and 'tabernacle' are similar words in Hebrew (respectively *miškab* and *miškan*). She no longer worships the King, the traditional title for the LORD in Jerusalem, but a pagan god (*Melek/Molek*). The high priests were no longer those who drew near to the LORD in a cloud of incense (Lev. 16.13), the image in Daniel's vision of the Man (Dan. 7.13); those who drew near were 'the sons of a sorceress, an adulterer and a harlot' (Isa. 57.3). The Hebrew words for 'incense cloud' and 'soothsayer' are written in the same way, *'nn*. These are all references to the new condition of the Jerusalem cult.

The Third Isaiah went on to compare the exclusion policies of the new cult to the worst practices of paganism: the high priestly sacrifice of a bull was as impure as human sacrifice; the cereal offering no better than pig's blood, burning frankincense as bad as worshipping an idol (Isa. 66.3):

What is this house that you would build for me,
and what is the place of my rest?
All these things my hand has made,
and so all these things are mine, says the LORD.
But this is the man to whom I will look,
he that is humble and contrite in spirit,
and trembles at my word. (Isa. 66.1–2)

He warned the people of Jerusalem: 'You shall leave your name to my chosen for a curse, and the LORD God will slay you; but his servants he will call by a different name' (Isa. 65.15). The Book of Enoch records the same events: 'And after that in the seventh week shall an apostate generation arise, and many shall be its deeds, and all its deeds shall be apostate' (*1 En.* 93.9).

This, then, was the harlot. To some she became known as Babylon because she had been built with Persian money by those who returned from Babylon. The compilers of the great Isaiah Scroll bewailed the fate of their city: 'How the faithful city has become a harlot, she that was full of justice' (Isa. 1.21). To them she had become Sodom (Isa. 1.10). The genius of Jerusalem was no longer Wisdom but Folly (see p. 208). Some remained faithful to her, but many were enticed into strange ways by the foreign harlot. The Book of Proverbs is full of warnings against the harlot and her new ways: 'My son, if you receive my words and treasure up my commandments ... you will be saved from the strange woman and from the foreign woman with her smooth words' (Prov. 2.1, 16). This harlot offers sacrifices before enticing the unwary to his death (Prov. 7.10–23) while Wisdom haunts her old territory, warning the simple what their fate will be (Prov. 1.20–33).

The Woman on the Scarlet Beast

The harlot in the vision is seated on many waters, on seven mountains and on a scarlet beast. This is the world of myth and symbol, and so the waters are not the real waters of Babylon, by which the people of Jerusalem 'sat down and wept when they remembered Zion' (Ps. 137.1). They are the waters of chaos and evil over which the LORD triumphed when he established Jerusalem:

The LORD sits enthroned over the flood;
the LORD sits enthroned as king for ever. (Ps. 29.10)

Just as the LORD overcame the primeval waters and reigned supreme among the powers of heaven, so his Anointed One ruled the waters and was supreme among the kings of the earth (Ps. 89.5–10, 20–27). Roaring waters and raging enemies were one and the same (Ps. 46): Jeremiah described the invading Philistines as rising waters and an overflowing torrent (Jer. 47.1) and he predicted that Babylon would be destroyed by enemies, covered with the waves of an angry sea (Jer. 51.42).

Hark! a cry from Babylon!
The noise of great destruction from the land of the Chaldeans!
For the LORD is laying Babylon waste,
and stilling her mighty voice.
Their waves roar like many waters,
the noise of their voice is raised;
for a destroyer has come upon her, upon Babylon. (Jer. 51.54–56)

Wisdom had been the queen consort of the LORD and had sat by the throne (*Wisd.* 9.4). She, too, must have been enthroned over the waters. The sun goddess at Ugarit had been known as the Great Lady who Tramples the Sea (KTU 1.3.v.40–41), her title Great Lady corresponding to the Hebrew title for the queen mother (e.g. 1 Kgs 15.13; Jer. 13.18; 29.2). Now the foreign harlot sits in her place, a parody of Wisdom, the Great Lady enthroned over the waters. The angel says that the harlot is seated on 'peoples and multitudes and nations and tongues' (17.15) which must have been a traditional phrase, for the Man in Daniel's vision was given dominion over 'peoples, nations and tongues' (Dan. 7.14).

The harlot holds a golden cup which was the symbol of the LORD's curse on her. In the Isaiah Targum, the phrase 'The oracle concerning Babylon' became 'The oracle of the cup of cursing to give to Babylon to drink' (Isa. 13.1; with similar expressions in the oracles against Moab 15.1, Damascus 17.1, and Egypt 19.1) The golden cup of abominations and impurities may be no more than a vivid description of the curse. It may, however, indicate the traditional punishment for an adulterous wife, with the harlot punished in the ways the Law prescribed for unfaithfulness. First, she drinks the cup of her abominations and impurities, the cup of God's wrath (17.4; 16.19). She is later depicted drunk with the blood of saints and martyrs (17.6), perhaps a later interpretation. The Law of Moses prescribed that any suspected adulteress should drink 'the water of bitterness that brings the curse'

(Num. 5.18). The priest prepared this by washing off the words of a curse into some water. If she was guilty, the curse would enter her body and 'cause her thigh to fall away' (Num. 5.27, whatever that meant!). Thus Ezekiel warned the harlot Jerusalem that she would drink a cup of horror and desolation: 'drink it and drain it out and pluck out your hair and tear your breasts' (Ezek. 23.33–34).

The Mishnah records what happened in the first century CE. The suspect was taken to the eastern gate of the temple where her clothes were torn and her hair unbound. She then drank the draught (*m. Sotah* 1.5). If the suspected adulteress was found guilty, the Law prescribed death by stoning (Deut. 22.23, cf. John 8.5), but in the case of a priest's daughter, death by burning (Lev. 21.9). Once she has been made drunk with the blood of saints and martyrs, the harlot is made desolate and naked and her flesh is devoured (17.16). It is significant that the harlot city is also burned (17.16). This may suggest a harlot of priestly lineage, perhaps the high priesthood itself (see p. 291), or perhaps, since Wisdom had been 'a minister in the holy tabernacle in Zion' (*Ben Sira* 24.10), she was the stranger who had replaced her as the genius of the second temple (see p. 204).

The harlot is dressed like the temple; arrayed in purple and scarlet, bedecked with gold and jewels and pearls (17.4). Josephus' description of the temple in his time gives some idea of its splendour: built of white marble and cedar wood, with its sanctuary doors covered in gold and a great curtain, a Babylonian tapestry, woven of blue, purple, scarlet and white. There were notices at its gates saying that no foreigner was allowed into the holy place (*War* 5.194). This was the harlot who had had the kings of the earth as her lovers: Herod adorned her with spoils taken from barbarous nations (*Ant.* 15.402). On her forehead was a name, perhaps a parody of the high priest's diadem which bore the Name, in which case her clothes might indicate the robes of the high priest. The vestments were of the same colours and fabric as the temple curtain, and his breastplate was made of gold and precious stones. They were also in the keeping of foreign rulers, Herod first and then the Romans, and only released to the high priest for the great festivals (*Ant.* 15.403–405), presumably to guarantee their co-operation and good behaviour (see p. 31). The harlot's finery was the gift of her fickle lovers.

The Great City

In later Christian interpretation, 'the woman that you saw is the great city which has dominion over the kings of the earth' (17.18), was said to be Rome. Although Jerusalem was a small city in comparison with Alexandria, Antioch or Rome, it had been part of the royal cult to proclaim the Davidic king as the greatest king on earth. The LORD had promised: 'I will make the nations your heritage, and the ends of the earth your possession' (Ps. 2.8) and 'I will make him the firstborn, the highest of the kings of the earth' (Ps. 89.27). The city of David was the city of the LORD, the great King (Ps. 48.2).

The image of the woman seated on a seven-headed beast must have been traditional because the angel explains what it means, in other words, what follows is a new interpretation in the manner of the Qumran commentaries. First, the seven heads are the seven mountains on which she sits (17.9). This has often been taken to mean that the harlot was Rome, since Rome was proverbially the city on seven hills, but seven mountains were a feature of the mythic geography of Jerusalem. Enoch saw them on his heavenly journey, seven mountains of precious stones 'but the middle one reached to heaven like the throne of God, of alabaster, and the summit of the throne was of sapphire' (*1 En.* 18.8). When he asked about these things, Enoch was told by the angel: 'This high mountain ... whose summit is like the throne of God, is his throne, where the Great Holy One, the LORD of Glory, the Eternal King, will sit when he shall come down to visit the earth with goodness' (*1 En.* 25.3). Since the throne was believed to be in the sanctuary of the temple: 'The LORD is in his holy temple, the LORD's throne is in heaven' (Ps. 11.4), there must have been seven mountains in the mythical geography of the temple, three on either side of the throne. The harlot was enthroned in the temple, presumably sharing the heavenly throne as the consort of the beast, just as Wisdom had shared the throne of the LORD (*Wisd.* 9.4). The temple was the throne of the beast mentioned in 16.10 (see p. 270).

The seven mountains were also seven kings (17.10), an identification which confirms that the mountains were those of the temple mythology, since this also described the great rulers of the earth as mountains. Jeremiah had described Babylon as a 'corrupted' (or destroying) 'mountain' which the LORD would roll down in flames and destroy (Jer. 51.25). When the prophets wanted to depict the future supremacy of the LORD over the whole earth, they said that 'his mountain' would be the highest: 'The mountain of [the house of*] the LORD shall be established as the highest of the mountains and shall be raised above the hills' (Isa. 2.2//Mic. 4.1).

The Isaiah Targum knew that mountains were kingdoms so that 'You shall thresh the mountains and crush them, and you shall make the hills like chaff', becomes 'You shall kill the Gentiles and destroy [them] and make the kingdoms like the chaff' (Isa. 41.15). Kings were mountains for anyone steeped in temple tradition.

Of the seven kings, five had fallen, one was reigning and the one yet to come would only reign for a short period (17.9). There have been many attempts to identify these kings; they were probably the Roman emperors who had dealings with Palestine. The five who had already fallen were Augustus (31 BCE–14 CE), Tiberias (14–37 CE), Caligula (37–41 CE), Claudius (41–54 CE) and Nero (54–68 CE), each of whom

*Probably a later addition as it is not in the LXX.

had had dealings with Palestine and would have been known to the people of Jerusalem. Augustus had divided the land between Herod's three sons (*War* 2.93–95), Tiberius had tried to have images brought into Jerusalem (*War* 2.169–71), Caligula ordered that his statue be erected in the temple (*Ant.* 18.261), Claudius gave additional territory to Agrippa I (*Ant.* 19.274) and Nero gave extra territory to Agrippa II (*War* 2.252). This interpretation of the seven kings must have been made in the time of the sixth king, Vespasian (69–79 CE) whose rise to power was 'prophesied' by Josephus (*War* 3.401).

There is also the beast, the symbol for any foreign ruler, but at the final stage in the growth of the Book of Revelation, identified as Nero whose number was 666 (13.18). He was assassinated in 68 CE, but rumours arose the year after his death that he would return from the east (Tacitus, *Histories* 2.8–9). Nero was thus the beast who 'was and is not and is to ascend from the bottomless pit' (17.8). Originally this had been the expected fate of Azazel – to be bound in the bottomless pit and then released before the final conflict and judgement (as in 20.1–3, 7–10; see also on 11.7). Nero was also the king who had belonged to the seven and would return as the eighth (17.11).

The ten horns are another mystery; in Daniel's prophecy they are the ten horns of the fourth beast, the kings who rule during the fourth empire (Dan. 7.24). The ten horns of the beast could have been the ten male heirs of Herod the Great who were granted titles such as tetrarch, but never had any real royal power. Their power depended on the favour of Rome 'their power and authority was given over to the beast' (7.13). Of Herod the Great's male hiers, 1) Antipater governed for a while jointly with his father, but was hated by all the people for his part in the death of his half brothers (*Ant.* 17.1), 2) Alexander and 3) Aristobulus were the sons of Mariamne the Hasmonean princess but were murdered before they could exercise any royal function (*Ant.* 16.394), 4) Herod, son of the second Mariamne, was named heir after Antipater, but never ruled (*Ant.* 17.53, 78), 5) Herod Philip and 6) Herod Antipas were tetrarchs not kings (*War.* 2.94), 7) Archelaus was ethnarch in Judea (*War.* 2.94), 8) Herod, brother of Agrippa I, had no royal title in Palestine (*War.* 2.217), 9) Agrippa I was given the title king of the tetrarchy but had no real power (*Ant.* 18.237), and 10) Agrippa II was only seventeen when his father died and deemed too young to be king over such a large area. A procurator, Cuspius Fadus, was put in charge of Judea and the whole kingdom (*Ant.* 19.362–63). These could have been the ten 'kings' who had not received power, who gave their power and authority to the beast, and who devoured Jerusalem before the final destruction.

It is impossible to know exactly what the interpreters of the vision had in mind; they intended their remarks to be cryptic: 'This calls for a mind with wisdom' (17.9). Modern ingenuity can devise almost anything to fit the texts, but, as we know far less about contemporary events than did the original interpreter, we must speculate only within reasonable limits. What information might have been available to the interpreters of prophecy in Palestine at that time? They would have known of the Roman emperors who had had direct dealings with Palestine, and they would have known about the Herods. The confused state of the text in this chapter suggests that something could have been lost or removed in transmission, and it is very likely that there are several different interpretations side by side. What is important is that the plan for history was unfolding and that the prophets were watching and counting. The beast and his horns were God's agents, like Assyria (Isa. 10.5–6) and the seventy shepherds described in *1 Enoch* 89.59–64. If they did more than God had permitted by way of punishment for the city, they would themselves be punished, cf. 13.5–7, where the beast is permitted to make war on the saints.

The beast and the harlot are good examples of the layering in the Book of Revelation. Several versions of the same theme occur, and several interpretations of each theme. Until the final prohibition was added, the original themes were used and reused by successive generations: 'I warn everyone who hears the words of the prophecy of this book: if anyone adds to them, God will add to him the plagues described in this book, and if anyone takes away from the words of the book of this prophecy, God will take away his share in the tree of life and in the holy city, which are described in this book' (22.18–19). The very fact that additions and excisions were prohibited shows that this was happening to prophetic texts. The beasts and the harlot, insofar as they are overtly political themes, would have attracted the greatest number of new interpretations.

The Angel with Great Authority

The angel who appears to announce the fall of Babylon comes as a great light which 'makes the earth bright with his splendour'. No other angel in the Book of Revelation is described in this way, but both the Man in 1.12 and the Mighty Angel in 10.1 have a face which shines like the sun. The angel in 18.1 sheds light all around him and, like the Mighty Angel in 10.1, he comes down from heaven. The people who walked in darkness had seen a great light (Isa. 9.2, see p. 160). This light symbolism must have been part of the Zealot ideology. The leader of the second revolt took Bar Kochba, 'Son of a Star' as his *nom de guerre* (c.f. Matt. 2.2) and Eusebius wrote of him: 'He paraded himself as a luminary come down from heaven to shine on their misery' (*History* 4.6).

In the list of portents which heralded the destruction of Jerusalem, Josephus described a phenomenon in the temple which must have been this angel appearing:

Thus it was that the wretched people were deluded at that time by charlatans and pretended messengers of the deity; while they neither heeded nor believed the manifest portents that foretold the coming desolation ... So again, before the revolt and commotion that led to war, at the time when the people were assembling for the feast of unleavened bread, on the eighth of the month Xanthicus, at the ninth hour of the night, so brilliant a light shone round the altar and the sanctuary that it seemed to be broad daylight; and this continued for half an hour. By the inexperienced, this was regarded as a good omen, but by the sacred scribes it was at once interpreted in accordance with after events. (*War* 6.288–90)

This phenomenon was widely reported; Tacitus described the prodigies which preceded the fall of Jerusalem, including 'fire from the clouds which illuminated the temple' (*Histories* 5.13). This was interpreted, said Josephus, as a messenger of the deity, i.e. it was said to be an angel, and the sacred scribes said it was a portent of disaster. This is the angel in 18.1, coming from heaven, i.e. from the holy of holies, and standing by the altar of incense to announce the fall of the city. This is where Amos had seen the LORD, although his vision was probably set in Bethel: 'I saw the LORD standing beside the altar and he said: "Smite the capitals until the thresholds shake, and shatter them on the heads of the people; and what are left of them I will slay with the sword; not one of them shall flee away, not one of them shall escape"' (Amos 9.1). Zechariah, the father of John the Baptist, saw an angel of the LORD standing by the altar of incense (Luke 1.11). The angel was named as Gabriel (Luke 1.19), but all the archangels were believed to be aspects of the one LORD: 'the LORD our God is One LORD' (Deut. 6.4). The angel announced the birth of John who was to herald the Day of the LORD 'that we should be saved from our enemies and from the hands of all that hate us' (Luke 1.71).

In 18.1 the light in the sanctuary, the bright angel coming from heaven, announces the fall of the city. The words are drawn from Isaiah and are allusions rather than quotations. It is impossible to know exactly how someone in the first century CE would have understood Isaiah 21.9, the first source, but it gives an extraordinary glimpse of an ancient seer in Jerusalem, and the experience of the seer of Revelation may well have been similar. He stands in his watch tower day and night (the holy of holies was often described as a tower, see p. 63) and he waits for news (Isa. 21.8). He hears an unnamed speaker announce 'Fallen, fallen is Babylon', and he then reports *what he has heard from the LORD*. The one who spoke to the seer in the holy of holies must have been the LORD. Habakkuk had the same experience: 'I will take my stand to watch, and station myself on the tower, and look forth to see what he will say to me ... And the LORD answered me: "Write the vision; make it plain upon tablets ..."' (Hab. 2.1–2). The seer of Revelation experienced the great light in the temple and must have been one of the sacred scribes who interpreted correctly what it meant. The LORD had spoken to him, and he reported what he had heard about the imminent disaster. The voice of the angel then alludes to Isaiah 34.10–15, the description of a devastated city which had become the home of wild birds and evil spirits. All these disasters were predicted,

said Isaiah, in the 'Book of the LORD', the lost text which was probably
the framework for Revelation 4–11 (see p. 67).

The Voice from Heaven

Josephus, Tacitus and Eusebius all record the voice from heaven which
said, 'Come out of her, my people'. This again was the voice of the
LORD, '*my* people', and a voice from heaven would mean a voice in
the holy of holies. Josephus records such a voice at Pentecost in the year
that the light had been seen at Passover: 'At the feast which is called
Pentecost, the priests on entering the inner court of the temple by night,
... reported that they were conscious first of a commotion and a din and
after that a voice as of a host, "We are departing hence"' (*War*
6.299–300). Tacitus wrote of a superhuman voice which cried, 'The
gods are departing and then the mighty stir of their going was heard'
(*Histories* 5.13). In 18.4 the seer of Revelation heard the voice from
heaven ... presumably he was one of the priests ministering in the
temple at Pentecost ... and the voice of the LORD told his people to leave
the doomed city. This was the original interpretation of the portent; that
the Christians should leave the city. Eusebius knew of this oracle:
'Members of the Jerusalem church, by means of an oracle given by revelation to acceptable persons there, were ordered to leave the city before
the war began and to settle in a town in Perea called Pella. To Pella those
who believed in Christ migrated from Jerusalem' (*History* 3.5).

Since the first Christians believed that Jesus was the LORD, the God
of Israel, their prophecies will also have begun: 'Thus says the LORD',
and this is one of those prophecies: 'Come out of her, my people, lest
you take part in her sins'. Then, in the manner of the classical
prophecies, the heavenly LORD speaks of himself in the third person:
'God has remembered her iniquities'. Compare the style of Isaiah; in
one oracle there is: 'I am he that comforts you', and then 'you have
forgotten the LORD ... I am the LORD your God' (Isa. 51.12–15). The
whole of chapter 18 is in the style of the ancient prophets, not because
the first-century prophets consciously imitated their style, but because
they too were prophets like Isaiah, Jeremiah and Ezekiel. The letters to
the seven churches are proof that the Jesus, the risen LORD, continued
to speak through his prophets.

The words used in this first-century oracle were those of the old
prophecies; closest are the oracles of Jeremiah:

Flee from the midst of Babylon,
let every man save his life!
Be not cut off in her punishment,
for this is the time of the LORD's vengeance,
the requital he is rendering her. (Jer. 51.6)

The words of Isaiah which precede the much quoted Servant Song were
probably in their minds also:

Depart, depart, go out thence,
touch no unclean thing;
go out from the midst of her, purify yourselves,
you who bear the vessels of the LORD. (Isa. 52.11)

Fragments of text found at Qumran show how the Hebrew prophets were being interpreted at that time with every word being scrutinized for hidden meanings. The Teacher of Righteousness was the greatest interpreter of all: 'They, the men of violence and the breakers of the covenant will not believe when they hear all that [ ] the final generation from the priest [ ] God sent [ ] that he might interpret all the words of his servants the prophets, through whom he foretold all that would happen to his people and ...' (1QpHab II). Jesus had warned his disciples that they would one day have to flee to the mountains, at the time of the desolating sacrilege (Mark 13.14), and his prophecy is echoed here. Someone who had received the Spirit of Truth (John 16.12–15) declared that Jesus' prophecy was about to be fulfilled.

God remembered the iniquities of the city. When Jerusalem had been handed over to the care of the seventy shepherds in the time of Isaiah, the Great Holy One appointed heavenly scribes to record their doings. The recording angels noted any excesses and reminded the LORD of the state of his people. The earliest reference to this is Isaiah 62.6–7, where the Watching Ones are called upon to give the LORD no rest until he restores Jerusalem. In *1 Enoch* their role is clearly described: 'Observe and mark everything that the shepherds will do to the sheep ... record against every individual shepherd all the destruction he effects. And read out before me ... that I may have this as a testimony against them' (*1 En.* 89.61–63). In the earliest Enoch material, the archangels report the sins on the earth to the great Holy One and he commands them to punish the evil doers and renew the earth (*1 En.* 9 and 10). Here in 18.5 the sins of Jerusalem, heaped up to heaven, are brought to the LORD's remembrance and he decrees punishment.

The command to punish Jerusalem is given to the avenging angels, with bitter echoes of the words of hope given to the exiles in Babylon. Isaiah had said:

Speak tenderly to Jerusalem and cry to her
that her warfare is ended,
that her iniquity is pardoned,
that she has received from the LORD's hand
double for all her sins. (Isa. 40.2)

In 18.6 the avenging angels are told exactly the opposite, to repay Jerusalem 'double for all she has done'. This is an oracle of judgement against Jerusalem, just as Isaiah and Jeremiah had uttered against Babylon (Isa. 47; Jer. 50 and 51) and Ezekiel against Tyre (Ezek. 27 and 28). There are echoes of all of them, but this is a new oracle against Jerusalem, classic in its form, matching offence and punishment.

Compare again the style of Isaiah who, in response to King Hezekiah's prayer, had received a word from the LORD concerning the Assyrians:

Because you have raged against me
and your arrogance has come to my ears,
I will put my hook in your nose
my bit in your mouth,
and I will turn you back on the way
by which you came. (Isa. 37.29)

A prophet in first-century Jerusalem, doubtless in response to prayers and doubtless also in the temple, received a word from the LORD about the situation in Jerusalem:

As she glorified herself and played the wanton,
so give her a like measure of torment and mourning.
Since in her heart she says, 'A queen I sit ...'
so shall her plagues come in a single day ...
and she shall be burned with fire. (Rev. 18.7–8)

The fate of the harlot is the fate of the high priest in 597 BCE, when Jerusalem was attacked by the Babylonians. He is easily recognizable as the high priest, despite his thin disguise as the king of Tyre, the result of a later reuse of the oracle. In Ezekiel 28 the figure full of wisdom who walks in the garden of God among the stones of fire (Ezek. 28.12–14) wears the jewels of the high priest's breastplate, as can be seen by comparing the LXX of Ezekiel 28.13 and the LXX of Exodus 28.17–20, which differ from the Hebrew. They give two identical lists of twelve precious stones for the high priest's breastplate and in the same order. The translator of the LXX knew that the splendid figure who walked in the garden of God was the high priest. The punishment of the harlot city would be like his because she too had become proud through wealth and was filled with violence.

Your heart was proud because of your beauty;
you corrupted your wisdom for the sake of your splendour.
I cast you to the ground;
I exposed you before kings,
to feast their eyes on you.
By the multitude of your iniquities,
in the unrighteousness of your trade
you profaned your sanctuaries;
so I brought forth fire from the midst of you;
it consumed you,
and I turned you to ashes on the earth
in the sight of all who saw you.
All who know you among the peoples are appalled at you;
you have come to a dreadful end
and shall be no more for ever. (Ezek. 28.17–19)

Compare these lines about the fallen high priest with the fate of the harlot city in Revelation 18: her heart was proud, 'she glorified herself and played the wanton' (18.7); she was exposed to kings, 'the kings of the earth who committed fornication with her ... will see the smoke of her burning' (18.9); her unrighteous trading, 'the merchants who gained wealth from her will stand far off weeping' (18.15); fire came from the midst of her, 'they saw the smoke of her burning' (18.18); and all who knew her were appalled at her dreadful end, 'they threw dust on their heads, as they wept and mourned, crying out, "Alas, alas, for the great city"' (18.19). The ideas and the sequence are similar.

The Wealth of the Harlot

The kings of the earth who have been her lovers weep when they see the harlot burning (18.9). The merchants weep as they see their business destroyed (18.11–17). The shipmasters and sailors weep for their lost cargoes (18.17–19). Who are these people and where are they standing as they watch the harlot burn?

Strabo gave an account of Palestine as it was towards the end of the first century BCE, and of the sea port of Joppa he wrote: 'The Judeans have used this place as a sea port when they gone down as far as the sea' (*Geographies* 16.2.28). He also observed that Jerusalem was visible from Joppa, so the merchants and seamen of Joppa could have seen the city burning. This could have been an eye-witness account of how the wealthy merchants reacted to the disaster, perhaps from some of the refugees who had been allowed to leave Jerusalem (see p. 74). Joppa itself had been razed to the ground during the war and a garrison had been left there (*War* 3.427), but its natural harbour would have been the nearest port for anyone from Jerusalem who wanted to leave the country, perhaps to go to Asia Minor (see p. 80).

Qumran materials give a glimpse of contemporary Jerusalem. The city is compared to Nineveh, and the text 'Nineveh is laid waste; who shall grieve over her?' (Nahum 3.7), is said to refer to those 'who seek smooth things, whose counsel shall perish, and whose congregation shall be dispersed' (4Q169 III). Two texts dating from the end of the first century BCE (but the originals could be older), show that the city and her priests were both wealthy and corrupt. A commentary on Nahum tells of 'the wealth which [ ] of Jerusalem have [ ] ...' (4Q169 I). A commentary on Habakkuk is better preserved and it interprets the passage which can be translated, 'the arrogant man seizes wealth without halting' (Hab. 2.5–6) as a reference to the Wicked Priest: 'When he ruled over Israel his heart became proud, and he forsook God, and betrayed the precepts for the sake of riches. He robbed and amassed the riches of the men of violence who rebelled against God, and he took the wealth of the peoples, heaping sinful iniquity upon himself' (1QpHab VIII). Of the verse, 'Because you have plundered many nations, all the remnant of the peoples shall plunder you' (Hab. 2.8) it says: 'Interpreted this concerns the last priests of Jerusalem, who shall amass money and wealth by plundering the peoples. But in the last days, their riches and booty shall be delivered into the hands of the army of the Kittim ...' (1QpHab IX) Josephus described the high priest Ananias (the Annas who had Jesus arrested, John 18.13) as 'a great hoarder up of money ... he also had servants who were very wicked ... and went to the threshing floors and took away the tithes that belonged to the priests by violence ... the other high priests acted in like manner' (*Ant.* 20.207).

The leaders in Jerusalem were described as 'scoffers, seekers of smooth things'. The Wicked Priest 'lived in the ways of abominations and every unclean defilement' (1QpHab VIII), like the harlot with her cup full of abominations and impurities. The Spouter of Lies 'led many astray that he might build his city of vanity with blood' (1QpHab X). There was a priest 'whose ignominy was greater than his glory, destined to drink the cup of the wrath of God' (1QpHab XI). The interpretation of 'the violence done to Lebanon shall overwhelm you ... because of the blood of men and the violence done to the land' (Hab. 2.17) is: 'This saying concerns the Wicked Priest ... As he himself plotted the destruction of the poor, so will God condemn him to destruction ... The city is Jerusalem where the Wicked Priest committed abominable deeds and defiled the temple of God. The violence done to the land: these are the cities of Judah where he robbed the poor of their possessions' (1QpHab XII). Nobody knows who first interpreted the prophecies in that way, or when, but the situation they described is exactly that of the harlot city.

There are also texts in *1 Enoch* which warn of judgement on the rich and corrupt. Although this had been a theme of the prophets since the time of Amos, and the passages in question draw freely on Amos and Isaiah, it is likely that these chapters of *1 Enoch* were written in the first century BCE when the words of Amos and Isaiah were thought to speak directly to that situation: 'Woe to those who build their houses with sin; for from their foundations they shall be overthrown. Woe to you, ye rich, for you have trusted in your riches and from your riches shall you depart' (*1 En.* 94.7–8). 'Woe to you, ye sinners, for your riches make you appear like the righteous ... Woe to you who devour the finest of the wheat' (*1 En.* 96.4–5). 'And in those days the prayer of the righteous shall reach unto the LORD, and for you the days of your judgement shall come' (*1 En.* 97.5).

The words of Jesus address this situation; he contrasted the rich and well-fed with those who would have a reward in heaven (Luke 6.20–26). He spoke of a fool who built yet bigger barns to store his grain surplus (Luke 12.16–20); his anger at the temple, which led to his arrest by the temple authorities, focused on its trading activities. He, too, foresaw that it was the wealth of the temple that would bring its ruin:

And he drew near [to Jerusalem] and saw the city and wept over it, saying, 'Would that even today you knew the things that made for peace! But now they are hid from your eyes. For the days shall come upon you when your enemies will cast up a bank about you and surround you, and hem you in on every side, and dash you to the ground, you and your children within you, and they will not leave one stone upon another in you; because you did not know the time of your visitation.' And he entered the temple and began to drive out those who sold, saying to them, 'It is written, "My house shall be a house of prayer"; but you have made it a den of robbers.' And he was teaching daily in the temple. The chief priests and the scribes and the principal men of the people sought to destroy him ... (Luke 19.41–47)

When Christian prophets spoke against the wealth of the harlot city, they were echoing the words of Jesus himself. This is the situation depicted by 'Isaiah' (see pp. 193–4), who described the corruption in Jerusalem in the years before the revolt. As the time of the Parousia drew near, there would be wicked elders and shepherds, people who loved office but lacked wisdom, and who exchanged the glorious robes of the saints for the robes of those who love money. There would be few true prophets and many would be led by the spirit of error into vainglory and love of money (*Asc. Isa.* 3.21–31). The letter of James, too, warned against the rich (Jas 5.1–6).

The situation in Judea in the first century CE is well documented in the works of Josephus. Even allowing for his pro-Roman stance, these depict a society riven with social and economic problems. After the Romans had assumed direct rule of Judea in 6 CE, they adopted their usual practice of employing the indigenous aristocracy to implement their rule. Most of these, including the high priests, had owed their money and position to the favour of Herod and to retain their power they needed the favour of Rome. Reflecting on what led up to the siege of Masada in 73 CE, Josephus wrote of 'men of power oppressing the multitude and the multitude earnestly labouring to destroy the men of power. The one part were desirous of tyrannizing over others; and the rest of offering violence to others and of plundering such as were richer than themselves' (*War* 7.261–62).

The centre of this discontent was Jerusalem itself, which Josephus describes as 'supreme, and presiding over the neighbouring country as the head does over the body' (*War* 3.54). It was the home of the wealthy aristocrats – archaeologists have discovered huge private houses in the city – and Herod and his family had used the wealth accumulated elsewhere in the kingdom to enrich the capital. It profited from the huge numbers of pilgrims who brought their offerings and taxes to the temple and then spent money in the city. The pious Tobit described his regular trips from Nineveh to Jerusalem; although purporting to describe the eighth century BCE it probably reflect conditions in the second century BCE: 'Taking the first fruits and tithes of my produce and the first shearings, I would give these to the priests, the sons of Aaron, at the altar. Of all my produce I would give a tenth to the sons of Levi who ministered in Jerusalem; a second tenth I would sell and I would go and spend the proceeds each year in Jerusalem; and the third tenth I would give to those to whom it was my duty' (*Tobit* 1.6–8).

The religious obligation of charity meant that many people eked out an existence in the city dependent on the alms given by pilgrims and on the riches of those they grew to hate, as witnessed by Jesus' parable of the rich man and Lazarus (Luke 16.19–31). Drought and famine in the 40s and early 60s had distorted the price of grain, and many peasants ran into debt, which must have heightened the fervour for the imminent tenth Jubilee. After burning the houses of the king and the high priest, the first act of the rebels in Jerusalem when the revolt began was to burn all the records of debts (*War* 2.427). As the war progressed, the rebels in the city burnt down the houses where corn was being stored, 'sufficient for a siege of many years' (*War* 5.25), thus precipitating famine in the city. Presumably these were the houses of merchants who had hoped to sell the corn at high prices.

The troubles were deep-rooted. When Herod the Great died in 4 BCE, an embassy of Jews had travelled to Rome to beg Caesar for a more reasonable ruler:

Herod ... was indeed in name a king but he had taken to himself an uncontrollable authority ... and had made use of that authority for the destruction of the Jews ... When he took the kingdom it was in an extraordinary flourishing condition but he had filled the nation with the utmost degree of poverty ... Though their nation had passed through many subversions and alterations of government, their history gave no account of any calamity they had ever been under that could be compared with this which Herod had had brought upon their nation. (*Ant.* 17.304, 311)

They were rewarded with Herod's son Archelaus whom the Romans deposed ten years later.

The harlot city prospered. She imported 'gold, silver, jewels and pearls, fine linen, purple, silk and scarlet, all kinds of scented wood, all articles of ivory, all articles of costly wood, bronze, iron and marble, cinnamon, spice, incense, myrrh, frankincense, wine, oil, fine flour and wheat, cattle and sheep, horse and chariots, and slaves, that is, human souls' (18.12–13). The list of merchandise may have been modelled on Ezekiel's list of the goods of Tyre, destroyed with the city which was also called a harlot (Isa. 23.16–17; Ezek. 27.12–36). Such luxury goods, however, would have been common to all the great cities of the Roman empire and cannot in themselves identify the city, as, for example, Rome. Most of the merchandise could have been destined for Jerusalem and even for the temple itself. No unclean animals are mentioned: no mules, even though they are included in the imports of Tyre, and no pigs, even though live pigs were imported into Rome for food. Cattle and sheep could be for sacrifices.

Of the goods which could not have been destined for the temple, there were horses, perhaps for the aristocracy and the military, but certainly for chariot racing. Herod built a theatre in Jerusalem and an amphitheatre nearby, where games and chariot races were held 'contrary to the Jewish customs' (*Ant.* 15.268). The chariots mentioned among the harlot's imports are not racing chariots, but the four-wheeled vehicles used for transport, again, perhaps for the Romanized aristocracy. Iron tools were forbidden in the temple, but the eastern gate of the inner court was reinforced with iron (*War* 6.293) and iron would have been necessary for the manufacture of weapons for the Roman soldiers. The articles of scented wood were probably furniture made of citron wood, a fashionable status symbol at this time and destined for Herod's palaces (*Ant.* 16.136–45; *War* 5.161–83). It is possible that the scented wood was aloes wood used for temple harps (see p. 261).

Slaves were bought and sold in Jerusalem. Jews could be sold if they were convicted of theft and unable to make restitution, but they could only be enslaved for a maximum of six years and only sold to a Jewish master. Or a male Jew could sell himself if hopelessly in debt, and then it became his family's responsibility to redeem him. A young woman could also be sold to a Jew as a wife. Herod, however, violated these customs by selling Jews convicted of theft to foreigners who would not have observed the Jewish law of release in the Sabbath year (Deut 15.12). This outraged the Jews (*Ant.* 16.1–2). Gentiles could also be bought and sold, but they fetched a higher price, since they did not have to be set free in the Sabbath year (Lev. 25.45–46). The high priest's slave Malchus, who was wounded by Peter when Jesus was arrested (John 18.10), was probably a Gentile; his name suggests he was a Nabatean.

Pearls and silk are not mentioned in connection with the temple, but the heavenly temple had gates of pearl (21.21) which indicates a place for pearls in temple symbolism even though the evidence has not survived. Trade in pearls was known in Palestine; Jesus told a parable about a pearl merchant (Matt. 13.45–46). Silk, too, was associated with the wealth of Jerusalem. Ezekiel described the unfaithful Jerusalem whom the Lord clothed in fine linen and silk (Ezek. 16.10), and the two fabrics are mentioned together in a lament over the fallen city, written towards the end of the first century CE:

Blessed is he who was not born,
or who was born and died.
But we, the living, woe to us,
because we have seen those afflictions of Zion,
and that which has befallen Jerusalem . . .
And you, virgins who spin fine linen,
and silk with gold of Ophir,
make haste and take all things and cast them into the fire
so that it may carry them to him who made them. (2 *Bar.* 10.6, 7, 19)

Ivory is not mentioned in the Scriptures in connection with the temple, but a small carved ivory knob from a temple servant's staff has been found.

All the other goods were used for the temple and its cult: in Herod's rebuilt temple, gold and silver had been used to cover the doors and gates, jewels were part of the high priest's regalia, linen, purple and scarlet were used for the vestments and the temple curtains (which Josephus described as 'Babylonian tapestry', *War* 5.212); costly wood could well have described the cedar imported for the ceiling (*War* 5.191); bronze was used for vessels used in the temple courtyard (1 Kgs 7.45; those taken into the temple were made of gold, 1 Kgs 7.48–50); marble was imported by Herod for the temple walls (*War* 5.190–91); the aromatics were ingredients of the various incenses: thirteen spices were blended together (*War* 5.218); wine, oil, fine flour, wheat, cattle and sheep all were used in the temple offerings (Lev. 1.2; 2.2; 2.14; *Ben Sira* 50.15).

Some idea of the wealth of the temple can be gleaned from Josephus' account of the looting; the detail is very similar to the list of the harlot's wealth:

They also burnt down the treasury chambers, in which was an immense quantity of money and an immense number of garments and other precious goods there deposited; and ... there it was that the entire riches of the Jews were heaped up together, while the rich people had there built themselves chambers. (*War* 6.282)

... one of the priests ... came out of the temple and delivered from the wall of the holy house two candlesticks like those that lay in the holy house, with tables and cisterns and vials all made of solid gold, and very heavy. He also delivered to him the veils and the garments with the precious stones and a great number of other precious vessels that belonged to their sacred worship. The treasurer of the temple also, whose name was Phineas, was seized on and showed Titus the coats and girdles of the priests, with a great quantity of purple and scarlet, which was there deposited for the use of the veil, as also a great deal of cinnamon and cassia with a large quantity of other sweet spices which used to be mixed together and offered as incense to God every day. (*War* 6.388–90)

Josephus records that some precious objects were concealed underground (*War* 6.432) and these, too, were looted.

The Copper Scroll (3Q15) is a list of huge amounts of treasure, some concealed in Jerusalem, some concealed in places to the east of the city. So vast are the sums described – it is estimated that there were 65 tons of silver and 26 tons of gold – that some scholars have dismissed it as a work of fiction. Others have suggested that the treasure was real because the deposits are so carefully listed and their location so accurately described. The question is: What treasure might it have been? It could have been collected to finance the rebuilding of the temple, or to support the second revolt in 135 CE. The most likely source, though, would have been the temple, especially as the treasure listed includes not only huge quantities of gold and silver but also sandalwood and priestly garments, offering vessels for cedar, resin and aloes, libation vessels, scrolls, money offerings and goods devoted to the temple.

After the Great Tribulation in the reign of Nero, John had received a prophecy about the imminent destruction of the temple (see p. 187).

Josephus knew of it and so it must have been public knowledge. This is when the temple treasure was hidden, perhaps removed from the city through the underground passages which Josephus described, through which some Zealots were able to escape during the siege (*War* 7.215).

Rejoicing in Heaven

Judgement is given against the great city, and a Mighty Angel, the LORD, throws a great stone into the sea. This is an acted prophecy like those described in the Hebrew Scriptures: Jeremiah broke a jar as he pronounced the LORD's judgement on Jerusalem (Jer. 19.11) and when he wrote the oracles of doom against Babylon, he asked Seraiah, one of King Zedekiah's servants, to take the book to Babylon:

> When you come to Babylon, see that you read all these words, and say, 'O LORD, thou hast said concerning this place that thou wilt cut it off, so that nothing shall dwell in it, neither man nor beast, and it shall be desolate for ever.' When you finish reading this book, bind a stone to it, and cast it into the midst of the Euphrates, and say, 'Thus shall Babylon sink, to rise no more, because of the evil I am bringing upon her.' (Jer. 51.61–64)

In the same way, the stone which the angel threw into the sea both symbolized the fall of the city and brought it about. Jeremiah recorded a similar oracle against Babylon:

> Behold I am against you, O destroying mountain, says the LORD,
> which destroys the whole earth;
> I will stretch out my hand against you,
> and roll you down from the crags,
> and make you a burnt mountain. (Jer. 51.25)

The Book of Lamentations described the fall of Jerusalem to the Babylonians in similar words: 'He [the LORD] has cast down from heaven to earth the splendour of Israel' (Lam. 2.1).

The angel's picture of the stricken city, with no music, no markets, no sounds of domestic life, recalls the ancient prophets' predictions for Jerusalem: Isaiah foresaw the city of chaos – his name for Jerusalem – without music and mirth (Isa. 24.8–9), and Jeremiah pronounced an oracle of doom from the LORD: 'And I will make to cease from the cities of Judah and from the streets of Jerusalem the voice of mirth and the voice of gladness, the voice of the bridegroom and the voice of the bride; for the land shall become a waste' (Jer. 7.34). The angel also speaks of the craftsmen and the merchants, a reference to the harlot's wealth, and of her sorcery, a reference, no doubt, to the infamous activities of Jewish magicians at that time (Acts 13.6 c.f. Rev. 21.8 and Rev. 22.15, no sorcerers in the heavenly Jerusalem).

The final reason for her punishment was 'the blood that had been shed within her walls'. Jesus had warned the scribes and Pharisees in Jerusalem that they were the sons of those who murdered the prophets and that their generation would be called to account: 'that upon you may come all the righteous blood shed on earth, from the blood of innocent Abel to the blood of Zechariah the son of Barachiah, whom you murdered between the sanctuary and the altar. Truly I say to you, all this will come upon this generation' (Matt. 23.35–36). The prophecies of Habakkuk foretold that the Spouter of Lies would 'build his city of vanity with blood', and that the city, where he did 'abominable deeds and defiled the temple', would meet a violent end (1QpHab X, XII). Josephus records many scenes of bloodshed in Jerusalem: Archelaus had some 3000 people killed after protesters had removed the golden image of an eagle from the temple gate (*War* 2.4–14); Pontius Pilate used temple funds to improve the city's water supply, and had the protesters killed (*War* 2.175–77); Gessius Florus, another Roman governor, took seventeen talents from the temple treasury and the ensuing protest was quelled with the slaughter of 3600 people (*War* 2.293–308). Jesus spoke of the Galileans, presumably in the temple, whose blood Pilate had mingled with their sacrifices (Luke 13.1).

With the harlot's judgement, God has 'avenged on her the blood of his servants' (19.2), showing that this judgement was the LORD returning to complete the Great Atonement, inaugurated by the sacrifice of the crucifixion. The Great High Priest had entered the holy of holies, heaven, carrying his own blood (the vision of the sacrificed Lamb in Rev. 5). After his enthronement he prepared to emerge again from the sanctuary and complete the atonement, purging the earth of evil and renewing the creation. This is clear in the longer version of Deuteronomy 32.43 (4QDeut^q) which differs from the MT (see p. 35). The *Assumption of Moses* 10, an expansion of this text, shows that the avenger was the LORD, the heavenly high priest who, in the Book of Revelation, has already received the incense of high priesthood (8.3) and emerged from the holy of holies in a cloud of incense (10.1). He is the Anointed One who has stayed in the holy of holies, in heaven, until the time appointed for the fulfilment of the prophecies and the renewal of the earth (Acts 3.18–21). The Letter to the Hebrews, which uses the imagery of the high priest more than any other New Testament writing, also uses the longer text of Deuteronomy 32.43 to describe the coming of Jesus: 'When he brings the first born into the world he says, "Let all God's angels worship him" ' (Heb. 1.6). The judgement of the harlot is the expected judgement for the death of the servants of God.

There may be another element in the destruction. Daniel had prophesied the destruction of Jerusalem, 'the decreed end poured out on the desolator' (Dan. 9.27), and this was to mark the Great Atonement, the fulfilment of the prophecies and visions, and the coming of everlasting righteousness (Dan. 9.24). It was to happen 490 years, ten jubilees, after the rebuilding of the city (see pp. 48–9) and during those years Jerusalem was under a curse, *herem* (see pp. 356–9). Jericho had been put under the *herem*, 'devoted to the LORD for destruction' (Josh.

6.17), and the burning of Jerusalem may have been seen as fulfilling this *ḥerem*. In the millennium kingdom which replaced the harlot, the curse was no more (22.3).

The multitude in heaven rejoice that their prayers have been answered, and they praise the LORD, exactly the scene in *1 Enoch* when the Man is enthroned:

> In those days shall have ascended the prayer of the righteous,
> and the blood of the righteous one from the earth before the LORD of Spirits.
> In those days the holy ones who dwell in the heavens
> shall unite with one voice . . .
> And give thanks and bless the name of the LORD of Spirits
> On behalf of the blood of the righteous ones that has been shed.
> That the prayer of the righteous
> may not be in vain before the LORD of Spirits.
> That judgement may be done unto them
> that they may not have to suffer for ever. (*1 En.* 47.1–2)

The voice from the throne commands the host of heaven to worship (19.5), just as in Deuteronomy 32.43 the angels are commanded to worship as the LORD emerges from heaven to avenge the blood of his servants. The sequence resumes at 19.11, when the heavenly warrior emerges from heaven, followed by his army of angels.

As the city burns, the host of heaven sing songs of praise to the LORD: 'Hallelujah! Salvation and glory and power belong to our God' (19.1); 'Hallelujah! The smoke from her goes up for ever and ever' (19.3); 'Amen! Hallelujah' (19.4); 'Hallelujah! For the LORD our God the Almighty reigns' (19.6), the only Hallelujahs in the Book of Revelation. The burning city is a great sacrifice, and the heavenly host sing the psalms that accompany a burnt offering. Amos spoke of songs and harps at the time of the offerings (Amos 5.23) and several psalms mention songs to accompany the sacrifice, e.g. Psalm 26.6–7 or Psalm 27.6. The Chronicler describes such a sacrifice in the time of Hezekiah when the desecrated temple had been cleansed and renewed:

> Then Hezekiah commanded that the burnt offering be offered on the altar. And when the burnt offering began, the song to the LORD began also, and the trumpets accompanied by the instruments of David, king of Israel. The whole assembly worshipped, and the singers sang, and the trumpets sounded; all this continued until the burnt offering was finished. (2 Chron. 29.27–28)

Fragments of heavenly hymns to accompany the Sabbath burnt offerings have been found among the Qumran material, evidence that sacrifices were still accompanied by songs at the end of the second temple period. These Songs of the Sabbath Sacrifice (4Q 400–407; 11Q 5–6) depict the worship of the angels in heaven, and the better preserved pieces enable us to see how closely their style resembles that of the hymns in the Book of Revelation: 'A psalm of praise by the tongue of the [ ] to the Warrior'; 'the voice of blessing from the chiefs of his sanctuary'; 'the King of Kings of all the eternal councils'; 'praises of exaltation for the king of glory' (4Q403); 'the cherubim prostrate themselves before him and bless. As they rise ... there is a roar of praise'; 'rivers of light ... the appearance of flames of fire' (4Q405).

The multitude in the heavenly sanctuary sang their praises, 'like the sound of many waters and like the sound of mighty thunderpeals' (19.6), and the temple burned. Josephus was there and recorded what he saw:

> The soldiers put fire to the gates, and the silver that was over them quickly carried the flames to the wood that was within it, whence it spread itself all on the sudden and caught hold of the cloisters ... As the flames went upwards, the Jews made a great clamour, such as so mighty as affliction required, and ran together to prevent it; and now they spared not their lives any longer nor suffered any thing to restrain their force, since that holy house was perishing ... (*War* 6.232, 253)

When the survivors reflected on the disaster, they could not believe it was a triumph for their enemies. The LORD, they said, had permitted the Romans to punish the evil city, just as the beast from the sea had been permitted to rage for a certain time. Writing as though describing the destruction of Jerusalem in 586 BCE, 'Baruch' wrote: 'Suddenly a strong spirit lifted me up and carried me above the wall of Jerusalem. And I saw, and behold, there were standing four angels at the four corners of the city, each of them with a burning torch in his hands'. The voice from heaven tells them to wait until the precious vessels have been removed from the temple and hidden: 'Now destroy the walls and overthrow them to their foundations so that the enemies do not boast and say, "We have overthrown the wall of Zion and we have burnt down the place of the mighty God"' (2 *Bar.* 6.3–4, 7.1).

Thus far, the Book of Revelation has been a reflection on history; the remaining chapters depict the future. It was not, however, the history of Jerusalem recorded in the Hebrew Scriptures. There had been other voices (Isa. 65.15). Those who preserved the Enoch traditions believed that the city's troubles began when the temple was 'reformed' (see p. 16). When the people abandoned the old ways and lost their vision (see p. 208), the LORD 'forsook the house and the tower' (1 *En.* 89.56) and handed his people over to foreign rulers – the seventy shepherds (see p. 226). Freedom from these shepherds, i.e. independence ('the Kingdom restored to Israel', Acts 1.6) entailed restoring the ancient temple cult. The vision of the future which forms the remaining chapters of Revelation depicts wisdom returning to her city and the priests returning to the Garden of Eden.

THE WARRIOR PRIEST

Then I saw heaven opened, and behold, a white horse! He who sat upon it is called Faithful and True, and in righteousness he judges and makes war. His eyes are like a flame of fire, and on his head are many diadems; and he has a name inscribed which no one knows but himself. He is clad in a robe sprinkled with blood, and the name by which he is called is The Word of God. And the armies of heaven, arrayed in fine linen, white and pure, followed him on white horses. From his mouth issues a sharp sword with which to smite the nations, and he will rule them with a rod of iron; he will tread the wine press of the fury of the wrath of God the Almighty. On his robe and on his thigh he has a name inscribed, King of kings and LORD of lords. (Rev. 19.11–16)

A portent had been seen in the sky a few days after Passover in 70 CE: 'Before sunset throughout all parts of the country, chariots were seen in the air and armed battalions hurtling through the clouds and encompassing the cities' (*War* 6.299). Josephus said this would have been thought unbelievable, but for the evidence of so many eyewitnesses and the calamities that followed. Tacitus also reported it: 'Contending hosts were seen meeting in the skies, arms flashed and suddenly the temple was illuminated with fire from the clouds' (*Histories* 5.13). It was the LORD appearing with his host, and 19.11–16 was the triumphant interpretation of this celestial sign, confirming to those besieged in Jerusalem that the summer of 70 CE was the last days before the end of the long-overdue tenth Jubilee.

In 14.1–5 there had been a glimpse of the Lamb on Zion with a host of warriors who followed him wherever he went. This was the preface to one account of the events, one interpretation of the portents seen in Jerusalem which culminated in the vision of the wine press. 19.11–16 is another sequence of prophecies following the portent of the warriors. Both were proclaiming the fulfilment of Isaiah's prophecy: 'The LORD of hosts will come down to fight upon Mount Zion and upon its hill. Like birds hovering, so the LORD of Hosts will protect Jerusalem; he will protect and deliver it, he will spare and rescue it' (Isa. 31.4–5). The host glimpsed on Mount Zion, 144,000 pure warriors, were coming down on white horses to fight against the enemies of Jerusalem.

The Blessing for the Prince of the Congregation described the Prince as a warrior, establishing the kingdom of his people, ravaging the earth with his sceptre and bringing death to the ungodly with the breath of his lips: 'May he make your horns of iron and your hooves of bronze, may you toss like a young bull . . .' (1QSb V). There is no way of knowing if this was a blessing for a historical figure. Like the vivid descriptions of warfare in the War Scroll, it could be a glimpse of the real hopes and aspirations of the time.

'Isaiah' (see pp. 193–4) knew that the armies of heaven were the first resurrected who would come on the Day of the LORD. 'With the LORD will come those whose spirits are clothed, they will descend and be present in the world, and the LORD will strengthen those who are found in the body, together with the saints in the robes of the saints' (*Asc. Isa.* 4.16).

The Divine Warrior

One of the oldest and most enduring images of the LORD was as the heavenly warrior. 'The LORD is a man of war', sang Moses, in his first Song, when Israel had come safely through the sea at the Exodus (Exod. 15.3). 'The LORD marched forth from Seir' to fight against the Canaanites (Judg. 5.4). Joshua saw a man with a drawn sword who was the commander of the army of the LORD. This must have been the LORD because Joshua worshipped him, and was told to take off his shoes as the place was holy (Josh. 5.14). Sometimes the LORD came from Sinai (Judg. 5.5), sometimes he rode on the clouds (Ps. 68.4), sometimes he emerged from the holy of holies (Isa. 26.21) which means he emerged from heaven. A terrifying passage in Habakkuk describes the LORD coming as the heavenly warrior to rescue his people and his Anointed One:

Thou didst bestride the earth in fury,
    thou didst trample the nations in anger.
Thou wentest forth for the salvation of thy people,
    for the salvation of thy anointed. (Hab. 3.12–13)

With pestilence and plague as his attendants, he 'measures' the earth and scatters the mountains, crushes the wicked and pierces his warriors. Always he comes to rescue his people, either in time of war, or from the hands of their oppressors.

Isaiah described the LORD coming to punish the inhabitants of the earth for their iniquity, in particular for all the blood that had been shed on the earth (Isa. 26.21) and he gave several pictures of the heavenly warrior: 'The LORD goes forth like a mighty man, like a man of war he stirs up his fury' (Isa. 42.13). He saw there was no justice for his people and put on his armour to redeem Zion (Isa. 59.15–20). His blood-spattered garments were compared to those of wine makers, and the wine press became an image of his anger on the day of vengeance and redemption (Isa. 63.1–6).

Most significant of all the warrior texts is the second Song of Moses and especially the fragment of a longer text found at Qumran. The LORD raises his hand to heaven and whets the lightning of his sword; then 'he avenges the blood of his sons and atones the land of his people' (Deut. 32.41, 43). As he emerges from heaven, the angels are commanded to worship him (see on 10.5–7). This text is important for two reasons: first because it shows that the warrior emerged on the Day of Atonement which was also the Day of the LORD, and second, because the text was used by the first Christians to describe Jesus (Heb. 1.6: 'Let all God's angels worship him', see p. 299). The Hebrews to whom this was written knew from their Scriptures that the warrior priest rode out of heaven, and in the letter they were reminded that the warrior was Jesus.

The heavenly warrior was to appear with his angel host. When he blessed Israel, Moses spoke of 'the LORD coming with ten thousands of holy ones' on the day he became king (Deut. 33.2, 5). These were the hosts which gave the ancient title 'the LORD of hosts' and they were often depicted as stars. They were the host who protected Elisha from the army of the king of Syria (2 Kgs 6.17), the host for whom Joel prayed: 'Bring down thy warriors, O LORD' (Joel 3.11). Zechariah prophesied a similar protection for Jerusalem, when the nations gathered against the city to attack and to plunder: 'Then the LORD will go forth and fight against those nations ... the LORD your God will come and all the holy ones with him' (Zech. 14.3, 5).

Heavenly warriors had appeared to protect Jerusalem from the tyranny of Antiochus Epiphanes in the years which preceded the Maccabean revolt in 167 BCE. Heliodorus was sent by Antiochus Epiphanes to rob the temple of its treasures, but a horseman wearing golden armour appeared before him and barred his way to the treasury. Heliodorus was struck down by the horse's hooves and then beaten back by the heavenly warrior's two attendants: 'And the temple, which a little while before was full of fear and disturbance, was filled with joy and gladness now that the Almighty LORD had appeared' (2 Macc. 3.22–30). When Antiochus invaded Egypt, there were apparitions of golden horsemen in the sky over Jerusalem for almost forty days: 'troops of horsemen drawn up ... the massing of spears, the hurling of missiles, the flash of golden trappings and armour of all sorts' (2 Macc. 5.2–4). The LORD himself was the heavenly warrior who emerged in time of crisis to protect his city.

The War Scroll from Qumran shows how vivid was this expectation of divine intervention in the first century CE. The human community had to observe the strictest rules of purity in preparation for fighting alongside the heavenly host (see on 14.4–5). The army was to be led by seven angel priests, dressed in white linen and battle vestments, with priestly turbans on their heads. The presence of the heavenly host assured the earthly warriors of victory, the battle on earth against the enemies of Israel being also the heavenly battle against Satan and his horde. This was the day appointed by God for the final defeat of wickedness:

This is the Day appointed by Him for the defeat and overthrow of the Prince of the Kingdom of Wickedness and he will send succour to the company of his redeemed by the might of the princely angel of the kingdom of Michael ... He will raise up the kingdom of Michael in the midst of the gods and the realm of Israel in the midst of all flesh. (1QM XVII)

'The war of the heavenly warriors', according to their hymn writer, 'would scourge the earth' and not end before the appointed destruction was complete (1QH XI, formerly III). The contemporary *Psalms of Solomon* describe the expected warrior as a king from the house of David to be revealed at the appointed time. He was to purge Jerusalem of Gentiles, smash the arrogance of sinners with an iron rod (Ps. 2.9) and destroy them with the word of his mouth before gathering in the holy people (*Pss Sol.* 17.21–24). The Benedictus, which Luke attributes to Zechariah the priest, shows that *the hope of a divine warrior to intervene and rescue his people was at the heart of the Christian messianic proclamation.* 'That we should be saved from our enemies, and from the hands of all that hate us ... that we being delivered from our enemies, might serve him without fear' (Luke 1.71, 74).

The War Scroll has various names for the heavenly warrior; he is the LORD, the King of Glory (1QM XII) but also the Prince of Light (1QM XIII) and angel prince Michael (1QM XVII). There is a problem about the names of the heavenly beings in the second temple period. The Second Isaiah had declared Israel's LORD to be no other than the High God El Elyon, and thus established belief in only one God, which is usually associated with the religion of the Hebrew Scriptures. The older faith of Israel, however, had not been monotheistic in that sense. It had recognized the existence of many divine beings who were the sons of El Elyon, God Most High (see p. 35). The study of the Israel's ancient angels is complicated by the poor state of many of the older texts, but from time to time they can be glimpsed. In texts such as the War Scroll, the double naming is quite clear; the guardian of Israel has his original name, the LORD, the King of Glory (1QM XII), but also his newer name, Michael, the guardian angel of Israel (1QM XVII). The same double naming appears in the Book of Revelation: the heavenly warrior is Michael, fighting with his angels against the dragon (12.7–9), but he is also the Servant/Lamb, the LORD of lords and King of kings, who conquers the ten kings and the beast (17.12–14), and The Word of God, King of kings and LORD of lords, who wages war on the beast and his armies (19.11–21).

The rider of the white horse is named Faithful and True (19.11), cf. the descriptions of the heavenly LORD in 1.5, 'the faithful witness'; 3.7, 'the true one'; 3.14 'the faithful and true witness'. He judges in righteousness, makes war, smites the nations with a rod of iron and treads the wine press of wrath. In his mouth is a sharp sword. In the Hebrew Scriptures, all these were descriptions of the LORD, the King. Jeremiah had spoken of the LORD as 'the true and faithful witness' (Jer. 42.5); the mouth of the Servant was 'like a sharp sword' (Isa. 49.2); the LORD had promised that the Davidic kings would 'break the nations with a rod of iron' (Ps. 2.9), and judge in right-eousness (Isa. 11.4). Revelation 19.15 gives the same curious translation of Psalm 2.9 as does the LXX, namely, 'he will shepherd the nations with a rod of iron'. Instead of 'break', they have 'shepherd'. This is best explained by the fact that some forms of the Hebrew verb 'to shepherd', *r'h* are identical to those of the verb 'to break', *r* ", so that both here and in 12.5 the one who was 'to break' with an iron rod has become 'a shepherd' with an iron rod.

It is possible that the seer himself combined all these images of the warrior, but more likely that he had in mind the messianic prophecy of Isaiah in the Targum; a branch from Jesse would be given the sevenfold spirit (see on 5.6) to 'judge with righteousness and smite the earth with the rod of his mouth' (Isa. 11.4). The Targum makes significant additions to the biblical text, and so includes all the warrior motifs which appear in 19.11–16. 'Behold the master of the world, the LORD of hosts, casts slaughter on his armies as grapes are trodden in the press' (*T. Isa.* 10.33); 'and a king shall come forth from the sons of Jesse and the Messiah from the sons of his sons' (*T. Isa.* 11.1). 'In truth he will judge the poor and reprove with *faithfulness for* the needy of the people; he shall strike the sinners of the land with the command of his mouth' (*T. Isa.* 11.4). 'He will raise an ensign for the peoples' (*T. Isa.* 11.12).

The warrior has his name – King of kings and LORD of lords – written on his robe and, apparently, on this thigh (19.16). This latter has always been a puzzle, and several solutions have been proposed, for example, that his horse had a tattoo on his leg (!). The most likely explanation is that an Aramaic word has been misread by the person who translated the book into Greek. The word for leg or foot is *rgl* and the word for standard or banner is *dgl*. Since the Aramaic letters *r* and *d* are very similar in form, such a confusion is possible. The original probably described an embroidered robe and a standard with the motto King of kings and LORD of lords, the banner being the 'ensign for the peoples' (*T. Isa.* 11.12). Elaborate standards (albeit using a different word for standard) are described in the War Scroll, some as much as 7 metres long. The War Scroll gives examples of several mottoes which were used, and they seem to have been part of the ritual of holy war. As they went into battle for example, the standard might have borne the words, 'Vengeance of God', and as they returned 'Victory of God' (1QM IV). The standard of the divine warrior, bearing the motto 'King of kings and LORD of lords', indicates the triumph which the warrior brings.

The rider of the white horse wears 'many diadems'; the high priest wore seven. What they were and how they were worn is not known, but a Qumran fragment describes the vesting of the high priest thus: 'the fifth crown ... the sixth crown ... the seventh crown ... the high priest is dressed ...' (11Q18). The rider also has a name 'written' which no one knows but himself (19.12). This could have been the Name worn by the high priest on his diadem (Exod. 28.36) known only to himself because none but he ever spoke the Name aloud. It is more likely, however, to have been the most secret Name, *'hyh 'šr 'hyh*, 'I am that I am', which the LORD revealed to Moses at the burning bush (Exod. 3.14). This was the Three Word Name by which the LORD spoke of himself, not the public form of the Name which was *yhwh* (see p. 125). This was the Three Word Name that Jesus claimed, and was probably what he said at his arrest when the soldiers 'drew back and fell to the ground' (John 18.6). When Thomas said that he could not compare Jesus to anyone (as in Isa. 40.18), Jesus took him aside and told him the Three Word Name which he claimed. 'When Thomas returned to his companions, they asked him. "What did Jesus say to you" ' and Thomas replied that if he revealed what had been said, they would stone him for blasphemy (*Thomas* 13, cf. John 10.31–33).

The Name had great power and was the bond of the creation. Evil angels tried to learn it from Michael to gain power over the creation because it was the key to heaven and earth (*1 En.* 69.14–21). The *Ascension of Isaiah* described Isaiah's ascent through the heavens with an angel guide who explained to him: 'in the seventh heaven, the One who is not named dwells, and his Chosen One, whose name is unknown and no heaven can learn his name ...' (*Asc. Isa.* 8.7). When Isaiah reached the seventh heaven he was told: 'This is your LORD, the LORD, the LORD Christ, who is to be called in the world Jesus, but you cannot hear his name until you have come up from the body' (*Asc. Isa.* 9.5).

This curious expression, that he has 'a Name written' (19.12), may indicate something other than the inscription on the diadem. In the Hekhalot Zutarti texts (which are only known at a later date but contain ancient material) there are passages where the *na'ar*, the Servant/young one, is said to be 'written' and 'sealed'. He was 'written by the one letter by which was created heaven and earth' (i.e. with the letter *tau* which was the sign of the Name), and 'sealed with I am that I am' (i.e. with *'hyh 'šr 'hyh*, #389). This same 'young one' is later introduced as the prince 'written with seven voices and seven letters and seventy names'. He has 'been appointed in the most secret and glorious places and serves before the fire that devours fire'. He (or more likely the Name) was not given to Adam, Shem, Abraham, Isaac or Jacob but only to Moses (#396). This confirms that it was the Three Word Name revealed at the burning bush, *'hyh 'šr 'hyh* (Exod. 3.14) with which the Servant was sealed. The rider on the white horse, 'written with the secret name', is probably early evidence for this curious expression, and the figure in Eden (Ezek. 28.12) the earliest evidence for the practice of 'sealing' the high priest (see p. 42).

'The name by which he is called is The Word of God' (19.13) means his public name in contrast with the Three Word Name known only to himself (19.12). An almost contemporary text described the Word as the mighty warrior who appeared on the night of the Exodus, in other words, this was a contemporary description of the LORD. The divine warrior was not just an image in the ancient texts. 'Thy all powerful Word leaped from heaven, from the royal throne, into the midst of the land that was doomed, a stern warrior, carrying the sharp sword of thy authentic command, and stood and filled all things with death ...' (*Wisd.* 18.15). Philo listed the many names of Israel's God, the Mighty Angel: he was 'the High Priest, his First Born, the Divine Word' (*Dreams* I.215), he was 'God's Firstborn, the Word, who holds the eldership among the angels, the ruler as it were. And many names are

his: for he is called the Beginning and the Name of God and the Man
after his Image' (*Tongues* 146). The *Prayer of Joseph*, a text quoted by
Origen and described by him as 'presently in use among the Hebrews',
describes the patriarch Jacob as having another, simultaneous existence
as the angel, Israel. The angel Israel, whose name means 'the one who
sees God', was 'the archangel of the power of the LORD, the chief
captain among the sons of God, the first minister before the face of God
who calls on God by the inextinguishable name' (*On John* 2.31).

The rider of the white horse has a robe 'dipped' in blood (some
ancient texts say 'sprinkled' with blood). This is the high priest
emerging after taking blood into the holy of holies. His robe has blood-
stains, not from the battle which has yet to begin, but from the
atonement sacrifice. His fiery eyes, like the Man in 1.14, show that he is
the Mighty Angel, the LORD who had appeared to Daniel on the bank
of the River Tigris as a fiery Man clothed in linen and a girdle of gold.
His body gleamed like molten metal and his eyes were like flaming
torches (Dan. 10.4–6). He was not Gabriel; Daniel had seen Gabriel in
an earlier vision and had not been overcome with fear (Dan. 9.20–23).
The fiery Man who appeared to Daniel on the river bank was far more
terrifying: 'So I was left alone and saw this great vision and no strength
was left in me; my radiant appearance was fearfully changed and I
retained no strength' (Dan. 10.8). Hippolytus, writing in Rome early in
the third century CE, said that Daniel had seen the LORD, 'but not yet
fully incarnate' (*On Daniel* 24). Ezekiel had seen the fiery Man,
enthroned over the four creatures, and Ezekiel, too, had fallen on his
face in fear because he had seen 'the likeness of the Glory of the LORD'
(Ezek. 1.26–28).

The Christians were expecting their LORD to return. As the older
generation began to die and the LORD had not returned, there was a
crisis in some communities. Paul addressed this in his first letter to the
church at Thessalonika, when he reassured them that 'we who are alive,
who are left until the coming of the LORD, shall not precede those who
have fallen asleep' (1 Thess. 4.15). He wrote much the same to Corinth
when he explained what was to happen in the near future; some would
die before the return and be resurrected but others would live to see the
return and be transformed from the perishable to the imperishable state:
'We shall not all sleep, but we shall all be changed, in a moment, in the
twinkling of an eye, at the last trumpet. For the trumpet will sound and
the dead will be raised imperishable, and we shall be changed' (1 Cor.
15.51–52). Paul does not say in what manner the LORD would return.
In his other letter to Thessalonika he said that the LORD would be
'revealed from heaven with his mighty angels in flaming fire, inflicting
vengeance upon those who do not know God and upon those who do
not obey the gospel of our LORD Jesus' (2 Thess. 1.7–8). How much of
this was primitive Christian teaching and how much Paul's own
interpretation we cannot say, but he went on to show considerable
knowledge of future events as predicted by the Palestinian prophets and

recorded in the Book of Revelation: 'for that day will not come unless rebellion comes first, and the man of lawlessness is revealed, the son of perdition ... For the mystery of lawlessness is already at work ... And then the lawless one will be revealed, and the LORD Jesus will slay him with the breath of his mouth and destroy him by his appearing and his coming' (2 Thess. 2.3, 7–8). There is no mention of a white horse or the many diadems, but Paul clearly has in mind the same warrior figure. He also knew of the seventh trumpet, i.e. the last trumpet, and the voices in heaven which would announce the establishment of the kingdom of God (see on 11.15).

Jesus spoke often of the Man who would come from heaven; he does not mention the white horse, or what he would be wearing, but he does speak of the Son of Man coming with power and great glory, sending out his angels with a loud trumpet call to gather his chosen ones (Matt. 24.31). He himself had come 'not to bring peace but a sword' (Matt. 10.34). Paul could write in 50 CE of 'waiting for God's Son from heaven ... who will descend with a cry of command, with the archangel's cry and with the sound of the trumpet of God' (1 Thess. 1.10; 4.16). He probably learnt this from the Palestinian church and they from Jesus who knew the traditional expectations of his people. His contemporaries at Qumran were looking for the Prince of Light to come from heaven and fight for them (1QM XIII) and they expected their army to be led by seven priests, fully vested in linen battle vestments (1QM VII) and by the high priest.

The Great Carnage

The armies of heaven emerged for the great battle against the beast and the kings of the earth (19.19). This was Armageddon, the battle at the holy mountain, when the vain conspiracy of the kings of the earth against the LORD's anointed (Ps. 2.2) would be destroyed (but see on 16.12–16). Before the battle began, 'one angel standing in the sun' summoned the birds of prey, probably the Dawn Angel (7.2) who had sealed the chosen ones before the wrath. He was the Glory of the LORD returning from the east (Ezek. 43.1–4), the Glory risen upon Jerusalem (Isa. 60.1) described as the Prince of Light(s) who ruled over the children of righteousness (1QM XIII, 1QS III). He commanded the Spirits of Truth and had been appointed in ancient times to help the people of the covenant. His antitype was the Angel of Malevolence who commanded the Angels of Destruction (1QM XIII), also known as Satan (CD V), the Angel of Darkness (1QS III) and Mastema (*Jubilees* 10.7) and his people were the Sons of the Pit (CD VI).

The angel in the sun summoned the birds of prey, just as the LORD had commanded Ezekiel to summon the birds and the beasts to a great sacrificial meal on the battlefield: 'You shall eat the flesh of the mighty and drink the blood of the princes of the earth' (Ezek. 39.17–18). The prophet had seen the hordes of Gog lying dead on the mountains of

Israel and so great was the slaughter that their weapons would make firewood for Israel for seven years and it would take seven months to bury all the dead. Ezekiel's vision of Gog and his destruction is not dated, but the material which follows is the prophet's Jubilee vision, dated in the twenty-fifth year of the exile, fourteen years after the conquest of the city, i.e. 572 BCE, on the tenth day of the first month of the year (Ezek. 40.1). This was the Day of Atonement in the old calendar. (It was later described as the seventh month when the year began to be reckoned from the spring, e.g. Lev. 23.27.) Ezekiel saw the city rebuilt and the priesthood restored (Ezek. 40–44), the glory of the LORD coming from the east and returning to the temple (Ezek. 43.1–5), the land restored to the twelve tribes (Ezek. 48) and a great river beginning to flow out of the temple (Ezek. 47.1–12). *Anyone reading this text in the first century CE would have expected the destruction of Gog to precede the Day of Atonement in the year of Jubilee.* Then the priesthood and the holy city would be restored, the LORD would return to his temple, the land be given back to the twelve tribes and a great river flow from the temple. Even though Gog is not mentioned in 19.17–21, *this sequence is followed in the final chapters of the Book of Revelation and was probably the literal expectation of the nationalists at the time of the war against Rome.*

The invasion of Gog and his horde was a sign of the last days. When Israel was dwelling securely, a great host from the north would cover the land like a cloud (Ezek. 38.16), but their expedition would be a disaster. The LORD would bring them to his land in order to judge them. Pestilence and bloodshed, rain, hail, fire and brimstone would show the whole world the holiness and greatness of the LORD. The LXX had translated Amos 7.1: 'The LORD God showed me, and behold a morning growth of locusts and behold one locust was Gog the king', and this was the inspiration for the cloud of locusts summoned by the fifth trumpet (see on 9.1–11) where their leader was Abaddon, the Angel of the Pit. In the War Scroll, the final battle against evil was a battle against the Kittim (the Romans), also described as the hordes of Gog (1QM XI).

Others had spoken of the LORD's great battle against the enemies of his people; Isaiah had described the miraculous deliverance of Jerusalem when 'the Angel of the LORD went forth and slew a hundred and eighty five thousand in the camp of the Assyrians' (Isa. 37.36). Elsewhere an interpretation was put upon such slaughter; it was a sacrifice. The destruction of Edom was 'a sacrifice in Bozra, a great slaughter in the land of Edom', when the sword of the LORD would be sated with blood and fat (Isa. 34.5–6). Jeremiah described a bloody battle in the north country by the River Euphrates as a sacrifice on the Day of the LORD (Jer. 46.10). Zephaniah gave the fullest interpretation when he described the fate of idolaters in Judah: 'The Day of the LORD is at hand, the LORD has prepared a sacrifice and consecrated the guests' (Zeph. 1.7). This was a gruesome communal meal to celebrate the Day of the LORD, rather than just corpses left on the battlefield for the birds of prey.

The Roman army slaughtered on the hills around Jerusalem was to be this sacrifice for the Day of the LORD, and the Targumist could well have had the Romans in mind when he expounded Isaiah 49.26: 'And I will make the flesh of those who are your oppressors food for every bird of the heavens, and just as they are drunk from sweet wine, so shall the beasts of the field be drunk with their blood. Then all the sons of flesh will know that I am the LORD your Saviour and your Redeemer, the Strong One of Jacob'. Isaiah 56.9 became: 'All the kings of the people who were gathered to distress you, Jerusalem, will be cast in your midst; they will be food for the beasts of the field – every beast of the forest will eat to satiety from them'.

The people of Palestine had good reason to look for such vengeance on the Romans. Gessius Florus, the Roman procurator of Judea whose brutality eventually drove the Jews to revolt, ordered an indiscriminate slaughter in Jerusalem in which 3600 citizens were killed (*War* 2.305–308). 'He killed every Jew in Caesarea: in one hour's time above twenty thousand Jews were killed and all Caesarea was emptied of its Jewish inhabitants; Florus caught such as ran away and sent them in bonds to the galleys' (*War* 2.457). Pogroms were instigated throughout the region; in Askelon, in Ptolemais, in Tyre, in Hippos and in Gadara. The prophets of the time looked for the day of retribution, 'for the everlasting destruction of all the company of Satan'. There would be a 'battle and terrible carnage before the God of Israel, for that shall be the day appointed from ancient times for the destruction of the sons of darkness' (1QM I). The last surviving section of the War Scroll seems to describe the victorious warriors going out on the morning after the great battle, to see where 'the warriors of the Kittim' fell.

The most ancient belief had been that LORD would defend Jerusalem against her enemies, but there were others who believed that the greatest enemy of the LORD's people was the wicked city herself. The sacrifice on the Day of the LORD would be Jerusalem, as prophesied by Daniel (Dan. 9.26), and the LORD's vengeance would be upon the city responsible for 'the blood of the LORD's servants, the blood of the prophets and the saints' (18.24; 19.2). These two incompatible themes stand side by side in the Book of Revelation: the invading army is destroyed by The Word of God and the armies of heaven, and yet the same army appears elsewhere as the sixth bowl of wrath poured out to destroy Jerusalem (16.12–16).

Jesus predicted the destruction of the city and warned the scribes, Pharisees and lawyers that the blood of the prophets would bring judgement on their generation (Luke 11.50). Another prediction was the cryptic remark about birds of prey when the Messiah returned: 'Wherever the body is, there the eagles will be gathered' (Matt. 24.28; Luke 17.37), i.e. the birds gathered to pick at the corpse would be Roman eagles picking at Jerusalem. Josephus described the terrible slaughter when the temple was taken: 'The ground was nowhere visible through the corpses but the soldiers had to clamber over heaps of bodies in pursuit of fugitives' (*War* 6.276). The Roman eagles were brought into the temple court and set up opposite the eastern gate. The victors offered sacrifice to their standards and then the priests who had been defending the holy of holies were executed (*War* 6.316–23).

The Lake of Fire

The beast and the false prophet were thrown alive into 'the lake of fire that burns with sulphur' (19.20), probably the burning valley which smelled of sulphur where the angels who had led mankind astray were burning (*1 En.* 67.6, see on 8.10–11). The Song of Moses described the fire kindled by the LORD's anger: 'It burns to the depths of Sheol, devours the earth and its increase, and sets on fire the foundations of the mountains' (Deut. 32.22), and Amos saw a great fire devouring the deep and eating the land (Amos 7.4). The fourth beast in Daniel's vision was killed first and then thrown into the fire (Dan. 7.11), but the beast and the false prophet did not die an ordinary death. They were condemned immediately to the second death in the lake of fire, the death from which there was no hope of resurrection (19.20; 20.14–15; also mentioned in the *T. Isa.* 22.14: 'This sin shall not be forgiven you until you die the second death)'.

John the Baptist had warned of the Day of the LORD when the grain would be threshed and the 'chaff burned with unquenchable fire' (Matt. 3.12). Jesus had spoken of 'the eternal fire prepared for the devil and his angels' (Matt. 25.41), and of the Son of Man sending his angels at the close of the age to burn all evil doers like weeds (Matt. 13.40–41). Cut away your hand or your foot or your eye, he taught, if it causes you to sin and so sends you 'to Gehenna, to the unquenchable fire' (Mark 9.42–48, see p. 255). He told of the selfish rich man who died and then suffered torments in a great fire (Luke 16.19–31). Paul believed that the fire awaited everyone on the Day of the LORD, when their evil works would be burned up and only the good survive (1 Cor. 3.13), and Jude warned those inclined to immorality that Sodom and Gomorrah were enduring a punishment of eternal fire (Jude 7).

Punishment by fire was an ancient belief. Isaiah had prophesied that on the day of Zion's redemption, rebels and sinners would be destroyed, and the Strong One, i.e. Azazel, and his works would burn (Isa. 1.31). He gave vivid descriptions of the Glory of the LORD becoming the fire of judgement (e.g. Isa. 10.16–17; 30.27–28), and this image was to persist. One of the Qumran hymns spoke of 'the light that became an eternal fountain and in its bright flames all the [ ] shall be consumed, [ ] a fire to devour all sinful men' (1 QH XIV, formerly VI) and *3 Enoch* described a river of fire from heaven that fell on the heads of the wicked (*3 En.* 33). This must have been the fiery river which both Enoch and Daniel saw flowing from the heavenly throne (*1 En.* 14.19; Dan. 7.10), and these later writers reveal where the river was flowing.

The greatest detail is found in the oldest parts of *1 Enoch*. Azazel was bound and imprisoned in the desert, then brought out at the judgement to be cast into the fire (*1 En.* 10.6), exactly as described in the Book of Revelation (see on 20.1–4, 10). In *1 Enoch* 10.11–13 it was Semḥaza and his associates who were bound for seventy generations and then taken to the abyss of fire at the judgement. There are several problems as to what these places of punishment were, and whether angels and humans suffered the same fate. In the first century CE, however, human sinners were condemned to the same fire as the angels, as can be seen from Jesus' parable of the sheep and the goats where the selfish were sent into the eternal fire 'prepared for the devil and his angels' (Matt. 25.41). Enoch describes this fire as a deep abyss, 'a horrible place', with columns of heavenly fire where the rebel angels were punished (*1 En.* 18.11–16; 21.7–10).

The undateable Parables of Enoch depict the kings and the mighty cast into a deep valley burning with fire. The angel explains to Enoch that on the Day, the earthly rulers would be punished for becoming subject to Satan and leading astray the people on earth (*1 En.* 54.1–6). Exactly the same accusation appears in the Book of Revelation. The beast and the false prophet, the agents of the dragon, are cast into the lake of fire because they have deceived people and led them astray to receive the mark of the beast and worship its image (19.20).

Binding the Strong One

An angel came down from heaven with the key to the bottomless pit and a great chain. He seized and bound the ancient serpent and then sealed him in the pit for a thousand years so that he could no longer deceive the world (20.1–3). The unnamed angel could have been Raphael who was commanded by the Great Holy One to bind Azazel and cast him into darkness (*1 En.* 10.4). The parallel account has Michael sent to bind Semḥaza (*1 En.* 10. 11).

When the Messiah was caught up to heaven (12.5), the ancient serpent was thrown down (12.9). Since then he had been terrorizing earth and sea, knowing that his time was short (12.12). He attempted to pursue the Woman with his flood and then, together with his agents the two beasts, went off to make war on her children. Revelation 12.7–20.3 describes this period of warfare, after the Ruler of this world had been cast out (John 12.31). It appears also in the Damascus Document: 'From the day of the gathering in of the Teacher of the Community until the end of all the men of war who deserted to the Liar there shall pass about forty years. And during that age the wrath of God shall be kindled against Israel ...' (CD XIV). Satan was unleashed against Israel at that time, fulfilling the prophecy of Isaiah 24.17: 'Terror and the pit and the snare are upon you, O inhabitant of the earth!' These were interpreted as the three nets by which Satan snared Israel, namely fornication, riches and profaning the temple (CD IV). All three feature in the teaching of Jesus; he even gave the same teaching about divorce and based it on the same text, 'God made them male and female' (Gen. 1.27; Mark 10.1–12, cf. CD IV).

Jesus spoke about binding the Strong One, an ancient description of Azazel (Isa. 1.31). His saying has survived in two forms, but the context of both is the same. When the Pharisees accused him of exorcizing because he was in league with Satan, Jesus said that his exorcisms were a sign that the kingdom of God had come. This he described as 'binding the Strong One' (Matt. 12.29) or 'overcoming him' (Luke 11.22), defeating the Strong One because he was even stronger. In the Book of Revelation, the LORD appears as the Strong/Mighty Angel (5.2, 10.1).

The oldest material in *1 Enoch* describes the binding of Azazel, and the place of his imprisonment was named Dudael, thought to be a corruption of Beth Hiddudo. This was the place near Jerusalem to which the scapegoat was led on the Day of Atonement (*m. Yoma* 6.8, see pp. 43–6). Azazel was to stay imprisoned until the Day of the LORD, when he would be cast into the fire. The Parables tell how Enoch saw great iron chains being made in a deep valley full of fire, and his angel guide told him they were being prepared for the host of Azazel, 'so that they may take them and cast them into the abyss ... as the LORD of Spirits commanded' (*1 En.* 54.5). A duplicate account described the binding of Semḥaza: first Gabriel was sent to stir up strife among the children of the fallen angels, so that they would destroy themselves in battle; then Michael was sent to bind Semḥaza and his associates for seventy generations 'when their sons have slain one another and they have seen the destruction of their beloved ones' (*1 En.* 10.12). (The *Book of Jubilees* tells a variant of this story; nine-tenths of the demons were imprisoned but their chief, here called Mastema, pleaded with the LORD to be allowed to keep one tenth of his horde.) There is an identical sequence in the Book of Revelation; first the beast, the false prophet and the kings of the earth are destroyed and then, after he has seen the destruction of his children, Satan is bound. After the seventy generations, the fallen angels were to be judged and taken to the abyss of fire (*1 En.* 10.12). Luke 3.23–37 implies knowledge of this as there are seventy generations between Enoch and Jesus.

The Deceiver was bound and sealed for a thousand years (20.2), but this was more than imprisonment. The motif of binding and sealing points to the ancient creation myth, when the hostile forces were bound and sealed with the Name before the LORD could order the creation. The *Prayer of Manasseh*, although attributed to the penitent king (2 Chron. 33.19), is likely to be a Jewish composition from the early Christian era and thus evidence for ideas current when the Book of Revelation was compiled. The *Prayer* describes the creation: 'O LORD God Almighty, thou who hast made heaven and earth with all their order, who hast shackled the sea by thy word of command, who hast confined the deep and sealed it with thy terrible and glorious Name ...' (*Prayer* 2–3). Job had spoken of the LORD 'stilling the sea and smiting Rahab' (Job 26.12), or shutting in the sea and setting bounds for it as the first act of creation (Job 38.8–11). The Babylonian Talmud was to tell of David sealing the abyss with the Name in order to prevent the waters of chaos from overwhelming Jerusalem (*b. Sukkah* 53b). This story is attributed to R. Johannan, a third-century rabbi, but the belief that the waters of chaos had been controlled by the Lord (or by the king) goes back to earliest times. Binding the ancient serpent was the first act of creation (see pp. 216–19) and here in 20.2–3 it is the first act of renewing the creation. The ancient serpent is kept in bonds, while the millennium kingdom is on earth, then he is destroyed in the lake of fire (20.10). Finally, there is a new heaven and a new earth with no more sea (21.1).

The LORD had established bounds for the hostile forces; they existed, but their power was limited and confined: 'Thou didst set a bound which they should not pass, so that they might not again cover the earth' (Ps. 104.9). Job had complained to the LORD: 'Am I the sea or a sea monster that thou settest a guard over me?' (Job 7.12). Both Jeremiah and Enoch knew that the sea was bound and limited by the sand: 'I placed the sand as a bound for the sea, a perpetual barrier which it cannot pass; though the waves toss, they cannot prevail, though they roar, they cannot pass over it' (Jer. 5.22). 'Through that oath the sea was created and to limit it [or perhaps, as its foundation] he set the sand' (*1 En.* 69.18). When the ancient serpent went to make war on the children of the Woman, 'he stood on the sand of the sea' (12.17). This detail told those who understood such things that his power was limited. When the LORD saw the wickedness of the earth in the time of Noah, however, he allowed the waters to return (Gen. 6.5–7), and it was prophesied that a 'flood' would destroy Jerusalem (Dan. 9.26).

The final Parable of Enoch describes this renewed creation and shows that the binding of the evil angels was its prelude (*1 En.* 69.13–21). Evil angels had tried to learn the hidden Name, which the Hekhalot Zutarti text shows was given to the Servant and was the power by which the earth was created and sealed. The evil angels had wanted this power for themselves, but they had failed. The text is obscure, but seems to say that the faithful were taught the Name of the Man, cf. the promise to the angel of Philadelphia, that he would be given the Name (3.12). The Man then sat on the throne of glory and destroyed those who had led the world astray. The evil ones were bound with chains and imprisoned, and then the whole earth was renewed; evil passed away and thereafter nothing perished (*1 En.* 69.26–29).

The Warrior sequence in the Book of Revelation derives from Israel's most ancient mythology. The Man vested with the hidden Name rides from heaven as the LORD coming to rescue his people. He triumphs over the kings and the mighty, and then binds the ancient serpent before he can restore the creation. Everything is ordained in the divine plan; the power of the dragon is limited, but so also is the power of the Messiah because the dragon has to be released at the end of one thousand years (20.3).

THE CITY OF THE SAINTS

Then came one of the seven angels who had the seven bowls full of the seven last plagues, and spoke to me, saying, 'Come, I will show you the Bride, the wife of the Lamb.' And in the Spirit he carried me away to a great, high mountain, and showed me the holy city Jerusalem coming down out of heaven from God, having the glory of God, its radiance like a most rare jewel, like a jasper, clear as crystal. (Rev. 21.9–11)

For they shall see the world that is now invisible to them, and they will see a time which is now hidden to them. And time will no longer make them older. For they will live in the heights of that world, and they will be like the angels and equal to the stars ... For the extents of Paradise will be spread out for them, and they will be shown the beauty of the majesty of the living beings under the throne, as well as all the hosts of angels. (2 *Bar.* 51.8–10, 11)

It is generally recognized that there are problems with the order of the text at this point in the Book of Revelation. After the Great Judgement described in 20.11–15 there still survive, apparently, the unclean and those who practise abomination and falsehood who have to be excluded from the heavenly city at the end of the next chapter (21.27). The millennium kingdom is announced but there is no description of it, nothing about the kingdom which had been central to the message of Jesus and the focus of the entire Book of Revelation.

I propose that at an early stage one loose folio of the text was turned over and then copied such that the second side became the first. The two passages in question, 20.4–21.8 and 21.9–22.5 are exactly the same length (2429 letters each). To restore the original order, it is necessary to insert 21.9–22.5 after 20.3, giving the sequence: the binding of Satan, the angel showing the jewelled heavenly city, the river of the water of life and the tree of life, the thrones and the millennium kingdom, the loosing of Satan and the final battle, the great throne and the Last Judgement, the new heaven and the new earth. It is likely that 21.5–8, which becomes the final paragraph with this re-ordering, was originally the first of the fragments collected at the end of the book, and that the body of the text ended at 21.5a: 'Behold I make all things new'.

If we assume that such a dislocation took place, it is possible to make further calculations. With a page size of 2429 letters, the dislocated page would have been the ninth leaf of the book, and the final fragments would have taken up only one side of the tenth leaf, clearly the final page. It is recognized that the Christians were the first to make extensive use of the codex rather than the scroll, perhaps because it was more economical to write on both sides of the sheet. The codex was in common use in Christian communities in the second century and almost certainly in the first century too. The basic form of a codex was four sheets stacked together and then folded to give eight leaves. This would explain why it was the 'ninth' leaf of the Book of Revelation which was misplaced, and probably at a very early stage in the history of its transmission.

The Marriage Supper

As the harlot city burns, the marriage of the Lamb is prepared. His Bride is not at first identified as the city. Only her dress is described: 'fine linen, white and pure, the righteous deeds of the saints' (19.8, see pp. 253, 263), an obvious contrast to the finery of the harlot dressed in purple and scarlet, gold, jewels and pearls (17.4). Later, when the Bride is revealed to be the city, her jewels are described (21.18–21). The Jubilee prophecy of Isaiah 61 underlies this description of the heavenly city:

He has clothed me with the garments of salvation,
he has covered me with the robe of righteousness,
as a bridegroom decks himself with a garland,
and as a bride adorns herself with her jewels. (Isa. 61.10)

The Bride appearing is the Jubilee manifestation of the city, as in Ezekiel's vision (Ezek. 40.1–43.5). The Isaiah Targum is even closer to the Book of Revelation, because it describes the Bridegroom as the high priest: 'as a bridegroom who prospers in his canopy, and as the high priest who is prepared in his garments, and as the bride who is adorned with her ornaments' (*T. Isa.* 61.10b). The warrior high priest rides from heaven wearing his many diadems and the Bride appears dressed as the Queen (see pp. 211, 318).

'The fine linen is the righteous deeds of the saints' may well have been an explanatory remark added for later hearers who no longer knew the temple tradition, but it was no innovation. It was the obvious way to understand Isaiah 61.10, and it passed into later Jewish tradition as the garments of the Shekinah. Whoever carried out the commandments was believed to clothe the Shekinah and cause her to appear on earth. The community for whom the Book of Revelation was written were 'the saints who keep the commandments of God' (14.12) whose deeds were to follow them into their rest, and here those deeds have become the garments which make the Bride visible on earth.

The sequence of the Bride and the Lamb, who then rides out as the Warrior, has been compared to Psalm 45, the royal wedding psalm. The king, girded with his sword, rides out to victory against his enemies and he is twice addressed as 'God': 'Your throne, O God, endures for ever, and Therefore, O God, your God has anointed you ...' (Ps. 45.6–7). The Hebrew text can bear other translations – e.g. 'your divine throne', but this is not how the early church understood the text, and Eusebius was quite clear what it meant. When the psalms spoke of the Anointed One they referred not simply to the king, but to the LORD anointed by his Father, El Elyon. Eusebius wrote: 'So the whole verse runs: Thou hast, O God, loved justice and hated impiety; therefore in return, O God, the highest and greatest God who is also thy God, had anointed you ... so that the Anointer, being the supreme God, is far above the Anointed, he being God in a different sense. And this would be clear to anyone who knew Hebrew. Therefore in these words you have it clearly stated that God was anointed and became the Christ' (*Proof of the Gospel* 4.15). The royal wedding psalm probably accompanied a temple ritual which enacted the LORD going forth against his enemies, and there stands at his right hand the queen, dressed in 'gold of Ophir' (Ps. 45.9).

This is the female figure who enables us to identify the Bride of the Lamb. She is the queen consort, who used to appear in ancient texts about the heavenly warrior. The Blessing of Moses tells how the LORD became king before all the tribes of Israel. He came in great glory from Sinai, with thousands of his holy ones, and at his right hand was Asherah, the Queen (see p. 205). The LORD is praised as the one who rides through the heavens to help his people and to drive out their enemies so that they can live in safety in a fertile land (Deut. 33.28). This is the sequence of the final part of the Book of Revelation: the Bride and the Warrior appear, he rides out to destroy the enemies of his people who are then able to live in his kingdom and reign with him for a thousand years. It is an Eden place of miraculous fertility, where the tree of life yields fruit all year long.

Jesus spoke of this wedding supper. Matthew records the parable of the wedding feast prepared by the king on the occasion of his son's wedding (Matt. 22.1–14). Luke has a similar parable, but he tells of a great banquet prepared by a man, rather than a wedding feast prepared by a king (Luke 14.15–24). Taking detail from both, it is possible to reconstruct Jesus' original, which must have been a parable about the inauguration of the kingdom by the heavenly warrior. Both agree that the parable depicts the kingdom, and that those for whom it was originally intended did not, in the end, enjoy it. Luke gives their excuses: one had recently bought a field, another had bought oxen and not yet tried them, another was recently married. These are very similar to the exemptions from holy war: 'If a man has built a new house and not dedicated it ... If a man has planted a vineyard and not enjoyed its fruit ... If a man has betrothed a wife and not married her ... let him go back to his house ...' (Deut. 20.5–7). The call to the wedding feast allowed no such exemptions, but reveals what may have been Jesus' characteristic teaching about his heavenly warriors. The guests at the feast would be the good and the bad (Matt. 22.10), the poor and the maimed, the blind and the lame (Luke 14.21). Ritual purity was not important (see p. 336). They would, however, need a wedding garment, the white robe which symbolized the resurrected state. Anyone not thus resurrected would be barred from the kingdom (Matt. 22.13), and those who had rejected the kingdom, who had abused and killed the king's messengers, would be punished. The king would send an army to destroy both them and their city (Matt. 22.7). The parable of the bridesmaids was also set at this wedding feast; the Bridegroom would return unexpectedly and some would find themselves excluded from the feast (Matt. 25.1–13).

The Jewelled City

Ezekiel had seen the new Jerusalem in his Jubilee vision. The hand of the LORD was upon him in a vision and brought him back from Babylon to Jerusalem. As he stood on a high mountain, he saw the city and then a man of bronze with a linen rope and a reed to measure it. Just as Moses had been shown the plan for the tabernacle (Exod. 25.40) and David the plan for the temple (1 Chron. 28.19), so Ezekiel was shown exactly how the temple was to be built: 'Declare all that you see to the house of Israel' (Ezek. 40.4). He was shown the building itself and also the regulations for the priesthood and sacrifices, who would be permitted to enter the holy of holies and serve there: 'The levitical priests, the sons of Zadok, who kept the charge of my holy of holies when the people of Israel went astray from me ... they shall enter my holy of holies' (Ezek. 44.16–17). This is significant as the vision in the Book of Revelation, like the Qumran texts, describes not only the new holy of holies but also its new priesthood.

The new city of Ezekiel's vision had not materialized for everyone. There was bitter division in Judea when the exiles began to return and rebuild the temple and then the city. Many who considered themselves to be equally heirs to the heritage of Jerusalem found they were excluded from the restored temple, from the rebuilt city and, ultimately, even from the canonical accounts of the history of the times (see p. 227). The excluded people described the cult of the new temple as impure and apostate (*1 En.* 93.9) and reckoned there would be seventy weeks of years until the destruction of the city 'from the going forth of the word to restore and build Jerusalem' (Dan. 9.25). The temple on the hill became the harlot's bed on the hill (Isa. 57.7) and those whom Abraham and Israel did not acknowledge (Isa. 63.16) began to look for another new Jerusalem, 'a city of joy and rejoicing' to be part of the new creation, when the land was restored to its Eden state (Isa. 65.17–25). Some early texts show the original messianic hope for a purified land after the judgement of the fallen angels (*1 En.* 10.16–19), some later texts looked for the Messiah to drive out the Gentiles from Jerusalem and purge Jerusalem so that it was holy again (*Pss Sol.* 17.30). The *Sibylline Oracles* from the end of the first century CE spoke of the Man from heaven who would destroy evil-doers and make 'a city more brilliant than stars or sun or moon ... and a holy temple exceedingly beautiful in its fair shrine ... an immense tower touching the clouds and visible to all', a place free from sin and strife, where the glory of the eternal God would be seen (*Sib.* 5.414–34).

Those, however, who deemed the second temple polluted and impure

(*1 En.* 89.73) looked for its total destruction. The LORD himself would bring a new one to set up in its place (*1 En.* 90.28–29). Jesus must be reckoned with these latter, as he prophesied the destruction of the temple (see p. 293). John's Jesus said that he himself would rebuild it (John 2.19, see p. 189), but Thomas' Jesus said, 'I shall destroy this house and no one will be able to rebuild it' (*Thomas* 71).

The seer of Revelation 21.9–27 saw this long-awaited city, *but without a temple* (see p. 337). One of the seven angels who poured the bowls of wrath took him on a spirit journey to 'a great high mountain to see the holy city Jerusalem coming down out of heaven from God' (21.10). So much in the holy city text bears the marks of Jesus' teaching that is could have been one of his visions. The early church knew that Jesus had had spirit journeys like Ezekiel. Origen and Jerome, for example, have preserved a quotation from the lost *Gospel of the Hebrews*: 'The Saviour himself says "Even now my mother the Holy Spirit took me and carried me up to the great mountain Thabor"' (Origen, *On Jeremiah Homily* 15.4; *On John* 2.12; Jerome, *On Micah* 7.6). 'The Hebrews' knew of another spirit journey like those described in the temptations in the wilderness, when the devil took Jesus to the holy city and set him on the pinnacle of the temple, or 'to a very high mountain to show him all the kingdoms of the world and the glory of them' (Matt. 4.8). These are similar to Ezekiel's spirit journeys; he also went to Jerusalem (Ezek. 8.3) and to a very high mountain opposite the city (Ezek. 40.2). Jesus refused the kingdoms of the world on the devil's terms, but John records a saying of the Baptist: 'He who has the bride is the bridegroom' (John 3.29). This implies that Jesus, at an early stage of his ministry, committed himself to the Bride, the New Jerusalem, rather than to the devil and the kingdoms of the world, and that *he talked about this commitment to his disciples*. The city whose light was the Glory of God and whose lamp was the Lamb (21.23) must have been the original context of the saying: 'You are the light of the world. A city set on a hill cannot be hid' (Matt. 5.14). This was the city to be revealed.

The vision of the harlot and the vision of the Bride form a pair; in each case the seer is taken in the Spirit by one of the bowl angels (17.1–3; 21.9–10). The harlot city is replaced by the heavenly Jerusalem. The harlot city wears linen, purple, scarlet gold, jewels and pearls* (18.16); the bride wears linen (19.8), gold, jewels and pearls** (21.11–21). The description of the city shows that she is the rejected Queen of Heaven, the Wisdom who had been rejected on earth and had returned to heaven, in contrast to the Unrighteousness who had been welcomed like rain in the desert (*1 En.* 42, see p. 208). Thus the harlot is seen in the desert but the queen descends to her rightful place. Like the figure on the heavenly throne, the city has the appearance of jasper (4.3, cf. 21.11), and like Wisdom, she has the radiance of the Glory of

---

*The 'earthly' vestments of the high priest (see p. 39).

**The 'heavenly' linen garments worn by the high priest in the holy of holies (see p. 39).

God (21.11, cf. *Wisd.* 6.12: 'Wisdom is radiant and unfading, easily discerned by those who love her', and *Wisd.* 7.25b: '[She is] a' pure emanation of the Glory of the Almighty)'. Nothing unclean can enter the city (21.27, cf. *Wisd.* 7.25c: 'Nothing defiled gains entrance into her'), and the city extends 12,000 stadia in each dimension, about 1500 miles (21.16, cf. *Wisd.* 8.1: 'She reaches mightily from one end of the earth to the other').

She is also the Wisdom who is both the sign and the means of resurrection, given to the righteous after the destruction of their enemies. *1 Enoch* describes how the LORD comes to execute judgement on the earth, how idols and their temples are burned and idolaters thrown into the fire of judgement, and how the righteous are then resurrected and given Wisdom (*1 En.* 91.7–10). The reappearance of Wisdom here in *1 Enoch* is identical to the reappearance of the true Jerusalem, the messianic kingdom, when the wicked temple is burned, sinners are thrown into the fire of judgement and the first resurrected reign in the millennium kingdom.

The Wisdom who is described in the *Wisdom of Solomon* bears a strong resemblance to the Bride of the Lamb and to the messianic kingdom of the resurrected that she embodies: 'Giving heed to her laws is assurance of immortality ... so the desire for Wisdom leads to a kingdom' (*Wisd.* 6.18, 20, cf. Rev. 20.4). 'Honour Wisdom that you may reign for ever' (*Wisd.* 6.21, cf. Rev. 22.5). 'She is a reflection of eternal light' (*Wisd.* 7.26, cf. Rev. 21.11). 'Compared with the light she is found to be superior, for it is succeeded by the night' (*Wisd.* 7.29–30, cf. Rev. 21.25). 'I desired to take her for my Bride' (*Wisd.* 8.2, cf. Rev. 21.9). 'I shall find rest with her ... and life with her has no pain' (*Wisd.* 8.16, cf. Rev. 21.4). 'Give me the Wisdom that sits by thy throne' (*Wisd.* 9.4). This is the Wisdom who was abandoned in the sixth week when the first temple was burned, and whose loss left the temple-dwellers blind and deprived of vision (*1 En.* 93.8). This is the Queen of Heaven whom the refugees from Jerusalem continued to honour in Egypt because, they said, 'since we left off burning incense to the queen of heaven, we have lacked everything and have been consumed by sword and famine' (Jer. 44.18).

The abandoned city/queen was vividly depicted by Isaiah, and her restoration was a sign that the covenant of peace stood firm (Isa. 54.10). She was to be put on her beautiful garments and be the holy city: 'There shall no more come into you the uncircumcised and the unclean' (Isa. 52.1). 'Arise and sit [on your throne'; Isa. 52.2, translating literally]. She was to be rebuilt as a city of gemstones, with foundations of sapphire, pinnacles of rubies,* gates of carbuncles and walls of precious stones (Isa. 54.11–12).

The Targum adds here that the timbers would be set in pearls, similar

---

*There are various suggestions for the meaning of *kadᵉkod*.

to the gates of pearl in the heavenly city (21.21). The city/queen is also a 'crown of beauty in the hand of the LORD, a royal diadem in the hand of God' (Isa. 62.3), doubtless a description of the holy city crowning the hill, just as Samaria had been described as the garland on the head of a drunkard (Isa. 28.1). The sons* of the holy city would marry her (Isa. 62.5), an allusion to the royal tradition that the king was both the son and the consort of Wisdom. This appears in the Book of Revelation as the son of the Woman (12.5) who later receives her as his Bride (19.7). Paul also mentions the heavenly city and her sons: 'The Jerusalem above is free and she is our mother' (Gal. 4.26–27), and he then quotes the prophecy in Isaiah 54.1 that the barren city would have many children.

Isaiah knew that the true Jerusalem was the heavenly city, and that any destruction on earth could not remove the heavenly reality: 'I have graven you on the palms of my hands, your walls are continually before me' (Isa. 49.16). When 'Baruch' was meditating on the destruction of Jerusalem in 70 CE, the LORD reassured him that the fallen city was not the eternal city engraved on the palms of his hands (2 *Bar.* 4.2). The LORD told Baruch that Adam had been shown the true Jerusalem before he sinned, but afterwards he was not able to see it. Abraham had glimpsed it when he made the covenant sacrifice (Gen. 15.7–21), presumably the tradition that Abraham had seen the end times (2 *Esdr.* 3.14), and Moses had seen it on Sinai (2 *Bar.* 4.3–6).

After the destruction of Jerusalem in 70 CE, 'Ezra' also received visions. In the third of them, an angel revealed to him the signs of the end times and the beginning of the messianic kingdom:

The city which now is not seen shall appear,** and the land which is now hidden shall be disclosed. And everyone who had been delivered from the evils that I have foretold shall see my wonders. For my son the Messiah shall be revealed with those who are with him and those who remain shall rejoice four hundred years. (2 *Esdr.* 7.26b–28)

This is the sequence in the Book of Revelation when the pages are reordered; first the city/bride appears, and then the messianic kingdom. In his fourth vision, 'Ezra' saw a Woman in deep mourning for the death of her son and at first he rebuked her for her selfish concerns: 'Zion the mother of us all is in deep grief and affliction ... You are sorrowing for one son, but we, the whole world, for our mother' (2 *Esdr.* 10.7–8). As he spoke to her, he saw her appearance change, 'her face suddenly shone exceedingly and her countenance flashed like lightning' (2 *Esdr.* 10.25). She gave a loud cry and when Ezra looked again, the woman had been transformed into a city. In his sixth vision, he saw the warrior Messiah rise up from the sea, carve for himself a great mountain and stand on it to defeat his enemies. The interpretation

---

*Sometimes inappropriately translated 'builders', the Hebrew consonants are identical, *bnym*.

**The Latin and Syriac texts have here: *the Bride shall appear, even the city appearing* ....

revealed to him was that the mountain was Zion which 'will come and be made manifest to all people, prepared and built, as you saw the mountain carved out without hands' (2 *Esdr.* 13.36).

The city from heaven is a cube (21.16), and has twelve gates, three in each wall (21.12–13). Each gate is a single pearl (21.21, cf. *b. Baba Bathra* 75a, 'huge pearls for the city gates'), and, like the city in Ezekiel's vision, each is inscribed with the name of one of the twelve tribes (Ezek. 48.30–34). Ezekiel names Reuben, Judah and Levi on the north side, Joseph, Benjamin and Dan on the east, Simeon, Issachar and Zebulun on the south and Gad, Asher and Naphtali on the west. The Temple Scroll has a different allocation, with the gates in the outer wall of the temple, not the city: Dan, Naphtali and Asher on the north side, Simeon, Judah and Levi on the east, Reuben, Joseph and Benjamin on the south and Issachar, Zebulun and Gad on the west (11QT XXXIX). The New Jerusalem Scroll seems to follow the Temple Scroll, but the text is very fragmented (4Q554). The Book of Revelation, like the Temple Scroll, implies that the temple and the city coincide.

At each gate of the city stood an angel (21.12), probably a memory of the ancient guardians of the city known to Isaiah, 'the watchmen set on the walls' (Isa. 62.6). These 'watchers' are concealed in many places in the Hebrew Scriptures, because the heirs of Josiah's temple purge were responsible for transmitting many ancient texts and when they removed the host of heaven from temple worship (2 Kgs 23.5) they also removed them from the Hebrew Scriptures. The *'rym*, 'watchers', can be seen in Isaiah 33.8, disguised as the witnesses, *'dym*, or cities, *'rym*, very similar words (Hebrew *d* and *r* look very similar), and in Daniel 4.13, where there is 'a watcher, a holy one'. When David tried to capture Jerusalem, the people of the city taunted him by saying, 'The blind and the lame will ward you off' (2 Sam. 5.6), but the blind and the lame conceal the ancient guardians of the city. 'The blind' were 'the watching ones', since the Hebrew verb *'wr* can mean to be blind or to be awake/aroused, and 'the lame' were the ones who guarded the thresholds of the city, the Hebrew verb *psḥ* meaning both 'to pass over' and 'to limp'. What David despised were not 'the blind and the lame' but the guardian angels of the city, the gates and doors who lift up their heads as the LORD enters (Ps. 24.7–9). In the vision of the heavenly city, the guardians of the gates and thresholds become the angels of the gates (21.12) and the twelve foundations become the apostles (21.14).

The heavenly city, however, is both city and temple, and so the angels of the temple gates are also a part of the picture. They can be seen in the Enochic Astronomy Book, a confused text of which some has survived in Ethiopic, but Aramaic fragments from Qumran show that there had been a fuller version. The temple and its courts were a microcosm of the universe and so when Enoch was taught about the calendar, he was shown the gates on the horizon through which the sun and moon rose and set. There were six in the east and six in the west (1 *En.* 72). These were also, however, the gates for the stars, which suggests that they were not just in the east and west, but the gates of the zodiac. These stars were the angels who had charge of the calendar (*1 En.* 75), the four great angels of the quarter days ensuring that the twelve months of thirty days each were divided by the angels of the quarters giving a solar year of 364 days (*1 En.* 82). The Temple Scroll shows that the plan of the ideal temple was, in fact, calendrical, the alignment of the gates in middle and outer walls on the eastern side coinciding with sunrise at the summer and winter solstices, and the central gate marking the equinoxes.

(Time was an important element in temple theology; the world beyond the veil was beyond historical time as it was beyond matter (see p. 20). The relationship between the ranks of angels, the LORD and God Most High was like the relationship between units of time. Just as one day is many hours, so one angel is many lesser spirits and all are part of the Great Holy One. The *Letter of Eugnostos* explained:

Time came to be as a type of the First Begetter, his son. [ ] came to be as a type of the [ ] twelve months came to be as a type of the twelve powers. The three hundred and sixty days of the year came to be as a type of the three hundred and sixty powers who were revealed by the Saviour. In relation to the angels who came from these without number, the hours and the moments of them came to be as a type. (*Eugnostos* CG III. 3.84)

One translation* of the *Book of Enoch* renders the title of God Most High as 'The Antecedent of Time' (*1 En.* 60. 2), which exactly describes the world beyond the veil. All this lore would have been known to the seers of the Book of Revelation, and must be read into their visions. It explains, for example, the multiple aspects of the one being which frequently appear, the seven angels who are the one LORD (16.2–21), or the three who are the one LORD (1.4–5).)

The angel guardians of the calendar explain the choice of precious stones. The foundations are adorned with jasper, sapphire, agate, emerald, onyx, carnelian, chrysolite, beryl, topaz, chrysoprase, jacinth and amethyst (21.19–20). A list of twelve precious stones immediately calls to mind the twelve stones set in the high priest's breastplate, engraved with the names of the twelve tribes (Exod. 28.17–21, 39.10–14). The list in 21.19–20 is very similar to the LXX list of the high priest's jewels; the names of eight of the stones are identical and the differences in the other four are probably due to the translator's guesswork. The first renders the Hebrew *nopek* a red stone, which the LXX gives as *anthrax*, a dark red stone, and Revelation as *chalkedon,* a word not known elsewhere but clearly meaning chalcedony, which can be red. The second is Hebrew *piṭᵉdah*, a yellow stone which the LXX gives as *topazion*, topaz and Revelation as *sardonux*, a striped agate. The third is the Hebrew *lešem,* a word whose meaning is unknown which the LXX renders *ligurion*, another word of unknown

*E. Isaac in *OTP* vol 1.

meaning, and Revelation gives as *chrusoprasos*, possibly a green-gold stone. The fourth is the Hebrew *šᵉbo*, a word of unknown meaning, which the LXX gives as *achates*, agate, and Revelation as *huakinthos*, a blue stone. Josephus, a priest, says that the twelve stones represented the twelve months, the twelve signs of the zodiac (*Ant.* 3.186), linking the twelve stones to Enoch's twelve calendar angels.

Tobit's prayer spoke of this jewelled city:

Let Jerusalem be built with sapphires and emeralds
her walls with precious stones
and her towers and battlements with pure gold.
The streets of Jerusalem will be inlaid
with beryl and ruby and stones of Ophir. (*Tobit* 13.16–17)

The New Jerusalem Text describes the streets paved with white stone, marble and jasper, and the walls built of *ḥašmal*, sapphire and ruby, with laths of gold (4Q554). The *ḥašmal* is the 'bronze' which Ezekiel saw in the midst of the fire of the chariot throne (Ezek. 1.4) and surrounding the fiery Man (Ezek. 1.27; 8.2). This is probably the wall of fire which Zechariah prophesied for Jerusalem: 'I will be to her a wall of fire round about, says the LORD, and I will be the glory within her' (Zech. 2.5).

Other texts confirm that the stones of the city were its people. Zechariah had spoken of the Day of the LORD, when he would save his flock and they would shine like jewels on his land (Zech. 9.16). The names of the apostles on the foundation stones (21.14) and the faithful priests as pillars (3.12) are but details of a wider picture. The community of saints were living stones built into a spiritual house (1 Pet. 2.5) whose foundation was the apostles and the prophets (Eph. 2.20–22). The Qumran Community described themselves in the same way: 'May the LORD bless you ... and set you as a splendid jewel in the midst of the congregation of the saints ... may you be as an angel of the presence' was the blessing for the sons of Zadok (1QSb IV). Ezekiel's fallen high priest was expelled from Eden, the garden of God where he had 'walked among the stones of fire' (Ezek. 28.14). Isaiah's jewelled city was interpreted as a description of the community: the sapphire foundations were the congregation of the elect and 'the ruby pinnacles the twelve [high priests] who gave judgement by Urim and Thummim'. The jewelled gates were the chiefs of the tribes of Israel (4Q164). Most remarkable of all are the Songs of the Sabbath Sacrifice, fragmented texts in which the holy of holies seems to be alive, literally a living temple. The pillars of the holy of holies sing praises (4Q403 I), the engraved tiles are the *'elohim* and holy angels of the innermost chamber (4Q405 19) and the doors and gates proclaim the glory of the King (4Q405 23).

The length, breadth and height of the city are equal (21.16). There was a similar belief about the second temple, that the greatest measurement of the temple building as a whole was 100 cubits in each direction (*m. Middoth* 4.6), but the elaborate details which follow (including the debate whether or not the scarecrow on the roof should be included in the height!) show that a perfect cube was not envisaged. A form of this tradition appears in the Talmud, attributed to R. Joḥannan: Jerusalem would be lifted up as high as her ground area, in other words, would be a cube (*b. Baba Bathra* 75b). A 'living holy of holies', however, would explain the shape of the jewelled city if its length, its breadth and its height were equal (21.16), i.e. it was a cube like the holy of holies (1 Kgs 6.20). The 'House of Holiness' is how the holy of holies is translated in the Qumran Targum of Leviticus 16.20 (4Q156.2), and so when the council of the community was described as a House of Holiness for Israel (1QS VIII, IX), it was proclaimed as the living holy of holies, 'a sanctuary of men built for himself that there they may send up, like the smoke of incense, the works of the Law' (4Q174). They were the ones who would fulfil the role of the LORD on the Day of the LORD, atoning the land and giving the wicked their reward. They were the precious cornerstone of the living temple: 'He has joined their assembly to the sons of heaven, to be a council of the community, a foundation of the building of holiness . . .' (1QS XI). This is a collective messianism just as we find in the Christian teaching about the body of Christ (1 Cor. 12.27), those who are in Christ (Gal. 3.27–28), who would share his throne (3.21), and rule in the millennium kingdom. The image of the temple is exactly that of the Letter to the Ephesians: the Christian community is 'built upon the foundation of the apostles and prophets, Christ Jesus being the cornerstone, in whom the whole structure is joined together and grows into a holy temple in the LORD; in whom you also are built into it for a dwelling place of God in the Spirit' (Eph. 2.20–22).

The angel who showed the city to the seer held a golden reed to measure the city. This must have been an ancient tradition: Ezekiel had a vision of a man 'whose appearance was like bronze' (Ezek. 40.3), holding a linen line and a measuring reed, and Zechariah saw a man with a measuring line (Zech. 2.1). The prophet learned that Jerusalem would be enlarged and prosper, and that the LORD himself would be the glory within her and a wall of fire round her. There was a man with a reed measuring the city in the fragmented New Jerusalem Text, and its dimensions are given in reeds and cubits: one street 6 reeds wide, another 10, and the gates 3 reeds across. The walls were 7 reeds high, the towers 10 and the 12 city gates each 6 reeds across (5Q15). The Temple Scroll has detailed prescriptions for the dimensions of the temple and its furnishings (11QT XXX–XXXIII), from which it is possible to see that at least some of the dimensions were of calendrical significance, and calculated such that they were only valid for Jerusalem. The position of the gates in the eastern walls, for example, marks the point of sunrise at the solstices, making allowance for the raised horizon of the Mount of Olives. These were real measurements for a real situation. The Mishnah, too, devotes a whole tractate to the measurements of the temple (*m. Middoth*).

The man with the golden reed measured the city, its gates and its walls (21.15), and they formed a cube of some 1500 miles. He also measured the wall as 144 cubits (approximately 216 feet or 65 metres), presumably the thickness of the outer wall as the height has already been given as 12,000 stadia. To have walls of such thickness would not have been out of proportion for the splendid city envisaged. The city of Babylon, which was 14 miles square, had walls 50 cubits thick (Herodotus, *Histories* 1.178), and the wall of the city described in the New Jerusalem scroll was 14 cubits (2 reeds) thick at its base (5Q15). The measurements were those of a 'man' 'that is, an angel' (21.17), an interesting piece of explanation for later hearers who had lost touch with the apocalyptists' convention of describing humans as animals, e.g. the Lamb, and angels as men.

Priests in Eden

The first temple had been the Garden of Eden and its high priest was Adam (see p. 20). When the temple was destroyed by the Babylonians, it was because the high priest had been expelled from the presence of God. In his pride he had corrupted his Wisdom and had desecrated his own holy of holies. The LORD brought fire to consume it (Ezek. 28.12–19). The story was retold for a new generation and Adam became Everyman, expelled from the presence of God and reduced to mortality (Gen. 2–3). The new generation had a new priesthood, regarded by some as impure and apostate, but those who remained loyal to the older faith looked forward to returning to their temple and their Eden. 'The perfect of way' would be taught the Wisdom of the sons of heaven: 'For God has chosen them for an everlasting covenant, and all the glory of Adam shall be theirs' (1QS IV).

The Third Isaiah was the voice of these people, and in his oracles we see the beginning of a hope which was fulfilled in the destruction of Jerusalem. He spoke of the Anointed One who would bring the Jubilee, 'to proclaim liberty to the captives, the year of the LORD's favour, the day of vengeance of our God' (Isa. 61.1–2), the prophecy which Jesus claimed to fulfil (Luke 4.21). He spoke of the new temple as a harlot (Isa. 57.7, see p. 281), of those who oppressed and excluded their brothers (Isa. 58.1–14; 63.16; 66.5). He spoke of the light of the LORD dawning again on his city (Isa. 60.1), and of the ousted priests being restored and recognized once more: 'You shall be called the priests of the LORD, men shall speak of you as the ministers of our God' (Isa. 61.6). The LORD, who hates robbery and wrong, would see them restored to their rightful heritage in the land, and Jerusalem would once again be the LORD's delight. There would be a new creation when Jerusalem would be a joy, with no more weeping or distress. Everyone would live to a great age in great prosperity, and Isaiah's prophecy of the messianic kingdom would be fulfilled: 'They shall not hurt or destroy in all my holy mountain' (Isa. 65.25, quoting Isa. 11.9). The new cult was condemned outright (Isa.66.3–4) and the new community was cursed and condemned to destruction: 'You shall leave your name to my chosen for a curse, and the LORD God will slay you' (Isa. 65.15). In the Isaiah Targum this became even more bitter: 'The LORD God will kill you with the second death', in other words, they would die with no hope of resurrection.

The description of the city from heaven in the Book of Revelation is the fulfilment of the Third Isaiah's prophecies, because his words had continued to inspire the dispossessed. The glory of the LORD would rise on the city (21.11). 'Nations shall come to your light and kings to the brightness of your rising' (Isa. 60.3) inspired, 'By its light shall the nations walk and the kings of the earth shall bring their glory into it' (21.24). 'Your gates shall be open continually' (Isa. 60.11) inspired, 'Its gates shall never be shut by day and there shall be no night there' (21.25). 'The sun shall no more be your light by day, nor for brightness shall the moon give you light at night; but the LORD will be your everlasting light and your God will be your glory' (Isa. 60.19) inspired, 'The city has no need of sun or moon to shine upon it, for the glory of God is its light and its lamp is the Lamb' (21.23). (When Isaiah spoke of 'the LORD' and 'your God' as sources of light, it is never suggested that two divinities were envisaged. Similarly, when the Book of Revelation speaks of God and the Lamb as sources of light, this is another indication that the Lamb is the LORD.)

Through the middle of the city flowed the river of the water of life, and there was also the tree of life, yielding its fruits throughout the year and leaves for the healing of the nations (22.1–2) This was Eden restored, and those who conquered (or 'were pure', see pp. 145, 261) would eat of the tree of life (2.7; 22.19) from which Adam and Eve had been barred (Gen. 3.22). The Genesis story describes one river in Eden which divided into four when it had left the garden (Gen. 2.10). There was 'every tree pleasant to the sight and good for food' and in the midst of the garden, the tree of life and the tree of knowledge. Adam was told that he could eat from any tree except the tree of knowledge (Gen. 2.9, 16–17) and he was barred from the tree of life only after his disobedience (Gen. 3.22–24). As the story is told, the fruit of the tree of life was originally a permitted food.

Behind Genesis is the older story known to Ezekiel the priest, but not to us. Ezekiel's description of the river flowing from the temple is his way of describing Eden come to earth. He describes all kinds of trees growing on the banks of the river, miraculous fruit trees which crop all through the year. Their leaves never wither and they have healing properties (Ezek. 47.7, 12). Elsewhere he describes Pharaoh as a mighty cedar tree with huge branches, watered by the rivers which flowed around its roots. Birds and beasts found shelter from its branches and all great nations lived in its shadow (Ezek. 31.2–9). In its beauty it surpassed all the trees in the garden of God. The miraculous properties of Ezekiel's fruit trees and the huge size of the royal tree appear in other texts as descriptions of the tree of life, which may be a memory of the older tradition: a huge tree, around whose roots flowed the river of life. Ezekiel compared Pharaoh to the great tree and the psalmist compared the righteous man to 'a tree planted by streams of water, that yields fruit in its season and its leaf does not wither' (Ps. 1.3). People as the trees of Eden is an important motif in later texts.

Another recurring motif in descriptions of the tree of life is its wonderful fragrance, the oldest example being in the account of Enoch's heavenly journeys. As he travelled he saw seven mountains and on the highest of them was a throne encircled by fragrant trees, with one tree more fragrant and more beautiful than all the others. When Enoch asked his angel guide about the tree, he was told:

This tall mountain . . . is his throne on which the holy and great LORD of Glory, the Eternal King, will sit when he descends to visit the earth with goodness. And as for this fragrant tree, not a single human being has the authority to touch it until the great judgement . . . It shall then be given to the righteous and the pious. And the elect will be presented with its fruit for life. He will plant it in the direction of the northeast, upon the holy place, in the direction of the house of the LORD, the Eternal King. (1 En. 25.3–5)

This was the tree of life. On another journey, Enoch saw a tree which was the Tree of Wisdom, 'its fruit like beautiful grape clusters and the fragrance of this tree travels far' (1 En. 32.4). Although there are two trees both in 1 Enoch and in Genesis, the original would have been a single tree of Wisdom whose fruit gave life. The gift of Wisdom, in temple theology, was the gift of life. Another Enoch text describes the beautiful fragrant tree in the third heaven, in the midst of Paradise (2 En. 8.1–4). The fragrant tree may explain Paul's phrase 'a fragrance from life to life' (2 Cor. 2.16).

The hope persisted that one day humankind would be permitted to return to their lost Eden. The *Testament of Levi* prophesied that in the time of the 'new priest', the saints would eat from the tree of life. After the decline of the priesthood in the seventh week, when priests became arrogant and lawless, idolaters, adulterers and money lovers who practised sodomy, a new priest would be raised up who would 'open the gates of Paradise, remove the sword that had threatened since Adam and grant to the saints to eat from the tree of life' (T. Levi 18.10–11). Enoch saw 'the holy ones in heaven . . . and the elect who dwell in the garden of life' (1 En. 61.12). The risen LORD in the seven letters promised the fruit of the tree of life 'to him who conquers' (2.7; or 'is pure') and threatened anyone who tampered with the prophecies that they would lose their share in the tree of life (22.19). 'Ezra' lamented that the promise of a future Paradise to be revealed, with its unspoiled fruit for healing, was no comfort to sinners who would not see it (2 Esdr. 7.123). He was told not to consider the fate of others, but to contemplate his own future: 'because it is for you that Paradise is opened, the tree of life is planted, the age to come is prepared, plenty is provided, a city is built, rest is appointed, goodness is established and Wisdom perfected beforehand' (2 *Esdr.* 8.52).

Above all, the return to Eden was the return to Wisdom, as the tree was one of her ancient symbols (see p. 203). Wisdom was 'the tree of life to those who grasped her' (Prov. 3.18), she took root in an honoured people and grew in their midst like a glorious, fragrant tree, 'Like cassia and camel's thorn I gave forth the aroma of spices, and like choice myrrh I spread a pleasant odour ... like the fragrance of frank-incense in the tabernacle' (*Ben Sira* 24.15). Wisdom spread her branches wide and offered her devotees food and drink.

Like a terebinth I spread out my branches,
and my branches are glorious and graceful,
Like a vine I caused loveliness to bud,
and my blossoms became glorious and abundant fruit,
Come to me, you who desire me, and eat your fill of my produce,
Those who eat of me will hunger for more,
and those who drink me will thirst for more. (*Ben Sira* 24.16–21)

She then described her streams, flowing out to water her garden and pouring out teaching like prophecy, cf. the prophecy of the Spirit in Joel, which Peter said was fulfilled at Pentecost: 'I will pour out my Spirit ... and your sons and your daughters shall prophesy' (Acts 2.17).

The text of Revelation 22.2 is not clear and so a variety of translations is offered. The problem is that the tree of life seems to be on both sides of the river. One solution might be that the tree bears its fruits 'on one side and the other', but it is more likely that the branches of the tree extend a great distance, or that the tree has its roots in the river, as did Ezekiel's great tree. The gist would then be that the tree stands in the middle of the city square and the river flows through the square and round the roots of the tree: 'The tree of life is in the midst of the square with the river [which flows all round it] on this side and that, bearing twelve fruits ...' Or perhaps the picture is of a huge tree in the midst of the river spreading out its branches on this side and that. Other first-century CE descriptions of the tree still emphasize the extent of its branches. 2 *Enoch* describes the tree of life in the midst of Paradise, surrounded by other fragrant fruit trees, but surpassing them all in size and fragrance: 'It covers the whole of Paradise and has something of every orchard tree and of every fruit' (2 *En.* 8.4). The Targum told of the Tree of Life whose height was a journey of 500 years (*T. Ps. Jon. Gen.* 2.19), and a later commentary on Genesis remembered the huge tree and the streams of Eden: 'The tree covered a five hundred years' journey and all the primeval waters branched out in streams under it' (*Gen. Rab.* XV 6).

The imagery of the first temple appears almost intact in the Egyptian gnostic texts, just as it does in the writings of Philo and other texts from the Jews in Egypt (see p. 206). One of these gnostic texts, whose modern name is *On the Origin of the World*, has a description of the tree of life: 'in the north of Paradise in order to give life to the immortal saints ... The colour of the tree of life is like the sun, and its branches are beautiful. Its leaves are like those of the cypress. Its fruit is like clusters of white grapes. Its height rises up to heaven' (CG II.5.110).

Contemporary texts show that the tree of life was also the place of the heavenly throne and so was itself the source of the waters. When God returned to Paradise on the chariot throne, it rested by the tree of life (*Ap. Ad.* 22).* In the first century CE the tree was believed to stand in the midst of Eden, 'at that place where the LORD takes his rest ... and two streams come forth, one a source of honey and milk, and a source which produces oil and wine. And it is divided into four parts ... (*2 En.* 8.3, 5). Thus the river, the tree of life and the throne described in 22.1–3 were part of the contemporary picture of Paradise.

The oldest descriptions of such a heavenly holy of holies are found in texts from the first temple period:

The children of men take refuge in the shadow of thy wings ...
For with thee is the fountain of life;
in thy light do we see light. (Ps. 36.7, 9)

There is a river whose streams make glad the city of God,
the holy habitation of the Most High. (Ps. 46.4)

But there the LORD in majesty will be for us
a place of broad rivers and streams ...
the LORD is our king; he will save us. (Isa. 33.21–22)

These are similar to the earlier Ugaritic texts which describe El in his palace at the source of the rivers (KTU 1.2.iii) and to several later texts. The Parables of Enoch, for example, describe the heavenly holy of holies as a place of streams: 'Wisdom is poured out like water' (*1 En.* 49.1), and fountains of righteousness and Wisdom flow from the place of the throne. The thirsty who drink from them are filled with Wisdom, i.e. they become resurrected, divine (*1 En.* 48.1). What follows at this point in *1 Enoch* resembles the sequence in the Book of Revelation: all who live on earth worship the Man who has been revealed to the Holy and Righteous Ones, then the kings and the mighty who possess the land face their doom and are handed over to the Chosen Ones for judgement. As they are judged, so a time of rest comes to the earth, and the Chosen Holy Ones enjoy eternal light. Another Parable describes how the Righteous Chosen Ones enjoy eternal light and peace after darkness has been destroyed (*1 En.* 58.1–6).

Ben Sira, too, pictures the streams of the holy of holies. The sequence begins as a poem in which Wisdom describes herself growing like a huge fragrant tree, but it changes abruptly into a eulogy of the Law of Moses. The imagery, however, is unmistakable. The Law flows like the rivers from Eden, the Pishon, the Tigris, the Euphrates and the Gihon (Gen.

---

*Justin knew a longer version of Ps. 96.10, 'The LORD reigns from the tree', (*Trypho* 73). *Xylon* corresponds to Hebrew '*s* and means tree or wood. The same line is alluded to in *Barnabas* 8.

2.10–14; *Ben Sira* 24.25–27 where the Jordan is added to the list!) and it fills men with Wisdom. Wisdom then resumes her poem and tells how she determined to water her garden, how her water course grew from a canal to a river and from a river to a sea, and how she poured out her teaching (*Ben Sira* 24.30–34). Isaiah had said something similar about the time of the Messiah: 'The earth shall be full of the knowledge of the LORD as the waters cover the sea' (Isa. 11.9).

Jesus used these Eden images in his teaching. He promised the Samaritan woman: 'Whoever drinks of the water that I shall give him will never thirst. The water that I give him will become in him a spring of water welling up to eternal life' (John 4.14). This is another way of speaking about the gift of Wisdom which resurrects and makes divine, and resembles a saying in the *Gospel of Thomas*: 'He who will drink from my mouth will become like me. I myself shall become he, and the things that are hidden will be revealed to him' (*Thomas* 108). Jesus stood in the temple at the Feast of Tabernacles and proclaimed, 'If anyone thirst let him come to me, and let him who believes in me drink. As the Scripture has said, Out of his heart shall flow rivers of living water' (John 7.37–38, alternative punctuation). John's Jesus speaks here as Wisdom, but also as the LORD who promised 'to pour out his Spirit like water on thirsty ground', and invited everyone to the waters (Isa. 44.3; 55.1). The evangelist explained that this water was in fact the gift of the Spirit, another indication that the hearers of the Johannine writings had lost touch with their temple context (John 7.39). Jesus also spoke of the kingdom of God as a mighty tree. The parable of the mustard seed draws its motifs from the tree of life, but Jesus emphasizes the smallness of its beginnings. The seed becomes great and puts forth large branches so that, like Ezekiel's tree, the birds can make nests in its shade (Mark 4.31–32).

The Qumran Hymns had exactly this picture of the Eden holy of holies. The community were priests in the place of light which was the true holy of holies, trees in the garden of God, planted beside the streams of Paradise:

And Thou wilt bring Thy glorious [ ] to all the men of Thy council, those who share a common lot with the angels of the Face. Among them shall be no mediator [ ] and no messenger [ ] ... They ... shall cause a shoot to grow into the boughs of an everlasting plant. It shall cover the whole [ ] with its shadow [ ] its roots [ ] to the Abyss. A source of light shall become an ever flowing fountain, and in its bright flames all the [ ] shall be consumed [ ] a fire to devour all sinful men in utter destruction. (1QH XIV, formerly VI)

Thou hast placed me, O my God, among the branches of the Council of Holiness ... I shall shine in a sevenfold light in [ ] Thee for Thy glory; for Thou art an everlasting light unto me and wilt establish my feet. (1 QH XV, formerly VII)

Thou hast placed me beside a fountain of streams in an arid land ... trees of life beside a mysterious fountain hidden among the trees by the water and they put out a shoot of the everlasting plant ... They sent out their roots to the watercourse that its stem might be open to the living waters and be one with the everlasting spring ... (1QH XVI, formerly VIII)

Thou hast caused [ ] to return that it may enter into a Covenant with Thee, and stand [ ] in the everlasting abode, illumined with perfect light for ever ... (1QH XXI, formerly XVIII)

The community was a plant of delight whose branches bore much fruit and supported the high heavens. None of its fruit was bad, and its roots could not be pulled up (4Q255).

They sang of their hidden plantation of trees, and of others whose roots did not reach to the true watercourse. No one entered their garden of everlasting trees to drink the holy waters who had not seen and believed in the Fountain of Life (1QH XVI, formerly VIII). Their hearts were open to the everlasting fountain (1QH XVIII, formerly X). They described themselves as the holy of holies, the Eternal Plantation, joined to the sons of heaven: 'My eyes have gazed on that which is eternal, on Wisdom concealed from men ... on a fountain of righteousness and on a storehouse of power ... on a spring of glory ... given to his Chosen Ones as an everlasting possession' (1QS X1). Anyone who betrayed the community and departed from the fountain of living waters would not find his name in the Book on the day of the Messiah (CD VIII). As they told their history, they wrote of the Scoffer who shed the waters of lies over Israel, and of the new plant that sprang up 390 years after the destruction of Jerusalem (CD I). Others described this as the end of the seventh week of Israel's history, when the elect Righteous from the eternal plant of righteousness would be given sevenfold instruction about the creation (1 En. 93.10).

The *Odes of Solomon* sang of the blessed as the trees of Paradise in the same way as did the Qumran hymns:

Their branches were flourishing
and their fruits were shining,
and their roots were from an immortal land.
And a river of gladness was irrigating them
and the region round about them in the land of eternal life ...
... blessed O Lord are they
who are planted in your land,
and who have a place in your Paradise
... and have passed from darkness into light. (*Ode* 11)

The Sons of Light

The city is the new holy of holies, and so it is Day One, before the sun and moon were created to give light to the material world (see p. 20). Jesus spoke of this light as 'the glory which I had with thee before the world was made' (John 17.5), and he prayed that his disciples might see this glory: 'Father I desire that they also, whom thou hast given me, may be with me where I am, to behold my glory which thou hast given me in thy love for me before the foundation of the world' (John 17.24). This is the marvellous light into which God calls his own people, his royal priesthood (1 Pet. 2.9), the servants of God-and-the-Lamb who stand before his throne in the holy of holies (22.3–4).

The Qumran Hymns sing of this: 'Thou hast revealed thyself to me in Thy power as perfect Light' (1QH XII, formerly IV). The one who had been placed 'among the branches' of the Council of Holiness knew that he would 'shine in a sevenfold light' (1QH XV, formerly VII; see p. 131). He would 'stand in the everlasting abode, illumined with perfect light for ever' (1QH XXI, formerly XVIII). The community defined themselves as 'the sons of light' who were ruled by 'the Prince of Light' (1QS III). Enoch spoke in his third Parable of 'the righteous and elect in the light of eternal life' (*1 En.* 58.3), and this was a vision of heaven. Jesus, however, spoke of the sons of this world who were more worldly wise than the sons of light (Luke 16.8), implying that the sons of light were already living alongside the sons of this world, that the kingdom was in some way present. John wrote in the same way of those who walk in the light and live in the light (1 John 1.7, 2.9) and have already passed from death to life (1 John 3.14). In other words, those who live in the light are already resurrected; they are the first-resurrected of the kingdom (see p. 338).

The clearest and most consistent use of these images of the holy of holies and Eden is found in the *Gospel of Thomas*. Since this is a collection of sayings, it is not possible to know if consecutive sayings are related ideas, but two sayings do seem to identify the place of light as the kingdom: 'Jesus said, "Blessed are the solitary and elect, for you will find the kingdom. For you are from it and to it you will return." Jesus said, "If they say to you, "Where did you come from?" say to them, "We came from the light, the place where the light came into being on its own accord" ' (*Thomas* 49, 50). The elect are from the kingdom and also from the place where light originated. In temple theology, this was the holy of holies, Day One, and in the Book of Revelation, this place is the holy of holies that comes from heaven as the new city, the millennium kingdom. Only those born from above, i.e. the first-resurrected, can either see or enter it (John 3.3–6).

Thomas' Jesus taught about the holy of holies as the place beyond time, Day One, but also the place from which the mystic could see all history (see p. 24). Those who entered the holy of holies were the resurrected because they had passed beyond the material world. 'Jesus said, "Have you discovered, then, the beginning, that you look for the end? For where the beginning is, there will the end be. Blessed is he who will take his place in the beginning, he will know the end and will not

---

*The implied fusion of the Sabbath and Day One is found in the early second century BCE. Aristobulus wrote: 'God ... gave us the seventh day for rest ... this could in reality also be called the first day' (in Eusebius *Preparation* 13.12).

experience death" ' (*Thomas* 18).* The next saying speaks of the trees of Paradise prepared for the chosen ones, another reference to the temple as Eden. The disciples later asked about the 'rest' and the coming of the new world, exactly the sequence at the end of the Book of Revelation, where the rest is the Sabbath 'day' of history, the millennium kingdom, and the new world is what follows after heaven and earth have passed away (see p. 363). 'His disciples said to him. "When will the rest of the dead come about, and when will the new world come?" He said to them, "What you look forward to has already come but you do not recognize it" ' (*Thomas* 51). This saying is similar to Logion 113: 'His disciples said to him, "When will the kingdom come?" ... It will not come by waiting for it ... rather, the kingdom of the Father is spread out upon the earth and men do not see it".' For some, the kingdom was already present; they were already resurrected and they were the ones who saw the kingdom before their physical death: 'There are some standing here who will not taste death before they see that the kingdom of God has come with power' (Mark 9.1).

The *Wisdom of Jesus Christ*, usually classed as a gnostic text, gave more detail: 'First Begetter Father is called Adam [ ] eye of the light because he came from the shining light [ ] his holy angels who are ineffable [and] shadowless ... [This is] the whole kingdom of the son of Man, the one who is called Son of God. It is full of ineffable and shadowless joy and unchanging jubilation because they rejoice over his imperishable glory (CG III.4.105–106).

John's Jesus spoke of the place of light where he had been in glory with the Father before the world was made (John 17.5), and he prayed that his disciples might come to that place to see his glory (John 17.24). Thus the servants of God-and-the-Lamb stand before his throne in the holy of holies and share his reign. He shines light upon them, and they see his face and have his Name on their foreheads (22.3–5). This was the ancient blessing of Aaron: 'The LORD bless you and keep you: The LORD make his face to shine upon you, and be gracious unto you: The LORD lift up his countenance upon you, and give you peace' (Num. 6.24–26).

The servants in the holy of holies worship God-and-the-Lamb and they 'see his face' (22.4), another indication that these are the traditions of the first temple. It was a hallmark of the Deuteronomists and their newer religion that nobody could see God. The older faith had known otherwise: those who ascended Sinai 'saw the God of Israel' (Exod. 24.10), Isaiah saw the LORD enthroned in the temple (Isa. 6.1) and spoke of those who would see the king in his beauty (Isa. 33.17). Ezekiel saw a fiery Man, 'the likeness of the glory of the LORD' (Ezek. 1.28). The Deuteronomists, however, were adamant that such things were not possible: when the commandments were given 'you heard the sound of words but saw no form, there was only a voice' (Deut. 4.12). Moses was told: 'You cannot see my face, for man shall not see me and live' (Exod. 33.20) even though the Pentateuch at this point also incorporates the older view: 'The LORD used to speak to Moses face to face' (Exod. 33.11). To see the face of the LORD was a priestly privilege granted to those who entered the holy of holies and stood before the throne. It was the experience which made mortals divine and, as Moses attracted to his story more and more elements of the older royal cult, so Philo described him entering the presence of God to be 'named God and King' (*Life of Moses* I, 158).

Jesus taught in this older royal tradition: 'Blessed are the pure in heart, for they shall see God' (Matt. 5.8). The pure in heart were his new priests, the royal priesthood purified by the blood of the Lamb (Rev. 1.5–6; 5.9). The summary of Jesus' teaching in Mark 7.21–23 describes the real defilement which issued from an impure heart: 'For from within, out of the heart of man, come evil thoughts, fornication, theft, murder, adultery, coveting, wickedness, deceit, licentiousness, envy, slander, pride, and foolishness. All these evil things come from within, and they defile a man'. There is no mention of the purity requirements of the Levitical priesthood, which excluded the disabled and the malformed as blemished and unfit for temple service (Lev. 21.17–23). There had always been other voices:

Who shall ascend the hill of the LORD,
And who shall stand in his holy place?
He who has clean hands and a pure heart,
who does not lift up his soul to what is false,
and does not swear deceitfully. (Ps. 24.3–4)

The Third Isaiah had promised a place in the temple to anyone who would keep the Sabbath and the covenant (Isa. 56.6). The Temple Scroll, however, envisaged the whole city as a temple area with the most rigorous traditional standards of purity. There was to be no sexual activity within the city, and no one who was blind, or afflicted with a skin disease, or who had touched a dead body, was permitted to enter. Only the purest of food and leather was permitted in the sacred city, and unclean birds were not permitted to fly overhead. No pollution was permitted because the LORD himself was there (11QT XLV). The Temple Scroll ruled that all the inhabitants of the city should observe the priestly purity laws and in this it coincided with the Book of Revelation. The different definition of impurity, though, reflected the characteristic teaching of Jesus, and suggests that the description of the heavenly city in the Book of Revelation may come from him.

Jesus' attitude to the ritually unclean can be seen in the parable of the Good Samaritan, who risked touching a dead body when the priest and the Levite had to pass by on the other side because of the purity laws (Luke 10.31–32); in the healing of the bleeding woman who was afraid because she had touched someone in her uncleanness (Luke 8.43–48); in his cleansing of lepers (Mark 1.40–44) and giving sight to the blind (Luke 18.35–43); and in his teaching about the nature of true blindness (Matt. 23.16–22).

Excluded from the jewelled city were 'common' things (21.27, cf. Acts 10.14, anything that is 'common or unclean'), which may reflect the practice of the Hebrew Christians who observed the food laws and expected Gentile Christians to do the same as a condition of table fellowship (Acts 15.29). Or something else may be intended in the light of Mark 7.18–19 which attributes to Jesus the teaching that all foods are clean. There is no problem, however, about the exclusion of those with an unclean lifestyle which was a sign of an impure heart: 'dogs and sorcerers and fornicators and murderers and idolaters and everyone who practises falsehood' (22.15, cf. 21.8), summarized in 21.27 as 'abomination and falsehood'. These were people who broke the Law of Moses: worshipping idols, committing murder, committing adultery, bearing false witness, practising witchcraft (forbidden in Exod. 22.18 and Deut. 18.10–12) and homosexual acts* (Lev. 20.13).

The new priests in the holy of holies are the pure in heart who see God, and so there are no divisions in the city to distinguish differing degrees of holiness. There is no temple with its graded courtyards, only a city/holy of holies whose gates are never shut, whose light is the glory of God. This is the kingdom of priests who reign for ever and ever.

---

*The Greek *kunes*, dogs, translates literally the Hebrew *kᵉlabim*, and so this could be a reference to the purity law which banned dogs from the sacred camp 'for they may eat some of the bones from the holy of holies to which meat is still attached' (4Q397). The word *kᵉlabim* also means sodomites (Deut. 23.18), and this is the more likely meaning here in a list of human sins; there were to be no such practices in the holy city. Other contemporary texts are similar: in the holy city there would be 'no illicit love of boys' (*Sib.* 5.430), and the wicked priests of the seventh week were condemned as 'pederasts who practised bestiality' (*T. Levi* 17.11).

THE MILLENNIUM KINGDOM

His servants shall worship him; they shall see his face and his name shall be on their foreheads. And night shall be no more; they need no light of lamp or sun, for the LORD God will be their light, and they shall reign for ever and ever.

Then I saw thrones, and seated on them those to whom judgement was committed. Also I saw the souls of those who had been beheaded for their testimony to Jesus and for the word of God ... They came to life and reigned with Christ for a thousand years ... This is the first resurrection ... they shall be priests of God and of Christ, and they shall reign with him a thousand years. (Rev. 22.3b–5; 20.4–6)

You are those who have continued with me in my trials; and I assign to you, as my Father assigned to me, a kingdom, that you may eat and drink at my table in my kingdom, and sit on thrones judging the twelve tribes of Israel. (Luke 22.28–30)

This is the new royal priesthood, fellow heirs with Christ who have suffered with him and entered his glory (Rom. 8.17). The leaders of the seven churches had been assured that they were the true priesthood, that those who were worthy would share the throne of Christ, just as he shared the throne of his Father (3.21). They would be safe from the second death (2.11) because their names were in the Book of Life (3.5). The new song of the elders round the throne had proclaimed them, the redeemed who were to reign on earth as a kingdom of priests (5.10). These are the martyrs from the Great Tribulation who serve before the throne in the temple (7.14–15), the firstborn (14.4) and the heavenly warriors of the King of kings and LORD of lords. They wear the Name on their foreheads and see his face (22.4).

The *Ascension of Isaiah* describes the coming of the kingdom; the saints will descend and come to earth with the LORD, together with those whose spirits are clothed. The LORD will strengthen those still alive, 'still found in the body', and then begin the judgement of the world. He will send out fire to consume the wicked 'and they will become as if they had not been created' (*Asc. Isa.* 4.16–18).

The First Resurrection

Belief in resurrection was fundamental in the early church, but the New Testament shows that this was not understood simply as a post-mortem experience. The faithful were reminded that they were already resurrected, 'raised with Christ' (Col. 3.1), and yet those who had been literally raised from the dead, such as the young man of Nain (Luke 7.11–17) and Jairus' daughter (Luke 8.40–48) did not, apparently, found a religious movement and attract disciples who thought themselves similarly resurrected. The Christian resurrection belief was not one of resuscitation, but of rebirth as a child of God. It developed in a context where there were many other beliefs about resurrection, and this led to confusion. Daniel 12.2–3 envisaged the dead being raised from the dust, some to punishment and others to everlasting life shining like stars. This implies more than a physical resuscitation; the righteous would be transfigured and become radiant in their resurrected state. The Book of Enoch gives details of how different places were reserved for the different categories of dead who were kept separate until the last judgement and then given what they deserved (*1 En.* 22.1–14). Jesus himself taught that the resurrected were 'equal to angels, sons of God, being sons of the resurrection' (Luke 20.36), and was at this point speaking of a future state after physical death.

Some of his contemporaries at Qumran thought themselves already resurrected: 'Thou hast cleansed a perverse spirit of great sin that it may stand with the host of the holy ones and that it may enter into community with the congregation of the sons of heaven' (1QH XI, formerly III). They believed they had been taken into the presence of God and transformed into angels. Their resurrection was not as disembodied spirits or immortal souls, but as whole human beings totally transformed into an angelic state. This is the scene described in 7.9, as 'a great multitude standing before the throne and before the Lamb, clothed in white robes'. They had resurrection bodies, what Paul called 'spiritual bodies, raised in power and imperishable' (1 Cor. 15.42–44).

What Paul meant by a spiritual body, *soma pneumatikon*, in contrast to the physical body, *soma psuchikon*, is best illustrated by comparison with Philo's account of the creation of Adam. This is not to suggest that Paul knew Philo, although it is likely that an educated Jew like Paul would have known the works of his distinguished older contemporary. Paul and Philo simply lived at the same time and knew the same ideas. Philo explained the two accounts of the creation (Gen. 1.1–2.4a and Gen. 2.4b–3.24) by saying that the first was the creation of the heavenly archetypes and the second of the material world. The earthly Adam, said Philo, was 'vastly different' from the man made in the image of God. The earthly man is an object of sense perception, he can be seen, consists of body and soul, *soma* and *psuche*, and is by nature mortal (*Creation* 135). These were also Paul's words, used in the context of what could and could not be seen. In contrast, said Philo, the man made after the image, the man of Genesis 1, was incorporeal, invisible, neither male nor female, and by nature incorruptible (*Creation* 134). When Paul used the term spiritual body, he referred to the human of Genesis 1, contrasted with the physical body, the humans of Genesis 2–3. Paul explained that the human situation reversed the order of creation; the earthly human can now return to his heavenly state, because he is resurrected (1 Cor. 15.42–50).

There is good reason to believe that Jesus saw himself as Son of God in this sense, already resurrected. His resurrection life began in the Jordan when he saw the heavens open and heard the voice telling him

that he was the Son of God. One version of Luke 3.22 has the voice at
the baptism say, 'You are my beloved son; today I have begotten you'
(Ps. 2.7), indicating a royal context for the resurrection experience as
this was a coronation psalm. Paul, who seems to be quoting a statement
of established belief, wrote that Jesus was designated Son of God with
power by the Holy Spirit by his resurrection from the dead (Rom. 1.4).
Either Paul is saying that Jesus was not a Son of God during his ministry
and that he did not become the Son until after the crucifixion, or, that
his 'resurrection' occurred earlier in his life and empowered him for his
ministry as Son of God.

The resurrection proof texts used of Jesus in the New Testament are
not post-mortem resuscitation texts such as Isaiah 26.19: 'Thy dead
shall live, their bodies shall rise', but texts which describe the mystical
ascent and enthronement of the king such as Psalm 2, or Psalm 110.
Other texts which speak of the king 'being raised up high' mean that he
was resurrected (i.e. what they understood by that word): 'The oracle of
the man who was raised on high,* the anointed ... (2 Sam. 23.1). The
same idea (but not the same word) occurs in Psalm 89.19–20: 'I have
raised on high one chosen from the people ... with my holy oil I have
anointed him'; and in Isaiah 52.14, 'my servant shall be exalted ...'

The resurrection of Melchizedek was known to the early church.
Comparing the priesthoods of Aaron and Melchizedek, the writer to the
Hebrews argues that if the rites of the current temple priesthood had
been effective there would have been no need for a priest 'to be resurrected in the manner of Melchizedek' (Heb. 7.11, translating literally),
rather than just inheriting the name of Aaron. Jesus is identified as this
new high priest, resurrected like Melchizedek, who has become a priest
'not by bodily descent, but by the power of an indestructible life' (Heb.
7.15–16). Summaries of the life of Jesus show that this was the original
understanding of his resurrection: 'God raised up his servant and sent
him to you' (Acts 3.26) and 'The God of our fathers raised up Jesus,
whom you killed ... God exalted him at his right hand' (Acts 5.30)
imply that Jesus was raised up before beginning his ministry and before
his final exaltation.

Paul spoke of Christians being already 'raised with Christ',
presumably repeating Jesus' experience of becoming sons of God and
angels at their baptism. He does not argue *for* this position, as though
it were some new idea; he argues *from* it, i.e. it is an established
Christian belief: 'If then you have been raised with Christ, seek the
things that are above where Christ is ...' (Col. 3.1). Paul also hoped for
a future resurrection when the dead would be raised at the sound of the
last trumpet (1 Cor. 15.51). Since he was writing to a Christian
community, this resurrection must correspond to the 'first resurrection'
of 20.5, the resurrection at the return of the LORD. Thus Paul, or
someone writing in his name to a leader of the church at Ephesus,

*Using the same word as Isa. 26.19, but clearly not intending a post-mortem resurrection.

dismissed the belief implied in baptismal resurrection as 'the godless chatter' of those who 'had swerved from the truth' (2 Tim. 2.16–17). They were upsetting the faithful, presumably those whose baptized loved ones had died. There had been a crisis in the church when the first generation who had been born again and raised with Christ, began to die either from old age or as martyrs. They had expected to see the return of the LORD in their lifetime, and so Paul assured the church at Thessalonika that those left alive at the LORD's return would have no advantage over those who had died. The dead in Christ would 'rise first', and then the living would be caught up with them to meet the LORD (1 Thess. 4.15–17). In each case, Paul implies that there had been a prophetic revelation, new teaching for a new situation. 'This we declare to you by the word of the LORD' (1 Thess. 4.15) and 'Lo! I tell you a mystery' (1 Cor. 15.51) presumably indicate oracles in answer to the question: What happens when the resurrected die? The answer was given: They would be raised in an additional, special resurrection, the first resurrection, to be with the LORD and enjoy the promised kingdom.

This additional revelation may explain the obvious addition in 20.4b–5. Those enthroned in the kingdom are joined by martyrs who live again and reign with Christ. These are the souls who had been beheaded for 'the witness of Jesus', souls who had neither worshipped the beast and its image nor received its mark (20.4). These are the saints who were exhorted to endure and keep 'the faith of Jesus' (14.12) and they were promised rest. The problem is that they were 'beheaded', the translation usually offered here for *pepelekismenos*. Little is known of the earliest martyrs, but hardly any seem to have died in that way. James bar Zebedee was killed with a sword in Jerusalem (Acts 12.2) and, when Peter was crucified in Rome, Paul is said to have been beheaded, presumably because he was a Roman citizen (Eusebius, *History* 2.25). The other martyrs in Nero's reign of terror died in the arena, or by crucifixion, or were burned to death (Tacitus, *Annals* 15.44). These are the multitude before the throne, 'coming out of the great tribulation', 7.14. There are no details of how Domitian's victims died, or even if they were Christians, since the charges were atheism and Jewish customs (*Dio Cassius Epitome* 67.14). He wanted to put to death the descendants of Jesus' family, but he let them live when he discovered they were only peasant farmers who believed that Christ's kingdom was in heaven and would appear at the end of the world (Hegesippus quoted in Eusebius, *History* 3.20). It is unlikely that all who shared the millennium kingdom with Christ were Roman citizens who had been put to death by execution. The word translated 'beheaded' means, literally, 'axed', and this may indicate which martyrs were the occasion of this vision. This type of axe, *pelekus*, was part of the standard battle equipment of a Roman soldier, in other words, it was a battle axe (*War* 3.95) Those who had been 'axed' were probably the faithful who died in the city after the exhortations of 14.12–13, and this is the vision of the rest promised to those who died in the LORD (14.13). Josephus describes the fate of 'poor women and children and a mixed multitude', who responded to the proclamation of a prophet. He told them that God had commanded them to go to the temple court on that very day and receive there the signs of salvation. This was the day when the Romans set fire to part of the temple, and all 6000 died, some in the flames, some attempting to escape (*War* 6.283–86). Some priests were trapped in the temple itself and took refuge on one of the broad walls of the sanctuary (*War* 6.279). There they remained for five days, until, driven by starvation, they came down. Titus refused to spare their lives and declared that priests should perish with their temple (*War* 6.322).

The priests of the first resurrection live and reign with Christ for one thousand years, and the martyrs participate in the priestly resurrection even after their physical death. The martyrs under the altar had already been declared part of the high priest's atonement sacrifice (see on 6.9–11). Their 'lot' is with the priests and they are blessed and holy (20.6), a word elsewhere rendered 'saint' (e.g. 1 Thess. 3.13, 'the saints'). Those whose lot is with the first-resurrected share the glory (John 17.22–24) and the promises in the seven letters show that this was understood as returning to Eden (2.7).

The 'lot' of the priests is reminiscent of the Melchizedek text (11QMelch), which describes the redeemed as the 'inheritance' of Melchizedek, the 'allotted portion' for whom atonement will be made at the end of the tenth Jubilee. Israel was the LORD's 'inheritance' (Deut. 32.9), and the 'priesthood of the LORD' was the inheritance of the Levites (Josh. 18.7). When he washed his disciples' feet, Jesus told Peter, 'If I do not wash you, you will have no inheritance with me' (John 13.8). The voice from the throne contrasted the heritage of those who conquer with that of the faithless who would die the second death (21.7), and the curse on anyone who altered the words of the Book of Revelation was to lose the inheritance it described (22.19).

The first-resurrected are the true priests, fulfilling Isaiah's Jubilee prophecy which is the recurring theme of the Melchizedek text, that the released would return to their heritage and 'be called the priests of the LORD, the ministers of our God', those with whom the eternal covenant would be made (Isa. 61.6, 8). Release, atonement, Jubilee and covenant appear in what remains of the Melchizedek text; true priesthood was probably a theme also, as it speaks of *the teachers who have been kept hidden and secret*. The Damascus Document draws all these themes and hopes together:

'With the remnant which held fast to the commandments of God' [cf. 12.17; 14.12, those who keep the commandments of God] 'he made his covenant with Israel for ever, revealing to them the hidden things in which all Israel had gone astray ... Those who hold fast to it are destined to live forever and all the glory of Adam shall be theirs. As God ordained for them by the hand of the prophet Ezekiel, saying, The Priests, the Levites and the sons of Zadok who kept the charge of my sanctuary when the children of Israel strayed from me, they shall offer me fat and blood. The priests are the converts of Israel who departed from the land of Judah, and [the Levites are] those who joined them. The sons of Zadok are the elect of Israel, the men called by name who shall stand at the end of days'. (CD III–IV)

Thrones Were Placed

Two judgements are described in the Book of Revelation: the Last Judgement before the great white throne, when the books are opened and the dead are judged (20.11–15), and the Day of the LORD, when he emerges from his holy place to complete the Great Atonement, to avenge the blood of his servants and atone the land of his people (Deut. 32.43). More than one judgement is implied in other contemporary texts, for example the *Testament of Abraham* A13 describes three judgements. First 'a wondrous man like a Son of God' passes sentence. He is identified as the Son of Adam (Son of Man? since *'adam* means man), and God has appointed him as judge (corresponding to the risen LORD throughout the Book of Revelation and the Man in Dan. 7.13–14). He is assisted by the angel of fire who tests souls (see p. 257). The second judgement is by the twelve tribes of Israel (corresponding to judgement by the first-resurrected, 20.4, or the saints Dan. 7.18, 27), and the third by the 'Master God of All' (corresponding to 20.11–14, or to Dan. 12.2–3).

Most of the prophecies and visions in the Book of Revelation describe the judgement on the Day of the LORD which was believed to be imminent, 'the revelation of Jesus Christ which God gave him to show to his servants what must soon take place' (1.1). Jesus had preached, 'The time is fulfilled, and the kingdom of God is at hand; repent, and believe in the gospel' (Mark 1.15). 'Repent', because the LORD was about to appear as the judge of all those living on earth. Not everyone would be fit to enter the Kingdom established on that Day (Matt. 7.21–23), the Day of the wrath of the Lamb from which there would be no escape (6.15–17). Baptism offered protection (see p. 155), and the characteristic of Christian baptism was that the Spirit was given and it was the moment of resurrection. Christians were 'sealed in the Holy Spirit for the day of redemption' (Eph. 4.30), the Holy Spirit which was, 'the guarantee of our inheritance until we acquire possession of it' (Eph. 1.14). Paul wrote of Christians being sealed, and given the Spirit as a guarantee (2 Cor. 1.22) of their place in the kingdom. Those who were waiting for the LORD Jesus Christ to appear knew they would be safe ('guiltless') on the Day of the LORD (1 Cor. 1.8). The judgement implied in 20.4 is the Day of the LORD, the Day of Atonement when Satan has been bound and the LORD has come with his saints to judge the living and to establish the kingdom. The only ones resurrected at this time are those to whom the kingdom was already promised, those baptized and sealed.

The servants of God who see his face and bear his name were to reign for ever, and so thrones were set in place, and on them sat those to whom/for whom judgement, *krima,* was given. The text here is not clear. It could mean that a verdict was given in their favour, but, if they were sitting on thrones, it is more likely to mean that they were appointed as judges. This is like Daniel's Man vision, when he saw the four beasts and then the Man ascending to heaven to be given everlasting dominion (Dan. 7.14). The angel explained the vision to Daniel, that the saints/holy ones of the Most High would be given into the power of the beast for 'a time, two times and half a time' (Dan. 7.25, see p. 186). Then the court would sit in judgement and take away his power; dominion would pass to the people of the holy ones of the Most High (Dan. 7.27). Daniel saw in his vision until 'the Ancient of Days came and judgement* was given to the saints of the Most High and the time came when the saints received the kingdom' (Dan. 7.22).

In the Book of Revelation, the saints receive the kingdom and reign for ever and ever (22.5), presumably until the end of time. This is similar to the saints in Daniel's vision receiving the 'greatness of the kingdoms under the whole heaven . . . an everlasting kingdom' (Dan. 7.27), but the theme of exaltation and receiving power was more widely known, and so Daniel's vision may not have been the direct source of the seer's inspiration. The exaltation of the afflicted Servant is the theme of the fourth Servant Song (Isa. 52.13–53.12) and a memory that the original Servant had been the king explains, for example, the belief elsewhere that the afflicted righteous would 'govern nations and peoples'. Not martyrdom but the injustice of life is the context here:

For though in the sight of men they were punished,
their hope is full of immortality.
. . . because God tested them and found them worthy of himself;
like gold in the furnace he tried them . . .
They will govern nations and rule over peoples,
and the LORD will reign over them for ever.
. . . because grace and mercy are upon his elect,
and he watches over his holy ones. (*Wisd.* 3.4–9)

Words attributed to Jesus show that he promised this exaltation to his followers: 'When the Son of Man sits on his glorious throne, you who have followed me will also sit on twelve thrones, judging the twelve tribes of Israel . . . and everyone who has left houses [or families] for my name's sake will . . . inherit eternal life' (Matt. 19.28–29). Paul, believed this, too: 'Do you not know that the saints will judge the world?' (1 Cor. 6.2), and there was a saying in the early church: 'If we have died with him we shall live with him; if we endure we shall also reign with

---

*There are two Greek texts of Daniel, the LXX, which translates this as *krisis,* an act of judging, implying that power was given to the saints, and Theodotion's version which has *krima,* the outcome of a judgement, a verdict, implying a verdict in favour of the saints. In practice, however, the words were virtually synonymous.

him' (2 Tim. 2.11–12). Thus the saints in the Book of Revelation were exhorted to endure; they knew they would reign with the LORD.

The two judgements, of the living and the first-resurrected on the Day of the LORD and of all the resurrected dead at the Last Judgement, soon coalesced in Christian thought. John 5.21–29 implies that the Son presides at the Last Judgement of the resurrected, as does 2 Timothy 4.1: 'in the presence of God and of Christ Jesus who is to judge the living and the dead ...' When Domitian had members of Jesus' family arrested, they explained that the kingdom of the Messiah was angelic and in heaven, and that he would judge 'the living and the dead' at the end of the world (Hegesippus in Eusebius, *History* 3.20), and eventually the Creeds declared, 'He shall come to judge the quick and the dead'. In the Book of Revelation, however, and in several other early texts, we glimpse the original hope of the Hebrew Christians. It was built on the ancient expectation of the LORD coming to avenge the blood of his servants and renew their land, but incorporated the more recent idea of a post-mortem resurrection at the end of time to give each person the reward or punishment which had not been received in life.

Peter's sermon in Solomon's Porch warned the assembled crowd that the process of the Day of the LORD had begun. 'Repent, therefore, and turn again that your sins may be blotted out', in preparation for the LORD's judgement of the living, 'that times of refreshing may come from the presence of the LORD', that the creation might be renewed on the Day, 'and that he may send the Messiah appointed for you, Jesus, whom heaven must receive until the time for establishing all that God spoke by the mouth of his holy prophets from of old' (Acts 3.19–21). Paul warned the people of Athens: 'God has fixed a Day on which he will judge the world in righteousness by a man whom he has appointed ...'(Acts 17.31), but he warned that Christians also would be judged by their deeds, an innovation. Although he could exhort on the basis of Christians being already raised with Christ (Col. 3.1), he also used the future resurrection and judgement to reinforce his moral teachings (Rom. 6.5–11). 'As I live, says the LORD, every knee shall bow to me', and so Paul warned, 'We shall all stand before the judgement seat of God' (i.e. the LORD, Rom. 14.10–11). He warned the Corinthian church: 'We must all appear before the judgement seat of Christ, so that each may receive good or evil according to what he has done in the body' (2 Cor. 5.10).

The Gospels show Jesus teaching about his future role as judge of the living on the Day of the LORD. This was the original context of the parable of the sheep and the goats (Matt. 25.31–46). The Son of Man comes with his angels and sits on his glorious throne. The nations gather before him and he, the King, separates them out. To the good he says: 'Come, O blessed of my Father, inherit the kingdom prepared for you from the foundation of the world'. The wicked are pronounced the angels of Satan and punished. The imagery is unmistakable; the Father and then his Son, the King, who presides at the judgement and decides who will enter the millennium kingdom. Jesus warned that on that Day (see pp. 354–6), he would not acknowledge as his own any people who had not done the will of his Father (Matt. 7.21–23). The Son of Man returning with his angels to bring judgement is another image of the Day of the LORD (Matt. 16.27 and parallels, cf. Deut. 33.2–5). The Son of Man had authority *on earth* to forgive sins (Luke 5.24). In the Book of Revelation, the harvest of the earth is the judgement of the living (14.15) and the Great Judgement on Jerusalem and the kings is wrought on earth, in history. The 'Hebrews' are assured that they have come to the heavenly Jerusalem 'to a judge who is God of all' (Heb. 12.23). This is ambiguous, but most probably refers to the Day of the LORD.

The Parables of Enoch have several descriptions of the Day of the LORD, the judgement of the living and the healing of the earth. In the first Parable, the congregation of the righteous appears and sinners are judged and driven from the earth. The Righteous One appears and the kings and the mighty perish (*1 En.* 38). There is no mention of resurrection. 'The congregation of the righteous' is the same as the saints of the Most High in Daniel's vision and the first-resurrected of the millennium kingdom. In the second Parable, the Elect One sits on the throne of glory and judges sinners; heaven and earth are transformed, the chosen ones live on earth and sinners are barred (*1 En.* 45). There is no mention of resurrection. In a place where there are fountains of Wisdom the Man is named (given the Name?), *all who dwell on earth worship him*, the kings of the earth and those who possess the land are downcast and handed over to the Chosen Ones for punishment, and then there is rest on the earth (*1 En.* 48). There is no mention of resurrection. (There is a separate account of the judgement of the resurrected in *1 En.* 51.1–5.) In the third Parable, the Elect One is seated on the throne of glory, and the kings and the mighty of the earth are judged. The Chosen Ones stand before him, but the rulers of the earth bow before him and beg for mercy. He hands them over to the angels of punishment, because they have oppressed his Chosen Ones (*1 En.* 62). The righteous receive their garments of glory, their resurrection bodies, and so they become like the first-resurrected of the millennium kingdom. The third Parable closes with a resumé of what has taken place: the cosmic covenant has been restored, the Son of Man has been revealed and has delivered his judgement, sinners and all who led the world astray have been destroyed from the earth, and there was to be no more corruption and decay (*1 En.* 69). There is no mention of resurrection.

Some of the earliest material in *1 Enoch* describes the three (or four, the text is corrupt) divisions in Sheol where the spirits of the dead wait for their resurrection *till the great judgement comes upon them* (*1 En.* 22.4). That judgement is never described. In the Dream Visions of Enoch, a judgement is described, but it is not the Last Judgement. After 'the sheep' had struggled against their enemies, perhaps a reference to the Maccabean revolt, the LORD of the sheep came to the earth in great wrath. His throne was erected in the land and books were opened before him. First the fallen angels and then their followers were judged and sent to the fiery abyss (1 En. 90.18–27). The temple was taken away and a new one erected, and then sheep became the rulers of the earth. Everyone in the community was 'able to see', in other words, they received the gift of Wisdom.

The first-resurrected on their thrones ruled with the Messiah for a thousand years (20.4). Theirs was the judgement that excluded the impure from the kingdom, and they were the sons of God revealed to release the creation from bondage to decay (Rom. 8.19–21) and restore the earth to its Eden state. Just as their blood had been part of the Great Atonement (see p. 154), so too the martyrs would be the royal priesthood who reigned with the Messiah: 'If we endure we shall also reign with him' (2 Tim. 2.12).

One Thousand Years

Jesus proclaimed the kingdom of God: 'The time is fulfilled and the kingdom of God is at hand' (Mark 1.15). *Whatever this has come to mean since that time, the kingdom of God in first-century Palestine must have meant the messianic millennium kingdom.* The Anointed One had originally been the Davidic king who reigned in Jerusalem, and the messianic kingdom was a sacral kingship where the person of the king guaranteed justice for his people and fertility for the land (Ps. 72). In the second temple period, the memory of sacral kingship was transformed into the hope for a future ruler who would restore justice and prosperity, and Jesus proclaimed that that time had come.

It is impossible to know how literally Jesus understood the idea of the kingdom of God. His enigmatic words to Pilate, 'My kingship is not of this world' (John 18.36), could have been spoken by one of the Davidic kings who also believed that their kingship came from heaven, that they were divine sons who had been raised up to the heavenly throne. This did not prevent their having an earthly kingdom, and many who followed Jesus expected this of him, also. After the miracle of the loaves and fishes, the crowd wanted to take Jesus and make him king (John 6.15). Even his closest disciples asked when he would restore the kingdom to Israel, and Jesus did not deny that the kingdom would be restored. He replied: 'It is not for you to know the times or seasons which the Father has fixed by his own authority' (Acts 1.6–7). The kingdom of God appears in the Book of Revelation as the one thousand year reign of the Messiah and his holy ones. The elders round the throne sang of the kingdom of priests who would reign on earth (5.10) and the fact that the kingdom lasts one thousand years indicates an earthly state since a heavenly kingdom would not have been measured in time.

Paul knew what was expected to happen in the near future; Christ had been raised first, and 'then at his coming, those who belong to Christ'. Only the Christian dead would rise to share the millennium kingdom. Christ would reign until he had overcome all his enemies, and when his triumph was complete, he would return the kingdom to his Father (1 Cor. 15.23–28). When the LORD Jesus appeared, he would battle with Satan and destroy him with the breath of his mouth (2 Thess. 2.8, cf. *Asc. Isa.* 4.14–18). These brief outlines broadly correspond to the sequence in the Book of Revelation. Christ would appear from heaven to establish his kingdom 'with the sword that issues from his mouth' (19.21), he would reign with those who belong to him (20.4–6) and overcome Satan and the nations who gather to battle against him (20.7–10).

There is a similar sequence in *1 Enoch*. The ancient Apocalypse of Weeks gives a stylized history of Israel in terms of 'weeks' or 'Sabbaths' which Enoch had learned from the words of the angels and the heavenly tablets (*1 En.* 91.12–17 and 93.1–14; the text is disordered here); it is the oldest text to describe a messianic kingdom in time followed by the eternal age. In the sixth week the people in the temple would become blind and forsake Wisdom, and then the temple would be burned. This was the end of the first temple period, and the blind were the temple 'reformers' in Josiah's reign (see p. 208). During the seventh week there would be an apostate generation, the restored priesthood, but towards the end of that week the chosen righteous would receive revelations of heavenly knowledge. The eighth week would be the initial struggle to establish the Messianic kingdom (corresponding to 19.11–21) culminating in a time of prosperity when the temple would be rebuilt (corresponding to the millennium kingdom, but John had been told that the temple would not be rebuilt, see p. 184). The ninth week was the time of judgement when the godless and their works were to be driven from the earth (corresponding to 20.4) and in the tenth week there would be the final judgement on the angels (corresponding to 20.7–10). Then the first heaven would pass away and a new heaven appear, when there would be no more time (corresponding to 20.11–21.4).

1 Enoch 10–11, some of the oldest material in the book, describes how Azazel/Semḥaza is bound for seventy generations, and during that time the earth is restored and healed. All oppression is cleansed from the earth and there are huge harvests. The 'storechambers of blessing are sent down onto the earth' and everyone lives in peace to a good old age (*1 En.* 11.1). This is the time of the kingdom. The *Book of Jubilees*, perhaps from the second century BCE, presents itself as Moses' account of what he learned on Sinai, the whole history of Israel until the LORD himself 'would descend and dwell with them in all the ages of eternity' (*Jub. 1.* 26). What follows is a description of the millennium kingdom, although not named as such: 'And [the LORD] said to the angel of the presence "Write for Moses from the first creation until my sanctuary is built in their midst for ever and ever. And the LORD will appear in the sight of all. And everyone will know that I am the God of Israel and the father of all the children of Jacob and king upon Mount Zion for ever and ever. And Zion and Jerusalem will be holy (*Jub.* 1.27–28).

Elsewhere there is a description of restored fertility after Satan has been banished: first there would be a time of decline and decay when people neglected the covenant and the sacred calendar, a time of war, poor crops and early death, but when people began to return to the covenant, their lives would be lengthened to almost one thousand years: 'And all of their days they will be complete, and live in peace and rejoicing, and there will be no Satan and no evil one who will destroy because all of their days will be days of blessing and healing. And then the LORD will heal his servants and they will rise up and see great peace and they will drive out their enemies ...' (*Jub.* 23.29–30). The days of the ancients had been 'as many as one thousand years and good' (*Jub.* 23.15) but Adam had lived only 930 years because he had eaten from the forbidden tree. Since it was written: 'In the day you eat from it you shall die' (Gen. 2.17), this 'day' must have been a day in the LORD's sight, namely one thousand years (*Jub.* 4.30; Ps. 90.4).

The recurring theme of healing and restoration is rooted in the atonement rites, when the earth was cleansed and healed at the start of the year. In the Book of Revelation this is the Great Atonement of the Sabbath year and Jubilee, when debt was remitted, slaves were released and land returned to its true owners. With the messianic age of Christ and his holy ones, the whole creation expected this release and renewal. Paul described the contrast between the present era of decay and the glorious future fertility of the messianic age, and the words he uses show the framework of his thinking. The earth, corrupted by the fallen angels, was to be restored when the sons of God appeared, those born of the Spirit, the first-resurrected. The argument of Romans 8 presupposes the sequence of events described in Revelation; the gift of the Spirit transforms the recipient into a son of God, a fellow heir with Christ who suffers with him (see p. 154) and then shares his glory in the messianic kingdom:

I consider that the sufferings of this present time are not worth comparing to the glory that is to be revealed to us. For the creation waits with eager longing for the revealing of the sons of God; for the creation was subjected to futility [i.e. nothingness, going nowhere], not of its own will but by the will of him who subjected it in hope; because the creation itself will be set free from its bondage to decay and obtain the glorious liberty of the children of God. (Rom. 8.18–21)

Here are all the themes: the divine plan to be endured, the present suffering, release from slavery and transformation from decay to fertility when the messianic kingdom is revealed.

There is evidence that Jesus taught about these events and expectations, particularly in writings associated with the church in Asia Minor. Additional material in a fifth-century copy of Mark's Gospel had Christ say to disciples: 'The limit of the years of the power of Satan is fulfilled. But other fearful things draw near, even on them for whom, because they had sinned, I was delivered to death that they might return to the truth and sin no more, that they might inherit the spiritual and incorruptible glory of righteousness which is in heaven, (MS Freer, Mark 16.14). This is the time after Satan has been bound, and the righteous enjoy their heavenly inheritance, the world beyond the veil. Papias, Bishop of Hierapolis early in the second century CE, recorded sayings of Jesus which he had learned from Aristion, a disciple of Jesus, and from the elder John (see p. 77). Now John compiled the Book of Revelation, and Aristion is said to have written the final section of Mark's Gospel, to replace the lost ending, and so may have been responsible for the material in the Freer text. These were the two who told Papias what Jesus had taught about the messianic kingdom, namely that after the resurrection of the dead there would be a period of a thousand years when Christ's kingdom would be set up on earth in material form (Eusebius, *History* 3.39).

Justin Martyr, a younger contemporary of Papias who lived for a while in Ephesus, was asked by Trypho if he really believed that Jerusalem would be rebuilt so that Christians could live there together with the patriarchs, prophets and saints of the Jews. Justin assured him that that was what he believed, even though some Christians did not: 'But I and every other completely orthodox Christian feel certain that there will be a resurrection of the flesh, followed by a thousand years in the rebuilt, embellished and enlarged City of Jerusalem, as was announced by the prophets Ezekiel, Isaiah and the others' (*Trypho* 80). The millennium, he said, would fulfil the prophecy of Isaiah 65.17–25, a time of fertility and a return to Eden, and this had been foretold also by John. He quoted what must have been the current understanding of Psalm 90.4: 'The Day of the LORD is as a thousand years'.

The fullest account of the millennium kingdom is found in the writings of Irenaeus, who also came originally from Asia Minor: 'For in as many days as this world was made, in so many thousand years shall it be concluded ... For the Day of the LORD is as a thousand years; and in six days created things were completed: it is evident therefore, that they will come to an end at the six thousandth year (*AH* 5.28). 'After the reign of the antichrist, then the LORD will come from heaven in the clouds ... bringing in for the righteous the times of the Kingdom, that is, the rest, the hallowed seventh day' (*AH* 5.30). He wrote of 'the mystery of the resurrection of the just and of the kingdom which is the commencement of incorruption ... For it is just that in that very creation in which they toiled or were afflicted ... they should receive the reward of their sufferings ... It is fitting, therefore, that the creation, being restored to its primeval condition, should without restraint be under the dominion of the righteous'. He then quotes Romans 8.19–21, that the creation itself is set free when the sons of God are revealed (*AH* 5.32). The kingdom was the seventh day, the true Sabbath, when all the prophesied blessings for the earth would appear: 'The predicted blessing, therefore, belongs unquestionably to the times of the kingdom, when the righteous shall bear rule upon their rising from the dead; when also the creation, having been renovated and set free, shall fructify with an abundance of all kinds of food ...' (*AH* 5.33). In the writings of Papias he had read sayings of Jesus passed on by John about the miraculous fertility of the millennium kingdom: 'The days will come when vineyards will grow each having ten thousand shoots and in one shoot ten thousand branches ... and upon every sprig ten thousand clusters, and in every cluster ten thousand grapes, and every grape when pressed shall yield twenty-five measures of wine'. Every grain of wheat would yield huge quantities of flour, fruit trees and grass would flourish and all animals would live at peace with each other. Judas refused to believe this, but Jesus told him: 'They shall see who come to that state of things' (*AH* 5.33).

This belief was attested also in first-century Palestine. *2 Baruch*, written in response to the fall of Jerusalem, has a similar account of the end times. The Messiah would begin to be revealed, then two monsters would appear, Behemoth from the land and Leviathan from the sea, who would be food for the people left in the land, cf. the beast from the sea and the beast from the land (Rev. 13.1, 11). Then there would be a time of miraculous fertility: 'The earth will yield fruits ten thousandfold, and on one vine will be a thousand branches and one branch will produce a thousand clusters, and one cluster will produce a thousand grapes, and one grape will produce a cor of wine' (*2 Bar.* 29.5).

2 Esdras, written in 100 CE 'thirty years after the fall of Jerusalem' (*2 Esdr.* 3.1), has a similar account of the end times. Although a Jewish text in origin with no traces of Christian belief, it was preserved by Christians, presumably because they recognized its similarity to their own prophecies in the Book of Revelation. The third vision gives a description of the messianic kingdom which is very similar to the millennium kingdom described in the Book of Revelation: 'The city that is now not seen shall appear and the land which is now hidden shall be disclosed. And everyone who has been delivered from the evils that I have foretold shall see my wonders. For my son the Messiah shall be revealed with those who are with him and those who remain shall rejoice for four hundred years' (*2 Esdr.* 7.26–28). This is not a Christian text. A Qumran text confirms that the Messiah was to be known as 'the Son of God Most High' (4Q246) and a later vision in *2 Esdras* also describes him as Son of God Most High (*2 Esdr.* 13.26–32). The high priest's question to Jesus, 'Are you the Messiah, the Son of the Blessed One?' (Mark 14.61) is not an impossible question for a Jew of that time to have asked. 'Ezra's' Messiah was to be revealed and reign with his people for 400 years: 'And after these years my Son the Messiah shall die, and all who draw human breath. And the world shall be turned back to primeval silence as it was in the first beginnings so that no one shall be left' (*2 Esdr.* 7.30–31). Everything was to return to the pre-created state. After seven days the earth and its chambers would give up their dead and the Most High be revealed on his throne as judge. At that time, the resurrected would be judged by their deeds; compassion and patience would have no place. The fire of hell and the joys of Paradise would be revealed and the nations would be required to recognize the One they had despised. In the Book of Revelation, this is the judgement before the great white throne (20.11–12).

There follows a long passage where 'Ezra' questions the Most High about the fate of sinners at the judgement, and is told that their fate is not his concern. He is promised the same reward as the faithful angels of the seven churches, and the resemblance to 21.3–4 is striking:

> Think of your own case and enquire of the glory of those who are like yourself. Because it is for you that Paradise is opened, the tree of life is planted, the age to come is prepared, plenty is provided, a city is built, rest is appointed and wisdom perfected beforehand. The root of evil is sealed up from you, illness is banished from you and death is hidden; hell has fled and corruption has been forgotten; sorrows have passed away and in the end the treasure of immortality is made manifest. (2 Esdr. 8.51–54)

'Ezra' is promised a place in the kingdom.

The Messiah and the first-resurrected were to reign for one thousand years, and it is unlikely that this figure was an innovation on the part of Jesus or the early church. The length of the messianic reign was matter for speculation and learned calculation at that time: seventy years was suggested on the basis of Isaiah 23.15, the seventy years when Tyre was forgotten; forty years on the basis of Deuteronomy 8.2 and Psalm 90.15, that forty years in the wilderness should be balanced by forty years of happiness; and similar reasoning was used of the 400 years slavery in Egypt (Gen. 15.13), giving the 400-year messianic reign in 2 Esdras. The figure of one thousand years had two bases: 'a thousand years in thy sight are as yesterday' (Ps. 90.4) and the seventh day as the Sabbath, the time of rest.

Seven thousand years as the total span of history was widely known at the end of the second temple period. 2 Enoch describes how Enoch, having been taken up to stand before the heavenly throne, was anointed and transformed into an angel and then instructed in the heavenly knowledge. He was shown the seven days of creation which were also apparently (the text is not clear) 7000 years of history. After the seventh day (and therefore millennium) of rest there was to be an eighth day which was beyond time, when no time was reckoned (2 En. 33.1–2), corresponding to Rev. 20.11–21.4. Pseudo-Philo described Moses' vision as he was about to die; Moses asked the LORD about the passage of time in history, 'how much has passed and how much remains'. He was told 'four and a half have passed, two and a half remain' (LAB 19.15). History was to be seven, presumably millennia. Kenaz had a vision of the creation and reported seeing the invisible creation and then images of men coming from the light of that invisible place. A voice told him that they would remain for 7000 years. Having seen the place of light, Kenaz exclaimed, 'If the repose of the just after they have died is like this, we must die to the corruptible world so as not to see sins' (LAB

28.8–10). For him the place of light was the place of rest, the place of the great Sabbath.

The *Letter of Barnabas*, written perhaps at the end of the first century CE, is attributed to the Levite from Cyprus (Acts 4.36) and is so steeped in Jewish tradition that this attribution is probably correct. He, too. argues from the six days of creation that 'He is going to bring the world to an end in six thousand years, since with him one day means a thousand years ... After that "he rested on the seventh" Day indicates that when his Son returns, he will put an end to the year of the Lawless One, pass sentence on the godless, transform the sun and moon and stars, and then on the seventh day, enter his true rest'. The great Sabbath will be kept holy because iniquity will be no more, and the LORD will have made all things new. 'Then we shall be able to keep it holy because we ourselves will have been made holy first' (*Barn.* 15).*
The acceptable Sabbath is not an observance of this present age but the one that 'after I have set all things at rest, is to usher in the eighth day, the commencement of the new world'. The 'rest' is the kingdom and eighth day begins the new creation, just as did the eighth day which was also the first day after Jesus' Sabbath rest in the tomb; cf. Hippolytus *On Daniel* 4. 'The Sabbath is a type and image of the future kingdom of the saints when they will reign with Christ'.

R. Eliezer ben Hyrcanus, at the end of the first century CE is said to have calculated one thousand years for the reign of the Messiah, on the basis of Psalm 90.4. He was a disciple of the great R. Johannan ben Zakkai (*m. Aboth* 2.9) and claimed that he only taught what he had learned from his master (*b. Sukkah* 28a). He was also accused of heresy because he listened with approval to what a disciple of Jesus was teaching. There is insufficient evidence for certainty, but there are some significant facts. There is no record of a figure *other than one thousand years* in pre-Christian sources, in other words, the great variety offered after the advent of Christianity may have been reaction to the Christians claiming the millennium kingdom. The idea of a Sabbath millennium is consistent with temple and Jubilee teaching about creation and renewal, which cannot be said of calculations based on the desert wanderings or the demise of Tyre. The bitter reaction to the terrible events of the war against Rome may explain why the rabbinic writings of the first six centuries CE have no quotation from Jewish apocalyptic writings, all of which were transmitted and preserved by Christians.

Jesus saw himself at work within the six-day scheme of history. When criticized by the Jews for healing on the Sabbath he replied: 'My Father is working still and I am working' (John 5.17). The implication is clear; he was thinking of the true Sabbath which lay in the future and thus he was still, with his Father, working to complete the creation. At the end of his sixth day, Good Friday, he declared, 'It is finished', or better 'It is

*In the Temple Scroll calendar (see p. 242) the Day of Atonement always falls on a Friday, the sixth day.

accomplished' (John 19.30) and then he rested on his Sabbath. The world would be 'completed' before the final conflict began (*Asc. Isa.* 4.2). The Letter to the Hebrews explains about the two concepts of Sabbath. Even though the work of creation was finished long ago, and God rested on the seventh day, it was also written that those who disregarded the ways of the LORD would never enter his rest (Ps. 95.11). 'So then there remains a Sabbath rest for the people of God, for whoever enters God's rest ceases from his labours as God also did from his' (Heb. 4.9–10). This was the rest promised to the faithful who endured (Rev. 14.12–13), not the sleep of death but the millennium Sabbath. The *Gospel of Thomas* shows how this belief developed after the literal hope for a millennium kingdom in the future had faded and John's new understanding of the return of the LORD had been accepted. Just as the LORD had returned already to his people, so too, the millennium kingdom was already present but only visible to the resurrected ones. The disciples ask Jesus, 'When will the repose of the dead come about and when will the new world come?' Jesus replies, 'What you look forward to has already come but you do not recognize it' (*Thomas* 51).

When Jesus taught about the kingdom he was speaking of the millennium. It was in the future, as he taught with the parable of wheat and the tares (Matt. 13.24–30, 36–43) and the parable of the great catch of fish (Matt. 13.47–50). Only the righteous would be part of the kingdom, and the evil ones would be destroyed in fire. It was also present insofar as those who were to be part of the kingdom were already being prepared, as he taught in the parables of the sower (Matt. 13.1–23) and parable of the seed growing in secret (Mark 4.26–29). For those who discovered the meaning of Jesus' teaching about the kingdom, it became the hidden treasure, the pearl beyond price (Matt. 13. 45–46). The kingdom was established after Satan had been driven out and so Jesus exorcized and spoke of binding the Strong One: 'If it is by the finger of God that I cast out demons, then the kingdom of God has come upon you' (Luke 11.20). The life of Jesus was thus a microcosm of the last times, just as his resurrection was deemed to be the first fruits of those who were sleeping (1 Cor. 15.20). Only those who had been born again, or born from above, would be able to enter the kingdom or to see it (John 3.3–5).

On that Day

The later texts which speak of miraculous fertility in the messianic age were developed from the older picture of sacral kingship, when the presence of the Anointed One ensured the prosperity of the kingdom. Psalm 72 prays that justice, *mišpaṭ*, and righteousness, *ṣedeq*, be given to the king, qualities which enable him to restore and maintain right order not only in human society but also in the world of nature:

May he judge thy people with righteousness,
and thy poor with justice!

Let the mountains bear prosperity for the people,
and the hills, in righteousness. (Ps. 72.2–3)

Isaiah's messianic prophecies spoke of the gift of the Spirit to transform both human society and the world of nature. The One on whom the Spirit rests would judge the poor with righteousness, slay the wicked with the breath of his lips and restore the whole earth to its Eden state (Isa. 11.1–9). This hope developed from the myth of the New Year ritual, when Azazel was bound and the earth was healed, when the LORD came forth from his holy place to take vengeance on his enemies and atone the land of his people (Deut. 32.43). Isaiah also described a time when the king would reign in righteousness and princes rule in justice (Isa. 32.1).

until the Spirit is poured upon us from on high,
and the wilderness becomes a fruitful field,
and the fruitful field is deemed a forest.
Then justice will dwell in the wilderness,
and righteousness abide in the fruitful field.
And the effect of righteousness will be peace,
and the result of righteousness,
quietness and trust for ever. (Isa. 32.15–17)

Vengeance and prosperity were both expected on the Day of the LORD, and as the prophetic texts were transmitted during the second temple period, descriptions of the longed-for Day were added to them. 'On that Day' indicates one of these texts. In the Book of Isaiah there are several examples of obvious additions, often collected together. 'On that Day' the Branch of the LORD would be glorious in Jerusalem, everyone in the city would be holy and recorded for life, and the glory of the LORD would shine over it (Isa. 4.2–6). This is the picture of the heavenly city in the Book of Revelation. 'On that Day' there would be the devastation of judgement – enemies, poor harvests – but afterwards prosperity (Isa. 7.18–25). 'On that Day' Israel would sing praises to the LORD (Isa. 12.1–6; 25.9). 'On that Day' cities would be deserted and people would abandon their idols (Isa. 17.7–9). 'On that Day' Judah would be more powerful than Egypt, there would be five cities in Egypt where the LORD was worshipped, and the Egyptians and the Assyrians would be at peace (Isa. 19.16–25). 'On that Day' the exiles would return to their land (Isa. 27.12–13). 'On that Day' the LORD would be the beautiful crown of the remnant of his people, giving justice, *mišpaṭ*, to their ruler and strength to their defenders (Isa. 28.5–6).

The Book of Amos records hopes for both judgement and prosperity. 'On that Day' the sun would go dark at noon and the young people would faint (Amos 8.9, 13, c.f. Mark 15.33). 'On that Day' prosperity would return to the house of David (Amos 9.11). Joel described the prosperity to follow the great harvest of wickedness: 'On that Day the mountains shall drip sweet wine, and the hills shall flow with milk, and all the stream beds of Judah shall flow with water; and a fountain shall

come forth from the house of the Lord, and water the valley of Shittim'
(the Dead Sea valley; Joel 3.18). Malachi wrote of the 'Day of his
coming', when the priests would be purified with fire and all evil-doers
would be judged (Mal. 3.2, 5; 4.1). For the righteous it would be a time
of triumph and healing, when the Sun of Righteousness would arise
with healing in her wings (Mal. 4.2, see p. 202).

The largest collection of these Day predictions is found in the last three
chapters of Zechariah. 'On that Day' Jerusalem would triumph over all
who come against her, and the LORD would put a shield around
Jerusalem (Zech. 12.8–9). The people of Jerusalem would look on the
one they had pierced, and they would mourn (Zech. 12.10, cf. Rev. 1.7).
'On that Day' a fountain in Jerusalem would cleanse the people from
their sin and uncleanness, and there would be no more idols or prophets
in the land (Zech. 13.1–4). 'On the Day of the LORD', nations would
gather for battle against Jerusalem, but the LORD himself would appear
on the Mount of Olives together with his holy ones (Zech. 14.1–5). 'On
that Day' it would be Day One, a return to the beginning of the creation
(see p. 18) before the sun and stars had been created. 'On that Day there
shall be no light and the glorious ones shall grow small, and it shall be
Day One' (Zech. 14.6–7a, translating literally). 'On that Day' living
waters would flow from Jerusalem and the LORD would become king
over the whole land/earth (Zech. 14.8–9). 'On that Day' plague and
panic would strike the enemies of Jerusalem (Zech. 14.12–15). 'On that
Day' everything in Jerusalem and Judah would be as sacred as the vessels
in the temple itself, even the bells on the horses and cooking pots. 'On that
Day' there would be no more traders in the temple (Zech. 14.20–21).

There is one other element in the picture. 'And they shall dwell in her
and there shall be no more curse of destruction* and Jerusalem shall
dwell in security' (Zech. 14.11, translating literally). Malachi, too,
threatened the LORD's *ḥerem* if there was no repentance (Mal. 4.6). The
implication of this is that Jerusalem had been put under a curse by
people who hoped to live there again on the Day of the LORD. These
must have been the people whose enemies were condemned by Isaiah:
'You shall leave your name to my Chosen for a curse' (Isa. 65.15,
šᵉbuʿah, a different word for curse); and whose history is recorded in *1
Enoch.* In the seventh week there was an apostate generation (*1 En.*
93.9) whose offerings were polluted and impure (*1 En.* 89.73, cf. Mal.
1.7: 'offering polluted food on my altar'). It was their polluted worship
which had put Jerusalem under the *ḥerem,* and when pure worship was
restored there would be no more *ḥerem.* Thus the sanctuary city in the
Book of Revelation is a place where there is no longer any curse,
because the throne of God-and-the-Lamb is there and his servants
worship him (22.3).

Jesus spoke of what would happen. *On that Day* many would claim

---

**ḥerem meaning something which has to be destroyed because it is unclean or hostile to the
LORD. Jericho was put under this ban of destruction (Josh. 6.17).

to be his followers but he would dismiss them (Matt. 7.21–23). *On that Day* the poor and the hungry would receive their reward (Luke 6.23). *On that Day* the towns that rejected his messengers would be judged (Luke 10.12). 'That Day' would come suddenly on all who dwell on the earth (Luke 21.34–35). At the Last Supper, Jesus told his disciples that he would not drink wine with them again until 'that Day', when he drank with them in the kingdom of his Father (Matt. 26.29).

The predictions of the Day in the Hebrew Scriptures and in the teaching of Jesus show how the picture of the millennium kingdom in the Book of Revelation had developed. It was the Day of the LORD when he became King over the whole land/earth, and his Day was known to be a thousand years. It was a time for judgement on enemies and for the restoration of Eden-like prosperity and fertility for the land of his Chosen Ones. It was a return to Day One, to the eternal/resurrected life of the holy of holies, and so the millennium kingdom enjoyed the cosmic light of the divine presence. Wisdom/Spirit flowed again, eyes were opened, and the entire city was as holy as the temple itself.

ALL THINGS NEW

Then comes the end, when he delivers the kingdom to God the Father after destroying every rule and every authority and power. For he must reign until he has put all his enemies under his feet. The last enemy to be destroyed is death. 'For he has put all things in subjection under his feet' [Ps. 8.6]. But when it says, 'All things are put in subjection under him', it is plain that he is excepted who put all things under him. When all things are subjected to him, then the Son himself will also be subjected to him who put all things under him, that God may be everything to everyone. (1 Cor. 15.24–28)

Paul's words to the Corinthian church are a good summary of the last part of the Book of Revelation and are proof that this teaching was not a minority concern. Paul, who differed from other Hebrew Christians on many matters, was at one with them when teaching about the future hope.

Satan Loosed

At the end of the millennium, Satan would be loosed from his prison and allowed to deceive the world again. These are predictions of future events: 'He will be loosed, he will come out and deceive' (20.7–8), but what follows is a report of past events: 'They marched over the land and surrounded the camp of the saints' (20.9). The most likely explanation of this is that a Hebrew original was imperfectly understood. The Hebrew system of verb tenses is differently nuanced from the Greek, and confusion of past and future is possible.

The loosing of the ancient serpent is not described in any other texts, but it probably derives from the ancient New Year rituals. Every year Azazel* was banished and, as the story is told in *1 Enoch*, imprisoned in a pit in the desert until the last judgement (*1 En.* 10.4–6). Since this was enacted every year, there must have been some account of his release/escape and reimprisonment. Here he emerges once again to deceive the nations. There is no account of his capture, only of his final fate in the lake of fire and sulphur (20.10) which corresponds to the account in the earliest part of *1 Enoch*. Azazel/Semḥaza and his fallen angels were to be imprisoned for seventy generations and then punished: 'On the day of the great judgement he shall be cast into the fire' (*1 En.* 10.6, cf. Isa. 1.31). Later Enochic material gives more detail and implies that the archangels brought Azazel before the throne of judgement where he was condemned to the fire. In this account the fallen angels are described as stars: 'And the judgement was held first

*For Azazel as Satan, see p. 215.

over the stars, and they were judged and found guilty and went to the place of condemnation and they were cast into an abyss, full of fire and flaming, and full of pillars of fire' (*1 En.* 90.24). Enoch had seen this place on his heavenly journey when Uriel had told him: 'This place is the prison of the angels and here they will be imprisoned forever' (*1 En.* 21.10). Jesus also spoke of it, 'the eternal fire prepared for the devil and his angels' (Matt. 25.41).

Satan was the deceiver of the whole world (12.9) and the nations he deceived prepare to attack Jerusalem. This seems to duplicate the accounts in 16.12–16, where the foul spirits like frogs assemble the kings of the whole world to fight at Armageddon, and they battle against the Word of God and the armies of heaven (19.19–21). That was clearly an earthly conflict as the birds were summoned to eat the flesh on the battlefield, a motif from the story of Gog, even though Gog is not mentioned. The 'duplicate' assault in 20.8–9, however, was probably angelic forces opposing the saints. Jesus described the resurrected as 'angels and sons of God' (Luke 20.36), and, since the people of the beloved city were the first-resurrected, they would have been angels engaged in heavenly warfare. The final battle against Gog and Magog is the defeat of supernatural evil and not its earthly manifestation which has already been defeated at Armageddon. These cannot have been the nations, but must have been the seventy shepherd-angels of the nations whom Enoch had seen destroyed by fire immediately after the judgement of Azazel. 'And those seventy shepherds were judged and found guilty and they were cast into that fiery abyss' (*1 En.* 90.25, see p. 227). This is what Paul described as destroying every rule and authority and power, the climax of the reign of Christ, before he hands the kingdom back to the Father (1 Cor. 15.24).

The horde of Gog and Magog 'went up over the land of open villages' and surrounded the camp of the saints and the beloved city (20.9). The Greek has 'went up', the usual term for a journey to Jerusalem, which occurs in the original account of Gog's invasion; he 'goes up' (Ezek. 38.9, 11, 16). 'The broad earth' is probably an over-literal translation of 'the land of open hamlets' through which Gog passed (Ezek. 38.11), the traditional description of a prosperous and secure land. Zechariah had compared the new Jerusalem to an open village because the LORD would defend her with a wall of fire (Zech. 2.4–5), and this is what happened in the final battle. The horde was destroyed by fire from heaven (20.9) because the LORD was reigning in his city: 'The LORD reigns ... fire goes before him and he burns up his adversaries round about' (Ps. 97.1, 3).

Jerusalem is the camp of 'the saints', the name adopted by the Christians to indicate their resurrected state (Rom. 1.7; 1 Cor. 1.2; 2 Cor. 1.1, etc.). The Damascus Covenant Community organized themselves into camps: 'If they live in camps according to the rule of the land ... they shall walk according to the Law' (CD VII). The 'elohim in the Songs of the Sabbath Sacrifice are 'in all the camps of God' (4Q405), and this is probably why the heavenly host was organized into huge camps, (3 *En.* 35.1–2). Those who broke the Law were 'cut off from the midst of the camp' (CD VIII). 'On the Sabbath day ... he shall not drink except in the camp ...' (CD X). There were rules for the assembly of the camps and for the 'bishop' (Guardian) of the camp (CD XII–XIII). The bishop of all the camps had to be a man of learning between thirty and fifty years old (i.e. like a priest, Num. 4.3) and his word was law (CD XIV). Jerusalem 'which he has chosen from all the tribes of Israel ... is the head of the camps of Israel' (4Q396, 397). Jerusalem was again 'the beloved city' and no longer the harlot, (cf. Pss 78.68; 87.2).

The Great White Throne

This is the Last Judgement when the dead are raised to be rewarded according to their deeds. The idea of the Last Judgement originated during the second temple period, when the belief in life after death developed in response to the problem of evil and injustice. It was the apparent triumph of the wicked in this life and the suffering of the righteous that necessitated such a judgement, when all the dead would be raised to answer for their deeds. Baruch complained to the LORD: if only this life exists, nothing could be more bitter (2 *Bar.* 21.13). The LORD revealed to him that judgement would come and the books would be opened (2 *Bar.* 24.1).

Two further developments complicated the picture of the last things: first, the memory of the anointed king gradually changed into the hope for a future anointed king and a future Paradise kingdom; and second, those who were influenced by the Deuteronomists and the Second Isaiah adopted a monotheism which fused into one deity God Most High ('God the Father') and the LORD ('God the Son'). For them, the Day of the LORD, which had formerly been an event in history when the creation was renewed, coalesced with the Last Judgement of the dead at the end of time, and the Messiah took on the role of God Most High.

This development can be seen in the role of the books at the judgement. The Day of the LORD was associated with the Book of the LORD, the Book of Life, which was a list of his faithful people. The Day of the LORD had originally been the time when the citizens of Zion were acknowledged; evil-doers were punished and excluded from the benefits of life in the city. Psalm 101 is the words of the king at this time as he promises to uphold the ways of the LORD in his city: 'I will destroy all the wicked in the land, cutting off all evildoers from the city of the LORD' (Ps. 101.8). The LORD registered the citizens of his beloved city (Ps. 87.6) and the psalmist prayed that his enemies might be excluded:

... may they have no acquittal from thee.
Let them be blotted out of the book of the living;
let them not be enrolled among the righteous. (Ps. 69.27–28)

What had been a memory, perhaps of a temple ceremony in the time of the kings, became part of the future hope. *On that Day* Jerusalem would be restored and all its citizens pure: 'On that Day ... he who is left in Zion and remains in Jerusalem will be called holy, every one who has been recorded for life in Jerusalem, when the LORD will have washed away the filth of the daughters of Zion and cleansed the blood-stains of Jerusalem' (Isa. 4.3–4). When the arrogant appeared blessed and evil-doers escaped all punishment, the faithful in Judah complain to the LORD that their good life is in vain: 'The LORD heeded and heard them, and a book of remembrance was written before him of those who feared the LORD and thought on his name. "They shall be mine", says the LORD of hosts, "my special possession on the day when I act, and I will spare them as a man spares his son who serves him"' (Mal. 3.16–17).

In addition there were 'the books', records of human conduct to be opened at the Last Judgement. These belonged originally in the story of the shepherd-angels, to whom the LORD committed the care of his people after the fall of Samaria, when Israel and Judah lost their independence (see p. 227). An angel was appointed to record all the deeds of the shepherd-angels and bring them before the LORD (*1 En.* 89.55–64). When his throne was set up near Jerusalem, the records were opened and the shepherd angels were punished, together with those who had helped them (*1 En.* 90.20–27). Recording angels first appear in the Hebrew Scriptures early in the second temple period, when Isaiah pleads with them to remind the LORD of the state of Jerusalem and to act (Isa. 62.6–7).

Deeds were thus an important element in both judgements, because it was a characteristic of Jesus' teaching that the purity requirements for his temple city and kingdom were not the ritual purities currently observed, but rather individual conduct. Thus he took the traditional motif of the condemned recognizing the true Messiah on the Day of the LORD (e.g. *1 En.* 62.2–13), and made of it the parable of the sheep and the goats, where the condemned have failed to recognize the Messiah in their fellow human beings (Matt. 25.41–46). At the Last Judgement, deeds had always been the issue, and a time of justice not mercy was expected: 'The Most High shall be revealed upon the seat of judgement, and compassion shall pass away, and patience shall be withdrawn, but only judgement shall remain, truth shall stand, and faithfulness shall grow strong. Recompense shall follow' (2 *Esdr.* 7.33–35). Pseudo-Philo is similar; at the end of time, 'I shall render to each according to his works and according to the fruits of his own devices ...' (LAB 3.10). This is the belief presupposed by Paul's argument in Romans 2, that God's kindness was for this life, and intended to lead to repentance (as in 2 Pet. 3.9), but the impenitent would discover God's righteous judgement on the day of wrath: 'For he will render to every man according to his works ... the doers of the law will be justified' (Rom. 2.6, 13). Peter wrote: 'If you invoke as Father him who judges each one impartially according to his deeds, conduct yourselves with fear throughout your time of exile' (1 Pet. 1.17).

The books were opened at the Last Judgement, 'the books in which are written the sins of all those who have sinned' (2 *Bar.* 24.1). 'When the seal is placed upon the age which is about to pass away ... the books shall be opened before the firmament' (2 *Esdr.* 6.20). 'Isaiah' saw these books in the seventh heaven, 'books but not like the books of this world ... and behold the deeds of the children of Israel were written there' (*Asc. Isa.* 9.22–23), and the *Testament of Abraham* had a realistic view of how large these books would need to be: 'On the table lay a book whose thickness was six cubits and its breadth was ten cubits' (*T. Abr.* A12.7). These texts are all contemporary with the Book of Revelation and so this is the picture in 20.12a, 'the dead standing before the throne and the books opened'.

The structure of 20.11–15, however, shows that two additions have been made to accommodate the belief in the first resurrection and make it a Christian text. Books were opened, but also another book which is the Book of Life. The latter looks like an addition, as does 20.14b–15 which explains the second death and then seems to contradict an earlier statement: 'The dead were judged by what was written in the books' (20.12) is very different from 'if anyone's name was not found written in the book of life, he was thrown into the lake of fire'. 20.11–14 was originally a vision of the Last Judgement, but it was expanded to accommodate the Christian hope for the Day of the LORD which had not come as soon as expected. The first-resurrected, both living and dead, had become the citizens of the heavenly Jerusalem and they had reigned for one thousand years. Then everything came to an end, heaven and earth passed away, including the heavenly Jerusalem and the millennium kingdom. Only the dead stood before the great white throne, and these must have included the first-resurrected. This is why in addition to the books of judgement, 'another book was opened which is the book of life' (20.12).

In the Book of Revelation, the book of life, or the Lamb's book of life (21.27) is the book of the LORD. Its role has not changed; it is still the register of the citizens of Jerusalem (now the heavenly Jerusalem), all who have never practised abomination and falsehood. Those whose names are inscribed know they will be safe at the Last Judgement, just as the risen LORD had promised the angel of the church at Sardis: 'He who conquers [or is pure] shall be clad in white garments, and I will not blot his name out of the book of life; I will confess his name before my Father and before his angels' (3.5). The names had been written in the book before the foundation of the world, and those not found there became worshippers of the beast and marvelled at him (13.8; 17.8). Those who 'entered the new covenant in the land of Damascus' had their names inscribed in a book, apparently the one described in Malachi 3.18: 'a book of reminder shall be written before him of them that fear God and worship his name, against the time when salvation and righteousness shall be revealed to them that fear God' (CD VIII). The Community Rule implies that those with names in the book were priests; it was forbidden to speak in anger against 'one of the priests inscribed in the book' (1QS VII). This may have been another element in Jesus' concept of the new priesthood; all written in the Lamb's book were the new priests who would be safe on the Day of the LORD.

A saying of Jesus in the Synoptic Gospels: 'Everyone who acknowledges me before men, I also will acknowledge before my Father who is in heaven' (Matt. 10.32; also Luke 12.8–9; Mark 8.38), must refer to the Last Judgement, when Jesus the LORD would claim his own and thus keep them safe. Paul knew that the names of his fellow workers were written in the book of life (Phil. 4.3), and the Hebrews were 'the assembly of the firstborn, enrolled in heaven' (Heb. 12.23). John must have had the Last Judgement in mind when he wrote: 'If anyone sins, we have an advocate with the Father, Jesus Christ the Righteous ...' (1 John 2.1). The problem of sins committed after baptism was very real, as can be seen from the harsh discipline imposed on the Hebrews: 'It is impossible to restore again to repentance those who have once been enlightened, who have tasted the heavenly gift and have become partakers of the Holy Spirit, if they then commit apostasy ...' (Heb. 6.4–5 also Heb. 10.26–31; 2 Pet. 2.21).

In Daniel the judgements are depicted differently, although the overall sequence is the same. The books are opened in front of the Ancient of Days and the beasts are judged *before* the Man ascends to be enthroned, and power passes to him and the saints (Dan. 7.9–27). Later, the Man clothed in linen, the LORD, reveals to Daniel that when Michael appears, there would be a time of trouble from which those written in the book would be safe. There would also be a resurrection to face judgement, some to eternal life and some to shame (Dan. 12.1–2).

The *Testament of Abraham* has a similar sequence of judgements (see p. 257), so it is clear that the chronology of the last times was a matter of great interest in the first century CE. In 'Ezra's' vision the LORD reveals the details of the last times and concludes: 'This is my judgement and its prescribed order; to you alone have I shown these things' (2 *Esdr.* 7.44). At the end of the reign of the Messiah (here 400 years, not one thousand), 'my son the Messiah shall die and all who draw human breath. And the world shall be turned back to primeval silence for seven days as it was at the first beginnings; so that none shall be left'. After this week, the world wakes again, everything corruptible perishes, the earth gives up its dead and God Most High appears on his judgement throne (2 *Esdr.* 7.29–33).

Other first-century Jewish texts have a similar picture of a new era after the end of time. God revealed to Enoch how there would be an eighth day, after the seven days of the creation. It would be both the eighth day and the first day of the new creation, and it would mark the beginning of 'a time not reckoned and unending', a time beyond time (2 *En.* 33.1–2). Enoch later instructed his children about that time: the whole creation, visible and invisible, would end, and each person would face the Last Judgement. All time would perish and all the righteous would gather together in the great age. There would be no more suffering or pain, 'no more darkness but instead a great light and Paradise ... for everything corruptible will pass away' (2 *En.* 65.6–10). Pseudo-Philo adds a remarkable passage to his account of the LORD's promise to Noah that while the earth remained, the natural order would be secure (Gen. 8.22): 'When the years appointed for the earth have been fulfilled, then light will cease and the darkness will fade away, and I will bring the dead to life and raise up those who are sleeping from the earth'. All will be judged according to their works, the world will cease to exist, death will be abolished. 'Then there will be another earth and another heaven, an everlasting dwelling place' (LAB 3.10).

These ideas were not new. Isaiah had contrasted the permanence of God's justice and the transience of the creation:

for the heavens will vanish like smoke,
the earth will wear out like a garment,
and they who dwell in it will die like gnats;
but my salvation will be for ever,
and my deliverance will never be ended. (Isa. 51.6)

Heaven and earth were created long ago, sang the psalmist, but they will wear out like a garment and pass away (Ps. 102.25–27). Jeremiah had seen the earth return to its pre-created state, without form and void (as in Gen. 1.1); the heavens had no light, the hills were moving, the birds had gone and there were no people left (Jer. 4.23–26). Jesus, too, knew that heaven and earth would pass away (Mark 13.31).

In the Book of Revelation, the seer stands before the great white throne, not the throne of 4.2–11, nor the thrones in 20.4 for the Messiah and his saints, but the throne of God Most High, which Enoch had glimpsed on his heavenly journey. At the end of the earth there were seven mountains, 'and the middle one reached to heaven like the throne of God, of alabaster, and the summit of the throne was of sapphire ...' (1 *En.* 18.8). The seer of the Book of Revelation saw the very end of time, when earth and sky had fled away, and the dead were standing before the throne. There are no details in this account: he does not say if the messianic kingdom has ended, if the Messiah and his saints have died, or if everything has returned to the pre-created state described in Jeremiah 4 and 2 *Esdras* 7. John, if John it was, was speaking to people who could have supplied these details for themselves.

This is a glimpse beyond time, after the world week has ended and the millennium Sabbath is over. If we follow Paul's chronology of the last times, the Messiah has reigned and all his enemies have been destroyed, 'every rule, power and authority put under his feet'. Then comes the end, says Paul, when he delivers the kingdom to God the Father (1 Cor. 15.24–25). Other Christian writers in the first century CE knew of this remote future, when the present creation would pass away. The seer of Revelation simply says that earth and sky fled from the presence of the One on the throne (20.11), but Peter described what would happen:

first, the Day of the LORD, 'and then the heavens will pass away with a loud noise, and the elements will be dissolved with fire, and the earth and the works that are upon it will be burned up' (2 Pet. 3.10). Barnabas wrote of the eighth day which followed the millennium Sabbath, when there would be a new world (*Barn.* 15).

The dead stand before the throne, the great resurrection for which the dead have been kept in waiting, and the sea, death and Hades give up their dead. Contemporary texts offer various descriptions of the resting places of the dead and some, but not all, distinguish between the place for the righteous and the place for the wicked as they wait for the Last Judgement. (This implies a preliminary sorting out before the Last Judgement, perhaps the scene envisaged in the *Testament of Abraham* A13.1–8.) The LORD described the resurrection to Baruch: 'Dust will be called and told Give back that which does not belong to you and raise up all that you have kept until its own time' (2 *Bar.* 42.8), and to Moses he said, 'I will give you rest in your slumber and bury you in peace ... until I visit the world, and I will raise up you and your fathers ... and you will come together and dwell in the immortal dwelling place that is not subject to time' (LAB 19.12). The earliest 'resurrection' texts had expected the dead to come back from the earth: 'the dwellers in the dust' would rise (Isa. 26.19), 'many of those who sleep in the dust of the earth shall awake, some to everlasting life, some to everlasting shame and contempt' (Dan. 12.2). Enoch saw their waiting places on his journey to Sheol and described how the righteous dead were separated from the wicked. He saw sinners who had not received their just reward in life, 'set apart in this great pain until the great day of judgement and punishment' (1 *En.* 22.10–11). The text breaks off before any details of the judgement are given. Later Enoch texts, however, distinguish between the earth and Sheol: 'In those days shall the earth give back that which has been entrusted to it and Sheol also shall give back that which it has received, and hell shall give back that which it owes' (1 *En.* 51.1), and the resurrection of the righteous only is envisaged in 1 *Enoch* 61.5, 'those who have been destroyed by the desert, those who have been devoured by the beasts, those who have been devoured by the fish of the sea'.

First-century texts also mention the chambers where the righteous waited for the Last Judgement, 'the fathers in their chambers of souls' (LAB 32.13). 'Did not the souls of the righteous in their chambers ask about these matters saying, How long are we to remain here and when will come the harvest of our reward? ... And the earth shall give up those who are asleep in it and the dust those who dwell silently in it; and the chambers shall give up the souls which have been committed to them' (2 *Esdr.* 4.35; 7.32). Other texts expected 'the treasuries of the souls to restore those enclosed in them' (2 *Bar.* 21.23, also 24.1), presumably what Jesus had in mind when he spoke of 'laying up treasure in heaven' (Matt. 6.20). Enoch explained that the Most High had appointed holy guardian angels for the righteous until the Last

Judgement (*1 En.* 100.5). The fallen angels were kept in gloomy pits until the judgement (2 Pet. 2.4), although Enoch had seen them in a pit of fire (*1 En.* 18.11).

The earth and the treasuries are not mentioned in 20.11–15 as giving up their dead, but this is implied because the resurrected dead are standing for the judgement before the sea, Death and Hades have given up their dead. Resurrection from the sea is an unusual idea, although implicit in *1 Enoch* 61.5, that the righteous who have been devoured by fish will be restored. The sea, Death and Hades may be synonymous here, as the sea is a symbol of evil in this tradition, and there is no sea in the new creation (21.1). Resurrection from hell, however, was a commonplace in the first century: 'I will bring the dead to life and raise up those who are sleeping from the earth. And hell will pay back its debt and the place of perdition will return its deposit so that I may render to each according to his works' (LAB 3.10). 'In Hades the chambers of the souls are like the womb . . . these places hasten to give back those things that were committed to them from the beginning' (2 *Esdr.* 4.41–42). 'Sheol also shall give back what it has received' (*1 En.* 51.1).

Death and Hades in 20.14 are evil powers, rather than places, just as they are in 6.8, riding on the pale horse. Here they are thrown into the lake of fire as the climax of the Last Judgement. The risen LORD holds the keys of Death and Hades (1.18), and the early church believed that the LORD had preached to the spirits in prison (1 Pet. 3.19) and had broken down the doors of hell to rescue the righteous dead. Contemporary texts, however, suggest another meaning for the keys. At the Last Judgement and before the new creation, 'death will be abolished and hell will shut its mouth' (LAB 3.10). 'Reprove the angel of death . . . and let the realm of death be sealed so that it may not receive the dead from this time . . .' (2 *Bar.* 21.23). The keys in the hands of the risen LORD may originally have meant that he had sealed up the realm of Death and Hades for ever, rather than opened them.

Death and Hades, together with anyone not found in the book of life, were thrown into the lake of fire, the second death. The risen LORD promised the angel of the church at Smyrna that if he was faithful he would not be hurt by the second death (2.11), and the first-resurrected in the millennium kingdom were also safe (20.6). The second death was the final death from which there was no resurrection. Jesus had warned his followers not to fear those who killed the body, but only him who could 'destroy both soul and body in Gehenna' (Matt. 10.32), the context for his assurance that he would acknowledge his own before his Father (Matt. 10.28). Although the second death is not mentioned by name elsewhere in the New Testament, the idea was well-known at the end of the second temple period. 'Surely this iniquity will not be forgiven you till you die' (Isa. 22.14) was altered by the Targum for the new situation where people believed in life after (ordinary) death. It became 'Surely this sin will not be forgiven you until you die the second death'. Isaiah had prophesied judgement against the people of the restored Jerusalem, who had corrupted the cult and excluded their own people from the temple (see p. 30), and the Targumist made it clear what this judgement would be: 'These [people] are a smoke in my nostrils that burns all day ... I will not keep silent but I will repay', became 'These, their anger is as smoke before me, their retribution is in Gehenna where the fire burns all the day ... I will not give them respite while they live, but theirs is the retribution of their sins. I will hand over their bodies to the second death' (*T. Isa.* 65.5b–6). The second prophecy: 'You shall leave your name to my chosen for a curse and the LORD God will slay you' became 'the LORD God will slay you with the second death' (*T. Isa.* 65.15). Immediately after the second death of the enemies of the Chosen Ones, the prophet heard the LORD proclaiming 'a new heavens and a new earth ... Jerusalem a rejoicing and her people a joy' (Isa. 65.17–18). Later tradition was to link the belief to Moses' blessing of Reuben: 'Let Reuben live and not die' (Deut. 33.6) was said to mean, 'Let Reuben live in this world and not die in the next', that is, not die the second death (b. *Sanhedrin* 92a).

A New Heaven and New Earth

The first heaven and the first earth have passed away (21.1; 20.11) and the sea is no more. The seer sees not 'the holy city Jerusalem' (21.10) which had been the millennium kingdom, but the 'holy city *new* Jerusalem' (21.2), coming from heaven. He does not attempt to describe this new state of existence beyond time and matter; all he says is that God now dwells with his people, and there will be no more tears, mourning, crying, pain or death (21.4). This must correspond to Peter's hope that after the heavens had dissolved and elements melted in fire, there would be 'new heavens and a new earth in which righteousness dwells' (2 Pet. 3.12–13). The Hebrews were taught that Haggai 2.6: 'Yet once more I will shake the heavens and the earth' was a prophecy of their own times. '"Yet once more" indicates the removal of what is shaken, as of what has been made, in order that what cannot be shaken may remain. Therefore let us be grateful for receiving a kingdom that cannot be shaken ... for our God is a consuming fire' (Heb. 12.27–29). This is the assurance of the first-resurrected who know they will be safe at the Last Judgement, and that their kingdom will not be destroyed. Paul gave an enigmatic description of the final state in 1 Corinthians 15.28: 'Then shall the Son also himself be subject unto him that put all things under him, that God may be all in all'. The AV's literal rendering here, 'all in all' implies a total reunion of God and his creation, which must be what is implied by 'the dwelling of God is with men'.

The dwelling, *skene*, is one of the words used for the tabernacle (e.g. Exod. 26.1, LXX) and the original tabernacle had been a copy of the whole creation which Moses had seen in his vision on Sinai (see p. 17). The true tabernacle, the tabernacle of God, was what Moses had seen in his vision, *the pre-created state outside time and matter*. The complex and obscure arguments in the Letter to the Hebrews seem to be making this point, that 'the first tabernacle' is symbolic of the present age (Heb. 9.8b, translating literally). When the new tabernacle of God comes from heaven, it is the new age, the eighth day, and a copy is no longer necessary because the tabernacle itself is with God's people. They no longer exist in the lower material and temporal state with its pain and finality.

Other writers expressed this idea in various ways. The *Book of Jubilees* has Moses write down what he sees on Sinai, the whole history of his people 'until I shall descend and dwell with them in all the ages of eternity' (*Jub.* 1.26). The angel of the presence is also told to write an account of everything 'from the first creation until my sanctuary is built in their midst for ever and ever' (*Jub.* 1.27). The most vivid contemporary accounts are in 2 *Enoch* and 2 *Esdras*, both of which are very similar to 21.1–4. 2 *Enoch* describes the ending of the visible and invisible creation, i.e. everything represented by the tabernacle, and then no more time. All the righteous souls assemble in the great eternal age 'with no weariness, sickness, affliction, worry, want, debilitation, night or darkness'. They would live in the great indestructible light and 'everything corruptible would pass away and the incorruptible come into being' (2 *En.* 65.9–10). 'Ezra' questioned the angel about the present evil age and was told: 'The Day of Judgement will be at the end of this age and the beginning of the immortal age to come, in which corruption has passed away ...' (2 *Esdr.* 7.113). Corruption in the moral sense was part of the corruptible material world, and so 'Ezra' was told there would be no place for sinful indulgence and unbelief in the new age. Uriel showed Enoch the movements of all the stars and their role in the calendar 'until the new creation which abides forever is created' (1 *En.* 72.1), i.e. until there was no more time and no further function for the calendar angels. The Apocalypse of Weeks concludes with a new heaven and the powers shining sevenfold, but no mention of the earth (1 *En.* 91.16).

The Fragments

If the pages are rearranged, 21.5a: 'Behold I make all things new' marks the end of the ordered text. 21.5b–8 and 22.6–20 are fragments which were not incorporated. Some are duplicates of oracles included elsewhere, which explains their position in the appendix, but the rest must have been left out for another reason.

The presence of these fragments is important evidence for the history of the text. First, that it was compiled from written sources which had authority and so could not be thrown away, and second, that the compiler of the Book of Revelation was reworking the material such that its final form was not identical with its original intent. The key to this reworking must lie in unduplicated material for which there was no place in the body of the text. 'Behold I am coming soon' (22.7), 'Behold

I am coming soon, bringing my recompense to repay everyone for what
he has done' (22.12), and 'He who testifies to these things says "Surely
I am coming soon" ' (22.20) are all sayings of the risen LORD, promising
his imminent return. *There was no place for these promises in the final
form of the text, because the hope of the imminent return faded with the
destruction of Jerusalem.*

The risen LORD had warned of his return in the early letters: 'I will
come soon and war against them with the sword of my mouth' (2.16),
'Hold fast what you have until I come' (2.25), 'I am coming soon; hold
fast what you have' (3.11), and the letters were already known to the
churches. Apart from the quotation in 16.15, the risen LORD does not
promise his return in the prophecies and visions in the present form of
the Book of Revelation. Even though these oracles had been given
through the prophets as words of the risen LORD, there was no place for
them after John had received the open scroll from the angel in the cloud
and learned that the return of the LORD would not be what he had
expected.

The other oracles can be placed: 21.5b–8 belongs with the heavenly
city oracles, with the promise of water for those who are worthy, as in
7.16–17, where those who serve before the throne do not thirst because
there are springs of living water. The words echo those of Isaiah (Isa.
55.1), of Wisdom (*Ben Sira* 24.19) and of Jesus (John 4.13–14; 6.35;
8.37–39). These springs are the fountains of Wisdom around the
throne, from which the thirsty drink (*1 En.* 48.1), and they appear in
the Qumran blessing for the faithful 'that keep his commandments ...
whom he has chosen for an eternal covenant'. The text is broken, but
'everlasting [ ] them that thirst' are clear (1QSb I). The hymn at the end
of the Community Rule depicts the same kingdom of priests as the Book
of Revelation, invited to drink from the fountain: 'My eyes have gazed
on that which is eternal ... on a fountain of righteousness ... on a
spring of glory ... God has given them to his chosen ones as an
everlasting possession, and has caused them to inherit the lot of his holy
ones. He has joined their assembly to the sons of heaven, a foundation
of the Building of Holiness' (i.e. the holy of holies, 1QS XI). Had
21.6b–7 been preserved in a cave at Qumran rather than at the end of
the Book of Revelation, scholars would not have found it a problem.
The Hymns are full of this imagery, e.g: 'Thou hast placed me beside a
fountain of streams ... trees of life beside a mysterious fountain ...'
'The well spring of life' and 'the waters of holiness' were not for anyone
who 'seeing has not discerned and considering has not believed' (1QH
XVI, formerly VIII). This oracle should probably be linked to 22.17:
'Let him who is thirsty come and take the water of life without price',
the invitation of 'the Spirit and the Bride'. Although the verb here is
plural ('they say'), the original may well have been the double naming
of a single subject such as appears elsewhere in the Book of Revelation,
giving rise to singular and plural readings at 6.17 (see p. 140). The Spirit
and the Bride were both designations for Wisdom, and here the LORD

as Wisdom (cf. 3.14–22, see p. 112) is inviting her children to drink (*Ben Sira* 24.21).

The promise to the Davidic kings: 'I will be his father and he shall be my son' (2 Sam. 7.14; Ps. 89.26) has become here the promise to everyone who has conquered (21.7, or was worthy), just as the angel of Thyatira was promised kingly rule (2.26–27) and the angel of Laodicea a share of the throne (3.21).

'These words are trustworthy and true' is duplicated at 22.6 and is very similar to 19.9b, 'These are true words of God'. This may have been a standard form of prophetic utterance, delivered at the end of an oracle.

'It is done' (21.6) has an unusual Greek form (a mixture of aorist and perfect tenses) and perhaps means 'they are done', i.e. the sayings are fulfilled.

'I am the Alpha and the Omega (21.6), occurs also at 1.8 and 22.13, 'the beginning and the end' also at 22.13.

22.8–9 is a duplicate of 19.10 where John was forbidden to worship the bowl angel who had revealed to him the fate of the harlot city. 22.8–9 could originally have been part of the second vision of the bowl angel, when John was shown the Bride city. In each case the angel is said to be a fellow servant. John is identified as one of the brothers who have the testimony/visions of Jesus (19.10), and as one of the brothers who are prophets and keep the words of this book (22.9). The prophets must have been those who 'had the visions of Jesus' (as in 12.7, where the same phrase is translated 'bear testimony to Jesus', RSV). Keep, *tereo*, means both to preserve and to observe closely (see p. 71); the prophets were the guardians of the visions and their interpretation, and they were blessed (1.3). 'Do not seal up the words of the prophecy of this book' (22.10) could have been the inspiration which led John to reveal the fulfilment of the fifth and sixth seals. The disastrous consequences of this revelation accounts for this appearing among the fragments.

Blessed are they who 'are washing their robes' (22.14) appears in some texts 'doing the commandments'. Since the Greek looks very similar: *plunontes tas stolas* and *poiountes tas entolas* (and even more similar in the ancient script with no spaces between the words!), it is easy to see how a scribe could have 'read' something which seemed to make more sense. Those who were coming from the Great Tribulation had 'washed their robes' and made them white in the blood of the Lamb (7.14). This was not necessarily an oracle for martyrs; the greeting to the seven churches described Jesus as the one who had freed us, *lusas*, from our sins by his blood or washed us, *lousas*, from our sins by his blood. It probably described those pure enough for the heavenly city, in contrast to those to be kept outside the gates, which were guarded by angels (21.12) who could still prevent access to the Tree of Life (Gen. 3.24).

The warning not to add to the prophecies nor to take anything away is a sign that they were regarded as holy writings; *they were already*

Scripture. No other book in the New Testament carries such a warning, but it does appear in Deuteronomy 4.2: 'You shall not add to the word which I command you nor take from it'. *1 Enoch* also concludes with a prediction that sinners would alter and pervert the words of Enoch (*1 En.* 104.10–13). Two texts other texts show how this prohibition was understood in the first century CE. When the LXX of the Law was translated, it was said, the priests and the elders agreed that it was an accurate translation and then:

pronounced a curse in accordance with their custom upon any one who should make any alteration either by adding anything or by changing in any way whatever any of the words which had been written, or by making any omission. This was a wise precaution, to ensure that the book might be preserved for all the future time unchanged. (*Aristeas* 311)

Josephus, too, explained the custom of his people in the matter of their holy books: 'No one has been so bold as either to add anything to them, or to make any change in them, but it becomes natural to all Jews, immediately and from their very birth, to esteem those books to contain divine doctrines ...' (*Against Apion* 8). This was the official position. In practice, however, changes had been made to the holy writings: Deuteronomy itself (the very name means the second law) was altering older ideas (see p. 17) and there was more than one Hebrew text of, for example, Deuteronomy and Isaiah, as shown by the Qumran texts. The Book of Revelation used the text of Scripture very freely, or else had a different text from any known today. The prohibition in 22.18 is a claim to inspiration, and the collection of fragments honours the belief that inspired writings could not be destroyed.

There are several speakers in the fragments, but the nature of the text means that it is not possible always to identify the speaker. 'John' speaks in 22.8, as in 1.9, but such a clear claim to authorship can be a sign of pseudepigraphy. 'Ezra' and 'Baruch' writing at this time were not Ezra and Baruch, nor was it Isaiah who wrote the *Ascension of Isaiah*. 'John' could have been a disciple, making his master's work available for the new situation in Asia Minor at the end of the first century, the traditional time for the 'publication' of the Book of Revelation. The warning in 22.18–19 probably came from 'John'.

The angel speaks in 22.9, but the other sayings seem to be attributed to the risen LORD. 'I am the Alpha and the Omega' (21.6) occurs also at 1.8 and 22.13, 'the beginning and the end' also at 22.13. He sits enthroned and passes judgement.

A comparison of 22.6 and 1.1 suggests that the one sent to show what must soon take place was, in each case, Jesus. 'The revelation of Jesus Christ which God gave him to show his servants what must soon take place' (1.1), and 'The LORD ... has sent his angel to show his servants what must soon take place' (22.6) implies that the angel of the LORD was Jesus, in other words, Jesus was the LORD made visible on earth (see p. 36). He appears in the Book of Revelation as the Mighty Angel.

That the LORD is the speaker in 22.6 is probably confirmed by 22.7, if these two originally belonged together: 'Behold, I am coming soon'. 22.10–13 is another cluster of sayings which seem to belong together and imply that the speaker is the risen LORD. He is coming soon to bring the judgement when evil-doers will be excluded from the kingdom, and he tells his prophet to reveal the words of the prophecies 'for the time is near'. This was the oracle that prompted John to declare the opening of the fifth and sixth seals, and 22.20 must come from the same period: 'He who testifies to these things says Surely I am coming soon'. 22.16 was probably the vision that prompted John to combine the letters and the visions and send them to the churches.

The New Testament records occasions when Jesus appeared and spoke to his disciples, apart from the Easter appearances. Paul saw Jesus on the road to Damascus, and recorded his words (Acts 9.5–6). The Spirit of Jesus did not allow Paul back into Asia Minor (Acts 16.7), and the LORD stood by Paul and spoke to him when he was in custody (Acts 23.11). It is inconceivable that these words of the risen LORD were not recorded and revered. It is the oracles given in such visions to John and the prophets in Jerusalem which are preserved at the end of the Book of Revelation.

'Come LORD Jesus' (22.20) has also been preserved in its original Aramaic 'Maranatha' (1 Cor. 16.22), followed in both cases by: 'The grace of the LORD Jesus be with you/all the saints'. This was the prayer of first-generation Christians looking for the Day of the LORD, and then the customary ending for a Christian letter (2 Cor. 13.14; Gal. 6.18; Eph. 6.24, etc.). After John had learned that the second coming would not be an event in the near future, the LORD returned to his people in the Eucharist.

EXCURSUS: PAROUSIA AND LITURGY

Although there are various possible translations of *Maranatha* (Our LORD comes, Our LORD has come), the fragments at the end of the Book of Revelation show that it was understood at that time to mean 'Come LORD'. The Lord himself assures his people that he is coming soon to bring the judgement (22.7, 12, 20), and the prayer reflects this hope of his imminent return. The position of these fragments at the end of the Book of Revelation suggests that they were no longer central to the message of the book. In other words, *Maranatha* was being understood in another way.

The same prayer appears elsewhere as the closing lines of a letter which give no indication of how it was understood (1 Cor. 16.22), but also at the close of an early eucharistic prayer, possibly the earliest known outside the New Testament, a very significant context (*Didache* 10). *This links the return of the LORD to the Eucharist.* Other lines of the Didache prayer are ambiguous: 'Let this present world pass away', for example, could imply either a literal understanding of the LORD's return or the present transforming effect of the Eucharist. *Maranatha in the Eucharist, however, must be the original epiklesis, praying for the coming of the LORD.* The Didache prayer has no reference to the words of institution at the Last Supper and no Passover imagery. As implied in John's account of the Last Supper (John 13.1–20), Jesus is 'Thy Servant Jesus', and thanks are offered for the knowledge, faith and everlasting life made known through him. The bread and wine are spiritual meat and drink (cf. John 6.25–58) which cause the Name to dwell in the hearts of those who have been fed. This could indicate that John's understanding of the Eucharist was the formative influence here, and that it was his new understanding of *Maranatha* which led to its transformation into the eucharistic *epiklesis*.

Passover or Day of Atonement?

Despite the apparently clear accounts of the Eucharist in the Synoptic Gospels, there are many problems as to its true origin and significance. *The Passover is the least likely context as this was the one sacrifice not offered by a priest* (*m. Pesaḥim* 5.6), and the earliest tradition remembers Jesus as the Great High Priest.* The words of institution known to the evangelists (Matt. 26.26–28; Mark 14.22–24; Luke 22.14–20) and Paul (1 Cor. 11.23–26) indicate as their context the priestly sacrifice of the Eternal Covenant, in other words, the Day of Atonement. The position of the Christian altar in a church building, beyond the boundary between

---

*In the Temple Scroll calendar, the Day of Atonement always falls on a Friday (see pp. 242, 353) but Passover always falls on a Tuesday.

earth and heaven, shows that it derived from the *kapporet* in the holy of holies, the place where the atonement blood was offered.

Even though Paul knew Christ as the paschal lamb (1 Cor. 5.7), he had also been taught that his death was 'for our sins in accordance with the scriptures' (1 Cor. 15.3). This indicates that the earliest interpretation of the death of Jesus was based on the fourth Servant Song, which, in the form known at Qumran, depicts a suffering Messiah figure who bears the sins of others (1QIsa^a 52.13–53.12). He was the high priest who sprinkled the atonement blood (Isa. 52.15) and *was himself the sacrifice* (Isa. 53.10). A similar expectation is found in Peter's temple sermon; the Servant, the Author of life, was about to return from heaven bringing 'times of refreshing' (Acts 3.13–21). Again, these texts indicate that the original understanding of the death of Jesus was the renewal of the Eternal Covenant on the Day of Atonement.

The original context of the Eucharist should be sought in the Day of Atonement, when the high priest took the blood into the holy of holies and then returned to complete the rite of atonement and renewal. At first the Christians had prayed for the literal return of the LORD to bring judgement on their enemies and to establish the kingdom. Their hopes for the history of their times were based on the ancient ritual pattern of the Day of Atonement. Jesus, the Great High Priest, had sacrificed himself as the atonement offering of the tenth Jubilee, had passed into heaven, the true holy of holies, and would emerge again to complete the atonement. When this did not literally happen, John learned in his vision of the returning high priest (Rev. 10) that the expectations of the church should return to the temple liturgy whence they had come. In the original temple ritual, the anointed high priest, even though he 'was' the LORD, had taken into the holy of holies the blood of a goat which represented his own life-blood. As he emerged, he sprinkled 'his' blood, i.e. he gave his life, to cleanse and consecrate the creation. This renewed on earth the kingdom of the LORD's anointed.

The Messiah, both high priest and victim, was the theme both of the Eucharist and of the Day of Atonement. Dix concluded:

From the days of Clement of Rome in the first century, for whom our Lord is 'the High-priest of our offerings' who is 'in the heights of the heavens (1 *Clem.* 36) it can be said with truth that this doctrine of the offering of the earthly eucharist by the heavenly Priest at the heavenly altar is to all intents and purposes the only conception of the eucharistic sacrifice which is known anywhere in the church … there is no pre-Nicene author Eastern or Western whose eucharistic doctrine is at all fully stated who does not regard the offering and consecration of the eucharist as the present action of the LORD Himself, the Second Person of the Trinity.*

Interpreting the Eucharist as the Day of Atonement offering, Origen wrote: 'You who came to Christ, the true High Priest, who made atonement for you … do not hold fast to the blood of the flesh. Learn

Shape of the Liturgy, p. 186.

rather the blood of the Word and hear him saying to you This is my blood which is poured out for you for the forgiveness of sins. He who is inspired by the mysteries knows both the flesh and the blood of the Word of God' (*On Leviticus* 9.10). Jerome, commenting on Zephaniah 3 wrote of 'the priests who pray at the Eucharist for the coming of the LORD'. He too went on to link the day of the LORD's coming to the Day of Atonement and 'Wait for me, for the day when I arise' (RSV, Zeph. 3.8) was read as 'Wait for me on the day of my resurrection'. This association of the two advents of the LORD with the Day of Atonement is found as early as the *Letter of Barnabas*, a Levite. As in Jerome, the earthly life of Jesus is compared to the role of the scapegoat who bore the sins, 'but the point of there being two similar goats is that when they see him coming on the Day, they are going to be struck with terror at the manifest parallel between him and the goat' (*Barn.* 7). The implication is that the blood of the goat being brought from the holy of holies was believed from the very earliest period to prefigure the Parousia and that the association of the Eucharist and the Day of Atonement was well known. Justin in the second century linked the sacrificed goat to the second coming (*Trypho* 40), and Cyril of Alexandria wrote some two centuries later: 'We must perceive the Immanuel in the slaughtered goat ... the two goats illustrate the mystery' (*Letter* 41).

In the Eucharist, the bishop or priest 'was' the high priest and therefore the LORD (e.g. Ignatius, *Magn.* 6: 'Let the bishop preside in the place of God'). He took into the holy of holies the bread and wine of the new bloodless sacrifice which became the body and blood of the LORD; this effected the atonement and renewal of the creation, and thus established on earth the expected kingdom. Hence the eschatological emphasis of the earliest eucharists. Dix again: 'The Eucharist is the contact of time with the eternal fact of the kingdom of God through Jesus. In it the church within time continually, as it were, enters into its own eternal being in that kingdom'.* In other words, it was the ancient high priestly tradition of entering the holy of holies beyond time and matter, the place of the heavenly throne. A fragment of this temple belief in the eternal present of events which humans have experienced as history, is to be found in the writings of the Deuteronomists who did so much to suppress the mystical elements of the ancient cult. The rebellious generation who had been at Sinai were told they would not live to enter the promised land (Num. 14.26–35); nevertheless, Moses reminded their children: 'Not with our fathers did the LORD make this covenant but with us who are all of us here alive this day' (Deut. 5.3).

Had the original understanding of the Eucharist derived from the Passover, we should have expected the Exodus imagery of liberation from slavery and becoming the chosen people. Instead, the expected benefits of the Eucharist were those of the Day of Atonement. Early evidence drawn from a variety of sources is consistent in this respect.

Shape, p. 225.

Bishop Sarapion's Prayer Book, for example, used in Egypt in the middle of the fourth century, speaks of 'the medicine of life to heal every sickness and not for condemnation', i.e. of the Eucharist bringing judgement and renewal which are the twin aspects of atonement. He prayed for angels to come and destroy the evil one, and for the establishment of the church, i.e. for the banishing of Azazel and the establishing of the kingdom. He prayed that the congregation would be made 'living men' (cf. *Thomas* 1 'the living', i.e. resurrected Jesus), able to speak of the unspeakable mysteries. 'Make us wise by the participation of the body and the blood.' This is the high priestly tradition of the temple, and the 'living men' are the first-resurrected who have become wise, the kingdom of priests reigning on earth after the evil one has been bound (Rev. 20.6). The *Liturgy of John Chrysostom* prays that the holy mysteries may bring remission of sins and forgiveness of transgressions, the gift of the Spirit, access to the LORD and a place in the kingdom, healing of soul and body, not judgement and condemnation. The *Anaphora of Addai and Mari* prays for enlightenment, and hopes for remission of sins, pardon of offences, hope of resurrection and new life in the kingdom. The *Liturgy of James* prays for peace and salvation, for forgiveness and protection from enemies. *All these themes derive from the covenant renewal of the Day of Atonement.*

There is a striking similarity between these prayers and the Qumran Hymns, and it would be easy to imagine the singer of the Hymns as the priest who had offered the eucharistic prayers. The singer knows the mysteries and has been purified from sin (1QH IX, formerly I and XII, formerly IV). He is one of the angels in the holy of holies (1QH XIV, formerly VI), he is strengthened by the Spirit (1QH XV, formerly VII), he has experienced light and healing (1QH XVII, formerly IX), he has been purified and become one of the holy ones, been resurrected and given understanding, he has stood in the assembly of the living, those with knowledge (1QH XIX, formerly XI). A creature of dust, he has been saved from the judgement, entered into the covenant and stands in the eternal place illumined by perfect light (1QH XXI, formerly XVIII).

A recurring theme of the liturgies is that of fear and awe. A homily on the mysteries attributed to Narsai (Homily XVII A, late fifth century) speaks of 'the dread mysteries ... let everyone be in fear and dread as they are performed ... the hour of trembling and great fear'. As the Spirit is summoned to the bread and wine, 'the priest worships with quaking and fear and harrowing dread'. The people stand in fear as the Spirit descends. In the mid-fourth century, Cyril of Jerusalem speaks of the 'most awful hour' when the priest begins the consecration and of 'the most awful sacrifice' (*Mystagogical Lectures* 5.4, 9). John Chrysostom has similar words to describe the coming of the Spirit (*On Priesthood* 6.4.34–36), and the people are commanded in the liturgy to 'stand in fear'. Perhaps the oldest example of all is the *Anaphora of Addai and Mari* which speaks of 'the great, fearful, holy, life-giving, divine mystery', before which the people stand in silence and awe. The priest prays as did Isaiah (Isa. 6.5): 'Woe is me ... for mine eyes have seen the LORD of hosts', and, in the manner of Moses in the tabernacle (Exod. 25.22): 'How dreadful is this place, for this day I have seen the LORD face to face ...'

Again, the setting is the holy of holies and the imagery drawn from the Day of Atonement. The earliest biblical account warns Aaron only to enter the holy of holies once a year, after elaborate preparation on the Day of Atonement. The LORD warns that he will appear in the cloud upon the *kapporet*, and Aaron might die (Lev. 16.2). The Mishnah records the fear of the high priest as he entered the holy of holies: he spent as little time as possible in the holy place (*m. Yoma* 5.1), and at the end of the ritual 'he made a feast for his friends because he had come safely out of the holy of holies' (*m. Yoma* 7.4). When the Glory of the LORD came to the desert tabernacle, Moses was not able to enter (Exod. 40.35) and when the Glory came to the temple, the priests were not able to continue their ministrations there (1 Kgs 8.10–11). The very purpose of the tabernacle was to provide a place where the LORD could dwell in the midst of his people (Exod. 25.8), and if this holy place was not pure, the LORD departed (Ezek. 8–11). John described the incarnation as the Glory dwelling on earth, the Word made flesh (John 1.14).

Theurgy and Apotheosis

Several passages in the Merkabah texts have suggested to scholars that drawing down the LORD into the temple was a major element of the temple service. 'The temple and the service performed there were thought of as able to attract the Shekinah' [the presence of the LORD] ... 'we can seriously consider the possibility that temple service was conceived as inducing the presence of the Shekinah in the Holy of Holies'.* The Hebrew Scriptures show that the LORD had been expected to appear in his temple (Num. 6.23–26; Isa. 64.1; Mal. 3.1), enthroned between the heavenly beings (Isa. 6.1–5), or to speak from above the cherubim of the *kapporet* (Exod. 25.22). The psalmist prayed that the Shepherd of Israel, enthroned upon the cherubim, would shine forth and come to save his people (Ps. 80.1–2, 3, 7, 19), that he would shine on his servant (Ps. 119.135). The psalmist also prayed for the LORD 'to arise' and come to help his people (e.g. Pss 3.7; 7.6; 68.1), and he was certain that the LORD would appear (Ps. 102.16).

The theurgical practices of pagan mysteries in the early years of Christianity are relatively well known. The Chaldean Oracles describe how to make an image of the goddess Hecate and how to draw her down into it. Certain words, materials and objects ('symbols') were believed to have a special affinity with a particular deity. 'The objects became receptacles of the gods because they had an intimate relationship with them and bore their signatures (*sunthemata*) in the manifest world'. The gods gave instructions how the rites were to be

*Idel, *Kabbalah*, p. 168.

performed and the ritual of invoking the deity was *theourgia* or *hierourgia*, divine or sacred work. 'The body of the theurgist became the vehicle through which the gods appeared in the physical world and through which he received their communion'.* The theurgic acts were believed to unite the soul to the will and activity of the deity, but not to effect complete union. It was believed that the divine order was impressed on the world. The symbols of theurgy functioned in an manner similar to Plato's forms in that both revealed the divine order. Plato had taught that the Demiurge 'completed the moulding of the world after the nature of the model' (*Timaeus* 39e). He, too, had been moulded after the nature of the model (Gen. 1.27).

Now this correspondence of heaven and earth is familiar from the temple and its rites, and it was far older than Plato. There is much in the *Timaeus*, for example, which seems to be dependent on the teachings of the Jerusalem priesthood of the first temple. The high priest, too, 'was' the LORD on earth when he wore the sacred seal which enabled him to 'bear' the sins of the people (Exod. 28.36–38). It has also been suggested that much of the Syrian Iamblichus' Chaldean theurgy, written early in the fourth century CE, derived directly from the practices of the Jewish temple mystics. Even his Semitic name invites speculation, deriving as it does from 'the LORD is king.'

Dionysius used the language of theurgy when he described the Christian mysteries in the *Ecclesiastical Hierarchy*. The bread and wine were the 'symbols' of Christ (437CD) whose original divine work had been to become a man. The bishop repeats the sacred work with the sacred symbols: 'He uncovers the veiled gifts ... he shows how Christ emerged from the hiddenness of his divinity to take on human form' (444C).

The mystery at the very heart of the first temple has been lost, but some texts invite speculation. When Solomon was enthroned as king *he became the* LORD, although the Chronicler does not explain the process (1 Chron. 29.20–23). Since the *kapporet* was the throne of the LORD, there must have been some link between the enthronement of the human king as the LORD and his being set on the place where the LORD used to appear. Origen implies that in the Day of Atonement ritual, the sacrificed goat was the LORD, the king (*Cels.* 6.43, PG XI 1364), and that the blood of this goat was sprinkled first on the 'throne' and then brought out from the holy of holies to effect the atonement by cleansing and healing the creation. In other words, the blood 'carried' the power of the divine life. In the bloodless sacrifice of the Christians, the wine was substituted for the blood of the goat (cf. Heb. 9.12), but the same process was believed to take place. The Christian altar, as we shall see, derived from the *kapporet* in the holy of holies, the 'throne' where the atonement blood was transformed and the LORD was present.

The royal psalms suggest that when the king entered the holy of holies he was 'born' in the glory of the holy ones and became the Melchizedek

*Shaw, *Theurgy*, pp. 48, 57.

priest, the LORD (Ps. 110). He was raised up, that is, resurrected to the heavenly life (Ps. 89.19; Heb. 7.15–17). This must have been the moment when he became king and was declared to be the Son (Ps. 2.7). Praying for the presence of the LORD in the holy of holies and in the person of the royal high priest at his inauguration, must have been the original context of the *Maranatha* prayer. Since, as the writer to the Hebrews knew, the high priest offered himself as the atonement sacrifice but was represented by the blood of the goat, the LORD must also have been invoked at every atonement sacrifice when the life of the royal high priest was represented by the blood of the goat. The first Christians, believing that they were seeing the ancient liturgy fulfilled in history, used the *Maranatha* prayer initially to pray for the Parousia in their own lifetime. After John's vision of the angel in the cloud, however, the prayer returned to its original setting as they prayed for the LORD to come to the bread and wine of the Eucharist.

The Epiklesis

When the Day of Atonement is recognized as the original context of the Eucharist, other elements in the tradition fall into place. The *epiklesis* derived from the *Maranatha* prayer. The earliest forms do keep the word 'come' and are addressed to the Second Person whereas later forms are prayers to the First Person to 'send'. Serapion's *epiklesis* preserves the older belief about the presence of the LORD dwelling in the holy of holies: 'O God of truth, let thy holy Logos come and dwell [*epidemesato*] upon this bread, that the bread may become the body of the Logos and upon this cup, that the cup may become the cup of the truth.' There is a long *epiklesis* in the *Acts of Thomas* 27 which calls on Christ to 'come'. All those who have been sealed with baptism perceive a human form and then receive the bread of the Eucharist. In the earlier period, the Spirit was understood to be the Logos (e.g. Justin, *Apology* 1.33: 'It is wrong to understand the Spirit and the Power of God as anything else than the Word who is also the firstborn of God, see p. 209)'. It was not until Cyril of Jerusalem (mid-fourth century) that the Third Person Spirit *epiklesis* began to be used, the prayer for the Father to send the Spirit onto the bread and wine.

The form in *Addai and Mari* is addressed to the Son: 'O my LORD, may thy Holy Spirit come and rest upon this offering', but other unique features of this prayer invite speculation as to its ultimate origin. The original form has no mention of God the Father or of the Trinity, of the crucifixion or resurrection of Jesus, it does not mention bread, wine, cup, Body or Blood, or the name of Jesus. There is no reference to partaking or communion. Dix again:

All these things ... are not of the framework of the prayer as they are the framework of the prayers that have been inspired by the systematic Greek theological tradition. Addai and Mari is a eucharistic prayer which is concentrated solely upon the experience of the eucharist ... Maranatha ... The ecstatic cry of the first pre-Pauline Aramaic speaking disciples is the summary of what it has to say.*

Was this derived from a temple prayer from the Day of Atonement? There were 'a great many of the priests obedient to the faith' in the earliest days in Jerusalem (Acts 6.7).

Several writers reveal that it was the Word which came into the bread and wine, but complications arise from the fact that *logos* can be understood to mean both the Word, the Second Person, or simply a prayer. Irenaeus, for example, argued 'if the cup which has been mixed and the bread which has been made receives the Word of God and becomes the Eucharist, the body and blood of Christ ...' (*AH* 5.2.3; PG 7.1125; also 1127). Origen, commenting on the Eucharist, said that the consecration was 'by the Word of God and prayer' (quoting 1 Tim. 4.5), where 'word' could be understood in either sense (*On Matt.* 11 PG 13.948–49), but his usage elsewhere suggests that he intended the Second Person. Athanasius taught that after great prayers and holy invocations, 'the Word comes down into the bread and wine and it becomes his body' (*Sermon to the Baptized*, PG 26.1325). As late as the early sixth century, Jacob of Serugh could write: 'Together with the priest, the whole people beseeches the Father that he will send his Son, that he may come down and dwell upon the oblation'.

The Traditions of the Priests

The mystery of the Eucharist was associated with Melchizedek. Eusebius wrote: 'Our Saviour Jesus, the Christ of God, even now performs through his ministers today sacrifices after the manner of Melchizedek' (*Proof* 5.3). Melchizedek is known in the Hebrew Scriptures only as the king of Salem, the priest of God Most High who brought out bread and wine to Abraham (Gen. 14.18), and as the royal high priest, the divine Son who would bring the Day of Judgement (Ps. 110). In the Qumran Melchizedek text, however, he is divine, the heavenly High Priest, the anointed prince who comes to Jerusalem to perform the Great Atonement at the end of the tenth Jubilee and to establish the kingdom. In the New Testament, Jesus is identified as this Melchizedek (Heb. 7.15), and the bread and wine of his sacrifice must have had some link to the bread and wine of Melchizedek.

What this was we can only guess, but the meal of bread and wine was associated with the vesting of the (high?) priest. The *Testament of Levi* describes how seven angels vested him and fed him 'bread and wine, the most holy things'** (*T. Levi* 8.5), suggesting that consuming bread and wine was a part of the consecration process. In the Hebrew Scriptures 'the most holy things' are the priests' portion of the offerings, and only the priests could consume them (e.g. Lev. 6.29; Ezek. 42.13; Ezra 2.63).

Shape, p. 252.
**Reading with R. H. Charles.

The 'most holy' was originally believed to communicate holiness (e.g. Exod. 29.37) but at the beginning of the second temple period there was a new ruling from the priests and only uncleanness was held to be contagious (Hag. 2.12). This is significant, as it suggests that the communication of holiness through consuming sacrificial offerings was a characteristic of the 'Melchizedek' cult of the first temple, but not of the second. It was, however, known to the author of the *Testament of Levi* and so this may have been how the elements of the Eucharist were originally understood.

The *Testament of Levi* also describes the priestly service of the archangels in the highest heaven; they offer atonement sacrifices before the Great Glory, and these offerings are described as bloodless and *logike,* literally 'logical' or 'intellectual' but commonly rendered 'reasonable', 'the reasonable and bloodless sacrifice' (*T. Levi* 3.6). It has been suggested, however, that *logike* in the context of liturgy indicates 'belonging to the Logos', just as it is used by Clement to describe the flock of the Good Shepherd who were not 'reasonable' sheep, but sheep of the Logos (*Instructor* III.112). The atonement sacrifice offered by the archangels in Levi's vision would then be the bloodless sacrifice of the Logos. What we cannot tell is whether or not this was a pre-Christian text and whether or not other references to the 'reasonable' sacrifice should be understood in this way.

There is nothing in the Hebrew Scriptures or in any related text which describes or explains the mystery of the holy of holies and how the presence of the LORD was believed to be present. This must, however, have been known to the priests who officiated there (see p. 28), and raises the question of what it was that Jesus the high priest is said to have transmitted secretly to a few of his disciples after his own experience of 'resurrection'. The evidence is consistent from the earliest period. Ignatius of Antioch wrote early in the second century that 'our own high priest is greater (than those of old)' for 'he has been entrusted with the holy of holies and to him alone are the secret things of God committed' (*Phil.* 9). Clement of Alexandria condemned people who were 'making a perverse use of divine words ... they do not enter in as we enter in, through the tradition of the LORD by drawing aside the curtain' (*Misc.* 7.17). The 'true teachers preserved the tradition of blessed doctrine derived directly from the holy apostles' (*Misc.* 1.1) and this tradition had 'been imparted unwritten by the apostles' (*Misc.* 6.7). There had been mysteries concealed in the Old Testament which the LORD revealed to the apostles and 'there were certainly among the Hebrews some things delivered unwritten' (*Misc.* 5.10).

The most likely mysteries to have been concealed in the Old Testament and transmitted unwritten are those of the priests, especially the secrets of the holy of holies. There is no known explanation of the rites of atonement; all that survive are the practical details of how the ritual was to be performed. The blood of the sacrifice had to be stirred by an attendant to prevent it clotting so that it could not be sprinkled (*m. Yoma* 4.3), but of the high priest's prayer in the temple no detail is given (*m. Yoma* 5.1). Only the public prayer is recorded (*m. Yoma* 6.2). Gardeners could buy the surplus blood for their gardens (*m. Yoma* 5.6), but no 'theology' of the blood sprinkling is offered.

Fragments of sanctuary lore, apart from the evidence in the Book of Revelation itself, have survived in Daniel 7 and the Parables of Enoch. In Daniel's vision, thought to be closely related to the royal rites of Psalm 2, the Man came in clouds (of incense?) before the One on the heavenly throne and 'was offered in sacrifice to him' (Dan. 7.13). The word usually rendered 'was presented before him' (*qrb*, literally 'brought near') is the term used for making a temple offering (and is implied in the Greek of Theodotion at this point). Given the temple context of this vision, 'offered as a sacrifice' is the more likely meaning. The one offered is then enthroned and given power over 'all peoples nations and languages'. In the Parables of Enoch, the blood of the Righteous One was taken up before the LORD of Spirits, together with the prayers of the righteous ones. The holy ones in heaven 'unite with one voice to pray and praise and give thanks and bless the name of the LORD of Spirits'. This is the thanksgiving element of the Eucharist. Then the books of the living were opened and read, and the 'number' of the righteous whose blood 'has been offered' was brought near to the throne (*1 En.* 47.4, where the Ethiopic implies the same word as in Dan. 7.13). This corresponds to the reading of the diptychs in the liturgy, the names of the living and the names of the dead who were remembered at the Eucharist. Then the Man was given the Name in the presence of the LORD of Spirits (i.e. he became the LORD), in the time and place before the stars and the heavens were created (i.e. in the holy of holies, Day One of creation). He became the staff of the righteous, the light of the Gentiles, and all on earth were to worship him. All these things were 'hidden before the creation of the world and for eternity', i.e. in the holy of holies (*1 En.* 48.6). Then the kings of the earth were judged, and 'the light of days' rested upon the holy and righteous ones. This is the establishing of the kingdom, the place of divine light (Rev. 22.5). The sequence is interesting and it must be related to the sequence in the Liturgy. It was certainly known to the early Christians: the Anointed One in human form (the Man) poured himself out, was raised up (into heaven), given the Name, and then worshipped (Phil. 2.6–11).

Origen, who knew *1 Enoch*, said that Jesus 'beheld these weighty secrets and made them known to a few' (*Cels.* 3.37). There were doctrines spoken in private to Jesus' genuine disciples but the words were not written down (*Cels.* 3.60, 6.6). 'If anyone is worthy to know the ineffable things he will learn the wisdom hidden in the mystery which God established before the ages' (*On Matt.* 7.2). 'Before the ages' in temple terminology means 'in the holy of holies'. Origen had contact with Jewish scholars when he lived in Caesarea and must have had good reason to write: 'The Jews used to tell of many things in accordance with secret traditions reserved to a few, for they had other knowledge than that which was common and made public' (*On John* 1.31).

Basil, also of Caesarea, writing in the middle of the fourth century, emphasized that some teachings of the church were drawn from written sources, but others were given secretly through apostolic tradition. If we attacked unwritten customs, he argued, claiming them to be of little importance, we would fatally mutilate the gospel. There was no written authority for signing with the cross, and none for praying facing towards the east, although Origen knew that this latter was linked to the Day of Atonement (*On Leviticus* 9.10). Above all Basil cited the words used in the Eucharist:

> Have any saints left for us in writing the words used in the invocation over the Eucharistic bread and the cup of blessing? As everyone knows we are not content in the liturgy simply to recite the words recorded by St Paul or the Gospels, but we add other words both before and after, words of great importance for this mystery. We have received these words from unwritten teaching ... which our fathers guarded in silence, safe from meddling and petty curiosity.

The uninitiated were not even allowed to be present at the mysteries, and this he linked to the custom of the temple: 'Only one chosen from all the priests was admitted to the innermost sanctuary ... so that he would be amazed by the novelty and strangeness of gazing on the holy of holies'. He went on to distinguish: 'Dogma is one thing, kerygma another; the first is observed in silence while the latter is proclaimed to the world' (*On the Holy Spirit* 66). Basil preserved the mystery he had received, but there are enough hints here to show he was speaking of the words of the *epiklesis*, and that these were associated with the holy of holies on the Day of Atonement.

Church and Temple

Later texts also indicate that the temple was the setting of the Eucharist, and the Day of Atonement its immediate model. Narsai (*Homily* XVII A) compared his contemplation of the mysteries of the Eucharist to Isaiah's vision of the LORD enthroned in the holy of holies. Only those who bore the mark like the temple priests were permitted to participate. They were also described as clad in garments of glory, and, like the guest without a wedding garment at the great wedding feast, outsiders were cast out (Matt. 22.13). The celebrating priest 'bore in himself the image of our LORD in that hour', and was warned to be worthy of that state, as were the temple priests who were warned not to bear the Name of the LORD in vain (Exod. 20.7). The curious situation of the one who represents the LORD offering elements which also represent the LORD exactly parallels the temple custom, where the high priest representing the LORD offered the blood of the goat which represented the LORD (Lev. 16.8, *lyhwh*, as the LORD, cf. Heb. 9.12 which implies this see p. 45).

Narsai offers two sets of symbolism, one derived from the death and burial of Jesus, but the other from the temple. This may reflect the differing emphases of Antioch and Alexandria, but it could also be a memory of the early church describing the earthly life of Jesus in terms of the high priestly traditions of the temple. There is evidence of this as early as Peter's temple sermon, where he describes the Parousia as the heavenly high priest emerging from the holy of holies to renew the creation (Acts 3.13–21). For Narsai the sanctuary of the church is 'a type of that kingdom which our LORD entered and into which he will bring with him all his friends' (cf. the holy of holies as the heavenly city, Rev. 21.16). The Christian altar is the symbol of the great and glorious throne (as was the *kapporet* above the ark in the holy of holies, Exod. 25.17–22). As on the Day of Atonement, so now, the priest 'trembles with fear for himself and for his people at that dread hour'. The people are exhorted to contemplate the Messiah enthroned in heaven who is also the one lying slain on the altar (cf. John's wordplay on the themes of crucifixion and exaltation: 'the Son of Man is lifted up', John 3.14; 8.28; 12.32, 34).

There follows a description of the scene in the sanctuary that evokes the descriptions of heavenly worship in the Songs of the Sabbath Sacrifice and the moment of silence which preceded the appearance of the Great High Priest (Rev. 8):

The priests are still and the deacons stand in silence, the whole people is quiet and still, subdued and calm ... the mysteries are set in order, the censers are smoking, the lamps are shining, and the deacons are hovering and brandishing [fans] in the likeness of the Watchers. Deep silence and peaceful calm settles on that place; it is filled and overflows with brightness and splendour, beauty and power.

The people join in the Sanctus, the song of the angels in Isaiah's throne vision and John's (Isa. 6.3; Rev. 4.8), and the priest speaks the words which 'the chosen apostles have not made known to us in the Gospels'. The Spirit comes to the bread and wine and 'the Spirit which raised him from the dead comes down now and celebrates the Mysteries of the resurrection of his body'. *The consecration is the moment of resurrection*, another remarkable link to the royal traditions of Israel, for the king was deemed to be resurrected (translated 'raised up', 2 Sam. 23.1) and he, too, became the LORD enthroned and he, too, was worshipped (1 Chron. 29.20–23), the LORD with his people.

The Anthem of the Sanctuary in the *Liturgy of Addai and Mari* describes a similar setting:

Thy throne, O God, endureth for ever. The cherubim compass the terrible seat of thy majesty and with fear moving their wings cover their faces for that they cannot lift up their eyes and behold the fire of thy Godhead. Thus art Thou glorified and dwellest among men, not to burn them up but to enlighten them. Great, O my LORD, is Thy mercy and Thy grace which thou hast showed to our race.

The ultimate source of this must be Isaiah 33.13–22, which contrasts the fear of sinners at the prospect of the everlasting fires, and the vision of the king in his beauty which awaits the upright. Compare also Enoch's account of the flaming fire around the heavenly throne, that no angels could enter because of the brightness (i.e. no ordinary priests could enter the holy of holies), and that no flesh could gaze upon the Glory. Enoch lay prostrate and trembling until invited to enter (*1 En.* 14.21–25).

Priests and deacons, 'thousands of Watchers and ministers of fire and spirit go forth' with the resurrected LORD, said Narsai, and the people rejoice 'when they see the Body setting forth from the midst of the altar'. This is exactly the procession described for the Day of the LORD, the Day of Judgement, when the LORD goes forth from his holy place with all his holy ones (Deut. 32.43, expanded in *Ass. Mos.* 10; Deut. 33.2–5). The effect of receiving the Body of the Risen LORD was that of the Day of Atonement, when the high priest emerged from the holy of holies, carrying the blood which cleansed and hallowed (Lev. 16.19), healing and renewing the creation which the temple represented. The Body of the Risen LORD, wrote Narsai, 'pardons debts, purifies blemishes, heals diseases, cleanses and purges stains with the hyssop of his mercy' (cf. Acts 3.19: 'times of refreshing come from the presence of the LORD' when the Anointed One returns).

Germanus of Constantinople (early eighth century) in his book *On the Divine Liturgy* presents the temple symbolism in great detail, alongside symbolism drawn from the life of Jesus. 'The church is an earthly heaven', he wrote, 'in which the super-celestial God dwells and walks about' (*Liturgy* 1). This must be the garden of Eden, which had been represented in the temple by the great hall. After comparing the apse to the cave of Christ's birth and burial and the table to the place where his dead body rested, he continues: 'The holy table is also the throne of God on which, borne by the cherubim, he rested in the body … The altar is and is called the heavenly and spiritual altar where the earthly and material priests who always assist and serve the LORD represent the spiritual, serving and hierarchical powers' (*Liturgy* 4, 6, also 41). The holy table, the spiritual altar, corresponds to the *kapporet* over the ark, the cherub throne where the blood of the LORD was offered by the high priest on the Day of Atonement. The chancel barriers correspond in function to the veil of the temple, separating 'the holy of holies accessible only to the priests' (*Liturgy* 9). The twenty-four presbyters are the seraphic powers (cf. Rev. 4.4) and the seven deacons are images of the angelic powers (cf. Rev. 4.5; *Liturgy* 16, but also the Qumran Songs of the Sabbath Sacrifice which describe the seven angels who are the ruling princes of the sanctuary and the account by John Chrysostom of an old man – presumably himself – who saw angels in shining robes around the altar, *On Priesthood* 6.4.45–50).

The priest before the altar speaks to God, as did Moses in the tabernacle, when the LORD spoke to him from above the *kapporet*, between

the cherubim (Exod. 25.22; *Liturgy* 41) and the priest sees the glory of
the LORD.

God truly spoke invisibly to Moses and Moses to God; so now the priest, standing
between the two cherubim in the sanctuary and bowing on account of the dreadful
and uncontemplable glory and brightness of the Godhead and contemplating the
heavenly liturgy, is initiated even into the splendour of the life-giving Trinity ...
(*Liturgy* 41)

The heavenly host in the sanctuary is represented by the deacons
holding fans 'in the likeness of the six winged seraphim and the many
eyed cherubim' (*Liturgy* 41), exactly as in the Hebrew Scriptures, where
the priests were the angels of the LORD (e.g. Mal. 2.7), and in the
Qumran Hymns and Blessings: e.g. 'may you attend upon the service in
the temple of the kingdom and decree destiny in company with the
angels of the presence ... may he consecrate you to the holy of holies'
(1QSb IV); '... standing with the host of the holy ones ... with the
congregation of the sons of heaven' (1QH XI, formerly III). The Songs
of the Sabbath Sacrifice speak of 'the priests of the inner temple,
ministers of the presence of the most holy king ... their expiations shall
obtain his goodwill for those who repent from sin ...' (4Q400), and of
the wings of the cherubim falling silent as they bless the heavenly throne
(4Q405). As in the liturgy, there are processions through the doors of
glory when the elohim and the holy angels enter and leave, proclaiming
the glory of the King (4Q405), cf. 'the Cherubic Hymn signified the
entrance of all the saints and righteous ahead of the cherubic powers
and the angelic hosts who run invisibly in advance of the Great King,
Christ ...' (*Liturgy* 37). *The Qumran Hymns and Blessings and the
Songs of the Sabbath Sacrifice must derive from the actual temple
services, which have survived as Christian Liturgy.*

The Sogitha on the Church of Edessa, composed in the mid-sixth
century, mentions 'the cherubim of its altar', a description (late fifth
century) of the church at Quartamin mentions a cherub over the altar
and the account of the Muslim capture of the church of St Jacob in
Aleppo alludes to the destruction of the cherubim above the altar, all
three indicating that the earliest Christian altars derived from the
kapporet. In Ethiopian churches, there is an ark in the sanctuary.

The Sacrifice

Perhaps the most striking parallel of all between the Day of Atonement
and the liturgy is the manner of preparing the bread. The central portion
of the loaf is removed in the manner of a sacrifice, and then known as
the holy bread or the Lamb. An exactly similar procedure was used for
the sin offering on the Day of Atonement in the first century CE,
according to the *Letter of Barnabas* which differs at this point from the
Mishnah. According to the latter, the high priest cut open the goat of
the sin offering and removed the sacrificial portions (the fat over the

entrails, the kidneys and a part of the liver, Lev. 3.12–16 and Lev. 4.31) and then burned them on the altar before sending the rest of the carcase to be burned outside the temple (*m. Yoma* 6.7; the comparison in Heb. 13.10–13 is confused). Barnabas, however, says that the goat was eaten: the people consumed the carcase, but the priests had the sacrificial portions, mixed with sour wine.

What does it say in the prophet?* Let them eat of the goat which is offered for their sins at the fast and, note this carefully, let all the priests but nobody else, eat of its inward parts, unwashed and with vinegar. Why was this? Because 'When I am about to give my body for the sins of this new people of mine, you will be giving me gall and vinegar to drink ...' (*Barn.* 7)

Barnabas, a Levite (Acts 4.36) interpreted the crucifixion as the sin offering and the vinegar which Jesus drank (John 19.29) as the vinegar of the sacrificial portion eaten by the priests. This must be the origin of the custom of removing the middle portion of the loaf and mixing it with wine.

The role of the bread in the temple is another mystery. Twelve loaves 'the Bread of the Presence' (literally 'the Face') were set on a golden table in the great hall of the temple, together with incense and flagons for drink offerings (Exod. 25.29–30). The bread became holy while it was in the temple: before being taken in it was placed on a marble table but when it was brought out it was placed on a table of gold because it had become holy (*m. Shekalim* 6.4). The loaves were eaten by the high priests every Sabbath, perhaps the origin of the weekly celebration of the Eucharist. The prothesis prayer in the liturgy of the Coptic Jacobites preserves the tradition of the Bread of the Face: 'LORD Jesus Christ ... the living bread which came down from heaven ... make thy face shine upon this bread and upon this cup which we have set upon this thy priestly table'.

The Older Testament?

There is much about the temple that is still unknown. There are also several texts in the Hebrew Scriptures which cannot be placed in any known context. Together, however, these texts have a certain consistency which at the very least invites speculation.

- Melchizedek, the priest of God Most High brought out bread and wine (Gen. 14.18). Until the discovery of the Melchizedek text at Qumran, Melchizedek was thought to be a relatively minor figure in the tradition; it is now clear that he was the Messiah, expected to make the final atonement sacrifice at the end of the tenth Jubilee.

*This reference cannot be identified, but it is not impossible that something relevant to Christian origins has dropped from the Hebrew Scriptures, as can be seen from the Qumran texts of Deuteronomy 32.8 (which mentions 'the sons of God' who have disappeared from the MT at this point) Deuteronomy 32.43 where the Qumran Hebrew corresponds to the longer LXX and Isaiah 52.14 (which identifies the Suffering Servant as 'the Anointed One' and not, as in the MT, the disfigured one).

Melchizedek was 'born' in the holy of holies among the holy ones (LXX, Ps. 110) and was the eternal priest, not by virtue of descent from Levi, but because he had been raised up, i.e. resurrected (Heb. 7.15–16).

- Moses, the high priests and the elders who stood before the heavenly throne, saw the God of Israel and *ate and drank* before him. They suffered no harm (Exod. 24.9–11). What was this meal?
- When Moses offered his own life for the sins of Israel he was told that such a sacrifice was not possible; each man bore his own sin (Exod. 32.30–33). What older view of atonement was excluded from the Hebrew Scriptures?
- The secret things belonged to the LORD and were no concern of humans (Deut. 29.29). What mattered was keeping the Law, and nobody needed to go up to heaven to receive that (Deut. 30.11–14). Who had gone up to heaven to learn secret things?
- Aaron was only permitted to enter the holy of holies once a year; had the earlier practice been different? (Lev. 16.2).
- Ezekiel knew that the mark of the LORD was a *tau*, at that period written as a diagonal cross (Ezek 9.4). This mark protected from the wrath.

When Eusebius described the re-establishment of the churches in the time of Constantine, he included an account of the oration delivered to Paulinus, Bishop of Tyre (*History* 10.4). The new building was compared to the tabernacle and the temple, its builder to Bezalel and Solomon. This could indicate that the church was deliberately adopting the temple as its model and that all temple elements in the later liturgies were a conscious imitation of the older rites. Origen, however, had known of the temple traditions a century earlier, and he had also known of the secret traditions of both Jews and Christians.

There is insufficient evidence for certainty, but such as there is indicates that the Great High Priest gave to his followers a new way of offering the sacrifice of atonement. *It was the very oldest understanding of the Day of Atonement, and was perpetuated in the Eucharist.*

NOTES

I used the critical edition of the Greek text in H. B. Swete, *The Apocalypse of St John* (London, 1906, 1917).

Introduction 'The mother of Christian theology' is Käsemann's now famous line from an article originally in *Zeitschrift für Theologie und Kirche* 57 (1960), ET 'The Beginnings of Christian Theology' in *New Testament Questions of Today* (London, 1969). The earlier date for the Book of Revelation in B. F. Westcott, *The Gospel According to St John* (London, 1894), p. lxxxvii; R. H. Lightfoot, *Biblical Essays* (London and New York, 1904), p. 52; F. J. A. Hort, *The Apocalypse of St John I–III* (London, 1903), p. xxxii. There is no evidence for Christian persecution in Asia Minor, Hort, *The Apocalypse of St John* p. xxi, S. R. F. Price, *Rituals and Power. The Roman Imperial Cult in Asia Minor* (Cambridge, 1984), p. 15.

Chapter 1 is developed from my *On Earth as it is in Heaven* (Edinburgh, 1995) and *The Risen* LORD (Edinburgh, 1996).

Chapter 2 is developed from my *The Gate of Heaven* (London, 1991) and 'Beyond the Veil of the Temple: The High Priestly Origins of the Apocalypses' in *Scottish Journal of Theology* 51.1 (1998), pp. 1–21. The quotation on icons is from R. Temple, *Icons; A Search for Inner Meaning* (London, 1982), p. 43.

Chapter 3 Hecataeus of Abdera in *Diodorus Siculus* xl 3:5–6. The material on Yeb is from B. Porten, *Archives from Elephantine. The Life of an Ancient Jewish Military Colony* (Berkeley 1968), on the economy of first-century Judea from M. Goodman, *The Ruling Class of Judaea. The Origins of the Jewish Revolt Against Rome* AD *66–70* (Cambridge, 1987) and on the eternal covenant from R. Murray, *The Cosmic Covenant* (London, 1992). The Great Angel is a summary of material in my *The Great Angel. A Study of Israel's Second God* (London, 1992) and my *The Gate of Heaven*. Most of the material on the Zealots was drawn from M. Hengel, *The Zealots. Investigations into the Jewish Freedom Movement in the Period from Herod I Until 70* AD (Edinburgh, 1989).

Chapter 4 Material on Ugarit is taken from N. Wyatt, *Religious Texts from Ugarit. The Words of Ilimilku and his Colleagues* (Sheffield, 1998), and from his 'The Stela of the Seated God from Ugarit', *Ugarit-Forschungen* 15 (1983), pp. 271–77, and 'Les Mythes des Dioscuri et l'idéologie royale dans les littératures d'Ougarit et d'Israel', *Revue Biblique* 103.4 (1996), pp. 481–516. Examples of Aramaic antecedents are taken from C. C. Torrey, *The Apocalypse of John* (Newhaven, 1958) and the list of Aramaized biblical book names from his 'The Aramaic Period of the Nascent Christian Church', *Zeitschrift für Neutestamentliche Wissenschaft* (1952–53), pp. 205–23. The sevenfold punishment as the priestly curse from Lev. 26 is from J. M. Ford, *Revelation* (New York, 1975).

Chapter 5 was developed from material in my books, *The Gate of Heaven* and *The Great Angel*, and from my article, 'The Veil of the Temple'.

Chapter 6 Some of the material on the Nikolaitans was drawn from W. C. van Manen, 'The Nikolaitans' in *Encyclopaedia Biblica,* ed. T. K. Cheyne and J. Sutherland Black (London, 1902). After reaching my conclusion about Amen/Amon, I discovered that L. Silbermann 'Farewell to O AMEN', *Journal of Biblical Literature* 82 (1963), pp. 213–15 had drawn the same conclusion albeit from different evidence. Much in the chapter is taken from my *The Risen* LORD.

Chapter 7 The Name meaning 'he who causes to be' was first suggested by W. F. Albright in a review in *Journal of Biblical Literature* 67 (1984), pp. 377–81. This was developed by W. H. Brownlee, 'The Ineffable Name of God' in *Bulletin of the American Schools of Oriental Research* 226 (1977), pp. 39–46.

Chapter 8 was developed from my *The Risen* LORD and from my 'Isaiah' in *Commentary 2000*, forthcoming (Grand Rapids, 2000). The reconstruction of Ps. 110 is from Wyatt 'Les Mythes des Dioscuri'.

Chapter 9 The suppression of knowledge/wisdom was developed from my *The Older Testament* (London, 1987). On the scroll of 5.1 being the scroll of 10.2, I agree with F. D. Mazzaferri, *The Genre of the Book of Revelation from a Source Critical Perspective*, BZNW (Berlin/New York, 1989), albeit arguing on a different basis and drawing different conclusions.

Chapter 11 Some of the material on the fifth and sixth trumpets was drawn from S. Giet, *L'Apocalypse et l'Histoire. Etude Historique sur l'Apocalypse Johannique* (Paris, 1957).

Chapter 12 The confusion over *soreg* was drawn from C. C. Torrey, *The Apocalypse of John. Oblias* meaning 'bond of the people' was drawn from P. Carrington, *The Meaning of Revelation* (London, 1931).

Chapter 13 The Ugaritic material was drawn from N. Wyatt, *Religious Texts from Ugarit,* 'The Stela of the seated God' and 'Les mythes des Dioscuri'. Some of the Daughter of Zion material was drawn from J. F. A. Sawyer, 'The Daughter of Zion and the Servant of the LORD in Isaiah. A Comparison', *Journal for the Study of the Old Testament* 44 (1989), pp. 89–107. The figurines: K. Kenyon, *Digging Up Jerusalem* (London, 1974). 'Wisdom' was developed from my *The Great Angel*, 'Asherah' from W. G. Dever, 'Asherah Consort of Yahweh. New Evidence from Kuntillet "Ajrud" ', *Bulletin of the American Schools of*

Oriental Research 255 (1984), pp. 21–37, and J. Day, 'Asherah in the Hebrew Bible and Northwest Semitic Literature', *Journal of Biblical Literature* 105/3 (1986), pp. 385–406. Someone must have suggested the obvious reading 'Asherah' at Deut. 33.2 and Isa. 6.13, but I have never come across it. The Yeb material was drawn from B. Porten, *Archives*, some of the Wisdom in Philo material from E. R. Goodenough, *By Light, Light. The Mystic Gospel of Hellenistic Judaism* (New Haven, 1935). The fate of Wisdom after the exile is from my *The Older Testament*, and the similarity of Wisdom and Logos from my *The Great Angel*. The Shekinah material was drawn from G. Scholem, *On the Kabbalah and its Symbolism* (New York, 1965).

Chapter 14 Material on the myth of the fallen angels and on the role of Third Isaiah as spokesman for the dispossessed community was drawn from my *The Older Testament*, Christian baptism material from my *The Risen* LORD. The high priest wearing the conquered snake was suggested in conversation by Crispin Fletcher-Louis.

Chapter 15 Josephus as the false prophet was developed from a suggestion in J. M. Ford, *Revelation*. 'Nero' in *DJD* II p. 101.

Chapter 16 Material on the Temple Scroll calendar was drawn from J. Maier, *The Temple Scroll* (Sheffield, 1985). The material on the Lamb and his army was developed from R. Bauckham, *The Climax of Prophecy: Studies in the Book of Revelation* (Edinburgh, 1993).

Chapter 17 The Eden symbolism of the temple was drawn from my *The Gate of Heaven*. The alternative meanings for *zk'*, and the 'harps of aloes wood' were drawn from C. C. Torrey, *The Apocalypse of John*. The evidence in later Jewish texts for hostility to the marble stones as water, the throne above the waters of the sea and the rainbow as the Glory, was drawn from D. Halperin, *The Faces of the Chariot. Early Jewish Responses to Ezekiel's Vision* (Tübingen, 1988); I realized that another interpretation of his evidence was possible in the light of my reading of the Book of Revelation. The plural identity of the LORD and 'mountains and islands' as concealing angel figures were drawn from my *The Great Angel*. Armageddon as the Mount of Assembly was drawn from Nestle, 'Har Magedon' in Hastings, *Dictionary of the Bible* (1899) 1910, citing Hommel (1890).

Chapter 18 Jerusalem as the harlot after the exile was drawn from my *The Older Testament*. The burning of the temple as the punishment of a priestly harlot was drawn from J. M. Ford, *Revelation*. The economic situation in Judea was developed from M. Goodman, *The Ruling Class of Judaea*. The ivory knob is described in the *Israel Museum Journal* VIII (1989), pp. 7–16, reprinted in *Biblical Archaeologist* 53/3 (1990), pp. 158–66. The Copper Scroll was first described in J. Allegro, *The Treasure of the Copper Scroll* (London, 1960).

Chapter 19 The multiple naming of angels is drawn from my *The Great Angel*. The possible confusion of *rgl* and *dgl* is from C. C. Torrey, *The*

Apocalypse of John. For the seven crowns of the high priest, see M. Chyutin, *The New Jerusalem Scroll from Qumran. A Comprehensive Reconstruction* (Sheffield, 1997). For the three-word Name in the *Gospel of Thomas*, see A. de Conick, *Seek to See Him* (Leiden, 1996). For the Enochic and angelic themes in Isaiah, see my *Isaiah: Commentary 2000*, forthcoming. For the place of Enoch in the cult of the first temple, see my *The Older Testament*.

Chapter 20 The first to suggest textual disorder at the end of the Book of Revelation was R. H. Charles, *A Critical and Exegetical Commentary on the Revelation of St John*, 2 vols, International Critical Commentary (Edinburgh, 1920). His was a complicated theory which offered no explanation as to how the disorder might have come about, but it prompted me to modify his theory and seek an explanation. The garments of the Shekinah was drawn from Scholem, *On the Kabbalah.* The material on the post-exilic situation and the evidence for the 'watchers' was drawn from my *The Older Testament*, the visions of Jesus from my *The Risen* LORD. The temple and the solar calendar was drawn from my 'The Temple Measurements and the Solar Calendar' in *Temple Scroll Studies*, ed. G. J. Brooke, JSPSup. 7 (Sheffield, 1989). On temple and time, see my 'Beyond the Veil'. The retelling of the Adam story and the role of the Deuteronomists in repressing the older cult were drawn from my *The Older Testament*.

Chapter 21 The first-resurrection material was developed from my *The Risen* LORD. I first read of the two judgements in R. H. Charles, *Revelation* and developed my suggestions from his.

Excursus I drew most of the factual information from:
J. M. Neale and R. F. Littledale, *The Liturgies of SS Mark, James, Clement, Chrysostom and Basil and the Church of Malabar* (London, 1859).
F. E. Brightman, *Liturgies Eastern and Western* (Oxford, 1896).
R. H. Connolly, *The Liturgical Homilies of Narsai* (Cambridge, 1909).
J. Wordsworth, *Bishop Sarapion's Prayer Book* (Connecticut, 1964).
C. Kucharek, *The Byzantine Slav Liturgy of St John Chrysostom* (Ontario, 1971).
G. Dix, *The Shape of the Liturgy* (London (1945) 1949). Quotations from pp. 186, 225, 252.
St Basil the Great, *On the Holy Spirit* (New York, 1980).
St Germanus of Constantinople on the Divine Liturgy. Translation Introduction and Commentary by P. Meyendorff (New York, 1984).
B. D. Spinks, *Prayers from the East* (Washington, 1993).
Temple theurgy in M. Idel, *Kabbalah New Perspectives* (New Haven and London, 1988), pp. 166–70.
Pagan theurgy compared to Christian in B. Lang, *Sacred Games. A History of Christian Worship* (New Haven and London, 1997), pp. 311–23.

Theurgy and Neoplatonism in H. Lewi, 'Chaldean Oracles and Theurgy', *Études Augustiniennes* (Paris, 1978) and G. Shaw, *Theurgy and the Soul. The Neoplatonism of Iamblichus* (Pennsylvania, 1995).
Chaldean Theurgy and Jewish Mysticism in J. Vanderspoel, 'Merkabah Mysticism and Chaldean Theurgy' in *Religion in the Ancient World*, ed. M. Dillon (Amsterdam, 1999), pp. 511–22.
The cherubim over the altar in K. E. McVey, 'The Domed Church as Microcosm: The Literary Roots of an Architectural Symbol', *Dumbarton Oaks Papers* 37 (1983).
Priestly ideas earlier than Plato in my 'Beyond the Veil of the Temple. The High Priestly Origins of the Apocalypses' in *Scottish Journal of Theology* 51.1 (1998), pp. 1–21.

SOURCES

Abbreviations

OTP The Old Testament Pseudepigrapha, 2 vols, ed. J. H. Charlesworth (New York and London, 1983, 1985).

ANF Ante-Nicene Fathers, ed. A. Roberts and J. Donaldson (Edinburgh 1868–72, reprinted Grand Rapids, 1950–52).

DJD Discoveries in the Judaean Desert, various editors (Oxford 1955–).

LCL Loeb Classical Library

Jewish Apocrypha and Pseudepigrapha

1 Enoch is extant in Ethiopic but Aramaic fragments have been found at Qumran and Greek fragments are also known. It has five sections: The Book of the Watchers, the Parables, the Astronomy Book, the Dreams Visions and the Admonitions. Fragments of all sections except the Parables have been found at Qumran. The earliest Qumran Enoch material dates from the third century BCE, but Enochic literature must be much older. The Book of Isaiah presupposes knowledge of something very similar. Jude, a member of Jesus' family, quoted from this text (Jude 14). English translation by E. Isaac in *OTP*, vol. 1, also R. H. Charles, *The Book of Enoch* (Oxford, 1912) and M. A. Knibb, *The Ethiopic Book of Enoch. A New Edition in the light of the Aramaic Dead Sea Fragments* (Oxford, 1978).

2 Enoch also known as *The Book of the Secrets of Enoch* is extant in Slavonic but, as most early religious texts in Slavonic were translated from Greek, *2 Enoch* was probably a Greek text. It is impossible to date, but affinities with ideas known in the first century CE suggest that its sources could be ancient. English translation by F. I. Andersen in *OTP*, vol. 1, also R. H. Charles and W. R. Morfill, *The Book of the Secrets of Enoch* (Oxford, 1896) and A. Vaillant, *Le livre des secrets d'Hénoch: texte slave et traduction francaise* (Paris (1952) 1976).

The *Book of Jubilees* also known as the *Little Genesis*, mentioned in the Damascus Document (CD XVI), is a writing with priestly interests possibly dating from early in the second century BCE. The fullest text has survived in Ethiopic but there are fragments in Greek, Syriac and Latin. The original was in Hebrew, and fragments have been found at Qumran and Masada. English translation by O. S. Wintermute in *OTP*, vol. 2.

The *Testaments of the Twelve Patriarchs* purports to be the final words of the twelve sons of Jacob, originating perhaps in the early years of the second century BCE, but with later Christian additions. The earliest surviving texts are in Greek, but Aramaic fragments of similar material have been found at Qumran. English translation by H. C. Kee in *OTP*, vol. 1, also R. H. Charles, *The Greek Versions of the Testaments of the Twelve Patriarchs* (Oxford, 1908) and *The Testaments of the Twelve Patriarchs* (London, 1908).

The *Assumption of Moses* also known as the *Testament of Moses*, purports to be Moses, final words to Joshua and as such is related to Deuteronomy 31–34. Only one Latin text is known which seems to have been translated from an earlier Greek. The original must have been written in Hebrew or Aramaic, probably in the first century CE, as there are thinly veiled references to Herod the Great in Chapter 7. English translation by J. Priest in *OTP*, vol. 1, also E. M. Laperrousaz, *Le Testament de Moïse (généralement appelé 'Assomption de Moïse')*. *Traduction avec introduction et notes* (Paris, 1970).

Apocalypse of Abraham is extant only in Slavonic, but certain names and phrases suggest a Hebrew original. It was probably written at the end of the first century CE as Abraham 'sees' the destruction of the temple. English translation by R. Rubinkiewicz in *OTP*, vol. 1, also G. H. Box and J. I. Landman, *The Apocalypse of Abraham* (London, 1918).

2 Baruch also known as *Syriac Baruch*, was translated from Greek into Syriac but probably had a Hebrew original. Written as though by Baruch, Jeremiah's scribe, after the first destruction of the temple in 597 BCE, it was in fact a reaction to the events of 70 CE. It is a composite work, and there is evidence of the variety of traditions and hopes for the temple and its rebuilding. English translation by A. F. J. Klijn in *OTP*, vol. 1, also P. Bogaert, *Apocalypse de Baruch. Introduction, traduction du Syriaque et commentaire* (Paris, 1969).

The *Testament of Abraham*, part of the *Testaments of the Three Patriarchs,* exists in Greek in a longer and a shorter form. The longer form is probably the original Alexandrian Greek and the shorter could be a translation from a Hebrew original. Scholars have suggested dates ranging from the second century BCE to the second century CE. Although a Jewish text, it was only preserved by Christians. English translation by E. P. Sanders in *OTP*, vol. 1, also G. H. Box, *The Testament of Abraham* (London, 1927) and M. E. Stone, *The Testament of Abraham: The Greek Recensions* (Montana, 1972).

The *Letter of Aristeas* was written in Greek, probably by an Alexandrian Jew, and describes the translation of the Septuagint in the mid-third century BCE. It also gives an account of the temple and the high priest. Josephus used it in *Antiquities* 12, but it is impossible to date the work. English translation by R. J. H. Shutt in *OTP*, vol. 2.

Sibylline Oracles There were Sibyls all over the ancient world – old women who gave oracles and prophecies. The most famous Sibyl was in Rome. Book 3 is an anthology of prophecies thought to have been compiled in Egypt. Some reflect Jewish interests in the temple and a saviour. Although composed over many years, the latest verses refer to Nero and events at the end of the first century CE. Book 5 is from the same period, with a heightened hostility to Rome and the hope of a king sent by God against Nero. English translation by J. J. Collins in *OTP*, vol. 1, also H. N. Bate, *The Sibylline Oracles Books III–V* (London, 1918).

Biblical Antiquities of Pseudo-Philo (*Liber Antiquitatum Biblicarum*, hence LAB) is extant in Latin but probably had a Hebrew original. LAB is a retelling of the Old Testament story from Adam to David, transmitted together with the Latin translations of Philo and at one time attributed to him (hence Pseudo-Philo). It was probably composed in the middle of the first century CE in Palestine as the author knew a Palestinian text of the Hebrew Scriptures. English translation by D. J. Harrington in *OTP*, vol. 2, also M. R. James, *The Biblical Antiquities of Philo* (London, 1917, reprinted New York, 1971).

Life of Adam and Eve is a Latin text which largely corresponds to a Greek text known as *The Apocalypse of Moses*. They elaborate on the story of Adam and Eve and probably derive from a Hebrew original written in the early second century CE. English translation by M. D. Johnson in *OTP*, vol. 2, also L. S. A. Wells in *The Apocrypha and Pseudepigrapha of the Old Testament*, vol. 2 ed. R. H. Charles (Oxford, 1913).

Psalms of Solomon are extant in Greek and Syriac and were listed in the fifth-century Codex Alexandrinus as following the Old and New Testaments and the Clementine Epistles. The codex is damaged and the text has not survived there. The original language was probably Hebrew as the psalms were written in response to Pompey's attack on Jerusalem in 63 BCE. They look for a true Messiah to rid them of corrupt and foreign rulers and to establish his everlasting kingdom. English translation by R. B. Wright in *OTP*, vol. 2, also G. B. Gray in *The Apocrypha and Pseudepigrapha of the Old Testament*, vol. 2, ed. R. H. Charles (Oxford, 1913) and H. S. Ryle and M. R. James, *Psalmoi Solomontos: Psalms of the Pharisees Commonly called the Psalms of Solomon* (Cambridge, 1891).

The *Lives of the Prophets* is extant in many languages and is a collection of legendary material about Isaiah, Jeremiah, Ezekiel and Daniel, the Twelve, and seven other prophets mentioned in the Hebrew Scriptures. The source material was probably in a Semitic language even though the final text was written in Greek, perhaps by a bilingual Jew in first-century Palestine. English translation by D. R. A. Hare in *OTP,* vol. 2, also C. C. Torrey, *The Lives of the Prophets. Greek Text and Translation* (Philadelphia, 1946).

Qumran Texts

English translations of most of the non-biblical texts in G. Vermes, *The Complete Dead Sea Scrolls in English* (London, 1997).

1QIsa[a], 'The Complete Isaiah Scroll' and 1QpHab, 'The Habakkuk Commentary' M. Burrows, J. C. Trever, W. H. Brownlee, *The Dead Sea Scrolls of St Mark's Monastery I* (New Haven, 1950).
1QSb, 'The Blessings' *DJD* I (1995).
1QH 'The Hymns' and 1QM, 'The War Scroll' E. L. Sukenik, *The Dead Sea Scrolls of the Hebrew University* (Jerusalem, 1954–5).
1QS, 'The Community Rule' M. Burrows, *The Dead Sea Scrolls of St Mark's Monastery II/2* (New Haven, 1951).
1Q14, 'Commentary on Micah', *DJD* I (1955).
3Q15, 'The Copper Scroll' J. M. Allegro, *The Treasure of the Copper Scroll* (London, 1960), *DJD* III (1962).
4QDeut[q], P. S. Skehan, 'A Fragment of the Song of Moses from Qumran', *Bulletin of the American Schools of Oriental Research* 136 (1954), pp. 12–15, *DJD* XIV (1995).
4Q En[g], J. T. Milik, *The Books of Enoch. The Aramaic Fragments of Qumran* Cave 4 (Oxford, 1976).
4Q 265–273, 5Q12, 6Q15, 'The Damascus Document'. The original Cairo Genizah text in S. Schechter, *Fragments of a Zadokite Work* (Cambridge, 1910). Qumran material in *DJD* XVIII (1996).
4Q156, 'The Targum of Leviticus', *DJD* VI (1977).
4Q400–407, 11Q17, 'The Songs of the Sabbath Sacrifice', *DJD* XI (1998).
4Q554–55, 5Q15, 1Q32, 2Q24, 4Q232, 11Q18, 'The New Jerusalem', M. Chyutin, *The New Jerusalem Scroll from Qumran* (Sheffield, 1997), *DJD* I (1955), III (1962), XXIII (1998).
11Q13, 'Melchizedek', *DJD* XXIII (1998).
11QT, 'The Temple Scroll' J. Maier, *The Temple Scroll* (Sheffield, 1985), *DJD* XXIII (1998).

Other Jewish Writers

Philo of Alexandria (about 20 BCE–50 CE) was from a wealthy and influential family; he himself headed the community's embassy to the Emperor Caligula in 40 CE. His brother Alexander was the governor of the Jews in Alexandria who paid for nine of the temple gates in Jerusalem to be overlaid with heavy plates of silver and gold (*War* 5.201–205) and may have been the Alexander mentioned in Acts 4.6. His brother's son, Tiberius Alexander, renounced his Judaism for service with the Romans and was made procurator of Judea in 46 CE (*Ant.* 20.100). He later became prefect of Egypt (*War* 2.309) where he persuaded the city to support Vespasian during the war against Jerusalem (*War* 4.616–18). He it was who brought the 2000 men from Alexandria to support the attack on Jerusalem (*War* 5.45) where he was a chief officer with Titus (*War* 5.510, 6.237). Philo's brother's other son, Marcus, married Berenice, the daughter of Herod Agrippa (*Ant.* 19.276ff.).

Jerome said that Philo was of a priestly family (*On Illustrious Men* XI) and he was probably correct. He was aware of the older priestly traditions of Israel, and much in his writings that is identified as Platonism, e.g. the heavenly archetypes, the second mediator God, is more likely to have originated in the priestly traditions of the first temple (see my 'Beyond the Veil of the Temple. The Priestly Origins of the Apocalypses' in *Scottish Journal of Theology* 51.1 (1998), pp. 1–21). The Greek text and English translation of his works by F. H. Colson, G. H. Whittaker, and R. Marcus in *LCL*, 12 vols (1929–63).

Joseph ben Matthias (about 35–100 CE) is usually known by his Roman name Flavius Josephus. He was of royal and high priestly blood, and at the start of the revolt against Rome he commanded troops in Galilee. When he was captured by the Romans, he changed sides and served as a translator for the Romans during the rest of the war. He later lived in Rome under the patronage of the emperor, and wrote *The Jewish War*, originally in Aramaic but only the Greek version survives. Although he was an eyewitness of much he described he was hardly an impartial observer. Greek text and English translation by H. St J. Thackeray, *LCL*, 3 vols (1927, 1997). He later wrote *The Antiquities of the Jews,* the first half of which was based on the Hebrew Scriptures and the remainder being a valuable source for the later period especially the era of the Herods. Greek text and English translation by R. Marcus, *LCL*, 9 vols (1963–69). Josephus also wrote an autobiography, *Life,* and an apologetic piece *Against Apion* which describes the antiquity of Israel and the ideals of the Law. Greek text and English translations by H. St. J. Thackeray in *LCL* (1956–65).

Rabbinic Texts

The Mishnah, a name derived perhaps from the Hebrew word for repeat or learn, perhaps from the fact that it was 'second' in relation to the Law, is the collection of religious law from the end of the second temple period attributed to R. Judah ha Nasi. The Mishnah comprises six sections, each subdivided into Tractates. English translation by H. Danby, *The Mishnah* (Oxford, 1933, 1989).

Gemara the 'completion' of the study, was added to each section of the Mishnah and thus the Talmud 'study' was formed. The Palestinian Talmud was probably compiled in Tiberias in the fifth century CE and the *Babylonian Talmud*, a longer work including other material taught in the rabbinic schools, was probably compiled in the early sixth century CE. English translation by I. Epstein, *The Babylonian Talmud*, 35 vols (London 1935–52, reprinted 1961).

The Mekhilta of R. Ishmael is a commentary on parts of Exodus, compiled perhaps in the second half of the third century CE, but preserving older material. Text and English translation by J. Z. Lauterbach, *Mekilta de Rabbi Ishmael*, 3 vols (Philadelphia, 1933–35).

Genesis Rabbah, a midrash compiled in Palestine perhaps in the early fifth century CE, became part of the medieval Midrash Rabbah, the Great Midrash. English translation, *Genesis Rabbah: The Judaic Commentary on Genesis: A New American Translation* by J. Neusner, 3 vols (Atlanta, 1985).

Numbers Rabbah is a composite work, the second part being older than the first. The older portion was probably in existence in the eighth century CE, the other in the twelfth century CE. English translation by J. J. Slotki in *Midrash Rabbah* (London, 1939, reprinted 1961).

The Targums are Aramaic translations of biblical texts. It is not possible to date them, because they are the written deposit of an oral tradition and contain material from many periods. There are English translations in the Aramaic Bible series published by T&T Clark, Edinburgh.
Vol. 1A, T. Neofiti, *Genesis* by M. McNamara (1992).
Vol. 1B, T. Pseudo Jonathan, *Genesis* by M. Maher (1992).
Vol. 11, *The Isaiah Targum* by B. Chilton (1987). The introduction to this volume is particularly important as background to 'The Revelation of Jesus Christ', as it gives evidence for Jesus' knowledge of the Isaiah Targum tradition and suggests that the interpretation in the Targum had itself the authority of prophecy. The tradition in the Talmud (*b. Meg.* 3a) is that the Targum of the Prophets was made by Jonathan ben Uzziel, a disciple of R. Hillel (and so a contemporary of the first Christians), and that he was helped by the prophets Haggai, Zechariah and Malachi. There are many similarities between interpretations in Isaiah Targum and those in the Book of Revelation which are the work of first-century Palestinian prophets.
Vol. 13, *The Ezekiel Targum* by S. H. Levey (1987).

There is an introduction to the Merkavah Texts in P. Schäfer, *The Hidden and Manifest God. Some Major Themes in Early Jewish Mysticism*, English translation by A. Pomerance (Albany, 1992).
3 Enoch also known as the *Hebrew Enoch* (but its original title was probably *Sepher Hekhalot*) contains material attributed to the early second-century CE R. Ishmael. It is the deposit of a school of tradition with Palestinian roots and probably reached its present form in the fifth/sixth century CE. English translation by P. Alexander in *OTP*, vol. 1.

Hekhalot Rabbati (The Greater Palaces) and *Hekhalot Zutarti* (The Lesser Palaces) are similar collections of texts which Schäfer holds to be earlier than *3 Enoch*. P. Schäfer, *Synopse zur Hekhalot Literatur* (Tübingen, 1981). I do not know of an English translation of these texts. Passages are identified by their paragraph number in this edition, e.g. # 123.

Early Christian Writers

The *Freer Logion*, from a fourth-century Greek MS found in Egypt and bought by Mr Freer, can be found in any critical edition of the Greek text of Mark, after Mark 16.14. English translation in M. R. James, *The Apocryphal New Testament* (Oxford, 1924, 1980), p. 34.

The *Ascension of Isaiah* is a composite work comprising the Martyrdom of Isaiah (chs. 1–5) and The Vision of Isaiah (chs. 6–11), but these sections are themselves composite. Although probably written in Hebrew and then translated into Greek and other languages, the entire text survives only in Ethiopic. A pre-Christian Hebrew text about the martyrdom of Isaiah has been expanded by Christian visionary material, some of which clearly describes the church in the first century. Given the significance of Isaiah in the teaching of Jesus and thus in the early church, it is no coincidence that an Isaiah text was expanded with Christian visionary material. The Christian additions show a remarkable similarity to the teaching attributed to James in Eusebius, *History* 2.23 and *Clementine Recognitions* 1.66–70. Epiphanius, *Panarion* I.36.16 attributes to James an otherwise unknown book used by the Ebionites, the *Ascents of James*, which has probably survived in these portions of the *Ascension of Isaiah*.

The *Odes of Solomon* are a collection of hymns on baptismal themes, written originally in Syriac or perhaps Hebrew at the end of the first century CE. There are similarities to the Qumran Hymns and to the Fourth Gospel. Text and English translation by J. H. Charlesworth, *The Odes of Solomon* (Oxford, 1973), translation only in OTP, vol. 2.

The *Letter of Barnabas*, written after the fall of Jerusalem in 70 CE, was traditionally attributed to Barnabas the Levite from Cyprus who was Paul's companion on his first missionary journey (Acts 4.36; 13.2). The Greek text was rediscovered in 1859 in the Sinai Codex. English translation by M. Staniforth in *Early Christian Writings. The Apostolic Fathers* (Harmondsworth, 1968).

Hermas was a visionary who lived in Rome and recorded his visions from c. 90 CE. *The Shepherd* (his guiding angel was dressed as a shepherd), was written in Greek and included in the Sinai Codex. Text and English translation by K. Lake in *The Apostolic Fathers*, vol. 2, LCL (1913, 1948).

Ignatius, the second Bishop of Antioch (Eusebius, *History* 3.36) c. 69 CE and died a martyr in Rome c. 107. En route to Rome he wrote seven letters to churches in Asia Minor, which were collected by Polycarp, Bishop of Smyrna (*Ep. Polycarp to the Philippians* 13.2). English translation by M. Staniforth in *Early Christian Writings. The Apostolic Fathers* (Harmondsworth, 1968).

Justin was born of a Roman family who lived near Shechem in Samaria. He lived for a while in Ephesus where his dialogue with the Jew Trypho is set, some time after the end of the Bar Kochbar revolt in 135 CE. He moved to Rome where he wrote his First Apology, addressed to the emperor Antoninus Pius, and his Second Apology addressed to the Roman senate. His defence of Christianity eventually led to his execution c.165 CE. English translation in *ANF*, vol. 1.

Irenaeus was born in Smyrna where he knew Polycarp and learned from him about the teachings of John. He studied in Rome and then went as bishop to Lyons. His work *The Demonstration of the Apostolic Preaching* was lost for centuries but an Armenian version was discovered in 1904. His major five-volume work, *Against Heresies,* is a refutation of gnosticism in all its aspects. It is extant in a Latin translation but fragments of the original Greek survive as quotations in other works. English translation in *ANF*, vol. 1.

Hippolytus (c. 160–235 CE), schismatic bishop at Rome who was exiled to Sardinia. He was the last major scholar in the Roman Church to write in Greek. English translation of *On the Holy Theophany* in *ANF*, vol. 5.

Clement of Alexandria (died c. 214 CE). According to Eusebius (*History* 6.6, 13) he settled in Alexandria as a pupil of Pantaenus and eventually succeeded him as head of the Catechetical School there, where he taught Origen. He fled to Asia Minor during the persecution of Severus in 202 CE. The English translation by W. Wilson of the eight books of the *Miscellanies* and the essay, *Who is the Rich Man?* in *ANF*, vol. 2.

Attributed to **Clement**, a bishop of Rome at the end of the first century CE, are the *Clementine Recognitions*, and the *Clementine Homilies* which describe how Clement was converted to Christianity and travelled with Peter. Opinions vary as to the date and value of the work. The original text has not survived, but there is a Latin translation by Rufinus (died 410 CE) and it was quoted by Origen in 231 CE. English translation by T. Smith in *ANF*, vol. 8.

The *Acts of Thomas*, originally written in Syriac early in the third century, were combined by the Manicheans with the *Acts of John*, the *Acts of Paul*, the *Acts of Peter* and the *Acts of Andrew*, as a substitute for the canonical Acts of the Apostles. English translation in M. R. James, *The Apocryphal New Testament* (Oxford, 1924, 1980).

Eusebius (c. 260–340 CE), Bishop of Caesarea, preserved in his writings quotations from many texts which no longer survive. The first draft of his *Church History* was written before he became a bishop c. 313 CE, but he revised the work in the light of later developments. The *Preparation of the Gospel* and its companion the *Proof of the Gospel* were written later in response to the philosopher Porphyry's attack on Christianity. Texts and English translation by K. Lake and J. E. L. Oulton as the *Ecclesiastical History* in *LCL*, 2 vols (1926, 1932), and by G. A. Williamson, *The History of the Church* (Harmondsworth, 1965); *The Preparation of the Gospel* by E. H. Gifford (Oxford, 1903).

Epiphanius became bishop of Salamis on Cyprus in 367 CE. He wrote the *Panarion*, meaning the Medicine Chest, against the eighty heresies which he believed were contrary to Nicene orthodoxy. It contains quotations from works which have not survived elsewhere. English translation by F. Williams, *Panarion Book 1* (1–46) (Leiden, 1987).

Jerome (c. 347–420) was head of a monastery near Bethlehem for over thirty years and was appointed by Pope Damasus to prepare a revised Latin text of the Bible, the Vulgate. Between 393 and 406 CE he wrote a series of commentaries on the Minor Prophets. Text of *On Micah* in *CCSL*, vols 72–80.

Cosmas *A Christian Topography*, English translation by J. W. McCrindle (London, 1897).

Gnostic Texts

Twelve papyrus books of gnostic texts and fragments of a thirteenth were found at Nag Hammadi in Egypt in 1945, and are known as the Coptic Gnostic Library. Most of the gnostic texts cited in this book are from this collection. There is still much to be learned about the so-called gnostics, and much to be unlearned. They regarded themselves as the guardians of true Christianity, and so the label 'heretic' should not be applied with too much confidence. The Book of Revelation condemns Pauline Christianity as a work of false prophecy and shows the priestly and temple setting of earliest Christianity. The Book of Revelation resembles much in the gnostic texts, not because it is a late text with gnostic corruption apparent, but because the original 'gnosticism' and the earliest Christianity were one and the same. The *Gospel of Thomas* shows Jesus in his original setting as a temple mystic, for example, and the pair of texts known as the *Letter of Eugnostos* and the *Wisdom of Jesus Christ* show how an older text, rooted in the priestly Wisdom tradition, was 'adopted' as the teaching of Jesus. The presupposition which makes Plato a major influence on Philo also masks the Hebrew roots of gnosticism (see my *The Great Angel*, 1992). English translations in *The Nag Hammadi Library in English*, ed. J. M. Robinson (Leiden, 1996). Critical editions of the original texts in *The Coptic Gnostic Library* (Leiden). Of the texts cited in this book:

Nag Hammadi Codex I, 2 vols, ed. H. W. Attridge (1985) contains the *Apocryphon of James* and the *Tripartite Tractate*.

Nag Hammadi Codex II.2–7, 2 vols, ed. B. Layton (1989) contains the *Gospel of Thomas*, the *Gospel of Philip*, the *Hypostasis of the Archons*, *On the Origin of the World*.

Nag Hammadi Codices II.1, III.1 and IV.1, ed. M. Waldstein and F. Wisse (1995) contains the *Apocryphon of John*.

Nag Hammadi Codices III.3–4 and V.1, ed. D. M. Parrott (1991) contains *Letter of Eugnostos* and the *Sophia of Jesus Christ*.

Nag Hammadi Codex III.5, ed. S. Emmel (1984) contains the *Dialogue of the Saviour*.

Ugaritic Texts

Texts from the late bronze age (c. 1550–1200 BCE) were recovered as the result of a chance find in 1928 near Ras Shamra on the coast of Syria. The ancient city of Ugarit yielded clay tablets in seven languages, one of them the hitherto unknown Ugaritic, akin to early Hebrew. The religious texts illuminate aspects of the Hebrew Scriptures. Fifty religious texts and commentary in N. Wyatt, *Religious Texts from Ugarit. The Words of Ilimilku and His Colleagues* (Sheffield, 1998).

Other Classical Texts

Herodotus of Halicarnassus (c. 485–425 BCE) was the first Greek historiographer and his *Histories* the earliest great prose work in European literature. English translation by A. de Sélincourt, *Herodotus. The Histories* (Harmondsworth, 1954, 1971. Greek text and English translation by A. D. Godley in *LCL*, 4 vols (1969).

Hecataeus of Abdera who lived in the fourth century BCE is quoted in Diodorus Siculus 40.3.5–6. Greek text and English translation by F. R. Walton in *LCL*, 12 vols (1967).

Pliny the elder (23–79 CE) died in the eruption of Vesuvius in 79 CE. His one surviving work is the *Natural History* in 37 books. Latin text and English translation by H. Rackham in *LCL*, 10 vols (1938, 1997).

Strabo wrote his *Geographies* in the closing years of the first century BCE. He lived in Rome but travelled widely and drew on other written sources in his work. Greek text and English translation by H. L. Jones in *LCL*, 8 vols (1924, 1967).

Tacitus was born about 55 CE and was proconsul of Asia about 112 CE. Little is known of his life. The fourteen books of *The Histories* cover the period from 69 CE to the death of Domitian in 96 CE. Latin text and English translation by J. Jackson, *LCL*, 4 vols (1962). His later work, the sixteen books of *The Annals* which cover the earlier period from 14 CE to 68 CE, was completed about 116 CE. Latin text and English translation by J. Jackson in *LCL*, 5 vols (1970).

Suetonius was writing early in the second century CE. His *Lives of the Caesars* are biographies rather than history. Latin text and English translation by J. C. Rolfe in *LCL*, 2 vols (1914, 1965).

Cassius Dio (c. 160–230 CE) wrote in Greek a *History of Rome* in eighty books, of which only parts survive. An *Epitome* of Dio was made in the eleventh century by Xiphilinus.

INDEX OF PERSONS, PLACES AND SUBJECTS

INDEX OF BIBLICAL AND ANCIENT TEXTS

Clement of Alexandria

Excerpts from Theodotus

Rich Man
42   75

Instructor
III.112   381

Hypotyposes (in Eusebius)   72, 183

Miscellanies
1.1   381
5.10   3, 381
6.7   3, 381
6.7–7.1   184
7.17   4, 22, 381

Origen

Celsus
3.37   4, 382
3.60   382
6.6   3, 72, 148, 182, 382
6.23   3
6.43   45, 378

On Leviticus
9.10   375, 383

On Jeremiah
Hom 15   320

On Ezekiel
Hom 1   127

On Matthew
7.2   382
11   380
16.6   75

On John
1.31   4, 383
2.12   209, 320
2.31   275, 308
13.33   72

Apostolic Constitutions
7.34–5   209
8.12   209

Eusebius

Preparation of the Gospel
9.29   141
13.12   334

Proof of the Gospel
4.15   110, 318
5.3   380

History of the Church
2.1   9, 72, 183
2.17   114, 138,
2.23   10, 11, 156, 192–4
2.25   341
3.5   74, 289
3.7   192–3
3.8   197
3.20   75, 76, 341, 345
3.24   9
3.31   10, 79, 99
3.39   77, 350
4.6   287
4.22   194
5.20   77
7.25   77
10.4   388

Athanasius

Sermon to the Baptised   380

Epiphanius

Panarion
I.29.4   10
I.30.16   193

Basil

On the Holy Spirit 66   2, 160, 184, 383

Sarapion

Prayer Book   375, 379

Cyril of Alexandria

Letter 41   375